Java Coding Problem

Second Edition

Become an expert Java programmer by solving over 250 brand-new, modern, real-world problems

Anghel Leonard

BIRMINGHAM—MUMBAI

Java Coding Problems
Second Edition

Senior Publishing Product Manager: Denim Pinto
Acquisition Editor – Peer Reviews: Gaurav Gavas
Project Editor: Namrata Katare
Senior Development Editor: Elliot Dallow
Copy Editor: Safis Editing
Technical Editor: Aniket Shetty
Proofreader: Safis Editing
Indexer: Rekha Nair
Presentation Designer: Ajay Patule
Developer Relations Marketing Executive: Vipanshu Parashar

First published: September 2019
Second edition: March 2024

Production reference: 2100424

Published by Packt Publishing Ltd.
Grosvenor House
11 St Paul's Square
Birmingham
B3 1RB, UK.

ISBN 978-1-83763-394-4

www.packt.com

Contributors

About the author

Anghel Leonard is a chief technology strategist with more than 20 years of experience in the Java ecosystem. In his daily work, he is focused on architecting and developing Java distributed applications that empower robust architectures, clean code, and high performance. He is passionate about coaching, mentoring, and technical leadership.

He is the author of several books and videos and dozens of articles related to Java technologies.

About the reviewers

George Adams is a senior software engineer at Microsoft and the Java Champion and steering committee chair at Eclipse Adoptium. He was a co-founder of AdoptOpenJDK in 2016 and, since then, has led its community outreach efforts. He was instrumental in moving the project to the Eclipse Foundation. George also contributes to both the Homebrew project and the Node.js Foundation, where he is a core collaborator and plays an active role in several of the workgroups.

Ivar Grimstad is a Jakarta EE developer advocate at the Eclipse Foundation. He is a Java Champion and JUG Leader based in Sweden. He contributes to the Jakarta EE specifications and is the PMC Lead for Eclipse Enterprise for Java (EE4J). He is also a specification lead for Jakarta MVC and represents the Eclipse Foundation on the JCP Executive Committee. Ivar is also involved in a wide range of open-source projects and communities and is a frequent speaker at international developer conferences.

David Vlijmincx is an Oracle ACE and a highly experienced Java developer with over 8 years of experience in the field. His main focus is on building scalable and high-quality applications using Java. He is passionate about sharing knowledge, has written a book about migrating Jakarta EE to the cloud, regularly blogs, and also speaks at conferences.

Join our community on Discord

Join our community's Discord space for discussions with the author and other readers:

https://discord.gg/8mgytp5DGQ

Table of Contents

Chapter 3: Working with Date and Time   **175**

Chapter 4: Records and Record Patterns   197

Chapter 8: Sealed and Hidden Classes   431

Chapter 9: Functional Style Programming — Extending APIs   459

Chapter 10: Concurrency — Virtual Threads and Structured Concurrency   527

Chapter 11: Concurrency – Virtual Threads and Structured Concurrency: Diving Deeper   581

Chapter 12: Garbage Collectors and Dynamic CDS Archives   647

Preface

The super-fast evolution of the JDK between versions 12 and 21 means two things: first, Java now has a host of powerful new features that you can adopt to solve a variety of modern-day problems; second, the learning curve of modern Java is becoming very steep.

This book enables you to take an objective approach to solving common problems by explaining the correct practices and decisions you need to make with respect to complexity, performance, readability, and more.

Java Coding Problems, Second Edition, will help you complete your daily tasks and meet deadlines, all while becoming a more proficient and self-sufficient Java developer. You can count on the 270+ (all brand-new for this edition) problems in this book to cover the most common and fundamental areas of interest: strings, numbers, arrays, collections, the Foreign Function and Memory API, data structures, date and time, pattern matching, sealed/hidden classes, functional programming, virtual threads, Structured Concurrency, Garbage Collectors, Dynamic CDS Archives, the Socket API, and Simple Web Server.

Put your skills on steroids with problems that have been carefully crafted to highlight and teach the core knowledge needed for daily work. In other words (no matter if your task is simple, middling, or complex), having this knowledge in your tool belt is a must, not an option.

By the end of this book, you will have gained a strong understanding of Java concepts, and you'll have the confidence to develop and choose the right solutions to all your Java problems.

While this book is entirely stand-alone, and you do not need anything else to get the most out of it, many of the topics covered in this book are also explored in *Java Coding Problems, First Edition*. If you haven't already read it, and you wish to get even more practice in, then consider picking that book up for a completely different set of Java problems.

Who this book is for

Java Coding Problems, Second Edition, is especially useful for late-beginner-to-intermediate Java developers looking to level-up their knowledge by solving real-world problems. However, the problems looked at within these pages will be encountered in the daily work of any Java developer, from beginner all the way to advanced practitioner.

Therefore, it is recommended that you are familiar with the Java fundamentals and have at least a foundational working knowledge of the language.

What this book covers

Chapter 1, Text Blocks, Locales, Numbers, and Math, includes 37 problems covering 4 main topics, text blocks, locales, numbers, and mathematical operations.

Chapter 2, Objects, Immutability, Switch Expressions, and Pattern Matching, includes 30 problems tackling, among other things, some less-known features of `java.util.Objects`, some interesting aspects of immutability, the newest features of `switch` expressions, and deep coverage of the pattern matching expressions; `instanceof` and `switch`.

Chapter 3, Working with Date and Time, includes 20 problems covering different date-time topics. These problems are mainly focused on the Calendar API and the JDK 8 Date/Time API. About the latter, we will cover some of the less-studied APIs like `ChronoUnit`, `ChronoField`, `IsoFields`, and `TemporalAdjusters`.

Chapter 4, Records and Record Patterns, includes 19 problems that cover in detail the Java records introduced in JDK 16 (JEP 395) and record patterns, which were introduced as a preview feature in JDK 19 (JEP 405), as a second preview feature in JDK 20 (JEP 432), and as a final feature in JDK 21 (JEP 440).

Chapter 5, Arrays, Collections, and Data Structures, includes 24 problems covering three main topics. We start with several problems meant to cover the new Vector API dedicated to data parallel processing. We continue with several data structures including Rope, Skip List, K-D Tree, Zipper, Binomial Heap, Fibonacci Heap, Pairing Heap, Huffman Coding, and so on. Finally, we discuss the three most popular join algorithms.

Chapter 6, Java I/O: Context-Specific Deserialization Filters, includes 13 problems related to Java serialization/deserialization processes. We start with classical problems like serializing/deserializing objects to `byte[]`, `String`, and XML formats. We then continue with JDK 9 deserialization filters meant to prevent deserialization vulnerabilities, and we finish with JDK 17 context-specific deserialization filters.

Chapter 7, Foreign (Function) Memory API, includes 28 problems covering the Foreign Function Memory API and Foreign Linker API. We start with the classical approaches for calling foreign functions, relying on the JNI API and the open-source JNA/JNR libraries. Next, we introduce the new approach delivered under the code name Project Panama. We dissect the most relevant APIs such as *Arena*, *MemorySegment*, *MemoryLayout*, and so on. Finally, we focus on the Foreign Linker API and the Jextract tool for calling foreign functions that have different types of signatures, including callback functions.

Chapter 8, Sealed and Hidden Classes, includes 13 problems covering Sealed and Hidden Classes. The first 11 recipes will cover Sealed Classes, a very cool feature brought in by JDK 17 to sustain closed hierarchies. The last two problems cover Hidden Classes, a JDK 15 feature that allows frameworks to create and use runtime (dynamic) classes hidden to the JVM.

Chapter 9, Functional Style Programming – Extending APIs, includes 24 problems covering a wide range of functional programming topics. We will start by introducing the JDK 16 `mapMulti()` and continue with a handful of problems for working with predicates (*Predicate*), functions, and collectors.

Chapter 10, Concurrency – Virtual Threads and Structured Concurrency, includes 16 problems briefly introducing *virtual threads* and *structured concurrency*.

Chapter 11, Concurrency – Virtual Threads and Structured Concurrency: Diving Deeper, includes 18 problems meant to dive deep into how *virtual threads* and *structured concurrency* work and how they should be harnessed in your applications.

Chapter 12, Garbage Collectors and Dynamic CDS Archives, includes 15 problems covering Garbage Collectors and Application Class-Data Sharing (AppCDS).

Chapter 13, Socket API and Simple Web Server, includes 11 problems covering the Socket API and 8 problems covering JDK 18's Simple Web Server. In the first 11 problems, we will discuss implementing socket-based applications such as blocking/non-blocking server/client applications, datagram-based applications, and multicast applications. In the second part of this chapter, we discuss Simple Web Server as a command-line tool.

To get the most out of this book

You should have a fundamental understanding of the Java language. You should also install the following:

- An IDE (the recommended, but not essential, choice is Apache NetBeans 20.x: `https://netbeans.apache.org/front/main/`).
- JDK 21 and the Maven latest release.
- Additional third-party libraries will need to be installed to fully follow along with some problems and chapters (nothing too difficult or special).

Download the example code files

The code bundle for the book is also hosted on GitHub at `https://github.com/PacktPublishing/Java-Coding-Problems-Second-Edition`. In case there's an update to the code, it will be updated on the existing GitHub repository.

We also have other code bundles from our rich catalog of books and videos available at `https://github.com/PacktPublishing/`. Check them out!

Download the color images

We also provide a PDF file that has color images of the screenshots/diagrams used in this book. You can download it here: `https://packt.link/gbp/9781837633944`.

Conventions used

There are a number of text conventions used throughout this book.

`CodeInText`: Indicates code words in text, database table names, folder names, filenames, file extensions, pathnames, dummy URLs, user input, and Twitter handles.

Here is an example: "For instance, let's add the `Patient` and `Appointment` records as well."

A block of code is set as follows:

```
if (staff instanceof Resident(String name, Doctor dr)) {
  return "Cabinet of " + dr.specialty() + ". Doctor: "
                       + dr.name() + ", Resident: " + name;
}
```

When we wish to draw your attention to a particular part of a code block, the relevant lines or items are highlighted:

```
if (staff instanceof Resident(String name, Doctor dr)) {
  return "Cabinet of " + dr.specialty() + ". Doctor: "
                       + dr.name() + ", Resident: " + name;
}
```

Any command-line input or output is written as follows:

```
2023-02-07T05:26:17.374159500Z
2023-02-07T05:26:17.384811300Z
2023-02-07T05:26:17.384811300Z
```

Bold: Indicates a new term, an important word, or words that you see onscreen. For example, words in menus or dialog boxes appear in the text like this. Here is an example: "The compiler recognizes a **Java record** via the **record** keyword."

Warnings or important notes appear like this.

Tips and tricks appear like this.

Get in touch

Feedback from our readers is always welcome.

General feedback: Email feedback@packtpub.com, and mention the book's title in the subject of your message. If you have questions about any aspect of this book, please email us at questions@packtpub.com.

Errata: Although we have taken every care to ensure the accuracy of our content, mistakes do happen. If you have found a mistake in this book we would be grateful if you would report this to us. Please visit, http://www.packtpub.com/submit-errata, selecting your book, clicking on the Errata Submission Form link, and entering the details.

Piracy: If you come across any illegal copies of our works in any form on the Internet, we would be grateful if you would provide us with the location address or website name. Please contact us at copyright@packtpub.com with a link to the material.

If you are interested in becoming an author: If there is a topic that you have expertise in and you are interested in either writing or contributing to a book, please visit http://authors.packtpub.com.

Share your thoughts

Once you've read *Java Coding Problems, Second Edition*, we'd love to hear your thoughts! Scan the QR code below to go straight to the Amazon review page for this book and share your feedback.

https://packt.link/r/1837633940

Your review is important to us and the tech community and will help us make sure we're delivering excellent quality content.

Download a free PDF copy of this book

Thanks for purchasing this book!

Do you like to read on the go but are unable to carry your print books everywhere?

Is your eBook purchase not compatible with the device of your choice?

Don't worry, now with every Packt book you get a DRM-free PDF version of that book at no cost.

Read anywhere, any place, on any device. Search, copy, and paste code from your favorite technical books directly into your application.

The perks don't stop there, you can get exclusive access to discounts, newsletters, and great free content in your inbox daily

Follow these simple steps to get the benefits:

1. Scan the QR code or visit the link below

https://packt.link/free-ebook/9781837633944

2. Submit your proof of purchase
3. That's it! We'll send your free PDF and other benefits to your email directly

1

Text Blocks, Locales, Numbers, and Math

This chapter includes 37 problems covering 4 main topics: text blocks, locales, numbers, and mathematical operations. We will start with text blocks (elegant multiline strings introduced in JDK 13 (JEP 355, preview)/ JDK 15 (JEP 378, final)), continue with problems for creating a Java `Locale`, including localized locales (JDK 19's `ofLocalizedPattern()`), and finish with problems about numbers and math, such as the Babylonian method for computing the square root and different corner cases of results overflows. The last part of the chapter is dedicated to JDK 17's (JEP 356, final) new API for pseudo-random generators.

By the end of this chapter, you'll be up to date with all the new and cool JDK features added that relate to these four topics.

 Throughout this book you will find references to the first edition. The role of these references is to provide you with the best resources for further reading related to certain topics. You can successfully go through this edition even if you haven't read the first one and don't intend to.

Problems

Use the following problems to test your string manipulation, Java locales, and mathematical corner case programming prowess. I strongly encourage you to give each problem a try before you turn to the solutions and download the example programs:

1. **Creating a multiline SQL, JSON, and HTML string:** Write a program that declares a multiline string (for instance, SQL, JSON, and HTML strings).

2. **Exemplifying the usage of text block delimiters:** Write a program that exemplifies step-by-step how the delimiters of a text block affect the resulting string.

3. **Working with indentation in text blocks:** Write a program that exemplifies different techniques to indent a text block. Explain the meaning of *incidental* and *essential* white spaces.

4. **Removing incidental white spaces in text blocks:** Highlight the main steps of the algorithm used by the compiler to remove the *incidental* white spaces of a text block.

5. **Using text blocks just for readability:** Write a program that creates a string looking like a text block (multiline string) but acts as a single-line string literal.

6. **Escaping quotes and line terminators in text blocks:** Write a program that exemplifies how to handle Java escape sequences (including quotes, \", and line terminators, \n and \r) in a text block.

7. **Translating escape sequences programmatically:** Write a program that has programmatic access for translating escape sequences in a text block. Consider that you have a text block containing embedded escape sequences, and you have to pass it to a function that gets a string that must not contain such sequences.

8. **Formatting text blocks with variables/expressions:** Write a program that exposes several techniques for formatting text blocks with variables/expressions. Comment on each technique from the readability perspective. Also, provide a **Java Microbenchmark Harness (JMH)** benchmark for these techniques.

9. **Adding comments in text blocks:** Explain how we can add comments in a text block.

10. **Mixing ordinary string literals with text blocks:** Write a program that mixes ordinary string literals with text blocks – for instance, via concatenation. Also, is an ordinary string literal and a text block equal if they have the same content?

11. **Mixing regular expression with text blocks:** Write an example of mixing regular expressions that have named groups with text blocks.

12. **Checking if two text blocks are isomorphic:** Write a program that checks if two text blocks are isomorphic. Two strings are considered isomorphic if we can map every character of the first string to every character of the second string in a one-to-one fashion (for instance, "xxyznnxiz" and "aavurraqu" are isomorphic).

13. **Concatenating strings vs. StringBuilder:** Write a JMH benchmark for comparing string concatenation (via the "+" operator) with the `StringBuilder` approach.

14. **Converting int to String:** Write a program that provides several common techniques for converting an `int` to a `String`. Also, for the proposed solutions, provide a JMH benchmark.

15. **Introducing string templates:** Explain and exemplify the usage of JDK 21's (JEP 430, preview) string templates feature.

16. **Writing a custom template processor:** Introduce an API for writing a user-defined template processor. Next, provide a few examples of custom template processors.

17. **Creating a Locale:** Write a program that reveals different approaches for creating a `Locale`. Also, create *language ranges* and *language priority lists*.

18. **Customizing localized date-time formats:** Write a program that exemplifies the usage of custom localized date-time formats.

19. **Restoring always-strict floating-point semantics:** Explain what the `strictfp` modifier is and how/where to use it in a Java application.

20. **Computing mathematical absolute value for int/long and a result overflow:** Write a program that exemplifies a corner case where applying the mathematical absolute value to an `int/long` leads to a result overflow. Also, provide a solution to this problem.

21. **Computing the quotient of the arguments and result overflow:** Write a program that exemplifies a corner case where computing the quotient of the arguments leads to a result overflow. Also, provide a solution to this problem.

22. **Computing the largest/smallest value that is less/greater than or equal to the algebraic quotient:** Write a program that relies on `java.util.Math` methods to compute the largest/smallest value that is less/greater than or equal to the algebraic quotient. Don't forget to cover the result overflow corner case as well.

23. **Getting integral and fractional parts from a double:** Write a program that exposes several techniques for getting the integral and fractional parts of a `double`.

24. **Testing if a double number is an integer:** Write a program that shows several approaches for testing if a `double` number is an integer. In addition, provide a JMH benchmark for the proposed solutions.

25. **Hooking Java (un)signed integers in a nutshell:** Explain and exemplify in code the usage of signed/unsigned integers in Java.

26. **Returning the flooring/ceiling modulus:** Define the *floor/ceil* modulus based on the *floor* and *ceil* operations, and exemplify the result in code lines.

27. **Collecting all prime factors of a given number:** A prime number is a number divisible by itself and 1 (for instance, 2, 3, and 5 are prime numbers). Write a program that collects all prime factors of a given positive number.

28. **Computing the square root of a number using the Babylonian method:** Explain the Babylonian method for computing the square root, elaborate a step-by-step algorithm for this method, and write the code based on this algorithm.

29. **Rounding a float number to specified decimals:** Write a program that contains several approaches for rounding a given `float` number to specified decimals.

30. **Clamping a value between min and max:** Provide a solution for clamping a given value between a given minimum and maximum.

31. **Multiply two integers without using loops, multiplication, bitwise, division, and operators:** Write a program that multiplies two integers without using loops, multiplication, bitwise, division, and operators. For instance, start from the *special binomial product formula*.

32. **Using TAU:** Explain the meaning of TAU in geometry/trigonometry, and write a program that solves the following problem: A circle has a circumference of 21.33 cm. What is the radius of the circle?

33. **Selecting a pseudo-random number generator:** Provide a short dissertation about the new API for generating pseudo-random numbers introduced in JDK 17 (JEP 356, final). Moreover, exemplify different techniques for selecting a pseudo-random number generator.

34. **Filling a long array with pseudo-random numbers:** Write a program that fills an array of long arrays with pseudo-random numbers in a parallel and non-parallel fashion.

35. **Creating a stream of pseudo-random generators:** Write a program that creates a stream of pseudo-random numbers and a stream of pseudo-random generators.

36. **Getting a legacy pseudo-random generator from new ones of JDK 17:** Write a program that instantiates a legacy pseudo-random generator (for instance, `Random`) that can delegate method calls to a JDK 17 `RandomGenerator`.

37. **Using pseudo-random generators in a thread-safe fashion (multithreaded environments):** Explain and exemplify the usage of pseudo-random generators in a multithreaded environment (for instance, using an `ExecutorService`).

The following sections describe solutions to the preceding problems. Remember that there usually isn't a single correct way to solve a particular problem. Also, remember that the explanations shown here include only the most interesting and important details needed to solve the problems. Download the example solutions to see additional details and to experiment with the programs at https://github.com/PacktPublishing/Java-Coding-Problems-Second-Edition/tree/main/Chapter01.

1. Creating a multiline SQL, JSON, and HTML string

Let's consider the following SQL multiline string:

```
UPDATE "public"."office"
SET ("address_first", "address_second", "phone") =
  (SELECT "public"."employee"."first_name",
          "public"."employee"."last_name", ?
   FROM "public"."employee"
   WHERE "public"."employee"."job_title" = ?
```

As is common knowledge, before JDK 8, we could wrap this SQL as a Java `String` (string literal) in several ways.

Before JDK 8

Probably the most common approach relies on straightforward concatenation via the well-known "+" operator. This way, we obtain a multiline string representation, as follows:

```
String sql =
 "UPDATE \"public\".\"office\"\n"
+ "SET (\"address_first\", \"address_second\", \"phone\") =\n"
+ "  (SELECT \"public\".\"employee\".\"first_name\",\n"
+ "          \"public\".\"employee\".\"last_name\", ?\n"
+ "   FROM \"public\".\"employee\"\n"
+ "   WHERE \"public\".\"employee\".\"job_title\" = ?";
```

The compiler should be (and usually is) smart enough to internally transform the "+" operations into a `StringBuilder`/`StringBuffer` instance and use the `append()` method to build the final string. However, we can use `StringBuilder` (not thread-safe) or `StringBuffer` (thread-safe) directly, as in the following example:

```
StringBuilder sql = new StringBuilder();
sql.append("UPDATE \"public\".\"office\"\n")
   .append("SET ...\n")
   .append("  (SELECT...\n")
   ...
```

Another approach (typically not so popular as the previous two) consists of using the `String.concat()` method. This is an immutable operation that basically appends a given string at the end of the current one. Finally, it returns the new combined string. Trying to append `null` values results in `NullPointerException` (in the previous two examples, we can append `null` values without getting any exceptions). Chaining `concat()` calls allows us to express multiline strings, as in the following example:

```
String sql = "UPDATE \"public\".\"office\"\n"
    .concat("SET...\n")
    .concat("  (SELECT...\n")
    ...
```

Furthermore, we have the `String.format()` method. By simply using the `%s` format specifier, we can concatenate multiple strings (including `null` values) in a multiline string, as follows:

```
String sql = String.format("%s%s%s%s%s%s",
    "UPDATE \"public\".\"office\"\n",
    "SET ...\n",
    "  (SELECT ...\n",
    ...
```

While these approaches are still popular these days, let's see what JDK 8 has to say about this topic.

Starting with JDK 8

Starting with JDK 8, we can use the `String.join()` method to represent multiline strings. This method is also specialized in string concatenation, and it allows us to have easy readability in our example. How so? This method takes as the first argument a delimiter, and it uses this between the strings that will be concatenated. So, if we consider that `\n` is our line delimiter, then it can be specified only once, as follows:

```
String sql = String.join("\n"
  ,"UPDATE \"public\".\"office\""
  ,"SET (\"address_first\", \"address_second\", \"phone\") ="
  ,"  (SELECT \"public\".\"employee\".\"first_name\","
  ,"           \"public\".\"employee\".\"last_name\", ?"
  ,"    FROM \"public\".\"employee\""
  ,"    WHERE \"public\".\"employee\".\"job_title\" = ?;");
```

Beside the `String.join()` method, JDK 8 also comes with `java.util.StringJoiner`. A `StringJoiner` supports a delimiter (as `String.join()`) but also supports a prefix and a suffix. Expressing our multiline SQL string doesn't require a prefix/suffix; therefore, the delimiter remains our favorite feature:

```
StringJoiner sql = new StringJoiner("\n");
sql.add("UPDATE \"public\".\"office\"")
    .add("SET (\"address_first\", ..., \"phone\") =")
    .add("  (SELECT \"public\".\"employee\".\"first_name\",")
    ...
```

Finally, we cannot mention JDK 8 without touching on its mighty Stream API. More precisely, we are interested in the `Collectors.joining()` collector. This collector works as `String.join()`, and in our case, it looks as follows:

```
String sql = Stream.of(
 "UPDATE \"public\".\"office\"",
 "SET (\"address_first\", \"address_second\", \"phone\") =",
 "  (SELECT \"public\".\"employee\".\"first_name\",",
 "          \"public\".\"employee\".\"last_name\", ?",
 "   FROM \"public\".\"employee\"",
 "   WHERE \"public\".\"employee\".\"job_title\" = ?;")
 .collect(Collectors.joining(String.valueOf("\n")));
```

All the previous examples have a bunch of shortcomings in common. The most important of these is that none of these examples represents a truly multiline string literal, and the degree of readability is seriously affected by the escaping characters and extra quotes needed for each line demarcation. Fortunately, starting with JDK 13 (as a future preview) and ending with JDK 15 (as a final feature), the new text blocks have become the standard for representing multiline string literals. Let's see how.

Introducing text blocks (JDK 13/15)

JDK 13 (JEP 355) offers a preview feature that aims to add support for multiline string literals. Over two versions, in JDK 15 (JEP 378), the text block feature has become final and permanent for use. But that's enough history; let's quickly see how text blocks shape our multiline SQL string:

```
String sql="""
           UPDATE "public"."office"
           SET ("address_first", "address_second", "phone") =
            (SELECT "public"."employee"."first_name",
                   "public"."employee"."last_name", ?
             FROM "public"."employee"
             WHERE "public"."employee"."job_title" = ?""";
```

This is so cool, right?! We immediately see that the readability of our SQL has been restored, and we didn't mess it up with delimiters, line terminators, and concatenations. The text block is concise, easy to update, and easy to understand. The footprint of extra code in our SQL string is zero, and the Java compiler will do the best to create a `String` in the most predictable way possible. Here is another example that embeds a piece of JSON information:

```
String json = """
              {
                "widget": {
                  "debug": "on",
                  "window": {
                    "title": "Sample Widget 1",
```

```
                    "name": "back_window"
                },
                "image": {
                    "src": "images\\sw.png"
                },
                "text": {
                    "data": "Click Me",
                    "size": 39
                }
            }
        }""";
```

How about representing a piece of HTML as a text block? Sure, here it is:

```
String html = """
            <table>
                <tr>
                    <thcolspan="2">Name</th>
                    <th>Age</th>
                </tr>
                <tr>
                    <td>John</td>
                    <td>Smith</td>
                    <td>22</td>
                </tr>
            <table>""";
```

So what is the syntax of a text block?

Hooking text blocks syntax

The syntax of text blocks is quite simple. No bells and whistles, no complicated things – there are just two aspects to keep in mind:

- A text block must start with """ (that is, three double quotation marks) and a newline. We refer to this construction as the *opening delimiter*.
- A text block must end with """ (that is, three double quotation marks). The """ can be on its own line (as a new line) or at the end of the last line of text (as in our example). We refer to this construction as the *closing delimiter*. However, there is a semantic difference between these two approaches (dissected in the next problem).

In this context, the following examples are syntactically correct:

```
String tb = """
            I'm a text block""";
```

```
String tb = """
          I'm a text block
          """;

String tb = """

          I'm a text block""";

String tb = """

          I'm a text block
          """;

String tb = """

          I'm a text block

          """;
```

On the other hand, the following examples are incorrect and lead to compiler errors:

```
String tb = """I'm a text block""";

String tb = "I'm a text block""";

String tb = """I'm a text block";

String tb = ""I'm a text block""";

String tb = """I'm a text block""";

String tb = ""I'm a text block
          """;
```

However, please consider the following best practice.

Important note

By looking on the previous snippets of code, we can shape a best practice for text blocks: use text blocks only when you have a multiline string; if the string fits a single line of code (as in the previous snippets), then use an ordinary string literal, since using text blocks doesn't add any significant value.

In the bundled code, you can practice all the examples from this problem on a piece of SQL, JSON, and HTML.

Important note

For third-party library support, please consider Apache Commons, `StringUtils.join()`, and Guava's `Joiner.on()`.

Next, let's focus on working with text block delimiters.

2. Exemplifying the usage of text block delimiters

Remember from the previous problem, *Creating a multiline SQL, JSON, and HTML string*, that a text block is syntactically delimited by an opening and a closing delimiter, represented by three double quotation marks, `"""`.

The best approach for exemplifying the usage of these delimiters consists of three simple steps: consider an example, inspect the output, and provide a conclusion. This being said, let's start with an example that imitates some of the JEP's examples:

```
String sql= """
           UPDATE "public"."office"
           SET ("address_first", "address_second", "phone") =
             (SELECT "public"."employee"."first_name",
                    "public"."employee"."last_name", ?
              FROM "public"."employee"
              WHERE "public"."employee"."job_title" = ?)""";
```

So by following the JEP examples, we have to align the content with the opening delimiter. It's probable that this alignment style is not consistent with the rest of our code and is not such a good practice. What will happen with the text block content if we rename the `sql` variable `updateSql`, `updateOfficeByEmployeeJobTitle`, or something else? Obviously, in order to preserve the alignment, this will push our content to the right even more. Fortunately, we can shift-left the content without affecting the final result, as follows:

```
String sql = """
  UPDATE "public"."office"
  SET ("address_first", "address_second", "phone") =
    (SELECT "public"."employee"."first_name",
           "public"."employee"."last_name", ?
     FROM "public"."employee"
     WHERE "public"."employee"."job_title" = ?)""";
```

Shifting right the opening/closing delimiters themselves will not affect the resulting `String`. It is unlikely that you'll have a good reason to do this, but just for the sake of completion, the following example produces the same result as the previous two examples:

```
String sql =                                    """
  UPDATE "public"."office"
  SET ("address_first", "address_second", "phone") =
    (SELECT "public"."employee"."first_name",
            "public"."employee"."last_name", ?
     FROM "public"."employee"
     WHERE "public"."employee"."job_title" = ?        """;
```

Now, let's see something more interesting. The opening delimiter doesn't accept content on the same line, while the closing delimiter sits to the right at the end of the content. However, what happens if we move the closing delimiter to its own line, as in the following two examples?

```
String sql= """
            UPDATE "public"."office"
            SET ("address_first", "address_second", "phone") =
              (SELECT "public"."employee"."first_name",
                      "public"."employee"."last_name", ?
               FROM "public"."employee"
               WHERE "public"."employee"."job_title" = ?
            """;

String sql= """
  UPDATE "public"."office"
  SET ("address_first", "address_second", "phone") =
    (SELECT "public"."employee"."first_name",
            "public"."employee"."last_name", ?
     FROM "public"."employee"
     WHERE "public"."employee"."job_title" = ?
  """;
```

This time, the resulting string contains a new line at the end of the content. Check the following figure (the text -- `BEFORE TEXT BLOCK` – and -- `AFTER TEXT BLOCK` -- are just guidelines added via `System.out.println()` to help you delimit the text block itself; they are not necessary and not part of the text block):

```
-- BEFORE TEXT BLOCK --
UPDATE "public"."office"
SET ("address_first", "address_second", "phone") =
  (SELECT "public"."employee"."first_name",
          "public"."employee"."last_name", ?
   FROM "public"."employee"
   WHERE "public"."employee"."job_title" = ?
-- AFTER TEXT BLOCK --
                    A
```

```
-- BEFORE TEXT BLOCK --
UPDATE "public"."office"
SET ("address_first", "address_second", "phone") =
  (SELECT "public"."employee"."first_name",
          "public"."employee"."last_name", ?
   FROM "public"."employee"
   WHERE "public"."employee"."job_title" = ?

-- AFTER TEXT BLOCK --
                    B
```

Figure 1.1: Move the closing delimiter to its own line, vertically aligned with the opening delimiter

In the left figure (*A*) the closing delimiter is at the end of the content. However, in the right figure (*B*), we moved the closing delimiter to its own line, and as you can see, the resulting `String` was enriched with a new line at the end.

Important note

Placing the closing delimiter on its own line will append a new line to the final `String`. Also, pay attention that vertically aligning the opening delimiter, the content, and the closing delimiter to the left margin may result later in extra work. If the variable name is modified, then manual re-indentation is needed to maintain this alignment.

So pay attention to how you place the closing delimiter.

Do you find this weird? Well, that's not all! In the previous example, the closing delimiter was placed on its own line but vertically aligned with the opening delimiter. Let's take a step forward and let's shift-left the end delimiter, as in the following example:

```
String sql= """
            UPDATE "public"."office"
            SET ("address_first", "address_second", "phone") =
              (SELECT "public"."employee"."first_name",
                      "public"."employee"."last_name", ?
               FROM "public"."employee"
               WHERE "public"."employee"."job_title" = ?
""";
```

The following figure reveals the effect of this action:

```
-- BEFORE TEXT BLOCK --
UPDATE "public"."office"
SET ("address_first", "address_second", "phone") =
  (SELECT "public"."employee"."first_name",
          "public"."employee"."last_name", ?
   FROM "public"."employee"
   WHERE "public"."employee"."job_title" = ?

-- AFTER TEXT BLOCK --
                        A
```

```
-- BEFORE TEXT BLOCK --
            UPDATE "public"."office"
            SET ("address_first", "address_second", "phone") =
              (SELECT "public"."employee"."first_name",
                      "public"."employee"."last_name", ?
               FROM "public"."employee"
               WHERE "public"."employee"."job_title" = ?

-- AFTER TEXT BLOCK --
                        B
```

Figure 1.2: Moving the closing delimiter to its own line and shifting it to the left

In the left figure (*A*), we have the closing delimiter on its own line and aligned with the opening delimiter. In the right figure (*B*), we have the effect of the previous code. Moving the closing delimiter to the left results in an additional indentation of the content to the right. The additional indentation depends on how much we shift-left the closing delimiter.

Important note

Placing the closing delimiter on its own line and shifting it to the left will append a new line and additional indentation to the final `String`.

On the other hand, if we move the closing delimiter to its own line and shift it to the right, it doesn't affect the final `String`:

```
String sql= """
             UPDATE "public"."office"
             SET ("address_first", "address_second", "phone") =
               (SELECT "public"."employee"."first_name",
                       "public"."employee"."last_name", ?
                FROM "public"."employee"
                WHERE "public"."employee"."job_title" = ?
                                                      """;
```

This code appends a new line to the final `String` but doesn't affect indentation. In order to better understand the behavior of opening/closing delimiters, you have to explore the next problem.

3. Working with indentation in text blocks

Indentation in text blocks is easy to understand if we have a clear picture of two terms:

- *Incidental* (or *unessential*) white spaces – represent the meaningless white spaces that result from code formatting (*leading* white spaces commonly added by the IDE) or are added intentionally/accidentally at the end of the text (*trailing* white spaces)
- *Essential* white spaces – represent the white spaces that we explicitly add, which are meaningful for the final string

In *Figure 1.3*, you can see the incidental versus essential white spaces in a JSON text block:

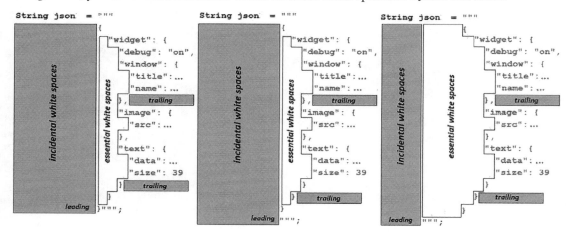

Figure 1.3: Incidental versus essential white spaces in a JSON text block

In the left figure, you can see the incidental versus essential white spaces when the closing delimiter is placed at the end of the content. In the middle figure, the closing delimiter was moved to its own line, while in the right figure, we also shifted to the left.

The incidental (unessential) white spaces are automatically removed by the Java compiler. The compiler removes all incidental trailing spaces (to enforce the same look in different text editors, which may automatically remove trailing white spaces) and uses a special internal algorithm (dissected in the next problem) to determine and remove the incidental leading white spaces. Also, it is important to mention that the line containing the closing delimiter is always part of this check (this is known as the *significant trailing line policy*).

The essential white spaces are preserved in the final string. Basically, as you can intuit from the previous figures, the essential white spaces can be added in two ways, as follows:

- By shifting the closing delimiter left (when this delimiter is on its own line)
- By shifting the content right (by explicitly adding white spaces or by using helper methods dedicated to controlling indentation)

Shifting the closing delimiter and/or the content

Let's start with the following code:

```
String json = """
-------------{
-------------++"widget": {
-------------++++"debug": "on",
-------------++++"window": {
-------------++++++"title": "Sample Widget 1",
-------------++++++"name": "back_window"
-------------++++},
-------------++++"image": {
-------------++++++"src": "images\\sw.png"
-------------++++},
-------------++++"text": {
-------------++++++"data": "Click Me",
-------------++++++"size": 39
-------------++++}
-------------++}
-------------}""";
```

The white spaces highlighted with the "–" sign represent incidental leading white spaces (there are no incidental trailing white spaces), while the white spaces highlighted with the "+" sign represent essential white spaces that you'll see in the resulting String. If we shift-right the whole content while the closing delimiter is at the end of the content, then the explicitly added white spaces are considered incidental and are removed by the compiler:

```
String json = """
---------------------{
---------------------++"widget": {
```

```
---------------------++++"debug": "on",
---------------------++++"window": {
---------------------++++++"title": "Sample Widget 1",
---------------------++++++"name": "back_window"
---------------------++++},
---------------------++++"image": {
---------------------++++++"src": "images\\sw.png"
---------------------++++},
---------------------++++"text": {
---------------------++++++"data": "Click Me",
---------------------++++++"size": 39
---------------------++++}
---------------------++}
---------------------}""";
```

However, if we move the closing delimiter to its own line (vertically aligned with the opening delimiter) and shift-right only the content, then we obtain essential white spaces that remain in the final string:

```
String json = """
--------------+++++++++{
--------------+++++++++++"widget": {
--------------+++++++++++++"debug": "on",
--------------+++++++++++++"window": {
--------------+++++++++++++++"title": "Sample Widget 1",
--------------+++++++++++++++"name": "back_window"
--------------+++++++++++++},
--------------+++++++++++++"image": {
--------------+++++++++++++++"src": "images\\sw.png"
--------------+++++++++++++},
--------------+++++++++++++"text": {
--------------+++++++++++++++"data": "Click Me",
--------------+++++++++++++++"size": 39
--------------+++++++++++++}
--------------+++++++++++}
--------------+++++++++}
              """;
```

Of course, we can add the same essential white spaces by left shifting the closing delimiter:

```
String json = """
-------+++++++{
-------+++++++++++"widget": {
-------+++++++++++++"debug": "on",
```

```
-------++++++++++++"window": {
-------+++++++++++++++"title": "Sample Widget 1",
-------+++++++++++++++"name": "back_window"
-------++++++++++++},
-------++++++++++++"image": {
-------+++++++++++++++"src": "images\\sw.png"
-------++++++++++++},
-------++++++++++++"text": {
-------+++++++++++++++"data": "Click Me",
-------+++++++++++++++"size": 39
-------++++++++++++}
-------++++++++++}
-------+++++++++}
        """;
```

Moreover, we can adjust each line of text by manually adding white spaces, as in the following example:

```
String json = """
--------------{
--------------++++"widget": {
--------------++++++++"debug": "on",
--------------++++++++"window": {
--------------++++++++++++++++++++++++++"title": "Sample Widget 1",
--------------+++++++++++++++++++++++++++"name": "back_window"
--------------++++++++},
--------------++++++++"image":  {
--------------++++++++++++++++++++++++++"src": "images\\sw.png"
--------------++++++++},
--------------++++++++"text":   {
--------------++++++++++++++++++++++++++"data": "Click Me",
--------------+++++++++++++++++++++++++++"size": 39
--------------++++++++}
--------------++++}
--------------}""";
```

Next, let's see some helper methods useful for indentation purposes.

Using indentation methods

Starting with JDK 12, we can add essential white spaces to a literal string via the String.indent(int n) method, where n represents the number of white spaces. This method can also be applied to indent the whole content of a text block, as follows:

```
String json = """
```

```
--------------********{
--------------********++"widget": {
--------------********++++"debug": "on",
--------------********++++"window": {
--------------********++++++"title": "Sample Widget 1",
--------------********++++++"name": "back_window"
--------------********++++},
--------------********++++"image": {
--------------********++++++"src": "images\\sw.png"
--------------********++++},
--------------********++++"text": {
--------------********++++++"data": "Click Me",
--------------********++++++"size": 39
--------------********++++}
--------------********++}
--------------********}""".indent(8);
```

Obviously, the white spaces added via indent() are not visible in the code editor of the IDE, but they are highlighted here via the "*" sign, just to illustrate the effect on the final string. However, when indent() is used, a new line is also appended, even if the closing delimiter is at the end of the content. In this context, moving the closing delimiter to its own line results in the same effect, so don't expect to see two new lines appended. Of course, feel free to practice the bundled code for the real experience.

The indent() method may be useful to align a block of content that contains lines of text placed at the same level of indentation, like the poem that follows:

```
String poem = """
            I would want to establish strength; root-like,
            anchored in the hopes of solidity.

            Forsake the contamination of instability.
            Prove I'm the poet of each line of prose.""";
```

If we manually add white spaces in front of each line of the poem, then the compiler will remove them, so no essential white spaces could be added globally. We can move the closing delimiter to its own line and shift it to the left, or shift-right the content to obtain the desired essential white spaces. However, in such a case, you still need to remove the new line that is added (as a result of moving the closing delimiter to its own line). The easiest way to do this is via the JDK 14 new escape sequence, \. By adding this escape sequence at the end of a line, we instruct the compiler to suppress appending a new line character to that line:

```
String poem = """
            I would want to establish strength; root-like,
            anchored in the hopes of solidity.
```

```
        Forsake the contamination of instability.
        Prove I'm the poet of each line of prose.\
    """;
```

While this escape sequence (\) is dissected in Problem 5, *Using text block just for readability*, let's see a few approaches based on a string API.

Before JDK 11, we can remove this line via a simple regular expression such as replaceFirst("\\s++$", ""), or rely on a third-party helper such as the Apache Commons StringUtils.stripEnd() method. However, starting with JDK 11, we can achieve this goal via String.stripTrailing(), as follows:

```
String poem = """
        I would want to establish strength; root-like,
        anchored in the hopes of solidity.

        Forsake the contamination of instability.
        Prove I'm the poet of each line of prose.
    """.stripTrailing();
```

Now, the content block is indented as a result of shifting the closing delimiter left, and the automatically added new line is removed thanks to the stripTrailing() method.

Important note

As well as stripTrailing(), JDK 11 also comes with stripLeading() and strip(). Also, starting with JDK 15, we have stripIndent(), which removes the leading and trailing white spaces exactly as the compiler does.

However, starting with JDK 12, we can use String.indent(int n), which saves us from adding white spaces manually:

```
String poem = """
        I would want to establish strength; root-like,
        anchored in the hopes of solidity.

        Forsake the contamination of instability.
        Prove I'm the poet of each line of prose."""
    .indent(6)
    .stripTrailing();
```

Now, it is time to move forward and dissect the algorithm for removing incidental white spaces.

4. Removing incidental white spaces in text blocks

Removing incidental white spaces in text blocks is typically a job accomplished by the compiler via a special algorithm. To understand the main aspects of this algorithm, let's go over it with the following example:

```
String json = """                      |Compiler:
----{                                   |Line 01: 4   lws
----++"widget": {                       |Line 02: 6   lws
----++++"debug": "on",                  |Line 03: 8   lws
----++++"window": {                     |Line 04: 8   lws
----++++++"title": "Sample Widget 1",   |Line 05: 10  lws
----++++++"name": "back_window"         |Line 06: 10  lws
----++++},                              |Line 07: 8   lws
----++++"image": {                      |Line 08: 8   lws
----++++++"src": "images\\sw.png"       |Line 09: 10  lws
----++++},                              |Line 10: 8   lws
----++++"text": {                       |Line 11: 8   lws
----++++++"data": "Click Me",           |Line 12: 10  lws
----++++++"size": 39                    |Line 13: 10  lws
----++++}                               |Line 14: 8   lws
----++}                                 |Line 15: 6   lws
----}                                   |Line 16: 4   lws
----""";                                |Line 17: 4   lws
```

We are especially interested in removing the incidental leading white spaces represented in the previous snippet of code, via the "–" sign.

To remove the incidental leading white spaces, the compiler has to inspect all non-blank lines (lines containing only white spaces), so in our case, it will inspect 17 lines. There are 16 lines of JSON code and the closing delimiter line.

The compiler scans each of these 17 lines and counts the number of leading white spaces. The character used to represent the white space is not relevant in this count – it could be simple space, tab, and so on. They all have the same weight of 1, so a single white space is the same as a single tab. This is needed because the compiler can't know how tab characters will be displayed in different text editors (for instance, a tab could be made of four or eight characters). Once this step of the algorithm is done, the compiler knows the exact number of leading white spaces for each of the inspected lines. For instance, line 1 has 4 **leading white spaces (lws)**, line 2 has 6 lws, line 3 has 8 lws, and so on (check the previous snippet of code to see all the numbers).

Important note

Let's quickly look at another text block best practice: Don't mix white spaces and tabs in the same text block. This way, you enforce indentation consistency and avoid any potential irregular indentation.

At this point, the compiler computes the minimum value of those numbers, and the result (in this case, 4) represents the number of incidental leading white spaces that should be removed from each of the 17 lines. So in the final result, at least one of the lines has no leading white space. Of course, the essential white space (an additional indentation represented via the "+" sign) remains untouched. For instance, in line 5, we have 10 lws – 4 incidental lws = 6 essential lws that remain untouched.

In the bundled code, you can find three more JSON examples that you can use to practice this algorithm. Now, we will tackle some text block readability aspects.

5. Using text blocks just for readability

Using text blocks just for readability can be translated as making a string look like a text block but act as a single-line string literal. This is especially useful for formatting long lines of text. For instance, we may want to have the following SQL string look like a text block (for readability purposes) but act as a single-line string literal (in the sense of being compact when we pass it to the database):

```
SELECT "public"."employee"."first_name"
FROM "public"."employee"
WHERE "public"."employee"."job_title" = ?
```

Starting with JDK 14, we can accomplish this goal via the new escape sequence, \ (a single backslash). By adding this escape sequence at the end of a line, we instruct the compiler to suppress appending a new line character to that line. So in our case, we can express the SQL as a single-line string literal, as follows:

```
String sql = """
            SELECT "public"."employee"."first_name" \
            FROM "public"."employee" \
            WHERE "public"."employee"."job_title" = ?\
            """;
```

Pay attention to not adding any white spaces after \ because you'll get an error.

If we throw this text block in a System.out.println(), then the output reveals the single-line string literal, as follows:

```
SELECT "public"."employee"."first_name" FROM "public"."employee" WHERE
"public"."employee"."job_title" = ?
```

Next, let's check out another example, as follows:

```
String sql = """
  UPDATE "public"."office" \
  SET ("address_first", "address_second", "phone") = \
    (SELECT "public"."employee"."first_name", \
            "public"."employee"."last_name", ? \
    FROM "public"."employee" \
    WHERE "public"."employee"."job_title" = ?\
  """;
```

This time, the resulting string is not exactly what we want because the essential white space is preserved. This means that the single-line string is sprinkled with sequences of spaces that we should reduce to a single space. This is where a regular expression can help:

```
sql.trim().replaceAll(" +", " ");
```

Done! Now, we have a single-line SQL string that looks like a text block in an IDE.

Next, let's assume that we want to print on a nice background the following poem wrapped in a text block:

```
String poem = """
              An old silent pond...
          A frog jumps into the pond,
             splash!! Silence again.
          """;
```

Adding a background to this poem will result in something like the following figure:

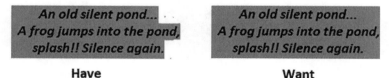

Have   **Want**

Figure 1.4: Adding a background to the poem

Important note

The colored background is just a guideline for alignment, as white on white would not be legible.

Since the compiler removes the trailing white space, we will obtain something as shown in the left figure. Obviously, we want something as shown in the right figure, so we need to find a way to preserve the trailing white space as essential. Starting with JDK 14, we can do that via the new escape sequence, \s.

We can repeat this escape sequence for every space as follows (we add three white spaces to the first line and two white spaces to the last line; this way, we obtain a symmetrical text block):

```
String poem = """
                An old silent pond...\s\s\s
            A frog jumps into the pond,
              splash!! Silence again.\s\s
            """;
```

Alternatively, we can manually add white spaces and a single \s at the end of the line. This is possible because the compiler preserves any white spaces in front of \s:

```
String poem = """
                An old silent pond...  \s
            A frog jumps into the pond,
              splash!! Silence again. \s
            """;
```

Done! Now, we have preserved white spaces, so when the background color is applied, we will obtain something as shown on the right side of *Figure 1.4*.

Next, let's focus on escaping characters.

6. Escaping quotes and line terminators in text blocks

Escaping double quotes is necessary only when we want to embed, in the text block, the sequence of three double quotes ("""), as follows:

```
String txt = """
            She told me
                \"""I have no idea what's going on\"""
            """;
```

Escaping """ can be done with \""". There is no need to write \"\"\".

The resulting string will look like this:

```
She told me
        """I have no idea what's going on"""
```

Whenever you need to embed " or "", simply do it as follows:

```
String txt = """
            She told me
                "I have no idea what's going on"
            """;

String txt = """
```

```
        She told me
                ""I have no idea what's going on""
    """;
```

So even if it works, don't do this, since is not necessary:

```
String txt = """
        She told me
                \"I have no idea what's going on\"
        """;
```

```
String txt = """
        She told me
                \"\"I have no idea what's going on\"\"
        """;
```

However, a construction such as """" (where the first " represents a double quote and the last """ represents the closing delimiter of the text block) will raise an error. In such a case, you can place a space as " """ or escape the double quote as \"""".

By definition, a text block represents string literals spanning multiple lines, so there is no need to explicitly escape line terminators (new lines), such as \n, \r, or \f. Just add new lines of text in the text block, and the compiler will take care of line terminators. Of course, this doesn't mean that using them doesn't work. For instance, obtaining a text block that has interleaved blank lines can be done via \n, as follows:

```
String sql = """
            SELECT "public"."employee"."first_name",\n
                    "public"."employee"."last_name", ?\n
            FROM "public"."employee"\n
            WHERE "public"."employee"."job_title" = ?
            """;
```

Using escape sequences (for example, \b, \t, \r, \n, \f, and so on) in text blocks can be done exactly like they would be done in old-school string literals. For instance, there is nothing wrong here:

```
String txt = """
            \b\bShe told me\n
        \t""I have no idea what's going on""
        """;
```

However, the same thing can be obtained without escape sequences (consider \t (tab) as eight white spaces):

```
String txt = """
            She told me
```

```
                    ""I have no idea what's going on""
        """;
```

You can practice all these examples in the bundled code.

Important note

Let's quickly look at another text block best practice: Adding escape sequences explicitly may negatively affect the readability of the text block, so use them carefully and only when they are really needed. For instance, explicit \n and \" are rarely necessary for text blocks.

Speaking about the \n line terminator (new line), it is important to be aware of the following note.

Important note

Probably the most used line terminator in Java is \n (Unix, **Line Feed (LF)**), but we can also use \r (Windows, **Carriage Return (CR)**) or \n\r (Windows, **Carriage Return Line Feed (CRLF)**). No matter which of these we prefer, Java text blocks always use \n (LF). First, the compiler normalizes all line breaks that are not added explicitly via escape sequences to \n (LF). Second, after the normalization of line terminators and managed indentation, the compiler handles all the explicit escape sequences (\n (LF), \f (FF), \r(CR), and so on), as in any string literal. Practically, this allows us to copy into a text block a legacy Java string containing escape sequences, obtaining the expected result without further modifications.

If you ever need to use the line terminator specific to your operating system, then you have to explicitly replace it after text block normalization via String.replaceAll(), as String::replaceAll("\n", System.lineSeparator()).

Embedding in a text block an escape sequence can be done as usual via the \\ construction. Here is an example of embedding the \" escape sequence as \\":

```
String sql = """
   SELECT \\"public\\".\\"employee\\".\\"first_name\\",
          \\"public\\".\\"employee\\".\\"last_name\\", ?
   FROM \\"public\\".\\"employee\\"
   WHERE \\"public\\".\\"employee\\".\\"job_title\\" = ?
   """;
```

You can check the output in the bundled code. Now, let's see how we can translate escape sequences programmatically.

7. Translating escape sequences programmatically

We already know that the compiler is responsible for the translation of escape sequences, and most of the time, there is no need to explicitly interfere in this process. But there are cases when we may need programmatic access to this process (for instance, to explicitly un-escape a string before passing it to a function).

Starting with JDK 15, we can accomplish this via `String.translateEscapes()`, which is capable of un-escape sequences such as \t, \n, \b, and so on, and octal numbers (\0–\377). However, this method doesn't translate Unicode escapes (\uXXXX).

We can perform an equality test in order to reveal how `translateEscapes()` works:

```
String newline = "\\n".translateEscapes();
System.out.println(("\n".equals(newline)) ? "yes" : "no");
```

As you can already intuit, the result is *yes*.

Next, let's assume that we want to use an external service that prints addresses on parcels. The function responsible for this task gets a string representing the address without containing escape sequences. The problem is that our customer's addresses pass through a formatting process that patches them with escape sequences, as in the following example:

```
String address = """
                 JASON MILLER (\\"BIGBOY\\")\\n
                 \\tMOUNT INC\\n
                 \\t104 SEAL AVE\\n
                 \\tMIAMI FL 55334 1200\\n
                 \\tUSA
                 """;
```

The following figure reveals how the resulting string will look if we don't translate escapes of the address (left side) and how it will look if we do (right side). Of course, our goal is to obtain the address from the right side and send it to print:

```
JASON MILLER (\"BIGBOY\")\n      JASON MILLER ("BIGBOY")
\tMOUNT INC\n
\t104 SEAL AVE\n                      MOUNT INC
\tMIAMI FL 55334 1200\n
\tUSA                                 104 SEAL AVE

                                      MIAMI FL 55334 1200

                                      USA
```

Figure 1.5: We want the string from the right side

Translation of escapes can be done programmatically via `String.translateEscapes()`, right before sending the result to the external service. Here is the code:

```
String translatedAddress = address.translateEscapes();
```

Now, `translatedAddress` can be passed to the external printing service. As an exercise, you can think about how to exploit this method to write a parser of source code, provided via Java or another programming language.

Important note

Similar results (of course, read the documentation to obtain the fine-grained information) can be obtained via Apache Commons' Lang third-party library support. Please consider `StringEscapeUtils.unescapeJava(String)`.

Next, let's talk about embedding expressions in text blocks.

8. Formatting text blocks with variables/expressions

In Java, it is a common practice to format string literals with variables/expressions to obtain dynamic strings. For instance, we can create a dynamic piece of XML string via the following well-known concatenation:

```
String fn = "Jo";
String ln = "Kym";


String str = "<user><firstName>" + fn
    + "</firstName><lastName>" + ln + "</lastName></user>";
```

```
// output
<user><firstName>Jo</firstName><lastName>Kym</lastName></user>
```

Of course, this tiny construction has serious issues from a readability perspective. XML code is human-readable if it is formatted and indented accordingly; otherwise, is really hard to follow its hierarchy. So, can we express this XML to look like the following figure?

```
<user>                              <user>
    <firstName>Jo</firstName>           <firstName>
    <lastName>Kym</lastName>             Jo
</user>                                 </firstName>
                                        <lastName>
                                         Kym
                                        </lastName>
                                    </user>
```

Figure 1.6: Formatted XML

Sure we can! By using some escape sequences (for instance, \n, \t, and \s), white spaces, and so on, we can construct a String to look like *Figure 1.6*. However, it would be better to express this concatenation via a text block. Maybe we can achieve the same readability in the IDE's code editor and console (at runtime). A possible approach looks like this:

```
String xml = """
            <user>
               <firstName>\
    """
+ fn
+ """
            </firstName>
               <lastName>\
    """
+ ln
+ """
            </lastName>
            </user>
    """;
```

So we can concatenate text blocks exactly like string literals via the "+" operator. Cool! The output of this code corresponds to the left side of *Figure 1.6*. On the other hand, the right side of *Figure 1.6* can be achieved as follows:

```
String xml = """
            <user>
               <firstName>
    """
+ fn.indent(4)
+ """
            </firstName>
               <lastName>
    """
+ ln.indent(4)
+ """
            </lastName>
            </user>
    """;
```

Well, while the resulting string looks good in both cases, we cannot say the same thing about the code itself. It still has a low readability rate.

Important note

By looking at the previous two snippets of code, we can easily conclude a best practice for text blocks: use them only when they significantly contribute to code clarity and the readability of multiline strings. Also, avoid declaring text blocks in complex expressions (for instance, in lambda expressions), since they may affect the readability of the entire expression. It is better to extract text blocks separately in static variables and refer to them in complex expressions.

Let's try another approach. This time, let's use a `StringBuilder` to obtain the result from the left side of *Figure 1.6*:

```
StringBuilder sbXml = new StringBuilder();

sbXml.append("""
        <user>
            <firstName>""")
    .append(fn)
    .append("""
        </firstName>
            <lastName>""")
    .append(ln)
    .append("""
        </lastName>
        </user>""");
```

Then, obtaining the result from the right side of *Figure 1.6* can be done as follows:

```
StringBuilder sbXml = new StringBuilder();

sbXml.append("""
        <user>
            <firstName>
        """)
    .append(fn.indent(4))
    .append("""
          </firstName>
          <lastName>
        """)
    .append(ln.indent(4))
    .append("""
          </lastName>
        </user>
        """);
```

So we can use text blocks in `StringBuilder`/`StringBuffer` exactly as we use string literals. While the resulting string corresponds to the examples from *Figure 1.6*, the code itself is still unsatisfactory from the readability perspective.

Let's give it another try via the JDK 1.4, `MessageFormat.format()`. First, let's shape the example from *Figure 1.6*, left side:

```
String xml = MessageFormat.format("""
                    <user>
                        <firstName>{0}</firstName>
                        <lastName>{1}</lastName>
                    </user>
                    """, fn, ln);
```

And obtaining the result from *Figure 1.6* (right side) can be done as follows:

```
String xml = MessageFormat.format("""
                    <user>
                        <firstName>
                         {0}
                        </firstName>
                        <lastName>
                         {1}
                        </lastName>
                    </user>
                    """, fn, ln);
```

The text blocks and `MessageFormat.format()` combo is a winning approach. The code readability is obviously better. But, let's go further, and let's give it a try in JDK 5 `String.format()`. As usual, *Figure 1.6* (left side) is first:

```
String xml = String.format("""
                    <user>
                        <firstName>%s</firstName>
                        <lastName>%s</lastName>
                    </user>
                    """, fn, ln);
```

And obtaining the result from *Figure 1.6* (right side) can be done as follows:

```
String xml = String.format("""
                    <user>
                        <firstName>
                         %s
                        </firstName>
                        <lastName>
```

```
                    %s
                </lastName>
            </user>
        """, fn, ln);
```

The text blocks and `String.format()` combo is another winning approach but is not the latest feature that we can exploit. Starting with JDK 15, `String.format()` has a more convenient companion named `formatted()`. Here is `String.formatted()` at work to reproduce *Figure 1.6* (left side):

```
String xml = """
        <user>
            <firstName>%s</firstName>
            <lastName>%s</lastName>
        </user>
        """.formatted(fn, ln);
```

And obtaining the result from *Figure 1.6* (right side) can be done as follows:

```
String xml = """
        <user>
            <firstName>
             %s
            </firstName>
            <lastName>
             %s
            </lastName>
        </user>
        """.formatted(fn, ln);
```

That is the best we can do. We managed to achieve the same level of readability in the IDE's code editor and runtime for a text block containing dynamic parts (variables). Cool, isn't it?!

From the performance perspective, you can find a benchmark of these approaches in the bundled code. In the following figure, you can see the results of this benchmark on an Intel® Core™ i7-3612QM CPU @ 2.10GHz machine with Windows 10, but feel free to test it on different machines, since the results are highly dependent on the machine.

Benchmark	Mode	Cnt	Score		Error	Units
Main.concatenation	avgt	5	0.670	±	0.004	ns/op
Main.messageFormat	avgt	5	3199.252	±	116.859	ns/op
Main.stringBuilder	avgt	5	318.641	±	9.198	ns/op
Main.stringFormat	avgt	5	1416.266	±	18.024	ns/op
Main.stringFormatted	avgt	5	1409.030	±	42.547	ns/op

Figure 1.7: Benchmark results

Conforming to these results, concatenation via the "+" operator is the fastest, while the `MessageFormat.format()` is the slowest.

9. Adding comments in text blocks

Question: Can we add comments in text blocks?

Official answer (according to the Java Language Specification): The lexical grammar implies that comments do not occur within character literals, string literals, or text blocks.

You might be tempted to try something like this, thinking it's a quick hack, but I really don't recommend it:

```
String txt = """
              foo   /* some comment */
              buzz //another comment
              """.replace("some_regex","");
```

Short answer: No, we cannot have comments in text blocks.

Let's move on and talk about mixing ordinary string literals with text blocks.

10. Mixing ordinary string literals with text blocks

Before mixing ordinary string literals with text blocks, let's consider the following statement: How different is an ordinary string literal from a text block? We can answer this question via the following snippet of code:

```
String str = "I love Java!";
String txt = """
              I love Java!""";


System.out.println(str == txt);       // true
System.out.println(str.equals(txt)); // true
```

Wow! So our snippet of code prints `true` twice. This means that an ordinary string literal and a text block are similar at runtime. We can define text blocks as string literals that span across multiple lines of text and use triple quotes as their opening and closing delimiter. How so? First, the instance produced from an ordinary string literal and a text block is of type `java.lang.String`. Second, we have to look at the compiler internals. Basically, the compiler adds strings to a special cached pool named a **String Constant Pool** (**SCP**) (more details about SCP are available in *Java Coding Problems*, *First Edition*, Problem 48, *Immutable string*) to optimize the memory usage, and starting with JDK 13, text blocks can be found in the same pool as strings.

Now that we know that there are no major differences in how ordinary string literals and text blocks are treated internally, we can be confident to mix them in a simple concatenation (basically, a text block can be used anywhere an ordinary string literal can be used):

```
String tom = "Tom";
String jerry = """
                Jerry""";


System.out.println(tom + " and " + jerry); // Tom and Jerry
```

Moreover, since a text block returns a String, we can use the entire arsenal of methods that we use for ordinary string literals. Here is an example:

```
System.out.println(tom.toUpperCase() + " AND "
    + jerry.toUpperCase()); // TOM AND JERRY
```

Also, as you just saw in *Problem 8*, *Formatting text blocks with variables/expressions*, text blocks can be used and mixed with ordinary string literals in StringBuilder(Buffer), MessageFormat.format(), String.format(), and String.formatted().

11. Mixing regular expression with text blocks

Regular expressions can be used with text blocks. Let's consider a simple string, as follows:

```
String nameAndAddress
    = "Mark Janson;243 West Main St;Louisville;40202;USA";
```

So here we have a name (Mark Janson) and some details about his address, delimited by a semicolon (;). It is a common scenario to pass such strings through regular expressions and extract the information as named groups. In this example, we can consider five named groups as follows:

- name: should contain the person's name (Mark Janson)
- address: should contain the person's street information (243 West Main St)
- city: should contain the person's city (Louisville)
- zip: should contain the city's zip code (40202)
- country: should contain the country's name (USA)

A regular expression that can match these named groups may look as follows:

```
(?<name>[ a-zA-Z]+);(?<address>[ 0-9a-zA-Z]+);(?<city>[ a-zA-Z]+);(?<zip>[\\
d]+);(?<country>[ a-zA-Z]+)$
```

This is a single-line string, so we can use it via the Pattern API, as follows:

```
Pattern pattern = Pattern.compile("(?<name>[ a-zA-Z]+);(?<address>[ 0-9a-zA-
Z]+);(?<city>[ a-zA-Z]+);(?<zip>[\\d]+);(?<country>[ a-zA-Z]+)$");
```

However, as you can see, writing our regex like this has a serious impact on readability. Fortunately, we can employ text blocks to solve this issue, as follows:

```
Pattern pattern = Pattern.compile("""
        (?<name>[ a-zA-Z]+);\
```

```
    (?<address>[ 0-9a-zA-Z]+);\
    (?<city>[ a-zA-Z]+);\
    (?<zip>[\\d]+);\
    (?<country>[ a-zA-Z]+)$""");
```

This is more readable, right? The only thing that we should take care of is to use the JDK 14 new escape sequence, \ (a single backslash), to remove the trailing line feed at the end of each line.

Next, you can simply match the address and extract the named groups, as follows:

```
if (matcher.matches()) {

  String name = matcher.group("name");
  String address = matcher.group("address");
  String city = matcher.group("city");
  String zip = matcher.group("zip");
  String country = matcher.group("country");
}
```

If you want just to extract the names of the groups, then you can rely on JDK 20's namedGroups():

```
// {country=5, city=3, zip=4, name=1, address=2}
System.out.println(matcher.namedGroups());
```

Actually, namedGroups() returns an unmodifiable Map<String, Integer>, where the key is the group name and the value is the group number. Furthermore, JDK 20 has also added the hasMatch() method, which returns true if the matcher contains a valid match from a previous match or find operation:

```
if (matcher.hasMatch()) { ... }
```

Note that hasMatch() will not attempt to trigger a match against the pattern as matches() does. When you need to check for valid matches in different places of your code, hasMatch() is preferable, since it will not perform matches. So, you can call matches() once, and in subsequent checks for valid matches, just call hasMatch().

Moreover, if you just need to extract the input subsequence captured for each named group by a given delimiter, then you can rely on JDK 21's splitWithDelimiters(CharSequence input, int limit). For instance, our string can be split by a semicolon (regex, ;+), as follows:

```
String[] result = Pattern.compile(";+")
  .splitWithDelimiters(nameAndAddress, 0);
```

The returned array contains the extracted data and the delimiters, as follows:

```
[Mark Janson, ;, 243 West Main St, ;,
Louisville, ;, 40202, ;, USA]
```

The second argument of `splitWithDelimiters()` is an integer representing how many times to apply the regex. If the `limit` argument is 0, then the pattern will be applied as many times as possible, and the trailing empty strings, whether substrings or delimiters, will be discarded. If it is positive, then the pattern will be applied, at most, the `limit` - 1 times, and if it is negative, the pattern will be applied as many times as possible.

12. Checking if two text blocks are isomorphic

Two text blocks are isomorphic if the resulting strings are isomorphic. Two string literals are considered isomorphic if we can map every character of the first string to every character of the second string in a one-to-one fashion.

For example, consider that the first string is "abbcdd" and the second string is "qwwerr". The one-to-one character mapping is shown in *Figure 1.8*:

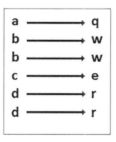

Figure 1.8: One-to-one character mapping between two strings

So as you can see in *Figure 1.8*, character "a" of the first string can be replaced by character "q" of the second string. Moreover, character "b" of the first string can be replaced by character "w" of the second string, character "c" by character "e", and character "d" by character "r". Obviously, vice versa is also true. In other words, these two strings are isomorphic.

How about the strings "aab" and "que"? These two strings are not isomorphic because "a" cannot be mapped to both "q" and "u".

If we extrapolate this logic to text blocks, then *Figure 1.9* is exactly what we need:

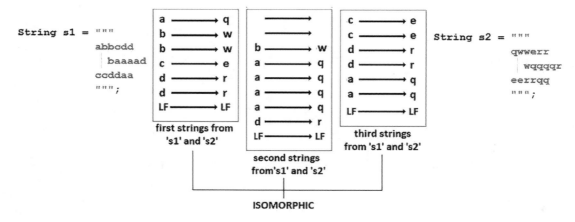

Figure 1.9: Two isomorphic text blocks

Two text blocks are isomorphic if their string lines are isomorphic in a one-to-one fashion. Moreover, notice that essential white spaces and **Line Terminators** (LF) should be mapped as well, while incidental leading/trailing white spaces are ignored.

The algorithm for ordinary string literals and text blocks is exactly the same, and it relies on *hashing* (more details about this topic are available in *Example 6: Hash table* in the *The Complete Coding Interview Guide in Java* book) and consists of the following steps:

1. Check if the two text blocks (s1 and s2) have the same length. If their lengths differ, then the text blocks are not isomorphic.
2. Create an empty map that will store mappings of the characters from s1 (as keys) to those of s2 (as values).
3. Pick up the first/next character from s1 (chs1) and s2 (chs2).
4. Check if chs1 is present as a key in the map.
5. If chs1 is present in the map as a key, then it has to be mapped to a value from s2 that is equal to chs2; otherwise, the text blocks are not isomorphic.
6. If chs1 is not present in the map as a key, then the map shouldn't contain chs2 as a value; otherwise, the text blocks are not isomorphic.
7. If chs1 is not present in the map as a key and the map doesn't contain chs2 as a value, then put (chs1 and chs2) in the map – chs1 as a key and chs2 as a value.
8. Repeat step 3 until the entire text block (s1) is processed.
9. If the entire text block (s1) was processed, then the text blocks are isomorphic.

In code lines, this O(n) algorithm can be expressed as follows:

```
public static boolean isIsomorphic(String s1, String s2) {

    // step 1
```

```
    if (s1 == null || s2 == null
                  || s1.length() != s2.length()) {
      return false;
    }


    // step 2
    Map<Character, Character> map = new HashMap<>();


    // step 3(8)
    for (int i = 0; i < s1.length(); i++) {


      char chs1 = s1.charAt(i);
      char chs2 = s2.charAt(i);


      // step 4
      if (map.containsKey(chs1)) {
        // step 5
        if (map.get(chs1) != chs2) {
          return false;
        }
      } else {
        // step 6
        if (map.containsValue(chs2)) {
          return false;
        }


        // step 7
        map.put(chs1, chs2);
      }
    }


    // step 9
    return true;
  }
```

Done! You can practice this example in the bundled code. This was the last problem covering text block topics. It is time to move on and discuss string concatenation.

13. Concatenating strings versus StringBuilder

Check out the following plain string concatenation:

```
String str1 = "I love";
```

```
String str2 = "Java";
String str12 = str1 + " " + str2;
```

We know that the `String` class is immutable (a created `String` cannot be modified). This means that creating `str12` requires an intermediary string that represents the concatenation of `str1` with white space. So after `str12` is created, we know that `str1 + " "` is just noise or garbage, since we cannot refer to it further.

In such scenarios, the recommendation is to use a `StringBuilder`, since it is a mutable class and we can append strings to it. So this is how the following statement was born: In Java, don't use the "+" operator to concatenate strings! Use `StringBuilder`, which is much faster.

Have you heard this statement before? I'm pretty sure you have, especially if you still run your applications on JDK 8 or even on a previous release. Well, this statement is not a myth, and it was true for sure at some moment in time, but is it still valid in the era of smart compilers?

For instance, consider the following two snippets of code that represent a simple concatenation of strings:

```
public static String concatViaPlus(          public static String concatViaStringBuilder(
      String str1, String str2,                     String str1, String str2,
      String str3, String str4) {                   String str3, String str4) {

   return str1 + str2 + str3 + str4;          StringBuilder sb = new StringBuilder();
}
                                              sb.append(str1)
                                                    .append(str2)
                                                    .append(str3)
                                                    .append(str4);

                                              return sb.toString();
                                           }
```

Figure 1.10: String concatenation vs. StringBuilder

In JDK 8, which approach (from *Figure 1.10*) is better?

JDK 8

Let's inspect the bytecode produced by these two snippets of code (use `javap -c -p` or Apache Commons **Byte Code Engineering Library** (**BCEL**); we have used the BCEL). The `concatViaPlus()` bytecode looks as follows:

```
JDK 8 bytecode of Strings#concatViaPlus()
-------------------------------------------------------
Code(maxStack = 2, maxLocals = 4, code_length = 27)
  0:    new                  <java.lang.StringBuilder> (14)
  3:    dup
  4:    invokespecial        java.lang.StringBuilder.<init> ()V (16)
  7:    aload_0
  8:    invokevirtual        java.lang.StringBuilder.append (Ljava/lang/String;)Ljava/lang/StringBuilder; (17)
 11:    aload_1
 12:    invokevirtual        java.lang.StringBuilder.append (Ljava/lang/String;)Ljava/lang/StringBuilder; (17)
 15:    aload_2
 16:    invokevirtual        java.lang.StringBuilder.append (Ljava/lang/String;)Ljava/lang/StringBuilder; (17)
 19:    aload_3
 20:    invokevirtual        java.lang.StringBuilder.append (Ljava/lang/String;)Ljava/lang/StringBuilder; (17)
 23:    invokevirtual        java.lang.StringBuilder.toString ()Ljava/lang/String; (21)
 26:    areturn
```

Figure 1.11: JDK 8 bytecode of concatViaPlus()

The JDK 8 compiler is smart enough to use a `StringBuilder` under the hood to shape our concatenation via the "+" operator. If you check the bytecode (skipped here for brevity) generated from `concatViaStringBuilder()`, then you'll see something more or less similar to *Figure 1.11*.

In JDK 8, the compiler knows when and how to optimize the bytecode via `StringBuilder`. In other words, the explicit usage of `StringBuilder` doesn't come with a significant benefit over plain concatenation via the "+" operator. There are many simple cases where this statement applies. What does a benchmark have to say about this? Check out the results:

Benchmark	Mode	Cnt	Score	Error	Units
Main.concatViaPlus	avgt	90	37.370 ± 0.215		ns/op
Main.concatViaStringBuilder	avgt	90	78.841 ± 1.000		ns/op

Figure 1.12: JDK 8 benchmark concatViaPlus() versus concatViaStringBuilder()

Obviously, concatenation via the "+" operator has won this game. Let's repeat this logic for JDK 11.

JDK 11

JDK 11 produces the following bytecode for `concatViaPlus()`:

```
JDK 11 bytecode of Strings#concatViaPlus()
-----------------------------------------------------------------
Code(maxStack = 4, maxLocals = 4, code_length = 10)
0:     aload_0
1:     aload_1
2:     aload_2
3:     aload_3
4:     invokedynamic      0:makeConcatWithConstants (Ljava/lang/String;Ljava/lang/String;
                                                     Ljava/lang/String;Ljava/lang/String;)
                                                     Ljava/lang/String; (14)       00

9:     areturn
```

Figure 1.13: JDK 11 bytecode of concatViaPlus()

We can immediately observe a big difference here. This time, the concatenation is accomplished via a call to `invokedynamic` (this is a dynamic call), which acts as a delegator for our code. Here, it delegates the code to `makeConcatWithConstants()`, which is a method of the `StringConcatFactory` class. While you can find this in the JDK documentation, pay attention that this class API was not created to be called directly. This class was specially created and designed to serve bootstrap methods for `invokedynamic` instructions. Before going further, let's look at an important note that you should consider.

> **Important note**
>
> The `invokedynamic` delegates/passes our concatenation code to be solved by code that is not part of the bytecode (this is why we cannot see the actual code (instructions) that solve our code). This is extremely powerful because it allows the Java engineers to continue the optimization process of the concatenation logic, while we can take advantage of it by simply moving to the next JDK. The code doesn't even need to be recompiled to take advantage of further optimizations.

Fun fact: The *indify* term comes from `invokedynamic`, also known as *indy*. It was introduced in JDK 7 and is used in JDK 8 lambda implementations. Since this instruction was quite useful, it becomes a solution for many other things, including JEP 280: *Indify String Concatenation*, introduced in JDK 9. I preferred to use it here with JDK 11, but this feature is available starting with JDK 9+, so you can give it a try in JDK 17 or 20, for example.

In a nutshell, `invokedynamic` works like this:

- The compiler appends an `invokedynamic` call at the point of concatenation.
- The `invokedynamic` call first executes the bootstrap method `makeConcat[WithConstants]`.
- The `invokedynamic` method calls `makeConcat[WithConstants]`, which is a bootstrap method meant to call the actual code responsible for concatenation.
- The `makeConcat[WithConstants]` uses an internal strategy to determine the best method of solving the concatenation.

- The method that fits the best is called, and the concatenation logic takes place.

This way, JEP 280 adds great flexibility, since JDK 10, 11, 12, 13, and so on can use different strategies and methods to accommodate string concatenation in the best possible way for our context.

How about the bytecode of `concatViaStringBuilder()`? This method doesn't take advantage of invokeddynamic (it relies on the classic invokevirtual instruction), as you can see here:

```
JDK 11 bytecode of Strings#concatViaStringBuilder()
--------------------------------------------------------------
Code(maxStack = 2, maxLocals = 5, code_length = 34)
0:    new                 <java.lang.StringBuilder> (18)
3:    dup
4:    invokespecial       java.lang.StringBuilder.<init> ()V (20)
7:    astore              %4
9:    aload               %4
11:   aload_0
12:   invokevirtual       java.lang.StringBuilder.append (Ljava/lang/String;)Ljava/lang/StringBuilder; (21)
15:   aload_1
16:   invokevirtual       java.lang.StringBuilder.append (Ljava/lang/String;)Ljava/lang/StringBuilder; (21)
19:   aload_2
20:   invokevirtual       java.lang.StringBuilder.append (Ljava/lang/String;)Ljava/lang/StringBuilder; (21)
23:   aload_3
24:   invokevirtual       java.lang.StringBuilder.append (Ljava/lang/String;)Ljava/lang/StringBuilder; (21)
27:   pop
28:   aload               %4
30:   invokevirtual       java.lang.StringBuilder.toString ()Ljava/lang/String; (25)
33:   areturn
```

Figure 1.14: JDK 11 bytecode of concatViaStringBuilder()

I'm sure that you're curious about which bytecode performs better, so here are the results:

```
Benchmark                          Mode   Cnt    Score     Error   Units
Main.concatViaPlus                 avgt    90   47.825 ± 0.177   ns/op
Main.concatViaStringBuilder        avgt    90   76.861 ± 0.451   ns/op
```

Figure 1.15: JDK 11, benchmark concatViaPlus() versus concatViaStringBuilder()

The results of these benchmarks were obtained on an Intel® Core™ i7-3612QM CPU @ 2.10GHz machine with Windows 10, but feel free to test it on different machines and different JDK versions, since the results are highly dependent on the machine.

Again, the `concatViaPlus()` wins this game. In the bundled code, you can find the complete code for this example. Moreover, you'll find the code for inspecting bytecode and benchmarking the concatenation in a loop via the "+" operator and StringBuilder. Give it a spin!

14. Converting int to String

As usual, in Java, we can accomplish a task in multiple ways. For instance, we can convert an int (primitive integer) to String via Integer.toString(), as follows:

```java
public String intToStringV1(int v) {
  return Integer.toString(v);
}
```

Alternatively, you can accomplish this task via a quite common hack (the code reviewer will raise his eyebrow here), consisting of concatenating an empty string with the integer:

```java
public String intToStringV2(int v) {
  return "" + v;
}
```

`String.valueOf()` can also be used as follows:

```java
public String intToStringV3(int v) {
  return String.valueOf(v);
}
```

A more esoteric approach via `String.format()` is as follows:

```java
public String intToStringV4(int v) {
  return String.format("%d", v);
}
```

These methods also work for a boxed integer and, therefore, for an `Integer` object. Since boxing and unboxing are costly operations, we strive to avoid them unless they are really necessary. However, you never know when an unboxing operation may sneak "behind the scenes" and ruin the performance of your application. To verify this statement, imagine that, for each of the previous methods, we also have its equal getting an `Integer` instead of an `int`. Here is one of them (the rest were skipped for brevity):

```java
public String integerToStringV1(Integer vo) {
  return Integer.toString(vo);
}
```

Benchmarking all these methods results in the following figure:

Benchmark	Mode	Cnt	Score	Error	Units
Main.intToStringV1	avgt	20	19.499	± 0.428	ns/op
Main.intToStringV2	avgt	20	20.145	± 0.243	ns/op
Main.intToStringV3	avgt	20	19.207	± 0.148	ns/op
Main.intToStringV4	avgt	20	171.027	± 0.641	ns/op
Main.integerToStringV1	avgt	20	27.255	± 0.207	ns/op
Main.integerToStringV2	avgt	20	29.618	± 0.056	ns/op
Main.integerToStringV3	avgt	20	27.231	± 0.064	ns/op
Main.integerToStringV4	avgt	20	166.432	± 0.337	ns/op

Figure 1.16: The results of benchmarking int to String conversion

There are two crystal-clear conclusions that we can derive from here:

- Using `String.format()` is very slow, and it should be avoided for `int` and `Integer`.
- All solutions that use an `Integer` are slower than those using an `int` primitive. So avoid unnecessary unboxing, even for such simple cases, since they may cause serious performance penalties.

The results of these benchmarks were obtained on an Intel® Core™ i7-3612QM CPU @ 2.10GHz machine with Windows 10, but feel free to test it on different machines, since the results are highly dependent on the machine.

Next, let's change the topic and talk about Java locales.

15. Introducing string templates

Until JDK 21, Java allows us to perform string composition for SQL, JSON, XML, and so on via different approaches, covered earlier in *Problem 8*. In that problem, you can see how to use text blocks and embedded expressions via simple concatenation, using the plus (+) operator, `StringBuilder.append()`, `String.format()`, `formatted()`, and so on. While using the plus (+) operator and `StringBuilder.append()` can be cumbersome and affect readability, the `String.format()` and `formatted()` may cause type mismatches. For instance, in the following example, it is quite easy to mess up the data types (`LocalDate`, `double`, and `String`) and the format specifiers (`%d`, `%s`, and `%.2f`):

```java
LocalDate fiscalDate = LocalDate.now();
double value = 4552.2367;
String employeeCode = "RN4555";

String jsonBlock = """
            {"sale": {
                "id": 1,
                "details": {
                    "fiscal_year": %d,
                    "employee_nr": "%s",
                    "value": %.2f
                }
            }
            """.formatted(
            fiscalDate.getYear(), employeeCode, value);
```

Moreover, any of these approaches doesn't cover input validity (as we don't know if the expressions are valid) and security issues (injections, which commonly affect SQL strings).

Starting with JDK 21, we can address these issues via *string templates* (JEP 430).

What's a string template?

String templates (template expressions) are a mechanism introduced as a preview feature in JDK 21 that can help us perform string interpolation efficiently and safely. This feature consists of three parts, as follows:

- A template processor (`RAW`, `STR`, `FMT`, user-defined, and so on)
- A dot character
- A string template containing the embedded expression(s) as `\{expression}`

RAW, STR, and FMT are the three *template processors* provided by JDK 21, but as you'll see, we can write our own template processors as well.

A *template processor* takes a string literal and the proper expressions, and it is capable of validating and interpolating it in a final result, which can be a string or other domain-specific object (for instance, a JSON object). If the template processor cannot successfully create the result, then an exception may be thrown.

The STR template processor

The STR template processor is available as a static field in java.lang.StringTemplate. Its goal is to serve simple string concatenation tasks. For instance, we can rewrite the previous example using STR, as follows:

```java
import static java.lang.StringTemplate.STR;


String jsonBlockStr = STR."""
        {"sale": {
            "id": 1,
            "details": {
                "fiscal_year": \{fiscalDate.getYear()},
                "employee_nr": "\{employeeCode}",
                "value": \{value}
            }
        }
        """;
```

Here, we have three embedded expressions (\{fiscalDate.getYear()}, \{employeeCode}, and \{value}) that STR will process in order to obtain the final string:

```
{"sale": {
    "id": 1,
    "details": {
        "fiscal_year": 2023,
        "employee_nr": "RN4555",
        "value": 4552.2367
    }
}
```

As you can see, the STR processor has replaced every embedded expression with the string value of that expression. The returned result is a String, and we can use any number of embedded expressions. If the expression is large, then you can split it in your IDE across multiple lines without introducing new lines in the final result.

The FMT template processor

In the previous example, we have the \{value} embedded expression, which is evaluated by STR to 4552.2367. This is correct, but we may like to format this value with two decimals, as 4552.24. In such cases, we need the FMT processor, which is available as a static field in java.util.FormatProcessor and is capable of interpreting the format specifiers present in embedded expressions (STR cannot do that). So using FMT to rewrite our example can be done as follows:

```
String jsonBlockFmt = FMT."""
        {"sale": {
            "id": 1,
            "details": {
                "fiscal_year": \{fiscalDate.getYear()},
                "employee_nr": "\{employeeCode}",
                "value": %.2f\{value}
            }
        }
        """;
```

Notice how the format specifier was added to the embedded expression (%.2f\{value}) before the backslash character. This will result in the following string:

```
...
"value": 4552.24
...
```

In the same manner, you can use any other format specifier. FMT will take each of them into account in order to return the expected result.

The RAW template processor

The RAW template processor is available as a static field of java.lang.StringTemplate. Calling RAW will return a StringTemplate instance that can be used later. For instance, here is a StringTemplate that we have extracted separately using RAW:

```
StringTemplate templateRaw = RAW."""
        "employee_nr": "\{employeeCode}",
        """;
```

Next, we can use templateRaw repeatedly, as in the following example:

```
LocalDate fiscalDate1 = LocalDate.of(2023, 2, 4);
LocalDate fiscalDate2 = LocalDate.of(2024, 3, 12);
double value1 = 343.23;
double value2 = 1244.33;

String jsonBlockRaw = STR."""
```

```
        {"sale": {
            "id": 1,
            "details": {
                "fiscal_year": \{fiscalDate1.getYear()},
                \{templateRaw.interpolate()}\
                "value": \{value1}
            }
        },
        {"sale": {
            "id": 2,
            "details": {
                "fiscal_year": \{fiscalDate2.getYear()},
                \{templateRaw.interpolate()}\
                "value": \{value2}
            }
        }
        """;
```

The \{templateRaw.interpolate()} expression calls the interpolate() method, which is responsible for processing the string defined in templateRaw. It is like calling interpolate(), as follows:

```
String employeeCodeString = templateRaw.interpolate();
```

The final result is the following string:

```
{"sale": {
    "id": 1,
    "details": {
        "fiscal_year": 2023,
        "employee_nr": "RN4555",
        "value": 343.23
    }
},
{"sale": {
    "id": 2,
    "details": {
        "fiscal_year": 2024,
        "employee_nr": "RN4555",
        "value": 1244.33
    }
}
```

The employee code is evaluated to an RN4555 string.

The character sequences that precede an embedded expression and the character sequence following the last embedded expression are known as *fragments*. If the string template begins with an embedded expression, then its fragment is zero-length. The same is true for directly adjacent embedded expressions. For instance, the fragments of templateRaw ("employee_nr": "\{employeeCode}",) are "employee_nr": " and ",. We have access to these fragments as a List<String> via the fragments() method.

```
List<String> trFragments = templateRaw.fragments();
```

Moreover, getting the results of the embedded expressions as a List<Object> can be done via the values() methods, as follows:

```
List<Object> trValues = templateRaw.values();
```

For templateRaw, this list will contain a single entry, RN4555.

In the bundled code, you can find more examples, including using STR, FMT, and RAW with simple strings (not text blocks).

16. Writing a custom template processor

The built-in STR and FMT can return only String instances and cannot throw exceptions. However, both of them are actually instances of the functional interface StringTemplate.Processor<R,E extends Throwable>, which defines the process() method:

```
R process(StringTemplate stringTemplate) throws E
```

By implementing the Processor<R,E extends Throwable> interface, we can write custom template processors that return R (any result type), not just String. Moreover, if something goes wrong during processing (for instance, validation issues are present), we can throw checked exceptions (E extends Throwable).

For instance, let's assume that we need to interpolate strings with expressions representing phone numbers. So we accept only the expressions that are phone numbers, matching the following regular expression:

```
private static final Pattern PHONE_PATTERN = Pattern.compile(
    "\\d{10}|(?:\\d{3}-){2}\\d{4}|\\(\\d{3}\\)\\d{3}-?\\d{4}");
```

In this case, the result is a String, so our custom template processor can be written as follows:

```
public class PhoneProcessor
    implements Processor<String, IllegalArgumentException> {

  private static final Pattern PHONE_PATTERN = ...;

  @Override
  public String process(StringTemplate stringTemplate)
    throws IllegalArgumentException {
```

```
      StringBuilder sb = new StringBuilder();
      Iterator<String> fragmentsIter
        = stringTemplate.fragments().iterator();

      for (Object value : stringTemplate.values()) {
        sb.append(fragmentsIter.next());

        if (!PHONE_PATTERN.matcher(
              (CharSequence) value).matches()) {
          throw new IllegalArgumentException(
            "This is not a valid phone number");
        }

        sb.append(value);
      }

      sb.append(fragmentsIter.next());

      return sb.toString();
    }
}
```

Now, we can test our processor with a simple message, as follows (here, we use valid phone numbers):

```
PhoneProcessor pp = new PhoneProcessor();
String workPhone = "072-825-9009";
String homePhone = "(040)234-9670";

String message = pp."""
    You can contact me at work at \{workPhone}
    or at home at \{homePhone}.
    """;
```

The resulting string is as follows:

```
You can contact me at work at 072-825-9009
or at home at (040)234-9670.
```

As you can see, our processor relies on a `StringBuilder` to obtain the final string. However, we can use the `StringTemplate.interpolate(List<String> fragments, List<?> values)` method as well and obtain a cleaner solution, as follows:

```
public class PhoneProcessor implements
    Processor<String, IllegalArgumentException> {
```

```
    private static final Pattern PHONE_PATTERN = ...;

    @Override
    public String process(StringTemplate stringTemplate)
        throws IllegalArgumentException {

      for (Object value : stringTemplate.values()) {

        if (!PHONE_PATTERN.matcher(
            (CharSequence) value).matches()) {
          throw new IllegalArgumentException(
            "This is not a valid phone number");
        }
      }

      return StringTemplate.interpolate(
        stringTemplate.fragments(), stringTemplate.values());
    }
}
```

However, as we said earlier, a template processor can return any type (R). For instance, let's assume that we shaped our previous message as a JSON string, as follows:

```
{
  "contact": {
    "work": "072-825-9009",
    "home": "(040)234-9670"
  }
}
```

This time, we want to interpolate strings with variables representing phone numbers and return a JSON object. More precisely, we want to return an instance of com.fasterxml.jackson.databind. JsonNode (here, we use the Jackson library, but it can be GSON, JSON-B, and so on):

```
@Override
public JsonNode process(StringTemplate stringTemplate)
    throws IllegalArgumentException {

  for (Object value : stringTemplate.values()) {

    if (!PHONE_PATTERN.matcher(
        (CharSequence) value).matches()) {
```

```
        throw new IllegalArgumentException(
          "This is not a valid phone number");
      }
    }

  ObjectMapper mapper = new ObjectMapper();

  try {
    return mapper.readTree(StringTemplate.interpolate(
      stringTemplate.fragments(), stringTemplate.values()));
  } catch (IOException ex) {
    throw new RuntimeException(ex);
  }
}
```

This time, the returned type is JsonNode:

```
PhoneProcessor pp = new PhoneProcessor();
String workPhone = "072-825-9009";
String homePhone = "(040)234-9670";

JsonNode jsonMessage = pp."""
  { "contact": {
      "work": "\{workPhone}",
      "home": "\{homePhone}"
      }
  }
  """;
```

In the bundled code, you can also find an example that uses a lambda expression for writing the previous custom template processor. Moreover, you can find an example in which instead of throwing an exception for invalid expressions we just replace the invalid values with a default value.

 Please note, a recent article *Update on String Templates* (*JEP 459*), which you can find at: `https://mail.openjdk.org/pipermail/amber-spec-experts/2024-March/004010.html`, suggests that processors, used in this way, will ultimately be replaced with simpler method calls.

17. Creating a Locale

A Java Locale (java.util.Locale) represents an object that wraps information about a specific geographical, political, or cultural region – that is, an object useful for internationalization purposes.

A Locale is typically used in conjunction with DateFormat/DateTimeFormatter to represent date-time in a format specific to a country, with NumberFormat (or its subclass, DecimalFormat) used to represent numbers in a format specific to a country (for instance, to represent an amount of money in a specific currency), or with MessageFormat to create formatted messages for a specific country.

For the most popular locales, Java provides a list of constants (for instance, Locale.GERMANY, Locale.CANADA, and so on). For locales that are not on this list, we have to use the formats defined in several RFCs. Most commonly, we use the *language* pattern (for instance, ro for Romanian) or the *language_country* pattern (for instance, ro_RO for Romania, en_US for United States, and so on). Sometimes, we may need the *language_country _variant* pattern, where *variant* is useful to map additional functionalities added by software vendors, such as browsers or operating systems (for instance, de_DE_WIN is a locale for German speakers in Germany, for Windows). However, two locales are treated as non-conforming: ja_JP_JP (which represents Japanese, as used in Japan) and th_TH_TH (which represents Thai, as used in Thailand, including Thai digits).

While you can learn more about Locale from its comprehensive documentation, let's mention that, before JDK 19, we can create a Locale via one of its three constructors – most commonly, via Locale(String language, String country), as follows:

```
Locale roDep = new Locale("ro", "RO"); // locale for Romania
```

Of course, if your Locale has already a defined constant, you can simply embed that constant where you need it in code or simply declare a Locale, as follows (here, for Germany):

```
Locale de = Locale.GERMANY; // de_DE
```

Another approach relies on Locale.Builder via a chain of setters:

```
Locale locale = new Locale.Builder()
  .setLanguage("ro").setRegion("RO").build();
```

Alternatively, this can be done via Locale.forLanguageTag() to follow the IETF BCP 47 standard language tags (which can be useful to represent complex tags such as China-specific Chinese, Mandarin, Simplified script, and "zh-cmn-Hans-CN"):

```
Locale locale = Locale.forLanguageTag("zh-cmn-Hans-CN");
```

Moreover, Java supports *language ranges*. This means that we can define a set of language tags that share some specific attributes. For instance, "de-*" represents a language range to recognize German in any region:

```
Locale.LanguageRange lr1
  = new Locale.LanguageRange("de-*", 1.0);
Locale.LanguageRange lr2
  = new Locale.LanguageRange("ro-RO", 0.5);
Locale.LanguageRange lr3
  = new Locale.LanguageRange("en-*", 0.0);
```

The previous `Locale.LanguageRange()` constructor takes two arguments: the language range and its weight (1.0, 0.5, 0.0). Typically, this weight reveals the user's preference (1.0 at the highest and 0.0 at the lowest). The weight is useful for defining *priority lists* as follows (we prefer Castilian Spanish (Spain) over Mexican Spanish and over Brazilian Portuguese):

```
String rangeString = "es-ES;q=1.0,es-MX;q=0.5,pt-BR;q=0.0";
List<Locale.LanguageRange> priorityList
  = Locale.LanguageRange.parse(rangeString);
```

Pay attention to defining a valid string of preferences so the `parse()` method can work.

Starting with JDK 19, the three constructors of `Locale` have been deprecated, and we can rely on three static `of()` methods instead. The equivalent of the previous code via the proper `of()` method is:

```
Locale ro = Locale.of("ro", "RO"); // ro_RO
```

Here are two more examples:

```
Locale de = Locale.of("de" ,"DE", "WIN");
Locale it = Locale.of("it"); // similar to Locale.ITALIAN
```

Using a `Locale` is straightforward. Here is an example of using the previous `ro` to format date-time via `DateFormat` for Romania and Italy:

```
// 7 ianuarie 2023, 14:57:42 EET
DateFormat rodf = DateFormat.getDateTimeInstance(
  DateFormat.LONG, DateFormat.LONG, ro);


// 7. Januar 2023 um 15:05:29 OEZ
DateFormat dedf = DateFormat.getDateTimeInstance(
  DateFormat.LONG, DateFormat.LONG, de);
```

In the next problem, we continue the locale journey.

18. Customizing localized date-time formats

Starting with JDK 8, we have a comprehensive date-time API containing classes such as `LocalDate`, `LocalTime`, `LocalDateTime`, `ZonedDateTime`, `OffsetDateTime`, and `OffsetTime`.

We can easily format the date-time output returned by these classes via `DateTimeFormatter.ofPattern()`. For instance, here, we format a `LocalDateTime` via the `y-MM-dd HH:mm:ss` pattern:

```
// 2023-01-07 15:31:22
String ldt = LocalDateTime.now()
  .format(DateTimeFormatter.ofPattern("y-MM-dd HH:mm:ss"));
```

More examples are available in the bundled code.

How about customizing our format based on a given locale – for instance, Germany?

```
Locale.setDefault(Locale.GERMANY);
```

We accomplish this via `ofLocalizedDate()`, `ofLocalizedTime()`, and `ofLocalizedDateTime()`, as in the following examples:

```
// 7. Januar 2023
String ld = LocalDate.now().format(
  DateTimeFormatter.ofLocalizedDate(FormatStyle.LONG));


// 15:49
String lt = LocalTime.now().format(
  DateTimeFormatter.ofLocalizedTime(FormatStyle.SHORT));


// 07.01.2023, 15:49:30
String ldt = LocalDateTime.now().format(
  DateTimeFormatter.ofLocalizedDateTime(FormatStyle.MEDIUM));
```

We may also use:

```
// Samstag, 7. Januar 2023 um 15:49:30
// Osteuropäische Normalzeit
String zdt = ZonedDateTime.now().format(
  DateTimeFormatter.ofLocalizedDateTime(FormatStyle.FULL));


// 07.01.2023, 15:49:30
String odt = OffsetDateTime.now().format(
  DateTimeFormatter.ofLocalizedDateTime(FormatStyle.MEDIUM));


// 15:49:30
String ot = OffsetTime.now().format(
  DateTimeFormatter.ofLocalizedTime(FormatStyle.MEDIUM));
```

A localized date, time, or date-time formatter supports four format styles:

- FULL: Format using all details.
- LONG: Format using lots of detail but not all.
- MEDIUM: Format with some detail.
- SHORT: Format as short as possible (typically numeric).

Depending on the combination between the localized artifact and format style, the code may end up with an exception such as *DateTimeException: Unable to extract.....* If you see such an exception, then it is time to consult the following table, which provides the accepted combos:

	ofLocalizedDate	ofLocalizedTime	ofLocalizedDateTime
LocalTime		MEDIUM, SHORT	
LocalDate	FULL, LONG, MEDIUM, SHORT		
LocalDateTime	FULL, LONG, MEDIUM, SHORT	MEDIUM, SHORT	MEDIUM, SHORT
ZonedDateTime	FULL, LONG, MEDIUM, SHORT	FULL, LONG, MEDIUM, SHORT	FULL, LONG, MEDIUM, SHORT
OffsetDateTime	FULL, LONG, MEDIUM, SHORT	MEDIUM, SHORT	MEDIUM, SHORT

Figure 1.17: Format style of a localized date, time, and date-time

Moreover, starting with JDK 19, we can use `ofLocalizedPattern(String pattern)` as well.

We can pass any pattern that is shown in *Figure 1.18*.

```
"G{0,5}" +          // Era
"y*" +              // Year
"Q{0,5}" +          // Quarter
"M{0,5}" +          // Month
"w*" +              // Week of Week Based Year
"E{0,5}" +          // Day of Week
"d{0,2}" +          // Day of Month
"B{0,5}" +          // Period/AmPm of Day
"[hHjC]{0,2}" +     // Hour of Day/AmPm (refer to LDML for 'j' and 'C')
"m{0,2}" +          // Minute of Hour
"s{0,2}" +          // Second of Minute
"[vz]{0,4}"         // Zone
```

Figure 1.18: Building a pattern for ofLocalizedPattern(String pattern)

This being said, let's change the current locale to Romania:

```
Locale.setDefault(Locale.of("ro", "RO"));
```

Let's also have some examples of `ofLocalizedPattern()`:

```
// 01.2023
String ld = LocalDate.now().format(
  DateTimeFormatter.ofLocalizedPattern("yMM"));

// 15:49
String lt = LocalTime.now().format(
  DateTimeFormatter.ofLocalizedPattern("Hm"));
```

```
// 01.2023, 15:49
String ldt = LocalDateTime.now().format(
  DateTimeFormatter.ofLocalizedPattern("yMMHm"));
```

And even more:

```
// 01.2023, 15:49:30 EET
String zdt = ZonedDateTime.now().format(
  DateTimeFormatter.ofLocalizedPattern("yMMHmsv"));

// 01.2023, 15:49:30
String odt = OffsetDateTime.now().format(
  DateTimeFormatter.ofLocalizedPattern("yMMHms"));

// 15:49:30
String ot = OffsetTime.now().format(
  DateTimeFormatter.ofLocalizedPattern("Hms"));
```

You can practice all these examples in the bundled code. Moreover, in the bundled code, you can find an application that uses locales and `NumberFormat` to format a royalty amount for different locales (currencies).

19. Restoring Always-Strict Floating-Point semantics

Floating-point calculations are not easy! Even some simple arithmetical properties don't apply to such calculations. For instance, floating-point addition or multiplication is not associative. In other words $(x + y) + z$ is not equal to $x + (y + z)$ where x, y, and z are real numbers. A quick example to test the associativity of multiplication follows:

```
double x = 0.8793331;
double y = 12.22933;
double z = 901.98334884433;

double m1 = (x * y) * z;   // 9699.617442382583
double m2 = (x * (y * z)); // 9699.617442382581

// m1 == m2 returns false
```

This means that floating-point arithmetic is a methodical approximation of real arithmetic. Computers have to approximate because of some limitations. For instance, exact floating-point outputs become very large quite quickly. Moreover, the exact inputs are not known, so with inexact inputs, it is difficult to obtain exact outputs.

To solve this problem, Java has to adopt a *rounding policy*. In other words, Java has to use a special kind of function capable of mapping from a real value to a floating-point value. These days, Java uses the so-called *round to nearest policy*. This policy attempts to round an inexact value to a value that is nearest to the *infinitely precise result*. In the case of equality (where the representable values are equally near to the inexact value), the value having the zero-most significant bit is the winner.

Moreover, floating-point calculations may produce different outputs on different platforms. In other words, running floating-point calculations on different chip architectures (for instance, 16-, 32-, or 64-bit processors) may lead to different results. Java solves this issue via the `strictfp` modifier. This keyword follows the IEEE 754 standards for floating-point calculations and was introduced in JDK 1.2.

Important note

The `strictfp` modifier represents all intermediate values in single/double-precision conforming to IEEE 754. However, some hardware-specific issues caused `strictfp` to become optional in JDK 1.2.

Let's assume that we have to implement a scientific calculator. Obviously, our calculator has to provide consistent results across platforms, so we rely on `strictfp`, as follows:

```java
public strictfp final class ScientificCalculator {

  private ScientificCalculator() {
    throw new AssertionError("Cannot be instantiated");
  }

  public static double multiply(
        final double v1, final double v2) {
    return v1 * v2;
  }

  public static double division(
        final double v1, final double v2) {
    return v1 / v2;
  }

  // more computational methods
}
```

The `strictfp` modifier used with the class guarantees that all member methods of this class take advantage of its effect. Now, we have consistent results across platforms. You can find this example in the bundled code.

Important note

The `strictfp` modifier can be used for classes (and is applied to nested classes as well), non-abstract methods, and interfaces. It cannot be used for variables, constructors, or abstract methods.

When the `strictfp` modifier is used on an interface, there are some important points to consider, as follows:

- It is not applied to the `abstract` methods declared in the interface.
- It is applied to the `default` methods declared in the interface.
- It is not applied to methods defined in classes that implement the interface.
- It is applied to all the methods declared in the inner classes of the interface.

For instance, consider the following `strictfp` interface:

```
public strictfp interface Rectangle {

  default double area(double length, double width) {
    ...
  }

  double diagonal(double length, double width);

  public class Trigonometry {

    public static double smallAngleOfDiagonals(
        double length, double width) {
      ...
    }

    public static double bigAngleOfDiagonals(
        double length, double width) {
      ...
    }
  }
}
```

Also, there is a non-`strictfp` class that implements the previous `strictfp` interface:

```
public class Main implements Rectangle {

  @Override
```

```java
  public double diagonal(double length, double width) {
    ...
  }

  public double perimeter(double length, double width) {
    ...
  }
}
```

To find out which artifacts are `strictfp`, let's run a little bit of Java reflection code that will reveal the modifiers of each method:

```java
public static void displayModifiers(
                        Class clazz, String member) {
  try {
    int modifiers = clazz.getDeclaredMethod(member,
      double.class, double.class).getModifiers();
    System.out.println(member + " has the following
    modifiers: " + Modifier.toString(modifiers));
  } catch (NoSuchMethodException | SecurityException e) {
    e.printStackTrace(System.out);
  }
}
```

Then, let's call this method:

```java
// public
displayModifiers(Main.class, "diagonal");

// public
displayModifiers(Main.class, "perimeter");

// public abstract
displayModifiers(Main.class.getInterfaces()[0], "diagonal");

// public strictfp
displayModifiers(Main.class.getInterfaces()[0], "area");

// public static strictfp
displayModifiers(Rectangle.Trigonometry.class,
  "smallAngleOfDiagonals");

// public static strictfp
```

```
displayModifiers(Rectangle.Trigonometry.class,
  "bigAngleOfDiagonals");
```

As you can see, the `strictfp` modifier is not present for all of our methods. So if we need `strictfp` on `perimeter()` and `diagonal()`, then we have to add it manually:

```
@Override
strictfp public double diagonal(double length, double width) {

  ...

}

strictfp public double perimeter(double length, double width) {


  ...

}
```

However, starting with JDK 17, there is some big news in this area.

> **Important note**
>
> Hardware has seriously evolved, and the issues causing `strictfp` to be optional in JDK 1.2 have been fixed, so the default floating-point semantics can be changed to consistently strict. In other words, starting with JDK 17, there is no need to explicitly use `strictfp`. JEP 306, *Restore Always-Strict Floating-Point Semantics*, provides this functionality out of the box everywhere. So starting with JDK 17, all floating-point operations are consistently strict.

Besides being good news for us as developers, JEP 306 also sustains several Java classes, such as `java.lang.Math` and `java.lang.StrictMath`, which become more robust and easy to implement.

20. Computing mathematical absolute value for int/long and result overflow

Mathematical absolute value is notated by placing the value between two pipe operators and is computed as follows:

```
|x| = x,  |-x| = x
```

It is commonly used for computing/expressing distances. For example, imagine that 0 represents the sea level and we have a scuba diver and a climber. The scuba diver is underwater at -45 ft (notice that we use negative numbers to express how deep in the water the scuba diver is). At the same time, the climber has climbed 30 ft high. Which of them is closer to the sea level (0)? We may think that since -45 < 30, the scuba diver is closer because its value is smaller. However, we can easily find the correct answer by applying the mathematical absolute, as follows:

```
|-45| = 45,  |30| = 30
45 > 30, so the climber is closer to the sea level (0)
```

58 Text Blocks, Locales, Numbers, and Math

Now, let's dive into the solution with the following example:

```
int x = -3;
int absofx = Math.abs(x); // 3
```

This is a very simple use case of `Math.abs()`, which returns the mathematical absolute value of the given integer. Now, let's apply this method to the following large numbers:

```
int x = Integer.MIN_VALUE; // -2,147,483,648
int absofx = Math.abs(x);  // -2,147,483,648
```

This is not good! The int domain was overflowed because of |Integer.MIN_VALUE| > |Integer.MAX_VALUE|. The expected result is the positive value of 2,147,483,648, which doesn't fit in the int domain. However, changing the x type from int to long will solve the problem:

```
long x = Integer.MIN_VALUE; // -2,147,483,648
long absofx = Math.abs(x);  // 2,147,483,648
```

But the problem will reappear if, instead of `Integer.MIN_VALUE`, there is `Long.MIN_VALUE`:

```
long y = Long.MIN_VALUE;// -9,223,372,036,854,775,808
long absofy = Math.abs(y); // -9,223,372,036,854,775,808
```

Starting with JDK 15, the Math class was enriched with two `absExact()` methods. There is one for int and one for long. These methods are very useful if the mathematical absolute result is prone to overflowing the int or long domain (for instance, the `Integer/Long.MIN_VALUE` values overflows the positive int/long range). In such cases, these methods throw `ArithmeticException` instead of returning a misleading result, as in the following example:

```
int absofxExact = Math.absExact(x);  // ArithmeticException
long absofyExact = Math.absExact(y); // ArithmeticException
```

In a functional style context, a potential solution will rely on the `UnaryOperator` functional interface, as follows:

```
IntUnaryOperator operatorInt = Math::absExact;
LongUnaryOperator operatorLong = Math::absExact;

// both throw ArithmeticException
int absofxExactUo = operatorInt.applyAsInt(x);
long absofyExactUo = operatorLong.applyAsLong(y);
```

When working with large numbers, also focus on `BigInteger` (immutable arbitrary-precision integers) and `BigDecimal` (immutable arbitrary-precision signed decimal numbers).

21. Computing the quotient of the arguments and result overflow

Let's start with two simple computations, as follows:

```
-4/-1 = 4, 4/-1 = -4
```

This is a very simple use case that works as expected. Now, let's keep the divisor as -1, and let's change the dividend to Integer.MIN_VALUE (-2,147,483,648):

```
int x = Integer.MIN_VALUE;
int quotient = x/-1; // -2,147,483,648
```

This time, the result is not correct. The int domain was overflowed because of |Integer.MIN_VALUE| > |Integer.MAX_VALUE|. It should be the positive 2,147,483,648, which doesn't fit in the int domain. However, changing the x type from int to long will solve the problem:

```
long x = Integer.MIN_VALUE;
long quotient = x/-1; // 2,147,483,648
```

But the problem will reappear if, instead of Integer.MIN_VALUE, there is Long.MIN_VALUE:

```
long y = Long.MIN_VALUE; // -9,223,372,036,854,775,808
long quotient = y/-1;    // -9,223,372,036,854,775,808
```

Starting with JDK 18, the Math class was enriched with two divideExact() methods. There is one for int and one for long. These methods are very useful if the division result is prone to overflowing the int or long (as Integer/Long.MIN_VALUE overflows the positive int/long range). In such cases, these methods throw ArithmeticException instead of returning a misleading result, as in the following example:

```
// throw ArithmeticException
int quotientExact = Math.divideExact(x, -1);
```

In a functional style context, a potential solution will rely on the BinaryOperator functional interface, as follows:

```
// throw ArithmeticException
BinaryOperator<Integer> operator = Math::divideExact;
int quotientExactBo = operator.apply(x, -1);
```

As we said in the previous problem as well, when working with large numbers, also focus on BigInteger (immutable arbitrary-precision integers) and BigDecimal (immutable arbitrary-precision signed decimal numbers).

22. Computing the largest/smallest value that is less/ greater than or equal to the algebraic quotient

By the largest value, we understand the value closest to positive infinity, while by the smallest value, we understand the value closest to negative infinity.

Computing the largest value that is less than or equal to the algebraic quotient can be done, starting with JDK 8, via `floorDiv(int x, int y)` and `floorDiv(long x, long y)`. Starting with JDK 9, we also have `floorDiv(long x, int y)`.

Computing the smallest value that is greater than or equal to the algebraic quotient can be done, starting with JDK 18, via `ceilDiv(int x, int y)`, `ceilDiv(long x, int y)`, and `ceilDiv(long x, long y)`.

However, none of these functions are capable of managing the corner case divisions presented in the previous problem, `Integer.MIN_VALUE/-1` and `Long.MIN_VALUE/-1`:

```
int x = Integer.MIN_VALUE; // or, x = Long.MIN_VALUE
Math.floorDiv(x, -1); // -2,147,483,648
Math.ceilDiv(x, -1);  // -2,147,483,648
```

Starting with JDK 18, whenever the result returned by `floorDiv()`/`ceilDiv()` is prone to overflowing the `int` or `long` domains, we can use `floorDivExact()` and `ceilDivExact()`. These methods come with flavors for `int` and `long` arguments. As you have probably intuited already, these methods throw `ArithmeticException` instead of returning a misleading result, as in the following example:

```
// throw ArtihmeticException
int resultFloorExact = Math.floorDivExact(x, -1);


// throw ArtihmeticException
int resultCeilExact = Math.ceilDivExact(x, -1);
```

In a functional style context, a potential solution will rely on the `BinaryOperator` functional interface, as follows:

```
// throw ArithmeticException
BinaryOperator<Integer> operatorf = Math::floorDivExact;
int floorExactBo = operatorf.apply(x, -1);


// throw ArithmeticException
BinaryOperator<Integer> operatorc = Math::ceilDivExact;
int ceilExactBo = operatorc.apply(x, -1);
```

Done! As you already know, when working with large numbers, also focus on `BigInteger` (immutable arbitrary-precision integers) and `BigDecimal` (immutable arbitrary-precision signed decimal numbers). These may save your day.

23. Getting integral and fractional parts from a double

You know those problems that are very easy if you know the solution and seem very difficult if you don't? This is exactly that kind of a problem. The solution is quite simple, as you can see in the following code:

```
double value = -9.33543545;

double fractionalPart = value % 1;
double integralPart = value - fractionalPart;
```

This was easy; I don't think you need further explanations. But this approach is not quite accurate. I mean, the integral part is -9, but this returns -9.0. Also, the fractional part is -0.33543545, but the returned value is -0.3354354500000003.

If we need a more accurate result, then using BigDecimal is more useful:

```
BigDecimal bd = BigDecimal.valueOf(value);
int integralPart = bd.intValue();
double fractionalPart = bd.subtract(
        BigDecimal.valueOf(integralPart)).doubleValue();
```

This time, the results are -9 and -0.33543545.

24. Testing if a double number is an integer

First of all, let's consider the following expected results (false means that the double is not an integer):

```
double v1 = 23.11;                       // false
double v2 = 23;                          // true
double v3 = 23.0;                        // true
double v4 = Double.NaN;                  // false
double v5 = Double.NEGATIVE_INFINITY;    // false
double v6 = Double.POSITIVE_INFINITY;    // false
```

Most probably, the first solution for testing if a double number is an integer consists of a simple cast as follows:

```
public static boolean isDoubleIntegerV1(double v) {

  return v == (int) v;
}
```

However, there are several other options. For instance, we can rely on modulus, as follows:

```
public static boolean isDoubleIntegerV2(double v) {

  return v % 1 == 0;
}
```

Alternatively, we can rely on the `Math.floor()` and `Double.isFinite()` methods. If the given double is a finite number and is equal to the result of `Math.floor()`, then it is an integer:

```
public static boolean isDoubleIntegerV3(double v) {

  return ((Math.floor(v) == v) && Double.isFinite(v));
}
```

We can also replace this equality via `Math.ceil()`:

```
public static boolean isDoubleIntegerV4(double v) {

  return (Math.floor(v) == Math.ceil(v)
                    && Double.isFinite(v));
}
```

Moreover, we can combine `Double.isFinite()` with `Math.rint()`, as follows:

```
public static boolean isDoubleIntegerV5(double v) {

  return ((Math.rint(v) == v) && Double.isFinite(v));
}
```

Finally, we can rely on Guava's `DoubleMath.isMathematicalInteger()`:

```
public static boolean isDoubleIntegerV6(double v) {

  return DoubleMath.isMathematicalInteger(v);
}
```

But which of these approaches has a better performance? Which one are you betting on? Well, let's see what a benchmark has to say:

Benchmark	(v)	Mode	Cnt	Score	Error	Units
Main.isDoubleIntegerV1	23.11	avgt	10	1.697	± 0.022	ns/op
Main.isDoubleIntegerV1	23	avgt	10	1.671	± 0.014	ns/op
Main.isDoubleIntegerV2	23.11	avgt	10	23.985	± 0.406	ns/op
Main.isDoubleIntegerV2	23	avgt	10	18.384	± 0.196	ns/op
Main.isDoubleIntegerV3	23.11	avgt	10	1.338	± 0.009	ns/op
Main.isDoubleIntegerV3	23	avgt	10	1.667	± 0.021	ns/op
Main.isDoubleIntegerV4	23.11	avgt	10	1.169	± 0.024	ns/op
Main.isDoubleIntegerV4	23	avgt	10	1.702	± 0.068	ns/op
Main.isDoubleIntegerV5	23.11	avgt	10	1.329	± 0.007	ns/op
Main.isDoubleIntegerV5	23	avgt	10	1.665	± 0.016	ns/op
Main.isDoubleIntegerV6	23.11	avgt	10	2.394	± 0.023	ns/op
Main.isDoubleIntegerV6	23	avgt	10	2.400	± 0.024	ns/op

Figure 1.19: Benchmark results

Based on these results, the conclusion is quite obvious – the solution that relies on modulus should be avoided. Also, the Guava solution seems to be slightly slower than the rest.

25. Hooking Java (un)signed integers in a nutshell

Signed values (or variables) such as signed integers or signed longs allow us to represent negative and positive numbers.

Unsigned values (or variables) such as unsigned integers or unsigned longs allow us to represent only positive numbers.

Signed and unsigned values (variables) of the same type share the same range. However, as you can see in the following figure, unsigned variables cover a larger magnitude number.

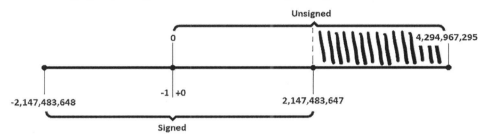

Figure 1.20: Signed and unsigned integers

The signed 32-bit integers range from –2,147,483,648 to 2,147,483,647 (around 4 billion values). Unsigned 32-bit integers range from 0 to 4,294,967,295 (also around 4 billion values).

So when we use signed integer variables, we can use 2 billion positive values, but when we use unsigned integer variables, we can use 4 billion positive values. The hatched part of the figure represents the extra 2 billion positive integer values.

Commonly, unsigned values are needed when we don't need negative values at all (for instance, to count something like an event occurrence) and we need to use values that reside in the hashed area in *Figure 1.20*.

Java supports only signed integers that use the popular *two's complement* representation in a signed system (for a detailed explanation of two's complement representation and bit manipulation, please check out *The Complete Coding Interview Guide in Java, Chapter 9, Bit Manipulation*). However, starting with JDK 8, we also have the *Unsigned Integer API*, which adds support for unsigned arithmetic.

Moreover, JDK 9, comes with a method named `Math.multiplyHigh(long x, long y)`. This method returns a `long`, representing the most significant 64 bits of the 128-bit product of two 64-bit factors. The following figure clarifies this statement:

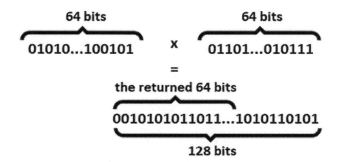

Figure 1.21: The most significant 64 bits of the 128-bit product of two 64-bit factors

For example:

```
long x = 234253490223L;
long y = -565951223449L;


long resultSigned = Math.multiplyHigh(x, y); // -7187
```

The returned result (-7187) is a signed value. The unsigned version of this method, unsignedMultiplyHigh(long x, long y), was introduced in JDK 18 and works as follows:

```
// 234253483036
long resultUnsigned = Math.unsignedMultiplyHigh(x, y);
```

So unsignedMultiplyHigh(long x, long y) returns a long representing the most significant 64 bits of the unsigned 128-bit product of two unsigned 64-bit factors.

However, remember that Java supports unsigned arithmetic, not unsigned values/variables. However, thanks to the Data Geekery company (very well known for the famous jOOQ), we have the **jOOU (Java Object Oriented Unsigned)** project, created to bring unsigned number types into Java. While you can explore this project at https://github.com/jOOQ/jOOU, here is an example of defining an unsigned long:

```
// using jOOU
ULong ux = ulong(234253490223L);   // 234253490223
ULong uy = ulong(-565951223449L); // 18446743507758328167
```

Here is its use in unsignedMultiplyHigh(long x, long y):

```
long uResultUnsigned = Math.unsignedMultiplyHigh(
    ux.longValue(), uy.longValue());
```

You can find these examples in the bundled code.

26. Returning the flooring/ceiling modulus

Having the *dividend / divisor = quotient* computation, we know that the *floor* operation applied to the (*dividend, divisor*) pair returns the largest integer that is less than or equal to the algebraic *quotient*. By the largest integer, we understand the integer closest to positive infinity. Starting with JDK 8, this operation can be obtained via Math.floorDiv() and, starting with JDK 18, Math.floorDivExact().

On the other hand, the *ceil* operation applied to the (*dividend, divisor*) pair returns the smallest integer that is greater than or equal to the algebraic *quotient*. By the smallest integer, we understand the integer closest to negative infinity. Starting with JDK 18, this operation can be obtained via Math.ceilDiv() and Math.ceilDivExact().

More details are available in *Problem 22*.

Now, based on the *floor* and *ceil* operations, we can define the following floor/ceil modulus relationships:

```
Floor_Modulus = dividend -
   (floorDiv(dividend, divisor) * divisor)
Ceil_Modulus = dividend -
   (ceilDiv(dividend, divisor) * divisor)
```

So we can write this in code as:

```
int dividend = 162;
int divisor = 42;    // 162 % 42 = 36

int fd = Math.floorDiv(dividend, divisor);
int fmodJDK8 = dividend - (fd * divisor); // 36

int cd = Math.ceilDiv(dividend, divisor);
int cmodJDK18 = dividend - (cd * divisor); // -6
```

Starting with JDK 8, floor modulus can be obtained via Math.floorMod(), as follows:

```
int dividend = 162;
int divisor = 42;

int fmodJDK8 = Math.floorMod(dividend, divisor); // 36
```

Here, we use floorMod(int dividend, int divisor). But we can also use two more flavors: floorMod(long dividend, long divisor) and, starting with JDK 9, floorMod(long dividend, int divisor).

If the *dividend % divisor* is 0, then floorMod() is 0. If *dividend % divisor* and floorMod() are not 0, then their result differs only if the signs of the parameters differ.

Starting with JDK 18, ceil modulus can be obtained via `Math.ceilMod()`, as follows:

```
int cmodJDK18 = Math.ceilMod(dividend, divisor); // -6
```

Here, we use `ceilMod(int dividend, int divisor)`. But we can also use two more flavors: `ceilMod(long dividend, int divisor)` and `ceilMod(long dividend, long divisor)`.

If the *dividend % divisor* is 0, then `ceilMod()` is 0. If *dividend % divisor* and `ceilMod()` are not 0, then their results differ only if the signs of the parameters are the same.

Moreover, the relationship between `floorMod()` and `floorDiv()` is as follows:

```
dividend == floorDiv(dividend, divisor) * divisor
             + floorMod(dividend, divisor)
```

Also, the relationship between `ceilMod()` and `ceilDiv()` is as follows:

```
dividend == ceilDiv(dividend, divisor) * divisor
             + ceilMod(dividend, divisor)
```

Notice that if the divisor is 0, then both `floorMod()` and `ceilMod()` throw `ArithmeticException`.

27. Collecting all prime factors of a given number

A prime number is a number divisible by itself and 1 (for instance, 2, 3, and 5 are prime numbers). Having a given number, we can extract its prime factors, as in the following figure:

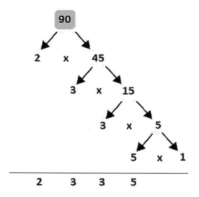

Figure 1.22: Prime factors of 90 are 2, 3, 3, and 5

The prime factors of 90 are 2, 3, 3, and 5. Based on *Figure 1.22*, we can create an algorithm to solve this problem, as follows:

1.   Define a `List` to collect prime factors of the given v.
2.   Initialize a variable s with 2 (the smallest prime number).
3.   If v % s is 0, collect s as a prime factor and compute the new v as v / s.
4.   If v % s is not 0, then increase s by 1.
5.   Repeat step 3 as long as v is greater than 1.

In code lines, this O(n) algorithm (O(log n) for composite numbers) can be expressed as follows:

```java
public static List<Integer> factors(int v) {

    List<Integer> factorsList = new ArrayList<>();
    int s = 2;

    while (v > 1) {
        // each perfect division give us a prime factor
        if (v % s == 0) {
            factorsList.add(s);
            v = v / s;
        } else {
            s++;
        }
    }

    return factorsList;
}
```

In the bundled code, you can find two more approaches. Moreover, you'll also find an application that counts the number of primes less than the given number, v (v should be positive).

28. Computing the square root of a number using the Babylonian method

Believe it or not, the ancient Babylonians (around 1500 BC) knew how to estimate square roots long before the popular method discovered by Newton.

Mathematically speaking, the Babylonian approach for estimating the square root of $v > 0$ is the recurrence relation from the following figure:

$$x_{n+1} = \frac{1}{2}\left(x_n + \frac{v}{x_n}\right) = F(x_n)$$

Figure 1.23: The recurrence relation of Babylonian square root approximation

The recurrence formula starts with an initial guess of x_0. Next, we calculate $x_1, x_2, ..., x_n$ by substituting x_{n-1} in the formula on the right-hand side and evaluating the expression.

For instance, let's try to apply this formula to estimate the square root of 65 (the result is 8.06). Let's start with x_0 as 65/2, so $x_0 = 32.5$, and let's calculate x_1 as:

$$x_1 = (x_0 + v/x_0)/2 \rightarrow x_1 = (32.5 + 65/32.5)/2 \rightarrow x_1 = 17.25$$

Having x_1, we can calculate x_2 as follows:

$$x_2 = (x_1 + v/x_1)/2 \rightarrow x_2 = (17.25 + 65/17.5)/2 \rightarrow x_2 = 10.25$$

Having x_2, we can calculate x_3 as follows:

$$x_3 = (x_2 + v/x_2)/2 \rightarrow x_3 = (10.25 + 65/10.5)/2 \rightarrow x_3 = 8.34$$

We are getting closer to the final result. Having x_3, we can calculate x_4 as follows:

$$x_4 = (x_3 + v/x_3)/2 \rightarrow x_4 = (8.34 + 65/8.34)/2 \rightarrow x_4 = 8.06$$

Done! After four iterations, we found that the square root of 65 is 8.06. Of course, being an approximation of the real value, we can continue until we reach the desired precision. More precision involves more iterations.

The algorithm that is based on the Babylonian approach to approximate the square root of v > 0 has several steps, as follows:

1. To start, choose an arbitrary positive value, x (the closer it is to the final result, the fewer iterations are needed). For instance, we start with x = v/2 as the initial guess.
2. Initialize y = 1, and choose the desired precision (for instance, e = 0.000000000001).
3. Until the precision (e) is achieved, do the following:

    1. Calculate the next approximation (xnext) as the average of x and y.
    2. Use the next approximation to set y as v/xnext.

So in code lines, we have the following snippet:

```
public static double squareRootBabylonian(double v) {

  double x = v / 2;
  double y = 1;
  double e = 0.000000000001; // precision

  while (x - y > e) {
    x = (x + y) / 2;
    y = v / x;
  }

  return x;
}
```

In the bundled code, you can also see an implementation that is useful if you know that v is a perfect square (for instance, 25, 144, 169, and so on).

29. Rounding a float number to specified decimals

Consider the following float number and the number of decimals that we want to keep:

```
float v = 14.9877655f;
int d = 5;
```

So the expected result after rounding up is 14.98777.

We can solve this problem in a straightforward manner in at least three ways. For instance, we can rely on the BigDecimal API, as follows:

```
public static float roundToDecimals(float v, int decimals) {

  BigDecimal bd = new BigDecimal(Float.toString(v));
  bd = bd.setScale(decimals, RoundingMode.HALF_UP);

  return bd.floatValue();
}
```

First, we create a BigDecimal number from the given float. Second, we scale this BigDecimal to the desired number of decimals. Finally, we return the new float value.

Another approach can rely on DecimalFormat, as follows:

```
public static float roundToDecimals(float v, int decimals) {

  DecimalFormat df = new DecimalFormat();
  df.setMaximumFractionDigits(decimals);

  return Float.parseFloat(df.format(v));
}
```

We define the format via setMaximumFractionDigits() and simply use this format on the given float. The returned String is passed through Float.parseFloat() to obtain the final float.

Finally, we can apply a more esoteric but self-explanatory approach, as follows:

```
public static float roundToDecimals(float v, int decimals) {

  int factor = Integer.parseInt(
               "1".concat("0".repeat(decimals)));

  return (float) Math.round(v * factor) / factor;
}
```

You can practice these examples in the bundled code. Feel free to add your own solutions.

30. Clamping a value between min and max

Let's assume that we have a pressure regulator that is capable of adjusting the given pressure in a certain range. For instance, if the passed pressure is below the minimum pressure, then the regulator increases the pressure to the minimum pressure. On the other hand, if the passed pressure is higher than the maximum pressure, then the regulator decreases the pressure to the maximum pressure. Moreover, if the passed pressure is between the minimum (inclusive) and maximum (inclusive) pressure, then nothing happens – this is the normal pressure.

Coding this scenario can be done in a straightforward manner, as follows:

```
private static final int MIN_PRESSURE = 10;
private static final int MAX_PRESSURE = 50;

public static int adjust(int pressure) {

  if (pressure < MIN_PRESSURE) {
    return MIN_PRESSURE;
  }

  if (pressure > MAX_PRESSURE) {
    return MAX_PRESSURE;
  }

  return pressure;
}
```

Neat! You can find different ways of expressing this code in shorter and smarter ways, but starting with JDK 21, we can accommodate solutions to this problem via the `Math.clamp()` method. One of the flavors of this method is `clamp(long value, int min, int max)`, which clamps the given `value` between the given `min` and `max`. For instance, we can rewrite the previous code via the `clamp()` method, as follows:

```
public static int adjust(int pressure) {

  return Math.clamp(pressure, MIN_PRESSURE, MAX_PRESSURE);
}
```

Cool, right!? The logic behind the `clamp()` method relies on the following code line:

```
return (int) Math.min(max, Math.max(value, min));
```

Other flavors of `clamp()` are `clamp(long value, long min, long max)`, `clamp(float value, float min, float max)`, and `clamp(double value, double min, double max)`.

31. Multiply two integers without using loops, multiplication, bitwise, division, and operators

The solution to this problem can start from the following algebraic formula, also known as the *special binomial product formula*:

$$(a+b)^2 = a^2 + b^2 + 2ab$$

$$\Downarrow$$

$$ab = ((a + b)^2 - a^2 - b^2)/2$$

Figure 1.24: Extracting a*b from a binomial formula

Now that we have the a*b product, there is only one issue left. The formula of a*b contains a division by 2, and we are not allowed to explicitly use the division operation. However, the division operation can be mocked in a recursive fashion, as follows:

```java
private static int divideByTwo(int d) {

    if (d < 2) {
        return 0;
    }

    return 1 + divideByTwo(d - 2);
}
```

Nothing can stop us now from using this recursive code to implement a*b, as follows:

```java
public static int multiply(int p, int q) {

    // p * 0 = 0, 0 * q = 0
    if (p == 0 || q == 0) {
        return 0;
    }

    int pqSquare = (int) Math.pow(p + q, 2);
    int pSquare = (int) Math.pow(p, 2);
    int qSquare = (int) Math.pow(q, 2);

    int squareResult = pqSquare - pSquare - qSquare;

    int result;

    if (squareResult >= 0) {
```

```
      result = divideByTwo(squareResult);
   } else {
      result = 0 - divideByTwo(Math.abs(squareResult));
   }

   return result;
}
```

In the bundled code, you can also practice a recursive approach to this problem.

32. Using TAU

What is TAU?

Short answer: It is the Greek letter τ.

Long answer: It is a Greek letter used to define the proportion of the circumference of a circle to its radius. Put simply, TAU is one turn of an entire circle, so 2*PI.

TAU allows us to express sinuses, cosines, and angles in a more intuitive and simple way. For instance, the well-known angles of 30^0, 45^0, 90^0, and so on can be easily expressed in radians via TAU as a fraction of a circle, as in the following figure:

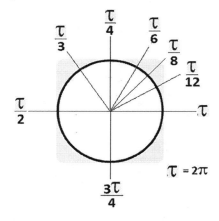

Figure 1.25: Angles represented using TAU

This is more intuitive than PI. It is like slicing a pie into equal parts. For instance, if we slice at TAU/8 (45^0), it means that we sliced the pie into eight equal parts. If we slice at TAU/4 (90^0), it means that we sliced the pie into four equal parts.

The value of TAU is 6.283185307179586 = 2 * 3.141592653589793. So the relationship between TAU and PI is TAU=2*PI. In Java, the well-known PI is represented via the Math.PI constant. Starting with JDK 19, the Math class was enriched with the Math.TAU constant.

Let's consider the following simple problem: A circle has a circumference of 21.33 cm. What is the radius of the circle?

We know that C = 2*PI*r, where C is the circumference and r is the radius. Therefore, r = C/(2*PI) or r = C/TAU. In code lines, we have:

```
// before JDK 19, using PI
double r = 21.33 / (2 * Math.PI);


// starting with JDK 19, using TAU
double r = 21.33 / Math.TAU;
```

Both approaches return a radius equal to 3.394.

33. Selecting a pseudo-random number generator

When we flip a coin or roll the dice, we say that we see "true" or "natural" randomness at work. Even so, there are tools that pretend they are capable of predicting the path of flipping a coin, rolling dice, or spinning a roulette wheel, especially if some contextual conditions are met.

Computers can generate random numbers using algorithms via the so-called **random generators**. Since algorithms are involved, the generated numbers are considered pseudo-random. This is known as "pseudo"-randomness. Obviously, pseudo-random numbers are also predictable. How so?

A pseudo-random generator starts its job by *seeding* data. This is the generator's secret (the *seed*), and it represents a piece of data used as the starting point to generate pseudo-random numbers. If we know how the algorithm works and what the *seed* was, then the output is predictable. Without knowing the *seed*, the rate of predictability is very low. So choosing the proper *seed* is a major step for every pseudo-random generator.

Until JDK 17, Java's API for generating pseudo-random numbers was a bit obtuse. Basically, we have a robust API wrapped in the well-known java.util.Random class, and two subclasses of Random: SecureRandom (cryptographically pseudo-random generator) and ThreadLocalRandom (not a thread-safe pseudo-random generator). From a performance perspective, the relationship between these pseudo-random generators is that SecureRandom is slower than Random, which is slower than ThreadLocalRandom.

As well as these classes, we have SplittableRandom. This is a non-thread-safe pseudo-generator capable of spinning a new SplittableRandom at each call of its split() method. This way, each thread (for instance, in a fork/join architecture) can use its own SplittableGenerator.

The class hierarchy of pseudo-random generators, up to JDK 17, is shown in the following figure:

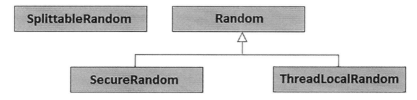

Figure 1.26: The class hierarchy of Java pseudo-random generators before JDK 17

As this architecture reveals, switching between pseudo-random generators or choosing between different types of algorithms is really cumbersome. Look at that SplittableRandom – is lost in no man's land.

Starting with JDK 17, we have a more flexible and powerful API for generating pseudo-random numbers. This is an interface-based API (released with JEP 356) that orbits the new RandomGenerator interface. Here is the enhanced class hierarchy of JDK 17:

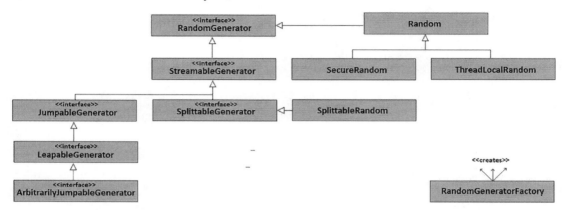

Figure 1.27: The class hierarchy of Java pseudo-random generators, starting with JDK 17

The RandomGenerator interface represents the climax of this API. It represents a common and uniform protocol for generating pseudo-random numbers. This interface has taken over the Random API and added a few more.

The RandomGenerator interface is extended by five sub-interfaces meant to provide special protocols for five different types of pseudo-random generators.

- StreamableGenerator can return streams of RandomGenerator objects
- SplittableGenerator can return a new generator from this one (split itself)
- JumpableGenerator can jump ahead a moderate number of draws
- LeapableGenerator can jump ahead a large number of draws
- ArbitrarilyJumpableGenerator can jump ahead an arbitrary number of draws

Getting the default RandomGenerator can be done as follows (this is the simplest approach to start generating pseudo-random numbers, but you have no control over what is chosen):

```
RandomGenerator defaultGenerator
  = RandomGenerator.getDefault();


// start generating pseudo-random numbers
defaultGenerator.nextInt/Float/...();
defaultGenerator.ints/doubles/...();
```

Besides these interfaces, the new API comes with a class (RandomGeneratorFactory), which is a factory of pseudo-random generators based on the selected algorithms. There are three groups of new algorithms (most probably, more are on the way); these groups are as follows:

- LXM group;

  - L128X1024MixRandom

  - L128X128MixRandom

  - L128X256MixRandom

  - **L32X64MixRandom**

  - L64X1024MixRandom

  - L64X128MixRandom

  - L64X128StarStarRandom

  - L64X256MixRandom

- Xoroshiro group:

  - Xoroshiro128PlusPlus

- Xoshiro group:

  - Xoshiro256PlusPlus

The highlighted algorithm is the default one (L32X64MixRandom).

Depending on the pseudo-random generator type, we can select all/some of the previous algorithms. For instance, the L128X256MixRandom algorithm can be used with SplittableGenerator, but it cannot be used with LeapableGenerator. A mismatch between the chosen algorithm and the pseudo-random generator results in IllegalArgumentException. The following figure can help you to decide which algorithm to use.

Name	Group	Ar. Jumpable	Deprecated	Hardware	Jumpable	Leapable	Splittable	Statistical	Stochastic	Streamable
L32X64MixRandom	LXM	false	false	false	false	false	true	true	false	true
L128X128MixRandom	LXM	false	false	false	false	false	true	true	false	true
L64X128MixRandom	LXM	false	false	false	false	false	true	true	false	true
L128X1024MixRandom	LXM	false	false	false	false	false	true	true	false	true
L64X128StarStarRandom	LXM	false	false	false	false	false	true	true	false	true
L64X256MixRandom	LXM	false	false	false	false	false	true	true	false	true
L128X256MixRandom	LXM	false	false	false	false	false	true	true	false	true
L64X1024MixRandom	LXM	false	false	false	false	false	true	true	false	true
SecureRandom	Legacy	false	false	false	false	false	false	false	true	false
Random	Legacy	false	false	false	false	false	false	true	false	false
SplittableRandom	Legacy	false	false	false	false	false	true	true	false	true
Xoroshiro128PlusPlus	Xoroshiro	false	false	false	true	true	false	true	false	true
Xoshiro256PlusPlus	Xoshiro	false	false	false	true	true	false	true	false	true

Figure 1.28: JDK 17 random generator algorithms and their properties

This figure was produced via the following code, which lists all the available algorithms and their properties (*streamable*, *leapable*, *statistical*, and so on):

```
Stream<RandomGeneratorFactory<RandomGenerator>> all
    = RandomGeneratorFactory.all();

Object[][] data = all.sorted(Comparator.comparing(
                 RandomGeneratorFactory::group))
    .map(f -> {
```

```
        Object[] obj = new Object[]{
          f.name(),
          f.group(),
          f.isArbitrarilyJumpable(),
          f.isDeprecated(),
          f.isHardware(),
          f.isJumpable(),
          f.isLeapable(),
          f.isSplittable(),
          f.isStatistical(),
          f.isStochastic(),
          f.isStreamable()
        };
        return obj;
    }).toArray(Object[][]::new);
```

Choosing an algorithm can be easily done by name or properties.

Choosing an algorithm by name

Choosing an algorithm by name can be done via a set of static of() methods. There is an of() method in RandomGenerator and RandomGeneratorFactory that can be used to create a pseudo-random generator for a specific algorithm, as follows:

```
RandomGenerator generator
  = RandomGenerator.of("L128X256MixRandom");


RandomGenerator generator
  = RandomGeneratorFactory.of("Xoroshiro128PlusPlus")
                          .create();
```

Next, we can generate pseudo-random numbers by calling a well-known API (ints(), doubles(), nextInt(), nextFloat(), and so on).

If we need a certain pseudo-random generator and algorithm, then we can use the of() method of that generator, as follows (here, we create a LeapableGenerator):

```
LeapableGenerator leapableGenerator
  = LeapableGenerator.of("Xoshiro256PlusPlus");


LeapableGenerator leapableGenerator = RandomGeneratorFactory
  .<LeapableGenerator>of("Xoshiro256PlusPlus").create();
```

In the case of SplittableRandom, you can use the constructor as well, but you cannot specify the algorithm:

```
SplittableRandom splittableGenerator = new SplittableRandom();
```

In the bundled code, you can see more examples.

Choosing an algorithm by property

As you saw in *Figure 1.28*, an algorithm has a set of properties (is *Jumpable*, is *Statistical*, and so on). Let's pick an algorithm that is *statistical* and *leapable*:

```
RandomGenerator generator = RandomGeneratorFactory.all()
  .filter(RandomGeneratorFactory::isLeapable)
  .filter(RandomGeneratorFactory::isStatistical)
  .findFirst()
  .map(RandomGeneratorFactory::create)
  .orElseThrow(() -> new RuntimeException(
      "Cannot find this kind of generator"));
```

The returned algorithm can be Xoshiro256PlusPlus.

34. Filling a long array with pseudo-random numbers

When we want to fill up a large array with data, we can consider the Arrays.setAll() and Arrays.parallelSetAll(). These methods can fill up an array by applying a generator function to compute each element of the array.

Since we have to fill up the array with pseudo-random data, we should consider that the generator function should be a pseudo-random generator. If we want to do this in parallel, then we should consider the SplittableRandom (JDK 8+)/SplittableGenerator (JDK 17+), which are dedicated to generating pseudo-random numbers in isolated parallel computations. In conclusion, the code may look as follows (JDK 17+):

```
SplittableGenerator splittableRndL64X256
  = RandomGeneratorFactory
      .<SplittableGenerator>of("L64X256MixRandom").create();

long[] arr = new long[100_000_000];
Arrays.parallelSetAll(arr,
                  x ->splittableRndL64X256.nextLong());
```

Alternatively, we can use SplittableRandom (this time, we cannot specify the algorithm, JDK 8+):

```
SplittableRandom splittableRandom = new SplittableRandom();

long[] arr = new long[100_000_000];
Arrays.parallelSetAll(arr, x ->splittableRandom.nextLong());
```

Next, let's see how we can create a stream of pseudo-random generators.

35. Creating a stream of pseudo-random generators

Before creating a stream of pseudo-random generators, let's create a stream of pseudo-random numbers. First thing first, let's see how to do it with the legacy Random, SecureRandom, and ThreadLocalRandom.

Since these three pseudo-random generators contain methods such as ints() returning IntStream, doubles() returning DoubleStream, and so on, we can easily generate an (in)finite stream of pseudo-random numbers, as follows:

```
Random rnd = new Random();
// the ints() flavor returns an infinite stream
int[] arrOfInts = rnd.ints(10).toArray(); // stream of 10 ints


// or, shortly
int[] arrOfInts = new Random().ints(10).toArray();
```

In our examples, we collect the generated pseudo-random numbers in an array. Of course, you can process them as you want. We can obtain similar results via SecureRandom, as follows:

```
SecureRandom secureRnd = SecureRandom.getInstanceStrong();
int[] arrOfSecInts = secureRnd.ints(10).toArray();


// or, shortly
int[] arrOfSecInts = SecureRandom.getInstanceStrong()
  .ints(10).toArray();
```

How about ThreadLocalRandom? Here it is:

```
ThreadLocalRandom tlRnd = ThreadLocalRandom.current();
int[] arrOfTlInts = tlRnd.ints(10).toArray();


// or, shortly
int[] arrOfTlInts = ThreadLocalRandom.current()
  .ints(10).toArray();
```

If you just need a stream of doubles between 0.0 and 1.0, then rely on Math.random(), which internally uses an instance of java.util.Random. The following example collects an array of doubles between 0.0 and 0.5. The stream will stop when the first double larger than 0.5 is generated:

```
Supplier<Double> doubles = Math::random;


double[] arrOfDoubles = Stream.generate(doubles)
    .takeWhile(t -> t < 0.5d)
    .mapToDouble(i -> i)
    .toArray();
```

How about using the new JDK 17 API? The RandomGenerator contains the well-known methods ints(), doubles(), and so on, and they are available in all its sub-interfaces. For instance, StreamableGenerator can be used, as follows:

```
StreamableGenerator streamableRnd
    = StreamableGenerator.of("L128X1024MixRandom");
int[] arrOfStRndInts = streamableRnd.ints(10).toArray();


// or, shortly
StreamableGenerator.of("L128X1024MixRandom")
    .ints(10).toArray();
```

Similarly, we can use JumpableGenerator, LeapableGenerator, and so on.

OK, now let's get back to our problem. How do we generate a stream of pseudo-random generators? All RandomGenerator sub-interfaces contain a method named rngs() that comes in different flavors. Without arguments, this method returns an infinite stream of new pseudo-random generators that implement the RandomGenerator interface. The following code generated five StreamableGenerator instances, and each of those generated 10 pseudo-random integers:

```
StreamableGenerator streamableRnd
    = StreamableGenerator.of("L128X1024MixRandom");

List<int[]> listOfArrOfIntsSG
    = streamableRnd.rngs(5) // get 5 pseudo-random generators
    .map(r -> r.ints(10))   // generate 10 ints per generator
    .map(r -> r.toArray())
    .collect(Collectors.toList());
```

We can accomplish the same thing with JumpableGenerator, but instead of rngs(), we may prefer jumps(), which implements the behavior specific to this type of generator:

```
JumpableGenerator jumpableRnd
    = JumpableGenerator.of("Xoshiro256PlusPlus");

List<int[]> listOfArrOfIntsJG = jumpableRnd.jumps(5)
    .map(r -> {
        JumpableGenerator jg = (JumpableGenerator) r;
        int[] ints = new int[10];
        for (int i = 0; i < 10; i++) {
            ints[i] = jg.nextInt();
            jg.jump();
        }

        return ints;
```

```
})
    .collect(Collectors.toList());
```

The same thing can be accomplished via `LeapableGenerator`. This time, we can use `rngs()` or `leaps()`, which implement the behavior specific to this type of generator:

```
LeapableGenerator leapableRnd
    = LeapableGenerator.of("Xoshiro256PlusPlus");


List<int[]> listOfArrOfIntsLG = leapableRnd.leaps(5)
    .map(r -> {
        LeapableGenerator lg = (LeapableGenerator) r;
        int[] ints = new int[10];
        for (int i = 0; i < 10; i++) {
            ints[i] = lg.nextInt();
            lg.leap();
        }

        return ints;
    })
    .collect(Collectors.toList());
```

Next, let's see how we can interleave legacy and new pseudo-random generators.

36. Getting a legacy pseudo-random generator from new ones of JDK 17

A legacy pseudo-random generator such as `Random`, `SecureRandom`, or `ThreadLocalRandom` can delegate method calls to a `RandomGenerator`, passed as an argument to `Random.from()`, `SecureRandom.from()`, or `ThreadLocalRandom.from()`, as follows:

```
Random legacyRnd = Random.from(
    RandomGenerator.of("L128X256MixRandom"));

// or, like his
Random legacyRnd = Random.from(RandomGeneratorFactory.
    of("Xoroshiro128PlusPlus").create());

// or, like this
Random legacyRnd = Random.from(RandomGeneratorFactory
    .<RandomGenerator.SplittableGenerator>of(
        "L128X256MixRandom").create());
```

The `from()` methods are available starting with JDK 19. In the bundled code, you can see more examples.

37. Using pseudo-random generators in a thread-safe fashion (multithreaded environments)

Random and SecureRandom instances are thread-safe. While this statement is true, pay attention that when a Random instance (or Math.random()) is used by multiple threads (multithreaded environment), your code is prone to thread contention because these threads share the same *seed*. Sharing the same seed involves synchronization of the *seed* access; therefore, it opens the door to thread contention. Obviously, thread contention leads to performance penalties, since threads may wait in the queue to gain access to the *seed*. Synchronization is typically expensive.

An alternative to Random is ThreadLocalRandom, which uses a Random instance for each thread and provides protection against thread contention, since it doesn't contain synchronized code or atomic operations. The downside is that ThreadLocalRandom uses an internal *seed* per thread that we cannot control or modify.

SplittableRandom is not thread-safe. Moreover, the new API consisting of implementations of RandomGenerator is not thread-safe.

This being said, a pseudo-random generator can be used in a multithread environment by using a thread-safe generator, or by splitting a new instance for each new thread. And when I say "splitting," I mean using SplittableGenerator.splits(long n), where n is the number of splits. Check out the code that uses 10 threads to populate a Java list with integers (each thread uses its own pseudo-random generator):

```
List<Integer> listOfInts = new CopyOnWriteArrayList<>();
ExecutorService executorService
  = Executors.newCachedThreadPool();

SplittableGenerator splittableGenerator
  = RandomGeneratorFactory
    .<SplittableGenerator>of("L128X256MixRandom").create();

splittableGenerator.splits(10)
  .forEach((anotherSplittableGenerator) -> {
    executorService.submit(() -> {
      int nextInt = anotherSplittableGenerator.nextInt(1_000);
      logger.info(() -> "Added in list "
          + nextInt + " by generator "
          + anotherSplittableGenerator.hashCode()
          + " running in thread"
          + Thread.currentThread().getName());
      listOfInts.add(nextInt);
    });
```

```
    });

    shutdownExecutor(executorService);
```

A snippet from the output:

```
INFO: Added in list 192 by generator 1420516714 running in threadpool-1-
thread-3
INFO: Added in list 366 by generator 1190794841 running in threadpool-1-
thread-8
INFO: Added in list 319 by generator 275244369 running in threadpool-1-thread-9
...
```

You can also use a `JumpableGenerator` or `LeapableGenerator`. The only difference is that instead of `splits()`, `JumpableGenerator` uses `jumps()` and `LeapableGenerator` uses `leaps()`.

Summary

This chapter collected 37 problems related to strings, locales, numbers, and math, intended to mix classical must-know problems with a bunch of problems solved via the latest JDK features, such as text blocks and pseudo-random generators. If you want to explore other similar problems, then consider *Java Coding Problems, First Edition*, which has a similar chapter (*Chapter 1*), covering another 39 problems.

Leave a review!

Enjoying this book? Help readers like you by leaving an Amazon review. Scan the QR code below for a 20% discount code.

Limited Offer

2

Objects, Immutability, Switch Expressions, and Pattern Matching

This chapter includes 30 problems, tackling, among others, some less-known features of `java.util.Objects`, some interesting aspects of immutability, the newest features of `switch` expressions, and deep coverage of the cool pattern matching capabilities of `instanceof` and `switch` expressions.

At the end of this chapter, you'll be up to date with all these topics, which are non-optional in any Java developer's arsenal.

Problems

Use the following problems to test your programming prowess on `Objects`, immutability, `switch` expressions, and pattern matching. I strongly encourage you to give each problem a try before you turn to the solutions and download the example programs:

38. **Explaining and exemplifying UTF-8, UTF-16, and UTF-32:** Provide a detailed explanation of what UTF-8, UTF-16, and UTF-32 are. Include several snippets of code to show how these work in Java.

39. **Checking a sub-range in the range from 0 to length:** Write a program that checks whether the given sub-range [*given start, given start + given end*) is within the bounds of the range from [*0, given length*). If the given sub-range is not in the [*0, given length*) range, then throw an `IndexOutOfBoundsException`.

40. **Returning an identity string:** Write a program that returns a string representation of an object without calling the overridden `toString()` or `hashCode()`.

41. **Hooking unnamed classes and instance main methods:** Give a quick introduction to JDK 21 unnamed classes and instance main methods.

42. **Adding code snippets in Java API documentation:** Provide examples of adding code snippets in Java API documentation via the new `@snippet` tag.

43. **Invoking default methods from** `Proxy` **instances:** Write several programs that invoke interface `default` methods from `Proxy` instances in JDK 8, JDK 9, and JDK 16.

44. **Converting between bytes and hex-encoded strings:** Provide several snippets of code for converting between bytes and hex-encoded strings (including byte arrays).

45. **Exemplify the initialization-on-demand holder design pattern:** Write a program that implements the initialization-on-demand holder design pattern in the classical way (before JDK 16) and another program that implements this design pattern based on the fact that, from JDK 16+, Java inner classes can have static members and static initializers.

46. **Adding nested classes in anonymous classes:** Write a meaningful example that uses nested classes in anonymous classes (pre-JDK 16, and JDK 16+).

47. **Exemplify erasure vs. overloading:** Explain in a nutshell what type erasure in Java and polymorphic overloading are, and exemplify how they work together.

48. **Xlinting default constructors:** Explain and exemplify the JDK 16+ hint for classes with default constructors, `-Xlint:missing-explicit-ctor`.

49. **Working with the receiver parameter:** Explain the role of the Java receiver parameter and exemplify its usage in code.

50. **Implementing an immutable stack:** Provide a program that creates an immutable stack implementation from zero (implement `isEmpty()`, `push()`, `pop()`, and `peek()` operations).

51. **Revealing a common mistake with Strings:** Write a simple use case of strings that contain a common mistake (for instance, related to the `String` immutability characteristic).

52. **Using the enhanced NullPointerException:** Exemplify, from your experience, the top 5 causes of `NullPointerException` and explain how JDK 14 improves NPE messages.

53. **Using yield in switch expressions:** Explain and exemplify the usage of the `yield` keyword with `switch` expressions in JDK 13+.

54. **Tackling the case null clause in switch:** Write a bunch of examples to show different approaches for handling `null` values in `switch` expressions (including JDK 17+ approaches).

55. **Taking on the hard way to discover equals():** Explain and exemplify how `equals()` is different from the `==` operator.

56. **Hooking instanceof in a nutshell:** Provide a brief overview with snippets of code to highlight the main aspect of the `instanceof` operator.

57. **Introducing pattern matching:** Provide a theoretical dissertation including the main aspects and terminology for *pattern matching* in Java.

58. **Introducing type pattern matching for instanceof:** Provide the theoretical and practical support for using the *type pattern matching* for `instanceof`.

59. **Handling the scope of a binding variable in type patterns for instanceof:** Explain in detail, including snippets of code, the scope of *binding variables* in *type patterns* for `instanceof`.

60. **Rewriting equals() via type patterns for instanceof:** Exemplify in code the implementation of `equals()` (including for generic classes) before and after *type patterns* for `instanceof` have been introduced.

61. **Tackling type patterns for instanceof and generics:** Provide several examples that use the combo *type patterns* for `instanceof` and generics.

62. **Tackling type patterns for instanceof and streams:** Can we use *type patterns* for `instanceof` and the Stream API together? If yes, provide at least an example.

63. **Introducing type pattern matching for switch:** *Type patterns* are available for `instanceof` but are also available for `switch`. Provide here the theoretical headlines and an example of this topic.

64. **Adding guarded pattern labels in switch:** Provide a brief coverage of *guarded pattern labels* in `switch` for JDK 17 and 21.

65. **Dealing with pattern label dominance in switch:** Pattern label dominance in `switch` is a cool feature, so exemplify it here in a comprehensive approach with plenty of examples.

66. **Dealing with completeness (type coverage) in pattern labels for switch:** This is another cool topic for `switch` expressions. Explain and exemplify it in detail (theory ad examples).

67. **Understanding the unconditional patterns and nulls in switch expressions:** Explain how `null` values are handled by unconditional patterns of `switch` expressions before and after JDK 19.

The following sections describe solutions to the preceding problems. Remember that there usually isn't a single correct way to solve a particular problem. Also remember that the explanations shown here include only the most interesting and important details needed to solve the problems. Download the example solutions to see additional details and to experiment with the programs at `https://github.com/PacktPublishing/Java-Coding-Problems-Second-Edition/tree/main/Chapter02`.

38. Explain and exemplifying UTF-8, UTF-16, and UTF-32

Character encoding/decoding is important for browsers, databases, text editors, filesystems, networking, and so on, so it's a major topic for any programmer. Check out the following figure:

Figure 2.1: Representing text with different char sets

In *Figure 2.1*, we see several Chinese characters represented in UTF-8, UTF-16, and ANSI on a computer screen. But, what are these? What is ANSI? What is UTF-8 and how did we get to it? Why don't these characters look normal in ANSI?

Well, the story may begin with computers trying to represent characters (such as letters from the alphabet or digits or punctuation marks). The computers understand/process everything from the real world as a binary representation, so as a sequence of 0 and 1. This means that every character (for instance, A, 5, +, and so on) has to be mapped to a sequence of 0 and 1.

The process of mapping a character to a sequence of 0 and 1 is known as *character encoding* or simply *encoding*. The reverse process of un-mapping a sequence of 0 and 1 to a character is known as *character decoding* or simply *decoding*. Ideally, an encoding-decoding cycle should return the same character; otherwise, we obtain something that we don't understand or we cannot use.

For instance, the Chinese character, 久, should be encoded in the computer's memory as a sequence of 0 and 1. Next, when this sequence is decoded, we expect back the same Chinese letter, 久. In *Figure 2.1*, this happens in the left and middle screenshots, while in the right screenshot, the returned character is ä[1].... A Chinese speaker will not understand this (actually, nobody will), so something went wrong!

Of course, we don't have only Chinese characters to represent. We have many other sets of characters grouped in alphabets, emoticons, and so on. A set of characters has well-defined content (for instance, an alphabet has a certain number of well-defined characters) and is known as a *character set* or, in short, a *charset*.

Having a charset, the problem is to define a set of rules (a standard) that clearly explains how the characters of this charset should be encoded/decoded in the computer memory. Without having a clear set of rules, the encoding and decoding may lead to errors or indecipherable characters. Such a standard is known as an *encoding scheme*.

One of the first encoding schemes was ASCII.

Introducing ASCII encoding scheme (or single-byte encoding)

ASCII stands for American Standard Code for Information Interchange. This encoding scheme relies on a 7-bit binary system. In other words, each character that is part of the ASCII charset (http://ee.hawaii.edu/~tep/EE160/Book/chap4/subsection2.1.1.1.html) should be representable (encoded) on 7 bits. A 7-bit number can be a decimal between 0 and 127, as in the next figure:

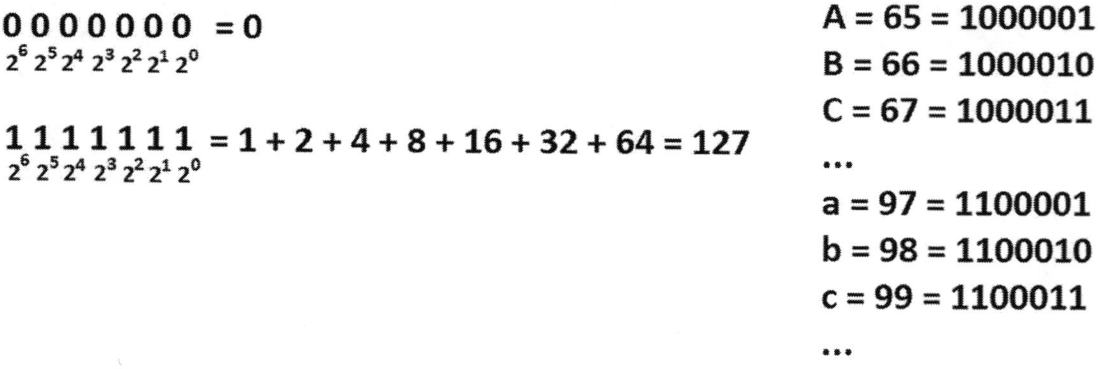

$$0\ 0\ 0\ 0\ 0\ 0\ 0 = 0$$
$$2^6\ 2^5\ 2^4\ 2^3\ 2^2\ 2^1\ 2^0$$

$$1\ 1\ 1\ 1\ 1\ 1\ 1 = 1 + 2 + 4 + 8 + 16 + 32 + 64 = 127$$
$$2^6\ 2^5\ 2^4\ 2^3\ 2^2\ 2^1\ 2^0$$

A = 65 = 1000001

B = 66 = 1000010

C = 67 = 1000011

...

a = 97 = 1100001

b = 98 = 1100010

c = 99 = 1100011

...

Figure 2.2: ASCII charset encoding

So, ASCII is an encoding scheme based on a 7-bit system that supports 128 different characters. But, we know that computers operate on bytes (octets) and a byte has 8 bits. This means that ASCII is a single-byte encoding scheme that leaves a bit free for each byte. See the following figure:

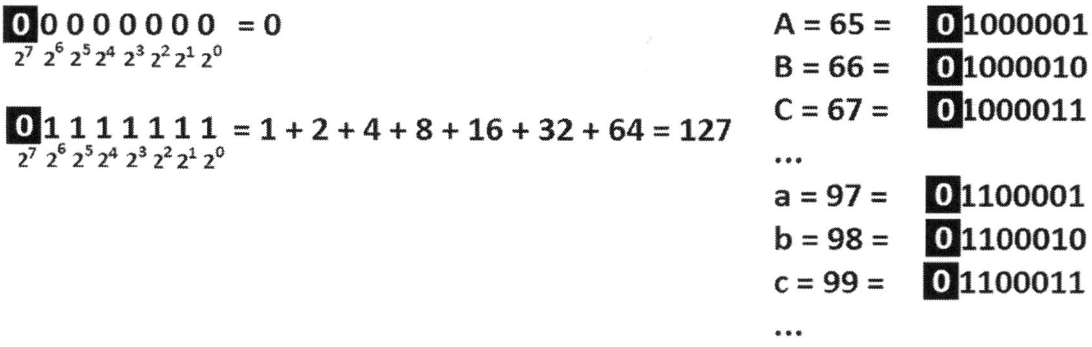

00 0 0 0 0 0 0 = 0
$2^7\ 2^6\ 2^5\ 2^4\ 2^3\ 2^2\ 2^1\ 2^0$

01 1 1 1 1 1 1 = 1 + 2 + 4 + 8 + 16 + 32 + 64 = 127
$2^7\ 2^6\ 2^5\ 2^4\ 2^3\ 2^2\ 2^1\ 2^0$

A = 65 = **0**1000001
B = 66 = **0**1000010
C = 67 = **0**1000011
...
a = 97 = **0**1100001
b = 98 = **0**1100010
c = 99 = **0**1100011
...

Figure 2.3: The highlighted bit is left free in ASCII encoding

In ASCII encoding, the letter A is 65, the letter B is 66, and so on. In Java, we can easily check this via the existing API, as in the following simple code:

```
int decimalA = "A".charAt(0); // 65
String binaryA = Integer.toBinaryString(decimalA); // 1000001
```

Or, let's see the encoding of the text *Hello World*. This time, we added the free bit as well, so the result will be 01001000 01100101 01101100 01101100 01101111 0100000 01010111 01101111 01110010 01101100 01100100:

```
char[] chars = "Hello World".toCharArray();
for(char ch : chars) {
  System.out.print("0" + Integer.toBinaryString(ch) + " ");
}
```

If we perform a match, then we see that 01001000 is *H*, 01100101 is *e*, 01101100 is *l*, 01101111 is *o*, 0100000 is space, 01010111 is *W*, 01110010 is *r*, and 01100100 is *d*. So, besides letters, the ASCII encoding can represent the English alphabet (upper and lower case), digits, space, punctuation marks, and some special characters.

Besides the core ASCII for English, we also have ASCII extensions, which are basically variations of the original ASCII to support other alphabets. Most probably, you've heard about the ISO-8859-1 (known as ISO Latin 1), which is a famous ASCII extension. But, even with ASCII extensions, there are still a lot of characters in the world that cannot be encoded yet. There are countries that have a lot more characters than ASCII can encode, and even countries that don't use alphabets. So, ASCII has its limitations.

I know what you are thinking ... let's use that free bit (2^7+127). Yes, but even so, we can go up to 256 characters. Still not enough! It is time to encode characters using more than 1 byte.

Introducing multi-byte encoding

In different parts of the world, people started to create multi-byte encoding schemes (commonly, 2 bytes). For instance, speaker of the Chinese language, which has a lot of characters, created Shift-JIS and Big5, which use 1 or 2 bytes to represent characters.

But, what happens when most of the countries come up with their own multi-byte encoding schemes trying to cover their special characters, symbols, and so on? Obviously, this leads to a huge incompatibility between the encoding schemes used in different countries. Even worse, some countries have multiple encoding schemes that are totally incompatible with each other. For instance, Japan has three different incompatible encoding schemes, which means that encoding a document with one of these encoding schemes and decoding with another will lead to a garbled document.

However, this incompatibility was not such a big issue before the Internet, since which documents have been massively shared all around the globe using computers. At that moment, the incompatibility between the encoding schemes conceived in isolation (for instance, countries and geographical regions) started to be painful.

It was the perfect moment for the Unicode Consortium to be created.

Unicode

In a nutshell, Unicode (`https://unicode-table.com/en/`) is a universal encoding standard capable of encoding/decoding every possible character in the world (we are talking about hundreds of thousands of characters).

Unicode needs more bytes to represent all these characters. But, Unicode didn't get involved in this representation. It just assigned a number to each character. This number is named a *code point*. For instance, the letter *A* in Unicode is associated with the code point 65 in decimal, and we refer to it as U+0041. This is the constant U+ followed by 65 in hexadecimal. As you can see, in Unicode, *A* is 65, exactly as in the ASCII encoding. In other words, Unicode is backward compatible with ASCII. As you'll see soon, this is big, so keep it in mind!

Early versions of Unicode contain characters having code points less than 65,535 (0xFFFF). Java represents these characters via the 16-bit char data type. For instance, the French ê (*e* with circumflex) is associated with the Unicode 234 decimal or U+00EA hexadecimal. In Java, we can use charAt() to reveal this for any Unicode character less than 65,535:

```
int e = "ê".charAt(0);              // 234
String hexe = Integer.toHexString(e); // ea
```

We also may see the binary representation of this character:

```
String binarye = Integer.toBinaryString(e); // 11101010 = 234
```

Later, Unicode added more and more characters up to 1,114,112 (0x10FFFF). Obviously, the 16-bit Java char was not enough to represent these characters, and calling charAt() was not useful anymore.

> **Important note**
>
> Java 19+ supports Unicode 14.0. The java.lang.Character API supports Level 14 of the **Unicode Character Database (UCD)**. In numbers, we have 47 new emojis, 838 new characters, and 5 new scripts. Java 20+ supports Unicode 15.0, which means 4,489 new characters for java.lang.Character.
>
> In addition, JDK 21 has added a set of methods especially for working with emojis based on their code point. Among these methods, we have boolean isEmoji(int codePoint), boolean isEmojiPresentation(int codePoint), boolean isEmojiModifier(int codePoint), boolean isEmojiModifierBase(int codePoint), boolean isEmojiComponent(int codePoint), and boolean isExtendedPictographic(int codePoint). In the bundled code, you can find a small application showing you how to fetch all available emojis and check if a given string contains emoji. So, we can easily obtain the code point of a character via Character.codePointAt() and pass it as an argument to these methods to determine whether the character is an emoji or not.

However, Unicode doesn't get involved in how these code points are encoded into bits. This is the job of special encoding schemes within Unicode, such as the **Unicode Transformation Format (UTF)** schemes. Most commonly, we use UTF-32, UTF-16, and UTF-8.

UTF-32

UTF-32 is an encoding scheme for Unicode that represents every code point on 4 bytes (32 bits). For instance, the letter *A* (having code point 65), which can be encoded on a 7-bit system, is encoded in UTF-32 as in the following figure next to the other two characters:

Byte 1	Byte 2	Byte 3	Byte 4
A = 00000000	00000000	00000000	01000001

wasted space

2^6 2^0

1+64=65 (code point)

Byte 1	Byte 2	Byte 3	Byte 4
暗 = 00000000	00000000	01100110	10010111

$2^{14}\,2^{13}$ $2^{10}\,2^9$ 2^7 2^4 $2^2\,2^1\,2^0$

wasted space

1+2+4+16+128+512+1024+8192+16384=26263 (code point)

Byte 1	Byte 2	Byte 3	Byte 4
☺ = 00000000	00000001	11110110	00001101

2^{16} $2^{15}\,2^{14}\,2^{13}\,2^{12}$ $2^{10}\,2^9$ $2^3\,2^2$ 2^0

wasted space

1+4+8+512+1024+4096+8192+16384+32768+65536=128525 (code point)

Figure 2.4: Three characters sample encoded in UTF-32

As you can see in *Figure 2.4*, UTF-32 uses 4 bytes (fixed length) to represent every character. In the case of the letter *A*, we see that UTF-32 wasted 3 bytes of memory. This means that converting an ASCII file to UTF-32 will increase its size by 4 times (for instance, a 1KB ASCII file is a 4KB UTF-32 file). Because of this shortcoming, UTF-32 is not very popular.

Java doesn't support UTF-32 as a standard charset but it relies on *surrogate pairs* (introduced in the next section).

UTF-16

UTF-16 is an encoding scheme for Unicode that represents every code point on 2 or 4 bytes (not on 3 bytes). UTF-16 has a variable length and uses an optional **Byte-Order Mark** (**BOM**), but it is recommended to use UTF-16BE (BE stands for Big-Endian byte order), or UTF-16LE (LE stands for Little-Endian byte order). While more details about Big-Endian vs. Little-Endian are available at https://en.wikipedia.org/wiki/Endianness, the following figure reveals how the orders of bytes differ in UTF-16BE (left side) vs. UTF-16LE (right side) for three characters:

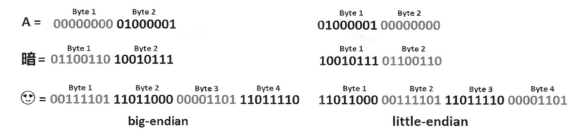

Figure 2.5: UTF-16BE (left side) vs. UTF-16LE (right side)

Since the figure is self-explanatory, let's move forward. Now, we have to tackle a trickier aspect of UTF-16. We know that in UTF-32, we take the *code point* and transform it into a 32-bit number and that's it. But, in UTF-16, we can't do that every time because we have code points that don't accommodate 16 bits. This being said, UTF-16 uses the so-called 16-bit *code units*. It can use 1 or 2 *code units* per *code point*. There are three types of code units, as follows:

- A code point needs a single code unit: these are 16-bit code units (covering U+0000 to U+D7FF, and U+E000 to U+FFFF)

- A code point needs 2 code units:

  - The first code unit is named *high surrogate* and it covers 1,024 values (U+D800 to U+DBFF)

  - The second code unit is named *low surrogate* and it covers 1,024 values (U+DC00 to U+DFFF)

A *high surrogate* followed by a *low surrogate* is named a *surrogate pair*. Surrogate pairs are needed to represent the so-called *supplementary* Unicode characters or characters having a code point larger than 65,535 (0xFFFF).

Characters such as the letter A (65) or the Chinese 暗 (26263) have a code point that can be represented via a single code unit. The following figure shows these characters in UTF-16BE:

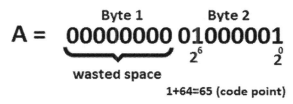

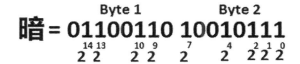

Figure 2.6: UTF-16 encoding of A and 暗

This was easy! Now, let's consider the following figure (encoding of Unicode, *Smiling Face with Heart-Shaped Eyes*):

Byte 1   **Byte 2**   **Byte 3**   **Byte 4**

😍 = **11011000 00111101 11011110 00001101**

$\underbrace{\quad}$ high $\underbrace{\quad}$ low

⇓

😍 = **00001111011000001101** = **1111011000001101**

$\quad 2^{15}\,2^{14}\,2^{13}\,2^{12}\quad 2^{10}\,2^{9}\qquad 2^{3}\,2^{2}\quad 2^{0}$

1+4+8+512+1024+4096+8192+16384+32768 =62989 +
                                      65536
                                      ————————
                                      128525 (code point)

Figure 2.7: UTF-16 encoding using a surrogate pair

The character from this figure has a code point of 128525 (or, 1 F60D) and is represented on 4 bytes.

Check the first byte: the sequence of 6 bits, 110110, identifies a high surrogate.

Check the third byte: the sequence of 6 bits, 110111, identifies a low surrogate.

These 12 bits (identifying the high and low surrogates) can be dropped and we keep the rest of the 20 bits: 00001111011000001101. We can compute this number as $2^0 + 2^2 + 2^3 + 2^9 + 2^{10} + 2^{12} + 2^{13} + 2^{14} + 2^{15} = 1 + 4 + 8 + 512 + 1024 + 4096 + 8192 + 16384 + 32768 = 62989$ (or, the hexadecimal, F60D).

Finally, we have to compute F60D + 0x10000 = 1 F60D, or in decimal 62989 + 65536 = 128525 (the code point of this Unicode character). We have to add 0x10000 because the characters that use 2 code units(a surrogate pair) are always of form 1 F...

Java supports UTF-16, UTF-16BE, and UTF-16LE. Actually, UTF-16 is the native character encoding for Java.

UTF-8

UTF-8 is an encoding scheme for Unicode that represents every code point on 1, 2, 3, or 4 bytes. Having this 1- to 4-byte flexibility, UTF-8 uses space in a very efficient way.

Important note

UTF-8 is the most popular encoding scheme that dominates the Internet and applications.

For instance, we know that the code point of the letter A is 65 and it can be encoded using a 7-bit binary representation. The following figure represents this letter encoded in UTF-8:

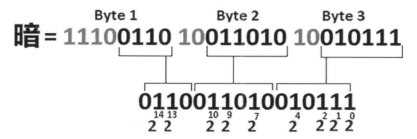

Figure 2.8: Letter A encoded in UTF-8

This is very cool! UTF-8 has used a single byte to encode A. The first (leftmost) 0 signals that this is a single-byte encoding. Next, let's see the Chinese character, 暗:

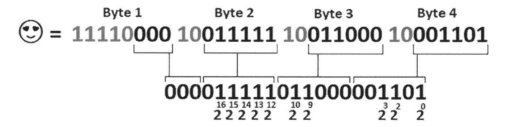

Figure 2.9: Chinese character, 暗, encoded in UTF-8

The code point of 暗 is 26263, so UTF-8 uses 3 bytes to represent it. The first byte contains 4 bits (1110) that signal that this is a 3-byte encoding. The next two bytes start with 2 bits of 10. All these 8 bits can be dropped and we keep only the remaining 16 bits, which gives us the expected code point.

Finally, let's tackle the following figure:

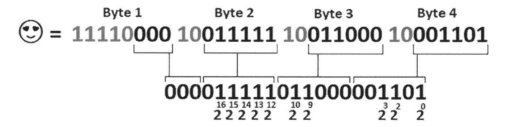

Figure 2.10: UTF-8 encoding with 4 bytes

This time, the first byte signals that this is a 4-byte encoding via 11110. The remaining 3 bytes start with 10. All these 11 bits can be dropped and we keep only the remaining 21 bits, 000011111011000001101, which gives us the expected code point, 128525.

In the following figure you can see the UTF-8 template used for encoding Unicode characters:

Number of bytes	First code point	Last code point	Byte 1	Byte 2	Byte 3	Byte 4
1	U+0000	U+007F	0xxxxxxx			
2	U+0080	U+07FF	110xxxxx	10xxxxxx		
3	U+0800	U+FFFF	1110xxxx	10xxxxxx	10xxxxxx	
4	U+10000	U+1FFFFF	11110xxx	10xxxxxx	10xxxxxx	10xxxxxx

Figure 2.11: UTF-8 template used for encoding Unicode characters

Did you know that 8 zeros in a row (00000000 – U+0000) are interpreted as NULL? A NULL represents the end of the string, so sending it "accidentally" will be a problem because the remaining string will not be processed. Fortunately, UTF-8 prevents this issue, and sending a NULL can be done only if we effectively send the U+0000 code point.

Java and Unicode

As long as we use characters with code points less than 65,535 (0xFFFF), we can rely on the charAt() method to obtain the code point. Here are some examples:

```
int cp1 = "A".charAt(0);                     // 65
String hcp1 = Integer.toHexString(cp1);      // 41
String bcp1 = Integer.toBinaryString(cp1);   // 1000001


int cp2 = "暗".charAt(0);                     // 26263
String hcp2 = Integer.toHexString(cp2);      // 6697
String bcp2 = Integer.toBinaryString(cp2);   // 1101100000111101
```

Based on these examples, we may write a helper method that returns the binary representation of strings having code points less than 65,535 (0xFFFF) as follows (you already saw the imperative version of the following functional code earlier):

```
public static String strToBinary(String str) {

    String binary = str.chars()
      .mapToObj(Integer::toBinaryString)
      .map(t -> "0" + t)
      .collect(Collectors.joining(" "));

    return binary;
}
```

If you run this code against a Unicode character having a code point greater than 65,535 (0xFFFF), then you'll get the wrong result. You'll not get an exception or any kind of warning.

So, charAt() covers only a subset of Unicode characters. For covering all Unicode characters, Java provides an API that consists of several methods. For instance, if we replace charAt() with codePointAt(), then we obtain the correct code point in all cases, as you can see in the following figure:

```
int a1 = "A".charAt(0);        // 65
int a2 = "A".codePointAt(0);   // 65

int b1 = "睄".charAt(0);        // 26263
int b2 = "睄".codePointAt(0);   // 26263

int c1 = "😊".charAt(0);        // 55357  - wrong
int c2 = "😊".codePointAt(0);   // 128525 - correct
```

Figure 2.12: charAt() vs. codePointAt()

Check out the last example, c2. Since codePointAt() returns the correct code point (128525), we can obtain the binary representation as follows:

```
String uc = Integer.toBinaryString(c2); // 11111011000001101
```

So, if we need a method that returns the binary encoding of any Unicode character, then we can replace the chars() call with the codePoints() call. The codePoints() method returns the code points of the given sequence:

```
public static String codePointToBinary(String str) {

    String binary = str.codePoints()
        .mapToObj(Integer::toBinaryString)
        .collect(Collectors.joining(" "));

    return binary;
}
```

The codePoints() method is just one of the methods provided by Java to work around code points. The Java API also includes codePointAt(), offsetByCodePoints(), codePointCount(), codePointBefore(), codePointOf(), and so on. You can find several examples of them in the bundled code next to this one for obtaining a String from a given code point:

```
String str1 = String.valueOf(Character.toChars(65)); // A
String str2 = String.valueOf(Character.toChars(128525));
```

The toChars() method gets a code point and returns the UTF-16 representation via a char[]. The string returned by the first example (str1) has a length of 1 and is the letter A. The second example returns a string of length 2 since the character having the code point 128525 needs a surrogate pair. The returned char[] contains both the high and low surrogates.

Finally, let's have a helper method that allows us to obtain the binary representation of a string for a given encoding scheme:

```java
public static String stringToBinaryEncoding(
        String str, String encoding) {

    final Charset charset = Charset.forName(encoding);
    final byte[] strBytes = str.getBytes(charset);
    final StringBuilder strBinary = new StringBuilder();

    for (byte strByte : strBytes) {
        for (int i = 0; i < 8; i++) {

            strBinary.append((strByte & 128) == 0 ? 0 : 1);
            strByte <<= 1;
        }

        strBinary.append(" ");
    }

    return strBinary.toString().trim();
}
```

Using this method is quite simple, as you can see in the following examples:

```java
// 00000000 00000000 00000000 01000001
String r = Charsets.stringToBinaryEncoding("A", "UTF-32");

// 10010111 01100110
String r = Charsets.stringToBinaryEncoding("暗",
            StandardCharsets.UTF_16LE.name());
```

You can practice more examples in the bundled code.

JDK 18 defaults the charset to UTF-8

Before JDK 18, the default charset was determined based on the operating system charset and locale (for instance, on a Windows machine, it could be windows-1252). Starting with JDK 18, the default charset is UTF-8 (`Charset.defaultCharset()` returns the string, UTF-8). Or, having a `PrintStream` instance, we can find out the used charset via the `charset()` method (starting with JDK 18).

But, the default charset can be explicitly set via the `file.encoding` and `native.encoding` system properties at the command line. For instance, you may need to perform such modification to compile legacy code developed before JDK 18:

```java
// the default charset is computed from native.encoding
```

```
java -Dfile-encoding = COMPAT
// the default charset is windows-1252
java -Dfile-encoding = windows-1252
```

So, since JDK 18, classes that use encoding (for instance, `FileReader`/`FileWriter`, `InputStreamReader`/ `OutputStreamWriter`, `PrintStream`, `Formatter`, `Scanner`, and `URLEncoder`/`URLDecoder`) can take advantage of UTF-8 out of the box. For instance, using UTF-8 before JDK 18 for reading a file can be accomplished by explicitly specifying this charset encoding scheme as follows:

```
try ( BufferedReader br = new BufferedReader(new FileReader(
    chineseUtf8File.toFile(), StandardCharsets.UTF_8))) {
    ...
}
```

Accomplishing the same thing in JDK 18+ doesn't require explicitly specifying the charset encoding scheme:

```
try ( BufferedReader br = new BufferedReader(
    new FileReader(chineseUtf8File.toFile()))) {
    ...
}
```

However, for `System.out` and `System.err`, JDK 18+ still uses the default system charset. So, if you are using `System.out/err` and you see question marks (?) instead of the expected characters, then most probably you should set UTF-8 via the new properties `-Dstdout.encoding` and `-Dstderr.encoding`:

```
-Dstderr.encoding=utf8 -Dstdout.encoding=utf8
```

Or, you can set them as environment variables to set them globally:

```
_JAVA_OPTIONS="-Dstdout.encoding=utf8 -Dstderr.encoding=utf8"
```

In the bundled code you can see more examples.

39. Checking a sub-range in the range from 0 to length

Checking that a given sub-range is in the range from 0 to the given length is a common check in a lot of problems. For instance, let's consider that we have to write a function responsible for checking if the client can increase the pressure in a water pipe. The client gives us the current average pressure (`avgPressure`), the maximum pressure (`maxPressure`), and the amount of extra pressure that should be applied (`unitsOfPressure`).

But, before we can apply our secret algorithm, we have to check that the inputs are correct. So, we have to ensure that none of the following cases happens:

- `avgPressure` is less than 0
- `unitsOfPressure` is less than 0
- `maxPressure` is less than 0

- The range [avgPressure, avgPressure + unitsOfPressure) is out of bounds represented by maxPressure

So, in code lines, our function may look as follows:

```
public static boolean isPressureSupported(
        int avgPressure, int unitsOfPressure, int maxPressure) {

    if(avgPresure < 0 || unitsOfPressure < 0 || maxPressure < 0
       || (avgPresure + unitsOfPressure) > maxPressure) {

        throw new IndexOutOfBoundsException(
              "One or more parameters are out of bounds");
    }

    // the secret algorithm
    return (avgPressure + unitsOfPressure) <
      (maxPressure - maxPressure/4);
}
```

Writing composite conditions such as ours is prone to accidental mistakes. It is better to rely on the Java API whenever possible. And, for this use case, it is possible! Starting with JDK 9, in java.util. Objects, we have the method checkFromIndexSize(int fromIndex, int size, int length), and starting with JDK 16, we also have a flavor for long arguments, checkFromIndexSize(int fromIndex, int size, int length). If we consider that avgPressure is fromIndex, unitsOfPressure is size, and maxPressure is length, then checkFromIndexSize() performs the arguments validation and throws an IndexOutOfBoundsException if something goes wrong. So, we write the code as follows:

```
public static boolean isPressureSupported(
        int avgPressure, int unitsOfPressure, int maxPressure) {

    Objects.checkFromIndexSize(
      avgPressure, unitsOfPressure, maxPressure);

    // the secret algorithm
    return (avgPressure + unitsOfPressure) <
      (maxPressure - maxPressure/4);
}
```

In the code bundle, you can see one more example of using checkFromIndexSize().

Besides checkFromIndexSize(), in java.util.Objects, we can find several other companions that cover common composite conditions such as checkIndex(int index, int length) – JDK 9, checkIndex(long index, long length) – JDK 16, checkFromToIndex(int fromIndex, int toIndex, int length) – JDK 9, and checkFromToIndex(long fromIndex, long toIndex, long length) – JDK 16.

And, by the way, if we switch the context to strings, then JDK 21 provides an overload of the well-known `String.indexOf()`, capable of searching a character/substring in a given string between a given begin index and end index. The signature is `indexOf(String str, int beginIndex, int endIndex)` and it returns the index of the first occurrence of `str`, or -1 if `str` is not found. Basically, this is a neat version of `s.substring(beginIndex, endIndex).indexOf(str) + beginIndex`.

40. Returning an identity string

So, what's an *identity string*? An identity string is a string built from an object without calling the over-ridden `toString()` or `hashCode()`. It is equivalent to the following concatenation:

```
object.getClass().getName() + "@"
  + Integer.toHexString(System.identityHashCode(object))
```

Starting with JDK 19, this string is wrapped in `Objects.toIdentityString(Object object)`. Consider the following class (`object`):

```
public class MyPoint {

  private final int x;
  private final int y;
  private final int z;
  ...

  @Override
  public String toString() {
    return "MyPoint{" + "x=" + x + ", y=" + y
                      + ", z=" + z + '}';
  }
}
```

By calling `toIdentityString()`, we obtain something as follows:

```
MyPoint p = new MyPoint(1, 2, 3);

// modern.challenge.MyPoint@76ed5528
Objects.toIdentityString(p);
```

Obviously, the overridden `MyPoint.toString()` method was not called. If we print out the hash code of p, we get 76ed5528, which is exactly what `toIdentityString()` returned. Now, let's override `hashCode()` as well:

```
@Override
public int hashCode() {
  int hash = 7;
  hash = 23 * hash + this.x;
```

```
    hash = 23 * hash + this.y;
    hash = 23 * hash + this.z;
    return hash;
}
```

This time, `toIdentityString()` returns the same thing, while our `hashCode()` returns `14ef3`.

41. Hooking unnamed classes and instance main methods

Imagine that you have to initiate a student in Java. The classical approach of introducing Java is to show the student a *Hello World!* Example, as follows:

```
public class HelloWorld {

  public static void main(String[] args) {
    System.out.println("Hello World!");
  }
}
```

This is the simplest Java example but it is not simple to explain to the student what `public` or `static` or `String[]` are. The ceremony involved in this simple example may scare the student – *if this is a simple example, then how is it a more complex one?*

Fortunately, starting with JDK 21 (JEP 445), we have *instance main methods*, which is a preview feature that allows us to shorten the previous example as follows:

```
public class HelloWorld {

  void main() {
    System.out.println("Hello World!");
  }
}
```

We can even go further and remove the explicit class declaration as well. This feature is known as *unnamed classes*. An unnamed class resides in the unnamed package that resides in the unnamed module:

```
void main() {
  System.out.println("Hello World!");
}
```

Java will generate the class on our behalf. The name of the class will be the same as the name of the source file.

That's all we need to introduce Java to a student. I strongly encourage you to read JEP 445 (and the new JEPs that will continue this JDK 21 preview feature work) to discover all the aspects involved in these features.

42. Adding code snippets in Java API documentation

I'm sure that you are familiar with generating **Java API documentation** (**Javadoc**) for your projects. We can do it via the `javadoc` tool from the command line, via IDE support, via the Maven plugin (`maven-javadoc-plugin`), and so on.

A common case in writing the Javadoc consists of adding snippets of code to exemplify the usage of a non-trivial class or method. Before JDK 18, adding snippets of code in documentation can be done via `{@code...}` or the `<pre>` tag. The added code is treated as plain text, is not validated for correctness, and is not discoverable by other tools. Let's quickly see an example:

```
/**
 * A telemeter with laser ranging from 0 to 60 ft including
 * calculation of surfaces and volumes with high-precision
 *
 * <pre>{@code
 *     Telemeter.Calibrate.at(0.00001);
 *     Telemeter telemeter = new Telemeter(0.15, 2, "IP54");
 * }</pre>
 */
public class Telemeter {
    ...
```

In the bundled code, you can see the full example. The Javadoc is generated at build time via the Maven plugin (`maven-javadoc-plugin`), so simply trigger a build.

Starting with JDK 18 (JEP 413 - *Code Snippets in Java API Documentation*), we have brand new support for adding snippets of code in documentation via the `{@snippet...}` tag. The code added via `@snippet` can be discovered and validated by third-party tools (not by the `javadoc` tool itself).

For instance, the previous snippet can be added via `@snippet` as follows:

```
/**
 * A telemeter with laser ranging from 0 to 60 ft including
 * calculation of surfaces and volumes with high-precision
 *
 * {@snippet :
 *     Telemeter.Calibrate.at(0.00001);
 *     Telemeter telemeter = new Telemeter(0.15, 2, "IP54");
 * }
 */
public class Telemeter {
    ...
```

A screenshot of the output is in the following figure:

A telemeter with laser ranging from 0 to 60 ft including calculation of surfaces and volumes with high-precision

```
Telemeter.Calibrate.at(0.00001);
Telemeter telemeter = new Telemeter(0.15, 2, "IP54");
```

Figure 2.13: Simple output from @snippet

The effective code starts from the newline placed after the colon (:) and ends before the closing right curly bracket (}). The code indentation is treated as in code blocks, so the compiler removes the incidental white spaces and we can indent the code with respect to the closing right curly bracket (}). Check out the following figure:

```
* {@snippet :
*       Telemeter.Calibrate.at(0.00001);
*       Telemeter telemeter = new Telemeter(
*           0.15,
*           2,
*           "IP54"
*       );
* }
```

```
Telemeter.Calibrate.at(0.00001);
Telemeter telemeter = new Telemeter(
    0.15,
    2,
    "IP54"
);
```

```
.* {@snippet :
.*       Telemeter.Calibrate.at(0.00001);
.*       Telemeter telemeter = new Telemeter(
.*           0.15,
.*           2,
.*           "IP54"
.*       );
*           }
```

```
Telemeter.Calibrate.at(0.00001);
Telemeter telemeter = new Telemeter(
    0.15,
    2,
    "IP54"
);
```

Figure 2.14: Indentation of code snippets

In the top example, the closing right curly bracket is aligned under the opening left curly bracket, while in the bottom example, we shifted the closing right curly bracket to the right.

Adding attributes

We can specify attributes for a @snippet via *name=value* pairs. For instance, we can provide a tip about the programming language of our snippet via the lang attribute. The value of the attribute is available to external tools and is present in the generated HTML. Here are two examples:

```
*  {@snippet lang="java" :
*      Telemeter.Calibrate.at(0.00001);
*      Telemeter telemeter = new Telemeter(0.15, 2, "IP54");
*  }
```

In the generated HTML, you'll easily identify this attribute as:

```
<code class="language-java"> … </code>
```

If the code is a structured text such as a *properties* file, then you can follow this example:

```
*  {@snippet lang="properties" :
*    telemeter.precision.default=42
*    telemeter.clazz.default=2
*  }
```

In the generated HTML, you'll have:

```
<code class="language-properties"></code>
```

Next, let's see how can we alter what is displayed in a snippet.

Using markup comments and regions

We can visually alter a snippet of code via *markup comments*. A markup comment occurs at the end of the line and it contains one or more *markup tags* of the form @name args, where args are commonly *name=value* pairs. Common markup comments include highlighting, linking, and content (text) modifications.

Highlighting

Highlighting a whole line can be done via @highlight without arguments, as in the following figure:

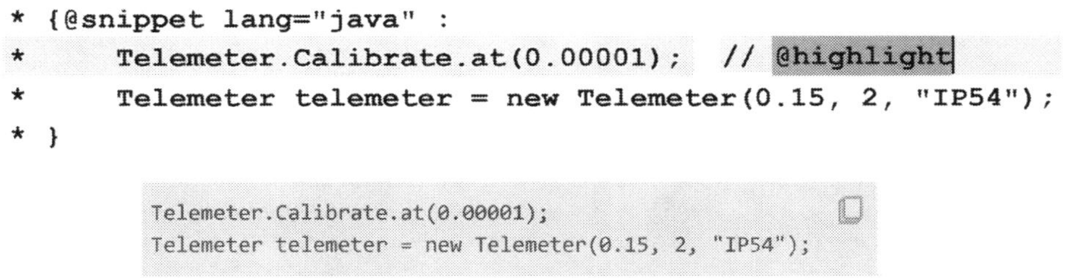

```
*  {@snippet lang="java" :
*      Telemeter.Calibrate.at(0.00001);   // @highlight
*      Telemeter telemeter = new Telemeter(0.15, 2, "IP54");
*  }
```

```
Telemeter.Calibrate.at(0.00001);
Telemeter telemeter = new Telemeter(0.15, 2, "IP54");
```

Figure 2.15: Highlighting a whole line of code

As you can see in this figure, the first line of code was bolded.

If we want to highlight multiple lines, then we can define *regions*. A region can be treated as anonymous or have an explicit name. An anonymous region is demarcated by the word `region` placed as an argument of the markup tag and the `@end` tag placed at the end of the region. Here is an example for highlighting two regions (an anonymous one and a named one (`R1`)):

```
* {@snippet lang="java" :
*     Telemeter.Calibrate.at(0.00001);
*     Telemeter telemeter = new Telemeter( // @highlight region
*         0.15,
*         2,
*         "IP54"                           // @end
*     );
* }

  {@snippet lang="java" :
      Telemeter.Calibrate.at(0.00001);
      Telemeter telemeter = new Telemeter( // @highlight region=R1
          0.15,
          2,
          "IP54"                           // @end region=R1
      );
  }
```

Figure 2.16: Highlighting a block of code using regions

Regular expressions allow us to highlight a certain part of the code. For instance, highlighting everything that occurs between quotes can be done via `@highlight regex='".*"'`. Or, highlighting only the word *Calibrate* can be done via the `substring="Calibrate"` argument, as in the following figure:

```
* {@snippet :
*   Telemeter.Calibrate.at(0.00001, "HIGH"); // @highlight substring="Calibrate" type=highlighted
* }
```

Figure 2.17: Highlighting only the word "Calibrate"

Next, let's talk about adding links in code.

Linking

Adding links in code can be done via the `@link` tag. The common arguments are `substring="…"` and `target="…"`. For instance, the following snippet provides a link for the text *Calibrate* that navigates in documentation to the description of the `Calibrate.at()` method:

Figure 2.18: Adding links in code

Next, let's see how we can modify the code's text.

Modifying the code's text

Sometimes we may need to alter the code's text. For instance, instead of `Telemeter.Calibrate.`
`at(0.00001, "HIGH");`, we want to render in documentation `Telemeter.Calibrate.at(eps, "HIGH");`.
So, we need to replace `0.00001` with `eps`. This is the perfect job for the `@replace` tag. Common arguments include `substring="…"` (or, `regex="…"`) and `replacement="..."`. Here is the snippet:

```
*   Telemeter.Calibrate.at(0.00001, "HIGH"); // @replace substring='0.00001' replacement="eps"
```

```
Telemeter.Calibrate.at(eps, "HIGH");  📋
```

Figure 2.19: Replacing the code's text

If you need to perform multiple replacements in a block of code, then rely on regions. In the following
example, we apply a regular expression to a block of code:

```
* Telemeter telemeter = new Telemeter( // @replace region regex="\d(?=\,)" replacement="..."
*     0.18,
*     7,
*     "IP54"                          // @end
* );
```

```
Telemeter telemeter = new Telemeter(  📋
    0.1...,
    ...,
    "IP54"
);
```

Figure 2.20: Applying multiple replacements via a simple regex and an anonymous region

If you need to perform more replacements on the same line, then just chain multiple `@replace` tags
(this statement applies to all tags such as `@highlight`, `@link`, and so on).

Using external snippets

So far, we have used only inlined snippets. But, there are scenarios when using inlined snippets is
not a convenient approach (for instance, if we need to repeat some parts of the documentation) or
it is not possible to use them (for instance, if we want to embed `/*…*/` comments, which cannot be
added in inlined snippets).

For such cases, we can use external snippets. Without any further configurations, JDK automatically recognizes external snippets if they are placed in a subfolder of the package (folder) containing the snippet tag. This subfolder should be named `snippet-files` and it can contain external snippets as Java sources, plain text files, or properties files. In the following figure, we have a single external file named `MainSnippet.txt`:

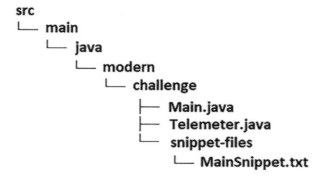

Figure 2.21: External snippets in snippet-files

If the external snippet is not a Java file, then it can be loaded via {@snippet file …} as follows:

```
{@snippet file = MainSnippet.txt}
{@snippet file = "MainSnippet.txt"}
{@snippet file = 'MainSnippet.txt'}
```

But, we can also customize the place and folder name of external snippets. For instance, let's place the external snippets in a folder named `snippet-src`, as follows:

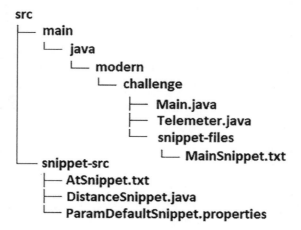

Figure 2.22: External snippets in a custom folder and place

This time, we have to instruct the compiler where to find the external snippets. This is done by passing the `--snippet-path` option to `javadoc`. Of course, you can pass it via the command line, via your IDE, or via `maven-javadoc-plugin`, as follows:

```
<additionalJOption>
    --snippet-path C:\...\src\snippet-src
</additionalJOption>
```

This path is relative to your machine, so feel free to adjust it accordingly in pom.xml.

Next, AtSnippet.txt and ParamDefaultSnippet.properties can be loaded exactly as you saw earlier for MainSnippet.txt. However, loading Java sources, such as DistanceSnippet.java, can be done via {@snippet class…}, as follows:

```
{@snippet class = DistanceSnippet}
{@snippet class = "DistanceSnippet"}
{@snippet class = 'DistanceSnippet'}
```

But, do not add explicitly the .java extension because you'll get an error such as *file not found on source path or snippet path: DistanceSnippet/java.java*:

```
{@snippet class = DistanceSnippet.java}
```

When using Java sources as external snippets, pay attention to the following note.

Important note

Even if the predefined snippet-files name is an invalid name for a Java package, some systems may treat this folder as being part of the package hierarchy. In such cases, if you place Java sources in this folder, you'll get an error such as *Illegal package name: "foo.buzz. snippet-files"*. If you find yourself in this scenario, then simply use another folder name and location for the documentation external snippets written in Java sources.

Regions in external snippets

The external snippets support regions via @start region=… and @end region=…. For instance, in AtSnippet.txt, we have the following region:

```
// This is an example used in the documentation
// @start region=only-code
    Telemeter.Calibrate.at(0.00001, "HIGH");
// @end region=only-code
```

Now, if we load the region as:

```
{@snippet file = AtSnippet.txt region=only-code}
```

We obtain only the code from the region without the text, *// This is an example used in the documentation*.

Here is another example of a properties file with two regions:

```
# @start region=dist
```

```
sc=[0,0]
ec=[0,0]
interpolation=false
# @end region=dist
# @start region=at
eps=0.1
type=null
# @end region=at
```

The region `dist` is used to show the default values for the arguments of the `distance()` method in the documentation:

```
   ...
 * <p><b>Defaults:</b></p>
 * {@snippet file = ParamDefaultSnippet.properties region=dist}
 */
public int distance(Point sc, Point ec, boolean interpolation) {
    ...
}
```

Defaults:

```
sc=[0,0]
ec=[0,0]
interpolation=false
```

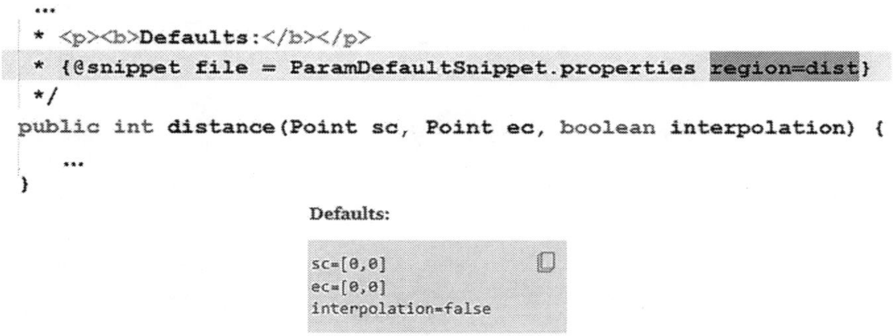

Figure 2.23: Using the dist region

And, the at region is used to show the default values for the arguments of the `at()` method in the documentation:

```
   ...
 * <p><b>Defaults:</b></p>
 * {@snippet file = ParamDefaultSnippet.properties region=at}
 *
 * PERFORM THE CALIBRATION BEFORE CREATING AN INSTANCE OF THIS CLASS
 */
public static boolean at(double eps, String type) {
    ...
}
```

Defaults:

```
eps=0.1
type=null
```

PERFORM THE CALIBRATION BEFORE CREATING AN INSTANCE OF THIS CLASS

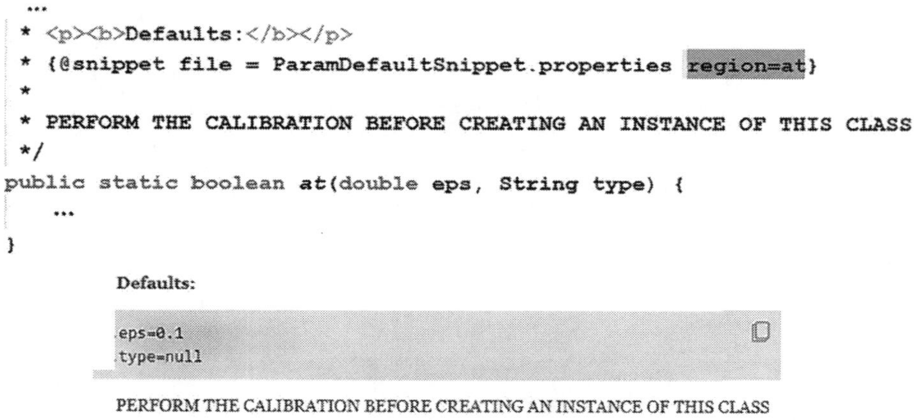

Figure 2.24: Using the "at" region

In external snippets, we can use the same tags as in the inlined snippets. For instance, in the following figure, you can see the complete source of AtSnippet.txt:

```
// This is an example used in the documentation
// @start region=only-code
                              // @highlight region substring="Calibrate" type=highlighted
Telemeter.Calibrate.at(0.00001, "HIGH"); // @replace substring='0.00001' replacement="eps" @replace substring='"HIGH"' replacement='"..."'
                              // @end
// @end region=only-code
```

Figure 2.25: Source of AtSnippet.txt

Notice the presence of @highlight and @replace.

> **Important note**
>
> Starting with JDK 19, the Javadoc search feature was also improved. In other words, JDK 19+ can generate a standalone search page for searching in the Javadoc API documentation. Moreover, the search syntax has been enhanced to support multiple search words.

You can practice these examples in the bundled code.

43. Invoking default methods from Proxy instances

Starting with JDK 8, we can define default methods in interfaces. For instance, let's consider the following interfaces (for brevity, all methods from these interfaces are declared as default):

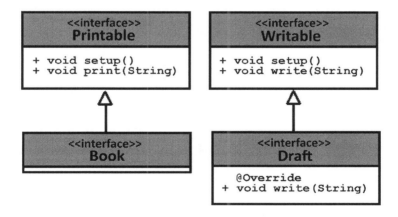

Figure 2.26: Interfaces: Printable, Writable, Draft, and Book

Next, let's assume that we want to use the Java Reflection API to invoke these default methods. As a quick reminder, the Proxy class goal is used to provide support for creating dynamic implementations of interfaces at runtime.

That being said, let's see how we can use the Proxy API for calling our default methods.

JDK 8

Calling a default method of an interface in JDK 8 relies on a little trick. Basically, we create from scratch a *package-private* constructor from the Lookup API. Next, we make this constructor accessible – this means that Java will not check the access modifiers to this constructor and, therefore, will not throw an `IllegalAccessException` when we try to use it. Finally, we use this constructor to wrap an instance of an interface (for instance, `Printable`) and use reflective access to the `default` methods declared in this interface.

So, in code lines, we can invoke the default method `Printable.print()` as follows:

```
// invoke Printable.print(String)
Printable pproxy = (Printable) Proxy.newProxyInstance(
  Printable.class.getClassLoader(),
  new Class<?>[]{Printable.class}, (o, m, p) -> {

    if (m.isDefault()) {
      Constructor<Lookup> cntr = Lookup.class
        .getDeclaredConstructor(Class.class);

      cntr.setAccessible(true);

      return cntr.newInstance(Printable.class)
                 .in(Printable.class)
                 .unreflectSpecial(m, Printable.class)
                 .bindTo(o)
                 .invokeWithArguments(p);
    }

    return null;
  });

// invoke Printable.print()
pproxy.print("Chapter 2");
```

Next, let's focus on the `Writable` and `Draft` interfaces. `Draft` extends `Writable` and overrides the default `write()`method. Now, every time we explicitly invoke the `Writable.write()` method, we expect that the `Draft.write()` method is invoked automatically behind the scenes. A possible implementation looks as follows:

```
// invoke Draft.write(String) and Writable.write(String)
Writable dpproxy = (Writable) Proxy.newProxyInstance(
 Writable.class.getClassLoader(),
  new Class<?>[]{Writable.class, Draft.class}, (o, m, p) -> {
```

```
    if (m.isDefault() && m.getName().equals("write")) {

      Constructor<Lookup> cntr = Lookup.class
        .getDeclaredConstructor(Class.class);

      cntr.setAccessible(true);

      cntr.newInstance(Draft.class)
          .in(Draft.class)
          .findSpecial(Draft.class, "write",
              MethodType.methodType(void.class, String.class),
              Draft.class)
          .bindTo(o)
          .invokeWithArguments(p);

      return cntr.newInstance(Writable.class)
          .in(Writable.class)
          .findSpecial(Writable.class, "write",
              MethodType.methodType(void.class, String.class),
              Writable.class)
          .bindTo(o)
          .invokeWithArguments(p);
    }

    return null;
  });

// invoke Writable.write(String)
dpproxy.write("Chapter 1");
```

Finally, let's focus on the `Printable` and `Book` interfaces. `Book` extends `Printable` and doesn't define any methods. So, when we call the inherited `print()` method, we expect that the `Printable.print()` method is invoked. While you can check this solution in the bundled code, let's focus on the same tasks using JDK 9+.

JDK 9+, pre-JDK 16

As you just saw, before JDK 9, the Java Reflection API provides access to non-public class members. This means that external reflective code (for instance, third-party libraries) can have deep access to JDK internals. But, starting with JDK 9, this is not possible because the new module system relies on strong encapsulation.

For a smooth transition from JDK 8 to JDK 9, we can use the `--illegal-access` option. The values of this option range from deny (sustains strong encapsulation, so no illegal reflective code is permitted) to permit (the most relaxed level of strong encapsulation, allowing access to platform modules only from unnamed modules). Between permit (which is the default in JDK 9) and deny, we have two more values: warn and debug. However, `--illegal-access=permit;` support was removed in JDK 17.

In this context, the previous code may not work in JDK 9+, or it might still work but you'll see a warning such as *WARNING: An illegal reflective access operation has occurred*.

But, we can "fix" our code to avoid illegal reflective access via `MethodHandles`. Among its goodies, this class exposes lookup methods for creating method handles for fields and methods. Once we have a `Lookup`, we can rely on its `findSpecial()` method to gain access to the `default` methods of an interface.

Based on `MethodHandles`, we can invoke the default method `Printable.print()` as follows:

```
// invoke Printable.print(String doc)
Printable pproxy = (Printable) Proxy.newProxyInstance(
    Printable.class.getClassLoader(),
    new Class<?>[]{Printable.class}, (o, m, p) -> {

      if (m.isDefault()) {
       return MethodHandles.lookup()
         .findSpecial(Printable.class, "print",
           MethodType.methodType(void.class, String.class),
           Printable.class)
         .bindTo(o)
         .invokeWithArguments(p);
      }

      return null;
  });

// invoke Printable.print()
pproxy.print("Chapter 2");
```

While in the bundled code, you can see more examples; let's tackle the same topic starting with JDK 16.

JDK 16+

Starting with JDK 16, we can simplify the previous code thanks to the new static method, `InvocationHandler.invokeDefault()`. As its name suggests, this method is useful for invoking `default` methods. In code lines, our previous examples for calling `Printable.print()` can be simplified via `invokeDefault()` as follows:

```
// invoke Printable.print(String doc)
Printable pproxy = (Printable) Proxy.newProxyInstance(
```

```
    Printable.class.getClassLoader(),
      new Class<?>[]{Printable.class}, (o, m, p) -> {

        if (m.isDefault()) {
          return InvocationHandler.invokeDefault(o, m, p);
        }

        return null;
    });

// invoke Printable.print()
pproxy.print("Chapter 2");
```

In the next example, every time we explicitly invoke the `Writable.write()` method, we expect that the `Draft.write()` method is invoked automatically behind the scenes:

```
// invoke Draft.write(String) and Writable.write(String)
Writable dpproxy = (Writable) Proxy.newProxyInstance(
  Writable.class.getClassLoader(),
    new Class<?>[]{Writable.class, Draft.class}, (o, m, p) -> {

    if (m.isDefault() && m.getName().equals("write")) {

      Method writeInDraft = Draft.class.getMethod(
        m.getName(), m.getParameterTypes());
      InvocationHandler.invokeDefault(o, writeInDraft, p);

      return InvocationHandler.invokeDefault(o, m, p);
    }

    return null;
  });

// invoke Writable.write(String)
dpproxy.write("Chapter 1");
```

In the bundled code, you can practice more examples.

44. Converting between bytes and hex-encoded strings

Converting bytes to hexadecimal (and vice versa) is a common operation in applications that manipulate fluxes of files/messages, perform encoding/decoding tasks, process images, and so on.

A Java byte is a number in the [-128, +127] range and is represented using 1 signed byte (8 bits). A hexadecimal (base 16) is a system based on 16 digits (0, 1, 2, 3, 4, 5, 6, 7, 8, 9, A, B, C, D, E, and F). In other words, those 8 bits of a byte value accommodate exactly 2 hexadecimal characters in the range 00 to FF. The decimal <-> binary <-> hexadecimal mapping is resumed in the following figure:

Decimal	0	1	2	3	4	5	6	7	8	9	10	11	12	13	14	15
Binary	0000	0001	0010	0011	0100	0101	0110	0111	1000	1001	1010	1011	1100	1101	1110	1111
Hex	0	1	2	3	4	5	6	7	8	9	A	B	C	D	E	F

Figure 2.27: Decimal to binary to hexadecimal conversion

For instance, 122 in binary is 01111010. Since 0111 is in hexadecimal 7, and 1010 is A, this results in 122 being 7A in hexadecimal (also written as 0x7A).

How about a negative byte? We know from the previous chapter that Java represents a negative number as *two's complement* of the positive number. This means that -122 in binary is 10000110 (retain the first 7 bits of positive 122 = 1111010, flip(1111010) = 0000101, add(0000001) = 00000110, and append sign bit 1, 10000110) and in hexadecimal, is 0x86.

Converting a negative number to hexadecimal can be done in several ways, but we can easily obtain the lower 4 bits as 10000110 & 0xF = 0110, and the higher four bits as (10000110>> 4) & 0xF = 1000 & 0xF = 1000 (here, the 0xF (binary, 1111) mask is useful only for negative numbers). Since, 0110 = 6 and 1000 = 8, we see that 10000110 is in hexadecimal 0x86.

If you need a deep coverage of bits manipulation in Java or you simply face issues in understanding the current topic, then please consider the book *The Complete Coding Interview Guide in Java*, especially *Chapter 9*.

So, in code lines, we can rely on this simple algorithm and `Character.forDigit(int d, int r)`, which returns the character representation for the given digit (d) in the given radix (r):

```java
public static String byteToHexString(byte v) {

  int higher = (v >> 4) & 0xF;
  int lower = v & 0xF;

  String result = String.valueOf(
    new char[]{
      Character.forDigit(higher, 16),
      Character.forDigit(lower, 16)}
    );

  return result;
}
```

There are many other ways to solve this problem (in the bundled code, you can see another flavor of this solution). For example, if we know that the `Integer.toHexString(int n)` method returns a string that represents the unsigned integer in base 16 of the given argument, then all we need is to apply the 0xFF (binary, 11111111) mask for negatives as:

```
public static String byteToHexString(byte v) {

    return Integer.toHexString(v & 0xFF);
}
```

If there is an approach that we should avoid, then that is the one based on `String.format()`. The `String.format("%02x ", byte_nr)` approach is concise but very slow!

How about the reverse process? Converting a given hexadecimal string (for instance, 7d, 09, and so on) to a byte is quite easy. Just take the first (d1) and second (d2) character of the given string and apply the relation, `(byte) ((d1 << 4) + d2)`:

```
public static byte hexToByte(String s) {

    int d1 = Character.digit(s.charAt(0), 16);
    int d2 = Character.digit(s.charAt(1), 16);

    return (byte) ((d1 << 4) + d2);
}
```

More examples are available in the bundled code. If you rely on third-party libraries, then check Apache Commons Codec (`Hex.encodeHexString()`), Guava (`BaseEncoding`), Spring Security (`Hex.encode()`), Bouncy Castle (`Hex.toHexString()`), and so on.

JDK 17+

Starting with JDK 17, we can use the `java.util.HexFormat` class. This class has plenty of static methods for handling hexadecimal numbers, including `String toHexDigits(byte value)` and `byte[] parseHex(CharSequence string)`. So, we can convert a byte to a hexadecimal string as follows:

```
public static String byteToHexString(byte v) {

    HexFormat hex = HexFormat.of();

    return hex.toHexDigits(v);
}
```

And, vice versa as follows:

```
public static byte hexToByte(String s) {

    HexFormat hex = HexFormat.of();
```

```
    return hex.parseHex(s)[0];
}
```

In the bundled code, you can also see the extrapolation of these solutions for converting an array of bytes (byte[]) to a String, and vice versa.

45. Exemplify the initialization-on-demand holder design pattern

Before we tackle the solution of implementing the initialization-on-demand holder design pattern, let's quickly recap a few ingredients of this solution.

Static vs. non-static blocks

In Java, we can have *initialization non-static blocks* and *static blocks*. An initialization non-static block (or simply, a non-static block) is automatically called every single time we instantiate the class. On the other hand, an initialization static block (or simply, a static block) is called a single time when the class itself is initialized. No matter how many subsequent instances of that class we create, the static block will never get executed again. In code lines:

```java
public class A {

  {
    System.out.println("Non-static initializer ...");
  }

  static {
    System.out.println("Static initializer ...");
  }
}
```

Next, let's run the following test code to create three instances of A:

```java
A a1 = new A();
A a2 = new A();
A a3 = new A();
```

The output reveals that the static initializer is called only once, while the non-static initializer is called three times:

```
Static initializer ...
Non-static initializer ...
Non-static initializer ...
Non-static initializer ...
```

Moreover, the static initializer is called before the non-static one. Next, let's talk about nested classes.

Nested classes

Let's look at a quick example:

```
public class A {
    private static class B { ... }
}
```

Nested classes can be static or non-static. A non-static nested class is referred to as an *inner class*; further, it can be a *local inner class* (declared in a method) or an *anonymous inner class* (class with no name). On the other hand, a nested class that is declared static is referred to as a *static nested class*. The following figure clarifies these statements:

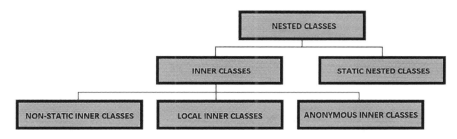

Figure 2.28: Java nested classes

Since B is a static class declared in A, we say that B is a static nested class.

Tackling the initialization-on-demand holder design pattern

The initialization-on-demand holder design pattern refers to a thread-safe lazy-loaded singleton (single instance) implementation. Before JDK 16, we can exemplify this design pattern in code as follows (we want a single thread-safe instance of Connection):

```
public class Connection { // singleton

  private Connection() {
  }

  private static class LazyConnection { // holder

    static final Connection INSTANCE = new Connection();

    static {
      System.out.println("Initializing connection ..."
        + INSTANCE);
    }
  }
```

```
  public static Connection get() {
    return LazyConnection.INSTANCE;
  }
}
```

No matter how many times a thread (multiple threads) calls `Connection.get()`, we always get the same instance of `Connection`. This is the instance created when we called `get()` for the first time (first thread), and Java has initialized the `LazyConnection` class and its statics. In other words, if we never call `get()`, then the `LazyConnection` class and its statics are never initialized (this is why we name it lazy initialization). And, this is thread-safe because static initializers can be constructed (here, `INSTANCE`) and referenced without explicit synchronization since they are run before any thread can use the class (here, `LazyConnection`).

JDK 16+

Until JDK 16, an inner class could contain static members as constant variables but it couldn't contain static initializers. In other words, the following code would not compile because of the static initializer:

```
public class A {

  public class B {

    {
      System.out.println("Non-static initializer ...");
    }

    static {
      System.out.println("Static initializer ...");
    }
  }
}
```

But, starting with JDK 16, the previous code is compiled without issues. In other words, starting with JDK 16, Java inner classes can have static members and static initializers.

This allows us to tackle the initialization-on-demand holder design pattern from another angle. We can replace the static nested class, `LazyConnection`, with a local inner class as follows:

```
public class Connection { // singleton

  private Connection() {
  }

  public static Connection get() {
```

```
    class LazyConnection { // holder

      static final Connection INSTANCE = new Connection();

      static {
        System.out.println("Initializing connection ..."
          + INSTANCE);
      }
    }

    return LazyConnection.INSTANCE;
  }
}
```

Now, the LazyConnection is visible only in its containing method, get(). As long as we don't call the get() method, the connection will not be initialized.

46. Adding nested classes in anonymous classes

In the previous problem, we had a brief overview of nested classes. As a quick reminder, an anonymous class (or, anonymous inner class) is like a local inner class without a name. Their purpose is to provide a more concise and expressive code. However, the code readability may be affected (look ugly), but it may be worth it if you can perform some specific task without having to do a full-blown class. For instance, an anonymous class is useful for altering the behavior of an existing method without spinning a new class. Java uses them typically for event handling and listeners (in GUI applications). Probably the most famous example of an anonymous class is this one from Java code:

```
button.addActionListener(new ActionListener() {
  public void actionPerformed(ActionEvent e) {
    ...
  }
}
```

Nevertheless, while local inner classes are actually class declarations, anonymous classes are expressions. To create an anonymous class, we have to extend an existing class or implement an interface, as shown in the following figure:

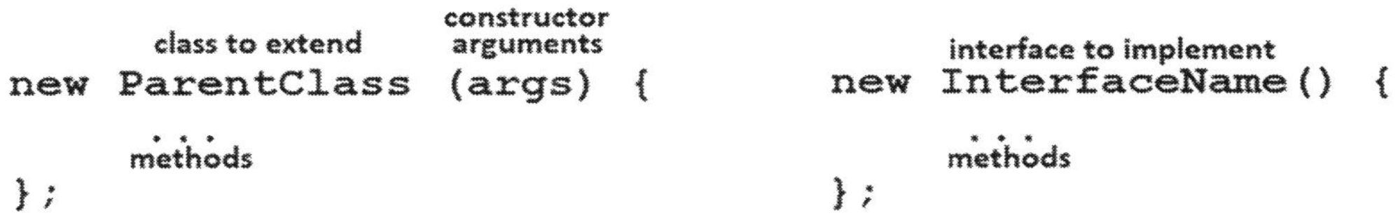

Figure 2.29: Anonymous class via class extension and interface implementation

Because they don't have names, anonymous classes must be declared and instantiated in a single expression. The resulting instance can be assigned to a variable that can be referred to later. The standard syntax for expressions looks like calling a regular Java constructor having the class in a code block ending with a semi-colon (;). The presence of a semi-colon is a hint that an anonymous class is an expression that must be part of a statement.

Finally, anonymous classes cannot have explicit constructors, be abstract, have a single instance, implement multiple interfaces, or be extended.

Next, let's tackle a few examples of nesting classes in anonymous classes. For instance, let's consider the following interface of a printing service:

```java
public interface Printer {

    public void print(String quality);
}
```

We use the `Printer` interface all over the place in our printing service, but we also want to have a helper method that is compact and simply tests our printer functions without requiring further actions or an extra class. We decided to hide this code in a static method named `printerTest()`, as follows:

```java
public static void printerTest() {

  Printer printer = new Printer() {

  @Override
  public void print(String quality) {

    if ("best".equals(quality)) {

      Tools tools = new Tools();

      tools.enableLaserGuidance();
      tools.setHighResolution();
    }

    System.out.println("Printing photo-test ...");
  }

class Tools {

    private void enableLaserGuidance() {
      System.out.println("Adding laser guidance ...");
    }
```

```
      private void setHighResolution() {
        System.out.println("Set high resolution ...");
      }
    }
  };
```

Testing the best quality print requires some extra settings wrapped in the inner Tools class. As you can see, the inner Tools class is nested in the anonymous class. Another approach consists of moving the Tools class inside the print() method. So, Tools becomes a local inner class as follows:

```
Printer printer = new Printer() {

  @Override
  public void print(String quality) {

    class Tools {

      private void enableLaserGuidance() {
        System.out.println("Adding laser guidance ...");
      }

      private void setHighResolution() {
        System.out.println("Set high resolution ...");
      }
    }

    if ("best".equals(quality)) {

      Tools tools = new Tools();

      tools.enableLaserGuidance();
      tools.setHighResolution();
    }

    System.out.println("Printing photo-test ...");
  }
};
```

The problem with this approach is that the Tools class cannot be used outside of print(). So, this strict encapsulation will restrict us from adding a new method (next to print()) that also needs the Tools class.

JDK 16+

But, remember from the previous problem that, starting with JDK 16, Java inner classes can have static members and static initializers. This means that we can drop the `Tools` class and rely on two static methods as follows:

```java
Printer printer = new Printer() {

  @Override
  public void print(String quality) {

    if ("best".equals(quality)) {
      enableLaserGuidance();
      setHighResolution();
    }

    System.out.println("Printing your photos ...");
  }

  private static void enableLaserGuidance() {
    System.out.println("Adding laser guidance ...");
  }

  private static void setHighResolution() {
    System.out.println("Set high resolution ...");
  }
};
```

If you find it more convenient to pick up these helpers in a static class, then do it:

```java
Printer printer = new Printer() {

  @Override
  public void print(String quality) {

    if ("best".equals(quality)) {
      Tools.enableLaserGuidance();
      Tools.setHighResolution();
    }

    System.out.println("Printing photo-test ...");
  }
```

```
    private final static class Tools {

      private static void enableLaserGuidance() {
        System.out.println("Adding laser guidance ...");
      }

      private static void setHighResolution() {
        System.out.println("Set high resolution ...");
      }
    }
  };
```

You can practice these examples in the bundled code.

47. Exemplify erasure vs. overloading

Before we join them in an example, let's quickly tackle erasure and overloading separately.

Erasure in a nutshell

Java uses *type erasure* at compile time in order to enforce type constraints and backward compatibility with old bytecode. Basically, at compilation time, all type arguments are replaced by Object (any generic must be convertible to Object) or type bounds (extends or super). Next, at runtime, the type erased by the compiler will be replaced by our type. A common case of type erasure implies generics.

Erasure of generic types

Practically, the compiler erases the unbound types (such as E, T, U, and so on) with the bounded Object. This enforces type safety, as in the following example of *class type erasure*:

```
public class ImmutableStack<E> implements Stack<E> {

  private final E head;
  private final Stack<E> tail;
  ...
```

The compiler applies type erasure to replace E with Object:

```
public class ImmutableStack<Object> implements Stack<Object> {

  private final Object head;
  private final Stack<Object> tail;
  ...
```

If the E parameter is bound, then the compiler uses the first bound class. For instance, in a class such as class Node<T extends Comparable<T>> {...}, the compiler will replace T with Comparable. In the same manner, in a class such as class Computation<T extends Number> {...}, all occurrences of T would be replaced by the compiler with the upper bound Number.

Check out the following case, which is a classical case of *method type erasure*:

```
public static <T, R extends T> List<T> listOf(T t, R r) {

  List<T> list = new ArrayList<>();

  list.add(t);
  list.add(r);

  return list;
}

// use this method
List<Object> list = listOf(1, "one");
```

How does this work? When we call listOf(1, "one"), we are actually passing two different types to the generic parameters T and R. The compiler type erasure has replaced T with Object. In this way, we can insert different types in the ArrayList and the code works just fine.

Erasure and bridge methods

Bridge methods are created by the compiler to cover corner cases. Specifically, when the compiler encounters an implementation of a parameterized interface or an extension of a parameterized class, it may need to generate a bridge method (also known as a synthetic method) as part of the type erasure phase. For instance, let's consider the following parameterized class:

```
public class Puzzle<E> {

  public E piece;

  public Puzzle(E piece) {
    this.piece = piece;
  }

  public void setPiece(E piece) {
    this.piece = piece;
  }
}
```

And, an extension of this class:

```
public class FunPuzzle extends Puzzle<String> {

  public FunPuzzle(String piece) {
    super(piece);
  }

  @Override
  public void setPiece(String piece) {
    super.setPiece(piece);
  }
}
```

Type erasure modifies `Puzzle.setPiece(E)` as `Puzzle.setPiece(Object)`. This means that the `FunPuzzle.setPiece(String)` method does not override the `Puzzle.setPiece(Object)` method. Since the signatures of the methods are not compatible, the compiler must accommodate the polymorphism of generic types via a bridge (synthetic) method meant to guarantee that sub-typing works as expected. Let's highlight this method in the code:

```
/* Decompiler 8ms, total 3470ms, lines 18 */
package modern.challenge;

public class FunPuzzle extends Puzzle<String> {
    public FunPuzzle(String piece) {
        super(piece);
    }

    public void setPiece(String piece) {
        super.setPiece(piece);
    }

    // $FF: synthetic method
    // $FF: bridge method
    public void setPiece(Object var1) {
        this.setPiece((String)var1);
    }
}
```

Now, whenever you see a bridge method in the stack trace, you will know what it is and why it is there.

Type erasure and heap pollution

Have you ever seen an unchecked warning? I'm sure you have! It's one of those things that is common to all Java developers. They may occur at compile-time as the result of type checking, or at runtime as a result of a cast or method call. In both cases, we talk about the fact that the compiler cannot validate the correctness of an operation, which implies some parameterized types. Not every unchecked warning is dangerous, but there are cases when we have to consider and deal with them.

A particular case is represented by *heap pollution*. If a parameterized variable of a certain type points to an object that is not of that type, then we are prone to deal with a code that leads to heap pollution. A good candidate for such scenarios involves methods with varargs arguments.

Check out this code:

```java
public static <T> void listOf(List<T> list, T... ts) {

  list.addAll(Arrays.asList(ts));
}
```

The listOf() declaration will cause this warning: *Possible heap pollution from parameterized vararg type T.* So, what's happening here?

The story begins when the compiler replaces the formal T... parameter into an array. After applying type erasure, the T... parameter becomes T[], and finally Object[]. Consequently, we opened a gate to possible heap pollution. But, our code just added the elements of Object[] into a List<Object>, so we are in the safe area.

In other words, if you know that the body of the varargs method is not prone to generate a specific exception (for example, ClassCastException) or to use the varargs parameter in an improper operation, then we can instruct the compiler to suppress these warnings. We can do it via the @SafeVarargs annotation as follows:

```java
@SafeVarargs
public static <T> void listOf(List<T> list, T... ts) {...}
```

The @SafeVarargs is a hint that sustains that the annotated method will use the varargs formal parameter only in proper operations. More common, but less recommended, is to use @SuppressWarnings({"unchecked", "varargs"}), which simply suppresses such warnings without claiming that the varargs formal parameter is not used in improper operations.

Now, let's tackle this code:

```java
public static void main(String[] args) {

  List<Integer> ints = new ArrayList<>();
  Main.listOf(ints, 1, 2, 3);

  Main.listsOfYeak(ints);
}
```

```java
public static void listsOfYeak(List<Integer>... lists) {

  Object[] listsAsArray = lists;

  listsAsArray[0] = Arrays.asList(4, 5, 6);
  Integer someInt = lists[0].get(0);

  listsAsArray[0] = Arrays.asList("a", "b", "c");
  Integer someIntYeak = lists[0].get(0); // ClassCastException
}
```

This time, the type erasure transforms the List<Integer>... into List[], which is a subtype of Object[]. This allows us to do the assignment: Object[] listsAsArray = lists;. But, check out the last two lines of code where we create a List<String> and store it in listsAsArray[0]. In the last line, we try to access the first Integer from lists[0], which obviously leads to a ClassCastException. This is an improper operation of using varargs, so it is not advisable to use @SafeVarargs in this case. We should have taken the following warnings seriously:

```java
// unchecked generic array creation for varargs parameter
// of type java.util.List<java.lang.Integer>[]
Main.listsOfYeak(ints);

// Possible heap pollution from parameterized vararg
// type java.util.List<java.lang.Integer>
public static void listsOfYeak(List<Integer>... lists) { ... }
```

Now, that you are familiar with type erasure, let's briefly cover polymorphic overloading.

Polymorphic overloading in a nutshell

Since *overloading* (also known as "ad hoc" polymorphism) is a core concept of **Object-Oriented Programming** (**OOP**), I'm sure you are familiar with Java method overloading, so I'll not insist on the basic theory of this concept.

Also, I'm aware that some people don't agree that overloading can be a form of polymorphism, but that is another topic that we will not tackle here.

We will be more practical and jump into a suite of quizzes meant to highlight some interesting aspects of overloading. More precisely, we will discuss *type dominance*. So, let's tackle the first quiz (wordie is an initially empty string):

```java
static void kaboom(byte b) { wordie += "a";}
static void kaboom(short s) { wordie += "b";}

kaboom(1);
```

What will happen? If you answered that the compiler will point out that there is no suitable method found for kaboom(1), then you're right. The compiler looks for a method that gets an integer argument, kaboom(int). Okay, that was easy! Here is the next one:

```
static void kaboom(byte b) { wordie += "a";}
static void kaboom(short s) { wordie += "b";}
static void kaboom(long l) { wordie += "d";}
static void kaboom(Integer i) { wordie += "i";}


kaboom(1);
```

We know that the first two kaboom() instances are useless. How about kaboom(long) and kaboom(Integer)? You are right, kaboom(long) will be called. If we remove kaboom(long), then kaboom(Integer) is called.

Important note

In primitive overloading, the compiler starts by searching for a one-to-one match. If this attempt fails, then the compiler searches for an overloading flavor taking a primitive broader domain than the primitive current domain (for instance, for an int, it looks for int, long, float, or double). If this fails as well, then the compiler checks for overloading taking boxed types (Integer, Float, and so on).

Following the previous statements, let's have this one:

```
static void kaboom(Integer i) { wordie += "i";}
static void kaboom(Long l) { wordie += "j";}


kaboom(1);
```

This time, wordie will be i. The kaboom(Integer) is called since there is no kaboom(int/long/float/ double). If we had a kaboom(double), then that method has higher precedence than kaboom(Integer). Interesting, right?! On the other hand, if we remove kaboom(Integer), then don't expect that kaboom(Long) will be called. Any other kaboom(boxed type) with a broader/narrow domain than Integer will not be called. This is happening because the compiler follows the inheritance path based on an IS-A relationship, so after kaboom(Integer), it looks for kaboom(Number), since Integer is a Number.

Important note

In boxed type overloading, the compiler starts by searching for a one-to-one match. If this attempt fails, then the compiler will not consider any overloading flavor taking a boxed type with a broader domain than the current domain (of course, a narrow domain is ignored as well). It looks for Number as being the superclass of all boxed types. If Number is not found, the compiler goes up in the hierarchy until it reaches the java.lang.Object, which is the end of the road.

Okay, let's complicate things a little bit:

```
static void kaboom(Object... ov) { wordie += "o";}
static void kaboom(Number n) { wordie += "p";}
static void kaboom(Number... nv) { wordie += "q";}


kaboom(1);
```

So, which method will be called this time? I know, you think kaboom(Number), right? At least, my simple logic pushes me to think that this is a common-sense choice. And it is correct!

If we remove kaboom(Number), then the compiler will call the varargs method, kaboom(Number...). This makes sense since kaboom(1) uses a single argument, so kaboom(Number) should have higher precedence than kaboom(Number...). This logic reverses if we call kaboom(1,2,3) since kaboom(Number) is no longer representing a valid overloading for this call, and kaboom(Number...) is the right choice.

But, this logic applies because Number is the superclass of all boxed classes (Integer, Double, Float, and so on).

How about now?

```
static void kaboom(Object... ov) { wordie += "o";}
static void kaboom(File... fv) { wordie += "s";}


kaboom(1);
```

This time, the compiler will "bypass" kaboom(File...) and will call kaboom(Object...). Based on the same logic, a call of kaboom(1, 2, 3) will call kaboom(Object...) since there is no kaboom(Number...).

Important note

In overloading, if the call has a single argument, then the method with a single argument has higher precedence than its varargs counterpart. On the other hand, if the call has more arguments of the same type, then the varargs method is called since the one-argument method is not suitable anymore. When the call has a single argument but only the varargs overloading is available, then this method is called.

This leads us to the following example:

```
static void kaboom(Number... nv) { wordie += "q";}
static void kaboom(File... fv) { wordie += "s";}


kaboom();
```

This time, kaboom() has no arguments and the compiler cannot find a unique match. This means that the reference to kaboom() is ambiguous since both methods match (kaboom(java.lang.Number...) in modern.challenge.Main and method kaboom(java.io.File...) in modern.challenge.Main).

In the bundled code, you can play even more with polymorphic overloading and test your knowledge. Moreover, try to challenge yourself and introduce generics in the equation as well.

Erasure vs. overloading

Okay, based on the previous experience, check out this code:

```
void print(List<A> listOfA) {
  System.out.println("Printing A: " + listOfA);
}

void print(List<B> listofB) {
  System.out.println("Printing B: " + listofB);
}
```

What will happen? Well, this is a case where overloading and type erasure collide. The type erasure will replace List<A> with List<Object> and List<B> with List<Object> as well. So, overloading is not possible and we get an error such as *name clash: print(java.util.List<modern.challenge.B>) and print (java.util.List<modern.challenge.A>) have the same erasure*.

In order to solve this issue, we can add a dummy argument to one of these two methods:

```
void print(List<A> listOfA, Void... v) {
  System.out.println("Printing A: " + listOfA);
}
```

Now, we can have the same call for both methods:

```
new Main().print(List.of(new A(), new A()));
new Main().print(List.of(new B(), new B()));
```

Done! You can practice these examples in the bundled code.

48. Xlinting default constructors

We know that a Java class with no explicit constructor automatically gets an "invisible" default constructor for setting default values of the instance variables. The following House class falls in this scenario:

```
public class House {

  private String location;
  private float price;
  ...
}
```

If this is exactly what we wanted, then it is no problem. But, if we are concerned about the fact that the default constructors are exposed by classes to publicly exported packages, then we have to consider using JDK 16+.

JDK 16+ added a dedicated *lint* meant to warn us about the classes that have default constructors. In order to take advantage of this *lint*, we have to follow two steps:

- Export the package containing that class
- Compile with -Xlint:missing-explicit-ctor (or -Xlint, -Xlint:all)

In our case, we export the package modern.challenge in module-info as follows:

```
module P48_XlintDefaultConstructor {
    exports modern.challenge;
}
```

Once you compile the code with -Xlint:missing-explicit-ctor, you'll see a warning like in the following figure:

```
public class Main {
```

```
[missing-explicit-ctor] class Main in exported package modern.challenge declares no explicit constructors,
                 thereby exposing a default constructor to clients of module P48_XlintDefaultConstructor
----
(Alt-Enter shows hints)
```

Figure 2.30: The warning produced by -Xlint:missing-explicit-ctor

Now, you can easily find out which classes have default constructors.

49. Working with the receiver parameter

Starting with JDK 8, we can enrich any of our instance methods with the optional *receiver parameter*. This is a purely syntactic parameter of enclosing type exposed via the this keyword. The following two snippets of code are identical:

```
public class Truck {

  public void revision1(Truck this) {
    Truck thisTruck = this;
    System.out.println("Truck: " + thisTruck);
  }

  public void revision2() {
    Truck thisTruck = this;
    System.out.println("Truck: " + thisTruck);
  }
}
```

Do not conclude that `revision2()` is an overloading of `revision1()`, or vice versa. Both methods have the same output, the same signature, and produce the same bytecode.

The receiver parameter can be used in inner classes as well. Here is an example:

```
public class PaymentService {

  class InvoiceCalculation {

    final PaymentService paymentService;

    InvoiceCalculation(PaymentService PaymentService.this) {
      paymentService = PaymentService.this;
    }
  }
}
```

Okay, but why use the receiver parameter? Well, JDK 8 introduced so-called *type annotations*, which are exactly as the name suggests: annotations that can be applied to types. In this context, the receiver parameter was added for annotating the type of object for which the method is called. Check out the following code:

```
@Target(ElementType.TYPE_USE)
public @interface ValidAddress {}

public String getAddress(@ValidAddress Person this) { ... }
```

Or, check this more elaborate example:

```
public class Parcel {

  public void order(@New Parcel this) {...}
  public void shipping(@Ordered Parcel this) {...}
  public void deliver(@Shipped Parcel this) {...}
  public void cashit(@Delivered Parcel this) {...}
  public void done(@Cashed Parcel this) {...}
}
```

Every client of a `Parcel` must call these methods in a precise sequence drawn via type annotations and receiver parameters. In other words, an order can be placed only if it is a new order, it can be shipped only if the order was placed, it can be delivered only if it was shipped, it can be paid only if it was delivered, and it can be closed only if it was paid.

At this moment, this strict sequence is pointed out only by these hypothetical annotations. But, this is the right road to implement further a static analysis tool that will understand the meaning of these annotations and trigger warnings every time a client of `Parcel` doesn't follow this precise sequence.

50. Implementing an immutable stack

A common coding challenge in interviews is this: Implement an immutable stack in Java.

Being an abstract data type, a stack needs at least this contract:

```java
public interface Stack<T> extends Iterable<T> {

  boolean isEmpty();

  Stack<T> push(T value);

  Stack<T> pop();

  T peek();
}
```

Having this contract, we can focus on the immutable implementation. Generally speaking, an immutable data structure stays the same until an operation attempts to change it (for instance, to add, put, remove, delete, push, and so on). If an operation attempts to alter the content of an immutable data structure, a new instance of that data structure must be created and used by that operation, while the previous instance remains unchanged.

Now, in our context, we have two operations that can alter the stack content: push and pop. The push operation should return a new stack containing the pushed element, while the pop operation should return the previous stack. But, in order to accomplish this, we need to start from somewhere, so we need an empty initial stack. This is a singleton stack that can be implemented as follows:

```java
private static class EmptyStack<U> implements Stack<U> {

  @Override
  public Stack<U> push(U u) {
    return new ImmutableStack<>(u, this);
  }

  @Override
  public Stack<U> pop() {
    throw new UnsupportedOperationException(
      "Unsupported operation on an empty stack");
  }

  @Override
  public U peek() {
    throw new UnsupportedOperationException (
```

```
          "Unsupported operation on an empty stack");
    }

    @Override
    public boolean isEmpty() {
      return true;
    }

    @Override
    public Iterator<U> iterator() {
      return new StackIterator<>(this);
    }
  }
}
```

The StackIterator is a trivial implementation of the Java Iterator. Nothing fancy here:

```
private static class StackIterator<U> implements Iterator<U> {

  private Stack<U> stack;

  public StackIterator(final Stack<U> stack) {
    this.stack = stack;
  }

  @Override
  public boolean hasNext() {
    return !this.stack.isEmpty();
  }

  @Override
  public U next() {

    U e = this.stack.peek();
    this.stack = this.stack.pop();

    return e;
  }

  @Override
  public void remove() {
  }
}
```

So far, we have the `Iterator` and an empty stack singleton. Finally, we can implement the logic of the immutable stack as follows:

```java
public class ImmutableStack<E> implements Stack<E> {

  private final E head;
  private final Stack<E> tail;

  private ImmutableStack(final E head, final Stack<E> tail) {
    this.head = head;
    this.tail = tail;
  }

  public static <U> Stack<U> empty(final Class<U> type) {
    return new EmptyStack<>();
  }

  @Override
  public Stack<E> push(E e) {
    return new ImmutableStack<>(e, this);
  }

  @Override
  public Stack<E> pop() {
    return this.tail;
  }

  @Override
  public E peek() {
    return this.head;
  }

  @Override
  public boolean isEmpty() {
    return false;
  }

  @Override
  public Iterator<E> iterator() {
    return new StackIterator<>(this);
  }
```

```
    // iterator code
    // empty stack singleton code
}
```

Creating a stack starts by calling theImmutableStack.empty() method, as follows:

```
Stack<String> s = ImmutableStack.empty(String.class);
```

In the bundled code, you can how this stack can be used further.

51. Revealing a common mistake with Strings

Everybody knows that String is an immutable class.

Even so, we are still prone to accidentally write code that ignores the fact that String is immutable. Check out this code:

```
String str = "start";
str = stopIt(str);

public static String stopIt(String str) {

  str.replace(str, "stop");

  return str;
}
```

Somehow, it is logical to think that the replace() call has replaced the text *start* with *stop* and now str is *stop*. This is the cognitive power of words (*replace* is a verb that clearly induces the idea that the text was replaced). But, String is immutable! Oh... we already know that! This means that replace() cannot alter the original str. There are many such silly mistakes that we are prone to accidentally make, so pay extra attention to such simple things, since they can waste your time in the debugging stage.

The solution is obvious and self-explanatory:

```
public static String stopIt(String str) {

  str = str.replace(str, "stop");

  return str;
}
```

Or, simply:

```
public static String stopIt(String str) {

  return str.replace(str, "stop");
}
```

Don't forget that `String` is immutable!

52. Using the enhanced NullPointerException

Take your time to dissect the following trivial code and try to identify the parts that are prone to cause a `NullPointerException` (these parts are marked as numbered warnings, which will be explained after the snippet):

```java
public final class ChainSaw {

  private static final List<String> MODELS
    = List.of("T300", "T450", "T700", "T800", "T900");

  private final String model;
  private final String power;
  private final int speed;

  public boolean started;

  private ChainSaw(String model, String power, int speed) {
    this.model = model;
    this.power = power;
    this.speed = speed;
  }

  public static ChainSaw initChainSaw(String model) {

    for (String m : MODELS) {
      if (model.endsWith(m)) {WARNING 3!
        return new ChainSaw(model, null, WARNING 5!
          (int) (Math.random() * 100));
      }
    }

    return null; WARNING 1,2!
  }

  public int performance(ChainSaw[] css) {

    int score = 0;
    for (ChainSaw cs : css) { WARNING 3!
      score += Integer.compare(
```

```
          this.speed,cs.speed); WARNING 4!
    }

    return score;
  }

  public void start() {
    if (!started) {
      System.out.println("Started ...");
      started = true;
    }
  }

  public void stop() {
    if (started) {
      System.out.println("Stopped ...");
      started = false;
    }
  }

  public String getPower() {
    return power; WARNING 5!
  }

  @Override
  public String toString() {
    return "ChainSaw{" + "model=" + model
      + ", speed=" + speed + ", started=" + started + '}';
  }
}
```

You noticed the warnings? Of course, you did! There are five major scenarios behind most **NullPointerException** (**NPEs**) and each of them is present in the previous class. Prior to JDK 14, an NPE doesn't contain detailed information about the cause. Look at this exception:

```
Exception in thread "main" java.lang.NullPointerException
    at modern.challenge.Main.main(Main.java:21)
```

This message is just a starting point for the debugging process. We don't know the root cause of this NPE or which variable is null. But, starting with JDK 14 (JEP 358), we have really helpful NPE messages. For example, in JDK 14+, the previous message looks as follows:

```
Exception in thread "main" java.lang.NullPointerException: Cannot invoke
"modern.challenge.Strings.reverse()" because "str" is null
    at modern.challenge.Main.main(Main.java:21)
```

The highlighted part of the message gives us important information about the root cause of this NPE. Now, we know that the `str` variable is `null`, so no need to debug further. We can just focus on how to fix this issue.

Next, let's tackle each of the five major root causes of NPEs.

WARNING 1! NPE when calling an instance method via a null object

Consider the following code written by a client of `ChainSaw`:

```
ChainSaw cs = ChainSaw.initChainSaw("QW-T650");
cs.start(); // 'cs' is null
```

The client passes a chainsaw model that is not supported by this class, so the `initChainSaw()` method returns `null`. This is really bad because every time the client uses the `cs` variable, they will get back an NPE as follows:

```
Exception in thread "main" java.lang.NullPointerException: Cannot invoke
"modern.challenge.ChainSaw.start()" because "cs" is null
    at modern.challenge.Main.main(Main.java:9)
```

Instead of returning `null`, it is better to throw an explicit exception that informs the client that they cannot continue because we don't have this chainsaw model (we can go for the classical `IllegalArgumentException` or, the more suggestive one in this case (but quite uncommon for `null` value handling), `UnsupportedOperationException`). This may be the proper fix in this case, but it is not universally true. There are cases when it is better to return an empty object (for example, an empty string, collection, or array) or a default object (for example, an object with minimalist settings) that doesn't break the client code. Since JDK 8, we can use `Optional` as well. Of course, there are cases when returning `null` makes sense but that is more common in APIs and special situations.

WARNING 2! NPE when accessing (or modifying) the field of a null object

Consider the following code written by a client of `ChainSaw`:

```
ChainSaw cs = ChainSaw.initChainSaw("QW-T650");
boolean isStarted = cs.started; // 'cs' is null
```

Practically, the NPE, in this case, has the same root cause as the previous case. We try to access the `started` field of `ChainSaw`. Since this is a primitive `boolean`, it was initialized by JVM with `false`, but we cannot "see" that since we try to access this field through a `null` variable represented by `cs`.

WARNING 3! NPE when null is passed in the method argument

Consider the following code written by a client of `ChainSaw`:

```
ChainSaw cs = ChainSaw.initChainSaw(null);
```

You are not a good citizen if you want a `null` `ChainSaw`, but who am I to judge? It is possible for this to happen and will lead to the following NPE:

```
Exception in thread "main" java.lang.NullPointerException: Cannot invoke
"String.endsWith(String)" because "model" is null
    at modern.challenge.ChainSaw.initChainSaw(ChainSaw.java:25)
    at modern.challenge.Main.main(Main.java:16)
```

The message is crystal clear. We attempt to call the `String.endWith()` method with a `null` argument represented by the `model` variable. To fix this issue, we have to add a guard condition to ensure that the passed `model` argument is not `null` (and eventually, not empty). In this case, we can throw an `IllegalArgumentException` to inform the client that we are here and we are guarding. Another approach may consist of replacing the given `null` with a dummy model that passes through our code without issues (for instance, since the model is a `String`, we can reassign an empty string, ""). However, personally, I don't recommend this approach, not even for small methods. You never know how the code will evolve and such dummy reassignments can lead to brittle code.

WARNING 4! NPE when accessing the index value of a null array/collection

Consider the following code written by a client of `ChainSaw`:

```
ChainSaw myChainSaw = ChainSaw.initChainSaw("QWE-T800");

ChainSaw[] friendsChainSaw = new ChainSaw[]{
  ChainSaw.initChainSaw("Q22-T450"),
  ChainSaw.initChainSaw("QRT-T300"),
  ChainSaw.initChainSaw("Q-T900"),
  null, // ops!
  ChainSaw.initChainSaw("QMM-T850"), // model is not supported
  ChainSaw.initChainSaw("ASR-T900")
};

int score = myChainSaw.performance(friendsChainSaw);
```

Creating an array of `ChainSaw` was quite challenging in this example. We accidentally slipped a `null` value (actually, we did it intentionally) and an unsupported model. In return, we get the following NPE:

```
Exception in thread "main" java.lang.NullPointerException: Cannot read field
"speed" because "cs" is null
```

```
    at modern.challenge.ChainSaw.performance(ChainSaw.java:37)
    at modern.challenge.Main.main(Main.java:31)
```

The message informs us that the cs variable is null. This is happening at line 37 in ChainSaw, so in the for loop of the performance() method. While looping the given array, our code iterated over the null value, which doesn't have the speed field. Pay attention to this kind of scenario: even if the given array/collection itself is not null, it doesn't mean that it cannot contain null items. So, adding a guarding check before handling each item can save us from an NPE in this case. Depending on the context, we can throw an IllegalArgumentException when the loop passes over the first null or simply ignore null values and don't break the flow (in general, this is more suitable). Of course, using a collection that doesn't accept null values is also a good approach (Apache Commons Collection and Guava have such collections).

WARNING 5! NPE when accessing a field via a getter

Consider the following code written by a client of ChainSaw:

```
ChainSaw cs = ChainSaw.initChainSaw("T5A-T800");
String power = cs.getPower();
System.out.println(power.concat(" Watts"));
```

And, the associated NPE:

```
Exception in thread "main" java.lang.NullPointerException: Cannot invoke
"String.concat(String)" because "power" is null
    at modern.challenge.Main.main(Main.java:37)
```

Practically, the getter getPower() returned null since the power field is null. Why? The answer is in the line return new ChainSaw(model, null, (int) (Math.random() * 100)); of the initChainSaw() method. Because we didn't decide yet on the algorithm for calculating the power of a chainsaw, we passed null to the ChainSaw constructor. Further, the constructor simply sets the power field as this. power = power. If it was a public constructor, then most probably we would have added some guarded conditions, but being a private constructor, it is better to fix the issue right from the root and not pass that null. Since the power is a String, we can simply pass an empty string or a suggestive string such as UNKNOWN_POWER. We also may leave a TODO comment in code such as // TODO (JIRA ####): replace UNKNOWN_POWER with code. This will remind us to fix this in the next release. Meanwhile, the code has eliminated the NPE risk.

Okay, after we fixed all these five NPE risks, the code has become the following (the added code is highlighted):

```
public final class ChainSaw {

  private static final String UNKNOWN_POWER = "UNKNOWN";

  private static final List<String> MODELS
    = List.of("T300", "T450", "T700", "T800", "T900");
```

```java
private final String model;
private final String power;
private final int speed;

public boolean started;

private ChainSaw(String model, String power, int speed) {
  this.model = model;
  this.power = power;
  this.speed = speed;
}

public static ChainSaw initChainSaw(String model) {

  if (model == null || model.isBlank()) {
   throw new IllegalArgumentException("The given model
            cannot be null/empty");
  }

  for (String m : MODELS) {
    if (model.endsWith(m)) {
      // TO DO (JIRA ####): replace UNKNOWN_POWER with code
      return new ChainSaw(model, UNKNOWN_POWER,
       (int) (Math.random() * 100));
      }
  }

  throw new UnsupportedOperationException(
    "Model " + model + " is not supported");
}

public int performance(ChainSaw[] css) {

  if (css == null) {
    throw new IllegalArgumentException(
      "The given models cannot be null");
  }

  int score = 0;
  for (ChainSaw cs : css) {
```

```java
      if (cs != null) {
        score += Integer.compare(this.speed, cs.speed);
      }
    }

    return score;
  }

  public void start() {
    if (!started) {
      System.out.println("Started ...");
      started = true;
    }
  }

  public void stop() {
    if (started) {
      System.out.println("Stopped ...");
      started = false;
    }
  }

  public String getPower() {
    return power;
  }

  @Override
  public String toString() {
    return "ChainSaw{" + "model=" + model
      + ", speed=" + speed + ", started=" + started + '}';
  }
}
```

Done! Now, our code is NPE-free. At least until reality contradicts us and a new NPE occurs.

53. Using yield in switch expressions

Here, we're going to look at how switch expressions have evolved in JDK 13+.

Java SE 13 added the new yield statement, which can be used instead of the break statement in switch expressions.

We know that a JDK 12+ switch expression can be written as follows (playerType is a Java enum):

```
return switch (playerType) {
  case TENNIS ->
    new TennisPlayer();
  case FOOTBALL ->
    new FootballPlayer();
  ...
};
```

Moreover, we know that a label's arrow can point to a curly-braces block as well (this works only in JDK 12, **not in JDK 13+**):

```
return switch (playerType) {
  case TENNIS -> {
    System.out.println("Creating a TennisPlayer ...");
    break new TennisPlayer();
  }
  case FOOTBALL -> {
    System.out.println("Creating a FootballPlayer ...");
    break new FootballPlayer();
  }
  ...
};
```

Since break can be confusing because it can be used in old-school switch statements and in the new switch expressions, JDK 13 added the yield statement to be used instead of break. The yield statement takes one argument representing the value produced by the current case. The previous examples can be written from JDK 13+ as follows:

```
return switch (playerType) {
  case TENNIS:
    yield new TennisPlayer();
  case FOOTBALL:
    yield new FootballPlayer();
  ...
};

return switch (playerType) {
  case TENNIS -> {
    System.out.println("Creating a TennisPlayer ...");
    yield new TennisPlayer();
  }
  case FOOTBALL -> {
```

```
      System.out.println("Creating a FootballPlayer ...");
      yield new FootballPlayer();
   }
   ...
};
```

In other words, starting with JDK 13+, a switch expression can rely on yield but not on break, and a switch statement can rely on break but not on yield.

54. Tackling the case null clause in switch

Before JDK 17, a null case in a switch was commonly coded as a guarding condition outside the switch, as in the following example:

```
private static Player createPlayer(PlayerTypes playerType) {

   // handling null values in a condition outside switch
   if (playerType == null) {
     throw new IllegalArgumentException(
       "Player type cannot be null");
   }

   return switch (playerType) {
     case TENNIS -> new TennisPlayer();
     case FOOTBALL -> new FootballPlayer();
     ...
   };
}
```

Starting with JDK 17+ (JEP 427), we can treat a null case as any other common case. For instance, here we have a null case that is responsible for handling the scenarios when the passed argument is null:

```
private static Player createPlayer(PlayerTypes playerType) {

   return switch (playerType) {
     case TENNIS -> new TennisPlayer();
     case FOOTBALL -> new FootballPlayer();
     case SNOOKER -> new SnookerPlayer();
     case null -> throw new NullPointerException(
                    "Player type cannot be null");
     case UNKNOWN -> throw new UnknownPlayerException(
                       "Player type is unknown");
     // default is not mandatory
     default -> throw new IllegalArgumentException(
```

```
                        "Invalid player type: " + playerType);
    };
}
```

In certain contexts, null and default have the same meaning, so we can chain them in the same case statement:

```
private static Player createPlayer(PlayerTypes playerType) {

  return switch (playerType) {
    case TENNIS -> new TennisPlayer();
    case FOOTBALL -> new FootballPlayer();
    ...
    case null, default ->
      throw new IllegalArgumentException(
        "Invalid player type: " + playerType);
  };
}
```

Or you might find it more readable like this:

```
...
case TENNIS: yield new TennisPlayer();
case FOOTBALL: yield new FootballPlayer();
...
case null, default:
  throw new IllegalArgumentException(
    "Invalid player type: " + playerType);
...
```

Personally, I suggest you think twice before patching your switch expressions with case null, especially if you plan to do it only for silently sweeping these values. Overall, your code may become brittle and exposed to unexpected behaviors/results that ignore the presence of null values. In the bundled code, you can test the complete examples.

55. Taking on the hard way to discover equals()

Check out the following code:

```
Integer x1 = 14; Integer y1 = 14;
Integer x2 = 129; Integer y2 = 129;

List<Integer> listOfInt1 = new ArrayList<>(
  Arrays.asList(x1, y1, x2, y2));
listOfInt1.removeIf(t -> t == x1 || t == x2);
```

```
List<Integer> listOfInt2 = new ArrayList<>(
  Arrays.asList(x1, y1, x2, y2));
listOfInt2.removeIf(t -> t.equals(x1) || t.equals(x2));
```

So, initially, `listOfInt1` and `listOfInt2` have the same items, [x1=14, y1=14, x2=129, y2=129]. But, what will contain `listOfInt1`/`listOfInt2` after executing the code based on `removeIf()` and `==`, respectively `equals()`?

The first list will remain with a single item, [129]. When t is x1, we know that x1 == x1, so 14 is removed. But, why is x2 removed? When t is y1, we know that y1 == x1 should be `false` since, via ==, we compare the object's references in memory, not their values. Obviously, y1 and x1 should have different references in the memory... or shouldn't they ? Actually, Java has an internal rule to cache integers in -127 ... 128. Since x1=14 is cached, y1=14 uses the cache so no new `Integer` is created. This is why y1 == x1 and y1 is removed as well. Next, t is x2, and x2 == x2, so x2 is removed. Finally, t is y2, but y2 == x2 returns `false`, since 129 > 128 is not cached, so x2 and y2 have different references in memory.

On the other hand, when we use `equals()`, which is the recommended approach for comparing the object's values, the resulting list is empty. When t is x1, x1 =x1, so 14 is removed. When t is y1, y1 =x1, so y1 is removed as well. Next, t is x2, and x2= x2, so x2 is removed. Finally, t is y2, and y2 =x2, so y2 is removed as well.

56. Hooking instanceof in a nutshell

Having an object (o) and a type (t), we can use the `instanceof` operator to test if o is of type t by writing o `instanceof` t. This is a `boolean` operator that is very useful to ensure the success of a subsequent casting operation. For instance, check the following:

```
interface Furniture {};
class Plywood {};
class Wardrobe extends Plywood implements Furniture {};
```

`instanceof` returns `true` if we test the object (for instance, `Wardrobe`) against the type itself:

```
Wardrobe wardrobe = new Wardrobe();
if(wardrobe instanceof Wardrobe) { } // true

Plywood plywood = new Plywood();
if(plywood instanceof Plywood) { } // true
```

`instanceof` returns true if the tested object (for instance, `Wardrobe`) is an instance of a subclass of the type (for instance `Plywood`):

```
Wardrobe wardrobe = new Wardrobe();
if(wardrobe instanceof Plywood) {} // true
```

instanceof returns true if the tested object (for instance, Wardrobe) implements the interface represented by the type (for instance, Furniture):

```
Wardrobe wardrobe = new Wardrobe();
if(wardrobe instanceof Furniture) {} // true
```

Based on this, consider the following note:

>
> **Important note**
>
> The logic behind instanceof relies on the IS-A relationship (this is detailed in *The Complete Coding Interview Guide in Java, Chapter 6, What is inheritance?*). In a nutshell, this relationship is based on interface implementation or class inheritance. For instance, wardrobe instanceof Plywood returns true because Wardrobe extends Plywood, so Wardrobe IS A Plywood. Similarly, Wardrobe IS A Furniture. On the other hand, Plywood IS-not-A Furniture, so plywood instanceof Furniture returns false. In this context, since every Java class extends Object, we know that foo instanceof Object returns true as long as foo is an instance of a Java class. In addition, null instanceof Object (or any other object) returns false, so this operator doesn't require an explicit null check.

Finally, keep in mind that instanceof works only with reified types (reified type information is available at runtime), which include:

- Primitive types (int, float)
- Raw types (List, Set)
- Non-generic classes/interfaces (String)
- Generic types with unbounded wildcards (List<?>, Map<?, ?>)
- Arrays of reifiable types (String[], Map<?, ?>[], Set<?>[])

This means that we cannot use the instanceof operator (or casts) with parameterized types because the type erasures alter all type parameters in generic code, so we cannot say which parameterized type for a generic type is in use at runtime.

57. Introducing pattern matching

JDK 16 has introduced one of the major and complex features of Java, referred to as *pattern matching*. The future is wide open for this topic.

In a nutshell, *pattern matching* defines a synthetic expression for checking/testing whether a given variable has certain properties. If those properties are met, then automatically extract one or more parts of that variable into other variables. From this point forward, we can use those extracted variables.

A pattern matching instance (pay attention, this has nothing to do with design patterns) is a structure made of several components as follows (this is basically the pattern matching terminology):

- The *target operand* or the argument of the predicate: This is a variable (or an expression) that we aim to match.

- The *predicate* (or *test*): This is a check that takes place at runtime and aims to determine if the given *target operand* does or doesn't have one or more properties (we match the *target operand* against the properties).

- One or more variables are referred to as *pattern variables* or *binding variables*: these variables are automatically extracted from the *target operand* if and only if the *predicate/test* succeeds.

- Finally, we have the *pattern* itself, which is represented by the *predicate* + *binding variables*.

Pattern Matching

```
|——————— PATTERN ———————|
TARGET OPERAND    PREDICATE    BINDING VARIABLE(S)
```

Figure 2.31: Pattern matching components

So, we can say that Java pattern matching is a synthetic expression of a complex solution composed of four components: target operand, predicate/test, binding variable(s), and pattern = predicate + binding variable(s).

The scope of binding variables in pattern matching

The compiler decides the scope (visibility) of the binding variables, so we don't have to bother with such aspects via special modifiers or other tricks. In the case of predicates that always pass (like an if(true) {}), the compiler scopes the binding variables exactly as for the Java *local variables*.

But, most patterns make sense precisely because the predicate may fail. In such cases, the compiler applies a technique called *flow scoping*. That is actually a combination of the *regular scoping* and *definitive assignment*.

The *definitive assignment* is a technique used by the compiler based on the structure of statements and expressions to ensure that a local variable (or blank final field) is definitely assigned before it is accessed by the code. In a pattern-matching context, a binding variable is assigned only if the predicate passes, so the *definitive assignment* aim is to find out the precise place when this is happening. Next, the regular block scope represents the code where the binding variable is in scope.

Do you want this as a simple important note? Here it is.

Important note

In pattern matching, the binding variable is flow-scoped. In other words, the scope of a binding variable covers only the block where the predicate passed.

We will cover this topic in *Problem 59*.

Guarded patterns

So far, we know that a pattern relies on a predicate/test for deciding whether the binding variables should be extracted from the target operand or not. In addition, sometimes we need to refine this predicate by appending to it extra boolean checks based on the extracted binding variables. We name this a *guarded pattern*. In other words, if the predicate evaluates to true, then the binding variables are extracted and they enter in further boolean checks. If these checks are evaluated to true, we can say that the target operand matches this guarded pattern.

We cover this in *Problem 64*.

Type coverage

In a nutshell, the switch expressions and switch statements that use null and/or pattern labels should be exhaustive. In other words, we must cover all the possible values with switch case labels.

We cover this in *Problem 66*.

Current status of pattern matching

Currently, Java supports type pattern matching for instanceof and switch, and record pattern-destructuring patterns for records (covered in *Chapter 4*). These are the final releases in JDK 21.

58. Introducing type pattern matching for instanceof

Can you name the shortcomings of the following classical snippet of code (this is a simple code used to save different kinds of artifacts on a USB device)?

```java
public static String save(Object o) throws IOException {

  if (o instanceof File) {
    File file = (File) o;
    return "Saving a file of size: "
      + String.format("%,d bytes", file.length());
  }

  if (o instanceof Path) {
    Path path = (Path) o;
    return "Saving a file of size: "
      + String.format("%,d bytes", Files.size(path));
  }

  if (o instanceof String) {
    String str = (String) o;
    return "Saving a string of size: "
      + String.format("%,d bytes", str.length());
```

```
    }

    return "I cannot save the given object";
}
```

You're right...type checking and casting are burdensome to write and read. Moreover, those check-cast sequences are error-prone (it is easy to change the checked type or the casted type and forget to change the type of the other object). Basically, in each conditional statement, we do three steps, as follows:

1. First, we do a type check (for instance, o `instanceof File`).
2. Second, we do a type conversion via cast (for instance, `(File) o`).
3. Third, we do a variable assignment (for instance, `File file =`).

But, starting with JDK 16 (JEP 394), we can use *type pattern matching for instanceof* to perform the previous three steps in one expression. The type pattern is the first category of patterns supported by Java. Let's see the previous code rewritten via the *type pattern*:

```java
public static String save(Object o) throws IOException {

    if (o instanceof File file) {
        return "Saving a file of size: "
            + String.format("%,d bytes", file.length());
    }

    if (o instanceof String str) {
        return "Saving a string of size: "
            + String.format("%,d bytes", str.length());
    }

    if (o instanceof Path path) {
        return "Saving a file of size: "
            + String.format("%,d bytes", Files.size(path));
    }

    return "I cannot save the given object";
}
```

In each `if`-then statement, we have a test/predicate to determine the type of `Object` o, a cast of `Object` o to `File`, `Path`, or `String`, and a destructuring phase for extracting either the length or the size from `Object` o.

The piece of code, (o `instanceof File file`) is not just some syntactic sugar. It is not just a convenient shortcut of the old-fashioned code to reduce the ceremony of conditional state extraction. This is a *type pattern* in action!

Practically, we match the variable o against File file. More precisely, we match the type of o against the type File. We have that o is the *target operand* (the argument of the predicate), instanceof File is the predicate, and the variable file is the *pattern* or *binding variable* that is automatically created only if instanceof File returns true. Moreover, instanceof File file is the *type pattern*, or in short, File file is the pattern itself. The following figure illustrates this statement:

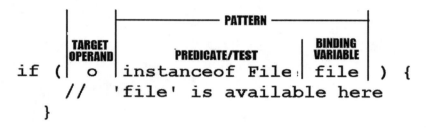

Figure 2.32: Type pattern matching for instanceof

In the type pattern for instanceof, there is no need to perform explicit null checks (exactly as in the case of plain instanceof), and no upcasting is allowed. Both of the following examples generate a compilation error in JDK 16-20, but not in JDK 14/15/21 (this is weird indeed):

```
if ("foo" instanceof String str) {}
if ("foo" instanceof CharSequence sequence) {}
```

The compilation error points out that the expression type cannot be a subtype of pattern type (no upcasting is allowed). However, with plain instanceof, this works in all JDKs:

```
if ("foo" instanceof String) {}
if ("foo" instanceof CharSequence) {}
```

Next, let's talk about the scope of binding variables.

59. Handling the scope of a binding variable in type patterns for instanceof

From *Problem 57*, we know the headlines of scoping the binding variables in pattern matching. Moreover, we know from the previous problem that in the type pattern for instanceof, we have a single binding variable. It is time to see some practical examples, so let's quickly crop this snippet from the previous problem:

```
if (o instanceof File file) {
  return "Saving a file of size: "
    + String.format("%,d bytes", file.length());
}

// 'file' is out of scope here
```

In this snippet, the `file` binding variable is visible in the `if`-then block. Once the block is closed, the `file` binding variable is out of scope. But, thanks to flow scoping, a binding variable can be used in the `if` statement that has introduced it to define a so-called *guarded pattern*. Here it is:

```
// 'file' is created ONLY if 'instanceof' returns true
if (o instanceof File file
    // this is evaluated ONLY if 'file' was created
    && file.length() > 0 && file.length() < 1000) {
  return "Saving a file of size: "
    + String.format("%,d bytes", file.length());
}


// another example
if (o instanceof Path path
      && Files.size(path) > 0 && Files.size(path) < 1000) {
  return "Saving a file of size: "
    + String.format("%,d bytes", Files.size(path));
}
```

The conditional part that starts with the `&&` short-circuit operator is evaluated by the compiler only if the `instanceof` operator is evaluated to `true`. This means that you cannot use the `||` operator instead of `&&`. For instance, is not logical to write this:

```
// this will not compile
if (o instanceof Path path
   || Files.size(path) > 0 && Files.size(path) < 1000) {...}
```

On the other hand, this is perfectly acceptable:

```
if (o instanceof Path path
   && (Files.size(path) > 0 || Files.size(path) < 1000)) {...}
```

We can also extend the scope of the binding variable as follows:

```
if (!(o instanceof String str)) {
  // str is not available here
  return "I cannot save the given object";
} else {
  return "Saving a string of size: "
    + String.format("%,d bytes", str.length());
}
```

Since we negate the `if`-then statement, the `str` binding variable is available in the `else` branch. Following this logic, we can use *early returns* as well:

```
public int getStringLength(Object o) {
```

```
  if (!(o instanceof String str)) {
    return 0;
  }

  return str.length();
}
```

Thanks to flow scoping, the compiler can set up strict boundaries for the scope of binding variables. For instance, in the following code, there is no risk of overlapping even if we keep using the same name for the binding variables:

```
private String strNumber(Object o) {

  if (o instanceof Integer nr) {
    return String.valueOf(nr.intValue());
  } else if (o instanceof Long nr) {
    return String.valueOf(nr.longValue());
  } else {
    // nr is out of scope here
    return "Probably a float number";
  }
}
```

Here, each nr binding variable has a scope that covers only its own branch. No overlapping, no conflicts! However, using the same name for the multiple binding variables can be a little bit confusing, so it is better to avoid it. For instance, we can use intNr and longNr instead of simple nr.

Another confusing scenario that is highly recommended to be avoided implies binding variables that hide fields. Check out this code:

```
private final String str
  = "   I am a string with leading and trailing spaces    ";

public String convert(Object o) {

  // local variable (binding variable) hides a field
  if (o instanceof String str) {
    return str.strip(); // refers to binding variable, str
  } else {
    return str.strip(); // refers to field, str
  }
}
```

So, using the same name for binding variables (this is true for any local variable as well) and fields is a bad practice that should be avoided.

In JDK 14/15, we cannot reassign binding variables because they are declared `final` by default. However, JDK 16+ solved the asymmetries that may occur between local and binding variables by removing the `final` modifier. So, starting with JDK 16+, we can reassign binding variables as in the following snippet:

```java
String dummy = "";
private int getLength(Object o) {
  if(o instanceof String str) {
      str = dummy; // reassigning binding variable

      // returns the length of 'dummy' not the passed 'str'
      return str.length();
  }

  return 0;
}
```

Even if this is possible, it is highly recommended to avoid such *code smells* and keep the world clean and happy by not re-assigning your binding variables.

60. Rewriting equals() via type patterns for instanceof

It is not mandatory to rely on `instanceof` to implement the `equals()` method, but it is a convenient approach to write something as follows:

```java
public class MyPoint {

  private final int x;
  private final int y;
  private final int z;

  public MyPoint(int x, int y, int z) {
    this.x = x;
    this.y = y;
    this.z = z;
  }

  @Override
  public boolean equals(Object obj) {

    if (this == obj) {
      return true;
    }

    if (!(obj instanceof MyPoint)) {
```

```
        return false;
    }

    final MyPoint other = (MyPoint) obj;

    return (this.x == other.x && this.y == other.y
      && this.z == other.z);
  }
}
```

If you are a fan of the previous approach for implementing equals(), then you'll love rewriting it via a type pattern for instanceof. Check out the following snippet:

```
@Override
public boolean equals(Object obj) {

  if (this == obj) {
    return true;
  }

  return obj instanceof MyPoint other
    && this.x == other.x && this.y == other.y
    && this.z == other.z;
}
```

If MyPoint is generic (MyPoint<E>) then simply use a wildcard as follows (more details are available in the next problem):

```
return obj instanceof MyPoint<?> other
  && this.x == other.x && this.y == other.y
  && this.z == other.z;
```

Cool, right?! However, pay attention that using instanceof to express the equals() contract imposes the usage of a final class of final equals(). Otherwise, if subclasses are allowed to override equals(), then instanceof may cause transitivity/symmetry bugs. A good approach is to pass equals() through a dedicated verifier such as equals verifier (https://github.com/jqno/equalsverifier), which is capable of checking the validity of the equals() and hashCode() contracts.

61. Tackling type patterns for instanceof and generics

Consider the following snippet of code that uses instanceof in the old-school fashion:

```
public static <K, V> void process(Map<K, ? extends V> map) {
  if (map instanceof EnumMap<?, ? extends V>) {
    EnumMap<?, ? extends V> books
      = (EnumMap<?, ? extends V>) map;
```

```
      if (books.get(Status.DRAFT) instanceof Book) {
        Book book = (Book) books.get(Status.DRAFT);
        book.review();
      }
    }
}

// use case
EnumMap<Status, Book> books = new EnumMap<>(Status.class);
books.put(Status.DRAFT, new Book());
books.put(Status.READY, new Book());

process(books);
```

As we know from *Problem 56*, we can combine instanceof with generic types via unbounded wild-cards, such as our EnumMap<?, ? extends V> (or EnumMap<?, ?>, but not EnumMap<K, ? extends V>, EnumMap<K, ?>, or EnumMap<K, V>).

This code can be written more concisely via the type pattern for instanceof as follows:

```
public static <K, V> void process(Map<K, ? extends V> map) {
  if (map instanceof EnumMap<?, ? extends V> books
    && books.get(Status.DRAFT) instanceof Book book) {
      book.review();
  }
}
```

In the example based on plain instanceof, we can also replace EnumMap<?, ? extends V> with Map<?, ? extends V>. But, as we know from *Problem 53*, this is not possible with type patterns because the expression type cannot be a subtype of pattern type (upcasting is allowed). However, this is not an issue anymore starting with JDK 21.

62. Tackling type patterns for instanceof and streams

Let's consider a List<Engine> where Engine is an interface implemented by several classes such as HypersonicEngine, HighSpeedEngine, and RegularEngine. Our goal is to filter this List and eliminate all RegularEngine classes that are electric and cannot pass our autonomy test. So, we can write code as follows:

```
public static List<Engine> filterRegularEngines(
            List<Engine> engines, int testSpeed) {

  for (Iterator<Engine> i = engines.iterator(); i.hasNext();){
    final Engine e = i.next();
    if (e instanceof RegularEngine) {
```

```
      final RegularEngine popularEngine = (RegularEngine) e;
      if (popularEngine.isElectric()) {
        if (!hasEnoughAutonomy(popularEngine, testSpeed)) {
          i.remove();
        }
      }
    }
  }

  return engines;
}
```

But, starting with JDK 8, we can safely remove from a List without using an Iterator via a default method from `java.util.Collection` named `public default boolean removeIf(Predicate<? super E> filter)`. If we combine this method (and, therefore, the Stream API) with type patterns for `instanceof`, then we can simplify the previous code as follows:

```
public static List<Engine> filterRegularEngines(
            List<Engine> engines, int testSpeed) {

  engines.removeIf(e -> e instanceof RegularEngine engine
    && engine.isElectric()
    && !hasEnoughAutonomy(engine, testSpeed));

  return engines;
}
```

So, whenever you have the chance to use type patterns with the Stream API, don't hesitate.

63. Introducing type pattern matching for switch

JDK 17 (JEP 406) added type pattern matching for `switch` as a preview feature. A second preview was available in JDK 18 (JEP 420). The final release is available in JDK 21 as JEP 441.

Type pattern matching for `switch` allows the *selector expression* (that is, o in `switch(o)`) to be of any type not just an enum constant, number, or string. By "any type," I mean any type (any object type, enum type, array type, record type, or sealed type)! The type pattern matching is not limited to a single hierarchy as it happens in the case of inheritance polymorphism. The `case` labels can have type patterns (referred to as case pattern labels or, simply, pattern labels), so the selector expression (o) can be matched against a type pattern, not only against a constant.

In the next snippet of code, we rewrote the example from *Problem 58* via a type pattern for `switch`:

```
public static String save(Object o) throws IOException {

  return switch(o) {
```

```
      case File file -> "Saving a file of size: "
              + String.format("%,d bytes", file.length());
      case Path path -> "Saving a file of size: "
              + String.format("%,d bytes", Files.size(path));
      case String str -> "Saving a string of size: "
              + String.format("%,d bytes", str.length());
      case null -> "Why are you doing this?";
      default -> "I cannot save the given object";
  };
}
```

The following figure identifies the main players of a switch branch:

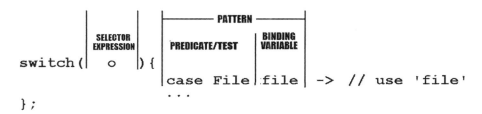

Figure 2.33: Type pattern matching for switch

The case for null is not mandatory. We have added it just for the sake of completeness. On the other hand, the default branch is a must, but this topic is covered later in this chapter.

64. Adding guarded pattern labels in switch

Do you remember that type patterns for instanceof can be refined with extra boolean checks applied to the binding variables to obtain fine-grained use cases? Well, we can do the same for the switch expressions that use pattern labels. The result is named *guarded pattern labels*. Let's consider the following code:

```
private static String turnOnTheHeat(Heater heater) {

  return switch (heater) {
    case Stove stove -> "Make a fire in the stove";
    case Chimney chimney -> "Make a fire in the chimney";
    default -> "No heater available!";
  };
}
```

Having a Stove and a Chimney, this switch decides where to make a fire based on pattern labels. But, what will happen if Chimney is electric? Obviously, we will have to plug Chimney in instead of firing it up. This means that we should add a guarded pattern label that helps us to make the difference between an electric and non-electric Chimney:

```java
return switch (heater) {
  case Stove stove -> "Make a fire in the stove";
  case Chimney chimney
    && chimney.isElectric() -> "Plug in the chimney";
  case Chimney chimney -> "Make a fire in the chimney";
  default -> "No heater available!";
};
```

Well, that was easy, wasn't it? Let's have another example that starts from the following code:

```java
enum FuelType { GASOLINE, HYDROGEN, KEROSENE }

class Vehicle {

  private final int gallon;
  private final FuelType fuel;

  ...

}
```

For each Vehicle, we know the fuel type and how many gallons of fuel fit in the tank. Now, we can write a switch that can rely on guarded pattern labels to try to guess the type of the vehicle based on this information:

```java
private static String theVehicle(Vehicle vehicle) {

  return switch (vehicle) {
    case Vehicle v && v.getFuel().equals(GASOLINE)
      && v.getGallon() < 120 -> "probably a car/van";
    case Vehicle v && v.getFuel().equals(GASOLINE)
      && v.getGallon() > 120 -> "probably a big rig";
    case Vehicle v && v.getFuel().equals(HYDROGEN)
      && v.getGallon() < 300_000 -> "probably an aircraft";
    case Vehicle v && v.getFuel().equals(HYDROGEN)
      && v.getGallon() > 300_000 -> "probably a rocket";
    case Vehicle v && v.getFuel().equals(KEROSENE)
      && v.getGallon() > 2_000 && v.getGallon() < 6_000
        -> "probably a narrow-body aircraft";
    case Vehicle v && v.getFuel().equals(KEROSENE)
      && v.getGallon() > 6_000 && v.getGallon() < 55_000
        -> "probably a large (B747-400) aircraft";
```

```
      default -> "no clue";
   };
}
```

Notice that the pattern labels are the same in all cases (`Vehicle v`) and the decision is refined via the guarded conditions. The previous examples work just fine in JDK 17 and 18, but they don't work starting with JDK 19+. Because the `&&` operator was considered confusing, starting with JDK 19+, we have to deal with a refinement syntax. Practically, instead of the `&&` operator, we use the new context-specific keyword `when` between the pattern label and the refining boolean checks. So, in JDK 19+, the previous code becomes:

```
return switch (vehicle) {
   case Vehicle v when (v.getFuel().equals(GASOLINE)
      && v.getGallon() < 120) -> "probably a car/van";
   case Vehicle v when (v.getFuel().equals(GASOLINE)
      && v.getGallon() > 120) -> "probably a big rig";
   ...
   case Vehicle v when (v.getFuel().equals(KEROSENE)
      && v.getGallon() > 6_000 && v.getGallon() < 55_000)
        -> "probably a large (B747-400) aircraft";
   default -> "no clue";
};
```

In the bundled code, you can find both versions for JDK 17/18, and JDK 19+.

65. Dealing with pattern label dominance in switch

The compiler matches the selector expression against the available pattern labels by testing the selector expression against each label starting from top to bottom (or, from the first to the last) in the exact order in which we wrote them in the `switch` block. This means that the first match wins. Let's assume that we have the following base class (`Pill`) and some pills (`Nurofen`, `Ibuprofen`, and `Piafen`):

```
abstract class Pill {}
class Nurofen extends Pill {}
class Ibuprofen extends Pill {}
class Piafen extends Pill {}
```

Hierarchically speaking, `Nurofen`, `Ibuprofen`, and `Piafen` are three classes placed at the same hierarchical level since all of them have the `Pill` class as the base class. In an IS-A inheritance relationship, we say that `Nurofen` is a `Pill`, `Ibuprofen` is a `Pill`, and `Piafen` is also a `Pill`. Next, let's use a `switch` to serve our clients the proper headache pill:

```
private static String headache(Pill o) {

   return switch(o) {
      case Nurofen nurofen -> "Get Nurofen ...";
```

```
      case Ibuprofen ibuprofen -> "Get Ibuprofen ...";
      case Piafen piafen -> "Get Piafen ...";

      default -> "Sorry, we cannot solve your headache!";
   };
}
```

Calling headache(new Nurofen()) will match the first pattern label, Nurofen nurofen. In the same manner, headache(new Ibuprofen()) matches the second pattern label, and headache(new Piafen()) matches the third one. No matter how we mix the order of these label cases, they will work as expected because they are on the same level and none of them dominate the others.

For instance, since people don't want headaches, they order a lot of Nurofen, so we don't have any anymore. We represent this by removing/comment the corresponding case:

```
return switch(o) {
  // case Nurofen nurofen -> "Get Nurofen ...";
  case Ibuprofen ibuprofen -> "Get Ibuprofen ...";
  case Piafen piafen -> "Get Piafen ...";

  default -> "Sorry, we cannot solve your headache!";
};
```

So, what happens when a client wants Nurofen? You're right ... the default branch will take action since Ibuprofen and Piafen don't match the selector expression.

But, what will happen if we modify the switch as follows?

```
return switch(o) {
  case Pill pill -> "Get a headache pill ...";
  case Nurofen nurofen -> "Get Nurofen ...";
  case Ibuprofen ibuprofen -> "Get Ibuprofen ...";
  case Piafen piafen -> "Get Piafen ...";
};
```

Adding the Pill base class as a pattern label case allows us to remove the default branch since we cover all possible values (this is covered in detail in *Problem 66*). This time, the compiler will raise an error to inform us that the Pill label case dominates the rest of the label cases. Practically, the first label case Pill pill dominates all other label cases because every value that matches any of the Nurofen nurofen, Ibuprofen ibuprofen, Piafen piafen patterns also matches the pattern Pill pill. So, Pill pill always wins while the rest of the label cases are useless. Switching Pill pill with Nurofen nurofen will give a chance to Nurofen nurofen, but Pill pill will still dominate the remaining two. So, we can eliminate the dominance of the base class Pill by moving its label case to the last position:

```
return switch(o) {
```

```
    case Nurofen nurofen -> "Get Nurofen ...";
    case Ibuprofen ibuprofen -> "Get Ibuprofen ...";
    case Piafenpiafen -> "Get Piafen ...";
    case Pill pill -> "Get a headache pill ...";
};
```

Now, every pattern label has a chance to win.

Let's have another example that starts from this hierarchy:

```
abstract class Drink {}
class Small extends Drink {}
class Medium extends Small {}
class Large extends Medium {}
class Extra extends Medium {}
class Huge extends Large {}
class Jumbo extends Extra {}
```

This time, we have seven classes disposed of in a multi-level hierarchy. If we exclude the base class `Drink`, we can represent the rest of them in a `switch` as follows:

```
private static String buyDrink(Drink o) {

    return switch(o) {
        case Jumbo j: yield "We can give a Jumbo ...";
        case Huge h: yield "We can give a Huge ...";
        case Extra e: yield "We can give a Extra ...";
        case Large l: yield "We can give a Large ...";
        case Medium m: yield "We can give a Medium ...";
        case Small s: yield "We can give a Small ...";
        default: yield "Sorry, we don't have this drink!";
    };
}
```

The order of pattern labels is imposed by the class hierarchy and is quite strict, but we can make some changes without creating any dominance issues. For instance, since `Extra` and `Large` are subclasses of `Medium`, we can switch their positions. Some things apply to `Jumbo` and `Huge` since they are both subclasses of `Medium` via `Extra`, respectively `Large`.

In this context, the compiler evaluates the selection expression by trying to match it against this hierarchy via an IS-A inheritance relationship. For instance, let's order a `Jumbo` drink while there are no more `Jumbo` and `Extra` drinks:

```
return switch(o) {
    case Huge h: yield "We can give a Huge ...";
    case Large l: yield "We can give a Large ...";
```

```
  case Medium m: yield "We can give a Medium ...";
  case Small s: yield "We can give a Small ...";
  default: yield "Sorry, we don't have this drink!";
};
```

If we order `Jumbo` (o is `Jumbo`), then we will get `Medium`. Why? The compiler matches `Jumbo` against `Huge` without success. The same result is obtained while matching `Jumbo` against `Large`. However, when it matches `Jumbo` against `Medium`, it sees that `Jumbo` is a `Medium` subclass via the `Extra` class. So, since `Jumbo` is `Medium`, the compiler chooses the `Medium` m pattern label. At this point, `Medium` matches `Jumbo`, `Extra`, and `Medium`. So, soon we will be out of `Medium` as well:

```
return switch(o) {
  case Huge h: yield "We can give a Huge ...";
  case Large l: yield "We can give a Large ...";
  case Small s: yield "We can give a Small ...";
  default: yield "Sorry, we don't have this drink!";
};
```

This time, any request for `Jumbo`, `Extra`, `Medium`, or `Small` will give us a `Small`. I think you get the idea.

Let's take a step further, and analyze this code:

```
private static int oneHundredDividedBy(Integer value) {

  return switch(value) {
    case Integer i -> 100/i;
    case 0 -> 0;
  };
}
```

Have you spotted the problem? A pattern label case dominates a constant label case, so the compiler will complain about the fact that the second case (`case 0`) is dominated by the first case. This is normal, since 0 is an `Integer` as well, so it will match the pattern label. The solution requires switching the cases:

```
  return switch(value) {
    case 0 -> 0;
    case Integer i -> 100/i;
  };
```

Here is another case to enforce this type of dominance:

```
enum Hero { CAPTAIN_AMERICA, IRON_MAN, HULK }

private static String callMyMarvelHero(Hero hero) {

  return switch(hero) {
```

```
    case Hero h -> "Calling " + h;
    case HULK -> "Sorry, we cannot call this guy!";
  };
}
```

In this case, the constant is HULK and it is dominated by the Hero h pattern label case. This is normal, since HULK is also a Marvel hero, so Hero h will match all Marvel heroes including HULK. Again, the fix relies on switching the cases:

```
return switch(hero) {
    case HULK -> "Sorry, we cannot call this guy!";
    case Hero h -> "Calling " + h;
};
```

Okay, finally, let's tackle this snippet of code:

```
private static int oneHundredDividedByPositive(Integer value){

  return switch(value) {
    case Integer i when i > 0 -> 100/i;
    case 0 -> 0;
    case Integer i -> (-1) * 100/i;
  };
}
```

You may think that if we enforce the Integer i pattern label with a condition that forces i to be strictly positive, then the constant label will not be dominated. But, this is not true; a guarded pattern label still dominates a constant label. The proper order places the constant labels first, followed by guarded pattern labels, and finally, by non-guarded pattern labels. The next code fixes the previous one:

```
return switch(value) {
  case 0 -> 0;
  case Integer i when i > 0 -> 100/i;
  case Integer i -> (-1) * 100/i;
};
```

Okay, I think you get the idea. Feel free to practice all these examples in the bundled code.

66. Dealing with completeness (type coverage) in pattern labels for switch

In a nutshell, switch expressions and switch statements that use null and/or pattern labels should be exhaustive. In other words, we must cover with explicit switch case labels all the possible values. Let's consider the following example:

```
class Vehicle {}
```

```
class Car extends Vehicle {}
class Van extends Vehicle {}

private static String whatAmI(Vehicle vehicle) {

  return switch(vehicle) {
    case Car car -> "You're a car";
    case Van van -> "You're a van";
  };
}
```

This snippet of code doesn't compile. The error is clear: *The switch expression does not cover all possible input values.* The compiler complains because we don't have a case pattern label for Vehicle. This base class can be legitimately used without being a Car or a Van, so it is a valid candidate for our switch. We can add a case Vehicle or a default label. If you know that Vehicle will remain an empty base class, then you'll probably go for a default label:

```
return switch(vehicle) {
    case Car car -> "You're a car";
    case Van van -> "You're a van";
    default -> "I have no idea ... what are you?";
  };
```

If we continue by adding another vehicle such as class Truck extends Vehicle {}, then this will be handled by the default branch. If we plan to use Vehicle as an independent class (for instance, to enrich it with methods and functionalities), then we will prefer to add a case Vehicle as follows:

```
return switch(vehicle) {
    case Car car -> "You're a car";
    case Van van -> "You're a van";
    case Vehicle v -> "You're a vehicle"; // total pattern
};
```

This time, the Truck class will match the case Vehicle branch. Of course, we can add a case Truck as well.

Important note

The Vehicle v pattern is named a *total type pattern*. There are two labels that we can use to match all possible values: the total type pattern (for instance, a base class or an interface) and the default label. Generally speaking, a total pattern is a pattern that can be used instead of the default label.

In the previous example, we can accommodate all possible values via the total pattern or the `default` label but not both. This makes sense since the `whatAmI(Vehicle vehicle)` method gets `Vehicle` as an argument. So, in this example, the selector expression can be only `Vehicle` or a subclass of `Vehicle`. How about modifying this method as `whatAmI(Object o)`?

```
private static String whatAmI(Object o) {

  return switch(o) {
    case Car car -> "You're a car";
    case Van van -> "You're a van";
    case Vehicle v -> "You're a vehicle"; // optional
    default -> "I have no idea ... what are you?";
  };
}
```

Now, the selector expression can be any type, which means that the total pattern `Vehicle v` is not total anymore. While `Vehicle v` becomes an optional ordinary pattern, the new total pattern is `case Object obj`. This means that we can cover all possible values by adding the `default` label or the `case Object obj` total pattern:

```
return switch(o) {
  case Car car -> "You're a car";
  case Van van -> "You're a van";
  case Vehicle v -> "You're a vehicle";  // optional
  case Object obj -> "You're an object"; // total pattern
};
```

I think you get the idea! How about using an interface for the base type? For instance, here is an example based on the Java built-in `CharSequence` interface:

```
public static String whatAmI(CharSequence cs) {

  return switch(cs) {
    case String str -> "You're a string";
    case Segment segment -> "You're a Segment";
    case CharBuffer charbuffer -> "You're a CharBuffer";
    case StringBuffer strbuffer -> "You're a StringBuffer";
    case StringBuilder strbuilder -> "You're a StringBuilder";
  };
}
```

Objects, Immutability, Switch Expressions, and Pattern Matching

This snippet of code doesn't compile. The error is clear: *The switch expression does not cover all possible input values*. But, if we check the documentation of `CharSequence`, we see that it is implemented by five classes: `CharBuffer`, `Segment`, `String`, `StringBuffer`, and `StringBuilder`. In our code, each of these classes is covered by a pattern label, so we have covered all possible values, right? Well, yes and no... "Yes" because we cover all possible values for the moment, and "no" because anyone can implement the `CharSequence` interface, which will break the exhaustive coverage of our `switch`. We can do this:

```
public class CoolChar implements CharSequence { ... }
```

At this moment, the `switch` expression doesn't cover the `CoolChar` type. So, we still need a `default` label or the total pattern, `case CharSequence charseq`, as follows:

```
return switch(cs) {
  case String str -> "You're a string";
  ...
  case StringBuilder strbuilder -> "You're a StringBuilder";

  // we have created this
  case CoolChar cool -> "Welcome ... you're a CoolChar";

  // this is a total pattern
  case CharSequence charseq -> "You're a CharSequence";

  // can be used instead of the total pattern
  // default -> "I have no idea ... what are you?";
};
```

Okay, let's tackle this scenario on the `java.lang.constant.ClassDesc` built-in interface:

```
private static String whatAmI(ConstantDesc constantDesc) {

  return switch(constantDesc) {
    case Integer i -> "You're an Integer";
    case Long l -> "You're a Long";
    case Float f -> " You're a Float";
    case Double d -> "You're a Double";
    case String s -> "You're a String";
    case ClassDesc cd -> "You're a ClassDesc";
    case DynamicConstantDesc dcd -> "You're a DCD";
    case MethodHandleDesc mhd -> "You're a MethodHandleDesc";
    case MethodTypeDesc mtd -> "You're a MethodTypeDesc";
  };
}
```

This code compiles! There is no `default` label and no total pattern but the `switch` expression covers all possible values. How so?! This interface is declared as sealed via the `sealed` modifier:

```
public sealed interface ClassDesc
    extends ConstantDesc, TypeDescriptor.OfField<ClassDesc>
```

Sealed interfaces/classes were introduced in JDK 17 (JEP 409) and we will cover this topic in *Chapter 8*. However, for now, it is enough to know that sealing allows us to have fine-grained control of inheritance so classes and interfaces define their permitted subtypes. This means that the compiler can determine all possible values in a `switch` expression. Let's consider a simpler example that starts as follows:

```
sealed interface Player {}
final class Tennis implements Player {}
final class Football implements Player {}
final class Snooker implements Player {}
```

And, let's have a `switch` expression covering all possible values for `Player`:

```
private static String trainPlayer(Player p) {

    return switch (p) {
        case Tennis t -> "Training the tennis player ..." + t;
        case Football f -> "Training the football player ..." + f;
        case Snooker s -> "Training the snooker player ..." + s;
    };
}
```

The compiler is aware that the `Player` interface has only three implementations and all of them are covered via pattern labels. We can add a `default` label or the total pattern `case Player player`, but you most probably don't want to do that. Imagine that we add a new implementation of the sealed `Player` interface named `Golf`:

```
final class Golf implements Player {}
```

If the `switch` expression has a `default` label, then `Golf` values will be handled by this `default` branch. If we have the total pattern `Player player`, then this pattern will handle the `Golf` values. On the other hand, if none of the `default` labels or total patterns are present, the compiler will immediately complain that the `switch` expression doesn't cover all possible values. So, we are immediately informed, and once we add a `case Golf g`, the error disappears. This way, we can easily maintain our code and have a guarantee that our `switch` expressions are always up to date and cover all possible values. The compiler will never miss the chance to inform us when a new implementation of `Player` is available.

A similar logic applies to Java enums. Consider the following enum:

```
private enum PlayerTypes { TENNIS, FOOTBALL, SNOOKER }
```

The compiler is aware of all the possible values for `PlayerTypes`, so the following `switch` expression compiles successfully:

```
private static String createPlayer(PlayerTypes p) {

  return switch (p) {
    case TENNIS -> "Creating a tennis player ...";
    case FOOTBALL -> "Creating a football player ...";
    case SNOOKER -> "Creating a snooker player ...";
  };
}
```

Again, we can add a `default` label or the total pattern, `case PlayerTypes pt`. But, if we add a new value in the enum (for instance, `GOLF`), the compiler will delegate the `default` label or the total pattern to handle it. On the other hand, if none of these are available, the compiler will immediately complain that the `GOLF` value is not covered, so we can add it (`case GOLF g`) and create a golf player whenever required.

So far, so good! Now, let's consider the following context:

```
final static class PlayerClub implements Sport {};
private enum PlayerTypes implements Sport
  { TENNIS, FOOTBALL, SNOOKER }

sealed interface Sport permits PlayerTypes, PlayerClub {};
```

The sealed interface `Sport` allows only two subtypes: `PlayerClub` (a class) and `PlayerTypes` (an enum). If we write a `switch` that covers all possible values for `Sport`, then it will look as follows:

```
private static String createPlayerOrClub(Sport s) {

  return switch (s) {
    case PlayerTypes p when p == PlayerTypes.TENNIS
      -> "Creating a tennis player ...";
    case PlayerTypes p when p == PlayerTypes.FOOTBALL
      -> "Creating a football player ...";
    case PlayerTypes p -> "Creating a snooker player ...";
    case PlayerClub p -> "Creating a sport club ...";
  };
}
```

We immediately observe that writing case `PlayerTypes p when p == PlayerTypes.TENNIS` is not quite neat. What we actually want is `case PlayerTypes.TENNIS` but, until JDK 21, this is not possible since qualified enum constants cannot be used in `case` labels. However, starting with JDK 21, we can use qualified names of enum constants as labels, so we can write this:

```
private static String createPlayerOrClub(Sport s) {

    return switch (s) {
      case PlayerTypes.TENNIS
        -> "Creating a tennis player ...";
      case PlayerTypes.FOOTBALL
        -> "Creating a football player ...";
      case PlayerTypes.SNOOKER
        -> "Creating a snooker player ...";
      case PlayerClub p
        -> "Creating a sport club ...";
    };
}
```

Done! Now you know how to deal with type coverage in `switch` expressions.

67. Understanding the unconditional patterns and nulls in switch expressions

Let's imagine that we use JDK 17 and we have the following code:

```
private static String drive(Vehicle v) {

    return switch (v) {
      case Truck truck -> "truck: " + truck;
      case Van van -> "van: " + van;
      case Vehicle vehicle -> "vehicle: " + vehicle.start();
    };
}

drive(null);
```

Notice the call, `drive(null)`. This call will hit the `Vehicle vehicle` total pattern, so even `null` values match total patterns. But, this means that the binding variable `vehicle` will also be `null`, which means that this branch is prone to `NullPointerException` (for instance, if we call a hypothetical method, `vehicle.start()`):

```
Exception in thread "main" java.lang.NullPointerException: Cannot invoke
"modern.challenge.Vehicle.start()" because "vehicle" is null
```

Because `Vehicle vehicle` matches all possible values, it is known as a total pattern but also as an *unconditional pattern* since it matches everything unconditionally.

But, as we know from *Problem 54*, starting with JDK 17+ (JEP 427), we can have a pattern label for `null` itself, so we can handle the previous shortcoming as follows:

```
return switch (v) {
    case Truck truck -> "truck: " + truck;
    case Van van -> "van: " + van;
    case null -> "so, you don't have a vehicle?";
    case Vehicle vehicle -> "vehicle: " + vehicle.start();
  };
```

Yes, everybody agrees that adding a `case null` between vehicles looks awkward. Adding it at the end is not an option since will raise a dominance issue. So, starting with JDK 19+, adding this `case null` is no longer needed in this kind of scenario. Basically, the idea remains the same meaning that the unconditional pattern still only matches `null` values so it will not allow the execution of that branch. Actually, when a `null` value occurs, the `switch` expressions will throw a `NullPointerException` without even looking at the patterns. So, in JDK 19+, this code will throw an NPE right away:

```
return switch (v) {
  case Truck truck -> "truck: " + truck;
  case Van van -> "van: " + van;

  // we can still use a null check
  // case null -> "so, you don't have a vehicle?";

  // total/unconditional pattern throw NPE immediately
  case Vehicle vehicle -> "vehicle: " + vehicle.start();
};
```

The NPE message reveals that `vehicle.start()` was never called. The NPE occurred much earlier:

```
Exception in thread "main" java.lang.NullPointerExceptionatjava.base/java.util.
Objects.requireNonNull(Objects.java:233)
```

We will expand on this topic later when we will talk about Java records.

Summary

That's all folks! This was a comprehensive chapter that covered four main topics, among others: `java.util.Objects`, immutability, `switch` expressions, and pattern matching for `instanceof` and `switch` expressions.

Join our community on Discord

Join our community's Discord space for discussions with the author and other readers:

https://discord.gg/8mgytp5DGQ

3

Working with Date and Time

This chapter includes 20 problems covering different date-time topics. These problems are mainly focused on the `Calendar` API and on the JDK Date/Time API. About the latter, we will cover some less popular APIs such as `ChronoUnit`, `ChronoField`, `IsoFields`, `TemporalAdjusters`, and so on.

At the end of this chapter, you'll have a ton of tips and tricks in your tool belt that will be very useful for solving a wide range of real-world date-time problems.

Problems

Use the following problems to test your programming prowess on date and time. I strongly encourage you to give each problem a try before you turn to the solutions and download the example programs:

68. **Defining a day period**: Write an application that goes beyond AM/PM flags and split the day into four periods: *night*, *morning*, *afternoon*, and *evening*. Depending on the given date-time and time zone generate one of these periods.

69. **Converting between Date and YearMonth**: Write an application that converts between `java.util.Date` and `java.time.YearMonth` and vice versa.

70. **Converting between int and YearMonth**: Let's consider that a `YearMonth` is given (for instance, 2023-02). Convert it to an integer representation (for instance, 24277) that can be converted back to `YearMonth`.

71. **Converting week/year to Date**: Let's consider that two integers are given representing a week and a year (for instance, week 10, year 2023). Write a program that converts 10-2023 to a `java.util.Date` via `Calendar` and to a `LocalDate` via the `WeekFields` API. Also, do vice versa: from a given `Date`/`LocalDate` extract the year and the week as integers.

72. **Checking for a leap year**: Let's consider that an integer is given representing a year. Write an application that checks if this year is a leap year. Provide at least three solutions.

73. **Calculating the quarter of a given date**: Let's consider that a `java.util.Date` is given. Write a program that returns the quarter containing this date as an integer (1, 2,3, or 4) and as a string (Q1, Q2, Q3, or Q4).

74. **Getting the first and last day of a quarter:** Let's consider that a `java.util.Date` is given. Write a program that returns the first and last day of the quarter containing this date. Represent the returned days as `Date` (implementation based on `Calendar`) and `LocalDate` (implementation based on the JDK 8 Date/Time API).

75. **Extracting the months from a given quarter:** Let's consider that a quarter is given (as an integer, a string (Q1, Q2, Q3, or Q4), or a `LocalDate`). Write a program that extracts the names of the months of this quarter.

76. **Computing pregnancy due date:** Write a pregnancy due date calculator.

77. **Implementing a stopwatch:** Write a program that implements a stopwatch via `System.nanoTime()` and via `Instant.now()`.

78. **Extracting the count of milliseconds since midnight:** Let's consider that a `LocalDateTime` is given. Write an application that counts the milliseconds passed from midnight to this `LocalDateTime`.

79. **Splitting a date-time range into equal intervals:** Let's assume that we have a date-time range given via two `LocalDateTime` instances, and an integer, n. Write an application that splits the given range into n equal intervals (n equal `LocalDateTime` instances).

80. **Explaining the difference between Clock.systemUTC() and Clock.systemDefaultZone():** Explain via meaningful examples what is the difference between `systemUTC()` and `systemDefaultZone()`.

81. **Displaying the names of the days of the week:** Display the names of the days of the week via the `java.text.DateFormatSymbols` API.

82. **Getting the first and last day of the year:** Let's consider that an integer representing a year is given. Write a program that returns the first and last day of this year. Provide a solution based on the `Calendar` API and one based on the JDK 8 Date/Time API.

83. **Getting the first and last day of the week:** Let's assume that we have an integer representing a number of weeks (for instance, 3 represents three consecutive weeks starting from the current date). Write a program that returns the first and last day of each week. Provide a solution based on the `Calendar` API and one based on the JDK 8 Date/Time API.

84. **Calculating the middle of the month:** Provide an application containing a snippet based on the `Calendar` API, and one based on the JDK 8 Date/Time API for calculating the middle of the given month as a `Date`, respectively as a `LocalDate`.

85. **Getting the number of quarters between two dates:** Let's consider that a date-time range is given via two `LocalDate` instances. Write a program that counts the number of quarters contained in this range.

86. **Converting Calendar to LocalDateTime:** Write a program that converts the given `Calendar` into a `LocalDateTime` (default time zone), respectively into a `ZonedDateTime` (for the Asia/Calcutta time zone).

87. **Getting the number of weeks between two dates:** Let's assume that we have a date-time range given as two `Date` instances or as two `LocalDateTime` instances. Write an application that returns the number of weeks contained in this range. For the `Date` range, write a solution based on the `Calendar` API, while for the `LocalDateTime` range, write a solution based on the JDK 8 Date/Time API.

The following sections describe solutions to the preceding problems. Remember that there usually isn't a single correct way to solve a particular problem. Also, remember that the explanations shown here include only the most interesting and important details needed to solve the problems. Download the example solutions to see additional details and to experiment with the programs at `https://github.com/PacktPublishing/Java-Coding-Problems-Second-Edition/tree/main/Chapter03`.

68. Defining a day period

Let's imagine that we want to say hello to a friend from another country (in a different time zone) via a message such as *Good morning*, *Good afternoon*, and so on based on their local time. So, having access to AM/PM flags is not enough, because we consider that a day (24 hours) can be represented by the following periods:

- 9:00 PM (or 21:00) – 5:59 AM = night
- 6:00 AM – 11:59 AM = morning
- 12:00 PM – 5:59 PM (or 17:59) = afternoon
- 6:00 PM (or 18:00) – 8:59 PM (or 20:59) = evening

Before JDK 16

First, we have to obtain the time corresponding to our friend's time zone. For this, we can start from our local time given as a `java.util.Date`, `java.time.LocalTime`, and so on. If we start from a `java.util.Date`, then we can obtain the time in our friend's time zone as follows:

```
LocalTime lt = date.toInstant().atZone(zoneId).toLocalTime();
```

Here, `date` is a `new Date()` and `zoneId` is `java.time.ZoneId`. Of course, we can pass the zone ID as a `String` and use the `ZoneId.of(String zoneId)` method to get the `ZoneId` instance.

If we prefer to start from `LocalTime.now()`, then we can obtain the time in our friend's time zone as follows:

```
LocalTime lt = LocalTime.now(zoneId);
```

Next, we can define the day periods as a bunch of `LocalTime` instances and add some conditions to determine the current period. The following code exemplifies this statement:

```
public static String toDayPeriod(Date date, ZoneId zoneId) {

  LocalTime lt = date.toInstant().atZone(zoneId).toLocalTime();

  LocalTime night = LocalTime.of(21, 0, 0);
  LocalTime morning = LocalTime.of(6, 0, 0);
  LocalTime afternoon = LocalTime.of(12, 0, 0);
  LocalTime evening = LocalTime.of(18, 0, 0);
  LocalTime almostMidnight = LocalTime.of(23, 59, 59);
  LocalTime midnight = LocalTime.of(0, 0, 0);
```

```
if((lt.isAfter(night) && lt.isBefore(almostMidnight))
 || lt.isAfter(midnight) && (lt.isBefore(morning))) {
 return "night";
 } else if(lt.isAfter(morning) && lt.isBefore(afternoon)) {
 return "morning";
 } else if(lt.isAfter(afternoon) && lt.isBefore(evening)) {
 return "afternoon";
 } else if(lt.isAfter(evening) && lt.isBefore(night)) {
 return "evening";
 }

 return "day";
}
```

Now, let's see how we can do this in JDK 16+.

JDK 16+

Starting with JDK 16+, we can go beyond AM/PM flags via the following strings: *in the morning, in the afternoon, in the evening,* and *at night.*

These friendly outputs are available via the new pattern, B. This pattern is available starting with JDK 16+ via DateTimeFormatter and DateTimeFormatterBuilder (you should be familiar with these APIs from *Chapter 1, Problem 18,* shown in *Figure 1.18*).

So, the following code uses the DateTimeFormatter to exemplify the usage of pattern B, representing a period of the day:

```
public static String toDayPeriod(Date date, ZoneId zoneId) {

 ZonedDateTime zdt = date.toInstant().atZone(zoneId);

 DateTimeFormatter formatter
    = DateTimeFormatter.ofPattern("yyyy-MMM-dd [B]");

 return zdt.withZoneSameInstant(zoneId).format(formatter);
}
```

Here is an output for Australia/Melbourne:

```
2023-Feb-04 at night
```

You can see more examples in the bundled code. Feel free to challenge yourself to adjust this code to reproduce the result from the first example.

69. Converting between Date and YearMonth

Converting a java.util.Date to JDK 8 java.time.YearMonth can be done based on YearMonth. from(TemporalAccessor temporal). A TemporalAccessor is an interface (more precisely, a framework-level interface) that exposes read-only access to any temporal object including date, time, and offset (a combination of these is also allowed). So, if we convert the given java.util.Date to java. time.LocalDate, then the result of the conversion can be passed to YearMonth.from() as follows:

```java
public static YearMonth toYearMonth(Date date) {

  return YearMonth.from(date.toInstant()
                .atZone(ZoneId.systemDefault())
                .toLocalDate());
}
```

Vice versa can be obtained via Date.from(Instant instant) as follows:

```java
public static Date toDate(YearMonth ym) {

  return Date.from(ym.atDay(1).atStartOfDay(
        ZoneId.systemDefault()).toInstant());
}
```

Well, that was easy, wasn't it?

70. Converting between int and YearMonth

Consider that we have YearMonth.now() and we want to convert it to an integer (for example, this can be useful for storing a year/month date in a database using a numeric field). Check out the solution:

```java
public static int to(YearMonth u) {

  return (int) u.getLong(ChronoField.PROLEPTIC_MONTH);
}
```

The *proleptic-month* is a java.time.temporal.TemporalField, which basically represents a date-time field such as *month-of-year* (our case) or *minute-of-hour*. The proleptic-month starts from 0 and counts the months sequentially from year 0. So, getLong() returns the value of the specified field (here, the proleptic-month) from this year-month as a long. We can cast this long to int since the proleptic-month shouldn't go beyond the int domain (for instance, for 2023/2 the returned int is 24277).

Vice versa can be accomplished as follows:

```java
public static YearMonth from(int t) {

  return YearMonth.of(1970, 1)
    .with(ChronoField.PROLEPTIC_MONTH, t);
}
```

You can start from any year/month. The 1970/1 (known as the *epoch* and the starting point for `java.time.Instant`) choice was just an arbitrary choice.

71. Converting week/year to Date

Let's consider the year 2023, week 10. The corresponding date is Sun Mar 05 15:15:08 EET 2023 (of course, the time component is relative). Converting the year/week to `java.util.Date` can be done via the `Calendar` API as in the following self-explanatory snippet of code:

```
public static Date from(int year, int week) {

  Calendar calendar = Calendar.getInstance();

  calendar.set(Calendar.YEAR, year);
  calendar.set(Calendar.WEEK_OF_YEAR, week);
  calendar.set(Calendar.DAY_OF_WEEK, 1);

  return calendar.getTime();
}
```

If you prefer to obtain a `LocalDate` instead of a `Date` then you can easily perform the corresponding conversion or you can rely on `java.time.temporal.WeekFields`. This API exposes several fields for working with *week-of-year*, *week-of-month*, and *day-of-week*. This being said, here is the previous solution written via `WeekFields` to return a `LocalDate`:

```
public static LocalDate from(int year, int week) {

  WeekFields weekFields = WeekFields.of(Locale.getDefault());

  return LocalDate.now()
                  .withYear(year)
                  .with(weekFields.weekOfYear(), week)
                  .with(weekFields.dayOfWeek(), 1);
}
```

On the other hand, if we have a `java.util.Date` and we want to extract the year and the week from it, then we can use the `Calendar` API. Here, we extract the year:

```
public static int getYear(Date date) {

  Calendar calendar = Calendar.getInstance();
  calendar.setTime(date);

  return calendar.get(Calendar.YEAR);
}
```

And here, we extract the week:

```java
public static int getWeek(Date date) {

  Calendar calendar = Calendar.getInstance();
  calendar.setTime(date);

  return calendar.get(Calendar.WEEK_OF_YEAR);
}
```

Getting the year and the week from a `LocalDate` is easy thanks to `ChronoField.YEAR` and `ChronoField.ALIGNED_WEEK_OF_YEAR`:

```java
public static int getYear(LocalDate date) {

  return date.get(ChronoField.YEAR);
}

public static int getWeek(LocalDate date) {

  return date.get(ChronoField.ALIGNED_WEEK_OF_YEAR);
}
```

Of course, getting the week can be accomplished via `WeekFields` as well:

```java
return date.get(WeekFields.of(
    Locale.getDefault()).weekOfYear());
```

Challenge yourself to obtain week/month and day/week from a `Date`/`LocalDate`.

72. Checking for a leap year

This problem becomes easy as long as we know what a leap year is. In a nutshell, a leap year is any year divisible by 4 (so, `year % 4 == 0`) that it is not a century (for instance, 100, 200, ..., n00). However, if the year represents a century that is divisible by 400 (so, `year % 400 == 0`), then it is a leap year. In this context, our code is just a simple chain of `if` statements as follows:

```java
public static boolean isLeapYear(int year) {

  if (year % 4 != 0) {
    return false;
  } else if (year % 400 == 0) {
    return true;
  } else if (year % 100 == 0) {
    return false;
  }
```

```
   return true;
}
```

But, this code can be condensed using the `GregorianCalendar` as well:

```
public static boolean isLeapYear(int year) {

  return new GregorianCalendar(year, 1, 1).isLeapYear(year);
}
```

Or, starting with JDK 8, we can rely on the `java.time.Year` API as follows:

```
public static boolean isLeapYear(int year) {

  return Year.of(year).isLeap();
}
```

In the bundled code, you can see more approaches.

73. Calculating the quarter of a given date

A year has 4 quarters (commonly denoted as Q1, Q2, Q3, and Q4) and each quarter has 3 months. If we consider that January is 0, February is 1, ..., and December is 11, then we can observe that January/3 = 0, February/3 =0, March/3 = 0, and 0 can represent Q1. Next, 3/3 = 1, 4/3 = 1, 5/3 = 1, so 1 can represent Q2. Based on the same logic, 6/3 = 2, 7/3 = 2, 8/3 = 2, so 2 can represent Q3. Finally, 9/3 = 3, 10/3 = 3, 11/3 = 3, so 3 represents Q4.

Based on this statement and the `Calendar` API, we can obtain the following code:

```
public static String quarter(Date date) {

  String[] quarters = {"Q1", "Q2", "Q3", "Q4"};

  Calendar calendar = Calendar.getInstance();
  calendar.setTime(date);
  int quarter = calendar.get(Calendar.MONTH) / 3;

  return quarters[quarter];
}
```

But, starting with JDK 8, we can rely on `java.time.temporal.IsoFields`. This class contains fields (and units) that follow the calendar system based on the ISO-8601 standard. Among these artifacts, we have the *week-based-year* and the one that we are interested in, *quarter-of-year*. This time, let's return the quarter as an integer:

```
public static int quarter(Date date) {
```

```
   LocalDate localDate = date.toInstant()
     .atZone(ZoneId.systemDefault()).toLocalDate();

   return localDate.get(IsoFields.QUARTER_OF_YEAR);
}
```

In the bundled code, you can see more examples including one that uses `DateTimeFormatter.ofPattern("QQQ")`.

74. Getting the first and last day of a quarter

Let's assume that we represent the first and last day of a quarter via this simple class:

```
public final class Quarter {

  private final Date firstDay;
  private final Date lastDay;
  ...
}
```

Next, we have a `java.util.Date` and we want the first and the last day of the quarter containing this date. For this, we can use JDK 8's `IsoFields.DAY_OF_QUARTER` (we introduced `IsoFields` in the previous problem). But, before we can use `IsoFields`, we have to convert the given `java.util.Date` to a `LocalDate` as follows:

```
LocalDate localDate = date.toInstant()
  .atZone(ZoneId.systemDefault()).toLocalDate();
```

Once we have the given `Date` as a `LocalDate`, we can easily extract the first day of the quarter via `IsoFields.DAY_OF_QUARTER`. Next, we add 2 months to this day to move into the last month of the quarter (a quarter has 3 months, so a year has 4 quarters) and we rely on `java.time.temporal.TemporalAdjusters`, more precisely on `lastDayOfMonth()` to obtain the last day of the quarter. Finally, we convert the two obtained `LocalDate` instances to `Date` instances. Here is the complete code:

```
public static Quarter quarterDays(Date date) {

  LocalDate localDate = date.toInstant()
    .atZone(ZoneId.systemDefault()).toLocalDate();

  LocalDate firstDay
    = localDate.with(IsoFields.DAY_OF_QUARTER, 1L);

  LocalDate lastDay = firstDay.plusMonths(2)
    .with(TemporalAdjusters.lastDayOfMonth());
```

```
    return new Quarter(
      Date.from(firstDay.atStartOfDay(
        ZoneId.systemDefault()).toInstant()),
      Date.from(lastDay.atStartOfDay(
        ZoneId.systemDefault()).toInstant())
    );
}
```

Of course, these conversions are not needed if you work directly with LocalDate. But, this way, you have a chance to learn more.

In the bundled code, you can find more examples, including one that relies entirely on the Calendar API.

75. Extracting the months from a given quarter

This problem becomes quite easy to solve if we are familiar with JDK 8's java.time.Month. Via this API, we can find the first month (0 for January, 1 for February, ...) of a quarter containing the given LocalDate as Month.from(LocalDate).firstMonthOfQuarter().getValue().

Once we have the first month, it is easy to obtain the other two as follows:

```
public static List<String> quarterMonths(LocalDate ld) {

  List<String> qmonths = new ArrayList<>();

  int qmonth = Month.from(ld)
    .firstMonthOfQuarter().getValue();

  qmonths.add(Month.of(qmonth).name());
  qmonths.add(Month.of(++qmonth).name());
  qmonths.add(Month.of(++qmonth).name());

  return qmonths;
}
```

How about passing the quarter itself as an argument? This can be done as a number (1, 2, 3, or 4) or as a string (Q1, Q2, Q3, or Q4). If the given quarter is a number, then the first month of the quarter can be obtained as quarter * 3 – 2, where the quarter is 1, 2, 3, or 4. This time, let's express the code in a functional style:

```
int qmonth = quarter * 3 - 2;
List<String> qmonths = IntStream.of(
        qmonth, ++qmonth, ++qmonth)
  .mapToObj(Month::of)
```

```
    .map(Month::name)
    .collect(Collectors.toList());
```

Of course, if you find it more concise, then you can use `IntStream.range(qmonth, qmonth+2)` instead of `IntStream.of()`. In the bundled, code you can find more examples.

76. Computing pregnancy due date

Let's start with these two constants:

```
public static final int PREGNANCY_WEEKS = 40;
public static final int PREGNANCY_DAYS = PREGNANCY_WEEKS * 7;
```

Let's consider the first day as a `LocalDate` and we want to write a calculator that prints the pregnancy due date, the number of remaining days, the number of passed days, and the current week.

Basically, the pregnancy due date is obtained by adding the `PREGNANCY_DAYS` to the given first day. Further, the number of remaining days is the difference between today and the given first day, while the number of passed days is `PREGNANCY_DAYS` minus the number of remaining days. Finally, the current week is obtained as the number of passed days divided by 7 (since a week has 7 days). Based on these statements, the code speaks for itself:

```java
public static void pregnancyCalculator(LocalDate firstDay) {

  firstDay = firstDay.plusDays(PREGNANCY_DAYS);
  System.out.println("Due date: " + firstDay);

  LocalDate today = LocalDate.now();
  long betweenDays =
    Math.abs(ChronoUnit.DAYS.between(firstDay, today));

  long diffDays = PREGNANCY_DAYS - betweenDays;

  long weekNr = diffDays / 7;
  long weekPart = diffDays % 7;

  String week = weekNr + " | " + weekPart;

  System.out.println("Days remaining: " + betweenDays);
  System.out.println("Days in: " + diffDays);
  System.out.println("Week: " + week);
}
```

See if you can think of a way to use this to calculate another important date.

77. Implementing a stopwatch

A classical implementation for a stopwatch relies on System.nanoTime(), System.currentTimeMillis(), or on Instant.now(). In all cases, we have to provide support for starting and stopping the stopwatch, and some helpers to obtain the measured time in different time units.

While the solutions based on Instant.now() and currentTimeMillis() are available in the bundled code, here we'll show the one based on System.nanoTime():

```
public final class NanoStopwatch {

  private long startTime;
  private long stopTime;
  private boolean running;

  public void start() {
    this.startTime = System.nanoTime();
    this.running = true;
  }

  public void stop() {
    this.stopTime = System.nanoTime();
    this.running = false;
  }

  //elaspsed time in nanoseconds
  public long getElapsedTime() {

    if (running) {
      return System.nanoTime() - startTime;
    } else {
      return stopTime - startTime;
    }
  }
}
```

If you need to return the measured time in milliseconds or seconds as well, then simply add the following two helpers:

```
//elaspsed time in millisecods
public long elapsedTimeToMillis(long nanotime) {

  return TimeUnit.MILLISECONDS.convert(
    nanotime, TimeUnit.NANOSECONDS);
```

```
  }

  //elaspsed time in seconds
  public long elapsedTimeToSeconds(long nanotime) {

    return TimeUnit.SECONDS.convert(
      nanotime, TimeUnit.NANOSECONDS);
  }
```

This approach is based on System.nanoTime() for measuring the elapsed time with high accuracy. This approach returns a high-resolution time in nanoseconds that doesn't rely on a system clock or any other wall clock (as Instant.now() or System.currentTimeMillis() does), so it is not exposed to common issues of wall clocks such as leap second, time uniformity, synchronicity issues, and so on.

Whenever you need a professional tool for measuring elapsed time, rely on Micrometer (https://micrometer.io/), JMH (https://openjdk.org/projects/code-tools/jmh/), Gatling (https://gatling.io/open-source/), and so on.

78. Extracting the count of milliseconds since midnight

So, we have a date-time (let's say a LocalDateTime or LocalTime) and we want to know how many milliseconds have passed from midnight to this date-time. Let's consider that the given date-time is right now:

```
LocalDateTime now = LocalDateTime.now();
```

Midnight is relative to now, so we can find the difference as follows:

```
LocalDateTime midnight = LocalDateTime.of(now.getYear(),
   now.getMonth(), now.getDayOfMonth(), 0, 0, 0);
```

Finally, compute the difference in milliseconds between midnight and now. This can be accomplished in several ways, but probably the most concise solution relies on java.time.temporal.ChronoUnit. This API exposes a set of units useful to manipulate a date, time, or date-time including milliseconds:

```
System.out.println("Millis: "
   + ChronoUnit.MILLIS.between(midnight, now));
```

In the bundled code, you can see more examples of ChronoUnit.

79. Splitting a date-time range into equal intervals

Let's consider a date-time range (bounded by a start date and an end date represented by two LocalDateTime instances) and an integer n. In order to split the given range into n equal intervals, we start by defining a java.time.Duration as follows:

```
Duration range = Duration.between(start, end);
```

Having this date-time range, we can rely on `dividedBy()` to obtain a copy of it divided by the specified n:

```
Duration interval = range.dividedBy(n - 1);
```

Finally, we can begin from the start date (the left head of the range) and repeatedly increment it with the interval value until we reach the end date (the right head of the range). After each step, we store the new date in a list that will be returned at the end. Here is the complete code:

```
public static List<LocalDateTime> splitInEqualIntervals(
        LocalDateTime start, LocalDateTime end, int n) {

  Duration range = Duration.between(start, end);
  Duration interval = range.dividedBy(n - 1);

  List<LocalDateTime> listOfDates = new ArrayList<>();
  LocalDateTime timeline = start;
  for (int i = 0; i < n - 1; i++) {
    listOfDates.add(timeline);
    timeline = timeline.plus(interval);
  }
  listOfDates.add(end);

  return listOfDates;
}
```

The resulting `listOfDates` will contain n dates at equal intervals.

80. Explaining the difference between Clock.systemUTC() and Clock.systemDefaultZone()

Let's start with the following three lines of code:

```
System.out.println(Clock.systemDefaultZone());
System.out.println(system(ZoneId.systemDefault()));
System.out.println(Clock.systemUTC());
```

The output reveals that the first two lines are similar. Both of them display the default time zone (in my case, Europe/Bucharest):

```
SystemClock[Europe/Bucharest]
SystemClock[Europe/Bucharest]
```

The third line is different. Here, we see Z time zone, which is specific to the UTC time zone and indicates the presence of a zone offset:

```
SystemClock[Z]
```

On the other hand, creating an `Instant` reveals that `Clock.systemUTC()` and `Clock.systemDefaultZone()` produce the same result:

```
System.out.println(Clock.systemDefaultZone().instant());
System.out.println(system(ZoneId.systemDefault()).instant());
System.out.println(Clock.systemUTC().instant());
```

The instant time is the same in all three cases:

```
2023-02-07T05:26:17.374159500Z
2023-02-07T05:26:17.384811300Z
2023-02-07T05:26:17.384811300Z
```

But, the difference occurs when we try to create a date, time, or date-time from these two clocks. For instance, let's create a `LocalDateTime` from `Clock.systemUTC()`:

```
// 2023-02-07T05:26:17.384811300
System.out.println(LocalDateTime.now(Clock.systemUTC()));
```

And, a `LocalDateTime` from `Clock.systemDefaultZone()`:

```
// 2023-02-07T07:26:17.384811300
System.out.println(LocalDateTime.now(
    Clock.systemDefaultZone()));
```

My time (default time zone, Europe/Bucharest) is 07:26:17. But, the time via `Clock.systemUTC()` is 05:26:17. This is because Europe/Bucharest is at an offset of UTC-2, so `systemUTC()` produces the date-time in the UTC time zone, while `systemDefaultZone()` produces the date-time in the current default time zone. However, both of them produce the same `Instant`.

81. Displaying the names of the days of the week

One of the hidden gems in Java is `java.text.DateFormatSymbols`. This class is a wrapper for date-time formatting data such as the names of the days of the week, and the names of the months. All these names are localizable.

Typically, you will use `DateFormatSymbols` via a `DateFormat` such as `SimpleDateFormat`, but in order to solve this problem, we can use it directly as in the following code:

```
String[] weekdays = new DateFormatSymbols().getWeekdays();

IntStream.range(1, weekdays.length)
    .mapToObj(t -> String.format("Day: %d -> %s",
        t, weekdays[t]))
    .forEach(System.out::println);
```

This code will output the weekdays' names as follows:

```
Day: 1 -> Sunday
...
Day: 7 -> Saturday
```

Challenge yourself to come up with another solution.

82. Getting the first and last day of the year

Getting the first and last day of the given year (as a numeric value) can be done via LocalDate and the handy TemporalAdjusters, firstDayOfYear(), and lastDayOfYear(). First, we create a LocalDate from the given year. Next, we use this LocalDate with firstDayOfYear()/lastDayOfYear() as in the following code:

```java
public static String fetchFirstDayOfYear(int year, boolean name) {

  LocalDate ld = LocalDate.ofYearDay(year, 1);
  LocalDate firstDay = ld.with(firstDayOfYear());

  if (!name) {
    return firstDay.toString();
  }

  return DateTimeFormatter.ofPattern("EEEE").format(firstDay);
}
```

And, for the last day, the code is almost similar:

```java
public static String fetchLastDayOfYear(int year, boolean name) {

  LocalDate ld = LocalDate.ofYearDay(year, 31);
  LocalDate lastDay = ld.with(lastDayOfYear());

  if (!name) {
    return lastDay.toString();
  }

  return DateTimeFormatter.ofPattern("EEEE").format(lastDay);
}
```

If the flag argument (name) is false, then we return the first/last day via LocalDate.toString(), so we will get something like 2020-01-01 (the first day of 2020) and 2020-12-31 (the last day of 2020). If this flag argument is true, then we rely on the EEEE pattern to return only the name of the first/last day of the year as Wednesday (the first day of 2020) and Thursday (the last day of 2020).

In the bundle code, you can also find a solution to this problem via the Calendar API.

83. Getting the first and last day of the week

Let's assume given an integer (nrOfWeeks) representing the number of weeks that we want to extract the first and last day of each week starting from now. For instance, for the given nrOfWeeks = 3 and a local date such as 06/02/2023, we want this:

```
[
Mon 06/02/2023,
Sun 12/02/2023,

Mon 13/02/2023,
Sun 19/02/2023,

Mon 20/02/2023,
Sun 26/02/2023
]
```

This is much easier than it might seem. We just need a loop from 0 to nrOfWeeks and two TemporalAdjusters to fit the first/last day of each week. More precisely, we need the nextOrSame(DayOfWeek dayOfWeek) and previousOrSame(DayOfWeek dayOfWeek) adjusters.

The nextOrSame() adjuster's role is to adjust the current date to the first occurrence of the given *day of week* after the date being adjusted (this can be *next or same*). On the other hand, the previousOrSame() adjuster's role is to adjust the current date to the first occurrence of the given *day of week* before the date being adjusted (this can be *previous or same*). For instance, if today is [Tuesday 07/02/2023], then previousOrSame(DayOfWeek.MONDAY) will return [Monday 06/02/2023], and nextOrSame(DayOfWeek.SUNDAY) will return [Sunday 12/02/2023].

Based on these statements, we can solve our problem via the following code:

```java
public static List<String> weekBoundaries(int nrOfWeeks) {

    List<String> boundaries = new ArrayList<>();
    LocalDate timeline = LocalDate.now();

    DateTimeFormatter dtf = DateTimeFormatter
        .ofPattern("EEE dd/MM/yyyy");
```

```
  for (int i = 0; i < nrOfWeeks; i++) {
    boundaries.add(dtf.format(timeline.with(
      previousOrSame(DayOfWeek.MONDAY))));
    boundaries.add(dtf.format(timeline.with(
      nextOrSame(DayOfWeek.SUNDAY))));
    timeline = timeline.plusDays(7);
  }

  return boundaries;
}
```

In the bundled code, you can also see a solution based on the `Calendar` API.

84. Calculating the middle of the month

Let's imagine that we have a `LocalDate` and we want to calculate from it another `LocalDate` representing the middle of the month. This can be achieved in seconds if we know that the `LocalDate` API has a method named `lengthOfMonth()`, which returns an integer representing the length of the month in days. So, all we have to do is calculate `lengthOfMonth()/2` as in the following code:

```
public static LocalDate middleOfTheMonth(LocalDate date) {

  return LocalDate.of(date.getYear(), date.getMonth(),
    date.lengthOfMonth() / 2);
}
```

In the bundled code, you can see a solution based on the `Calendar` API.

85. Getting the number of quarters between two dates

This is just another problem that requires us to have a deep grasp of the Java Date/Time API. This time, we talk about `java.time.temporal.IsoFields`, which was introduced in *Problem 73*. One of the ISO fields is `QUARTER_YEARS`, which is a temporal unit representing the concept of a *quarter-year*. So, having two `LocalDate` instances, we can write this:

```
public static long nrOfQuarters(
    LocalDate startDate, LocalDate endDate) {

  return IsoFields.QUARTER_YEARS.between(startDate, endDate);
}
```

Feel free to challenge yourself to provide a solution for `java.util.Date/Calendar`.

86. Converting Calendar to LocalDateTime

In *Problem 68*, you saw that converting a java.util.Date (date) to a LocalTime can be done as follows:

```
LocalTime lt = date.toInstant().atZone(zoneId).toLocalTime();
```

In the same manner, we can convert a java.util.Date to a LocalDateTime (here, zoneId was replaced with ZoneId.systemDefault()):

```
LocalDateTime ldt = date.toInstant().atZone(
    ZoneId.systemDefault()).toLocalDateTime();
```

We also know that we can obtain a java.util.Date from a Calendar via the getTime() method. So, by gluing the pieces of the puzzle together, we obtain the following code:

```
public static LocalDateTime
        toLocalDateTime(Calendar calendar) {

  Date date = calendar.getTime();

  return date.toInstant().atZone(
    ZoneId.systemDefault()).toLocalDateTime();
}
```

The same result but following a shorter path can be obtained like this:

```
return LocalDateTime.ofInstant(Instant.ofEpochMilli(
    calendar.getTimeInMillis()), ZoneId.systemDefault());
```

Or, even shorter, like this:

```
return LocalDateTime.ofInstant(
    calendar.toInstant(), ZoneId.systemDefault());
```

But, this code assumes that the time zone of the given Calendar is the default time zone. If the calendar has a different time zone (for instance, Asia/Calcutta), then we might expect back a ZonedDateTime instead of a LocalDateTime. This means that we should adjust the previous code accordingly:

```
public static ZonedDateTime
        toZonedDateTime(Calendar calendar) {

  Date date = calendar.getTime();

  return date.toInstant().atZone(
    calendar.getTimeZone().toZoneId());
}
```

Again, some shorter versions are available, but we've not shown these as they are less expressive:

```
return ZonedDateTime.ofInstant(
  Instant.ofEpochMilli(calendar.getTimeInMillis()),
    calendar.getTimeZone().toZoneId());


return ZonedDateTime.ofInstant(calendar.toInstant(),
    calendar.getTimeZone().toZoneId());
```

Done!

87. Getting the number of weeks between two dates

If the given two dates are instances of LocalDate(Time), then we can rely on java.time.temporal. ChronoUnit. This API exposes a set of units useful to manipulate a date, time, or date-time and we have used it before in *Problem 78*. This time, let's use it again to compute the number of weeks between two dates:

```
public static long nrOfWeeks(
    LocalDateTime startLdt, LocalDateTime endLdt) {

  return Math.abs(ChronoUnit.WEEKS.between(
    startLdt, endLdt));
}
```

On the other hand, if the given dates are java.util.Date, then you can choose to convert them to LocalDateTime and use the previous code or to rely on the Calendar API. Using the Calendar API is about looping from the start date to the end date while incrementing the calendar date week by week:

```
public static long nrOfWeeks(Date startDate, Date endDate) {

  Calendar calendar = Calendar.getInstance();
  calendar.setTime(startDate);

  int weeks = 0;
  while (calendar.getTime().before(endDate)) {
    calendar.add(Calendar.WEEK_OF_YEAR, 1);
    weeks++;
  }

  return weeks;
}
```

When the calendar date is after the end date, we have the number of weeks.

Summary

Mission accomplished! I hope you enjoyed this short chapter filled to the brim with tips and tricks about manipulating date-time in real-world applications. I strongly encourage you to also read the homologous chapter from *Java Coding Problems, First Edition*, which contains another 20 problems covering other date-time topics.

Join our community on Discord

Join our community's Discord space for discussions with the author and other readers:

https://discord.gg/8mgytp5DGQ

4

Records and Record Patterns

This chapter includes 19 problems that cover, in detail, the Java records introduced in JDK 16 (JEP 395), and record patterns introduced as a preview feature in JDK 19 (JEP 405), as a second preview feature in JDK 20 (JEP 432), and as a final feature in JDK 21 (JEP 440).

We start by defining a simple Java record. We continue by analyzing a record's internals, what it can and cannot contain, how to use records in streams, how they improve serialization, and so on. We are also interested in how we can use records in Spring Boot applications, including JPA and jOOQ technologies.

Next, we focus on record patterns for `instanceof` and `switch`. We will talk about nested record patterns, guarded record patterns, handling `null` values in record patterns, and so on.

At the end of this chapter, you'll have mastered Java records. This is great because records are a must-have for any Java developer who wants to adopt the coolest Java features.

Problems

Use the following problems to test your programming prowess on Java records. I strongly encourage you to give each problem a try before you turn to the solutions and download the example programs:

88. **Declaring a Java record:** Write an application that exemplifies the creation of a Java record. Moreover, provide a short description of the artifacts generated by the compiler for a record behind the scenes.

89. **Introducing the canonical and compact constructors for records:** Explain the role of the built-in record's canonical and compact constructors. Provide examples of when it makes sense to provide such explicit constructors.

90. **Adding more artifacts in a record:** Provide a meaningful list of examples about adding explicit artifacts in Java records (for instance, adding instance methods, static artifacts, and so on).

91. **Iterating what we cannot have in a record:** Exemplify what we cannot have in a record (for instance, we cannot have explicit `private` fields) and explain why.

92. **Defining multiple constructors in a record:** Exemplify several approaches for declaring multiple constructors in a record.

93. **Implementing interfaces in records:** Write a program that shows how to implement interfaces in records.

94. **Understanding record serialization:** Explain in detail and exemplify how record serialization works behind the scenes.

95. **Invoking the canonical constructor via reflection:** Write a program that exemplifies how to invoke, via reflection, the canonical constructor of a record.

96. **Using records in streams:** Write several examples to highlight the usage of records for simplifying functional expressions relying on the Stream API.

97. **Introducing record patterns for instanceof:** Write a bunch of examples that introduce *record patterns* for instanceof, including *nested record patterns*.

98. **Introducing record patterns for switch:** Write a bunch of examples that introduce *record patterns* for switch.

99. **Tackling guarded record patterns:** Write several snippets of code to exemplify *guarded record patterns* (guarded conditions based on the binding variables).

100. **Using generic records in record patterns:** Write an application that highlights the declaration and usage of generic records.

101. **Handling nulls in nested record patterns:** Explain and exemplify how to deal with null values in record patterns (explain the edge case of null values in nested record patterns as well).

102. **Simplifying expressions via record patterns:** Imagine that you have an expression (arithmetic, string-based, Abstract Syntax Tree (AST), and so on). Write a program that uses record patterns to simplify the code for evaluating/transforming this expression.

103. **Hooking unnamed patterns and variables:** Explain and exemplify the JDK 21 preview feature covering unnamed patterns and variables.

104. **Tackling records in Spring Boot:** Write several applications for exemplifying different use cases of records in Spring Boot (for instance, using records in templates, using records for configurations, and so on).

105. **Tackling records in JPA:** Write several applications for exemplifying different use cases of records in JPA (for instance, using records and constructor expressions, using records and result transformers, and so on).

106. **Tacking records in jOOQ:** Write several applications for exemplifying different use cases of records in jOOQ (for instance, using records and the MULTISET operator).

The following sections describe solutions to the preceding problems. Remember that there usually isn't a single correct way to solve a particular problem. Also, remember that the explanations shown here include only the most interesting and important details needed to solve the problems. Download the example solutions to see additional details and to experiment with the programs at https://github.com/PacktPublishing/Java-Coding-Problems-Second-Edition/tree/main/Chapter04.

88. Declaring a Java record

Before diving into Java records, let's think a little bit about how we commonly hold data within a Java application. You're right … we define simple classes containing the needed instance fields populated with our data via the constructors of these classes. We also expose some specific getters, and the popular `equals()`, `hashCode()`, and `toString()` methods. Further, we create instances of these classes that wrap our precious data and we pass them around to solve our tasks all over our application. For instance, the following class carries data about melons like the melon types and their weights:

```java
public class Melon {

    private final String type;
    private final float weight;

    public Melon(String type, float weight) {
        this.type = type;
        this.weight = weight;
    }

    public String getType() {
        return type;
    }

    public float getWeight() {
        return weight;
    }

    // hashCode(), equals(), and to String()
}
```

You should be pretty familiar with this kind of traditional Java class and this tedious ceremony, so there is no need to go over this code in detail. Now, let's see how we can accomplish the exact same thing but using Java record syntactical sugar that drastically reduces the previous ceremony:

```java
public record MelonRecord(String type, float weight) {}
```

Java records were delivered as a feature preview starting with JDK 14, and it was released and closed in JDK 16 as JEP 395. This single line of code gives us the same behavior as the previous one, the `Melon` class. Behind the scenes, the compiler provides all the artifacts, including two `private final` fields (type and weight), a constructor, two accessor methods having the same names as the fields (`type()` and `weight()`), and the trilogy containing `hashCode()`, `equals()`, and `toString()`. We can easily see the code generated by the compiler by calling the `javap` tool on the `MelonRecord` class:

```
public final class modern.challenge.MelonRecord extends java.lang.Record {
    public modern.challenge.MelonRecord(java.lang.String, float);
    public final java.lang.String toString();
    public final int hashCode();
    public final boolean equals(java.lang.Object);
    public java.lang.String type();
    public float weight();
}
```

Figure 4.1: The code of a Java record

Pay attention that these accessor's names don't follow the Java Bean convention, so there is no `getType()` or `getWeight()`. There is `type()` and `weight()`. However, you can explicitly write these accessors or explicitly add the `getType()`/`getWeight()` getters – for instance, for exposing defensive copies of fields.

All these things are built based on the parameters given when we declare a record (`type` and `weight`). These parameters are also known as the components of the record and we say that a record is built on the given components.

The compiler recognizes a Java record via the `record` keyword. This is a special type of class (exactly like `enum` is a special type of Java class) declared as `final` and automatically extending `java.lang.Record`.

Instantiating `MelonRecord` is the same as instantiating the `Melon` class. The following code creates a `Melon` instance and a `MelonRecord` instance:

```
Melon melon = new Melon("Cantaloupe", 2600);
MelonRecord melonr = new MelonRecord("Cantaloupe", 2600);
```

Java records are not an alternative to mutable Java Bean classes. Moreover, you may think that a Java record is just a plain transparent approach for carrying immutable data or an immutable state (we say "transparent" because it fully exposes its state, and we say "immutable" because the class is `final`, it has only `private final` fields, and no setters). In this context, we may think that Java records are not quite useful because they just overlap the functionality that we can obtain via Lombok or Kotlin. But as you'll see in this chapter, a Java record is more than that, and it provides several features that are not available in Lombok or Kotlin. Moreover, if you benchmark, you'll notice that using records has significant advantages in the performance context.

89. Introducing the canonical and compact constructors for records

In the previous problem, we created the `MelonRecord` Java record and we instantiated it via the following code:

```
MelonRecord melonr = new MelonRecord("Cantaloupe", 2600);
```

How is this possible (since we didn't write any parameterized constructor in `MelonRecord`)? The compiler just followed its internal protocol for Java records and created a default constructor based on the components that we provided in the record declaration (in this case, there are two components, `type` and `weight`).

This constructor is known as the *canonical constructor* and it is always aligned with the given components. Every record has a canonical constructor that represents the only way to create instances of that record.

But, we can redefine the canonical constructor. Here is an explicit canonical constructor similar to the default one – as you can see, the canonical constructor simply takes all the given components and sets the corresponding instance fields (also generated by the compiler as private final fields):

```
public MelonRecord(String type, float weight) {

  this.type = type;
  this.weight = weight;
}
```

Once the instance is created, it cannot be changed (it is immutable). It will only serve the purpose of carrying this data around your program. This explicit canonical constructor has a shortcut known as the *compact constructor* – this is specific to Java records. Since the compiler knows the list of given components, it can accomplish its job from this compact constructor, which is equivalent to the previous one:

```
public MelonRecord {}
```

Pay attention to not confuse this compact constructor with the one without arguments. The following snippets are not equivalent:

```
public MelonRecord {}    // compact constructor
public MelonRecord() {} // constructor with no arguments
```

Of course, it doesn't make sense to write an explicit canonical constructor just to mimic what the default one does. So, let's examine several scenarios when redefining the canonical constructor makes sense.

Handling validation

At this moment, when we create a MelonRecord, we can pass the type as null, or the melon's weight as a negative number. This leads to corrupted records containing non-valid data. Validating the record components can be handled in an explicit canonical constructor as follows:

```
public record MelonRecord(String type, float weight) {

  // explicit canonical constructor for validations
  public MelonRecord(String type, int weight) {

    if (type == null) {
      throw new IllegalArgumentException(
        "The melon's type cannot be null");
    }
```

```
    if (weight < 1000 || weight > 10000) {
      throw new IllegalArgumentException("The melon's weight
        must be between 1000 and 10000 grams");
    }

    this.type = type;
    this.weight = weight;
  }
}
```

Or, via the compact constructor as follows:

```
public record MelonRecord(String type, float weight) {

  // explicit compact constructor for validations
  public MelonRecord {

    if (type == null) {
      throw new IllegalArgumentException(
        "The melon's type cannot be null");
    }

    if (weight < 1000 || weight > 10000) {
      throw new IllegalArgumentException("The melon's weight
        must be between 1000 and 10000 grams");
    }
  }
}
```

Validation handling is the most common use case for explicit canonical/compact constructors. Next, let's see two more lesser-known use cases.

Reassigning components

Via an explicit canonical/compact constructor, we can reassign components. For instance, when we create a `MelonRecord`, we provide its type (for instance, Cantaloupe) and its weight in grams (for instance, 2600 grams). But, if we want to use weight in kilograms (2600 g = 2.6 kg), then we can provide this conversion in an explicit canonical constructor as follows:

```
// explicit canonical constructor for reassigning components
public MelonRecord(String type, float weight) {

  weight = weight/1_000; // overwriting the component 'weight'
```

```
    this.type = type;
    this.weight = weight;
}
```

As you can see, the `weight` component is available and reassigned before the `weight` field is initialized with the new reassigned value. In the end, the `weight` component and the `weight` field have the same value (2.6 kg). How about this snippet of code?

```
public MelonRecord(String type, float weight) {

    this.type = type;
    this.weight = weight/1_000;
}
```

Well, in this case, in the end, the `weight` field and the `weight` component will have different values. The `weight` field is 2.6 kg, while the `weight` component is 2600 g. Pay attention that most probably this is not what you want. Let's check another snippet:

```
public MelonRecord(String type, float weight) {

    this.type = type;
    this.weight = weight;

    weight = weight/1_000;
}
```

Again, in the end, the `weight` field and the `weight` component will have different values. The `weight` field is 2600 g, while the `weight` component is 2.6 kg. And again, pay attention—most probably this is not what you want.

Of course, the cleanest and most simple approach relies on the compact constructor. This time, we cannot sneak in any accidental reassignments:

```
public record MelonRecord(String type, float weight) {

    // explicit compact constructor for reassigning components
    public MelonRecord {

        weight = weight/1_000; // overwriting the component 'weight'
    }
}
```

Finally, let's tackle the third scenario.

Defensive copies of the given components

We know that a Java record is immutable. But this doesn't mean that its components are immutable as well. Think of components such as arrays, lists, maps, dates, and so on. All these components are mutable. In order to restore total immutability, you'll prefer to work on copies of these components rather than modify the given components. And, as you may have already intuited, this can be done via the explicit canonical constructor.

For instance, let's consider the following record that gets a single component representing the retail prices for a set of items as a `Map`:

```java
public record MarketRecord(Map<String, Integer> retails) {}
```

This record shouldn't modify this `Map`, so it relies on an explicit canonical constructor for creating a defensive copy that will be used in subsequent tasks without any risks of modification (`Map.copyOf()` returns an unmodifiable copy of the given `Map`):

```java
public record MarketRecord(Map<String, Integer> retails) {

  public MarketRecord {
    retails = Map.copyOf(retails);
  }
}
```

Basically, this is just a flavor of component reassignment.

Moreover, we can return defensive copies via the accessor methods:

```java
public Map<String, Integer> retails() {
  return Map.copyOf(retails);
}

// or, getter in Java Bean style
public Map<String, Integer> getRetails() {
  return Map.copyOf(retails);
}
```

You can practice all these examples in the bundled code.

90. Adding more artifacts in a record

So far, we know how to add an explicit canonical/compact constructor into a Java record. What else can we add? Well, for example, we can add instance methods as in any typical class. In the following code, we add an instance method that returns the `weight` converted from grams to kilograms:

```java
public record MelonRecord(String type, float weight) {

  public float weightToKg() {
```

```
      return weight / 1_000;
   }
}
```

You can call `weightToKg()` exactly as you call any other instance method of your classes:

```
MelonRecord melon = new MelonRecord("Cantaloupe", 2600);

// 2600.0 g = 2.6 Kg
System.out.println(melon.weight() + " g = "
  + melon.weightToKg() + " Kg");
```

Besides instance methods, we can add `static` fields and methods as well. Check out this code:

```
public record MelonRecord(String type, float weight) {

  private static final String DEFAULT_MELON_TYPE = "Crenshaw";
  private static final float DEFAULT_MELON_WEIGHT = 1000;

  public static MelonRecord getDefaultMelon() {

    return new MelonRecord(
      DEFAULT_MELON_TYPE, DEFAULT_MELON_WEIGHT);
  }
}
```

Calling `getDefaultMelon()` is done as usual via class name:

```
MelonRecord defaultMelon = MelonRecord.getDefaultMelon();
```

Adding nested classes is also possible. For example, here we add a `static` nested class:

```
public record MelonRecord(String type, float weight) {

  public static class Slicer {

    public void slice(MelonRecord mr, int n) {
      start();
      System.out.println("Slicing a " + mr.type() + " of "
        + mr.weightToKg() + " kg in " + n + " slices ...");
      stop();
    }

    private static void start() {
```

```
      System.out.println("Start slicer ...");
    }

    private static void stop() {
      System.out.println("Stop slicer ...");
    }
  }
}
```

And, calling `Slicer` can be done as usual:

```
MelonRecord.Slicer slicer = new MelonRecord.Slicer();
slicer.slice(melon, 10);
slicer.slice(defaultMelon, 14);
```

But, even if it is allowed to add all these artifacts in a Java record, I strongly suggest you think twice before doing this. The main reason is that Java records should be about data and only data, so it is kind of weird to pollute a record with artifacts that involve additional behavior. If you hit such a scenario, then you probably need a Java class, not a Java record.

In the next problem, we will see what we cannot add to a Java record.

91. Iterating what we cannot have in a record

There are several artifacts that we cannot have in a Java record. Let's tackle the top 5 one by one.

A record cannot extend another class

Since a record already extends `java.lang.Record` and Java doesn't support multiple inheritances, we cannot write a record that extends another class:

```
public record MelonRecord(String type, float weight)
  extends Cucurbitaceae {…}
```

This snippet doesn't compile.

A record cannot be extended

Java records are `final` classes, so they cannot be extended:

```
public class PumpkinClass extends MelonRecord {…}
```

This snippet doesn't compile.

A record cannot be enriched with instance fields

When we declare a record, we also provide the components that become the instance fields of the record. Later, we cannot add more instance fields as we could in a typical class:

```
public record MelonRecord(String type, float weight) {
```

```
   private String color;
   private final String color;
}
```

Adding color as a final or non-final separate field doesn't compile.

A record cannot have private canonical constructors

Sometimes we create classes with `private` constructors that expose `static` factories for creating instances. Basically, we call the constructor indirectly via a `static` factory method. This practice is not available in a Java record because `private` canonical/compact constructors are not allowed:

```
public record MelonRecord(String type, float weight) {

  private MelonRecord(String type, float weight) {

    this.type = type;
    this.weight = weight;
  }

  public static MelonRecord newInstance(
      String type, float weight) {
    return new MelonRecord(type, weight);
  }
}
```

This snippet doesn't compile. However, you can have `public` canonical constructors and `private` non-canonical constructors that first invoke one of the `public` canonical constructors.

A record cannot have setters

As you saw, a Java record exposes a getter (accessor method) for each of its components. These getters have the same names as components (for type we have `type()`, not `getType()`). On the other hand, we cannot have setters since the fields corresponding to the given components are `final`:

```
public record MelonRecord(String type, float weight) {

  public void setType(String type) {
    this.type = type;
  }

  public void setWeight(float weight) {
    this.weight = weight;
  }
}
```

This snippet doesn't compile. Well, the list of artifacts that cannot be added to a Java record remains open, but these are the most common.

92. Defining multiple constructors in a record

As you know, when we declare a Java record, the compiler uses the given components to create a default constructor known as the canonical constructor. We can also provide an explicit canonical/compact constructor, as you saw in *Problem 89*.

But, we can go even further and declare more constructors with a different list of arguments. For example, we can have a constructor with no arguments for returning a default instance:

```
public record MelonRecord(String type, float weight) {

  private static final String DEFAULT_MELON_TYPE = "Crenshaw";
  private static final float DEFAULT_MELON_WEIGHT = 1000;

  MelonRecord() {
    this(DEFAULT_MELON_TYPE, DEFAULT_MELON_WEIGHT);
  }
}
```

Or, we can write a constructor that gets only the melon's type or the melon's weight as an argument:

```
public record MelonRecord(String type, float weight) {

  private static final String DEFAULT_MELON_TYPE = "Crenshaw";
  private static final float DEFAULT_MELON_WEIGHT = 1000;

  MelonRecord(String type) {
    this(type, DEFAULT_MELON_WEIGHT);
  }

  MelonRecord(float weight) {
    this(DEFAULT_MELON_TYPE, weight);
  }
}
```

Moreover, we can add arguments that don't fit any component (here, country):

```
public record MelonRecord(String type, float weight) {

  private static Set<String> countries = new HashSet<>();

  MelonRecord(String type, int weight, String country) {
```

```
      this(type, weight);
      MelonRecord.countries.add(country);
   }
}
```

What do all these constructors have in common? They all call the canonical constructor via the `this` keyword. Remember that the only way to instantiate a Java record is via its canonical constructor, which can be called directly or, as you saw in the previous examples, indirectly. So, keep in mind that all explicit constructors that you add to a Java record must first call the canonical constructor.

93. Implementing interfaces in records

Java records cannot extend another class but they can implement any interface exactly like a typical class. Let's consider the following interface:

```
public interface PestInspector {

  public default boolean detectPest() {
    return Math.random() > 0.5d;
  }

  public void exterminatePest();
}
```

The following snippet of code is a straightforward usage of this interface:

```
public record MelonRecord(String type, float weight)
      implements PestInspector {

  @Override
  public void exterminatePest() {

    if (detectPest()) {
      System.out.println("All pests have been exterminated");
    } else {
      System.out.println(
        "This melon is clean, no pests have been found");
    }
  }
}
```

Notice that the code overrides the `abstract` method `exterminatePest()` and calls the `default` method `detectPest()`.

94. Understanding record serialization

In order to understand how Java records are serialized/deserialized, let's have a parallel between classical code based on plain Java classes and the same code but expressed via the Java record's syntactical sugar.

So, let's consider the following two plain Java classes (we have to explicitly implement the Serializable interface because, in the second part of this problem, we want to serialize/deserialize these classes):

```java
public class Melon implements Serializable {

  private final String type;
  private final float weight;

  public Melon(String type, float weight) {

    this.type = type;
    this.weight = weight;
  }

  // getters, hashCode(), equals(), and toString()
}
```

And, the MelonContainer class that uses the previous Melon class:

```java
public class MelonContainer implements Serializable {

  private final LocalDate expiration;
  private final String batch;
  private final Melon melon;

  public MelonContainer(LocalDate expiration,
      String batch, Melon melon) {

    ...
    if (!batch.startsWith("ML")) {
      throw new IllegalArgumentException(
        "The batch format should be: MLxxxxxxxx");
    }
    ...

    this.expiration = expiration;
    this.batch = batch;
    this.melon = melon;
```

```
    }

    // getters, hashCode(), equals(), and toString()
}
```

If we express this code via Java records, then we have the following code:

```
public record MelonRecord(String type, float weight)
   implements Serializable {}

public record MelonContainerRecord(
   LocalDate expiration, String batch, Melon melon)
   implements Serializable {

   public MelonContainerRecord {
     ...
     if (!batch.startsWith("ML")) {
       throw new IllegalArgumentException(
         "The batch format should be: MLxxxxxxxx");
     }
     ...
   }
}
```

Notice that we have explicitly implemented the Serializable interface since, by default, Java records are not serializable.

Next, let's create a MelonContainer instance:

```
MelonContainer gacContainer = new MelonContainer(
   LocalDate.now().plusDays(15), "ML9000SQA0",
     new Melon("Gac", 5000));
```

And, a MelonContainerRecord instance:

```
MelonContainerRecord gacContainerR = new MelonContainerRecord(
   LocalDate.now().plusDays(15), "ML9000SQA0",
     new Melon("Gac", 5000));
```

To serialize these objects (gacContainer and gacContainerR), we can use the following code:

```
try ( ObjectOutputStream oos = new ObjectOutputStream(
   new FileOutputStream("object.data"))) {
     oos.writeObject(gacContainer);
}
```

```
try ( ObjectOutputStream oos = new ObjectOutputStream(
    new FileOutputStream("object_record.data"))) {
        oos.writeObject(gacContainerR);
}
```

And, the deserialization can be accomplished via the following code:

```
MelonContainer desGacContainer;
try ( ObjectInputStream ios = new ObjectInputStream(
    new FileInputStream("object.data"))) {
    desGacContainer = (MelonContainer) ios.readObject();
}


MelonContainerRecord desGacContainerR;
try ( ObjectInputStream ios = new ObjectInputStream(
    new FileInputStream("object_record.data"))) {
    desGacContainerR = (MelonContainerRecord) ios.readObject();
}
```

Before exploiting these snippets of code for a practical examination of serialization/deserialization, let's try a theoretical approach meant to provide some hints for these operations.

How serialization/deserialization works

The serialization/deserialization operations are represented in the following diagram:

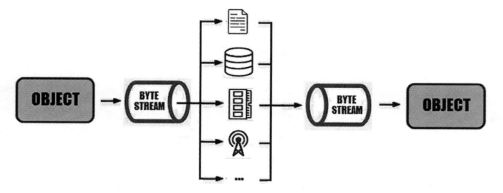

Figure 4.2: Java serialization/deserialization operations

In a nutshell, *serialization* (or serializing an object) is the operation of extracting the state of an object as a byte stream and representing it as a persistent format (a file, a database, in memory, over the network, and so on). The reverse operation is called *deserialization* (or deserializing an object) and represents the steps of reconstructing the object state from the persistent format.

In Java, an object is serializable if it implements the Serializable interface. This is an empty interface with no state or behavior that acts as a marker for the compiler. In the absence of this interface, the compiler assumes that the object is not serializable.

The compiler uses its internal algorithm for the serialization of objects. This algorithm relies on every trick in the book, like special privileges (ignoring accessibility rules) to access objects, malicious reflection, constructors bypassing, and so on. It is beyond our purpose to bring light to this dark magic, so as a developer, it is enough to know that:

- If a part of an object is not serializable then you'll get a runtime error
- You can alter the serialization/deserialization operations via the writeObject()/readObject() API

Ok, now let's see what's going on when an object is serialized.

Serializing/deserializing gacContainer (a typical Java class)

The gacContainer object is an instance of MelonContainer, which is a plain Java class:

```
MelonContainer gacContainer = new MelonContainer(
    LocalDate.now().plusDays(15), "ML9000SQA0",
        new Melon("Gac", 5000));
```

After serializing it in a file called *object.data*, we obtain the byte stream representing the gacContainer state. While you can inspect this file in the bundled code (use a hex editor such as https://hexed. it/), here is a human-readable interpretation of its content:

```
OBJECT_A
    class_name:MelonContainer
    class_data [
     field:expiration, type:LocalDate, value:2023-02-26
     field:batch, type:String, value:ML9000SQA0
     field: melon, type:Melon, value:
        OBJECT_B
            class_name:Melon
            class_data [
             field:type, type:String, value:Gac
             field:weight, type:float, value:5000.0
            ]
    ]
```

Figure 4.3: Human-readable interpretation of gacContainer serialization

The deserialization operation takes place by building the object graph from the top down. When the class name is known, the compiler creates an object by calling the non-arguments constructor of the first superclass of MelonContainer that is non-serializable. In this case, that is the non-argument constructor of java.lang.Object. So, the compiler is not calling the constructor of MelonContainer.

Next, the fields are created and set to the default values, so the created object has `expiration`, `batch`, and `melon` as `null`. Of course, this is not the correct state of our object, so we continue processing the serialization stream to extract and populate the fields with the correct values. This can be seen in the following diagram (on the left side, the created object has default values; on the right side, the fields have been populated with the correct state):

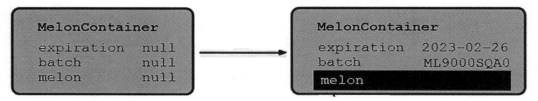

Figure 4.4: Populating the created object with the correct state

When the compiler hits the `melon` field, it must perform the same steps to obtain the `Melon` instance. It sets the fields (`type` and `weight` to `null`, respectively, `0.0f`). Further, it reads the real values from the stream and sets the correct state for the `melon` object.

Finally, after the entire stream is read, the compiler will link the objects accordingly. This is shown in the following figure (1, 2, and 3 represent the steps of the deserialization operation):

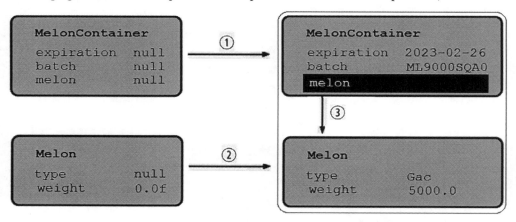

Figure 4.5: Linking the objects to obtain the final state

At this point, the deserialization operation has been done and we can use the resulting object.

Deserializing a malicious stream

Providing a malicious stream means altering the object state before deserialization. This can be done in many ways. For instance, we can manually modify the *object.data* instance in an editor (this is like an untrusted source) as in the following figure where we replaced the valid batch `ML9000SQA0` with the invalid batch `0000000000`:

Original stream

```
00000080   6D 6F 64 65 72 6E 2F 63  68 61 6C 6C 65 6E 67 65    modern/challenge
00000090   2F 4D 65 6C 6F 6E 3B 78  70 74 00 0A 4D 4C 39 30    /Melon;xpt..ML90
000000A0   30 30 53 51 41 30 73 72  00 0D 6A 61 76 61 2E 74    00SQA0sr..java.t
```

Malicious stream

```
00000080   6D 6F 64 65 72 6E 2F 63  68 61 6C 6C 65 6E 67 65    modern/challenge
00000090   2F 4D 65 6C 6F 6E 3B 78  70 74 00 0A 30 30 30 30    /Melon;xpt..0000
000000A0   30 30 30 30 30 30 73 72  00 0D 6A 61 76 61 2E 74    000000sr..java.t
```

Figure 4.6: Modify the original stream to obtain a malicious stream

If we deserialize the malicious stream (in the bundle code, you can find it as the object_malicious. data file) then you can see that the corrupted data has "successfully" landed in our object (a simple call of toString() reveals that batch is 0000000000):

```
MelonContainer{expiration=2023-02-26,
    batch=0000000000, melon=Melon{type=Gac, weight=5000.0}}
```

The guarding conditions from Melon/MelonContainer constructors are useless since the deserialization doesn't call these constructors.

So, if we summarize the shortcomings of serializing/deserializing a Java class, we must highlight the presence of the window of time that occurs when the objects are in an improper state (waiting for the compiler to populate fields with the correct data and to link them in the final graph) and the risk of dealing with malicious states. Now, let's pass a Java record through this process.

Serializing/deserializing gacContainerR (a Java record)

In a nutshell, the minimalist design of declaring Java records and their semantic constraints allows the serialization/deserialization operations to act differently from a typical Java class. And when I say "differently," I should actually say much better and more robust. How so? Well, the serialization of a Java record is based only on its component's state, while deserialization relies on the single point of entry for a Java record, its canonical constructor. Remember that the only way to create a Java record is to directly/indirectly call its canonical constructor? This applies to deserialization as well, so this operation can no longer bypass the canonical constructor.

That being said, the gacContainerR object is a MelonContainerRecord instance:

```
MelonContainerRecord gacContainerR = new MelonContainerRecord(
    LocalDate.now().plusDays(15), "ML9000SQA0",
      new Melon("Gac", 5000));
```

After serializing it in a file called `object_record.data`, we obtain the byte stream representing the `gacContainerR` state. While you can inspect this file in the bundled code (use a hex editor such as `https://hexed.it/`), here is a human-readable interpretation of its content:

```
OBJECT_A
    class_name:MelonContainerRecord
    class_data [
     field:expiration, type:LocalDate, value:2023-02-26
     field:batch, type:String, value:ML9000SQA0
     field: melon, type:Melon, value:
        OBJECT_B
            class_name:Melon
            class_data [
             field:type, type:String, value:Gac
             field:weight, type:float, value:5000.0
            ]
    ]
```

Figure 4.7: Human-readable interpretation of MelonContainerRecord serialization

Yes, you're right—with the exception of the class name (`MelonContainerRecord`), the rest is the same as in *Figure 4.3*. This sustains the migration from ordinary/regular Java classes to Java records. This time, the compiler can use the accessors exposed by the record, so no dark magic is needed.

Ok, so nothing got our attention here, so let's examine the deserialization operation.

Remember that for regular Java classes, the deserialization builds the object graph from the top down. In the case of Java records, this operation takes place from the bottom up, so in reverse order. In other words, this time, the compiler reads first the fields (primitives and reconstructed objects) from the stream and stores them in memory. Next, having all the fields in its hands, the compiler tries to match these fields (their names and values) against the components of the record. Any field from the stream that doesn't match a component (name and value) is dropped from the deserialization operation. Finally, after the match is successfully performed, the compiler calls the canonical constructor to reconstruct the record object state.

Deserializing a malicious stream

In the bundled code, you can find a file named `object_record_malicious.data` where we replaced the valid batch `ML9000SQA0` with the invalid batch `0000000000`. This time, deserializing this malicious stream will result in the exception from the following figure:

```
Exception in thread "main" java.io.InvalidObjectException: The batch format should be: MLxxxxxxxx
        at java.base/java.io.ObjectInputStream.readRecord(ObjectInputStream.java:2386)
        at java.base/java.io.ObjectInputStream.readOrdinaryObject(ObjectInputStream.java:2274)
        at java.base/java.io.ObjectInputStream.readObject0(ObjectInputStream.java:1760)
        at java.base/java.io.ObjectInputStream.readObject(ObjectInputStream.java:538)
        at java.base/java.io.ObjectInputStream.readObject(ObjectInputStream.java:496)
        at modern.challenge.Main.main(Main.java:61)
Caused by: java.lang.IllegalArgumentException: The batch format should be: MLxxxxxxxx
        at modern.challenge.MelonContainerRecord.<init>(MelonContainerRecord.java:16)
        at java.base/java.io.ObjectInputStream.readRecord(ObjectInputStream.java:2384)
        ... 5 more
```

Figure 4.8: Deserializing a malicious stream causing an exception

As you already know, this exception originates in our guarding condition added in the explicit canonical constructor of our Java record.

It is obvious that Java records significantly improve serialization/deserialization operations. This time, there is no moment when the reconstructed objects are in a corrupted state, and the malicious streams can be intercepted by guarding conditions placed in the canonical/compact constructor.

In other words, the record's semantic constraints, their minimalist design, the state accessible only via the accessor methods, and the object creation only via the canonical constructors sustain the serialization/deserialization as a trusted process.

Refactoring legacy serialization

Serialization/deserialization via Java records is awesome, but what can we do in the case of legacy code, such as `MelonContainer`? We cannot take all our legacy classes that act as carriers of data and rewrite them as Java records. It will consume a lot of work and time.

Actually, there is a solution backed in the serialization mechanism that requires us to add two methods named `writeReplace()` and `readResolve()`. By following this reasonable refactoring step, we can serialize legacy code as records and deserialize it back into legacy code.

If we apply this refactoring step to `MelonContainer`, then we start by adding the `writeReplace()` method in this class as follows:

```
@Serial
private Object writeReplace() throws ObjectStreamException {
    return new MelonContainerRecord(expiration, batch, melon);
}
```

The `writeReplace()` method must throw an `ObjectStreamException` and return an instance of `MelonContainerRecord`. The compiler will use this method for serializing `MelonContainer` instances as long as we mark it with the `@Serial` annotation. Now, the serialization of a `MelonContainer` instance will produce the *object.data* file containing the byte stream corresponding to a `MelonContainerRecord` instance.

Next, the readResolve() method must be added to the MelonContainerRecord as follows:

```
@Serial
private Object readResolve() throws ObjectStreamException {
  return new MelonContainer(expiration, batch, melon);
}
```

The readResolve() method must throw an ObjectStreamException and return an instance of MelonContainer. Again, the compiler will use this method for deserializing MelonContainerRecord instances as long as we mark it with the @Serial annotation.

When the compiler deserializes an instance of MelonContainerRecord, it will call the canonical constructor of this record, so it will pass through our guarding conditions. This means that a malicious stream will not pass the guarding conditions, so we avoid creating corrupted objects. If the stream contains valid values, then the readResolve() method will use them to reconstruct the legacy MelonContainer.

Hey, Kotlin/Lombok, can you do this? No, you can't!

In the bundled code, you can find a file named object_malicious.data that you can use to practice the previous statement.

95. Invoking the canonical constructor via reflection

It is not a daily task to invoke the canonical constructor of a Java record via reflection. However, this can be accomplished quite easily starting with JDK 16, which provides in java.lang.Class the RecordComponent[] getRecordComponents() method. As its name and signature suggest, this method returns an array of java.lang.reflect.RecordComponent representing the components of the current Java record.

Having this array of components, we can call the well-known getDeclaredConstructor() method to identify the constructor that gets as arguments exactly this array of components. And that is the canonical constructor.

The code that puts these statements into practice is provided by the Java documentation itself, so there is no need to reinvent it. Here it is:

```
// this method is from the official documentation of JDK
// https://docs.oracle.com/en/java/javase/19/docs/api/
// java.base/java/lang/Class.html#getRecordComponents()
public static <T extends Record> Constructor<T>
      getCanonicalConstructor(Class<T> cls)
          throws NoSuchMethodException {
  Class<?>[] paramTypes
    = Arrays.stream(cls.getRecordComponents())
            .map(RecordComponent::getType)
            .toArray(Class<?>[]::new);
```

```
    return cls.getDeclaredConstructor(paramTypes);
  }
```

Consider the following records:

```
public record MelonRecord(String type, float weight) {}
public record MelonMarketRecord(
  List<MelonRecord> melons, String country) {}
```

Finding and calling the canonical constructors for these records via the previous solution can be done as follows:

```
Constructor<MelonRecord> cmr =
    Records.getCanonicalConstructor(MelonRecord.class);
MelonRecord m1 = cmr.newInstance("Gac", 5000f);
MelonRecord m2 = cmr.newInstance("Hemi", 1400f);

Constructor<MelonMarketRecord> cmmr =
    Records.getCanonicalConstructor(MelonMarketRecord.class);
  MelonMarketRecord mm = cmmr.newInstance(
      List.of(m1, m2), "China");
```

If you need deep coverage of Java reflection principles, then consider *Java Coding Problems, First Edition, Chapter 7.*

96. Using records in streams

Consider the MelonRecord that we have used before:

```
public record MelonRecord(String type, float weight) {}
```

And a list of melons as follows:

```
List<MelonRecord> melons = Arrays.asList(
  new MelonRecord("Crenshaw", 1200),
  new MelonRecord("Gac", 3000),
  new MelonRecord("Hemi", 2600),
  ...
);
```

Our goal is to iterate this list of melons and extract the total weight and the list of weights. This data can be carried by a regular Java class or by another record as follows:

```
public record WeightsAndTotalRecord(
    double totalWeight, List<Float> weights) {}
```

Populating this record with data can be done in several ways, but if we prefer the Stream API then most probably we will go for the `Collectors.teeing()` collector. We won't go into too much detail here, but we'll quickly show that it is useful for merging the results of two downstream collectors. (If you're interested, you can find more details about this particular collector in *Java Coding Problems, First Edition, Chapter 9, Problem 192*.)

Let's see the code:

```
WeightsAndTotalRecord weightsAndTotal = melons.stream()
  .collect(Collectors.teeing(
      summingDouble(MelonRecord::weight),
      mapping(MelonRecord::weight, toList()),
      WeightsAndTotalRecord::new
));
```

Here, we have the `summingDouble()` collector, which computes the total weight, and the `mapping()` collector, which maps the weights in a list. The results of these two downstream collectors are merged in `WeightsAndTotalRecord`.

As you can see, the Stream API and records represent a very nice combo. Let's have another example starting from this functional code:

```
Map<Double, Long> elevations = DoubleStream.of(
      22, -10, 100, -5, 100, 123, 22, 230, -1, 250, 22)
  .filter(e -> e > 0)
  .map(e -> e * 0.393701)
  .mapToObj(e -> (double) e)
  .collect(Collectors.groupingBy(
      Function.identity(), counting()));
```

This code starts from a list of elevations given in centimeters (based on sea level being 0). First, we want to keep only the positive elevations (so, we apply `filter()`). Next, these will be converted to inches (via `map()`) and counted (via the `groupingBy()` and `counting()` collectors).

The resulting data is carried by `Map<Double, Long>`, which is not very expressive. If we pull this map out of the context (for instance, we pass it as an argument into a method), it is hard to say what `Double` and `Long` represent. It would be more expressive to have something such as `Map<Elevation, ElevationCount>`, which clearly describes its content.

So, `Elevation` and `ElevationCount` can be two records as follows:

```
record Elevation(double value) {

  Elevation(double value) {
    this.value = value * 0.393701;
  }
}
```

```
record ElevationCount(long count) {}
```

To simplify the functional code a little bit, we also moved to convert from centimeters to inches in the Elevation record, inside its explicit canonical constructor. This time, the functional code can be rewritten as follows:

```
Map<Elevation, ElevationCount> elevations = DoubleStream.of(
      22, -10, 100, -5, 100, 123, 22, 230, -1, 250, 22)
   .filter(e -> e > 0)
   .mapToObj(Elevation::new)
   .collect(Collectors.groupingBy(Function.identity(),
         Collectors.collectingAndThen(counting(),
            ElevationCount::new)));
```

Now, passing Map<Elevation, ElevationCount> to a method dispels any doubt about its content. Any team member can inspect these records in the blink of an eye without losing time reading our functional implementation in order to deduce what Double and Long represent. We can be even more expressive and rename the Elevation record as PositiveElevation.

97. Introducing record patterns for instanceof

In order to introduce *record patterns*, we need a more complex record than the one we've used so far, so here's one:

```
public record Doctor(String name, String specialty)
   implements Staff {}
```

This record implements the Staff interface as any other employee of our hospital. Now, we can identify a certain doctor in the old-fashioned style via instanceof as follows:

```
public static String cabinet(Staff staff) {

   if (staff instanceof Doctor) {
     Doctor dr = (Doctor) staff;
     return "Cabinet of " + dr.specialty()
        + ". Doctor: " + dr.name();
   }
   ...
}
```

But, as we know from *Chapter 2, Problems 58-67*, JDK has introduced *type patterns* that can be used for instanceof and switch. So, in this particular case, we can rewrite the previous code via type patterns as follows:

```
public static String cabinet(Staff staff) {
```

```
    if (staff instanceof Doctor dr) { // type pattern matching
      return "Cabinet of " + dr.specialty()
          + ". Doctor: " + dr.name();
    }
    ...
}
```

Nothing is new so far! The binding variable `dr` can be used to call the record accessor's `specialty()` and `name()`, to add checks, computations, and so on. But, the compiler knows very well that the `Doctor` record was built based on two components (`name` and `specialty`) so the compiler should be able to deconstruct this object and give us these components directly as binding variables instead of accessing them via `dr`.

This is exactly what *record pattern matching* is all about. Record pattern matching appeared as a preview feature in JDK 19 (JEP 405), as a second preview feature in JDK 20 (JEP 432), and as a final release in JDK 21 (JEP 440).

Record pattern matching is exactly the syntax of declaring `name` and `specialty` as binding variables by following the same declaration syntax as in the record itself (or like in the canonical constructor). Here is the previous code written via record patterns:

```
public static String cabinet(Staff staff) {

    // record pattern matching
    if (staff instanceof Doctor(String name, String specialty)){
      return "Cabinet of " + name + ". Doctor: " + specialty;
    }
    ...
}
```

Very simple, isn't it?

Now, `name` and `specialty` are the binding variables that can be used directly. We simply put this syntax in place of the type pattern. In other words, we replaced the type pattern with a record pattern.

Important note

The compiler exposes the record's components via the corresponding binding variables. This is accomplished by deconstructing records in pattern matching, which is referred to as *record patterns*. In other words, the deconstruction patterns allow us to access the components of an object in a very handy, intuitive, and readable way.

In record patterns, it is the compiler's responsibility to initialize binding variables such as `name` and `specialty`. In order to accomplish this, the compiler calls the accessors of the corresponding components. This means that if you have some extra code in these accessors (for example, return defensive copies, perform validations or apply constraints, and so on), then this code is properly executed.

Let's go further and work with some nested records.

Nested records and record patterns

Let's assume that besides the Doctor record, we also have the following record:

```
public record Resident(String name, Doctor doctor)
  implements Staff {}
```

Each resident has a coordinator, which is a doctor, so a Resident nests a Doctor. This time, we have to nest the record patterns accordingly as in the following code:

```
public static String cabinet(Staff staff) {

  if (staff instanceof Resident(String rsname,
      Doctor(String drname, String specialty))) {

    return "Cabinet of " + specialty + ". Doctor: "
                    + drname + ", Resident: " + rsname;
  }
  ...
}
```

Both the resident and the doctor, have a name component. But we cannot use the binding variable name twice in this context since it will cause a conflict. This is why we have rsname and drname. Notice that the names of the binding variables don't have to mirror the names of the components. This is possible because the compiler identifies components by position not by their names. But, of course, when it is possible, mirroring the name reduces the confusion and keeps the readability of the code high.

If there is no need to deconstruct the Doctor record, then we can write it like this:

```
if (staff instanceof Resident(String name, Doctor dr)) {
  return "Cabinet of " + dr.specialty() + ". Doctor: "
                    + dr.name() + ", Resident: " + name;
}
```

Adding more nested records follows the same principle. For instance, let's add the Patient and Appointment records as well:

```
public record Appointment(LocalDate date, Doctor doctor) {}
public record Patient(
  String name, int npi, Appointment appointment) {}
```

Now, we can write the following beauty:

```
public static String reception(Object o) {
  if (o instanceof Patient(var ptname, var npi,
              Appointment(var date,
```

```
                Doctor (var drname, var specialty)))) {

    return "Patient " + ptname + " (NPI: " + npi
           + ") has an appointment at "
           + date + " to the doctor " + drname
           + " (" + specialty + ").";
  }
  ...
}
```

Or, if we don't want to deconstruct Appointment and use var:

```
if (o instanceof Patient(
    var ptname, var npi, var ap)) {

    return "Patient " + ptname + " (NPI: " + npi
         + ") has an appointment at "
         + ap.date() + " to the doctor " + ap.doctor().name()
         + " (" + ap.doctor().specialty() + ").";
}
```

Notice that, this time, we have used var instead of explicit types. Feel free to do the same since var fits very well in this case. If you are not familiar with type inference, then consider *Java Coding Problems, First Edition, Chapter 4,* which contains detailed explanations and best practices. More details about argument type inference in record patterns are available later in this chapter in *Problem 100.*

I think you got the idea!

98. Introducing record patterns for switch

You already know that type patterns can be used for instanceof and switch expressions. This statement is true for record patterns as well. For instance, let's reiterate the Doctor and Resident records:

```
public record Doctor(String name, String specialty)
  implements Staff {}
public record Resident(String name, Doctor doctor)
  implements Staff {}
```

We can easily use these two records via record patterns in a switch expression as follows:

```
public static String cabinet(Staff staff) {

 return switch(staff) {
   case Doctor(var name, var specialty)
     -> "Cabinet of " + specialty + ". Doctor: " + name;
   case Resident(var rsname, Doctor(var drname, var specialty))
```

```
        -> "Cabinet of " + specialty + ". Doctor: "
                    + drname + ", Resident: " + rsname;
    default -> "Cabinet closed";
  };
}
```

Adding more nested records follows the same principle. For instance, let's add the `Patient` and `Appointment` records as well:

```
public record Appointment(LocalDate date, Doctor doctor) {}
public record Patient(
  String name, int npi, Appointment appointment) {}
```

Now, we can write the following beauty:

```
public static String reception(Object o) {

  return switch(o) {
    case Patient(String ptname, int npi,
        Appointment(LocalDate date,
        Doctor (String drname, String specialty))) ->
          "Patient " + ptname + " (NPI: " + npi
              + ") has an appointment at "
              + date + " to the doctor " + drname + " ("
              + specialty + ").";
    default -> "";
  };
}
```

Or, without deconstructing `Appointment` and using `var`:

```
return switch(o) {
  case Patient(var ptname, var npi, var ap) ->
    "Patient " + ptname + " (NPI: "
    + npi + ") has an appointment at "
    + ap.date() + " to the doctor " + ap.doctor().name()
    + " (" + ap.doctor().specialty() + ").";
  default -> "";
};
```

Notice that the topics covered in *Chapter 2*, such as dominance, completeness, and unconditional patterns, remain valid for record patterns with `switch` as well. Actually, there are some important things to highlight about unconditional patterns, but that is covered later, in *Problem 101*.

99. Tackling guarded record patterns

Exactly as in the case of type patterns, we can add guarding conditions based on the binding variables. For instance, the following code uses guarding conditions with `instanceof` for determining if the Allergy cabinet is open or closed (you should be familiar with the `Doctor` record from the previous two problems):

```
public static String cabinet(Staff staff) {

  if (staff instanceof Doctor(String name, String specialty)
      && (specialty.equals("Allergy")
      && (name.equals("Kyle Ulm")))) {
    return "The cabinet of " + specialty
      + " is closed. The doctor "
      + name + " is on holiday.";
  }

  if (staff instanceof Doctor(String name, String specialty)
      && (specialty.equals("Allergy")
      && (name.equals("John Hora")))) {
    return "The cabinet of " + specialty
      + " is open. The doctor "
      + name + " is ready to receive patients.";
  }

  return "Cabinet closed";
}
```

If we add into the equation the `Resident` record as well, then we can write this:

```
if (staff instanceof Resident(String rsname,
    Doctor(String drname, String specialty))
      && (specialty.equals("Dermatology")
      && rsname.equals("Mark Oil"))) {
  return "Cabinet of " + specialty + ". Doctor "
    + drname + " and resident " + rsname
    + " are ready to receive patients.";
}
```

And, if we add the `Patient` and `Appointment` records as well, then we can check if a certain patient has an appointment as follows:

```
public static String reception(Object o) {
```

```
   if (o instanceof Patient(var ptname, var npi,
                  Appointment(var date,
                  Doctor (var drname, var specialty)))
      && (ptname.equals("Alicia Goy") && npi == 1234567890
      && LocalDate.now().equals(date))) {

      return "The doctor " + drname + " from " + specialty
                        + " is ready for you " + ptname;
   }

   return "";
}
```

When we are using record patterns with guarded conditions in switch expressions, things are straightforward. The mention consists of using the when keyword (not the && operator) as in the following code:

```
public static String cabinet(Staff staff) {

  return switch(staff) {
    case Doctor(var name, var specialty)
      when specialty.equals("Dermatology")
        -> "The cabinet of " + specialty
              + " is currently under renovation";
    case Doctor(var name, var specialty)
      when (specialty.equals("Allergy")
      && (name.equals("Kyle Ulm")))
        -> "The cabinet of " + specialty
              + " is closed. The doctor " + name
              + " is on holiday.";
    case Doctor(var name, var specialty)
      when (specialty.equals("Allergy")
      && (name.equals("John Hora")))
        -> "The cabinet of " + specialty
              + " is open. The doctor " + name
              + " is ready to receive patients.";
    case Resident(var rsname,
        Doctor(var drname, var specialty))
      when (specialty.equals("Dermatology")
      && rsname.equals("Mark Oil"))
        -> "Cabinet of " + specialty + ". Doctor "
              + drname + " and resident " + rsname
              + " are ready to receive patients.";
```

```
      default -> "Cabinet closed";
   };
}
```

And, if we add the `Patient` and `Appointment` records as well, then we can check if a certain patient has an appointment as follows:

```
public static String reception(Object o) {

  return switch(o) {

    case Patient(String ptname, int npi,
        Appointment(LocalDate date,
        Doctor (String drname, String specialty)))
      when (ptname.equals("Alicia Goy")
      && npi == 1234567890 && LocalDate.now().equals(date))
        -> "The doctor " + drname + " from " + specialty
          + " is ready for you " + ptname;
    default -> "";
  };
}
```

The JDK 19+ context-specific keyword `when` is added between the pattern label and the checks (the boolean expressions representing the guarding conditions) this avoids the confusion of using the `&&` operator.

100. Using generic records in record patterns

Declaring a generic record for mapping fruit data can be done as follows:

```
public record FruitRecord<T>(T t, String country) {}
```

Now, let's assume a `MelonRecord`, which is a fruit (actually, there is some controversy over whether a melon is a fruit or a vegetable, but let's say that it is a fruit):

```
public record MelonRecord(String type, float weight) {}
```

We can declare a `FruitRecord<MelonRecord>` as follows:

```
FruitRecord<MelonRecord> fruit =
  new FruitRecord<>(new MelonRecord("Hami", 1000), "China");
```

This `FruitRecord<MelonRecord>` can be used in record patterns with `instanceof`:

```
if (fruit instanceof FruitRecord<MelonRecord>(
    MelonRecord melon, String country)) {
  System.out.println(melon + " from " + country);
}
```

Or, in switch statements/expressions:

```
switch(fruit) {
  case FruitRecord<MelonRecord>(
      MelonRecord melon, String country) :
    System.out.println(melon + " from " + country); break;
  default : break;
};
```

Next, let's see how we can use type argument inference.

Type argument inference

Java supports inference of type arguments for record patterns, so we can re-write the previous examples as follows:

```
if (fruit instanceof FruitRecord<MelonRecord>(
    var melon, var country)) {
  System.out.println(melon + " from " + country);
}
```

Or, if we want more concise code, then we can drop the type arguments as follows:

```
if (fruit instanceof FruitRecord(var melon, var country)) {
  System.out.println(melon + " from " + country);
}
```

The same works for switch:

```
switch (fruit) {
  case FruitRecord<MelonRecord>(var melon, var country) :
    System.out.println(melon + " from " + country); break;
  default : break;
};
```

Or, more concise:

```
switch (fruit) {
  case FruitRecord(var melon, var country) :
    System.out.println(melon + " from " + country); break;
  default : break;
};
```

Here, the type for melon is inferred as MelonRecord, and the type for country as String.

Now, let's assume the following generic record:

```
public record EngineRecord<X, Y, Z>(X x, Y y, Z z) {}
```

The generics X, Y, and Z can be anything. For instance, we can define an engine by its type, horsepower, and cooling system as follows:

```
EngineRecord<String, Integer, String> engine
  = new EngineRecord("TV1", 661, "Water cooled");
```

Next, we can use the engine variable and instanceof as follows:

```
if (engine instanceof EngineRecord<String, Integer, String>
    (var type, var power, var cooling)) {
  System.out.println(type + " - " + power + " - " + cooling);
}

// or, more concise
if (engine instanceof EngineRecord(
    var type, var power, var cooling)) {
  System.out.println(type + " - " + power + " - " + cooling);
}
```

And, with switch as follows:

```
switch (engine) {
  case EngineRecord<String, Integer, String>(
      var type, var power, var cooling) :
    System.out.println(type + " - "
                             + power + " - " + cooling);
  default : break;
};

// or, more concise
switch (engine) {
  case EngineRecord(var type, var power, var cooling) :
    System.out.println(type + " - "
                             + power + " - " + cooling);
  default : break;
};
```

In both examples, we rely on inferred types for arguments. The type inferred for the type argument is String, for power is Integer, and for cooling is String.

Type argument inference and nested records

Let's assume the following record:

```
public record ContainerRecord<C>(C c) {}
```

And the following nested container:

```
ContainerRecord<String> innerContainer
  = new ContainerRecord("Inner container");
ContainerRecord<ContainerRecord<String>> container
  = new ContainerRecord(innerContainer);
```

Next, we can use container as follows:

```
if (container instanceof
    ContainerRecord<ContainerRecord<String>>(
      ContainerRecord(var c))) {
  System.out.println(c);
}
```

Here, the type argument for the nested pattern ContainerRecord(var c) is inferred to be String, so the pattern itself is inferred to be ContainerRecord<String>(var c).

More concise code can be obtained if we drop the type arguments in the outer record pattern as follows:

```
if (container instanceof ContainerRecord(
    ContainerRecord(var c))) {
      System.out.println(c);
}
```

Here, the compiler will infer that the entire instanceof pattern is ContainerRecord<ContainerReco rd<String>>(ContainerRecord<String>(var c)).

Or, if we want the outer container, then we write the following record pattern:

```
if (container instanceof
    ContainerRecord<ContainerRecord<String>>(var c)) {
  System.out.println(c);
}
```

In the bundled code, you can find these examples for switch as well.

Important note

Pay attention that type patterns don't support the implicit inference of type arguments (for instance, the type pattern List list is always treated as a raw type pattern).

So, Java Generics can be used in records exactly as in regular Java classes. Moreover, we can use them in conjunction with record patterns and instanceof/switch.

101. Handling nulls in nested record patterns

From *Chapter 2, Problem 54, Tackling the case null clause in switch,* we know that starting with JDK 17 (JEP 406), we can treat a null case in switch as any other common case:

```
case null -> throw new IllegalArgumentException(...);
```

Moreover, from *Problem 67*, we know that, when type patterns are involved as well, a total pattern matches everything unconditionally including null values (known as an unconditional pattern). Solving this issue can be done by explicitly adding a null case (as in the previous snippet of code) or relying on JDK 19+. Starting with JDK 19, the unconditional pattern still matches null values only it will not allow the execution of that branch. The switch expressions will throw a NullPointerException without even looking at the patterns.

This statement partially works for record patterns as well. For instance, let's consider the following records:

```
public interface Fruit {}


public record SeedRecord(String type, String country)
  implements Fruit {}
public record MelonRecord(SeedRecord seed, float weight)
  implements Fruit {}
public record EggplantRecord(SeedRecord seed, float weight)
  implements Fruit {}
```

And, let's consider the following switch:

```
public static String buyFruit(Fruit fruit) {

  return switch(fruit) {
    case null -> "Ops!";
    case SeedRecord(String type, String country)
      -> "This is a seed of " + type + " from " + country;
    case EggplantRecord(SeedRecord seed, float weight)
      -> "This is a " + seed.type() + " eggplant";
    case MelonRecord(SeedRecord seed, float weight)
      -> "This is a " + seed.type() + " melon";
    case Fruit v -> "This is an unknown fruit";
  };
}
```

If we call buyFruit(null), then we will get the message *Ops!*. The compiler is aware that the selector expression is null and that there is a case null, therefore it will execute that branch. If we remove that case null, then we immediately get a NullPointerException. The compiler will not evaluate the record patterns; it will simply throw a NullPointerException.

Next, let's create an eggplant:

```
SeedRecord seed = new SeedRecord("Fairytale", "India");
EggplantRecord eggplant = new EggplantRecord(seed, 300);
```

This time, if we call buyFruit(seed), we get the message *This is a seed of Fairytale from India*. The call matches the case SeedRecord(String type, String country) branch. And, if we call buyFruit(eggplant), then we get the message *This is a Fairytale eggplant*. The call matches the case EggplantRecord(SeedRecord seed, float weight) branch. There are no surprises so far!

Now, let's have an edge case. We assume that SeedRecord is null and we create the following "bad" eggplant:

```
EggplantRecord badEggplant = new EggplantRecord(null, 300);
```

The buyFruit(badEggplant) call will return a NullPointerException containing the following crystal clear message: *java.lang.NullPointerException: Cannot invoke "modern.challenge.SeedRecord.type()" because "seed" is null*. As you can see, in the case of nested null, the compiler cannot prevent the execution of the corresponding branch. The nested null doesn't short-circuit the code and hits the code of our branch (case EggplantRecord(SeedRecord seed, float weight)) where we call seed.type(). Since seed is null, we get a NullPointerException.

We cannot cover this edge case via a case such as case EggplantRecord(null, float weight). This will not compile. Obviously, a deeper or wider nesting will complicate these edge cases even more. However, we can add a guard to prevent the issue and cover this case as follows:

```
case EggplantRecord(SeedRecord seed, float weight)
    when seed == null -> "Ops! What's this?!";
```

Let's see what happens in the case of using instanceof instead of switch. So, the code becomes:

```
public static String buyFruit(Fruit fruit) {

  if (fruit instanceof SeedRecord(
      String type, String country)) {
    return "This is a seed of " + type + " from " + country;
  }

  if (fruit instanceof EggplantRecord(
      SeedRecord seed, float weight)) {
    return "This is a " + seed.type() + " eggplant";
  }

  if (fruit instanceof MelonRecord(
      SeedRecord seed, float weight)) {
    return "This is a " + seed.type() + " melon";
```

```
    }

    return "This is an unknown fruit";
}
```

In the case of instanceof, there is no need to add explicit null checks. A call such as buyFruit(null) will return the message *This is an unknown fruit*. This happens since no if statement will match the given null.

Next, if we call buyFruit(seed), we get the message *This is a seed of Fairytale from India*. The call matches the if (fruit instanceof SeedRecord(String type, String country)) branch. And, if we call buyFruit(eggplant), then we get the message *This is a Fairytale eggplant*. The call matches the case if (fruit instanceof EggplantRecord(SeedRecord seed, float weight)) branch. Again, there are no surprises so far!

Finally, let's bring in front the badEggplant via the buyFruit(badEggplant) call. Exactly as in the case of the switch example, the result will consist of an NPE: *Cannot invoke "modern.challenge.SeedRecord. type()" because "seed" is null*. Again, the nested null cannot be intercepted by the compiler and the if (fruit instanceof EggplantRecord(SeedRecord seed, float weight)) branch is executed leading to a NullPointerException because we call seed.type() while seed is null.

Trying to cover this edge case via the following snippet of code will not compile:

```
if (fruit instanceof EggplantRecord(null, float weight)) {
  return "Ops! What's this?!";
}
```

However, we can add a guard to cover this case as follows:

```
if (fruit instanceof EggplantRecord(
    SeedRecord seed, float weight) && seed == null) {
  return "Ops! What's this?!";
}
```

So, pay attention that nested patterns don't take advantage of case null or of the JDK 19+ behavior that throws an NPE without even inspecting the patterns. This means that null values can pass through a case (or instanceof check) and execute that branch leading to NPEs. So, avoiding null values or adding extra checks (guards) as much as possible should be the way to a smooth road ahead.

102. Simplifying expressions via record patterns

Java records can help us to simplify snippets of code meant to handle/evaluate different expressions (mathematical, statistical, string-based, **Abstract Syntax Tree** (**AST**), and so on) a lot. Typically, evaluating such expressions implies a lot of conditions and checks that can be implemented via if and/ or switch statements.

For example, let's consider the following records meant to shape string-based expressions that can be concatenated:

```
interface Str {}

record Literal(String text) implements Str {}
record Variable(String name) implements Str {}

record Concat(Str first, Str second) implements Str {}
```

Some parts of the string expression are literals (`Literal`) while others are provided as variables (`Variable`). For brevity, we can evaluate these expressions only via the concatenation operation (`Concat`), but feel free to add more operations.

During the evaluation, we have an intermediary step for simplifying the expression by removing/replacing irrelevant parts. For example, we can consider that the terms of the expression that are empty strings can be safely removed from the concatenation process. In other words, a string expression such as t + " " can be simplified as t, since the second term of our expression is a blank string.

The code meant to perform this kind of simplification can rely on type patterns and `instanceof` as follows:

```
public static Str shortener(Str str) {

  if (str instanceof Concat s) {
    if (s.first() instanceof Variable first
        && s.second() instanceof Literal second
        && second.text().isBlank()) {
          return first;
    } else if (s.first() instanceof Literal first
        && s.second() instanceof Variable second
        && first.text().isBlank()) {
          return second;
    }
  }

  return str;
}
```

This code will become quite verbose if we continue to add more rules for simplifying the given `str`. Fortunately, we can increase the readability of this code by using record patterns and `switch`. This way, the code becomes more compact and expressive. Check this out:

```
public static Str shortener(Str str) {

  return switch (str) {
    case Concat(Variable(var name), Literal(var text))
      when text.isBlank() -> new Variable(name);
```

```
      case Concat(Literal(var text), Variable(var name))
        when text.isBlank() -> new Variable(name);
      default -> str;
   };
}
```

How cool is this?

103. Hooking unnamed patterns and variables

One of the most remarkable preview features of JDK 21 is JEP 443 or *unnamed patterns and variables*. In other words, via unnamed patterns and variables, JDK 21 provides support for representing record components and local variables that we are not using in our code (we don't care about them) as an underscore character (_).

Unnamed patterns

Deconstructing a record allows us to express record patterns, but we do not always use all the resulting components. Unnamed patterns are useful for indicating the record components that we don't use but we have to declare for the sake of syntax. For instance, let's have the following example (the Doctor, Resident, Patient, and Appointment records were introduced earlier, in *Problem 97* and *98*, so, for brevity, I'll skip their declarations here):

```
if (staff instanceof Doctor(String name, String specialty)) {
  return "The cabinet of " + specialty
        + " is currently under renovation";
}
```

In this example, the Doctor record was deconstructed as Doctor(String name, String specialty) but we are using only the specialty component while we don't need the name component. However, we cannot write Doctor(String specialty) since this doesn't respect the Doctor record signature. Alternatively, we can simply replace the String name with an underscore as follows:

```
if (staff instanceof Doctor(_, String specialty)) {
  return "The cabinet of " + specialty
        + " is currently under renovation";
}
```

The unnamed pattern is shorthand for the type pattern var _, so we can write if (staff instanceof Doctor(var _, String specialty)) as well.

Let's consider another use case:

```
if (staff instanceof Resident(String name, Doctor dr)) {
  return "The resident of this cabinet is : " + name;
}
```

In this case, we use the `name` of the `Resident` but we don't care about the `Doctor`, so we can simply use an underscore as follows:

```
if (staff instanceof Resident(String name, _)) {
  return "The resident of this cabinet is : " + name;
}
```

Here is another example that ignores the specialty of the doctor:

```
if (staff instanceof Resident(String rsname,
       Doctor(String drname, _))) {
    return "This is the cabinet of doctor " + drname
         + " and resident " + rsname;
}
```

Next, let's add the `Patient` and `Appointment` records as well:

```
if (o instanceof Patient(var ptname, var npi,
                   Appointment(var date,
                   Doctor (var drname, var specialty)))) {

  return "Patient " + ptname
       + " has an appointment for the date of " + date;
}
```

In this example, we don't need the `npi` component and the `Doctor` component so we can replace them with an underscore:

```
if (o instanceof Patient(var ptname, _,
                   Appointment(var date, _))) {

  return "Patient " + ptname
       + " has an appointment for the date of " + date;
}
```

And, here is a case that needs only the patient's name:

```
if (o instanceof Patient(var ptname, _, _)) {

  return "Patient " + ptname + " has an appointment";
}
```

Of course, in such cases, you may prefer to rely on type pattern matching and express the code as follows:

```
if (o instanceof Patient pt) {
```

```
    return "Patient " + pt.name() + " has an appointment";
}
```

I think you got the idea! When you don't need a record component and you want to clearly communicate this aspect while typing your code faster, just replace that component with an underscore (_).

Unnamed patterns can be used with switch as well. Here is an example:

```
// without unnamed patterns
return switch(staff) {
  case Doctor(String name, String specialty) ->
      "The cabinet of " + specialty
    + " is currently under renovation";
  case Resident(String name, Doctor dr) ->
      "The resident of this cabinet is : " + name;
  default -> "Cabinet closed";
};

// with unnamed patterns
return switch(staff) {
  case Doctor(_, String specialty) ->
      "The cabinet of " + specialty
    + " is currently under renovation";
  case Resident(String name, _) ->
      "The resident of this cabinet is : " + name;
  default -> "Cabinet closed";
};
```

Nested records and unnamed patterns can significantly reduce the code length. Here is an example:

```
// without unnamed patterns
return switch(o) {
  case Patient(String ptname, int npi,
               Appointment(LocalDate date,
               Doctor (String drname, String specialty))) ->
      "Patient " + ptname + " has an appointment";
  default -> "";
};

// with unnamed patterns
return switch(o) {
  case Patient(String ptname, _, _) ->
      "Patient " + ptname + " has an appointment";
```

```
    default -> "";
  };
```

Now, let's focus on another use case of unnamed variables, and let's assume the following starting point:

```
public sealed abstract class EngineType
  permits ESSEngine, DSLEngine, LPGEngine {}


public final class ESSEngine extends EngineType {}
public final class DSLEngine extends EngineType {}
public final class LPGEngine extends EngineType {}


public record Car<E extends EngineType>(E engineType) {}
```

So, we have a sealed class (EngineType) extended by three final classes (ESSEngine, DSLEngine, and LPGEngine), and a record (Car). Next, we want to write the following switch:

```
public static String addCarburetor(Car c) {

  return switch(c) {
    case Car(DSLEngine dsl), Car(ESSEngine ess)
      -> "Adding a carburetor to a ESS or DSL car";
    case Car(LPGEngine lpg)
      -> "Adding a carburetor to a LPG car";
  };
}
```

Check out the first case label. We have grouped the first two patterns in one case label since the DSL and ESS cars can have the same type of carburetor. However, this will not compile and will result in an error: *illegal fall-through from a pattern*. Since both patterns can match is erroneous to name the components. In such cases, we can elide the components via unnamed variables as follows:

```
public static String addCarburetor(Car c) {

  return switch(c) {
    case Car(DSLEngine _), Car(ESSEngine _)
      -> "Adding a carburetor to a ESS or DSL car";
    case Car(LPGEngine lpg)
      -> "Adding a carburetor to a LPG car";
  };
}
```

This compiles and works fine. Moreover, the second case label can be written as case Car(LPGEngine _) as well since we don't use the lpg name on the right-hand side.

If you need to add a *guard* to a case label with multiple patterns, then keep in mind that the guard applies to the multiple patterns as a whole not to each individual pattern. For instance, the following code is correct:

```
public static String addCarburetor(Car c, int carburetorType){

  return switch(c) {
    case Car(DSLEngine _), Car(ESSEngine _)
      when carburetorType == 1
        -> "Adding a carburetor of type 1 to a ESS or DSL car";
    case Car(DSLEngine _), Car(ESSEngine _)
        -> "Adding a carburetor of tpye "
          + carburetorType + " to a ESS or DSL car";
    case Car(LPGEngine lpg) -> "Adding a carburetor "
          + carburetorType + " to a LPG car";
  };
}
```

Next, let's tackle unnamed variables.

Unnamed variables

Along with **unnamed patterns** (specific to the deconstruction of record components), JDK 21 introduces *unnamed variables*. An unnamed variable is also represented by an underscore (_) and is useful to highlight which variables we don't need/use. Such variables can occur in one of the following contexts.

In a catch block

Whenever you don't use the exception parameter of a catch block, you can replace it with an underscore. For instance, in the following snippet of code, we catch an ArithmeticException but we log a friendly message that doesn't use the exception parameter:

```
int divisor = 0;
try {
  int result = 1 / divisor;
  // use result
} catch (ArithmeticException _) {
  System.out.println("Divisor " + divisor + " is not good");
}
```

The same technique can be applied to multi-catch cases.

In a for loop

Unnamed variables can be used in a simple for loop. For instance, in the following snippet of code, we call logLoopStart() but we don't use the returned result:

```java
int[] arr = new int[]{1, 2, 3};
for (int i = 0, _ = logLoopStart(i); i < arr.length; i++) {
  // use i
}
```

Unnamed variables can be used in an enhanced for loop as well. In the following snippet of code, we iterate the cards list via an enhanced for loop but we don't use the cards:

```java
int score = 0;
List<String> cards = List.of(
   "12 spade", "6 diamond", "14 diamond");
for (String _ : cards) {
  if (score < 10) {
    score ++;
  } else {
    score --;
  }
}
```

So, here, we don't care about the cards' values, so instead of writing for (String card : cards) {…}, we simply write for (String _ : cards) {…}.

In an assignment that ignores the result

Let's consider the following code:

```java
Files.deleteIfExists(Path.of("/file.txt"));
```

The deleteIfExists() method returns a boolean result indicating if the given file was successfully deleted or not. But, in this code, we didn't capture that result, so it is not clear if we want to ignore the result or if we just forgot about it. If we assume that we forgot about it, then most probably we wanted to write this:

```java
boolean success = Files.deleteIfExists(Path.of("/file.txt"));
if (success) { ... }
```

But, if we just wanted to ignore it, then we can clearly communicate it via an unnamed variable (this signals that we are aware of the result but we don't want to take further actions based on its value):

```java
boolean _ = Files.deleteIfExists(Path.of("/file.txt"));
var _ = Files.deleteIfExists(Path.of("/file.txt"));
```

The same technique applies every time you want to ignore the result of the expression on the right-hand side.

In try-with-resources

Sometimes, we don't use the resource opened in a *try-with-resources* block. We just need the context of this resource and we want to benefit from the fact that it is `AutoCloseable`. For instance, when we call `Arena.ofConfined()`, we may need the `Arena` context without explicitly using it. In such cases, unnamed variables can help us as in the following example:

```
try (Arena _ = Arena.ofConfined()) {
  // don't use arena
}
```

Or, using var:

```
try (var _ = Arena.ofConfined()) {
  // don't use arena
}
```

The `Arena` API is part of the Foreign (Function) Memory API introduced in *Chapter 7*.

In lambda expressions

When a lambda parameter is not relevant for our lambda expression, we can simply replace it with an underscore. Here is an example:

```
List<Melon> melons = Arrays.asList(…);

Map<String, Integer> resultToMap = melons.stream()
  .collect(Collectors.toMap(Melon::getType, Melon::getWeight,
    (oldValue, _) -> oldValue));
```

Done! Don't forget that this is a preview feature in JDK 21, so use `--enable-preview`.

104. Tackling records in Spring Boot

Java records fit perfectly in Spring Boot applications. Let's have several scenarios where Java records can help us increase readability and expressiveness by squeezing the homologous code.

Using records in controllers

Typically, a Spring Boot controller operates with simple POJO classes that carry our data back over the wire to the client. For instance, check out this simple controller endpoint returning a list of authors, including their books:

```
@GetMapping("/authors")
public List<Author> fetchAuthors() {

  return bookstoreService.fetchAuthors();
}
```

Here, the Author (and Book) can be simple carriers of data written as POJOs. But, they can be replaced by records as well. Here it is:

```
public record Book(String title, String isbn) {}
public record Author(
    String name,  String genre, List<Book> books) {}
```

That's all! The Jackson library (which is the default JSON library in Spring Boot) will automatically marshal instances of type Author/Book into JSON. In the bundled code, you can practice the complete example via the localhost:8080/authors endpoint address.

Using records with templates

Thymeleaf (https://www.thymeleaf.org/) is probably the most used templating engine in Spring Boot applications. Thymeleaf pages (HTML pages) are typically populated with data carried by POJO classes, which means that Java records should work as well.

Let's consider the previous Author and Book records, and the following controller endpoint:

```
@GetMapping("/bookstore")
public String bookstorePage(Model model) {

    model.addAttribute("authors",
        bookstoreService.fetchAuthors());

    return "bookstore";
}
```

The List<Author> returned via fetchAuthors() is stored in the model under a variable named authors. This variable is used to populate bookstore.html as follows:

```
...
<ul th:each="author : ${authors}">
  <li th:text="${author.name} + ' ('
              + ${author.genre} + ')'" />
  <ul th:each="book : ${author.books}">
    <li th:text="${book.title}" />
  </ul>
</ul>
...
```

Done!

Using records for configuration

Let's assume that in `application.properties` we have the following two properties (they could be expressed in YAML as well):

```
bookstore.bestseller.author=Joana Nimar
bookstore.bestseller.book=Prague history
```

Spring Boot maps such properties to POJO via `@ConfigurationProperties`. But, a record can be used as well. For instance, these properties can be mapped to the `BestSellerConfig` record as follows:

```
@ConfigurationProperties(prefix = "bookstore.bestseller")
public record BestSellerConfig(String author, String book) {}
```

Next, in `BookstoreService` (a typical Spring Boot service), we can inject `BestSellerConfig` and call its accessors:

```
@Service
public class BookstoreService {

  private final BestSellerConfig bestSeller;

  public BookstoreService(BestSellerConfig bestSeller) {
    this.bestSeller = bestSeller;
  }

  public String fetchBestSeller() {

    return bestSeller.author() + " | " + bestSeller.book();
  }
}
```

In the bundled code, we have added a controller that uses this service as well.

Record and dependency injection

In the previous examples, we have injected the `BookstoreService` service into `BookstoreController` using the typical mechanism provided by SpringBoot – dependency injection via constructor (it can be done via `@Autowired` as well):

```
@RestController
public class BookstoreController {

  private final BookstoreService bookstoreService;

  public BookstoreController(
```

```
        BookstoreService bookstoreService) {
    this.bookstoreService = bookstoreService;
}


@GetMapping("/authors")
public List<Author> fetchAuthors() {

    return bookstoreService.fetchAuthors();
}
}
```

But, we can compact this class by re-writing it as a record as follows:

```
@RestController
public record BookstoreController(
        BookstoreService bookstoreService) {

@GetMapping("/authors")
public List<Author> fetchAuthors() {

    return bookstoreService.fetchAuthors();
}
}
```

The canonical constructor of this record will be the same as our explicit constructor. Feel free to challenge yourself to find more use cases of Java records in Spring Boot applications.

105. Tackling records in JPA

If you are a fan of JPA (I cannot see why, but who am I to judge), then you'll be more than happy to find out that Java records can be helpful in JPA. Typically, Java records can be used as DTOs. Next, let's see several scenarios when records and JPA make a delightful combo.

DTO via record constructor

Let's assume that we have a JPA typical Author entity that maps author data such as id, name, age, and genre.

Next, we want to write a query that fetches the authors of a certain genre. But, we don't need to fetch authors as entities because we don't plan to modify this data. This is a read-only query returning only the name and age of each author of the given genre. So, we need a DTO that can be expressed via records as follows:

```
public record AuthorDto(String name, int age) {}
```

Next, a typical Spring Data JPA, `AuthorRepository` powered by the Spring Data Query Builder mechanism, can take advantage of this record as follows:

```
@Repository
public interface AuthorRepository
   extends JpaRepository<Author, Long> {

  @Transactional(readOnly = true)
  List<AuthorDto> findByGenre(String genre);
}
```

Now, the generated query fetches the data and Spring Boot will map it accordingly to be carried around by the `AuthorDto`.

DTO via record and JPA constructor expression

Another flavor of the previous scenario can rely on a JPA query that uses a constructor expression as follows:

```
@Repository
public interface AuthorRepository
     extends JpaRepository<Author, Long> {

  @Transactional(readOnly = true)
  @Query(value = "SELECT
         new com.bookstore.dto.AuthorDto(a.name, a.age)
         FROM Author a")
  List<AuthorDto> fetchAuthors();
}
```

The `AuthorDto` is the same record listed in the previous example.

DTO via record and result transformer

If working with Hibernate 6.0+ result transformers is not on your "to-do" list, then you can simply jump to the next topic.

Let's consider the following two records:

```
public record BookDto(Long id, String title) {}

public record AuthorDto(Long id, String name,
      int age, List<BookDto> books) {

  public void addBook(BookDto book) {
    books().add(book);
```

```
    }
}
```

This time, we have to fetch a hierarchical DTO represented by `AuthorDto` and `BookDto`. Since an author can have several books written, we have to provide, in `AuthorDto`, a component of the type `List<BookDto>` and a helper method for collecting the books of the current author.

In order to populate this hierarchical DTO, we can rely on an implementation of `TupleTransformer`, `ResultListTransformer` as follows:

```java
public class AuthorBookTransformer implements
        TupleTransformer, ResultListTransformer {

  private final Map<Long, AuthorDto>
    authorsDtoMap = new HashMap<>();

  @Override
  public Object transformTuple(Object[] os, String[] strings){

    Long authorId = ((Number) os[0]).longValue();

    AuthorDto authorDto = authorsDtoMap.get(authorId);

    if (authorDto == null) {
      authorDto = new AuthorDto(((Number) os[0]).longValue(),
            (String) os[1], (int) os[2], new ArrayList<>());
    }

    BookDto bookDto = new BookDto(
      ((Number) os[3]).longValue(), (String) os[4]);

    authorDto.addBook(bookDto);

    authorsDtoMap.putIfAbsent(authorDto.id(), authorDto);

    return authorDto;
  }

  @Override
  public List<AuthorDto> transformList(List list) {
    return new ArrayList<>(authorsDtoMap.values());
  }
}
```

You can find the complete application in the bundled code.

DTO via record and JdbcTemplate

If working with SpringBoot JdbcTemplate is not on your "to-do" list, then you can simply jump to the next topic.

The JdbcTemplate API has been a huge success among those who love to work with JDBC. So, if you are familiar with this API, then you'll be very happy to find out that it can be combined with Java records quite nicely.

For instance, having the same AuthorDto and BookDto as in the previous scenario, we can rely on JdbcTemplate to populate this hierarchical DTO as follows:

```
@Repository
@Transactional(readOnly = true)
public class AuthorExtractor {

  private final JdbcTemplate jdbcTemplate;

  public AuthorExtractor(JdbcTemplate jdbcTemplate) {
    this.jdbcTemplate = jdbcTemplate;
  }

  public List<AuthorDto> extract() {

    String sql = "SELECT a.id, a.name, a.age, b.id, b.title "
    + "FROM author a INNER JOIN book b ON a.id = b.author_id";

    List<AuthorDto> result = jdbcTemplate.query(sql,
     (ResultSet rs) -> {

      final Map<Long, AuthorDto> authorsMap = new HashMap<>();
      while (rs.next()) {
        Long authorId = (rs.getLong("id"));
        AuthorDto author = authorsMap.get(authorId);
        if (author == null) {
          author = new AuthorDto(rs.getLong("id"),
            rs.getString("name"),
              rs.getInt("age"), new ArrayList());
        }

        BookDto book = new BookDto(rs.getLong("id"),
          rs.getString("title"));
```

```
            author.addBook(book);
            authorsMap.putIfAbsent(author.id(), author);
        }

        return new ArrayList<>(authorsMap.values());
    });

    return result;
    }
}
```

You can find the complete application in the bundled code.

Team up Java records and @Embeddable

Hibernate 6.2+ allows us to define Java records as embeddable. Practically, we start with an embeddable class defined as follows:

```
@Embeddable
public record Contact(
    String email, String twitter, String phone) {}
```

Next, we use this embeddable in our Author entity as follows:

```
@Entity
public class Author implements Serializable {

    private static final long serialVersionUID = 1L;

    @Id
    @GeneratedValue(strategy = GenerationType.IDENTITY)
    private Long id;

    @Embedded
    private Contact contact;

    private int age;
    private String name;
    private String genre;
    ...
}
```

And, in our `AuthorDto` DTO as follows:

```
public record AuthorDto(
  String name, int age, Contact contact) {}
```

Next, a classical Spring Data JPA `AuthorRepository` powered by the Spring Data Query Builder mechanism can take advantage of this record as follows:

```
@Repository
public interface AuthorRepository
    extends JpaRepository<Author, Long> {

  @Transactional(readOnly = true)
  List<AuthorDto> findByGenre(String genre);
}
```

Now, the generated query fetches the data and Spring Boot will map it accordingly to be carried around by the `AuthorDto`. If we print one of the fetched authors to the console, we will see something like this:

```
[AuthorDto[name=Mark Janel, age=23,
   contact=Contact[email=mark.janel@yahoo.com,
              twitter=@markjanel, phone=+40198503]]
```

The highlighted part represents our embeddable.

106. Tackling records in jOOQ

The more you learn about JPA, the more you'll love jOOQ. Why? Because jOOQ represents the best way to write SQL in Java. Flexibility, versatility, dialect agnostic, rock-solid SQL support, a small learning curve, and high performance are just a few of the attributes that make jOOQ the most appealing persistence technology for modern applications.

Being part of the modern technology stack, jOOQ is the new persistence trend that respects all standards of a mature, robust, and well-documented technology.

If you are not familiar with jOOQ, then please consider my book *jOOQ Masterclass*.

That being said, let's assume that we have a database schema consisting of two tables, `Productline` and `Product`. A product line contains multiple products, so we can shape this one-to-many relationship via two records as follows:

```
public record RecordProduct(String productName,
  String productVendor, Integer quantityInStock) {}
public record RecordProductLine(String productLine,
  String textDescription, List<RecordProduct> products) {}
```

In jOOQ, we can populate this model via a simple query based on the `MULTISET` operator:

```
List<RecordProductLine> resultRecord = ctx.select(
```

```
PRODUCTLINE.PRODUCT_LINE, PRODUCTLINE.TEXT_DESCRIPTION,
  multiset(
    select(
        PRODUCT.PRODUCT_NAME, PRODUCT.PRODUCT_VENDOR,
        PRODUCT.QUANTITY_IN_STOCK)
      .from(PRODUCT)
      .where(PRODUCTLINE.PRODUCT_LINE.eq(
            PRODUCT.PRODUCT_LINE))
    ).as("products").convertFrom(
        r -> r.map(mapping(RecordProduct::new))))
      .from(PRODUCTLINE)
      .orderBy(PRODUCTLINE.PRODUCT_LINE)
      .fetch(mapping(RecordProductLine::new));
```

How cool is this? jOOQ can produce any nested collection value of jOOQ Records or DTOs (POJO/Java records) in a fully type-safe manner, with zero reflections, no N+1 risks, no de-duplications, and no accidental Cartesian products. This allows the database to perform nesting and optimize the query execution plan.

In the bundled code, you can see another example that fetches a many-to-many relationship in a record model. Moreover, in the bundled code, you can find an example that relies on the jOOQ MULTISET_AGG() function. This is a synthetic aggregate function that can be used as an alternative to MULTISET.

Summary

The goal of this chapter was to deeply cover Java records and record patterns. We have assigned the same importance to both the theoretical and the practical parts so that, in the end, there are no secrets regarding the use of these two topics. And, just in case you wonder why we didn't cover the topic regarding record patterns appearing in the header of an enhanced for statement, then please notice that this was added as a preview in JDK 20 but it was removed in JDK 21. This feature may be re-proposed in a future JEP.

Leave a review!

Enjoying this book? Help readers like you by leaving an Amazon review. Scan the QR code below for a 20% discount code.

*Limited Offer

5

Arrays, Collections, and Data Structures

This chapter includes 24 problems covering three main topics. We start with several problems related to the new Vector API dedicated to parallel data processing. We continue with several data structures, including Rope, Skip List, K-D Tree, Zipper, Binomial Heap, Fibonacci Heap, Pairing Heap, Huffman Coding, and so on. Finally, we discuss the three most popular join algorithms.

At the end of this chapter, you'll know how to write code for exploiting data parallel processing, exploiting a bunch of cool and lesser-known data structures, and how join operations work. And, as a bonus, you'll be familiar with the JDK 21 Sequenced Collections API.

Problems

Use the following problems to test your programming prowess on Java arrays, collections, and data structures. I strongly encourage you to give each problem a try before you turn to the solutions and download the example programs:

107. **Introducing parallel computations with arrays**: Explain in a few paragraphs what data parallel processing is and how it works.

108. **Covering the Vector API's structure and terminology**: Explain with examples the Vector API terminology. Cover notions such as element type, shape, species, lanes, and so on.

109. **Summing two arrays via the Vector API**: Write an application that uses the Vector API for summing up two Java arrays.

110. **Summing two arrays unrolled via the Vector API**: Write an application that uses the Vector API for summing two Java arrays using the *unrolled* technique.

111. **Benchmarking the Vector API**: Given two arrays, x[] and y[], write an application that benchmarks the computation z[] = x[] + y[], w[] = x[] * z[] * y[], k[] = z[] + w[] * y[] using plain Java and the Vector API.

112. **Applying the Vector API to compute FMA:** Provide a Vector API implementation of the famous Fused Multiply Add (FMA).

113. **Multiplying matrices via the Vector API:** Write a Vector API implementation for multiplying two matrices.

114. **Hooking the image negative filter with the Vector API:** Write a program that uses the Vector API to apply the negative filter to an image.

115. **Dissecting factory methods for collections:** Exemplify several approaches for creating unmodifiable/immutable maps, lists, and sets in Java.

116. **Getting a list from a stream:** Provide several snippets of code useful for collecting `Stream` content into a Java `List`.

117. **Handling map capacity:** Explain what the capacity of a Java `Map` is and how it can be used to control the number of effective mappings.

118. **Tackling Sequenced Collections:** Provide in-depth dive into the JDK 21 Sequenced Collections API. Exemplify this API on your favorite Java collections and explain what the alternatives before this API are.

119. **Introducing the Rope data structure:** Explain what the Rope data structure is and provide a Java implementation for its main operations (index, insert, delete, concatenation, and split).

120. **Introducing the Skip List data structure:** Explain and exemplify the Skip List data structure.

121. **Introducing the K-D Tree data structure:** Provide a brief introduction of K-D Trees and a Java implementation for 2-D Trees.

122. **Introducing the Zipper data structure:** Explain and exemplify on a tree the Zipper data structure.

123. **Introducing the Binomial Heap data structure:** Provide a deep coverage of a Binomial Heap data structure. Explain its main operations and exemplify them in a Java implementation.

124. **Introducing the Fibonacci Heap data structure:** Explain and exemplify the Fibonacci Heap data structure.

125. **Introducing the Pairing Heap data structure:** Explain and exemplify the Pairing Heap data structure.

126. **Introducing the Huffman Coding data structure:** The Huffman Coding algorithm was developed by David A. Huffman in 1950. Explain its usage and exemplify it via a Java implementation.

127. **Introducing the Splay Tree data structure:** A Splay Tree is a flavor of **Binary Search Tree (BST)**. Explain what its particularities are and provide an implementation of its main operations.

128. **Introducing the Interval Tree data structure:** An Interval Tree is another flavor of **Binary Search Tree (BST)**. Highlight its usage and exemplify it via a Java implementation.

129. **Introducing the Unrolled Linked List data structure:** Explain and exemplify the Unrolled Linked List data structure.

130. **Implementing join algorithms:** There are three famous join algorithms: Nested Loop Join, Hash Join, and Sort Merge Join. Explain and exemplify each of them in two tables that are involved in a one-to-many relationship.

The following sections describe solutions to the preceding problems. Remember that there usually isn't a single correct way to solve a particular problem. Also, remember that the explanations shown here include only the most interesting and important details needed to solve the problems. Download the example solutions to see additional details and to experiment with the programs at `https://github.com/PacktPublishing/Java-Coding-Problems-Second-Edition/tree/main/Chapter05`.

107. Introducing parallel computations with arrays

There was a time when CPUs were only capable of performing operations on data in the traditional mode known as **Single Instruction, Single Data (SISD)** or von Neumann architecture. In other words, one CPU cycle can process a single instruction and a single piece of data. The processor applies that instruction to that data and returns a result.

Modern CPUs are capable of performing parallel computations and working in a mode known as **Single Instruction, Multiple Data (SIMD)**. This time, one CPU cycle can apply a single instruction on multiple pieces of data simultaneously, which theoretically should speed things up and improve performance. The following diagram highlights these statements:

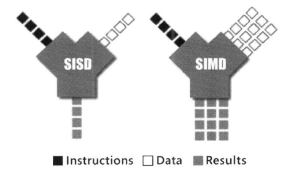

Figure 5.1: SISD vs. SIMD

If we add two arrays X and Y via an SISD-based CPU, then we expect that each CPU cycle will add an element from X with an element from Y. If we do the same task on a SIMD-based CPU, then each CPU cycle will simultaneously perform the addition on chunks from X and Y. This means that an SIMD CPU should complete the task faster than the SISD CPU.

This is the big picture! When we come closer, we see that CPU architectures come in many flavors, so it is quite challenging to develop an application capable of leveraging the best performance of a specific platform.

The two big competitors in the market, Intel and AMD, come with different SIMD implementations. It is not our goal to dissect this topic in detail, but it can be useful to know that the first popular desktop SIMD was introduced in 1996 by Intel under the name MMX (x86 architecture). In response, the AIM alliance (made up of Apple, IBM, and Freescale Semiconductor) promoted AltiVec – an integer and single-precision floating-point SIMD implementation. Later on, in 1999, Intel introduced the new SSE system (using 128-bit registers).

Since then, SIMD has evolved via extensions such as Advanced Vector Extensions (AVX, AVX2 (256-bit registers) and AVX-512 (512-bit registers)). While AVX and AVX2 are supported by Intel and AMD, the AVX-512 introduced in 2022 is supported only by the latest Intel processors. The following figure helps illustrate all of this:

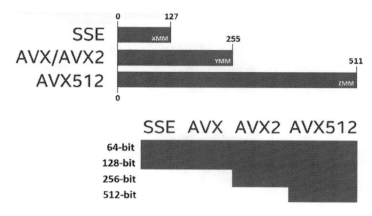

Figure 5.2: SIMD implementation history

Figure 5.2 is just the SIMD representation of a CPU structure. In reality, the platforms are much more complex and come in many flavors. There is no silver bullet and each platform has its strong and weak points. Trying to explore the strong points and avoid the weaknesses is a real challenge for any programming language trying to leverage the performance of a specific platform with high expectations.

For instance, what is the proper set of instructions that JVM should generate in order to squeeze out the best performance from a specific platform on computations that involve vectors (arrays)? Well, starting with JDK 16 (JEP 338), Java provides an incubator module, jdk.incubator.vector, known as the Vector API. The goal of this API is to allow developers to express, in a very platform-agnostic way, vector computations that are transformed at runtime in optimal vector hardware instructions on supported CPU architectures.

Starting with JDK 21 (JEP 448), the Vector API reached the sixth incubator, so we can try out some examples that take advantage of data-parallel accelerated code in contrast to scalar implementation. Running examples based on this incubator API can be done by adding the --add-modules=jdk.incubator.vector and --enable-preview VM options.

But, before that, let's cover the Vector API structure and terminology.

108. Covering the Vector API's structure and terminology

The Vector API is mapped by the jdk.incubator.vector module (and a package with the same name). A jdk.incubator.vector.Vector instance starts from a generic abstract combination characterized by a *type* and a *shape*. A vector is an instance of the Vector<E> class.

The vector element type

A Vector<E> has an *element type* (ETYPE), which is one of the Java primitive types: byte, float, double, short, int, or long. When we write Vector<E>, we say that E is the boxed version of ETYPE (for instance, when we write Vector<Float>, E is Float, and ETYPE is float). For more convenience, Java declares a specialized subtype for each *element type*, as shown in the following figure:

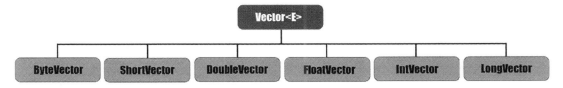

Figure 5.3: Specialized vector subtypes

Even if E is a boxed type, there is no boxing-unboxing overhead because Vector<E> works internally on ETYPE and thus on primitive types.

Besides the *element type*, a vector is also characterized by a *shape*.

The vector shape

A vector is also characterized by a *shape* (also referred to as VSHAPE) representing the size or capacity in bits of the vector. It can be 64, 128, 256, or 512 bits. Each of these values is wrapped by the VectorShape enumeration (for instance, the S_128_BIT enum item represents a shape of length 128 bits) next to an extra enum item representing the maximum length supported on the platform (S_Max_BIT). This is determined automatically on the currently running Java platform.

The vector species

A vector characterized by its *element type* and *shape* determines a unique *vector species,* which is a fixed instance of VectorSpecies<E>. This instance is shared by all vectors having the same shape and ETYPE. We can think of VectorSpecies<E> as a factory used to create vectors of the required *element type* and *shape*. For instance, we can define a factory for creating vectors of the double type having a size of 512 bits as follows:

```
static final VectorSpecies<Double> VS = VectorSpecies.of(
    double.class, VectorShape.S_512_BIT);
```

If you just need a factory for vectors of the maximal bit-size supported by the current platform independent of the element type, then rely on S_Max_BIT:

```
static final VectorSpecies<Double> VS = VectorSpecies.of(
    double.class, VectorShape.S_Max_BIT);
```

If you just need the largest vector *species* for your *element type* (here, double) for the current platform, then rely on ofLargestShape(). This vector *species* is chosen by the platform and it has a *shape* with the largest possible bit-size for your *element type* (don't confuse this with S_Max_BIT, which is independent of the *element type*):

```
static final VectorSpecies<Double> VS =
  VectorSpecies.ofLargestShape(double.class);
```

Or, maybe you need the vector *species* preferred by the current platform for your *element type*. This can be achieved via ofPreferred() as follows:

```
static final VectorSpecies<Double> VS =
  VectorSpecies.ofPreferred(double.class);
```

The preferred *species* is the most convenient approach when you don't want to bother specifying an explicit *shape*.

 Important note

The preferred *species* is the most optimal *shape* for the given *element type* on the current platform (runtime).

Moreover, for convenience, each specialized vector (IntVector, FloatVector, and so on) defines a set of static fields for covering all possible *species*. For example, the static field DoubleVector.SPECIES_512 can be used for *species* representing DoubleVector instances of 512-bit size (VectorShape.S_512_BIT):

```
static final VectorSpecies<Double> VS =
  DoubleVector.SPECIES_512;
```

If you want the maximal *species*, then rely on SPECIES_MAX:

```
static final VectorSpecies<Double> VS =
  DoubleVector.SPECIES_MAX;
```

Or, if you want the preferred *species*, then rely on SPECIES_PREFERRED:

```
static final VectorSpecies<Double> VS =
  DoubleVector.SPECIES_PREFERRED;
```

You can easily inspect the *element type* and *shape* of a VectorSpecies instance via the elementType() and vectorShape() methods as follows:

```
System.out.println("Element type: " + VS.elementType());
System.out.println("Shape: " + VS.vectorShape());
```

So far, you know how to create vector *species* (vector factories). But, before starting to create vectors and apply operations on them, let's talk about vector *lanes*.

Vector lanes

A Vector<E> is like a fixed-sized Java array made of *lanes*. The *lane count* is returned by the length() method and is called VLENGTH. The *lane count* is equal to the number of scalar elements stored in that vector.

If you know the *element size* and the *shape* of the vector, then you can compute the number of *lanes* as (*shape/element size*). You should get the same result as returned by length(). The *element size* is returned by elementSize(), and the *shape* is returned by vectorBitSize() or vectorShape().vectorBitSize().

For instance, a vector whose *shape* is 256 bits with an *element type* of float (which is 32 bits (4 bytes) in Java) holds 8 float scalar elements, so it has 8 *lanes*. The following figure illustrates this statement:

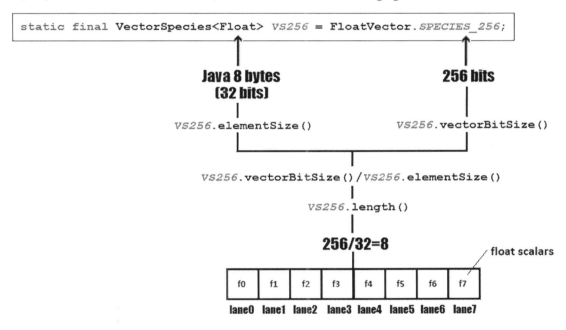

Figure 5.4: Computing the number of lanes

Based on this example, you can easily compute the number of *lanes* for any other vector configuration. Next, let's see why it is important to know about *lanes*.

Vector operations

Applying operations on vectors is the climax of our efforts. The number of *lanes* estimates the SIMD performance because vector operations operate on *lanes*. A single vector operation affects a *lane* as a unit of work. For instance, if our vector has 8 *lanes*, it means that SIMD will perform 8 *lanewise* operations at once.

In the following figure, you can see a comparison of SISD vs. SIMD in this context:

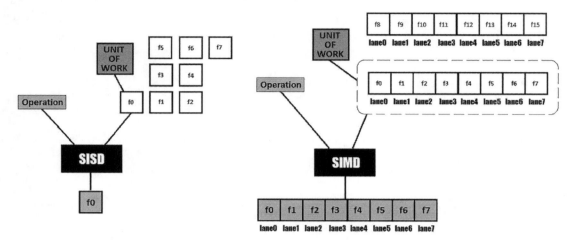

Figure 5.5: SISD vs. SIMD

While SISD has a single scalar as a unit of work, SIMD has 8 scalars (8 *lanes*), which explains why SIMD offers a significant performance bump over SISD.

So, a Vector<E> is operated on *lanes*. Mainly, we have *lanewise* operations (such as addition, division, and bit shifts) and *cross-lane* operations that reduce all *lanes* to a single scalar (for instance, summing all *lanes*). The following figure depicts these statements:

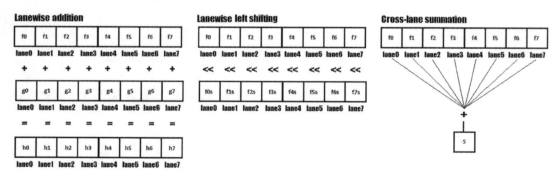

Figure 5.6: Lanewise and cross-lane operations

Moreover, a Vector<E> can be operated on with a VectorMask<E>. This is a sequence of boolean values that can be used by some vector operations to filter the selection and operation of lane elements of the given input vectors. Check out the following figure (the addition operation is applied only when the mask contains 1):

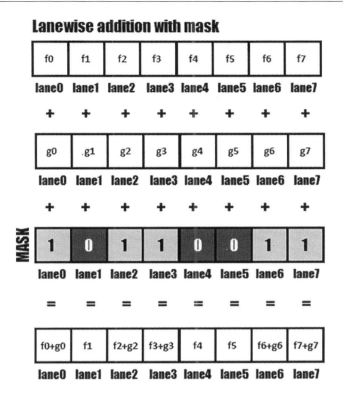

Figure 5.7: Lanewise addition with mask

Important note

Note that masks are not supported by all CPUs. A CPU that doesn't support masks may face degradation in performance.

Speaking about vector operations, you should definitely take a look at the Vector and VectorOperators documentation. In the Vector class, we have methods that apply operations between two vectors. For instance, we have methods for binary operations (such as add(), div(), sub(), and mul()), for comparisons (such as eq(), lt(), and compare()), for mathematical operations (such as abs()), and so on. Moreover, in VectorOperators we have a bunch of nested classes (for instance, VectorOperators. Associative) and several constants representing *lanewise* operations such as trigonometric functions (SIN, COS, and so on), bitwise shifting operations (LSHL and LSHR), mathematical operations (ABS, SQRT, and POW), and so on.

In the following problems, you'll see a part of these operations at work, but for now let's touch on the last essential topic, creating vectors.

Creating vectors

We already know that having a VectorSpecies is like having a factory for creating vectors of the required *element type* and *shape*. Now, let's see how we can use such a factory to effectively create vectors (fill them up with scalars) that get involved in solving real problems.

Let's assume the following *species* (a vector of 8 *lanes*, 32*8=256):

```
static final VectorSpecies<Integer> VS256
  = IntVector.SPECIES_256;
```

Next, let's create the most common types of vectors.

Creating vectors of zeros

Let's assume that we need a vector containing only zeros. A quick approach relies on the zero() method as follows:

```
// [0, 0, 0, 0, 0, 0, 0, 0]
Vector<Integer> v = VS256.zero();
```

This produced a vector with 8 *lanes* of 0.0. The same thing can be obtained from the specialized IntVector class as well via zero(VectorSpecies<Integer> species):

```
IntVector v = IntVector.zero(VS256);
```

You can easily extrapolate this example to FloatVector, DoubleVector, and so on.

Creating vectors of the same primitive value

Creating a vector and loading it up with a primitive value can quickly be accomplished via the broadcast() method as follows:

```
// [5, 5, 5, 5, 5, 5, 5, 5]
Vector<Integer> v = VS256.broadcast(5);
```

The same thing can be obtained from the specialized IntVector class as well via broadcast(VectorSpecies<Integer> species, int e) or broadcast(VectorSpecies<Integer> species, long e):

```
IntVector v = IntVector.broadcast(VS256, 5);
```

Of course, we can use it to broadcast a vector of zeros as well:

```
// [0, 0, 0, 0, 0, 0, 0, 0]
Vector<Integer> v = VS256.broadcast(0);
IntVectorv = IntVector.broadcast(VS256, 0);
```

Finally, let's see the most common use case for creating a vector.

Creating vectors from Java arrays

Creating vectors from Java arrays is the most common use case. Practically, we start from a Java array and call the fromArray() method name.

Using fromArray() from VectorSpecies

The `fromArray()` method is available in `VectorSpecies` as `fromArray(Object a, int offset)`. Here is an example of creating a vector from an array of integers:

```
int[] varr = new int[] {0, 1, 2, 3, 4, 5, 6, 7};
Vector<Integer> v = VS256.fromArray(varr, 0);
```

Since the `varr` length (8) is equal to the vector length and we start from index 0, the resulting vector will contain all the scalars from the array. This is no longer true in the following example where the last 4 scalars will not be part of the resulting vector:

```
int[] varr = new int[] {0, 1, 2, 3, 4, 5, 6, 7, 8, 9, 10, 11};
Vector<Integer> v = VS256.fromArray(varr, 0);
```

The scalars 8, 9, 10, and 11 are not present in the resulting array. Here is another example, using `offset = 2`:

```
int[] varr = new int[] {0, 1, 2, 3, 4, 5, 6, 7, 8, 9, 10, 11};
Vector<Integer> v = VS256.fromArray(varr, 2);
```

This time, the scalars 0, 1, 10, and 11 are not present in the resulting array.

Pay attention that the length of the Java array shouldn't be less than the vector's length. For instance, the following example will cause an exception:

```
int[] varr = new int[]{0, 1, 2, 3, 4, 5};
IntVector v = IntVector.fromArray(VS256, varr, 0);
```

Since the Java array length is 6 (less than 8), this will cause a `java.lang.IndexOutOfBoundsException` instance. So, the minimum accepted length for `varr` is 8.

Using fromArray() from specialized vectors

Each specialized vector class provides a bunch of `fromArray()` flavors. For instance, the `IntVector` exposes the popular `fromArray(VectorSpecies<Integer> species, int[] a, int offset)` method, which can be used in a straightforward way:

```
int[] varr = new int[] {0, 1, 2, 3, 4, 5, 6, 7};
IntVector v = IntVector.fromArray(VS256, varr, 0);
```

If we prefer the `fromArray(VectorSpecies<Integer> species, int[] a, int offset, VectorMask<Integer> m)` flavor, then we can filter the selected scalars from the Java array via `VectorMask`. Here is an example:

```
int[] varr = new int[]{0, 1, 2, 3, 4, 5, 6, 7};
boolean[] bm = new boolean[]{
    false, false, true, false, false, true, true, false};

VectorMask m = VectorMask.fromArray(VS256, bm, 0);
IntVector v = IntVector.fromArray(VS256, varr, 0, m);
```

Based on a one-to-one match, we can easily observe that the resulting vector will fetch only the scalars 2, 5, and 6. The resulting vector will be: [0, 0, 2, 0, 0, 5, 6, 0].

Another flavor of `fromArray()` is `fromArray(VectorSpecies<Integer> species, int[] a, int offset, int[] indexMap, int mapOffset)`. This time, we use a map of indexes to filter the selected scalars:

```
int[] varr = new int[]{11, 12, 15, 17, 20, 22, 29};
int[] imap = new int[]{0, 0, 0, 1, 1, 6, 6, 6};


IntVector v = IntVector.fromArray(VS256, varr, 0, imap, 0);
```

The resulting array will be: [11, 11, 11, 12, 12, 29, 29, 29]. We have 11 from index 0, 12 from index 1, and 29 from index 6.

In addition, we can apply `VectorMask` to the previous index map via `fromArray(VectorSpecies<Integer> species, int[] a, int offset, int[] indexMap, int mapOffset, VectorMask<Integer> m)`:

```
int[] varr = new int[]{11, 12, 15, 17, 20, 22, 29};
boolean[] bm = new boolean[]{
  false, false, true, false, false, true, true, false};
int[] imap = new int[]{0, 0, 0, 1, 1, 6, 6, 6};


VectorMask m = VectorMask.fromArray(VS256, bm, 0);
IntVector v = IntVector.fromArray(VS256, varr, 0, imap, 0, m);
```

The resulting vector is: [0, 0, 11, 0, 0, 29, 29, 0].

Creating vectors from memory segments

Memory segments are a topic covered in detail in *Chapter 7* as part of the Foreign Function and Memory API, but as a quick teaser, here is an example of creating a vector from a memory segment via `IntVector.fromMemorySegment()`:

```
IntVector v;
MemorySegment segment;
try (Arena arena = Arena.ofConfined()) {
  segment = arena.allocate(32);
  segment.setAtIndex(ValueLayout.JAVA_INT, 0, 11);
  segment.setAtIndex(ValueLayout.JAVA_INT, 1, 21);
  // continue set: 12, 7, 33, 1, 3
  segment.setAtIndex(ValueLayout.JAVA_INT, 7, 6);
```

```
  v = IntVector.fromMemorySegment(VS256, segment,
    0, ByteOrder.nativeOrder());
}
```

The created vector is: [11, 21, 12, 7, 33, 1, 3, 6].

In the bundled code, you can find several more examples for manipulating data across lane boundaries such as slicing, un-slicing, shuffling/rearranging, compressing, expanding, converting, casting, and reinterpreting shapes.

In the next problem, we start creating complete examples that exploit what we've learned so far.

109. Summing two arrays via the Vector API

Summing two arrays is the perfect start for applying what we've learned in the preceding two problems. Let's assume that we have the following Java arrays:

```
int[] x = new int[]{1, 2, 3, 4, 5, 6, 7, 8};
int[] y = new int[]{4, 5, 2, 5, 1, 3, 8, 7};
```

For computing z=x+y via the Vector API, we have to create two Vector instances and rely on the add() operation, z=x.add(y). Since the Java arrays hold integer scalars, we can use the IntVector specialization as follows:

```
IntVector xVector = IntVector.fromArray(
  IntVector.SPECIES_256, x, 0);
IntVector yVector = IntVector.fromArray(
  IntVector.SPECIES_256, y, 0);
```

In Java, an integer needs 4 bytes, so 32 bits. Since x and y hold 8 integers, we need 8*32=256 bits to represent them in our vector. So, relying on SPECIES_256 is the right choice.

Next, we can apply the add() operation as follows:

```
IntVector zVector = xVector.add(yVector);
```

Done! It is time for JVM to generate the optimal set of instructions (data-parallel accelerated code) that will compute our addition. The result will be a vector as [5, 7, 5, 9, 6, 9, 15, 15].

This was a simple case but not quite realistic. Who would employ parallel computational capabilities for summing up two arrays having a couple of elements?! In the real world, x and y may have much more than 8 elements. Most probably, x and y have millions of items and are involved in multiple calculation cycles. That is exactly when we can leverage the power of parallel computation.

But, for now, let's assume that x and y are as follows:

```
x = {3, 6, 5, 5, 1, 2, 3, 4, 5, 6, 7, 8, 3, 6, 5, 5, 1, 2, 3,
     4, 5, 6, 7, 8, 3, 6, 5, 5, 1, 2, 3, 4, 3, 4};
y = {4, 5, 2, 5, 1, 3, 8, 7, 1, 6, 2, 3, 1, 2, 3, 4, 5, 6, 7,
     8, 3, 6, 5, 5, 1, 2, 3, 4, 5, 6, 7, 8, 2, 8};
```

If we apply the previous code (based on SPECIES_256), the result will be the same because our vectors can accommodate only the first 8 scalars and will ignore the rest. If we apply the same logic but use SPECIES_PREFERRED, then the result is unpredictable since the vector's shape is specific to the current platform. However, we can intuit that we will accommodate the first n (whatever that n is) scalars but not all.

This time, we need to chunk the arrays and use a loop to traverse the arrays and compute z_chunk = x_chunk + y_chunk. The result of summing two chunks is collected in a third array (z) until all chunks are processed. We define a method that starts as follows:

```
public static void sum(int x[], int y[], int z[]) {
    ...
```

But, how big should a chunk be? The first challenge is represented by the loop design. The loop should start from 0, but what are the upper bound and the step? Typically, the upper bound is the length of x, so 34. But, using x.length is not exactly useful because it doesn't guarantee that our vectors will accommodate as many scalars as possible from the arrays. What we are looking for is the largest multiple of VLENGTH (vector's length) that is less than or equal to x.length. In our case, that is the largest multiple of 8 that is less than 34, so 32. This is exactly what the loopBound() method returns, so we can write the loop as follows:

```
private static final VectorSpecies<Integer> VS256
  = IntVector.SPECIES_256;

int upperBound = VS256.loopBound(x.length);
for (int i = 0; i < upperBound; i += VS256.length()) {
    ...
}
```

The loop step is the vector's length. The following diagram pre-visualizes the code:

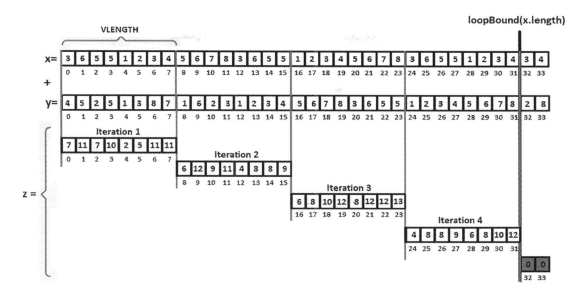

Figure 5.8: Computing z = x + y in chunks

So, at the first iteration, our vectors will accommodate the scalars from index 0 to 7. At the second iteration, the scalars are from index 8 to 15, and so on. Here is the complete code:

```
private static final VectorSpecies<Integer> VS256
  = IntVector.SPECIES_256;


public static void sum(int x[], int y[], int z[]) {

  int upperBound = VS256.loopBound(x.length);
  for (int i = 0; i < upperBound; i += VS256.length()) {

    IntVector xVector = IntVector.fromArray(VS256, x, i);
    IntVector yVector = IntVector.fromArray(VS256, y, i);
    IntVector zVector = xVector.add(yVector);

    zVector.intoArray(z, i);
  }
}
```

The `intoArray(int[] a, int offset)` transfers the scalars from a vector to a Java array. This method comes in different flavors next to `intoMemorySegment()`.

The resulting array will be: [7, 11, 7, 10, 2, 5, 11, 11, 6, 12, 9, 11, 4, 8, 8, 9, 6, 8, 10, 12, 8, 12, 12, 13, 4, 8, 8, 9, 6, 8, 10, 12, 0, 0]. Check out the last two items ... they are equal to 0. These are the items that result from `x.length - upperBound` = 34 – 32 = 2. When the largest multiple of `VLENGTH` (vector's length) is equal to `x.length`, this difference will be 0, otherwise, we will have the rest of the items that have not been computed. So, the previous code will work as expected only in the particular case when `VLENGTH` (vector's length) is equal to `x.length`.

Covering the remaining items can be accomplished in at least two ways. First, we can rely on a `VectorMask` as in the following code:

```java
public static void sumMask(int x[], int y[], int z[]) {

  int upperBound = VS256.loopBound(x.length);
  int i = 0;
  for (; i < upperBound; i += VS256.length()) {

    IntVector xVector = IntVector.fromArray(VS256, x, i);
    IntVector yVector = IntVector.fromArray(VS256, y, i);
    IntVector zVector = xVector.add(yVector);

    zVector.intoArray(z, i);
  }

  if (i <= (x.length - 1)) {
    VectorMask<Integer> mask
        = VS256.indexInRange(i, x.length);

    IntVector zVector = IntVector.fromArray(VS256, x, i, mask)
        .add(IntVector.fromArray(VS256, y, i, mask));

    zVector.intoArray(z, i, mask);
  }
}
```

The `indexInRange()` computes a mask in the range [`i`, `x.length-1`]. Applying this mask will result in the following z array: [7, 11, 7, 10, 2, 5, 11, 11, 6, 12, 9, 11, 4, 8, 8, 9, 6, 8, 10, 12, 8, 12, 12, 13, 4, 8, 8, 9, 6, 8, 10, 12, 5, 12]. Now, the last two items are computed as expected.

Important note

As a rule of thumb, avoid using `VectorMask` in loops. They are quite expensive and may lead to a significant degradation in performance.

Another approach for dealing with these remaining items is to go for a piece of traditional Java code as follows:

```java
public static void sumPlus(int x[], int y[], int z[]) {

  int upperBound = VS256.loopBound(x.length);
  int i = 0;
  for (; i < upperBound; i += VS256.length()) {

    IntVector xVector = IntVector.fromArray(VS256, x, i);
    IntVector yVector = IntVector.fromArray(VS256, y, i);
    IntVector zVector = xVector.add(yVector);

    zVector.intoArray(z, i);
  }

  for (; i < x.length; i++) {
    z[i] = x[i] + y[i];
  }
}
```

Practically, we sum up the remaining items in a Java traditional loop outside the vectors loop. You can check these examples in the bundled code.

110. Summing two arrays unrolled via the Vector API

In this problem, we take the example of summing two arrays from the previous problem and re-write the loop in an *unrolled* fashion.

Loop unrolling can be applied manually (as we will do here) or by the compiler, and it stands for an optimization technique meant to reduce the loop iteration count.

In our case, in order to reduce the loop iteration count, we use more vectors to repeat the sequence of loop body statements that are responsible for summing the items. If we know that our arrays are long enough to always require at least 4 loop iterations, then rewriting the code as follows will reduce the loop iterations by 4 times:

```java
public static void sumUnrolled(int x[], int y[], int z[]) {
```

```
int width = VS256.length();
int i = 0;
for (; i <= (x.length - width * 4); i += width * 4) {

  IntVector s1 = IntVector.fromArray(VS256, x, i)
      .add(IntVector.fromArray(VS256, y, i));
  IntVector s2 = IntVector.fromArray(VS256, x, i + width)
      .add(IntVector.fromArray(VS256, y, i + width));
  IntVector s3 = IntVector.fromArray(VS256, x, i + width * 2)
      .add(IntVector.fromArray(VS256, y, i + width * 2));
  IntVector s4 = IntVector.fromArray(VS256, x, i + width * 3)
      .add(IntVector.fromArray(VS256, y, i + width * 3));

  s1.intoArray(z, i);
  s2.intoArray(z, i + width);
  s3.intoArray(z, i + width * 2);
  s4.intoArray(z, i + width * 3);
  }

  for (; i < x.length; i++) {
  z[i] = x[i] + y[i];
  }
}
```

Consider the following x and y vectors:

```
x = {3, 6, 5, 5, 1, 2, 3, 4, 5, 6, 7, 8, 3, 6, 5, 5, 1, 2, 3,
     4, 5, 6, 7, 8, 3, 6, 5, 5, 1, 2, 3, 4, 3, 4};
y = {4, 5, 2, 5, 1, 3, 8, 7, 1, 6, 2, 3, 1, 2, 3, 4, 5, 6, 7,
     8, 3, 6, 5, 5, 1, 2, 3, 4, 5, 6, 7, 8, 2, 8};
int[] z = new int[x.length];
```

Calling the sumPlus(x, y, z) method written in the previous problem will require 4 loop iterations to complete. Calling sumUnrolled(x, y, z) will require a single iteration to complete.

111. Benchmarking the Vector API

Benchmarking the Vector API can be accomplished via JMH. Let's consider three Java arrays (x, y, z) each of 50,000,000 integers, and the following computation:

```
z[i] = x[i] + y[i];
w[i] = x[i] * z[i] * y[i];
k[i] = z[i] + w[i] * y[i];
```

So, the final result is stored in a Java array named k. And, let's consider the following benchmark containing four different implementations of this computation (using a mask, no mask, *unrolled*, and plain scalar Java with arrays):

```
@OutputTimeUnit(TimeUnit.MILLISECONDS)
@BenchmarkMode({Mode.AverageTime, Mode.Throughput})
@Warmup(iterations = 3, time = 1)
@Measurement(iterations = 5, time = 1)
@State(Scope.Benchmark)
@Fork(value = 1, warmups = 0,
    jvmArgsPrepend = {"--add-modules=jdk.incubator.vector"})
public class Main {

  private static final VectorSpecies<Integer> VS
    = IntVector.SPECIES_PREFERRED;
  ...
  @Benchmark
  public void computeWithMask(Blackhole blackhole) {…}

  @Benchmark
  public void computeNoMask(Blackhole blackhole) {…}

  @Benchmark
  public void computeUnrolled(Blackhole blackhole) {…}

  @Benchmark
  public void computeArrays(Blackhole blackhole) {…}
}
```

Running this benchmark on an Intel(R) Core(TM) i7-3612QM CPU @ 2.10GHz machine running Windows 10 produced the following results:

Benchmark	(length)	Mode	Cnt	Score	Error	Units
Main.computeArrays	50000000	thrpt	5	0.009 ±	0.001	ops/ms
Main.computeNoMask	50000000	thrpt	5	0.019 ±	0.001	ops/ms
Main.computeUnrolledNoMask	50000000	thrpt	5	0.019 ±	0.001	ops/ms
Main.computeWithMask	50000000	thrpt	5	0.019 ±	0.001	ops/ms
Main.computeArrays	50000000	avgt	5	114.407 ±	3.544	ms/op
Main.computeNoMask	50000000	avgt	5	51.316 ±	1.638	ms/op
Main.computeUnrolledNoMask	50000000	avgt	5	51.215 ±	1.088	ms/op
Main.computeWithMask	50000000	avgt	5	51.667 ±	0.736	ms/op

Figure 5.9: Benchmark results

Overall, executing the computation using data-parallel capabilities gives the best performance, highest throughput, and best average time.

112. Applying the Vector API to compute FMA

In a nutshell, **Fused Multiply Add** (**FMA**) is the mathematical computation (a*b) + c, which is heavily exploited in matrix multiplications. That's all we need to cover for this problem, but if you need a primer on FMA, consider *Java Coding Problems, First Edition, Chapter 1, problem 38*.

Implementing FMA via the Vector API can be done via the fma(float b, float c) or fma(Vector<Float> b, Vector<Float> c) operation, the latter is the one you'll see in an example shortly.

Let's assume that we have the following two arrays:

```
float[] x = new float[]{1f, 2f, 3f, 5f, 1f, 8f};
float[] y = new float[]{4f, 5f, 2f, 8f, 5f, 4f};
```

Computing FMA(x, y) can be expressed as the following sequence: $4+0=4 \rightarrow 10+4=14 \rightarrow 6+14=20 \rightarrow 40+20=60 \rightarrow 5+60=65 \rightarrow 32+65=97$. So, FMA(x, y) = 97. Expressing this sequence via the Vector API can be done as shown in the following code:

```
private static final VectorSpecies<Float> VS
  = FloatVector.SPECIES_PREFERRED;

public static float vectorFma(float[] x, float[] y) {

  int upperBound = VS.loopBound(x.length);
  FloatVector sum = FloatVector.zero(VS);
  int i = 0;
  for (; i < upperBound; i += VS.length()) {

    FloatVector xVector = FloatVector.fromArray(VS, x, i);
    FloatVector yVector = FloatVector.fromArray(VS, y, i);
    sum = xVector.fma(yVector, sum);
  }

  if (i <= (x.length - 1)) {
    VectorMask<Float> mask = VS.indexInRange(i, x.length);

    FloatVector xVector = FloatVector.fromArray(
      VS, x, i, mask);
    FloatVector yVector = FloatVector.fromArray(
      VS, y, i, mask);
    sum = xVector.fma(yVector, sum);
  }
```

```
    float result = sum.reduceLanes(VectorOperators.ADD);

    return result;
}
```

Have you noticed the code line `sum = xVector.fma(yVector, sum)`? This is equivalent to `sum = xVector.mul(yVector).add(sum)`.

The novelty here consists of the following line:

```
    float result = sum.reduceLanes(VectorOperators.ADD);
```

This is an associative *cross-lane* reduction operation (see *Figure 5.6*). Before this line, the sum vector looks as follows:

```
    sum= [9.0, 42.0, 6.0, 40.0]
```

By applying the `reduceLanes(VectorOperators.ADD)`, we sum the values of this vector and reduce it to the final result, 97.0. Cool, right?!

113. Multiplying matrices via the Vector API

Let's consider two matrices of 4x4 denoted as X and Y. Z=X*Y is as follows:

$$\begin{pmatrix} 1 & 2 & 5 & 4 \\ 5 & 4 & 3 & 7 \\ 2 & 2 & 6 & 2 \\ 4 & 1 & 2 & 5 \end{pmatrix} \cdot \begin{pmatrix} 3 & 4 & 1 & 8 \\ 7 & 4 & 9 & 9 \\ 5 & 6 & 7 & 3 \\ 5 & 8 & 7 & 7 \end{pmatrix} = \begin{pmatrix} 62 & 74 & 82 & 69 \\ 93 & 110 & 111 & 134 \\ 60 & 68 & 76 & 66 \\ 54 & 72 & 62 & 82 \end{pmatrix}$$

$$\mathbf{X} \qquad\qquad \mathbf{Y} \qquad\qquad \mathbf{Z}$$

Figure 5.10: Multiplying two matrices (X * Y = Z)

Multiplying X with Y means multiplying the first row from X with the first column from Y, the second row from X with the second column from Y, and so on. For instance, (1 x 3) + (2 x 7) + (5 x 5) + (4 x 5) = 3 + 14 + 25 + 20 = 62. Basically, we repeatedly apply FMA computation and fill up Z with the results.

In this context, and based on the previous problem about computing FMA, we can produce the following code for multiplying X with Y:

```
private static final VectorSpecies<Float> VS
    = FloatVector.SPECIES_PREFERRED;

public static float[] mulMatrix(
    float[] x, float[] y, int size) {

    final int upperBound = VS.loopBound(size);
    float[] z = new float[size * size];
```

```
  for (int i = 0; i < size; i++) {
    for (int k = 0; k < size; k++) {
      float elem = x[i * size + k];
      FloatVector eVector = FloatVector.broadcast(VS, elem);
      for (int j = 0; j < upperBound; j += VS.length()) {
        FloatVector yVector = FloatVector.fromArray(
            VS, y, k * size + j);
        FloatVector zVector = FloatVector.fromArray(
            VS, z, i * size + j);
        zVector = eVector.fma(yVector, zVector);
        zVector.intoArray(z, i * size + j);
      }
    }
  }

  return z;
}
```

In the bundled code, you can find this example next to another one using SPECIES_512.

114. Hooking the image negative filter with the Vector API

An image is basically a matrix of pixels represented in the **Alpha, Red, Green, Blue** (**ARGB**) spectrum. For instance, an image of 232x290 can be represented as a matrix of 67,280 pixels. Applying specific filters (sepia, negative, grayscale, and so on) to an image typically requires processing each pixel from this matrix and performing certain calculations. For instance, the algorithm for applying the negative filter to an image can be used as follows:

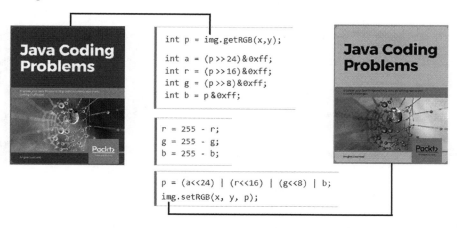

Figure 5.11: Apply the negative filter effect to an image

For each pixel, we extract the color components A, R, G, and B. We subtract the R, G, and B values from 255, and finally, we set the new value to the current pixel.

Let's assume that we have an array (pixel[]) containing all pixels of an image. Next, we want to pass pixel[] as an argument to a method powered by the Vector API capable of applying the negative filter and setting the new values directly in pixel[].

Here is a possible implementation:

```
private static final VectorSpecies<Integer> VS
  = IntVector.SPECIES_PREFERRED;


public static void negativeFilter(
   int pixel[], int width, int height) {

  for (int i = 0; i <= (width * height - VS.length());
          i += VS.length()) {

    IntVector alphaVector = IntVector.fromArray(VS, pixel, i)
      .lanewise(VectorOperators.LSHR, 24).and(0xff);
    IntVector redVector = IntVector.fromArray(VS, pixel, i)
      .lanewise(VectorOperators.LSHR, 16).and(0xff);
    IntVector greenVector = IntVector.fromArray(VS, pixel, i)
      .lanewise(VectorOperators.LSHR, 8).and(0xff);
    IntVector blueVector = IntVector.fromArray(VS, pixel, i)
      .and(0xff);


    IntVector subAlphaVector
      = alphaVector.lanewise(VectorOperators.LSHL, 24);
    IntVector subRedVector = redVector.broadcast(255)
      .sub(redVector).lanewise(VectorOperators.LSHL, 16);
    IntVector subGreenVector = greenVector.broadcast(255)
      .sub(greenVector).lanewise(VectorOperators.LSHL, 8);
    IntVector subBlueVector
      = blueVector.broadcast(255).sub(blueVector);


    IntVector resultVector = subAlphaVector.or(subRedVector)
      .or(subGreenVector).or(subBlueVector);


    resultVector.intoArray(pixel, i);
  }
}
```

In the first part, we extract A, R, G, and B into four vectors (`alphaVector`, `redVector`, `greenVector`, and `blueVector`) by applying the `LSHR` *lanewise* operation. Afterward, we subtract R, G, and B from 255 and compute the new R, G, and B by applying the `LSHL` *lanewise* operation. Next, we compute the new color by applying the bitwise logical disjunction (|) between the new A, R, G, and B values. Finally, we set the new color in the `pixel[]` array.

115. Dissecting factory methods for collections

Using factory methods for collections is a must-have skill. It is very convenient to be able to quickly and effortlessly create and populate unmodifiable/immutable collections before putting them to work.

Factory methods for maps

For instance, before JDK 9, creating an unmodifiable map could be accomplished like this:

```
Map<Integer, String> map = new HashMap<>();
map.put(1, "Java Coding Problems, First Edition");
map.put(2, "The Complete Coding Interview Guide in Java");
map.put(3, "jOOQ Masterclass");

Map<Integer, String> imap = Collections.unmodifiableMap(map);
```

This is useful if, at some point in time, you need an unmodifiable map from a modifiable one. Otherwise, you can take a shortcut as follows (this is known as the *double-brace initialization* technique and, generally, an anti-pattern):

```
Map<Integer, String> imap = Collections.unmodifiableMap(
  new HashMap<Integer, String>() {
    {
      put(1, "Java Coding Problems, First Edition");
      put(2, "The Complete Coding Interview Guide in Java");
      put(3, "jOOQ Masterclass");
    }
  });
```

If you need to return an unmodifiable/immutable map from a `Stream` of `java.util.Map.entry` then here you go:

```
Map<Integer, String> imap = Stream.of(
  entry(1, "Java Coding Problems, First Edition"),
  entry(2, "The Complete Coding Interview Guide in Java"),
  entry(3, "jOOQ Masterclass"))
  .collect(collectingAndThen(
   toMap(e -> e.getKey(), e -> e.getValue()),
   Collections::unmodifiableMap));
```

Moreover, let's not forget the empty and singleton maps (quite useful to return a map from a method instead of null):

```
Map<Integer, String> imap = Collections.emptyMap();
Map<Integer, String> imap = Collections.singletonMap(
  1, "Java Coding Problems, First Edition");
```

Starting with JDK 9, we can rely on a more convenient approach for creating unmodifiable/immutable maps thanks to JEP 269: *Convenience Factory Methods for Collections*. This approach consists of Map.of(), which is available from 0 to 10 mappings or, in other words, is overloaded to support 0 to 10 key-value pairs. Here, we use Map.of() for three mappings:

```
Map<Integer, String> imap = Map.of(
  1, "Java Coding Problems, First Edition",
  2, "The Complete Coding Interview Guide in Java",
  3, "jOOQ Masterclass"
);
```

Maps created via Map.of() don't allow null keys or values. Such attempts will end up in a NullPointerException.

If you need more than 10 mappings then you can rely on static <K,V> Map<K,V> ofEntries(Entry<? Extends K,? extends V>... entries) as follows:

```
import static java.util.Map.entry;
...
Map<Integer, String> imap2jdk9 = Map.ofEntries(
  entry(1, "Java Coding Problems, First Edition"),
  entry(2, "The Complete Coding Interview Guide in Java"),
  entry(3, "jOOQ Masterclass")
);
```

Finally, creating an unmodifiable/immutable map from an existing one can be done via static <K,V> Map<K,V> copyOf(Map<? extends K,? extends V> map):

```
Map<Integer, String> imap = Map.copyOf(map);
```

If the given map is unmodifiable then Java will most probably not create a copy and will return an existing instance. In other words, imap == map will return true. If the given map is modifiable then most probably the factory will return a new instance, so imap == map will return false.

Factory methods for lists

Before JDK 9, a modifiable List could be used for creating an unmodifiable List with the same content as follows:

```
List<String> list = new ArrayList<>();
list.add("Java Coding Problems, First Edition");
```

```
list.add("The Complete Coding Interview Guide in Java");
list.add("jOOQ Masterclass");

List<String> ilist = Collections.unmodifiableList(list);
```

A common approach for creating a List consists of using Arrays.asList():

```
List<String> ilist = Arrays.asList(
  "Java Coding Problems, First Edition",
  "The Complete Coding Interview Guide in Java",
  "jOOQ Masterclass"
);
```

However, keep in mind that this is a fixed-size list, not an unmodifiable/immutable list. In other words, operations that attempt to modify the list size (for instance, ilist.add(…)) will result in UnsupportedOperationException, while operations that modify the current content of the list (for instance, ilist.set(…)) are allowed.

If you need to return an unmodifiable/immutable List from a Stream then here you go:

```
List<String> ilist = Stream.of(
  "Java Coding Problems, First Edition",
  "The Complete Coding Interview Guide in Java",
  "jOOQ Masterclass")
.collect(collectingAndThen(toList(),
        Collections::unmodifiableList));
```

Moreover, creating an empty/singleton list can be done as follows:

```
List<String> ilist = Collections.emptyList();
List<String> ilist = Collections.singletonList(
  "Java Coding Problems, First Edition");
```

Starting with JDK 9+, it is more convenient to rely on the List.of() factory methods available for 0 to 10 elements (null elements are not allowed):

```
List<String> ilist = List.of(
  "Java Coding Problems, First Edition",
  "The Complete Coding Interview Guide in Java",
  "jOOQ Masterclass");
```

If you need a copy of an existing list then rely on List.copyOf():

```
List<String> ilist = List.copyOf(list);
```

If the given list is unmodifiable then Java will most probably not create a copy and will return an existing instance. In other words, ilist == list will return true. If the given list is modifiable then the factory will most likely return a new instance, so ilist == list will return false.

Factory methods for sets

Creating Set instances follows the same path as List instances. However, note that there is no singletonSet(). To create a singleton set, simply call singleton():

```
Set<String> iset = Collections.singleton(
    "Java Coding Problems, First Edition");
```

You can find more examples in the bundled code. You may also be interested in *Problem 109* from *Java Coding Problems, First Edition*, which covers unmodifiable versus immutable collections. Moreover, please consider the next problem presented here as well, since it provides more info on this context.

116. Getting a list from a stream

Collecting a Stream into a List is a popular task that occurs all over the place in applications that manipulate streams and collections.

In JDK 8, collecting a Stream into a List can be done via the toList() collector as follows:

```
List<File> roots = Stream.of(File.listRoots())
    .collect(Collectors.toList());
```

Starting with JDK 10, we can rely on the toUnmodifiableList() collector (for maps, use toUnmodifiableMap(), and for sets, toUnmodifiableSet()):

```
List<File> roots = Stream.of(File.listRoots())
    .collect(Collectors.toUnmodifiableList());
```

Obviously, the returned list is an unmodifiable/immutable list.

JDK 16 has introduced the following toList() default method in the Stream interface:

```
default List<T> toList() {
    return (List<T>) Collections.unmodifiableList(
        new ArrayList<>(Arrays.asList(this.toArray())));
}
```

Using this method to collect a Stream into an unmodifiable/immutable list is straightforward (pay attention that this is not like Collectors.toList(), which returns a modifiable list):

```
List<File> roots = Stream.of(File.listRoots()).toList();
```

In the bundled code, you can also find an example of combining flatMap() and toList().

117. Handling map capacity

Let's assume that we need a List capable of holding 260 items. We can do it as follows:

```
List<String> list = new ArrayList<>(260);
```

The array underlying `ArrayList` is created directly to accommodate 260 items. In other words, we can insert 260 items without worrying about resizing or enlarging the list several times in order to hold these 260 items.

Following this logic, we can reproduce it for a map as well:

```
Map<Integer, String> map = new HashMap<>(260);
```

So, now we can assume that we have a map capable of accommodating 260 mappings. Actually, no, this assumption is not true! A `HashMap` works on the *hashing* principle and is initialized with an initial capacity (16 if no explicit initial capacity is provided) representing the number of internal buckets and a default *load factor* of 0.75. What does that mean? It means that when a `HashMap` reaches 75% of its current capacity, it is doubled in size and a rehashing takes place. This guarantees that the mappings are evenly distributed in the internal buckets. But, for significantly large maps, this is an expensive operation. Javadoc states that *"creating a HashMap with a sufficiently large capacity will allow the mappings to be stored more efficiently than letting it perform automatic rehashing as needed to grow the table."*

In our case, it means that a map can hold 260 x 0.75 = 195 mappings. In other words, when we insert the 195th mapping, the map will be automatically resized to 260 * 2 = 520 mappings.

To create a `HashMap` for 260 mappings, we have to calculate the initial capacity as the number of mappings/load factor: 260 / 0.75 = 347 mappings:

```
// accommodate 260 mappings without resizing
Map<Integer, String> map = new HashMap<>(347);
```

Or, if we want to express it as a formula, we can do it as follows:

```
Map<Integer, String> map = new HashMap<>(
   (int) Math.ceil(260 / (double) 0.75));
```

Starting with JDK 19, this formula has been hidden behind the `static <K,V> HashMap<K,V> newHashMap(int numMappings)` method. This time, `numMappings` represents the number of mappings, so we can write this:

```
// accommodate 260 mappings without resizing
Map<Integer, String> map = HashMap.newHashMap(260);
```

Analog methods exist for `HashSet`, `LinkedHashSet`, `LinkedHashMap`, and `WeakHashMap`.

118. Tackling Sequenced Collections

The Sequenced Collections API was added as a final feature in JDK 21 under JEP 431. Its main goal is to make the navigation of Java collections easier by providing a common API to all collections having a well-defined encounter order.

A Java collection with a well-defined encounter order has a well-defined first element, second element, and so on, until the last element. The encounter order is the order in which an `Iterator` will iterate the elements of a collection (list, set, sorted set, map, and so on). The encounter order can take advantage of stability over time (lists) or not (sets).

This API consists of 3 interfaces named SequencedCollection (valid for any collection that has a well-defined encounter order), SequencedSet (extends SequencedCollection and Set to provide support for Java sets), and SequencedMap (extends Map to give support to any Java map that has a well-defined encounter order). In the following diagram, you can see the locations of these 3 interfaces in the collections type hierarchy:

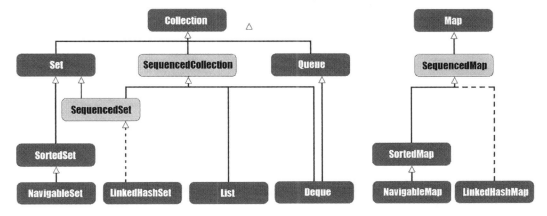

Figure 5.12: The location of the Sequenced Collections API in the collections type hierarchy

The SequencedCollection API targets four main operations on a collection: getting the first/last element, adding a new element in the first/last position, removing the first/last element, and reversing a collection.

The SequencedCollection API defines 7 methods, as follows:

- getFirst() gets the first element of the current collection
- getLast() gets the last element of the current collection
- addFirst(E e) adds the given element e as the first element of the current collection
- addLast(E e) adds the given element e as the last element of the current collection
- removeFirst() removes the first element of the current collection
- removeLast() removes the last element of the current collection
- reversed() returns the reverse collection of the current collection

SequencedSet extends SequencedCollection and overrides the reversed() method to return SequencedSet.

SequencedMap defines the following methods:

- firstEntry() returns the first entry (first key-value mapping) from the current map
- lastEntry() returns the last entry (last key-value mapping) from the current map
- putFirst(K k, V v) attempts to insert (or replace) the given key-value mapping as the first mapping in the current map
- putLast(K k, V v) attempts to insert (or replace) the given key-value mapping as the last mapping in the current map

- pollFirstEntry() removes and returns the first entry (first key-value mapping) from the current map (if no entry is present then it returns null)
- pollLastEntry() removes and returns the last entry (last key-value mapping) from the current map (if no entry is present then it returns null)
- reversed() returns the reverse map of the current map
- sequencedEntrySet() returns a SequencedSet view of the entry set (entrySet()) of the current map
- sequencedKeySet() returns a SequencedSet view of the key set (keyset()) of the current map
- sequencedValues() returns a SequencedCollection view of the values (values()) of the current map

The well-defined encounter order is a property spread across the collections type hierarchy, so we have to consider that the Sequenced Collections API works completely with some collections, partially with others, and not at all with yet others. Let's tackle a few common collections and try out this new API.

Applying the Sequenced Collections API to lists

Java lists (implementations of List) rely on indexes to support a well-defined (stable) encounter order, so they are a perfect candidate for the Sequenced Collections API.

Next, let's see how we can exploit the Sequenced Collections API for two of the most popular implementations of List. Obviously, we are talking about ArrayList and LinkedList. ArrayList and LinkedList implement SequencedCollection.

Applying the Sequenced Collections API to ArrayList and LinkedList

Let's assume that we have the following ArrayList and LinkedList:

```
List<String> list = new ArrayList<>(
  Arrays.asList("one", "two", "three", "four", "five"));


List<String> linkedlist = new LinkedList<>(
  Arrays.asList("one", "two", "three", "four", "five"));
```

Getting the first element from ArrayList is quite simple. The first element is at index 0, so calling get(0) is all we need to do:

```
String first = list.get(0); // one
```

Getting the last element is a little trickier. We don't know the index of the last element but we know the size of the list, so we can write this (it is not neat, but it works):

```
String last = list.get(list.size() - 1); // five
```

On the other hand, if we rely on the JDK 21 Sequenced Collections API then we can get the first and last elements as follows:

```
String first = list.getFirst(); // one
String last = list.getLast();  // five
```

That's really neat and applies to the LinkedList as well! We don't involve any explicit indexes.

Adding an element in the first position means adding an element at index 0 via the well-known add(index, element). Moreover, adding an element in the last position means calling the add(element) method without an explicit index as follows:

```
list.add(0, "zero"); // add on the first position
list.add("six");     // add on the last position
```

Adding the same elements via the Sequenced Collections API can be done as follows:

```
list.addFirst("zero");
list.addLast("six");
```

Removing the first/last element can be done via the remove() method and the proper indexes as follows:

```
list.remove(0);                 // remove the first element
list.remove(list.size() - 1);   // remove the last element
```

If we know the value of the last element then we can remove it without an explicit index as follows:

```
list.remove("five");
```

Removing the same elements via the Sequenced Collections API can be done as follows:

```
list.removeFirst();
list.removeLast();
```

So, using the Sequenced Collections API is straightforward. No arguments are involved. And, this works for LinkedList as well.

Reversing the list can be done via the Collections.reverse() helper. This method reverses the given list:

```
Collections.reverse(list);
```

On the other hand, the Sequenced Collections API returns a new list representing the reverse of the given list as follows:

```
List<String> reversedList = list.reversed();
```

Again, the same code works for LinkedList as well. So, the Sequenced Collections API works perfectly for lists.

Applying the Sequenced Collections API to sets

Java sets (implementations of Set) can be split into two categories. We have sorted sets (implementations of SortedSet) that support a well-defined (stable) encounter order and sets that make no guarantees as to the iteration order (HashSet).

A SortedSet has an order dictated by the logic of a comparator (*natural ordering* or Comparator). When we insert a new element in a sorted set, the comparator logic decides where this element will land, so we don't know the index value of an element. However, a sorted set has the notion of first and last elements and an Iterator will iterate the elements in the order settled by the comparator.

On the other hand, a set such as HashSet has no guarantees as to the iteration order. The elements of a HashSet are ordered by its internal hashing algorithms. An Iterator over a HashSet iterates its elements in no particular order and, when we insert a new element, we have no idea where this element will land in the HashSet.

Next, let's see how we can exploit the Sequenced Collections API for three of the most popular sets. We choose HashSet (an implementation of Set), LinkedHashSet (an extension of HashSet), and TreeSet (an implementation of NavigableSet that extends SortedSet).

Applying the Sequenced Collections API to HashSet

A HashSet iterates its elements in no particular order, which means that a HashSet has no idea (stability) of the first, second, or last elements. Iterating the same HashSet multiple times may result in different outputs. In this context, we can add an element to a set via the add(E e) method. The element will be added only if it doesn't exist already and will land in a position computed by the HashSet internal hashing algorithms. Moreover, we can remove an element by its value via remove(Object o). Since the order of elements is not stable, it doesn't make sense to reverse HashSet. In this context, the Sequenced Collections API doesn't work at all, so HashSet doesn't take advantage of this API.

Applying the Sequenced Collections API to LinkedHashSet

A LinkedHashSet is a HashSet that relies on a doubly-linked list to maintain a well-defined encounter order. A LinkedHashSet implements SequencedSet, so it can take advantage of the Sequenced Collections API. Let's deep dive into the following LinkedHashSet:

```
SequencedSet<String> linkedhashset = new LinkedHashSet<>(
  Arrays.asList("one", "two", "three", "four", "five"));
```

The LinkedHashSet doesn't expose an API for getting the first/last elements. However, we can rely on the well-defined encounter order and on the Iterator (or Stream) API to get the first element as follows:

```
linkedhashset.iterator().next();
linkedhashset.stream().findFirst().get();
```

This is not neat, and for the last element it is even worse:

```
linkedhashset.stream().skip(
  linkedhashset.size() - 1).findFirst().get();
String last = (String) linkedhashset.toArray()
  [linkedhashset.size() - 1];
```

Fortunately, JDK 21 simplifies this task via the getFirst() and getLast() methods:

```
linkedhashset.getFirst();
linkedhashset.getLast();
```

Adding an element into LinkedHashSet is possible only if that element doesn't exist. This is normal since sets don't accept doubles as lists. However, adding on the first position is not an easy task (we can do it if we transform LinkedHashSet into another collection, add the element on the first position, and convert back to LinkedHashSet) so we skipped that here. Adding an element to the last position is easy via the add() method:

```
// cannot add on first position
linkedhashset.add("six"); // add on last position
```

But if we rely on the Sequenced Collections API, then we can add on the first/last position via addFirst()/addLast():

```
linkedhashset.addFirst("zero");
linkedhashset.addLast("six");
```

Removing the first/last element is possible only if we know the values of those elements:

```
linkedhashset.remove("one");
linkedhashset.remove("five");
```

Obviously, this approach is not robust and safe and you'll prefer to get the first/last elements as you saw earlier via Iterator/Stream, and call remove() on those elements afterward. However, the more appropriate option is to rely on the Sequenced Collections API:

```
linkedhashset.removeFirst();
linkedhashset.removeLast();
```

There is no other straightforward solution to reverse LinkedHashSet than using the Sequenced Collections API:

```
SequencedSet<String> reversedLhs = linkedhashset.reversed();
```

So, as you can see, the Sequenced Collections API really simplifies the usage of LinkedHashSet. Cool!

Applying the Sequenced Collections API to TreeSet

A TreeSet is a sorted set that implements NavigableSet (an extension of SortedSet) so it takes advantage of all methods of a sorted set plus some navigation methods. It also implements SequencedCollection and SequencedSet.

Let's consider the following TreeSet:

```
SortedSet<String> sortedset = new TreeSet<>(
  Arrays.asList("one", "two", "three", "four", "five"));
```

Relying on the default comparator for strings (that is, natural ordering, which compares two strings lexicographically), the sorted set will be *five, four, one, three, two*. So, the first element is *five*, and the last element is *two*. Getting the first/last element of a sorted set can be done via the first() and last() methods:

```
sortedset.first();
sortedset.last();
```

So, the Sequenced Collections API doesn't bring significant value in this case:

```
sortedset.getFirst();
sortedset.getLast();
```

Adding a new element to the first/last position in a sorted set is not possible. Since the order of elements is dictated by a comparator (natural ordering or an explicit Comparator), we cannot guarantee that an added element will land in the first or last position. For instance, the following code will not add the elements as we may expect (zero as the first element, and six as the last element):

```
sortedset.add("zero");
sortedset.add("six");
```

After applying the lexicographical criteria, the resulting sorted set will be *five, four, one, six, three, two, zero*. So, *zero* is actually the last element and *six* is the fourth element.

Trying to apply the Sequenced Collections API (addFirst()/addLast()) will throw an UnsupportedOperationException exception.

How about removing the first/last elements from a sorted set? Since we can get the first/last elements of a tree set, we can also remove them as follows:

```
String first = sortedset.first();
sortedset.remove(first);

String last = sortedset.last();
sortedset.remove(last);
```

The Sequenced Collections API implementation represents a shortcut of the previous code:

```
sortedset.removeFirst();
sortedset.removeLast();
```

Reversing a sorted set can be done via descendingSet() or descendingIterator(). Both of them are available in TreeSet, so here is the usage of descendingSet():

```
SortedSet<String> reversedSortedSet
    = new TreeSet<>(sortedset).descendingSet();
```

It is much neater to rely on the Sequenced Collections API as follows:

```
SortedSet<String> reversedSortedSet = sortedset.reversed();
```

Cool, right?!

Applying the Sequenced Collections API to maps

Java maps (implementations of Map) may have a well-defined encounter order (for instance, LinkedHashMap (implementation of Map and SequencedMap), TreeMap (implementation of SortedMap and SequencedMap)) or an unstable order over time (for instance, HashMap implementation of Map). Exactly as in the case of HashSet, HashMap cannot take advantage of the Sequenced Collections API.

Applying the Sequenced Collections API to LinkedHashMap

LinkedHashMap is a map with a well-defined encounter order. Here is an example:

```
SequencedMap<Integer, String> linkedhashmap
  = new LinkedHashMap<>();
linkedhashmap.put(1, "one");
linkedhashmap.put(2, "two");
linkedhashmap.put(3, "three");
linkedhashmap.put(4, "four");
linkedhashmap.put(5, "five");
```

Getting the first entry (Map.Entry) from a linked hash map can be done via the Iterator/Stream API as follows:

```
linkedhashmap.entrySet().iterator().next();
linkedhashmap.entrySet().stream().findFirst().get();
```

The same logic can be applied to get the first key (via keyset()) or the first value (via values()):

```
linkedhashmap.keySet().iterator().next();
linkedhashmap.keySet().stream().findFirst().get();

linkedhashmap.values().iterator().next();
linkedhashmap.values().stream().findFirst().get();
```

Getting the last entry/key/value requires code that is even uglier than the previous code:

```
linkedhashmap.entrySet().stream()
  .skip(linkedhashmap.size() - 1).findFirst().get();
Entry<Integer, String> lastEntryLhm = (Entry<Integer, String>)
  linkedhashmap.entrySet().toArray()[linkedhashmap.size() - 1];

linkedhashmap.keySet().stream()
  .skip(linkedhashmap.size() - 1).findFirst().get();
Integer lastKeyLhm = (Integer) linkedhashmap.keySet()
  .toArray()[linkedhashmap.size() - 1];

linkedhashmap.values().stream()
```

```
  .skip(linkedhashmap.size() - 1).findFirst().get();
String lastValueLhm = (String) linkedhashmap.values()
  .toArray()[linkedhashmap.size() - 1];
```

In this case, the Sequenced Collections API is really useful for avoiding such painful and cumbersome code. For instance, getting the first element from `LinkedHashMap` via the Sequenced Collections API can be done via `firstEntry()`/`lastEntry()` as follows:

```
Entry<Integer, String> fe = linkedhashmap.firstEntry();
Entry<Integer, String> le = linkedhashmap.lastEntry();
```

While there is no `firstKey()`/`lastKey()` or `firstValue()`/`lastValue()`, we can get the first key/value via `sequencedKeySet()` and `sequencedValues()` as follows:

```
SequencedSet<Integer> keysLinkedHashMap
  = linkedhashmap.sequencedKeySet();
keysLinkedHashMap.getFirst();
keysLinkedHashMap.getLast();

SequencedCollection<String> valuesLinkedHashMap
  = linkedhashmap.sequencedValues();
valuesLinkedHashMap.getFirst();
valuesLinkedHashMap.getLast();
```

The same logic can be applied for entries as well via `sequencedEntrySet()`:

```
SequencedSet<Entry<Integer, String>> entriesLinkedHashMap
  = linkedhashmap.sequencedEntrySet();
entriesLinkedHashMap.getFirst();
entriesLinkedHashMap.getLast();
```

But, obviously, using `firsEntry()`/`lastEntry()` is neater.

Adding a new entry on the last position is possible by simply calling `put(K key, V value)`. However, adding a new entry to the first position cannot be done that easily. But, we can create a new `LinkedHashMap` and put the new entry into it. Afterwards, we copy the entries from the original `LinkedHashMap` as follows:

```
SequencedMap<Integer, String> slinkedhashmap
  = new LinkedHashMap<>();
slinkedhashmap.put(0, "zero"); // add the first entry
slinkedhashmap.putAll(linkedhashmap);
slinkedhashmap.put(6, "six");  // add the last entry
```

The resulting `slinkedhashmap` will contain the following entries: *0=zero, 1=one, 2=two, 3=three, 4=four, 5=five, 6=six.*

Obviously, this is far from an optimal and elegant approach. We would do better to rely on the Sequenced Collections API's putFirst()/putLast() as follows:

```
linkedhashmap.putFirst(0, "zero");
linkedhashmap.putLast(6, "six");
```

That's quite neat!

Removing the first/last entry can be done in two steps. First, we get the first/last entry from LinkedHashMap via the Iterator/Stream APIs. Second, we rely on the remove() method as follows:

```
Entry<Integer, String> firstentrylhm
  = linkedhashmap.entrySet().iterator().next();
linkedhashmap.remove(firstentrylhm.getKey());
// or, like this
linkedhashmap.remove(
  firstentrylhm.getKey(), firstentrylhm.getValue());

Entry<Integer, String> lastEntryLhm
  = linkedhashmap.entrySet().stream().skip(
      linkedhashmap.size() - 1).findFirst().get();
linkedhashmap.remove(lastEntryLhm.getKey());
// or, like this
linkedhashmap.remove(
  lastEntryLhm.getKey(), lastEntryLhm.getValue());
```

Wow! That's ugly, right?! Fortunately, the Sequenced Collections API exposes pollFirstEntry()/pollLastEntry() precisely for this purpose:

```
linkedhashmap.pollFirstEntry();
linkedhashmap.pollLastEntry();
```

Reversing LinkedHashMap is also tricky. There are multiple cumbersome approaches, one of which is to create a new LinkedHashMap. Then, employ the descendingIterator() API to iterate the original LinkedHashMap from end to start while adding to the new LinkedHashMap:

```
SequencedMap<Integer, String> reversedlinkedhashmap
  = new LinkedHashMap<>();
Set<Integer> setKeys = linkedhashmap.keySet();
LinkedList<Integer> listKeys = new LinkedList<>(setKeys);
Iterator<Integer> iterator = listKeys.descendingIterator();

while (iterator.hasNext()) {
  Integer key = iterator.next();
  reversedlinkedhashmap.put(key, linkedhashmap.get(key));
}
```

This code is hard to digest! It would be better to use the Sequenced Collections API, which exposes the reversed() method:

```
SequencedMap<Integer, String> reversedMap
  = linkedhashmap.reversed();
```

That's simple!

Applying the Sequenced Collections API to SortedMap (TreeMap)

SortedMap extends SequencedMap and keeps its entries sorted by the natural ordering or by an explicit Comparator. Let's give it a try on a TreeMap implementation of SortedMap:

```
SortedMap<Integer, String> sortedmap = new TreeMap<>();
sortedmap.put(1, "one");
sortedmap.put(2, "two");
sortedmap.put(3, "three");
sortedmap.put(4, "four");
sortedmap.put(5, "five");
```

Getting the first/last entry from TreeMap can be done via the firstKey() and lastKey() methods respectively, like this:

```
Integer fkey = sortedmap.firstKey(); // first key
String fval = sortedmap.get(fkey);   // first value

Integer lkey = sortedmap.lastKey();  // last key
String lval = sortedmap.get(lkey);   // last value
```

If we prefer the Sequenced Collections API, then we can use firstEntry()/lastEntry():

```
sortedmap.firstEntry();
sortedmap.firstEntry().getKey();
sortedmap.firstEntry().getValue();

sortedmap.lastEntry();
sortedmap.lastEntry().getKey();
sortedmap.lastEntry().getValue();
```

In addition, sorted maps can take advantage of sequencedKeySet(), sequencedValues(), and sequencedEntrySet() as follows:

```
SequencedSet<Integer> keysSortedMap
  = sortedmap.sequencedKeySet();
keysSortedMap.getFirst();
keysSortedMap.getLast();

SequencedCollection<String> valuesSortedMap
```

```
    = sortedmap.sequencedValues();
valuesSortedMap.getFirst();
valuesSortedMap.getLast();


SequencedSet<Entry<Integer, String>> entriesSortedMap
    = sortedmap.sequencedEntrySet();
entriesSortedMap.getFirst();
entriesSortedMap.getLast();
```

Since a sorted map keeps its entries ordered based on the natural ordering or an explicit Comparator, we cannot add an entry on the first/last position. In other words, what we want to insert on the first/last position may land anywhere in the sorted map depending on the Comparator logic. In this context, the Sequenced Collections API represented by putFirst()/putLast() will throw UnsupportedOperationException:

```
sortedmap.putFirst(0, "zero"); //UnsupportedOperationException
sortedmap.putLast(6, "six");   //UnsupportedOperationException
```

Removing the first/last entry can be done via the remove() methods as follows:

```
Integer fkey = sortedmap.firstKey();
String fval = sortedmap.get(fkey);

Integer lkey = sortedmap.lastKey();
String lval = sortedmap.get(lkey);

sortedmap.remove(fkey);
sortedmap.remove(fkey, fval);
sortedmap.remove(lkey);
sortedmap.remove(lkey, lval);
```

The Sequenced Collections API can significantly reduce this code via pollFirstEntry() and pollLastEntry():

```
sortedmap.pollFirstEntry();
sortedmap.pollLastEntry();
```

Reversing a sorted map can be done via descendingMap() (or descendingKeySet()):

```
NavigableMap<Integer, String> reversednavigablemap
    = ((TreeMap) sortedmap).descendingMap();
```

Or, we can keep things simple via the Sequenced Collections API, which exposes the reversed() method:

```
SortedMap<Integer, String> reversedsortedmap
    = sortedmap.reversed();
```

Done! As you have just seen, the Sequenced Collections API is quite useful and easy to use. Feel free to exploit it on other collections as well.

119. Introducing the Rope data structure

Prerequisite: Starting with this problem, we will cover a bunch of complex data structures that require previous experience with binary trees, lists, heaps, queues, stacks, and so on. If you are a novice in the data structure field, then I strongly recommend you postpone the following problems until you manage to read *The Complete Coding Interview Guide in Java*, which provides deep coverage of these preliminary topics.

When we need to handle large amounts of text (for instance, if we were developing a text editor or a powerful text search engine), we have to deal with a significant number of complex tasks. Among these tasks, we have to consider appending/concatenating strings and memory consumption.

The Rope data structure is a special binary tree that aims to improve string operations while using memory efficiently (which is especially useful for large strings). Its Big O goals are listed in the following figure:

Operation	Rope	String
Index	O(log n)	O(1)
Insert	O(log n) no rebalancing O(n) worst case	O(n)
Delete	O(log n)	O(n)
Concat	O(log n) no rebalancing O(n) worst case	O(n)
Split	O(log n)	O(1)

Figure 5.13: Big O for Rope

Being a binary tree, a Rope can be shaped via the classical Node class as follows:

```java
public static class Node {

  private Node left;
  private Node right;

  private int weight;
  private String str;

  public Node(String str) {
    this(null, null, str.length(), str);
  }

  public Node(Node left, Node right, int weight) {
```

```
      this(left, right, weight, null);
   }

   public Node(Node left, Node right, int weight, String str) {
      this.left = left;
      this.right = right;
      this.str = str;
      this.weight = weight;
   }
}
```

Each node holds pointers to its children (left and right) and the total weight of the nodes in its left subtree (weight). Leaf nodes store small chunks of the large string (str). Here is a Rope for the text *I am a very cool rope*:

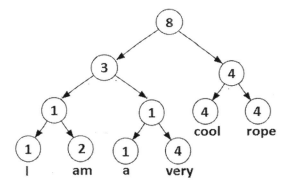

Figure 5.14: Rope sample

Next, let's implement the main operations of a Rope, starting with searching by index. Rope is a static class containing all the following operations.

Implementing indexAt(Node node, int index)

The indexAt(Node node, int index) method attempts to find the character at the given index. This is a recursive process based on a simple rule, as follows:

- If index > (weight - 1) then index = index - weight and move to the right node.
- If index < weight then just move to the left node.

These two steps are repeated until we hit a leaf node and we return the character at the current index.

Let's assume that we want to return the character from index 5, which is e (see *Figure 5.14*):

- Starting from the root, we have index = 5, index < 8, so we move left.
- Next, index = 5, 5 > 3, so index = 5 – 3 = 2 and we move right.
- Next, index = 2, 2 > 1, so index = 2 – 1 = 1 and we move right.

- The right node is a leaf node, so we return charAt(1), which is e.

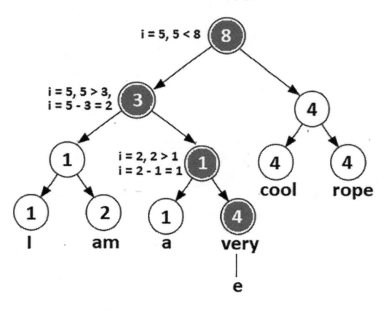

Figure 5.15: Implementing indexAt()

In code form, this algorithm is quite simple:

```java
public static char indexAt(Node node, int index) {

    if (index > node.weight - 1) {
      return indexAt(node.right, index - node.weight);
    } else if (node.left != null) {
      return indexAt(node.left, index);
    } else {
      return node.str.charAt(index);
    }
}
```

Next, let's talk about concatenating two Ropes.

Implementing concat(Node node1, Node node2)

Concatenating two Ropes (node1 and node2) is a straightforward step-by-step algorithm:

- Create a new root node that has the weight of the leaf nodes in node1.
- The new root node has node1 as its left child and node2 as its right child.
- Optional rebalancing (this isn't implemented here, but takes the form of classic binary tree rebalancing).

The following diagram represents the concatenation of two Ropes:

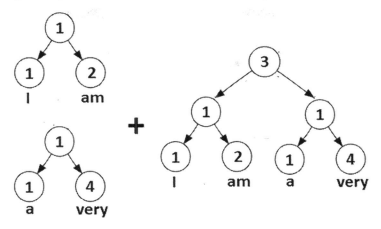

Figure 5.16: Concatenating two Ropes

In code form, we have the following:

```
public static Node concat(Node node1, Node node2) {
  return new Node(node1, node2, getLength(node1));
}

private static int getLength(Node node) {

  if (node.str != null) {
    return node.weight;
  } else {
    return getLength(node.left) + (node.right == null ?
      0 : getLength(node.right));
  }
}
```

Next, let's insert a new node.

Implementing insert(Node node, int index, String str)

In order to insert a piece of a string at a certain index in the original string, we have to split the original string and perform two concatenations. The algorithm has three steps, as follows:

- Split the original string at a given index into two strings, s1 and s2.
- Concatenate s1 and the given str into s3.
- Concatenate s1 with the new s3.

In code form, we get the following implementation:

```java
public static Node insert(Node node, int index, String str) {

  List<Node> splitRopes = Rope.split(node, index);
  Node insertNode = new Node(null, null, str.length(), str);
  Node resultNode;

  if (splitRopes.size() == 1) {
    if (index == 0) {
      resultNode = Rope.concat(insertNode, splitRopes.get(0));
    } else {
      resultNode = Rope.concat(splitRopes.get(0), insertNode);
    }
  } else {
    resultNode = Rope.concat(splitRopes.get(0), insertNode);
    resultNode = Rope.concat(resultNode, splitRopes.get(1));
  }

  return resultNode;
}
```

Next, let's see how to delete a substring.

Implementing delete(Node node, int start, int end)

Deleting a substring from the original string between start and end requires two splits and one concatenation. The algorithm consists of three steps, as follows:

- Split the original string at start into s1 and s2.
- Split s2 at end into s3 and s4.
- Concatenate s1 and s4.

In code form, we have the following implementation:

```java
public static Node delete(Node node, int start, int end) {

  Node beforeNode = null;
  Node afterNode;

  List<Node> splitRopes1 = Rope.split(node, start);

  if (splitRopes1.size() == 1) {
    afterNode = splitRopes1.get(0);
```

```
  } else {
    beforeNode = splitRopes1.get(0);
    afterNode = splitRopes1.get(1);
  }

  List<Node> splitRopes2 = Rope.split(afterNode, end - start);
  if (splitRopes2.size() == 1) {
    return beforeNode;
  }

  return beforeNode == null ? splitRopes2.get(1) :
    Rope.concat(beforeNode, splitRopes2.get(1));
}
```

Finally, let's talk about splitting a Rope.

Implementing split(Node node, int index)

Splitting a Rope into two Ropes is an operation that should come with two considerations:

- The split should take place at the last character (index).
- The split should take place at the middle character (index).

Both of these cases are considered in the implementation listed in the bundled code. Since this code is simple but quite large, we skipped it here for brevity.

120. Introducing the Skip List data structure

The Skip List data structure is a probabilistic data structure built on top of a linked list. A Skip List uses an underlying linked list to keep a sorted list of items, but it also provides the capability to skip certain items in order to speed up operations such as insert, delete, and find. Its Big O goals are listed in the following figure:

Operation	Average	Worst
Search	O(log n)	O(n)
Insert	O(log n)	O(n)
Delete	O(log n)	O(n)

Figure 5.17: Big (O) for Skip List

A Skip List has two types of layers. The base layer (or the lower layer, or layer 0) consists of a regular linked list that holds the sorted list of all items. The rest of the layers contain sparse items and act as an "express line" meant to speed up the search, insert, and delete items. The following figure helps us to visualize a Skip List with three layers:

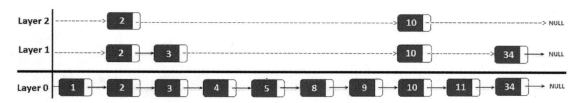

Figure 5.18: Skip List sample

So, this Skip List holds on layer 0 the items 1, 2, 3, 4, 5, 8, 9, 10, 11, and 34 and has two express lines (layer 1 and layer 2) containing sparse items. Next, let's see how we can find a certain item.

Implementing contains(Integer data)

Searching certain items starts on layer n, continues layer n-1, and so on until layer 0. For instance, let's assume that we want to find item 11.

We start on layer 2 and continue running on this layer until we find a node >= 11. Since the value 11 doesn't exist on layer 2, we search for an item less than 11 and we find 10.

We get down on layer 1 and continue searching. Based on the same logic we find item 10 again. Layer 1 doesn't contain item 11 either. If it had contained it, then we would have stopped the search.

We go down again, this time to layer 0 (the base layer containing all items), and continue searching until we find item 11. The following figure depicts our search path:

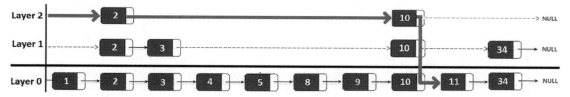

Figure 5.19: Finding an item in a Skip List

By following the highlighted path, we can see that we skipped a significant number of items until we found item 11.

In code form, this operation can be implemented as follows:

```
public boolean contains(Integer data) {

  Node cursorNode = head;

  for (int i = topLayer - 1; i >= 0; i--) {
    while (cursorNode.next[i] != null) {
      if (cursorNode.next[i].getData() > data) {
        break;
      }
```

```
      if (cursorNode.next[i].getData().equals(data)) {
        return true;
      }

      cursorNode = cursorNode.next[i];
    }
  }

  return false;
}
```

Next, let's see how we can insert a new item.

Implementing insert(Integer data)

Inserting a new item takes place on a randomly chosen layer. In other words, the layer of an item is chosen randomly at insertion time. We can insert it into an existing layer or create a new layer specially for this new item. We can create new layers until we hit an arbitrary chosen MAX_NUMBER_OF_LAYERS (we have MAX_NUMBER_OF_LAYERS = 10).

During the insertion algorithm, we apply the following steps to search for the proper place for the item to insert:

- If the item of the next node is less than the item to insert, then we continue moving forward on the same layer.
- If the item of the next node is greater than the item to insert, then we save the pointer to the current node and continue by moving one layer down. The search continues from here.
- At some point, we will reach the base layer (layer 0). Since this layer holds all items, we know for sure that we will find a slot here for the new item.

In the following figure, item 7 was inserted on Layer 1:

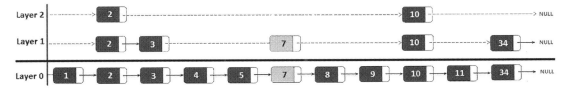

Figure 5.20: Inserting an item in a Skip List

The implementation is straightforward:

```
public void insert(Integer data) {

    int layer = incrementLayerNo();
```

```
    Node newNode = new Node(data, layer);

    Node cursorNode = head;

    for (int i = topLayer - 1; i >= 0; i--) {
      while (cursorNode.next[i] != null) {
        if (cursorNode.next[i].getData() > data) {
          break;
        }

        cursorNode = cursorNode.next[i];
      }

      if (i <= layer) {
        newNode.next[i] = cursorNode.next[i];
        cursorNode.next[i] = newNode;
      }
    }

    size++;
}
```

The `incrementLayerNo()` is a method that randomly decides the layer on which the new item will be inserted.

Implementing delete(Integer data)

Deleting an item is a simple operation. We start from the top layer, find the item to delete, and then delete it. The challenge is to pay attention to only eliminating the item by correctly linking the remaining nodes. The implementation is simple:

```
public boolean delete(Integer data) {

  Node cursorNode = head;
  boolean deleted = false;

  for (int i = topLayer - 1; i >= 0; i--) {
    while (cursorNode.next[i] != null) {

      if (cursorNode.next[i].getData() > data) {
        break;
      }
```

```
        if (cursorNode.next[i].getData().equals(data)) {
          cursorNode.next[i] = cursorNode.next[i].next[i];
          deleted = true;
          size--;

          break;
        }

        cursorNode = cursorNode.next[i];
      }
    }

    return deleted;
  }
```

Challenge yourself to implement a Skip List on top of the Java built-in `LinkedList`. It will be fun and give you the chance to explore the Skip List data structure a step further.

121. Introducing the K-D Tree data structure

A K-D Tree (also referred to as a K-dimensional tree) is a data structure that is a flavor of **Binary Search Tree (BST)** dedicated to holding and organizing points/coordinates in a K-dimensional space (2-D, 3-D, and so on). Each node of a K-D Tree holds a point representing a multi-dimensional space. The following snippet shapes a node of a 2-D Tree:

```java
private final class Node {

  private final double[] coords;

  private Node left;
  private Node right;

  public Node(double[] coords) {
    this.coords = coords;
  }
  ...
}
```

Instead of a `double[]` array, you may prefer `java.awt.geom.Point2D`, which is dedicated to representing a location in *(x, y)* coordinate space.

Commonly, K-D Trees are useful for performing different kinds of searches such as nearest-neighbor searches and range queries. For instance, let's assume a 2-D space and a bunch of *(x, y)* coordinates in this space:

```
double[][] coords = {
    {3, 5}, {1, 4}, {5, 4}, {2, 3}, {4, 2}, {3, 2},
    {5, 2}, {2, 1}, {2, 4}, {2, 5}
};
```

We can represent these coordinates using the well-known X-Y coordinates system, but we can also store them in a K-2D Tree as in the following figure:

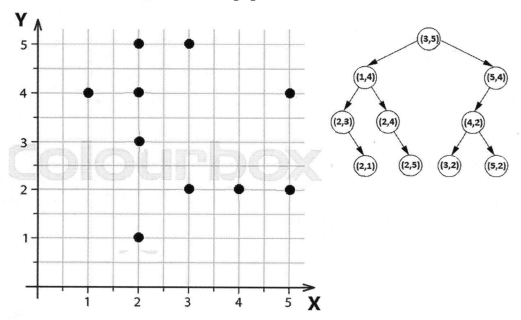

Figure 5.21: A 2D space represented in X-Y coordinates system and K-2D Tree

But, how did we build the K-D Tree?

Inserting into a K-D Tree

We insert our coordinates (cords) one by one starting with coords[0] = (3,5). The (3,5) pair becomes the root of the K-D Tree. The next pair of coordinates is (1,4). We compare *x* of the root with *x* of this pair and we notice that 1 < 3, which means that (1,4) becomes the left child of the root. The next pair is (5,4). At the first level, we compare the *x* of the root with 5 and we see that 5 > 3, so (5,4) becomes the right child of the root. The following figure illustrates the insertion of (3,5), (1,4), and (5,4).

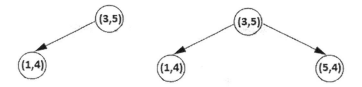

Figure 5.22: Inserting (3,5), (1,4), and (5,4)

Next, we insert the pair (2,3). We compare the x components of (2,3) and (3,5) and we see that 2 < 3, so (2,3) goes to the left of the root. Next, we compare the y component of (2,3) and (1,4) and we see that 3 < 4, so (2,3) goes to the left of (1,4).

Next, we insert the pair (4,2). We compare the x components of (4,2) and (3,5) and we see that 4 > 3, so (4,2) goes to the right of the root. Next, we compare the y component of (4,2) and (5,4) and we see that 2 < 4, so (4,2) goes to the left of (5,4). The following figure illustrates the insertion of (2, 3), and (4,2).

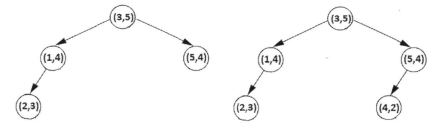

Figure 5.23: Inserting (2,3) and (4,2)

Next, we insert the pair (3,2). We compare the x components of (3,2) and (3,5) and we see that 3 = 3, so (3,2) goes to the right of the root. Next, we compare the y component of (3,2) and (5,4) and we see that 2 < 4, so (3,2) goes to the left of (5,4). Next, we compare the x component of (3,2) and (4,2) and we see that 3 < 4, so (3,2) goes to the left of (4,2).

Next, we insert the pair (5,2). We compare the x components of (5,2) and (3,5) and we see that 5 > 3, so (5,2) goes to the right of the root. Next, we compare the y component of (5,2) and (5,4) and we see that 2 < 4, so (5,2) goes to the left of (5,4). Next, we compare the x component of (5,2) and (4,2) and we see that 5 > 4, so (5,2) goes to the right of (4,2). The following figure outlines the insertion of (3,2), and (5,2).

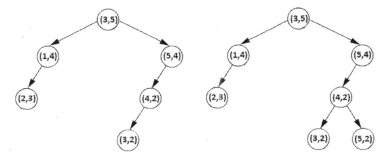

Figure 5.24: Inserting (3,2) and (5,2)

Next, we insert the pair (2,1). We compare the *x* components of (2,1) and (3,5) and we see that 2 < 3, so (2,1) goes to the left of the root. Next, we compare the *y* component of (2,1) and (1,4) and we see that 1 < 4, so (2,1) goes to the left of (1,4). Next, we compare the *x* component of (2,1) and (2,3) and we see that 2 = 2, so (2,1) goes to the right of (2,3).

Next, we insert the pair (2,4). We compare the *x* components of (2,4) and (3,5) and we see that 2 < 3, so (2,4) goes to the left of the root. Next, we compare the *y* component of (2,4) and (1,4) and we see that 4 = 4, so (2,4) goes to the right of (1,4).

Finally, we insert the pair (2,5). We compare the *x* components of (2,5) and (3,5) and we see that 2 < 3, so (2,5) goes to the left of the root. Next, we compare the *y* component of (2,5) and (1,4) and we see that 5 > 4, so (2,5) goes to the right of (1,4). Next, we compare the *x* component of (2,5) and (2,4) and we see that 2 = 2, so (2,5) goes to the right of (2,4). The following figure illustrates the insertion of (2,1), (2,4), and (2,5).

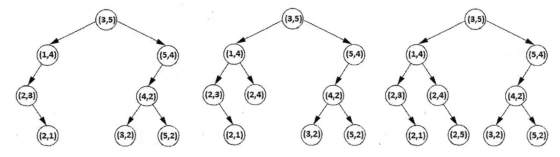

Figure 5.25: Inserting (2,1), (2,4), and (2,5)

Done! So inserting has two simple rules:

- We compare components alternatively starting with *x*. At level one, we compare *x*, at level two, we compare *y*, at level three we compare *x*, at level four we compare *y*, and so on.
- When comparing (*x1*, *y1*) with (*x2*, *y2*), if *x2* >= *x1* or *y2* >= *y1* (depending on which component is being compared) then the (*x2*,*y2*) node goes to the right (*x1*,*y1*), otherwise to the left.

Based on these statements, the implementation of a 2-D model is straightforward:

```
public void insert(double[] coords) {
  root = insert(root, coords, 0);
}


private Node insert(Node root, double[] coords, int depth) {

  if (root == null) {
    return newNode(coords);
  }

  int cd = depth % 2;
```

Chapter 5   305

```
    if (coords[cd] < root.coords[cd]) {
      root.left = insert(root.left, coords, depth + 1);
    } else {
      root.right = insert(root.right, coords, depth + 1);
    }

    return root;
}
```

Another approach for inserting in a K-D Tree relies on a sorting algorithm for sorting the coordinates. This implementation is not provided here.

Finding the nearest neighbor

Finding the nearest neighbor is the classical operation performed on a K-D Tree. We have a given point (x,y), and we want to know what the nearest point is from the K-D Tree. For instance, we may want to find the nearest neighbor of (4,4) – check the following figure:

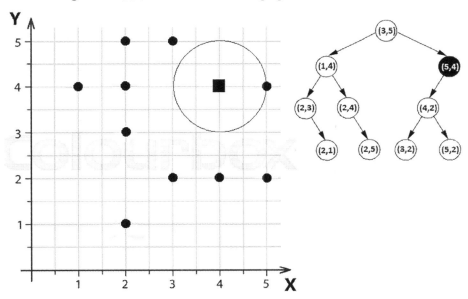

Figure 5.26: Find the nearest neighbor of (4,4)

The nearest neighbor of (4,4) is (5,4). In a nutshell, finding the nearest neighbor is about finding the shortest distance from the given point to any other point present in the K-D Tree. We start from the root and compute the distance between the given point (or target node) and the current node. The shortest distance wins. The implementation starts like this:

```
public double[] findNearest(double[] coords) {

    Node targetNode = newNode(coords);
```

```
  visited = 0;
  foundDistance = 0;
  found = null;


  nearest(root, targetNode, 0);


  return found.coords.clone();
}
```

The nearest() method is a recursive solution for finding the minimum distance:

```
private void nearest(Node root, Node targetNode, int index) {

  if (root == null) {
    return;
  }


  visited++;
  double theDistance = root.theDistance(targetNode);

  if (found == null || theDistance < foundDistance) {
    foundDistance = theDistance;
    found = root;
  }


  if (foundDistance == 0) {
    return;
  }


  double rootTargetDistance = root.get(index) -
    targetNode.get(index);
  index = (index + 1) % 2;


  nearest(rootTargetDistance > 0 ?
    root.left : root.right, targetNode, index);


  if (rootTargetDistance *
          rootTargetDistance >= foundDistance) {
    return;
  }


  nearest(rootTargetDistance > 0 ?
```

```
        root.right : root.left, targetNode, index);
    }
```

In the bundled code, you can find the missing parts of the preceding code, such as the method for computing the distance between two points.

Searching and deleting items from a K-D Tree is similar to performing these operations on a BST, so nothing new.

Challenge yourself to implement a 3-D Tree.

122. Introducing the Zipper data structure

The Zipper data structure is meant to facilitate cursor-like navigation capabilities over another data structure such as a tree. Moreover, it may provide capabilities for manipulating the tree like adding nodes, removing nodes, and so on.

The Zipper is created on the top of a tree and is characterized by the current position of the cursor and the current range or the current visibility area. At any moment, the Zipper doesn't see or act on the entire tree; its actions are available only on a subtree or a range of the tree relative to its current position. The modification accomplished via the Zipper is visible only in this range, not in the entire tree.

In order to navigate and determine the current range, a Zipper must be aware of the tree structure. For instance, it must be aware of all the children of each node, which is why we start from an interface that must be implemented by any tree that wants to take advantage of a Zipper:

```java
public interface Zippable {

    public Collection<? extends Zippable> getChildren();
}
```

A tree that implements `Zippable` ensures that it exposes its children to the Zipper. For instance, a tree `Node` implementation can be done as follows:

```java
public class Node implements Zippable {

    private final String name;
    private final List<Node> children;

    public Node(final String name, final Node... children) {

        this.name = name;
        this.children = new LinkedList<>(Arrays.asList(children));
    }

    public String getName() {
        return name;
    }
}
```

```
    @Override
    public Collection<Node> getChildren() {
      return this.children;
    }

    @Override
    public String toString() {
      return "Node{" + "name=" + name
        + ", children=" + children + '}';
    }
}
```

The following figure illustrates the characteristics of a Zipper at some moment in time:

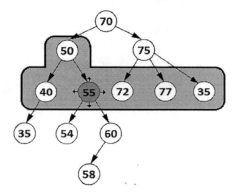

Figure 5.27: The Zipper position and range on an arbitrary tree

The Zipper's current position is represented by the node labeled 55 – the Zipper cursor is on position 55. The highlighted gray area is the zipper's current range/visibility. Everything that happens in this area is invisible outside of it. From the current position, the Zipper can move down(), up(), left(), and right(). Every move will refine the Zipper range accordingly.

When the Zipper is applied to a tree, each node of the tree (Node) becomes a Zipper-node, represented here by the ZipNode class. As you can see in the following code, a ZipNode acts as a wrapper of a Node and represents the unit of work for the Zipper:

```
public final class ZipNode<T extends Zippable>
      implements Zippable {

  private static final Zippable[] DUMMY = new Zippable[0];

  private final T node;        // wrap the original tree node
  private Zippable[] children; // list of children
```

```
// wrap a ZipNode without children
protected ZipNode(final T node) {
  this(node, DUMMY);
}


// wrap a ZipNode and its children
protected ZipNode(final T node, Zippable[] children) {

  if (children == null) {
    children = new Zippable[0];
  }

  this.node = node;
  this.children = children;
}
```

The remaining code handles the initialization of children in a lazy fashion (on demand):

```
@Override
public Collection<? extends Zippable> getChildren() {
  lazyGetChildren();
  return (children != null) ?
    new LinkedList<>(Arrays.asList(children)) : null;
}


// return the original node
public T unwrap() {
  return node;
}

public boolean isLeaf() {
  lazyGetChildren();
  return children == null || children.length == 0;
}

public boolean hasChildren() {
  lazyGetChildren();
  return children != null && children.length > 0;
}

protected Zippable[] children() {
```

```
      lazyGetChildren();
      return children;
  }


  protected ZipNode<T> replaceNode(final T node) {
    lazyGetChildren();
    return new ZipNode<>(node, children);
  }


  // lazy initialization of children
  private void lazyGetChildren() {

    if (children == DUMMY) {
      Collection<? extends Zippable> nodeChildren
        = node.getChildren();
      children = (nodeChildren == null) ?
        null : nodeChildren.toArray(Zippable[]::new);
    }
  }


  @Override
  public String toString() {
    return node.toString(); // call the original toString()
  }
}
```

All the Zipper operations act on a ZipNode, not on a Node.

Next, we have the Zipper range implementation, which basically defines the gray part of *Figure 5.27*. We have the parent node and the left/right siblings of the current range:

```
final class ZipperRange {

  private final ZipperRange parentRange;
  private final ZipNode<?> parentZipNode;
  private final Zippable[] leftSiblings;
  private final Zippable[] rightSiblings;

  protected ZipperRange(final ZipNode<?> parentZipNode,
      final ZipperRange parentRange, final Zippable[]
      leftSiblings, final Zippable[] rightSiblings) {

    this.parentZipNode = parentZipNode;
```

```
      this.parentRange = parentRange;
      this.leftSiblings = (leftSiblings == null) ?
        new Zippable[0] : leftSiblings;
      this.rightSiblings = (rightSiblings == null) ?
        new Zippable[0] : rightSiblings;
    }


    // getters omitted for brevity
  }
```

ZipperRange works in tandem with Cursor, which contains the implementation of the Zipper actions (down(), up(), left(), right(), rightMost(), leftMost(), clear(), add(), addAll(), insertLeft(), insertRight(), remove(), removeLeft(), removeRight(), and so on):

```
public final class Cursor<T extends Zippable> {

  private final ZipNode<T> zipNode;
  private final ZipperRange range;

  protected Cursor(final ZipNode<T> zipNode,
                   final ZipperRange range) {

    this.zipNode = zipNode;
    this.range = range;
  }
  ...
}
```

Since this code is significantly large, the remainder was skipped here. You can find it in the bundled code.

Finally, we have the Zipper class. This class is used for creating a Zipper via the createZipper() method. It is also used for recreating/updating the tree based on the modifications done via the Zipper. This is done in the unwrapZipper() method as follows:

```
public final class Zipper {

  public static <T extends Zippable>
      Cursor<T> createZipper(final T node) {
    return new Cursor<>(new ZipNode<>(node),
      new ZipperRange(null, null, null, null)); // root range
  }


  public static <T extends Zippable> T unwrapZipper(
```

```
        final Cursor<T> tree) {
    return Zipper.<T>unwrapZipper(tree.root().zipNode());
  }


  private static <T extends Zippable> T unwrapZipper(
        final Zippable node) {

    if (node instanceof ZipNode<?>) {

      ZipNode<T> zipNode = (ZipNode<T>) node;
      T original = zipNode.unwrap();

      if (!zipNode.isLeaf()) {
        Collection<T> children
          = (Collection<T>) original.getChildren();
        original.getChildren().clear();

        for (Zippable zipped : zipNode.children()) {
          children.add((T) unwrapZipper(zipped));
        }
      }

    return original;
    } else {

      return (T) node;
    }
  }
}
```

In the bundled code, you can find the complete implementation and an example of using the Zipper on a given tree.

123. Introducing the Binomial Heap data structure

A Binomial Heap data structure is a set composed of Binomial Trees. Each Binomial Tree is a Min Heap, which means that it follows the *min-heap* property. In a nutshell, a heap is a Min Heap if its items are in descending order, meaning that the minimum item is the root (more details are available in *The Complete Coding Interview Guide in Java* book).

In a nutshell, a Binomial Tree is ordered and typically defined in a recursive fashion. It is denoted as B_k, where k implies the following properties:

- A Binomial Tree has 2^k nodes.
- The height of a Binomial Tree is equal to k.
- The root of a Binomial Tree has the degree k, which is the greatest degree.

A B_0 Binomial Tree has a single node. A B_1 Binomial Tree has two B_0 Trees, and one of them is a left subtree of the other one. A B_2 Tree has two B_1, one of which is the left subtree of the other. In general, a B_k Binomial Tree contains two B_{k-1} Binomial Trees, one of which is the left subtree of the other (two B_{k-1} Trees are linked to the composed B_k). In the following figure, you can see B_0, B_1, B_2, B_3, and B_4:

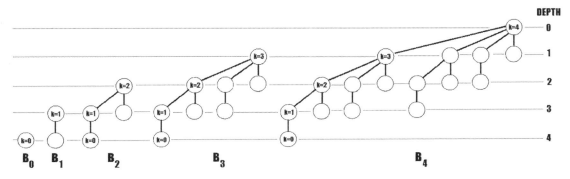

Figure 5.28: B_0-B_4 Binomial Trees

The goals of a Binomial Heap from a Big O perspective are listed in the following figure:

Operation	Worst
Insert	O(log n)
Find minimum key	O(log n)
Extract minimum key	O(log n)
Decreasing a key	O(log n)
Deleting a node	O(log n)
Union or merging	O(log n)

Figure 5.29: Big O for Binomial Heap

In the following figure, you can see a sample of a Binomial Heap. The roots of the Binomial Trees (here, 9, 1, and 7) within a Binomial Heap are represented via a linked list referred to as the *root list*.

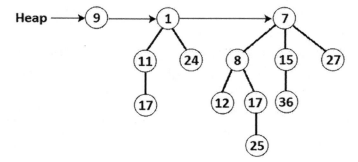

Figure 5.30: Binomial Heap sample

In other words, as you can easily intuit from this figure, a Binomial Heap is an extension (or a flavor) of a Binary Heap, which provides high performance for merging or unioning two heaps and is a perfect fit for the task of implementing priority queues.

Based on this figure, we can define the skeleton of a Binomial Heap as follows:

```
public class BinomialHeap {

  private Node head;

  private final class Node {

    private int key;
    private int degree;
    private Node parent;
    private Node child;
    private Node sibling;

    public Node() {
      key = Integer.MIN_VALUE;
    }

    public Node(int key) {
      this.key = key;
    }
    ...
  }
  ...
}
```

If we represent the relevant part of a Node as a diagram, we obtain the following figure (here, you can see the internal structure of a Node for items 11 and 25):

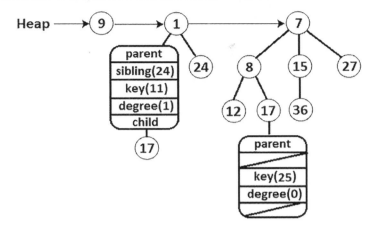

Figure 5.31: Expanding a Node

Now that we have the main structure of a Binomial Heap, let's cover several operations.

Implementing insert(int key)

Inserting a new key into a Binomial Heap is a two-step operation. In the first step, we create a new heap containing only the given key (a Node wrapping the given key). Second, we union the current heap with this newly created heap as follows:

```
public void insert(int key) {
   Node node = new Node(key);
   BinomialHeap newHeap = new BinomialHeap(node);

   head = unionHeap(newHeap);
}
```

The union operation is depicted as the last operation of this problem.

Implementing findMin()

Finding the minimum key of a Binomial Heap requires us to loop through the *root list* (which is a linked list) and find the smallest key. This can be optimized from *O(log n)* to *O(1)* if we decide to maintain a pointer to the minimum root. However, the *O(log n)* approach is listed here:

```
public int findMin() {

   if (head == null) {
      return Integer.MIN_VALUE;
   } else {
```

```
    Node min = head;
    Node nextNode = min.sibling;

    while (nextNode != null) {
      if (nextNode.key < min.key) {
        min = nextNode;
      }
      nextNode = nextNode.sibling;
    }

    return min.key;
  }
}
```

Since our Binomial Heap holds primitive integers, we use `Integer.MIN_VALUE` as an equivalent to "no value." If you adjust the implementation to use `Integer` or generic `T`, then you can replace `Integer.MIN_VALUE` with `null`.

Implementing extractMin()

Before extracting the minimum key, we have to find it. Afterward, we delete it. Finally, we have to union the resulting subtrees as follows:

```
public int extractMin() {

  if (head == null) {
    return Integer.MIN_VALUE;
  }

  Node min = head;
  Node minPrev = null;
  Node nextNode = min.sibling;
  Node nextNodePrev = min;

  while (nextNode != null) {
    if (nextNode.key < min.key) {
      min = nextNode;
      minPrev = nextNodePrev;
    }

    nextNodePrev = nextNode;
    nextNode = nextNode.sibling;
  }
```

```
    deleteTreeRoot(min, minPrev);


    return min.key;
}
```

The `deleteTreeRoot()` is a helper method useful for deleting the given root and performing a union on the remaining sub-trees:

```
private void deleteTreeRoot(Node root, Node previousNode) {

    if (root == head) {
      head = root.sibling;
    } else {
      previousNode.sibling = root.sibling;
    }


    Node unionHeap = null;
    Node child = root.child;
    while (child != null) {
      Node nextNode = child.sibling;
      child.sibling = unionHeap;
      child.parent = null;
      unionHeap = child;
      child = nextNode;
    }


  BinomialHeap toUnionHeap = new BinomialHeap(unionHeap);

    head = unionHeap(toUnionHeap);
}
```

Implementing decreaseKey(int key, int newKey)

Decreasing a key value means replacing an existing key with a smaller one. When this operation happens, the new key may be smaller than the key of its parent, which means that the *min-heap* property is violated. This scenario requires us to swap the current node with its parent, its parent with its grandparent, and so on until we reestablish compliance with the *min-heap* property. The implementation starts as follows:

```
public void decreaseKey(int key, int newKey) {

    Node found  = findByKey(key);
    if (found != null) {
```

```
      decreaseKey(found, newKey);
  }
}


private void decreaseKey(Node node, int newKey) {

  node.key = newKey;
  goUp(node, false);
}
```

The goUp() method is a helper method used to reestablish the *min-heap* property:

```
private Node goUp(Node node, boolean goToRoot) {

  Node parent = node.parent;
  while (parent != null && (goToRoot
      || node.key < parent.key)) {

    int t = node.key;
    node.key = parent.key;
    parent.key = t;

    node = parent;
    parent = parent.parent;
  }

  return node;
}
```

As you will see next, this helper is useful for deleting a node as well.

Implementing delete(int key)

Deleting a key is done by first finding the corresponding Node and decreasing it to the minimum (Integer.MIN_VALUE). Next, we delete the minimum from the heap and connect the remaining subtrees. The implementation relies on the goUp() and deleteTreeRoot() helpers listed in the previous sections:

```
public void delete(int key) {

  Node found = findByKey(key);
  if (found != null) {
```

```
      delete(found);
  }
}

private void delete(Node node) {

  node = goUp(node, true);

  if (head == node) {
    deleteTreeRoot(node, null);
  } else {
    Node previousNode = head;
    while (previousNode.sibling.key != node.key) {
      previousNode = previousNode.sibling;
    }
    deleteTreeRoot(node, previousNode);
  }
}
```

Finally, let's talk about union heaps.

Implementing unionHeap(BinomialHeap heap)

Consider two Binomial Heaps (H1 and H2). The goal of the union operation is to create H3 by unifying H1 with H2. Let's assume that H1 (having a conventional string representation used by our application as 31 22 [40] 8 [13 [24] 11]) and H2 (55 24 [45] 3 [7 [29 [40] 9] 5 [37] 18]) are those from the following figure:

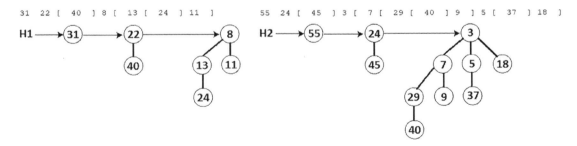

Figure 5.32: Two Binomial Heaps, H1 and H2

The contract of unification starts with an initial merging of H1 and H2 in the order of their degrees. In our case, the merge operation produces the following output:

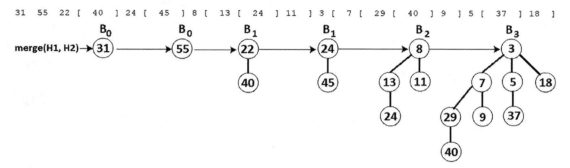

31   55   22 [40   ] 24 [45   ] 8 [13 [24   ] 11   ] 3 [7 [29 [40   ] 9   ] 5 [37   ] 18   ]

Figure 5.33: Merging H1 and H2

This operation is performed by the following helper method:

```
private Node merge(BinomialHeap h1, BinomialHeap h2) {

  if (h1.head == null) {
    return h2.head;
  } else if (h2.head == null) {
    return h1.head;
  } else {
    Node headIt;
    Node h1Next = h1.head;
    Node h2Next = h2.head;

    if (h1.head.degree <= h2.head.degree) {
      headIt = h1.head;
      h1Next = h1Next.sibling;
    } else {
      headIt = h2.head;
      h2Next = h2Next.sibling;
    }

    Node tail = headIt;
```

```
    while (h1Next != null && h2Next != null) {
      if (h1Next.degree <= h2Next.degree) {
        tail.sibling = h1Next;
        h1Next = h1Next.sibling;
      } else {
        tail.sibling = h2Next;
        h2Next = h2Next.sibling;
      }

      tail = tail.sibling;
    }

    if (h1Next != null) {
      tail.sibling = h1Next;
    } else {
      tail.sibling = h2Next;
    }

    return headIt;
  }
}
```

Next, we need to combine the Binomial Trees of the same order. While we traverse the roots of the merged heaps (here, 31, 55, 22, 24, 8, and 3), we use three pointers denoted as PREV-X (the previous node of the current node), X (the current node), and NEXT-X (the next node of the current node). These pointers help us to solve the following four cases:

- *Case 1*: X and NEXT-X have different orders. In this case, we just move the X pointer ahead.
- *Case 2*: X, NEXT-X, and NEXT-NEXT-X have the same order. In this case, we just move the X pointer ahead.
- *Case 3*: X and NEXT-X have the same order, different from NEXT-NEXT-X. And if X.KEY<= NEXT-X.KEY, then NEXT-X becomes the child of X.
- *Case 4*: X and NEXT-X have the same order, different from NEXT-NEXT-X. And if X.KEY>NEXT-X. KEY, then X becomes the child of NEXT-X.

If we apply these four cases to our example, we notice that after merging H1 and H2, we are in *Case 3* since X and NEXT-X have the same order (B_0), which is different from the order of NEXT-NEXT-X (which is B_1) and X.KEY = 31 < 55 = NEXT-X.KEY. So, NEXT-X becomes the child of X, as in the following figure:

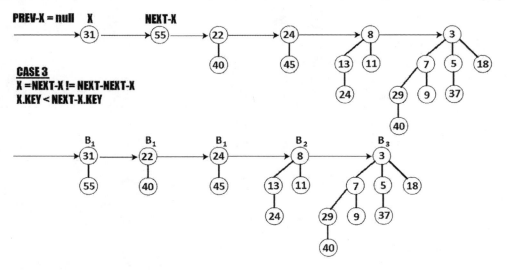

Figure 5.34: Applying Case 3

Going further, we notice that X, NEXT-X, and NEXT-NEXT-X have the same order B_1. This means that we are in *Case 2*, so we have to move the X pointer forward, as in the following figure:

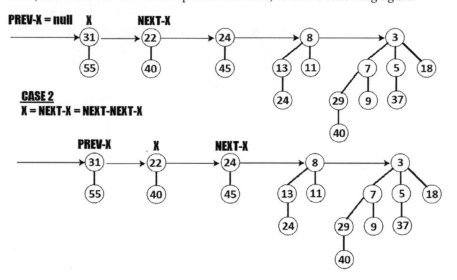

Figure 5.35: Applying Case 2

Next, we are in *Case 3* again. We see that X and NEXT-X have the same order (B_1), which is different from the order of NEXT-NEXT-X (B_2). And, we also see that X.KEY = 22 < 24 = NEXT-X.KEY, so NEXT-X becomes the child of X, as in the following figure:

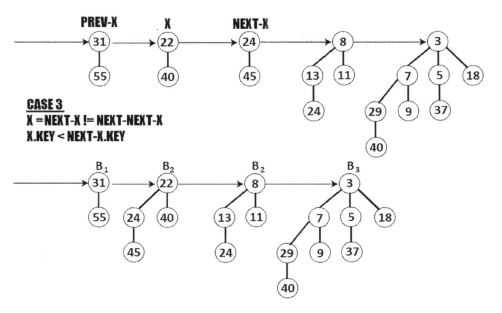

Figure 5.36: Applying Case 3 again

Next, we are in *Case 4*. We see that X and NEXT-X have the same order (B₂) which is different from the order of NEXT-NEXT-X (B₃). And, we also see that X.KEY = 22 > 8 = NEXT-X.KEY, so X becomes the child of NEXT-X, as in the following figure:

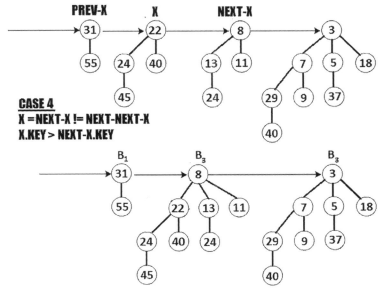

Figure 5.37: Applying Case 4

Next, we are in *Case 4* again. We see that X and NEXT-X have the same order (B_3), which is different from the order of NEXT-NEXT-X (null). And, we also see that X.KEY = 8 > 3 = NEXT-X.KEY, so X becomes the child of NEXT-X, as in the following figure:

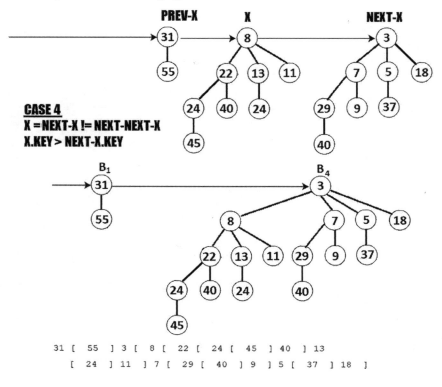

```
31 [  55  ] 3 [  8 [  22 [  24 [  45  ] 40  ] 13
   [  24  ] 11  ] 7 [  29 [  40  ] 9  ] 5 [  37  ] 18  ]
```

Figure 5.38: Applying Case 4 again

At this point, none of the four cases is valid so this is the final form of the Binomial Heap.

Based on this example, we can implement the union operation as follows (notice the highlighted cases in the following code):

```java
private Node unionHeap(BinomialHeap heap) {

    Node mergeHeap = merge(this, heap);

    head = null;
    heap.head = null;

    if (mergeHeap == null) {
        return null;
    }

    Node previousNode = null;
```

```
    Node currentNode = mergeHeap;
    Node nextNode = mergeHeap.sibling;


    while (nextNode != null) {
      if (currentNode.degree != nextNode.degree
          || (nextNode.sibling != null
          && nextNode.sibling.degree == currentNode.degree)) {
[C:1,2] previousNode = currentNode;
[C:1,2] currentNode = nextNode;
      } else {
        if (currentNode.key < nextNode.key) {
[C:3]     currentNode.sibling = nextNode.sibling;
[C:3]     linkNodes(currentNode, nextNode);
[C:4]   } else {
[C:4]     if (previousNode == null) {
[C:4]       mergeHeap = nextNode;
[C:4]     } else {
[C:4]       previousNode.sibling = nextNode;
[C:4]     }
[C:4]
[C:4]     linkNodes(nextNode, currentNode);
[C:4]     currentNode = nextNode;
        }
      }

    nextNode = currentNode.sibling;
  }


  return mergeHeap;
}
```

The `linkNodes()` method is a helper method that links the current node with the next node:

```
private void linkNodes(Node minNodeTree, Node other) {

  other.parent = minNodeTree;
  other.sibling = minNodeTree.child;
  minNodeTree.child = other;
  minNodeTree.degree++;

}
```

Done! You can find the complete application in the bundled code.

124. Introducing the Fibonacci Heap data structure

A Fibonacci Heap is a flavor of Binomial Heap with excellent performance in *amortized time* for operations such as insert, extract minimum, and merge. It is an optimal choice for implementing priority queues. A Fibonacci Heap is made of trees, and each tree has a single root and multiple children arranged in a heap-ordered fashion. The root node with the smallest key is always placed at the beginning of the list of trees.

It is called a Fibonacci Heap because each tree of order k has at least F_{k+2} nodes, where F_{k+2} is the $(k+2)^{th}$ Fibonacci number.

In the following figure, you can see a Fibonacci Heap sample:

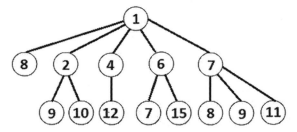

Figure 5.39: Fibonacci Heap sample

The main operations in a Fibonacci Heap are (Big O represents the *amortized time*): insert (O(1)), decrease key (O(1)), find the minimum (O(1)), extract minimum (O(log n)), deletion (O(log n)), and merge (O(1)). You can find an implementation of these operations in the bundled code.

125. Introducing the Pairing Heap data structure

The Pairing Heap is a flavor of Binomial Heap with the capability of self-adjusting/rearranging to keep itself balanced. It has very good performance in *amortized time* and is a good fit for the task of implementing priority queues.

A Pairing Heap is a pairing tree with a root and children. Each heap of a Pairing Heap represents a value and has a set of children that are also heaps. The value of a heap is always less than (*min-heap* property) or greater than (*max-heap* property) the value of its children heaps.

In the following figure, you can see a Min Pairing Heap:

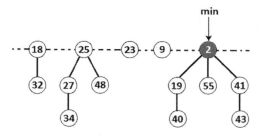

Figure 5.40: A Min Pairing Heap sample

The main operations in a Pairing Heap are: insert (O(1)), decrease key (actual time: O(1), amortized time O(log n)), find the minimum (O(1)), extract the minimum (actual time: O(n), amortized time (O (log n)), and merge (actual time: O(1), amortized time (O(log n)). You can find an implementation of these operations in the bundled code.

126. Introducing the Huffman Coding data structure

The Huffman Coding algorithm was developed by David A. Huffman in 1950 and can easily be understood via an example. Let's assume that we have the string shown in the following figure.

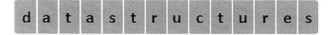

Figure 5.41: Initial string

Let's assume that each character needs 8 bits to be represented. Since we have 14 characters, we can say that we need 8*14=112 bits to send this string over a network.

Encoding the string

The idea of Huffman Coding is to compress (shrink) such strings to a smaller size. For this, we create a tree of character frequencies. A Node of this tree can be shaped as follows:

```
public class Huffman {

    private Node root;
    private String str;
    private StringBuilder encodedStr;
    private StringBuilder decodedStr;

    private final class Node {

        private Node left;
        private Node right;

        private final Character character;
        private final Integer frequency;

        // constructors
    }
    ...
}
```

For instance, the following figure shows the calculation of the frequency of each character from our string in ascending order:

Figure 5.42: Calculating the frequency of each character

After sorting, these characters are stored in a **priority queue** (PQ). Each character will become a leaf node in a tree by following several steps:

- *Step 1*: Create a node with two children (a partial tree). The left child holds the minimum frequency, and the right child holds the next minimum frequency. The node itself holds the sum of its left and right children.
- *Step 2*: Remove these two frequencies from the PQ.
- *Step 3*: Insert this partial tree into the PQ.
- *Step 4*: Repeat steps 1-3 until the PQ is empty and we obtain a single tree from these partial trees.

If we apply *steps 1-3* twice, we obtain the following figure:

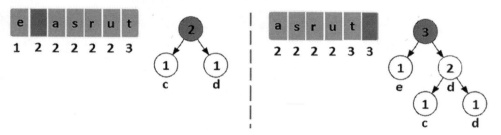

Figure 5.43: Applying steps 1-3 twice

In code form, these steps appear as follows:

```
public void tree(String str) {

    this.str = str;
    this.root = null;
    this.encodedStr = null;
    this.decodedStr = null;


    Map<Character, Integer> frequency = new HashMap<>();


    for (char character : str.toCharArray()) {
      frequency.put(character,
            frequency.getOrDefault(character, 0) + 1);
```

```
    }

    PriorityQueue<Node> queue = new PriorityQueue<>(
        Comparator.comparingInt(ch -> ch.frequency));

    for (Entry<Character, Integer> entry : frequency.entrySet()) {
        queue.add(new Node(entry.getKey(), entry.getValue()));
    }

    while (queue.size() != 1) {

        Node left = queue.poll();
        Node right = queue.poll();

        int sum = left.frequency + right.frequency;

        queue.add(new Node(null, sum, left, right));
    }

    this.root = queue.peek();
}
```

By repeating these steps until the PQ is empty, we obtain the final tree. Next, for each node of this tree that is not a leaf, we assign the value 0 to the left edge and 1 to the right edge. This is the encoding step that can be coded as follows:

```
public String encode() {

    Map<Character, String> codes = new HashMap<>();
    encode(this.root, "", codes);

    this.encodedStr = new StringBuilder();
    for (char character : this.str.toCharArray()) {
        this.encodedStr.append(codes.get(character));
    }

    return this.encodedStr.toString();
}

private void encode(Node root, String str,
                    Map<Character, String> codes) {

    if (root == null) {
```

```
    return;
  }


  if (isLeaf(root)) {
    codes.put(root.character, str.length() > 0 ? str : "1");
  }


  encode(root.left, str + '0', codes);
  encode(root.right, str + '1', codes);
}
```

The final result looks like this:

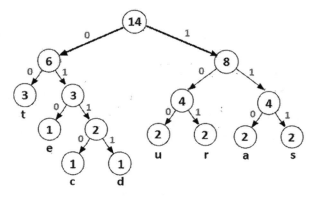

Figure 5.44: The final tree

Now, sending this tree over the network will send the compressed string. The next figure gives us the new size of this string:

Character	Frequency	Code	Bits
a	2	110	6
c	1	0110	4
d	1	0111	4
e	1	010	3
r	2	101	6
s	2	111	6
t	3	00	6
u	2	100	6
			41

Figure 5.45: The size of the compressed string

So, we reduce the size of the string from 112 bits to 41 bits. This is the compressed or encoded string.

Decoding the string

Decoding the string is a simple step. We take each code and traverse the tree to find the assigned character. For instance, we take *0111* and we find *d*, we take *110* and we find *a*, and so on. Decoding can be implemented as follows:

```java
public String decode() {

  this.decodedStr = new StringBuilder();

  if (isLeaf(this.root)) {
    int copyFrequency = this.root.frequency;
    while (copyFrequency-- > 0) {
      decodedStr.append(root.character);
    }
  } else {
    int index = -1;
    while (index < this.encodedStr.length() - 1) {
      index = decode(this.root, index);
    }
  }

  return decodedStr.toString();
}

private int decode(Node root, int index) {

  if (root == null) {
    return index;
  }

  if (isLeaf(root)) {
    decodedStr.append(root.character);
    return index;
  }

  index++;
  root = (this.encodedStr.charAt(index) == '0')
    ? root.left : root.right;
```

```
    index = decode(root, index);

    return index;
}


private booleanisLeaf(Node root) {
  return root.left == null && root.right == null;
}
```

After processing all of the code, we should obtain the decoded string.

127. Introducing the Splay Tree data structure

A Splay Tree is a flavor of **Binary Search Tree (BST)**. Its particularity consists of the fact that it is a self-balancing tree that places the recently accessed items at the root level.

The *splaying* operation or *splaying* an item is a process that relies on tree rotations meant to bring the item to the root position. Every operation on the tree is followed by *splaying*.

So, the goal of *splaying* is to bring the most recently used item closer to the root. This means that subsequent operations on these items will be performed faster.

The *splaying* operation relies on six rotations:

- Zig rotation – the tree rotates to the right (every node rotates to the right)
- Zag rotation – the tree rotates to the left (every node rotates to the left)
- Zig-Zig rotation – double Zig rotation (every node moves twice to the right)
- Zag-Zag rotation – double Zag rotation (every node moves twice to the left)
- Zig-Zag rotation – a Zig rotation followed by a Zag
- Zag-Zig rotation – a Zag rotation followed by a Zig

In the bundled code, you can find an implementation of a Splay Tree. Moreover, you can use this visualizer: https://www.cs.usfca.edu/~galles/visualization/SplayTree.html.

128. Introducing the Interval Tree data structure

An Interval Tree is a flavor of **Binary Search Tree (BST)**. Its particularity consists of the fact that it holds intervals of values. Beside the interval itself, a Node of an Interval Tree holds the maximum value of the current interval and the maximum value of the subtree rooted with this Node.

In code form, an Interval Tree is shaped as follows:

```
public class IntervalTree {

  private Node root;
```

```java
public static final class Interval {

  private final int min, max;

  public Interval(int min, int max) {
    this.min = min;
    this.max = max;
  }
  ...
}

private final class Node {

  private final Interval interval;
  private final Integer maxInterval;

  private Node left;
  private Node right;

  private int size;
  private int maxSubstree;

  Node(Interval interval, Integer maxInterval) {

    this.interval = interval;
    this.maxInterval = maxInterval;

    this.size = 1;
    this.maxSubstree = interval.max;
  }
}
...
}
```

Let's consider that we have the following intervals of integers: [4, 7], [1, 10], [7, 23], [6, 8], [9, 13], and [2, 24].

Implementing insert(Interval interval)

The first interval ([4, 7]) becomes the root of the tree. Next, we compare the interval [1, 10] to [4, 7] by comparing the left side of the interval. Since 1 < 4, the interval [1, 10] goes to the left of the root.

Next, we compare the interval [7, 23] with [4, 7]. Since 7 > 4, the interval [7, 23] goes to the right of [4, 7]. Applying the same logic for the rest of the interval will result in the following tree:

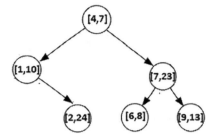

Figure 5.46: The interval tree

The previous logic (insert operation, O(log n)) is materialized in code form as follows:

```
public void insert(Interval interval) {
  root = insert(root, interval);
}


private Node insert(Node root, Interval interval) {

  if (root == null) {
    return new Node(interval, interval.max);
  }

  if (interval.min < root.interval.min) {
    root.left = insert(root.left, interval);
  } else {
    root.right = insert(root.right, interval);
  }

  if (root.maxSubstree < interval.max) {
    root.maxSubstree = interval.max;
  }


  return root;
}
```

Other operations specific to an interval tree are searching the intervals that overlap the given interval (O(log n)) and deleting (O (log n)). You can find the implementations in the bundled code.

129. Introducing the Unrolled Linked List data structure

An Unrolled Linked List is a flavor of a linked list that stores arrays (multiple items). Each node of an Unrolled Linked List can store an array. It is like combining the powers of an array with those of a linked list. In other words, an Unrolled Linked List is a data structure with a low memory footprint and high performance on insertion and deletion.

Insertion and deletion from an Unrolled Linked List have different implementations.

For instance, we can insert arrays (`insert(int[] arr)`), which means that for each insertion, we create a new node and insert that array into it.

Deleting an item is equivalent to removing the item from the specified index in the proper array. If, after deletion, the array is empty, then it is removed from the list as well.

Another approach assumes that the Unrolled Linked List has a fixed capacity (each node holds an array of this capacity). Further, we insert items one by one by following a low-water mark of 50%. This means that if we insert an item that cannot be added to the current node (array), then we create a new node and insert into it half of the original node's items plus this item.

Deleting an item uses the reverse logic. If the number of items in a node drops below 50%, then we move the items from the neighboring array over to get back to a low-water mark above 50%. If the neighboring array also drops below 50%, then we have to merge these two nodes.

You can find both approaches in the bundled code. On the other hand, you can challenge yourself to provide an Unrolled Linked List implementation that extends the JVM Collections API. You can start from either of the following two approaches:

```
public class UnrolledLinkedList<E>
        extends AbstractList<E>
        implements List<E>, Serializable { ... }


public class UnrolledLinkedList<E>
        extends AbstractSequentialList<E>
        implements Deque<E>, Cloneable, Serializable { ... }
```

Add this implementation to your GitHub portfolio and you'll impress your interviewer.

130. Implementing join algorithms

Join algorithms are typically used in databases, mainly when we have two tables in a one-to-many relationship and we want to fetch a result set containing this mapping based on a join predicate. In the following figure, we have the author and book tables. An author can have multiple books and we want to join these tables to obtain a result set as the third table.

The author table

authorId	name
1	Author_1
2	Author_2
3	Author_3
4	Author_4
5	Author_5

The book table

bookId	title	authorId
1	Book_1	1
2	Book_2	1
3	Book_3	2
4	Book_4	3
5	Book_5	3
6	Book_6	3
7	Book_7	4
8	Book_8	5
9	Book_9	5

author JOIN book

authorId	name	title	bookId
1	Author_1	Book_1	1
1	Author_1	Book_2	2
2	Author_2	Book_3	3
3	Author_3	Book_4	4
3	Author_3	Book_5	5
3	Author_3	Book_6	6
4	Author_4	Book_7	7
5	Author_5	Book_8	8
5	Author_5	Book_9	9

Figure 5.47: Joining two tables (author and book)

There are three popular join algorithms for solving this problem: Nested Loop Join, Hash Join, and Sort Merge Join. While databases are optimized to choose the most appropriate join for the given query, let's try to implement them in plain Java on the following two tables expressed as records:

```
public record Author(int authorId, String name) {}
public record Book(int bookId, String title, int authorId) {}


List<Author> authorsTable = Arrays.asList(
  new Author(1, "Author_1"), new Author(2, "Author_2"),
  new Author(3, "Author_3"), new Author(4, "Author_4"),
  new Author(5, "Author_5"));


List<Book> booksTable = Arrays.asList(
  new Book(1, "Book_1", 1), new Book(2, "Book_2", 1),
  new Book(3, "Book_3", 2), new Book(4, "Book_4", 3),
  new Book(5, "Book_5", 3), new Book(6, "Book_6", 3),
  new Book(7, "Book_7", 4), new Book(8, "Book_8", 5),
  new Book(9, "Book_9", 5));
```

Our goal is to join the Author and Book records by matching the Author.authorId and Book.authorId attributes. The result should be a projection (ResultRow) that contains authorId, name, title, and bookId:

```
public record ResultRow(int authorId, String name,
                        String title, int bookId) {}
```

Next, let's talk about Nested Loop Join.

Nested Loop Join

The Nested Loop Join algorithm relies on two loops that traverse both relations to find records that match the joining predicate:

```
public static List<ResultRow> nestedLoopJoin(
    List<Author> authorsTable, List<Book> booksTable) {

  List<ResultRow> resultSet = new LinkedList();

  for (Author author : authorsTable) {
    for (Book book : booksTable) {
      if (book.authorId() == author.authorId()) {
        resultSet.add(new ResultRow(
        author.authorId(), author.name(),
          book.title(), book.bookId()));
      }
    }
  }

  return resultSet;
}
```

The time complexity of this algorithm is O(n*m) where n is the size of authorsTable and m is the size of booksTable. This is quadratic complexity, which makes this algorithm useful only for small datasets.

Hash Join

As the name suggests, Hash Join relies on *hashing*. So, we have to create a hash table from the authors table (the table with fewer records) and afterward we loop through the books table to find their authors in the created hash table as follows:

```
public static List<ResultRow> hashJoin(
    List<Author> authorsTable, List<Book> booksTable) {

  Map<Integer, Author> authorMap = new HashMap<>();

  for (Author author : authorsTable) {
    authorMap.put(author.authorId(), author);
  }
```

```
List<ResultRow> resultSet = new LinkedList();

for (Book book : booksTable) {
  Integer authorId = book.authorId();
  Author author = authorMap.get(authorId);

  if (author != null) {
    resultSet.add(new ResultRow(author.authorId(),
      author.name(), book.title(), book.bookId()));
  }
}

return resultSet;
}
```

The time complexity of this algorithm is O(n+m), where *n* is the size of authorsTable and *m* is the size of booksTable. So, this is better than Nested Loop Join.

Sort Merge Join

As the name suggests, Sort Merge Join starts by sorting the two tables by the attribute of the join. Afterward, we loop the two tables and apply the join predicate as follows:

```
public static List<ResultRow> sortMergeJoin(
    List<Author> authorsTable, List<Book> booksTable) {

  authorsTable.sort(Comparator.comparing(Author::authorId));

  booksTable.sort((b1, b2) -> {
    int sortResult = Comparator
          .comparing(Book::authorId)
          .compare(b1, b2);

    return sortResult != 0 ? sortResult : Comparator
          .comparing(Book::bookId)
          .compare(b1, b2);
  });

  List<ResultRow> resultSet = new LinkedList();

  int authorCount = authorsTable.size();
  int bookCount = booksTable.size();
```

```
    int p = 0;
    int q = 0;

    while (p <authorCount && q < bookCount) {
      Author author = authorsTable.get(p);
      Book book = booksTable.get(q);

      if (author.authorId() == book.authorId()) {
        resultSet.add(new ResultRow(author.authorId(),
          author.name(), book.title(), book.bookId()));
        q++;
      } else {
        p++;
      }
    }

    return resultSet;
}
```

The time complexity of the Sort Merge Join algorithm is O(nlog(n) + mlog(m)) where n is the size of authorsTable and m is the size of booksTable. So, this is better than Nested Loop Join and Hash Join.

Summary

In this chapter, we covered a lot of interesting topics. We started with the new Vector API for empowering parallel data processing, then we continued with a bunch of cool data structures like Zipper, K-D Trees, Skip List, Binomial Heap, and so on. We finished with a nice overview of the three main join algorithms. Moreover, we've covered the JDK 21 Sequenced Collections API.

Join our community on Discord

Join our community's Discord space for discussions with the author and other readers:

```
https://discord.gg/8mgytp5DGQ
```

6

Java I/O: Context-Specific Deserialization Filters

This chapter includes 13 problems related to Java serialization/deserialization processes. We start with classical problems like serializing/deserializing objects to byte[], String, and XML. We continue with JDK 9 deserialization filters meant to prevent deserialization vulnerabilities, and we finish with JDK 17 (JEP 415, final) context-specific deserialization filters.

At the end of this chapter, you'll be skilled in solving almost any problem related to serializing/deserializing objects in Java.

Problems

Use the following problems to test your programming prowess on Java serialization/deserialization. I strongly encourage you to give each problem a try before you turn to the solutions and download the example programs:

131. **Serializing objects to byte arrays:** Write a Java application that exposes two helper methods for serializing/deserializing objects to/from byte[].

132. **Serializing objects to strings:** Write a Java application that exposes two helper methods for serializing/deserializing objects to/from String.

133. **Serializing objects to XML:** Exemplify at least two approaches for serializing/deserializing objects to/from XML format.

134. **Introducing JDK 9 deserialization filters:** Provide a brief introduction to JDK 9 deserialization filters including some insights into the ObjectInputFilter API.

135. **Implementing a custom pattern-based ObjectInputFilter:** Provide an example of implementing and setting a custom pattern-based filter via the ObjectInputFilter API.

136. **Implementing a custom class ObjectInputFilter:** Exemplify the creation of an ObjectInputFilter via a class implementation.

137. **Implementing a custom method ObjectInputFilter:** Exemplify the creation of an `ObjectInputFilter` via a method implementation.

138. **Implementing a custom lambda ObjectInputFilter:** Exemplify the creation of an `ObjectInputFilter` via a lambda expression.

139. **Avoiding StackOverflowError at deserialization:** First, write a snippet of code that can be successfully serialized but, in the deserialization phase, causes a `StackOverflowError`. Second, write a filter that avoids this unpleasant scenario.

140. **Avoiding DoS attacks at deserialization:** First, write a snippet of code that can be successfully serialized but, in the deserialization phase, causes a DoS attack. Second, write a filter that avoids this unpleasant scenario.

141. **Introducing JDK 17 easy filter creation:** Explain and exemplify the usage of the JDK 17 `allowFilter()` and `rejectFilter()` methods.

142. **Tackling context-specific deserialization filters:** Explain and exemplify the usage of JDK 17 Filter Factories.

143. **Monitoring deserialization via JFR:** Exemplify the usage of **Java Flight Recorder** (JFR) for monitoring a deserialization event.

The following sections describe solutions to the preceding problems. Remember that there usually isn't a single correct way to solve a particular problem. Also, remember that the explanations shown here include only the most interesting and important details needed to solve the problems. Download the example solutions to see additional details and to experiment with the programs at `https://github.com/PacktPublishing/Java-Coding-Problems-Second-Edition/tree/main/Chapter06`.

131. Serializing objects to byte arrays

In *Chapter 4, Problem 94*, we talked about the serialization/deserialization of Java records, so you should be pretty familiar with these operations. In a nutshell, serialization is the process of transforming an in-memory object into a stream of bytes that can also be stored in memory or written to a file, network, database, external storage, and so on. Deserialization is the reverse process, that is, recreating the object state in memory from the given stream of bytes.

A Java object is serializable if its class implements `java.io.Serializable` (or, `java.io.Externalizable`). Accomplishing serialization/deserialization takes place via the `java.io.ObjectOutputStream` and `java.io.ObjectInputStream` classes and `writeObject()`/`readObject()` methods.

For instance, let's assume the following `Melon` class:

```
public class Melon implements Serializable {

  private final String type;
  private final float weight;


  // constructor, getters
}
```

And, an instance of `Melon`:

```
Melon melon = new Melon("Gac", 2500);
```

Serializing the `melon` instance into a byte array can be accomplished as follows:

```
public static byte[] objectToBytes(Serializable obj)
        throws IOException {

  try (ByteArrayOutputStream baos
            = new ByteArrayOutputStream();
        ObjectOutputStream ois
            = new ObjectOutputStream(baos)) {
    ois.writeObject(obj);

    return baos.toByteArray();
  }
}
```

Of course, we can use this helper to serialize any other object, but for the `melon` instance, we call it as follows:

```
byte[] melonSer = Converters.objectToBytes(melon);
```

Deserialization is done via another helper that uses `readObject()` as follows:

```
public static Object bytesToObject(byte[] bytes)
        throws IOException, ClassNotFoundException {

  try ( InputStream is = new ByteArrayInputStream(bytes);
        ObjectInputStream ois = new ObjectInputStream(is)) {
    return ois.readObject();
  }
}
```

We can use this helper to deserialize any other object from a byte array, but for the `melonSer`, we call it as follows:

```
Melon melonDeser = (Melon) Converters.bytesToObject(melonSer);
```

The returned `melonDeser` restores the initial object state even if it is not the same instance. In the bundled code, you can also see an approach based on Apache Commons Lang.

132. Serializing objects to strings

In the previous problem, you saw how to serialize objects to byte arrays. If we work a little bit on a byte array, we can obtain a string representation of serialization. For instance, we can rely on `java.util.Base64` to encode a byte array to `String` as follows:

```
public static String objectToString(Serializable obj) throws IOException {

    try ( ByteArrayOutputStream baos = new ByteArrayOutputStream();
          ObjectOutputStream ois = new ObjectOutputStream(baos)) {
        ois.writeObject(obj);

        return Base64.getEncoder().encodeToString(baos.toByteArray());
    }
}
```

A possible output looks like this:

```
rO0ABXNyABZtb2Rlcm4uY2hhbGxlbmdlLk1lbG9u2WrnGA2MxZ4CAAJGAAZ3ZWlnaHRMAAR0eXBldAAST
GphdmEvbGFuZy9TdHJpbmc7eHBFHEAAdAADR2Fj
```

And, the code to obtain such a String is as follows:

```
String melonSer = Converters.objectToString(melon);
```

The reverse process relies on the `Base64` decoder as follows:

```
public static Object stringToObject(String obj)
            throws IOException, ClassNotFoundException {

  byte[] data = Base64.getDecoder().decode(obj);
  try ( ObjectInputStream ois = new ObjectInputStream(
        new ByteArrayInputStream(data))) {
   return ois.readObject();
  }
}
```

Calling this method is straightforward:

```
Melon melonDeser = (Melon)
      Converters.stringToObject(melonSer);
```

The `melonDeser` object is the result of deserializing the previous string.

133. Serializing objects to XML

Serializing/deserializing objects to XML via the JDK API can be accomplished via java.beans.
XMLEncoder, respectively XMLDecoder. The XMLEncoder API relies on Java Reflection to discover the
object's fields and write them in XML format. This class can encode objects that respect the Java Beans
contract (https://docs.oracle.com/javase/tutorial/javabeans/writing/index.html). Basically,
the object's class should contain a public no-arguments constructor and public getters and setters for
private/protected fields/properties. Implementing Serializable is not mandatory for XMLEncoder/
XMLDecoder, so we can serialize/deserialize objects that don't implement Serializable. Here, it is
a helper method that encodes the given Object to XML:

```
public static String objectToXML(Object obj)
            throws IOException {

  ByteArrayOutputStream baos = new ByteArrayOutputStream();

  try ( XMLEncoder encoder = new XMLEncoder(
                new BufferedOutputStream(baos))) {
    encoder.writeObject(obj);
  }

  baos.close();

  return new String(baos.toByteArray());
}
```

The reverse process (deserialization) uses the XMLDecoder as follows:

```
public static Object XMLToObject(String xml)
            throws IOException {

  try ( InputStream is
    = new ByteArrayInputStream(xml.getBytes());
   XMLDecoder decoder = new XMLDecoder(is)) {

   return decoder.readObject();
  }
}
```

The XMLEncoder/XMLDecoder is much more flexible than the writeObject()/readObject() API. For
instance, if a field/property is added/removed/renamed or its type has changed, then the decoding
process skips everything it cannot decode and tries to decode as much as possible without throwing
an exception.

Another common approach relies on the third-party library Jackson 2.x, which comes with XmlMapper. This library should be added as a dependency (of course, if you don't have it already present in your project):

```
<dependency>
  <groupId>com.fasterxml.jackson.dataformat</groupId>
  <artifactId>jackson-dataformat-xml</artifactId>
  <version>2.x</version>
</dependency>
```

Next, we create an instance of XmlMapper:

```
XmlMapper xmlMapper = new XmlMapper();
```

Via XmlMapper, we can serialize objects as XML as follows (there is no problem if the object's class doesn't implement Serializable and/or it doesn't contain setters):

```
public static String objectToXMLJackson(Object obj)
            throws JsonProcessingException {

  XmlMapper xmlMapper = new XmlMapper();

  if (xmlMapper.canSerialize(obj.getClass())) {
   return xmlMapper.writeValueAsString(obj);
  }

  return "";
}
```

Calling this method can be done as follows (melon is an instance of the Melon class):

```
String melonSer = Converters.objectToXMLJackson(melon);
```

The reverse process can rely on readValue() as follows:

```
public static <T> T XMLToObjectJackson(
        String xml, Class<T> clazz)
            throws JsonProcessingException {

  XmlMapper xmlMapper = new XmlMapper();

  return xmlMapper.readValue(xml, clazz);
}
```

Calling this method can be done as follows:

```
Melon melonDeser = Converters
    .XMLToObjectJackson(melonSer, Melon.class);
```

Take your time to explore the XmlMapper API since it has a lot more to offer. For now, consider running the bundled code to see the XML produced by each of these two approaches.

If you plan to serialize/deserialize an object to JSON, then consider *Java Coding Problems*, *First Edition*, *Problem 141*, for a comprehensive set of examples based on JSONB, Jackson, and Gson.

134. Introducing JDK 9 deserialization filters

As you know from *Chapter 4*, *Problem 94*, deserialization is exposed to vulnerabilities that may cause serious security issues. In other words, between serialization–deserialization cycles, an untrusted process (attacker) can modify/alter the serialization form to execute arbitrary code, sneak in malicious data, and so on.

In order to prevent such vulnerabilities, JDK 9 has introduced the possibility of creating restrictions via filters meant to accept/reject deserialization based on specific predicates. A deserialization filter intercepts a stream that expects to be deserialized and applies to it one or more predicates that should be successfully passed in order to proceed with deserialization. If a predicate fails, then deserialization doesn't even start and the stream is rejected.

There are two kinds of filters:

- **JVM-wide filters:** Filters applied to every deserialization that takes place in the JVM. The behavior of these filters is tightly coupled with how they are combined with other filters (if any).
- **Stream filters:** Filters that operate on all ObjectInputStream instances of an application (*stream-global filters*) or on certain ObjectInputStream instances (*stream-specific filters*).

We can create the following types of filters:

- Filters based on patterns (known as *pattern-based filters*): These filters can be used to filter modules, packages, or classes via string patterns. They can be applied without touching the code (as JVM-wide filters) or they can be created via the ObjectInputFilter API (as *pattern-based stream filters*).
- Filters based on the ObjectInputFilter API: This API allows us to define filters directly in code. Usually, such filters are defined based on string patterns or Java Reflection.

Pattern-based filters

Let's see several filters based on string patterns. For instance, this filter accepts all classes from the foo package (and from any other package that is not buzz) and rejects all classes from the buzz package (a class that passes a pattern that starts with ! is rejected):

```
foo.*;!buzz.*
```

Patterns are delimited via semicolons (;) and white spaces are considered as part of the pattern.

The following filter rejects only the modern.challenge.Melon class:

```
!modern.challenge.Melon
```

The following filter rejects the Melon class from the modern.challenge package and accepts all other classes from this package (the * is the wildcard used to represent unspecified class/package/module names):

```
!modern.challenge.Melon;modern.challenge.*;!*
```

The following filter accepts all classes from the foo package and its sub-packages (notice the ** wild-card):

```
foo.**
```

The following filter accepts all classes starting with Hash:

```
Hash*
```

Besides filtering classes, packages, and modules, we can also define the so-called *resource filters*, which allow us to accept/reject resources based on an object's graph complexity and size. In this context, we have maxdepth (the maximum graph depth), maxarray (the maximum array size), maxrefs (the maximum number of references between objects of a graph), and maxbytes (the maximum number of stream bytes). Here is an example:

```
maxdepth=5;maxarray=1000;maxrefs=50 foo.buzz.App
```

Now, let's see how we can use such filters.

Applying a pattern-based filter per application

If we want to apply a *pattern-based filter* to a single run of an application, then we can rely on the jdk.serialFilter system property. Without touching the code, we use this system property at the command line as in the following example:

```
java -Djdk.serialFilter=foo.**;Hash* foo.buzz.App
```

A system property replaces a Security Property value.

Applying a pattern-based filter to all applications in a process

To apply a *pattern-based filter* to all applications in a process, we should follow two steps (again, we don't touch the application code):

1. In an editor (for instance, Notepad or Wordpad), open the java.security file. In JDK 6-8, this file is located in $JAVA_HOME/lib/security/java.security, while in JDK 9+, it is in $JAVA_HOME/conf/security/java.security.

2. Edit this file by appending the pattern to the jdk.serialFilter Security Property.

Done!

ObjectInputFilter-based filters

Via the `ObjectInputFilter` API, we can create custom filters based on string patterns and Java Reflection. These filters can be applied to certain streams (*stream-specific filters*) or to all streams (*stream-global filters*) and can be implemented as *pattern-based filters*, as classes, methods, or lambda expressions.

First, we implement the filter via the `ObjectInputFilter` API. Second, we set the filter on all/certain `ObjectInputStream` instances. Setting the filter as a *stream-global filter* is done via `ObjectInputFilter.Config.setSerialFilter(ObjectInputFilter filter)`. On the other hand, setting the filter as a *stream-specific filter* can be done via `ObjectInputStream.setObjectInputFilter(ObjectInputFilter filter)`.

For instance, creating a *pattern-based filter* via this API can be done by calling the `Config.createFilter(String pattern)` method.

A custom filter defined as a class is done by implementing the `ObjectInputFilter` functional interface and overriding the `Status checkInput(FilterInfo filterInfo)` method.

A custom filter defined as a method is commonly done via a static method as `static ObjectInputFilter.Status someFilter(FilterInfo info) {…}`.

And, a custom filter defined as a lambda expression is commonly expressed as `ois.setObjectInputFilter(f -> (…))`, where `f` is `ObjectInputFilter` and `ois` is an instance of `ObjectInputStream`.

A filter returns a *status* (`java.io.ObjectInputFilter.Status`), which can be `ALLOWED`, `REJECTED`, or `UNDECIDED`.

In the next problems, we will explore these statements via examples.

135. Implementing a custom pattern-based ObjectInputFilter

Let's assume that we already have the `Melon` class and the helper methods for serializing/deserializing objects to/from byte arrays from *Problem 131*.

Creating a *pattern-based filter* via the `ObjectInputFilter` API can be done by calling the `Config.createFilter(String pattern)` method. For instance, the following filter rejects the `modern.challenge.Melon` class:

```
ObjectInputFilter melonFilter = ObjectInputFilter.Config
    .createFilter("!modern.challenge.Melon;");
```

We can set this filter as a *stream-global filter* via `setSerialFilter()` as follows:

```
ObjectInputFilter.Config.setSerialFilter(melonFilter);
```

If we need to get access to a *stream-global filter*, then we can call `getSerialFilter()`:

```
ObjectInputFilter serialFilter =
  ObjectInputFilter.Config.getSerialFilter();
```

Any stream deserialization in this application will pass through this filter, which will reject any instance of `modern.challenge.Melon`. You can practice this filter in the bundled code.

On the other hand, if we want to set this on a specific stream, then we can modify our `Converters.bytesToObject()` method to accept a filter as follows:

```
public static Object bytesToObject(byte[] bytes,
               ObjectInputFilter filter)
                 throws IOException, ClassNotFoundException {

  try ( InputStream is = new ByteArrayInputStream(bytes);
       ObjectInputStream ois = new ObjectInputStream(is)) {

    // set the filter
    ois.setObjectInputFilter(filter);

    return ois.readObject();
    }
}
```

If we pass `null` as `filter`, then the filter will not be applied. Otherwise, the passed filter will be applied to the current stream:

```
Melon melon = new Melon("Gac", 2500);

// serialization works as usual
byte[] melonSer = Converters.objectToBytes(melon);

// here, we pass the melonFilter, which rejects the instances
// of modern.challenge.Melon, so deserialization is rejected
Melon melonDeser = (Melon) Converters.bytesToObject(
      melonSer, melonFilter);
```

In this example, the `melonFilter` will reject deserialization and the output will be as follows:

```
Exception in thread "main" java.io.InvalidClassException: filter status:
REJECTED
...
```

You can also practice this filter in the bundled code.

136. Implementing a custom class ObjectInputFilter

Let's assume that we already have the Melon class and the helper methods for serializing/deserializing objects to/from byte arrays from *Problem 131*.

An ObjectInputFilter can be written via a dedicated class by implementing the ObjectInputFilter functional interface as in the following example:

```
public final class MelonFilter implements ObjectInputFilter {

  @Override
  public Status checkInput(FilterInfo filterInfo) {

  Class<?> clazz = filterInfo.serialClass();
  if (clazz != null) {
   // or, clazz.getName().equals("modern.challenge.Melon")
   return
    !(clazz.getPackage().getName().equals("modern.challenge")
      && clazz.getSimpleName().equals("Melon"))
      ? Status.ALLOWED : Status.REJECTED;
  }

  return Status.UNDECIDED;
  }
}
```

This filter is exactly the same as the *pattern-based filter*, !modern.challenge.Melon, only that it is expressed via Java Reflection.

We can set this filter as a *stream-global filter* as follows:

```
ObjectInputFilter.Config.setSerialFilter(new MelonFilter());
```

Or, as a *stream-specific filter* as follows:

```
Melon melonDeser = (Melon) Converters.bytesToObject(
  melonSer, new MelonFilter());
```

Of course, the bytesToObject() accepts an argument of type ObjectInputFilter and sets this filter accordingly (ois is the specific ObjectInputStream):

```
ois.setObjectInputFilter(filter);
```

In this example, the MelonFilter will reject deserialization and the output will be as follows:

```
Exception in thread "main" java.io.InvalidClassException: filter status:
REJECTED
…
```

You can practice both approaches (*stream-global* and *stream-specific*) in the bundled code.

137. Implementing a custom method ObjectInputFilter

Let's assume that we already have the Melon class and the helper methods for serializing/deserializing objects to/from byte arrays from *Problem 131*.

An ObjectInputFilter can be written via a dedicated method as in the following example:

```
public final class Filters {

  private Filters() {
   throw new AssertionError("Cannot be instantiated");
  }

  public static ObjectInputFilter.Status melonFilter(
              FilterInfo info) {

  Class<?> clazz = info.serialClass();
  if (clazz != null) {
   // or, clazz.getName().equals("modern.challenge.Melon")
   return
     !(clazz.getPackage().getName().equals("modern.challenge")
       && clazz.getSimpleName().equals("Melon"))
       ? Status.ALLOWED :Status.REJECTED;
  }

  return Status.UNDECIDED;
  }
}
```

Of course, you can add more filters in this class.

We can set this filter as a *stream-global filter* as follows:

```
ObjectInputFilter.Config
              .setSerialFilter(Filters::melonFilter);
```

Or, as a *stream-specific filter* as follows:

```
Melon melonDeser = (Melon) Converters.bytesToObject(
   melonSer, Filters::melonFilter);
```

Of course, the bytesToObject() accepts an argument of type ObjectInputFilter and sets this filter accordingly (ois is the specific ObjectInputStream):

```
ois.setObjectInputFilter(filter);
```

In this example, the `Filters::melonFilter` will reject deserialization and the output will be as follows:

```
Exception in thread "main" java.io.InvalidClassException: filter status:
REJECTED
...
```

You can check out both approaches (*stream-global* and *stream-specific*) in the bundled code. Moreover, you can also practice another example that rejects all instances of `Melon` and its subclasses based on a *stream-global filter*.

138. Implementing a custom lambda ObjectInputFilter

Let's assume that we already have the `Melon` class and the helper methods for serializing/deserializing objects to/from byte arrays from *Problem 131*.

An `ObjectInputFilter` can be written via a dedicated lambda and set as a *stream-global filter* as follows:

```
ObjectInputFilter.Config
   .setSerialFilter(f -> ((f.serialClass() != null)
   // or, filter.serialClass().getName().equals(
   //     "modern.challenge.Melon")
   && f.serialClass().getPackage()
                  .getName().equals("modern.challenge")
   && f.serialClass().getSimpleName().equals("Melon"))
   ? Status.REJECTED : Status.UNDECIDED);
```

Or, as a *stream-specific filter* as follows:

```
Melon melonDeser = (Melon) Converters.bytesToObject(melonSer,
   f -> ((f.serialClass() != null)
    // or, filter.serialClass().getName().equals(
    //      "modern.challenge.Melon")
   && f.serialClass().getPackage()
                  .getName().equals("modern.challenge")
   && f.serialClass().getSimpleName().equals("Melon"))
   ? Status.REJECTED : Status.UNDECIDED);
```

You can practice these examples in the bundled code.

139. Avoiding StackOverflowError at deserialization

Let's consider the following snippet of code:

```
// 'mapOfSets' is the object to serialize/deserialize
HashMap<Set, Integer> mapOfSets = new HashMap<>();
Set<Set> set = new HashSet<>();
mapOfSets.put(set, 1);
set.add(set);
```

We plan to serialize the `mapOfSets` object as follows (I assume that `Converters.objectToBytes()` is well-known from the previous problems):

```
byte[] mapSer = Converters.objectToBytes(mapOfSets);
```

Everything works just fine until we try to deserialize `mapSer`. At that moment, instead of a valid object, we will get a `StackOverflowError` as follows:

```
Exception in thread "main" java.lang.StackOverflowError
  at java.base/java.util.HashMap$KeyIterator
    .<init>(HashMap.java:1626)
  at java.base/java.util.HashMap$KeySet
    .iterator(HashMap.java:991)
  at java.base/java.util.HashSet
    .iterator(HashSet.java:182)
  at java.base/java.util.AbstractSet
    .hashCode(AbstractSet.java:120)
  at java.base/java.util.AbstractSet
    .hashCode(AbstractSet.java:124)
  ...
```

The deserialization process got stuck in the `hashCode()` method of `Set`. The solution is to create a filter that will reject deserialization if the object has a graph depth bigger than 2. This can be a *pattern-based filter* as follows:

```
ObjectInputFilter filter = ObjectInputFilter.Config
  .createFilter("maxdepth=2;java.base/*;!*");
```

Next, call the deserialization process with this filter:

```
HashMap mapDeser = (HashMap) Converters
  .bytesToObject(mapSer, filter);
```

I assume that `Converters.bytesToObject()` is well-known from the previous problems. This time, instead of getting `StackOverflowError`, the deserialization is rejected by the filter.

140. Avoiding DoS attacks at deserialization

Denial-of-service (DoS) attacks are typically malicious actions meant to trigger, in a short period of time, a lot of requests to a server, application, and so on. Generally speaking, a DoS attack is any kind of action that intentionally/accidentally overwhelms a process and forces it to slow down or even crash. Let's see a snippet of code that is a good candidate for representing a DoS attack in the deserialization phase:

```
ArrayList<Object> startList = new ArrayList<>();

List<Object> list1 = startList;
List<Object> list2 = new ArrayList<>();

for (int i = 0; i < 101; i++) {

  List<Object> sublist1 = new ArrayList<>();
  List<Object> sublist2 = new ArrayList<>();

  sublist1.add("value: " + i);

  list1.add(sublist1);
  list1.add(sublist2);

  list2.add(sublist1);
  list2.add(sublist2);

  list1 = sublist1;
  list2 = sublist2;
}
```

We plan to serialize the startList object as follows (I assume that Converters.objectToBytes() is well-known from the previous problems):

```
byte[] startListSer = Converters.objectToBytes(startList);
```

Everything works just fine until we try to deserialize startListSer. At that moment, instead of a valid object, we will get…nothing! Actually, the application starts normally, but it just hangs there in the deserialization phase. The system slows down and, after a while, it will eventually crash.

The object graph is too deep to be deserialized and that leads to a behavior similar to a DoS attack. The solution is to create a filter that will reject deserialization if the object has a graph depth bigger than a safe value. This can be a *pattern-based filter* as follows:

```
ObjectInputFilter filter = ObjectInputFilter.Config
  .createFilter("maxdepth=10;java.base/*;!*");
```

Next, call the deserialization process with this filter:

```
ArrayList startListDeser = (ArrayList)
  Converters.bytesToObject(startListSer, filter);
```

I assume that `Converters.bytesToObject()` is well-known from the previous problems. This time, the deserialization is rejected by the filter and the DoS attack is prevented.

141. Introducing JDK 17 easy filter creation

Starting with JDK 17, we can express filters more intuitively and readably via two convenient methods named `allowFilter()` and `rejectFilter()`. And, since the best way to learn is with an example, here is a usage case of these two convenient methods:

```java
public final class Filters {

 private Filters() {
  throw new AssertionError("Cannot be instantiated");
 }

 public static ObjectInputFilter allowMelonFilter() {

  ObjectInputFilter filter = ObjectInputFilter.allowFilter(
   clazz -> Melon.class.isAssignableFrom(clazz),
         ObjectInputFilter.Status.REJECTED);

  return filter;
 }

 public static ObjectInputFilter rejectMuskmelonFilter() {

  ObjectInputFilter filter = ObjectInputFilter.rejectFilter(
   clazz -> Muskmelon.class.isAssignableFrom(clazz),
         ObjectInputFilter.Status.UNDECIDED);

  return filter;
 }
}
```

The `allowMelonFilter()` relies on `ObjectInputFilter.allowFilter()` to allow only objects that are instances of `Melon` or subclasses of `Melon`. The `rejectMuskmelonFilter()` relies on `ObjectInputFilter.rejectFilter()` to reject all objects that are instances of `Muskmelon` or subclasses of `Muskmelon`.

We can use each of these filters as you already know from the previous problems, so let's tackle another use case. Let's assume that we have the following hierarchy of classes:

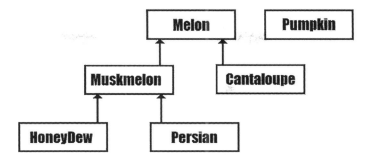

Figure 6.1: An arbitrary hierarchy of classes

Let's assume that we want to deserialize only objects that are instances of `Melon` or subclasses of `Melon` but they are not `Muskmelon` or subclasses of `Muskmelon`. In other words, we allow deserializing instances of `Melon` and `Cantaloupe`.

If we apply the `allowMelonFilter()`, then we will deserialize instances of `Melon`, `Muskmelon`, `Cantaloupe`, `HoneyDew`, and `Persian` since all these are `Melon`.

On the other hand, if we apply `rejectMuskmelonFilter()`, then we will deserialize instances of `Melon`, `Cantaloupe`, and `Pumpkin` since these are not `Muskmelon`.

But, if we apply `rejectMuskmelonFilter()` after applying `allowMelonFilter()`, then we will deserialize only `Melon` and `Cantaloupe`, which is exactly what we want.

Intuitively, we may think to chain our filters by writing something like this (ois is the current `ObjectInputStream`):

```
ois.setObjectInputFilter(Filters.allowMelonFilter());
ois.setObjectInputFilter(Filters.rejectMuskmelonFilter());
```

But, this will not work! It will cause a `java.lang.IllegalStateException`: *filter cannot be set more than once.*

The solution relies on `ObjectInputFilter.merge(filter, anotherFilter)`, which returns a filter that merges the status of these two filters by applying the following logic:

1. Call `filter` and get the returned `status`
2. If the returned `status` is `REJECTED`, then return it
3. Call `anotherFilter` and get the returned `otherStatus`
4. If `anotherStatus` is `REJECTED`, then return it
5. If either `status` or `otherStatus` is `ALLOWED`, then return `ALLOWED`
6. Otherwise, return `UNDECIDED`

Nevertheless, if `anotherFilter` is `null`, the filter is returned.

Based on this logic, we can merge the status of `Filters.allowMelonFilter()` with the status of `Filters.rejectMuskmelonFilter()` as follows:

```
public static Object bytesToObject(byte[] bytes,
        ObjectInputFilter allowFilter,
        ObjectInputFilter rejectFilter)
        throws IOException, ClassNotFoundException {

  try ( InputStream is = new ByteArrayInputStream(bytes);
        ObjectInputStream ois = new ObjectInputStream(is)) {

    // set the filters
    ObjectInputFilter filters = ObjectInputFilter.merge(
      allowFilter, rejectFilter);
    ois.setObjectInputFilter(filters);

    return ois.readObject();
  }
}
```

Next, let's talk about JDK 17 Filter Factories.

142. Tackling context-specific deserialization filters

JDK 17 enriched the deserialization filter capabilities with the implementation of JEP 415, *Context-Specific Deserialization Filters*.

Practically, JDK 17 added the so-called Filter Factories. Depending on the context, a Filter Factory can dynamically decide what filters to use for a stream.

Applying a Filter Factory per application

If we want to apply a Filter Factory to a single run of an application, then we can rely on the `jdk.serialFilterFactory` system property. Without touching the code, we use this system property at the command line as in the following example:

```
java -Djdk.serialFilterFactory=FilterFactoryName YourApp
```

The `FilterFactoryName` is the fully qualified name of the Filter Factory, which is a public class that can be accessed by the application class loader, and it was set before the first deserialization.

Applying a Filter Factory to all applications in a process

To apply a Filter Factory to all applications in a process, we should follow two steps (again, we don't touch the application code):

1. In an editor (for instance, Notepad or Wordpad), open the java.security file. In JDK 6-8, this file is located in $JAVA_HOME/lib/security/java.security, while in JDK 9+, it is in $JAVA_HOME/conf/security/java.security.

2. Edit this file by appending the Filter Factory to the jdk.serialFilterFactory Security Property.

Applying a Filter Factory via ObjectInputFilter.Config

Alternatively, a Filter Factory can be set directly in code via ObjectInputFilter.Config as follows:

```
ObjectInputFilter.Config
  .setSerialFilterFactory(FilterFactoryInstance);
```

The FilterFactoryInstance argument is an instance of a Filter Factory. This Filter Factory will be applied to all streams from the current application.

Implementing a Filter Factory

A Filter Factory is implemented as a BinaryOperator<ObjectInputFilter>. The apply(ObjectInputFilter current, ObjectInputFilter next) method provides the *current filter* and the *next* or *requested filter*.

In order to see how it works, let's assume that we have the following three filters:

```
public final class Filters {

  private Filters() {
   throw new AssertionError("Cannot be instantiated");
  }

  public static ObjectInputFilter allowMelonFilter() {

   ObjectInputFilter filter = ObjectInputFilter.allowFilter(
    clazz -> Melon.class.isAssignableFrom(clazz),
          ObjectInputFilter.Status.REJECTED);

   return filter;
  }

  public static ObjectInputFilter rejectMuskmelonFilter() {

   ObjectInputFilter filter = ObjectInputFilter.rejectFilter(
    clazz -> Muskmelon.class.isAssignableFrom(clazz),
          ObjectInputFilter.Status.UNDECIDED);

   return filter;
```

```
    }

    public static ObjectInputFilter packageFilter() {

      return ObjectInputFilter.Config.createFilter(
            "modern.challenge.*;!*");
    }
}
```

The `Filters.allowMelonFilter()` is set as a *stream-global filter* as follows:

```
ObjectInputFilter.Config.setSerialFilter(
    Filters.allowMelonFilter());
```

The `Filters.rejectMuskmelonFilter()` is set as a *stream-specific filter* as follows:

```
Melon melon = new Melon("Melon", 2400);

// serialization
byte[] melonSer = Converters.objectToBytes(melon);

// deserialization
Melon melonDeser = (Melon) Converters.bytesToObject(
    melonSer, Filters.rejectMuskmelonFilter());
```

And, the `Filters.packageFilter()` is set in the Filter Factory as follows:

```
public class MelonFilterFactory implements
        BinaryOperator<ObjectInputFilter> {

    @Override
    public ObjectInputFilter apply(
            ObjectInputFilter current, ObjectInputFilter next) {

      System.out.println();
      System.out.println("Current filter: " + current);
      System.out.println("Requested filter: " + next);

      if (current == null && next != null) {
        return ObjectInputFilter.merge(
            next, Filters.packageFilter());
      }
```

```
    return ObjectInputFilter.merge(next, current);
  }
}
```

The `MelonFilterFactory` is set via `ObjectInputFilter.Config` before any deserialization takes place:

```
MelonFilterFactory filterFactory = new MelonFilterFactory();
ObjectInputFilter.Config
                 .setSerialFilterFactory(filterFactory);
```

Now that everything is in place, let's see what's happening. The `apply()` method is called twice. The first time it is called is when the `ObjectInputStream ois` is created, and we obtain the following output:

```
Current filter: null

Requested filter:
predicate(modern.challenge.Filters$$Lambda$4/0x000000080
1001800@ba8a1dc, ifTrue: ALLOWED,ifFalse: REJECTED)
```

The *current filter* is null, and the *requested filter* is `Filters.allowMelonFilter()`. Since the *current filter* is null and the *requested filter* is not null, we decided to return a filter as the result of merging the status of the *requested filter* with the status of the `Filters.packageFilter()`.

The second time the `apply()` method is called happens when the `ois.setObjectInputFilter(filter)` is called in `Converters.bytesToObject(byte[] bytes, ObjectInputFilter filter)`. We have the following output:

```
Current filter: merge(predicate(modern.challenge.
Filters$$Lambda$4/0x0000000801001800@ba8a1dc, ifTrue: ALLOWED,
ifFalse:REJECTED), modern.challenge.*;!*)

Requested filter: predicate(modern.challenge.
Filters$$Lambda$10/0x0000000801002a10@484b61fc, ifTrue: REJECTED,
ifFalse:UNDECIDED)
```

This time, the *current* and *requested filters* are not null, so we merge their statuses again. Finally, all filters are successfully passed and the deserialization takes place.

143. Monitoring deserialization via JFR

Java Flight Recorder (JFR) is an event-based tool for the diagnosis and profiling of Java applications. This tool was initially added in JDK 7 and, since then, it has been constantly improved. For instance, in JDK 14, JFR was enriched with event streaming, and in JDK 19, with filtering event capabilities, and so on. You can find all JFR events listed and documented per JDK version at https://sap.github.io/SapMachine/jfrevents/.

Among its rich list of events, JFR can monitor and record deserialization events (the deserialization event). Let's assume a simple application like the one from *Problem 131* (the first problem of this chapter). We start configuring JFR for monitoring the deserialization of this application by adding deserializationEvent.jfc into the root folder of the application:

```xml
<?xml version="1.0" encoding="UTF-8"?>
<configuration version="2.0" description="test">
  <event name="jdk.Deserialization">
    <setting name="enabled">true</setting>
    <setting name="stackTrace">false</setting>
  </event>
</configuration>
```

Practically, this file instructs JFR to monitor and record the deserialization events.

Next, we use -XX:StartFlightRecording=filename=recording.jfr to instruct JFR to record output in a file named recording.jfr, and we continue with settings=deserializationEvent.jfc to point out the configuration file listed previously.

So, the final command is the one from this figure:

```
Command Prompt                                                          —  □  ×
C:\SBPBP\GitHub\Java-Coding-Problems-Second-Edition\Chapter06\P143_MonitoringDeserializationJfr>
java -XX:StartFlightRecording=filename=recording.jfr,settings=deserializationEvent.jfc -classpat
h target\classes modern.challenge.Main
```

Figure 6.2: Running JFR

After this command is executed, you'll see an output as in *Figure 6.3*:

```
Command Prompt                                                          —  □  ×
C:\SBPBP\GitHub\Java-Coding-Problems-Second-Edition\Chapter06\P143_MonitoringDeserializationJfr>
java -XX:StartFlightRecording=filename=recording.jfr,settings=deserializationEvent.jfc -classpat
h target\classes modern.challenge.Main
[0.703s][info][jfr,startup] Started recording 1. No limit specified, using maxsize=250MB as defa
ult.
[0.703s][info][jfr,startup]
[0.703s][info][jfr,startup] Use jcmd 13728 JFR.dump name=1 to copy recording data to file.
Serialization: [-84, -19, 0, 5, 115, 114, 0, 22, 109, 111, 100, 101, 114, 110, 46, 99, 104, 97,
108, 108, 101, 110, 103, 101, 46, 77, 101, 108, 111, 110, -39, 106, -25, 24, 13, -116, -59, -98,
2, 0, 2, 70, 0, 6, 119, 101, 105, 103, 104, 116, 76, 0, 4, 116, 121, 112, 101, 116, 0, 18, 76,
106, 97, 118, 97, 47, 108, 97, 110, 103, 47, 83, 116, 114, 105, 110, 103, 59, 120, 112, 69, 28,
64, 0, 116, 0, 3, 71, 97, 99]

Deserialization: Melon{type=Gac, weight=2500.0}
```

Figure 6.3: The output of our application

JFR has produced a file named `recording.jfr`. We can easily view the content of this file via the JFR CLI. The command (`jfr print recording.jfr`) and the output are available in *Figure 6.4*:

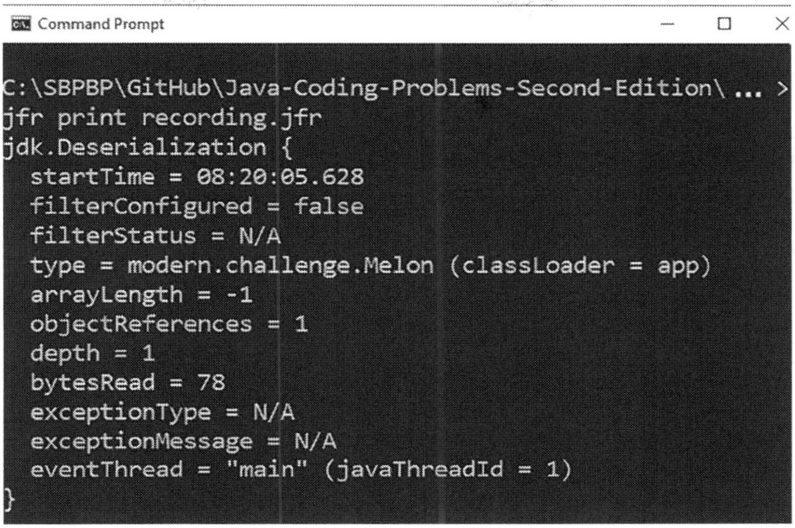

Figure 6.4: The output of JFR containing deserialization information

JFR produced a single deserialization event since our application has performed a single serialization/deserialization cycle of a `Melon` object. You can see the type of the object (here, `Melon`) via the `type` field. Since the `Melon` instance is not an array, the `arrayLength` was set to -1, which means that arrays are not applicable. The `objectReferences` represents the first object reference in the stream (so, 1) and the `bytesRead` represents the number of bytes read from this stream (in this case, 78 bytes). We also see that there was no filter present, `filterConfigured = false`, and `filterStatus = N/A` (not applicable). Moreover, `exceptionType` and `exceptionMessage` are N/A. They are not applicable because there is no filter present. They are useful for capturing any exceptions caused by a potential filter.

Besides the JFR CLI, you can use more powerful tools for consuming the deserialization event such as JDK Mission Control (`https://www.oracle.com/java/technologies/jdk-mission-control.html`) and the well-known Advanced Management Console (`https://www.oracle.com/java/technologies/advancedmanagementconsole.html`).

Summary

In this chapter, we covered a bunch of problems dedicated to handling Java serialization/deserialization processes. We started with classical problems and moved on to cover JDK 17 context-specific deserialization filters passing through JDK 9 deserialization filters on the way.

Join our community on Discord

Join our community's Discord space for discussions with the author and other readers:

https://discord.gg/8mgytp5DGQ

7

Foreign (Function) Memory API

This chapter includes 28 problems covering the Foreign Memory API and Foreign Linker API. We'll start with the classical approaches for calling foreign functions relying on the JNI API and the open-source JNA/JNR libraries. Next, we'll introduce the new approach delivered under the code name Project Panama (third review in JDK 21 and final release in JDK 22 as JEP 454). We'll dissect the most relevant APIs, such as Arena, MemorySegment, MemoryLayout, and so on. Finally, we'll focus on the Foreign Linker API and the Jextract tool for calling foreign functions with different types of signatures, including callback functions.

By the end of this chapter, you'll be skilled in putting JNI, JNA, JNR, and, of course, Project Panama to work and you'll be able to confidently answer any interview questions with this topic on the menu.

Problems

Use the following problems to test your programming prowess in manipulating off-heap memory and calling native foreign functions from Java. I strongly encourage you to give each problem a try before you turn to the solutions and download the example programs:

144. **Introducing Java Native Interface (JNI):** Write a Java application that calls a C/C++ native foreign function via the JNI API (for instance, implement in C a function with the following signature: long sumTwoInt(int x, int y)).

145. **Introducing Java Native Access (JNA):** Write a Java application that calls a C/C++ native foreign function via the JNA API.

146. **Introducing Java Native Runtime (JNR):** Write a Java application that calls a C/C++ native foreign function via the JNR API.

147. **Motivating and introducing Project Panama:** Provide a theoretical and meaningful transition from classical approaches of manipulating off-heap memory and foreign functions to the new Project Panama.

148. **Introducing Panama's architecture and terminology:** Provide a brief description of Project Panama, including architecture, terminology, and the main API components.

149. **Introducing Arena and MemorySegment:** Explain and exemplify via snippets of code the `Arena` and `MemorySegment` APIs.

150. **Allocating arrays into memory segments:** Write several approaches for allocating arrays into memory segments (via `Arena` and `MemorySegment`).

151. **Understanding addresses (pointers):** Exemplify the usage of memory addresses (pointers) in Java (`ValueLayout.ADDRESS`).

152. **Introducing the sequence layout:** Explain and exemplify the usage of the sequence layout. Moreover, introduce the `PathElement` and `VarHandle` APIs.

153. **Shaping C-like structs into memory segments:** Exemplify the approach of shaping C-like structs via Java memory layouts (`StructLayout`).

154. **Shaping C-like unions into memory segments:** Exemplify the approach of shaping C-like unions via Java memory layouts (`UnionLayout`).

155. **Introducing PaddingLayout:** Provide a detailed explanation and meaningful examples for explaining padding layout (introduce *size*, *alignment*, *stride*, *padding*, and *order* of bytes).

156. **Copying and slicing memory segments:** Exemplify different approaches for copying and slicing parts of a memory segment, including `asOverlappingSlice()` and `segmentOffset()`.

157. **Tackling the slicing allocator:** Exemplify the usage of the slicing allocator (`SegmentAllocator`).

158. **Introducing the slice handle:** Explain and exemplify the usage of `sliceHandle()`.

159. **Introducing layout flattening:** Consider a hierarchical memory layout (for instance, two nested sequence layouts). Explain and exemplify how to flatten this model.

160. **Introducing layout reshaping:** Provide an example that reshapes a hierarchical sequence layout.

161. **Introducing the layout spreader:** Provide a brief explanation and a simple example of using the layout spreader (`asSpreader()`).

162. **Introducing the memory segment view VarHandle:** Exemplify the usage of `MethodHandles.memorySegmentViewVarHandle(ValueLayout layout)` for creating a `VarHandle` that can be used to access a memory segment.

163. **Streaming memory segments:** Write several snippets of code for combining memory segments with the Java Stream API.

164. **Tackling mapped memory segments:** Provide a brief introduction of mapped memory segments and exemplify them in Java code.

165. **Introducing the Foreign Linker API:** Provide a brief description of the Foreign Linker API, including `Linker`, `SymbolLookup`, *downcall*, and *upcall*.

166. **Calling the sumTwoInt() foreign function:** Write a Java application that calls the `sumTwoInt()` method (the `long sumTwoInt(int x, int y)` implemented in *Problem 144*) via the Foreign Linker API.

167. **Calling the modf() foreign function:** Use the Foreign Linker API to call the `modf()` foreign function – this function is part of the C standard library.

168. **Calling the strcat() foreign function:** Use the Foreign Linker API to call the `strcat()` foreign function – this function is part of the C standard library.

169. **Calling the bsearch() foreign function**: Use the Foreign Linker API to call the bsearch() foreign function – this function is part of the C standard library.

170. **Introducing Jextract**: Provide a brief description of the Jextract tool, including the main options.

171. **Generating native binding for modf()**: Exemplify the combination of Jextract and the Foreign Linker API to call the modf() foreign function.

The following sections describe solutions to the preceding problems. Remember that there usually isn't a single correct way to solve a particular problem. Also, remember that the explanations shown here include only the most interesting and important details needed to solve the problems. Download the example solutions to see additional details and to experiment with the programs at https://github.com/PacktPublishing/Java-Coding-Problems-Second-Edition/tree/main/Chapter07.

144. Introducing Java Native Interface (JNI)

Java Native Interface (JNI) was the first Java API meant to act as a bridge between JVM bytecode and native code written in another programming language (typically C/C++).

Let's suppose that we plan to call via JNI a C function on a Windows 10, 64-bit machine.

For instance, let's consider that we have a C function for summing two integers called sumTwoInt(int x, int y). This function is defined in a C shared library named math.dll. Calling such functions from Java (generally speaking, functions implemented by native shared libraries) starts with loading the proper shared native library via System.loadLibrary(String library). Next, we declare the C function in Java via the native keyword. Finally, we call it with the following code:

```
package modern.challenge;

public class Main {

  static {
    System.loadLibrary("math");
  }

  private native long sumTwoInt(int x, int y);

  public static void main(String[] args) {
    long result = new Main().sumTwoInt(3, 9);

    System.out.println("Result: " + result);
  }
}
```

Next, we focus on C implementation. We need the header file (the .h file) and the source file that implements this method (the .cpp file).

Generating the header (.h) file

The header file (definition of the method) can be obtained by running javac with the –h option against our Main.java source, as in the following figure (before JDK 9, use javah):

```
C:\SBPBP\GitHub\Java-Coding-Problems-Second-Edition\Chapter07\P144_EngagingJNI>
 javac -h src/main/java/modern/challenge/cpp -d target/classes src/main/java/modern/challenge/Main.java
```

Figure 7.1: Running javac –h to compile source code and generate the .h file

Or, as plain text:

```
C:\SBPBP\GitHub\Java-Coding-Problems-Second-Edition\Chapter07\P144_EngagingJNI>
   javac -h src/main/java/modern/challenge/cpp -d target/classes src/main/java/
modern/challenge/Main.java
```

This command compiles our code (Main.java) and places the resulting class in the target/classes folder. In addition, this command generates the C header modern_challenge_Main.h in jni/cpp. The important code of this file is listed here:

```
/*
 * Class:      modern_challenge_Main
 * Method:     sumTwoInt
 * Signature: (II)J
 */
JNIEXPORT jlong JNICALL Java_modern_challenge_Main_sumTwoInt
  (JNIEnv *, jobject, jint, jint);
```

The function name was generated as Java_modern_challenge_Main_sumTwoInt. Moreover, we have here the following artifacts:

- JNIEXPORT – the function is marked as exportable
- JNICALL – sustains JNIEXPORT to guarantee that the function can be found by JNI
- JNIEnv – represents a pointer to the JNI environment for accessing JNI functions
- jobject – represents a reference to this Java object

Implementing the modern_challenge_Main.cpp

Next, we provide the C implementation in src/main/java/modern/challenge/cpp as follows:

```
#include <iostream>
#include "modern_challenge_Main.h"


JNIEXPORT jlong JNICALL Java_modern_challenge_Main_sumTwoInt
  (JNIEnv* env, jobject thisObject, jint x, jint y) {
    std::cout << "C++: The received arguments are : "
      << x << " and " << y << std::endl;
```

```
    return (long)x + (long)y;
}
```

This is a simple snippet of C code that prints a message and returns x + y as a `long` result.

Compiling the C source code

So far, we have the C source code (the .cpp file) and the generated header (.h). Next, we have to compile the C source code, and for this, we need a C compiler. There are many options, like Cygwin, MinGW, and so on.

We decided to install MinGW (https://sourceforge.net/projects/mingw-w64/) for 64-bit platforms and use the G++ compiler.

Having G++ in our hands, we have to trigger a specific command for compiling the C code, as in the following figure:

```
C:\SBPBP\GitHub\Java-Coding-Problems-Second-Edition\Chapter07\P144_EngagingJNI>

    g++ -c "-I%JAVA_HOME%\include" "-I%JAVA_HOME%\include\win32"

    src/main/java/modern/challenge/cpp/modern_challenge_Main.cpp

    -o jni/cpp/modern_challenge_Main.o
```

Figure 7.2: Compiling the C source code

Or, as plain text:

```
C:\SBPBP\GitHub\Java-Coding-Problems-Second-Edition\Chapter07\P144_EngagingJNI>
    g++ -c "-I%JAVA_HOME%\include" "-I%JAVA_HOME%\include\win32"
    src/main/java/modern/challenge/cpp/modern_challenge_Main.cpp
    -o jni/cpp/modern_challenge_Main.o
```

Next, we have to pack everything in `math.dll`.

Generating the native shared library

It is time to create the native shared library, `math.dll`. For this, we use G++ again, as in the following figure:

```
C:\SBPBP\GitHub\Java-Coding-Problems-Second-Edition\Chapter07\P144_EngagingJNI>

    g++ -shared -o jni/cpp/math.dll jni/cpp/modern_challenge_Main.o

    -static -m64 -Wl,--add-stdcall-alias
```

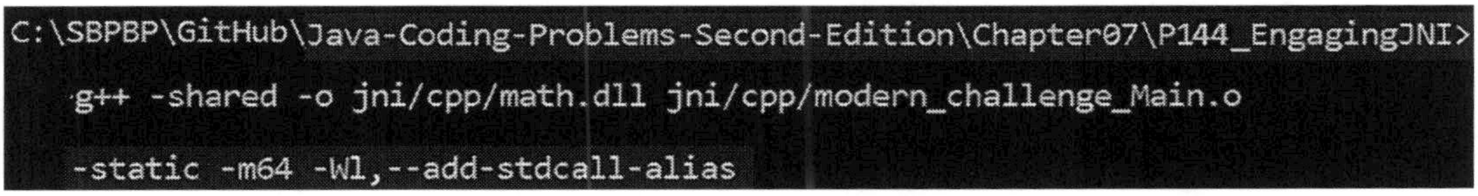

Figure 7.3: Creating the math.dll

Or, as plain text:

```
C:\SBPBP\GitHub\Java-Coding-Problems-Second-Edition\Chapter07\P144_EngagingJNI>
   g++ -shared -o jni/cpp/math.dll jni/cpp/modern_challenge_Main.o
   -static -m64 -Wl,--add-stdcall-alias
```

Notice that we have used the –static option. This option instructs G++ to add in math.dll all dependencies. If you dislike this approach, then you may need to manually add the dependencies in order to avoid java.lang.UnsatisfiedLinkError errors. To find out the missing dependencies, you can use a DLL dependency walker such as this one: https://github.com/lucasg/Dependencies.

Finally, run the code

Finally, we can run the code. Keep your fingers crossed and execute the command in the following figure:

```
C:\SBPBP\GitHub\Java-Coding-Problems-Second-Edition\Chapter07\P144_EngagingJNI>

   java -Djava.library.path=jni/cpp -classpath target/classes modern.challenge.Main


   C++: The received arguments are : 3 and 9
   Result: 12
```

Figure 7.4: Executing the Java code

Or, as plain text:

```
C:\SBPBP\GitHub\Java-Coding-Problems-Second-Edition\Chapter07\P144_EngagingJNI>
   java -Djava.library.path=jni/cpp
   -classpath target/classes modern.challenge.Main
```

Notice that we should set the library path; otherwise, Java will not be able to load math.dll. If everything worked fine, then you should see the output from this figure.

Well, as you can easily conclude, JNI is not easy to use. Imagine doing all this work for an entire C library like TensorFlow, which has 200+ functions. Besides being hard to use, JNI also faces a lot of shortcomings, for example, it is error-prone, hard to maintain, and brittle, it has poor exception support, JNI errors can crash the JVM, it has a maximum off-heap of 2 GB allocated via ByteBuffer that cannot be directly free (we have to wait for the garbage collector to do it), and many more. Despite all this, it is still worth learning this technique because, as you'll surely know, management is often not quick to adopt new ways of doing things.

With this in mind, the community came up with other approaches that we will discuss in the next problems.

145. Introducing Java Native Access (JNA)

Java Native Access (JNA) is a brave open-source attempt to address JNI complexity via a more intuitive and easy-to-use API. Being a third-party library, JNA must be added as a dependency in our project:

```
<dependency>
  <groupId>net.java.dev.jna</groupId>
  <artifactId>jna-platform</artifactId>
  <version>5.8.0</version>
</dependency>
```

Next, let's try to call the same `sumTwoInt()` method from *Problem 144*. This function is defined in a C native shared library named `math.dll` and stored in our project in the `jna/cpp` folder.

We start by writing a Java interface that extends JNA's `Library` interface. This interface contains declarations of methods and types that we plan to call from Java and are defined in native code. We write the `SimpleMath` interface containing the `sumTwoInt()` declaration as follows:

```
public interface SimpleMath extends Library {
  long sumTwoInt(int x, int y);
}
```

Next, we have to instruct JNA to load the `math.dll` library and generate a concrete implementation of this interface so we can call its methods. For this, we need the `jna.library.path` system property and JNA's `Native` class, as follows:

```
package modern.challenge;

public class Main {

  public static void main(String[] args) {

    System.setProperty("jna.library.path", "./jna/cpp");

    SimpleMath math = Native.load(Platform.isWindows()
      ? "math" : "NOT_WINDOWS", SimpleMath.class);

    long result = math.sumTwoInt(3, 9);
    System.out.println("Result: " + result);
  }
}
```

Here, we instruct JNA to load `math.dll` from `jna/cpp` via `System.setProperty()`, but you can also do it from a terminal via `–Djna.library.path=jna/cpp`.

Next, we call `Native.load()`, which takes two arguments. First, it takes the native library name, which in our case is `math` (without the `.dll` extension). Second, it takes the Java interface containing the declaration of the methods, which in our case is `SimpleMath.class`. The `load()` method returns a concrete implementation of `SimpleMath` that we use to call the `sumTwoInt()` method.

The JNA `Platform` helper allows us to provide the name of the native library specific to the current operating system. We have only `math.dll` for Windows.

Implementing the .cpp and .h files

This time, there is no naming convention from the `.cpp` and `.h` files, so let's name them `Arithmetic.cpp` and `Arithmetic.h` (the header file is optional). The source code of `Artihmetic.cpp` is basically plain C code:

```cpp
#include <iostream>
#include "Arithmetic.h"

long sumTwoInt(int x, int y) {
  std::cout << "C++: The received arguments are : " << x <<
     " and " << y << std::endl;
  return (long)x + (long)y;
}
```

As you can see, with JNA, there is no need to patch our code with the JNI-specific bridge code. It is only plain C code. The `Arithmetic.h` is optional and we can write it as follows:

```cpp
#ifndef FUNCTIONS_H_INCLUDED
#define FUNCTIONS_H_INCLUDED

  long sumTwoInt(int x, int y);

#endif
```

Next, we can compile our code.

Compiling the C source code

Compiling the C source code is done via the G++ compiler with the command from the following figure:

```
C:\SBPBP\GitHub\Java-Coding-Problems-Second-Edition\Chapter07\P145_EngagingJNA>

    g++ -c "-I%JAVA_HOME%\include" "-I%JAVA_HOME%\include\win32"

    src/main/java/modern/challenge/cpp/Arithmetic.cpp

    -o jna/cpp/Arithmetic.o
```

Figure 7.5: Compiling the C++ code

Or, as plain text:

```
C:\SBPBP\GitHub\Java-Coding-Problems-Second-Edition\Chapter07\P145_EngagingJNA>
    g++ -c "-I%JAVA_HOME%\include" "-I%JAVA_HOME%\include\win32"
    src/main/java/modern/challenge/cpp/Arithmetic.cpp
    -o jna/cpp/Arithmetic.o
```

Next, we can generate the proper native library.

Generating the native shared library

It is time to create the native shared library, `math.dll`. For this, we use G++ again as in the following figure:

```
C:\SBPBP\GitHub\Java-Coding-Problems-Second-Edition\Chapter07\P145_EngagingJNA>
    g++ -shared -o jna/cpp/math.dll jna/cpp/Arithmetic.o -static -m64 -Wl,--add-stdcall-alias
```

Figure 7.6: Generating math.dll

Or, as plain text:

```
C:\SBPBP\GitHub\Java-Coding-Problems-Second-Edition\Chapter07\P145_
EngagingJNA>g++ -shared -o jna/cpp/math.dll jna/cpp/Arithmetic.o -static -m64
-Wl,--add-stdcall-alias
```

At this point, you should have `math.dll` in the `jna/cpp` folder.

Finally, run the code

Finally, we can run the code. If everything worked fine, then you're done. Otherwise, if you get an exception such as `java.lang.UnsatisfiedLinkError`: *Error looking up function 'sumTwoInt': The specified procedure could not be found*, then you have to fix it.

But what happened? Most probably, the G++ compiler has applied a technique referred to as *name mangling* (or, *name decoration*) – `https://en.wikipedia.org/wiki/Name_mangling`. In other words, the G++ compiler has renamed the `sumTwoInt()` method to something else that is not known to JNA.

Solving this issue can be done in two steps. First, we need to inspect `math.dll` with a DLL dependency walker such as this one, `https://github.com/lucasg/Dependencies`. As you can see in the following figure, G++ has renamed `sumTwoInt` to `_Z9sumTwoIntii` (of course, on your computer, it could be another name):

▣C	18 (0x0012)	N/A	_Unwind_SetIP	0x0000bf90	None
▣C	19 (0x0013)	N/A	_Z9sumTwoIntii	0x000013b0	Demumble
▣C	20 (0x0014)	N/A	__emutls_get_address	0x0000c570	None

Figure 7.7: G++ has renamed sumToInt to _Z9sumTwoIntii

Second, we have to tell JNA about this name (_Z9sumTwoIntii). Basically, we need to define a Map containing the corresponding mapping of names and pass this map to a flavor of Native.load() that takes this map as the last argument. The code is straightforward:

```java
public class Main {

  private static final Map MAPPINGS;

  static {
    MAPPINGS = Map.of(
      Library.OPTION_FUNCTION_MAPPER,
      new StdCallFunctionMapper() {
      Map<String, String> methodNames
        = Map.of("sumTwoInt", "_Z9sumTwoIntii");

      @Override
      public String getFunctionName(
            NativeLibrary library, Method method) {
        String methodName = method.getName();
        return methodNames.get(methodName);
      }
    });
  }

  public static void main(String[] args) {

    System.setProperty("jna.library.path", "./jna/cpp");

    SimpleMath math = Native.load(Platform.isWindows()
      ? "math" : "NOT_WINDOWS", SimpleMath.class, MAPPINGS);

    long result = math.sumTwoInt(3, 9);
    System.out.println("Result: " + result);
  }
}
```

Done! Now, you should obtain the result of 3+9. Feel free to explore JNA further, and attempt to use C/C++ structures, unions, and pointers.

146. Introducing Java Native Runtime (JNR)

Java Native Runtime (JNR) is another open-source attempt to address JNI's complexity. It is a serious competitor for JNA, having a more intuitive and powerful API than JNI.

We can add it as a dependency as follows:

```xml
<dependency>
    <groupId>com.github.jnr</groupId>
    <artifactId>jnr-ffi</artifactId>
    <version>2.2.13</version>
</dependency>
```

Let's assume that we have the exact same C method (`sumTwoInt()`) and the native shared library (`math.dll`) from *Problem 145*.

We start by writing a Java interface containing the declarations of methods and types that we plan to call from Java and are defined in native code. We write the `SimpleMath` interface containing the `sumTwoInt()` declaration as follows:

```java
public interface SimpleMath {

  @IgnoreError
  long sumTwoInt(int x, int y);

}
```

The `@IgnoreError` annotation instructs JNR to not save the *errno value* (`https://www.geeksforgeeks.org/errno-constant-in-c/`).

Next, we have to instruct JNR to load the `math.dll` library and generate a concrete implementation of this interface so we can call its methods. For this, we need the `LibraryLoader` and the following intuitive code:

```java
public class Main {

  public static void main(String[] args) {

    LibraryLoader<SimpleMath> loader =
            FFIProvider.getSystemProvider()
    .createLibraryLoader(SimpleMath.class)
    .search("./jnr/cpp")
    .map("sumTwoInt", "_Z9sumTwoIntii");

    loader = loader.map("sumTwoInt", "_Z9sumTwoIntii");

    if (Platform.getNativePlatform().getOS()
    == Platform.OS.WINDOWS) {

      SimpleMath simpleMath = loader.load("math");
```

```
    long result = simpleMath.sumTwoInt(3, 9);

    System.out.println("Result: " + result);
   }
  }
 }
```

Via the `LibraryLoader` API, we prepare the playground. We instruct JNR that our library is located in `jnr/cpp` via the `search()` method. Moreover, we provide the proper mapping of the method's names via the `map()` method (remember from *Problem 145* that G++ renames the method via *name mangling* (or, *name decoration*) from `sumTwoInt` to `_Z9sumTwoIntii`).

Finally, we load the library via the `load()` method and call the `sumTwoInt()` method.

JNR provides many other features that you can exploit starting from `https://github.com/jnr`. You may also be interested in JavaCPP, which is another alternative to JNI (`https://github.com/bytedeco/javacpp`).

147. Motivating and introducing Project Panama

Project Panama, or the Foreign Function & Memory (FFM) API, is an elegant way of saying goodbye to JNI. This project started in JDK 17 as JEP 412 (first incubator). It continued in JDK 18 as JEP 419 (second incubator), JDK 19 as JEP 424 (first preview), JDK 20 as JEP 434 (second preview), and JDK 21 as JEP 442 (third preview). This is where things are at the time of writing.

To understand the goals of this project, we have to talk about accessing **off-heap** memory from Java applications. By off-heap memory, we mean the memory that is outside the JVM heap and is not managed by the garbage collector.

Surfing off-heap is the job of JNI, JNA, and JNR. In one way or another, these APIs can work in off-heap land to handle different tasks. Among these tasks, we can enumerate the following:

- Use native libraries (for instance, some common libraries are Open CL/GL, CUDA, TensorFlow, Vulkan, OpenSSL, V8, BLAS, cuDNN, and so on)
- Share memory across different processes
- Serialize/deserialize memory content to the so-called *mmaps*

The Java *de facto* API for accomplishing these kinds of tasks is `ByteBuffer`, or better, the so-called *allocated direct buffers*, which are more efficient in accessing off-heap memory. Alternatively, we can use JNI, or as you saw, third-party libraries such as JNA and JNR.

However, `ByteBuffer` and JNI have a lot of shortcomings that make them useful only in a limited number of scenarios. A few of their drawbacks are listed below:

- `ByteBuffer`:
  - Brittle and error-prone

- Unstable memory addresses
- Backed by an array that can be manipulated by the garbage collector
- Allocated direct buffers
- Cannot scale when used as a general off-heap API
- Works well only if used by power users who deeply understand its use
- No solution for deallocation/free memory

- JNI:

  - As you saw in *Problem 144*, JNI is hard to use (even for simple cases)
  - It is brittle and error-prone
  - It is difficult/expensive to maintain
  - There is poor error checking
  - It can crash the JVM

These shortcomings and much more are behind the reason for the creation of Project Panama. The goal of this project is to become the new *de facto* API for interoperating with foreign data, functions, and memory in Java. To accomplish this goal, Project Panama has two main features:

- A future-proof API (low-level, efficient, robust, and safe) to replace the old-school API based on byte buffers – this is referred to as the memory access API and is capable of accessing on-heap and off-heap memory.
- A brand-new paradigm replaces the JNI concepts and mechanisms, so now we have an intuitive, easy-to-use, and robust solution for creating Java bindings for native libraries. This is referred to as the Foreign Linker API.

In the next problems, we will dive deeper into this project.

148. Introducing Panama's architecture and terminology

When we talk about architecture, it helps to present a meaningful diagram, so here it is:

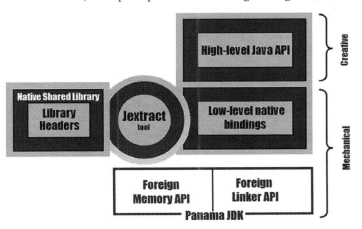

Figure 7.8: Project Panama architecture

This diagram reveals the interoperability of Panama's components. The climax of this diagram is the Jextract tool. As you'll see in this chapter, Jextract is a very handy tool capable of consuming the headers of native libraries and producing low-level Java native bindings. These bindings are the unit of work for two major APIs of Project Panama:

- Foreign Memory API – used to allocate/deallocate off-heap/on-heap memory
- Foreign Linker API – used to call foreign functions directly from Java and vice versa

The process described so far is entirely mechanical. When these APIs and the low-level Java native bindings are not enough for our tasks, then we can take things a step further and create a set of higher-level Java bindings. Of course, this is not a task for novices, but it is very powerful. For instance, you may have an existing automation tool for generating JNI bindings and now you want to modernize your tool to generate a higher level of pure Java bindings in Panama's style.

Among the abstractions used by Project Panama, we have the following:

- `java.lang.foreign.MemorySegment`: This API shapes a heap or native memory segment. A heap segment accesses on-heap memory, while a native segment accesses off-heap memory. In both cases, we're talking about a contiguous region of memory that has a lifespan bounded by space and time.
- `java.lang.foreign.Arena` (or `MemorySession` in JDK versions earlier than 20): This API can control the memory segment's lifespan.
- `java.lang.foreign.MemorySegment.Scope`: This API represents the scope of a memory segment.
- `java.lang.foreign.MemoryLayout`: This API describes the content of memory segments as *memory layouts*. For instance, among the available memory layouts, in the context of basic Java data types (`int`, `double`, `long`, and so on), we have *memory value layouts* (`java.lang.foreign.ValueLayout`).

Of course, next to these three pillars, we have many other classes and helpers. In the next problems, we will cover several scenarios meant to get us familiar with the major aspects of using Project Panama's APIs.

149. Introducing Arena and MemorySegment

A `MemorySegment` shapes a heap or native memory segment. A heap segment accesses on-heap memory, while a native segment accesses off-heap memory. In both cases, we talk about a contiguous region of memory that has a lifespan bounded by space and time.

Among its characteristics, a memory segment has a *size* in bytes, an *alignment* of bytes, and a *scope*. The scope is shaped via the `java.lang.foreign.MemorySegment.Scope` sealed interface and represents the lifespan of the memory segment. A native memory segment lifespan is controlled by a `java.lang.foreign.Arena` instance. An `Arena` has a scope that can be:

The *arena global scope* (or *global arena*): The memory segments with the arena global scope are always accessible. In other words, the regions of memory allocated to these segments are never deallocated and their global scope remains alive forever.

Attempting to close (`close()`) this scope will result in `UnsupportedOperationException`. Here is an example of creating a native memory segment of 8 bytes in the arena global scope:

```
MemorySegment globalSegment = Arena.global().allocate(8);
```

The *arena auto scope*: The memory segments with the arena automatic scope are managed by the garbage collector. In other words, the garbage collector determines when the regions of memory backing these segments can be safely deallocated.

Attempting to close (`close()`) this scope will result in an `UnsupportedOperationException`. Here is an example of creating a native memory segment of 8 bytes in the auto scope:

```
MemorySegment autoSegment = Arena.ofAuto().allocate(8);
```

The *arena confined scope* (or, *confined arena*): Strict control of the memory segment's lifespan (allocation/deallocation and lifetime) can be obtained via a confined arena. Typically, this scope lives in a `try-with-resources` block. When the `Arena` is closed (by explicitly calling `close()`, or by simply leaving the arena's `try-with-resources` block), its scope is closed, all memory segments associated with this scope are destroyed, and memory is deallocated automatically. A confined arena is opened via `ofConfined()` and is owned by the current thread – the memory segments associated with the scope of a confined arena can only be accessed by the thread that created the arena.

In code lines, a confined arena can be created as follows:

```
try (Arena arena = Arena.ofConfined()) {
  // current thread work with memory segments (MS1, MS2, …)
}

// here, memory segments MS1, MS2, …, have been deallocated
```

The *arena shared scope* (or, *shared arena*): A shared arena is typically opened in a `try-with-resources` block via `ofShared()` and can be shared by multiple threads – the memory segments associated with the scope of the shared arena can be accessed by any thread (for instance, this can be useful for performing parallel computations on memory segments). When the `Arena` is closed (by explicitly calling `close()`, or by simply leaving the arena's `try-with-resources` block), its scope is closed, all memory segments associated with this scope are destroyed, and memory is deallocated automatically.

In code lines, a confined arena can be created as follows:

```
try (Arena arena = Arena.ofShared()) {
  // any thread work with memory segments (MS1, MS2, …)
}

// here, memory segments MS1, MS2, …, have been deallocated
```

By calling `arena.scope()`, we obtain the `MemorySegment.Scope` of the arena, and by calling `arena.scope().isAlive()`, we can find out if the current scope is alive or not. A memory segment is accessible only if its scope is alive, so as long as the arena's scope is alive.

Here, we have a memory segment of 8 bytes in the arena scope:

```
try (Arena arena = Arena.ofConfined()) {

    MemorySegment arenaSegment = arena.allocate(8);
}
```

Summarizing the main characteristics of arena scopes in a table can be done as follows:

Arena's scope	Bounded lifespan	Explicitly closeable	Multiple threads
Arena.global()	no	no	yes
Arena.ofAuto()	yes	no	yes
Arena.ofConfined()	yes	yes	no
Arena.ofShared()	yes	yes	yes

Figure 7.9: Summarizing the main characteristics of arena scopes

If you want to monitor the allocated native memory, then this article will help you to do so: `https://www.morling.dev/blog/tracking-java-native-memory-with-jdk-flight-recorder/`. Before going further, let's briefly introduce *memory layouts*.

Introducing memory layouts (ValueLayout)

Memory layouts are shaped by the `java.lang.foreign.MemoryLayout` interface and their goal is to describe the content of memory segments.

We have *simple memory layouts*, including `ValueLayout` and `PaddingLayout`, but we also have *complex memory layouts* for describing complex memory segments such as `SequenceLayout`, `StructLayout`, `UnionLayout`, and `GroupLayout`. The complex layouts are useful to model hierarchical user-defined data types such as C-like sequences, structures, unions, and so on.

Allocating memory segments of value layouts

For now, we are interested in `ValueLayout`. This is a simple memory layout that is useful to represent basic Java data types such as `int`, `float`, `double`, `char`, `byte`, and so on. In an API-specific example, a `ValueLayout.JAVA_LONG` is a layout whose *carrier* is `long.class`, a `ValueLayout.JAVA_DOUBLE` is a layout whose *carrier* is `double.class`, and so on. The *carrier* of a value layout can be obtained via the `carrier()` method.

For instance, let's assume that we have a confined arena and need a memory segment for storing a single `int` value. We know that a Java `int` needs 4 bytes, so our segment can be allocated as follows (the first argument of `allocate()` is the `int` *byte size*, and the second argument is the `int` *byte alignment*):

```
MemorySegment segment = arena.allocate(4, 4);
```

But we can achieve the same thing via `ValueLayout` as follows (here, we use `allocate(MemoryLayout layout)` and `allocate(long byteSize, long byteAlignment)`):

```
MemorySegment segment = arena.allocate(ValueLayout.JAVA_INT);
MemorySegment segment = arena
  .allocate(ValueLayout.JAVA_INT.byteSize(),
          ValueLayout.JAVA_INT.byteAlignment());
```

Or, without specifying the *byte alignment*, via allocate(long byteSize):

```
MemorySegment segment = arena.allocate(4);
MemorySegment segment = arena
  .allocate(ValueLayout.JAVA_INT.byteSize());
```

Here is another example of allocating a memory segment for storing a Java double using the *byte alignment* specific to ValueLayout.JAVA_DOUBLE:

```
MemorySegment segment
  = arena.allocate(ValueLayout.JAVA_DOUBLE);
MemorySegment segment = arena.allocate(
  ValueLayout.JAVA_DOUBLE.byteSize(),
  ValueLayout.JAVA_DOUBLE.byteAlignment());
```

Or, allocating a memory segment for storing a Java char can be done as follows:

```
MemorySegment segment = arena.allocate(ValueLayout.JAVA_CHAR);
MemorySegment segment = MemorySegment.allocate(
  ValueLayout.JAVA_CHAR.byteSize(),
  ValueLayout.JAVA_CHAR.byteAlignment());
```

Now that we know how to allocate a memory segment to different data types, let's see how we can set/get some values.

Setting/getting the content of a memory segment

The Arena API provides a set of allocate() methods inherited from SegmentAllocator that can be used to allocate a memory segment and set its content in the same line of code (in the previous section, we used only the allocate() flavors that allocate memory segments but don't set their content). For instance, calling allocate(OfInt layout, int value) allocates a memory segment for storing an int and sets that int to the given value (OfInt is an interface that extends ValueLayout). Here, we consider the int as being Integer.MAX_VALUE:

```
MemorySegment segment = arena.allocate(
  ValueLayout.JAVA_INT, Integer.MAX_VALUE);
```

Or, here we allocate a memory segment for a char and set that char to a (allocate(OfChar layout, char value)):

```
MemorySegment segment = arena.allocate(
  ValueLayout.JAVA_CHAR, 'a');
```

But if we want to set the content of a memory segment later (not at the same time as the allocation), then we can use the `MemorySegment.set()` or `setAtIndex()` method.

For instance, we can set the `Integer.MAX_VALUE` via `set(OfInt layout, long offset, int value)` as follows:

```
MemorySegment segment = ...;
segment.set(ValueLayout.JAVA_INT, 0, Integer.MAX_VALUE);
```

The second argument is the `offset` (0, 4, 8, 12, ...), which in this case must be 0. Alternatively, we can use `setAtIndex(OfInt layout, long index, int value)` as follows:

```
segment.setAtIndex(
    ValueLayout.JAVA_INT, 0, Integer.MAX_VALUE);
```

Here, the second argument represents an index exactly as in an array (0, 1, 2, 3...). In this case, it must be 0 since we have a single integer stored in the memory segment.

Getting content from a certain offset can be done via `get()` and from a certain index via `getAtIndex()` methods. For instance, getting the `int` stored at a certain offset can be done via `get(OfInt layout, long offset)`:

```
int val = segment.get(ValueLayout.JAVA_INT, 0);
```

And, the `int` stored at a certain index via `getAtIndex(OfInt layout, long index)`, as follows:

```
int val = segment.getAtIndex(ValueLayout.JAVA_INT, 0);
```

In the next problems, you'll see more examples of using these methods.

Working with Java strings

Allocating a memory segment for storing a Java `String` is a special case. If we have an `Arena` instance, then we can allocate a memory segment and set its content as a Java `String` via `allocateUtf8String(String str)` as follows (here, the Java string is abcd):

```
MemorySegment segment = arena.allocateUtf8String("abcd");
```

The `allocateUtf8String(String str)` converts a Java `String` into a C-like string that is UTF-8-encoded and `null`-terminated. The size of the memory segment is obtained as `str.length + 1`. This means that we can allocate a segment for the abcd string as follows:

```
MemorySegment segment = arena.allocate(5);
```

Or, more expressive:

```
MemorySegment segment = arena.allocate("abcd".length() + 1);
```

Having the allocated memory segment, we can set the string via `setUtf8String(long offset, String str)` as follows:

```
segment.setUtf8String(0, "abcd");
```

Offset 0 means exactly at the start of the memory segment. Since this memory segment has the size computed to fit exactly the string abcd, we cannot have an offset other than 0. For instance, the following snippet results in an IndexOutOfBoundsException:

```
segment.setUtf8String(1, "abcd");
```

Getting the string stored in a memory segment can be done via MemorySegment.getUtf8String(long offset), so we can do it as follows:

```
String str = segment.getUtf8String(0);
```

You can practice all these examples in the bundled code.

150. Allocating arrays into memory segments

Now that we know how to create memory segments for storing single values, let's take it a step further and try to store an array of integers. For instance, let's define a memory segment for storing the following array: [11, 21, 12, 7, 33, 1, 3, 6].

A Java int needs 4 bytes (32 bits) and we have 8 integers, so we need a memory segment of 4 bytes x 8 = 32 bytes = 256 bits. If we try to represent this memory segment, then we can do it as in the following figure:

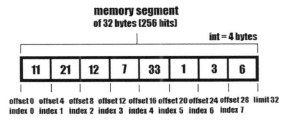

Figure 7.10: A memory segment of 8 integers

In code lines, we can allocate this memory segment via any of the following approaches (arena is an instance of Arena):

```
MemorySegment segment = arena.allocate(32);
MemorySegment segment = arena.allocate(4 * 8);
MemorySegment segment = arena.allocate(
   ValueLayout.JAVA_INT.byteSize() * 8);
MemorySegment segment = arena.allocate(Integer.SIZE/8 * 8);
MemorySegment segment = arena.allocate(Integer.BYTES * 8);
```

Next, we can use the set(OfInt layout, long offset, int value) method to populate the memory segment as follows:

```
segment.set(ValueLayout.JAVA_INT, 0, 11);
segment.set(ValueLayout.JAVA_INT, 4, 21);
segment.set(ValueLayout.JAVA_INT, 8, 12);
```

```
segment.set(ValueLayout.JAVA_INT, 12, 7);
segment.set(ValueLayout.JAVA_INT, 16, 33);
segment.set(ValueLayout.JAVA_INT, 20, 1);
segment.set(ValueLayout.JAVA_INT, 24, 3);
segment.set(ValueLayout.JAVA_INT, 28, 6);
```

Or, we can use the `setAtIndex(OfInt layout, long index, int value)` method as follows:

```
segment.setAtIndex(ValueLayout.JAVA_INT, 0, 11);
segment.setAtIndex(ValueLayout.JAVA_INT, 1, 21);
segment.setAtIndex(ValueLayout.JAVA_INT, 2, 12);
segment.setAtIndex(ValueLayout.JAVA_INT, 3, 7);
segment.setAtIndex(ValueLayout.JAVA_INT, 4, 33);
segment.setAtIndex(ValueLayout.JAVA_INT, 5, 1);
segment.setAtIndex(ValueLayout.JAVA_INT, 6, 3);
segment.setAtIndex(ValueLayout.JAVA_INT, 7, 6);
```

We already know that we can access any of these integers via `get()` using the offset or via `getAtIndex()` using the index. This time, let's try to use this memory segment to populate an `IntVector` (introduced in *Chapter 5*). The code should look as follows:

```
IntVector v = IntVector.fromMemorySegment(
    VS256, segment, 0, ByteOrder.nativeOrder());
```

So, the Vector API exposes the `fromMemorySegment()` method, especially to populate a vector from a memory segment. The `ByteOrder` can be `nativeOrder()`, which means the platform's native order of bytes, `BIG_ENDIAN` (big-endian byte order), or `LITTLE_ORDER` (little-endian byte order).

A more convenient approach for populating the memory segment relies on a suite of `Arena.allocateArray()` methods inherited from `SegmentAllocator`. These methods create and populate the memory segment in a single line of code, as follows:

```
MemorySegment segment = arena.allocateArray(
    ValueLayout.JAVA_INT, 11, 21, 12, 7, 33, 1, 3, 6);

// or, like this
MemorySegment segment = arena.allocateArray(
    ValueLayout.JAVA_INT,
    new int[]{11, 21, 12, 7,  33, 1, 3,  6});
```

Or, here it is a `char[]` array:

```
MemorySegment segment = arena.allocateArray(
    ValueLayout.JAVA_CHAR,"abcd".toCharArray());
```

All these examples allocate an off-heap memory segment. If we need an on-heap memory segment, then we can rely on MemorySegment.ofArray(), as follows:

```
MemorySegment segment = MemorySegment
    .ofArray(new int[]{11, 21, 12, 7, 33, 1, 3, 6});
```

For complete examples, please consider the bundled code.

151. Understanding addresses (pointers)

A memory segment has a memory address (*pointer*) expressed as a long number. An off-heap memory segment has a *physical address* that points out the memory region that backs the segment (*base address*). Each memory layout stored in this segment has its own memory address as well. For instance, here is an example of querying the *base address* of a memory segment via the address() method (arena is an instance of Arena):

```
MemorySegment segment = arena
    .allocate(ValueLayout.JAVA_INT, 1000);
long addr = segment.address(); // 2620870760384
```

On the other hand, an on-heap memory segment has a *non-physical stable virtualized* address typically representing an offset within the memory region of that segment (the client sees a stable address while the garbage collector can reallocate the region of memory inside the heap). For instance, an on-heap segment created via one of the ofArray() factory methods has an address of 0.

Next, let's focus only on off-heap memory segments. Let's consider the following three memory segments containing integer values (arena is an instance of Arena):

```
MemorySegment i1 = arena.allocate(ValueLayout.JAVA_INT, 1);
MemorySegment i2 = arena.allocate(ValueLayout.JAVA_INT, 3);
MemorySegment i3 = arena.allocate(ValueLayout.JAVA_INT, 2);
```

Each of these segments has a memory address. Next, let's create a segment containing their addresses (like a segment of pointers). First, we allocate such a segment via ValueLayout.ADDRESS as follows:

```
MemorySegment addrs = arena
    .allocateArray(ValueLayout.ADDRESS, 3);
```

Since each address is a long value, the size of addrs is 24 bytes. We can use the set() method and the offsets 0, 8, and 16 to set the addresses of i1, i2, and i3, or we can use the setAtIndex() and refer to offsets as indexes 0, 1, and 2:

```
addrs.setAtIndex(ValueLayout.ADDRESS, 0, i1);
addrs.setAtIndex(ValueLayout.ADDRESS, 1, i2);
addrs.setAtIndex(ValueLayout.ADDRESS, 2, i3);
```

We can represent this in the following diagram:

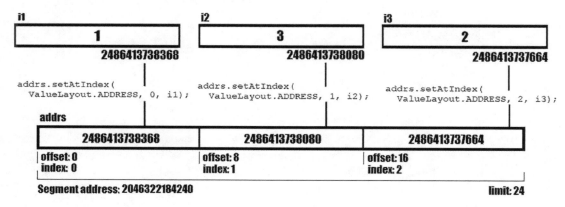

Figure 7.11: Storing i1, i2, and i3 addresses in an array of addresses

In other words, we set the address of i1 at offset 0 in addrs, the address of i2 at offset 8, and the address of i3 at offset 16. The addrs segment doesn't hold the data of i1, i2, and i3. It is just a segment of pointers that points to the memory addresses of i1, i2, and i3.

If we call get()/getAtIndex(), we will get an address:

```
MemorySegment addr1 = addrs.getAtIndex(ValueLayout.ADDRESS, 0);
MemorySegment addr2 = addrs.getAtIndex(ValueLayout.ADDRESS, 1);
MemorySegment addr3 = addrs.getAtIndex(ValueLayout.ADDRESS, 2);
```

We can represent this in the following diagram:

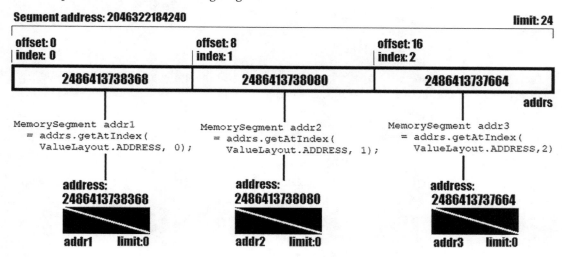

Figure 7.12: Getting addresses from the array of addresses

But check out the return type. It is not a long value! It is a MemorySegment. The returned native memory segments (addr1, addr2, and addr3) are automatically associated with the *global scope*. They have the size 0 (*limit: 0*) and each of them wraps the returned address of the given offset/index (the long value is available via addr1/2/3.address()). However, in the case of an *unbounded* address layout, the size is expected to be Long.MAX_VALUE (9223372036854775807).

This means that we shouldn't do this:

```
addr1.get(ValueLayout.JAVA_INT, 0); DON'T DO THIS!
```

This causes an IndexOutOfBoundsException since addr1 has a size of 0 bytes – this is known as a *zero-length memory segment*. Getting the integer value associated with an address can be done via the ofAddress() and a flavor of the reinterpret() methods, as follows:

```
int v1 = MemorySegment.ofAddress(addr1.address())
    .reinterpret(ValueLayout.JAVA_INT.byteSize())
    .get(ValueLayout.JAVA_INT, 0);
```

First, we call ofAddress() and pass the addr1 address. This will create a native memory segment with the size 0. Next, we call the reinterpret() method and pass the size of the int type. This will return a new memory segment (a reinterpreted memory segment) with the same address and scope as this segment, but with the given size (4 bytes). Finally, we read the integer value stored at this address at offset 0. The same thing can be done for addr2 and addr3:

```
int v2 = MemorySegment.ofAddress(addr2.address())
    .reinterpret(ValueLayout.JAVA_INT.byteSize())
    .get(ValueLayout.JAVA_INT, 0);
int v3 = MemorySegment.ofAddress(addr3.address())
    .reinterpret(ValueLayout.JAVA_INT.byteSize())
    .get(ValueLayout.JAVA_INT, 0);
```

Before using the reinterpret() or withTargetLayout() methods, please consider the following note:

> **Important note**
>
> The reinterpret() method (and all other methods for working with zero-length memory segments) is considered a *restricted* method. It should be used with caution since any mistake can lead to a VM crash when trying to access the memory segment.

We can check whether two long addresses are equal via the == operator:

```
addr1.address() == i1.address() // true
```

Or, via equals():

```
addr1.equals(i1) // true
```

At this point, we have that i1=1, i2=3, and i3=2. Let's manipulate only the addresses to obtain i1=1, i2=2, and i3=3. So, we want to switch the integer values of i2 and i3 by switching the addresses, not the values. First, we store the i2 address as a long:

```
long i2Addr = i2.address();
```

Next, we set the i2 address as the i3 address:

```
i2 = MemorySegment.ofAddress(i3.address())
    .reinterpret(ValueLayout.JAVA_INT.byteSize());
```

Finally, we set the address of i3 as the address of i2:

```
i3 = MemorySegment.ofAddress(i2Addr)
    .reinterpret(ValueLayout.JAVA_INT.byteSize());
```

Done! Now, i1=1, i2=2, and i3=3. I hope you found this exercise useful for understanding how to manipulate values, offsets, and memory addresses.

152. Introducing the sequence layout

In *Problem 149*, we already covered the ValueLayout for basic data types. Next, let's talk about the *sequence layout* (java.lang.foreign.SequenceLayout).

But before introducing the sequence layout, let's take a moment to analyze the following snippet of code:

```
try (Arena arena = Arena.ofConfined()) {

  MemorySegment segment = arena.allocate(
    ValueLayout.JAVA_DOUBLE.byteSize() * 10,
    ValueLayout.JAVA_DOUBLE.byteAlignment());

  for (int i = 0; i < 10; i++) {
    segment.setAtIndex(ValueLayout.JAVA_DOUBLE,
      i, Math.random());
  }

  for (int i = 0; i < 10; i++) {
    System.out.printf("\nx = %.2f",
      segment.getAtIndex(ValueLayout.JAVA_DOUBLE, i));
  }
}
```

We start by creating a native memory segment for storing 10 double values. Next, we rely on setAtIndex() to set these double values. Finally, we print them.

So, basically, we repeat the ValueLayout.JAVA_DOUBLE 10 times. When an *element layout* is repeated *n* times (a finite number of times), we can express the code via a sequence layout (java.lang.foreign. SequenceLayout). In other words, a sequence layout represents a repetition/sequence of a given *element layout* for a finite number of times.

The following code uses SequenceLayout to shape the previous snippet:

```
SequenceLayout seq = MemoryLayout.sequenceLayout(
    10, ValueLayout.JAVA_DOUBLE);
```

The number of repetitions (*element count*) is 10, and the repeated *element layout* is ValueLayout.JAVA_DOUBLE.

But how do we set the values of a sequence layout? There are at least two approaches, and one of them relies on a combination of the java.lang.invoke.VarHandle API and the java.lang.foreign. MemoryLayout.PathElement API.

Introducing PathElement

In a nutshell, the PathElement API exposes a friendly approach for navigating a hierarchal memory layout via the so-called *layout path*. By chaining path elements in a layout path, we can locate an element layout, which can be a sequence layout (located via sequence path elements) or, as you'll see in other problems, a group layout (which can be a struct layout or a union layout located via group path elements). Sequence layouts are traversed via PathElement.sequenceElement(), while group layouts via PathElement.groupElement(). Each element layout has a number of elements referred to as the *element count* (obtained via a method named elementCount()).

Introducing VarHandle

VarHandle is not new to town. It was introduced in JDK 9. A VarHandle is a dynamic, immutable, non-visible-state, strongly typed reference to a variable that cannot be subclassed. Its goal is to provide read/write access to the handled variables under certain circumstances.

A VarHandle is characterized by two aspects:

- The type of variables represented by this VarHandle as a generic type (T)
- A list of Coordinate Types (denoted CT) used to locate variables referenced by this VarHandle

The CT list may be empty.

Typically, a VarHandle method gets a variable number of Object arguments. Argument(s) checking is accomplished at runtime (static argument(s) checking is disabled). Different methods of VarHandle expect to have a variable number of arguments of different types.

Putting PathElement and VarHandle together

The path elements (layout path) are arguments of the MemoryLayout.varHandle() method, which is capable of returning a VarHandle that can be used to access a memory segment at the layout located via this layout path. The path is considered rooted in this layout.

So, in our simple case, we can obtain a VarHandle for seq as follows:

```
// VarHandle[varType=double,
// coord=[interface java.lang.foreign.MemorySegment, long]]
VarHandle sphandle = seq.varHandle(
  PathElement.sequenceElement());
```

Our path layout is just a simple navigation via PathElement.sequenceElement(). The returned VarHandle represents variables of the type double and contains a CT of (MemorySegment and long).

The MemorySegment represents the memory segment from this sequence layout and the long value represents the index in this memory segment. This means that we can set 10 double values, as follows:

```
try (Arena arena = Arena.ofConfined()) {

  MemorySegment segment = arena.allocate(seq);

  for (int i = 0; i < seq.elementCount(); i++) {
    sphandle.set(segment, i, Math.random());
  }
  ...
```

Getting these 10 double values can be done as follows:

```
  for (int i = 0; i < seq.elementCount(); i++) {
    System.out.printf("\nx = %.2f", sphandle.get(segment, i));
  }
}
```

A VarHandle can be created via arrayElementVarHandle(int... shape) as well. This method creates a VarHandle for accessing a memory segment as a multi-dimensional array (this is known as a *strided var handler*). The varargs argument, shape, represents the size of each nested array dimension. You can find this example in the bundle code.

Next, let's complicate things a little bit.

Working with nested sequence layouts

Let's consider the following sequence layout of 400 bytes (5 * 10 * 8 bytes):

```
SequenceLayout nestedseq = MemoryLayout.sequenceLayout(5,
  MemoryLayout.sequenceLayout(10, ValueLayout.JAVA_DOUBLE));
```

So, here we have 5 sequence layouts of 10 ValueLayout.JAVA_DOUBLE each. Navigating to the ValueLayout.JAVA_DOUBLE requires a layout path obtained by chaining two calls of sequenceLayout(), as follows:

```
// VarHandle[varType=double, coord=[interface
```

```
// java.lang.foreign.MemorySegment, long, long]]
VarHandle nphandle = nestedseq.varHandle(
  PathElement.sequenceElement(),
  PathElement.sequenceElement());
```

Besides the memory segment, the VarHandle accepts two long values. The first long corresponds to the outer sequence layout, and the second long corresponds to the inner sequence layout. The number of elements (element count) for the outer sequence is 5, and it can be obtained as follows:

```
long outer = nestedseq.elementCount();
```

The element count of the inner sequence is 10, and it can be obtained via the select() method, as follows:

```
long inner = ((SequenceLayout) nestedseq.select(
  PathElement.sequenceElement())).elementCount();
```

Now, outer fits the first long argument in the coordinate's types of nphandle, while inner fits the second long argument. So, we can get/set the double values of our sequence as follows:

```
try (Arena arena = Arena.ofConfined()) {

  MemorySegment segment = arena.allocate(nestedseq);

  long outer = nestedseq.elementCount();
  long inner = ((SequenceLayout) nestedseq.select(
    PathElement.sequenceElement())).elementCount();

  for (int i = 0; i < outer; i++) {
    for (int j = 0; j < inner; j++) {
      nphandle.set(segment, i, j, Math.random());
    }
  }

  for (int i = 0; i < outer; i++) {
    System.out.print("\n-----" + i + "-----");
    for (int j = 0; j < inner; j++) {
      System.out.printf("\nx = %.2f",
        nphandle.get(segment, i, j));
    }
  }
}
```

In the bundled code, you can see an example relying on ValueLayout.JAVA_DOUBLE. arrayElementVarHandle(5, 10) as well.

153. Shaping C-like structs into memory segments

Let's consider the C-like struct from the following figure:

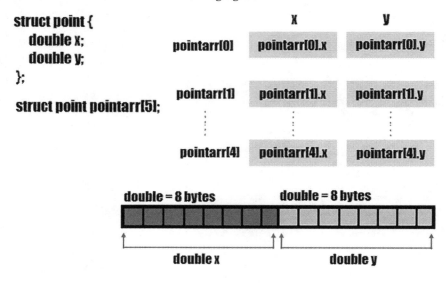

Figure 7.13: A C-like structure

So, in *Figure 7.13*, we have a C-like struct named point to shape an (x, y) pair of double values. Moreover, we have 5 such pairs declared under the name pointarr. We can try to shape a memory segment to fit this model as follows (arena is an instance of Arena):

```
MemorySegment segment = arena.allocate(
  2 * ValueLayout.JAVA_DOUBLE.byteSize() * 5,
  ValueLayout.JAVA_DOUBLE.byteAlignment());
```

Next, we should set (x, y) pairs into this segment. For this, we can visualize it as follows:

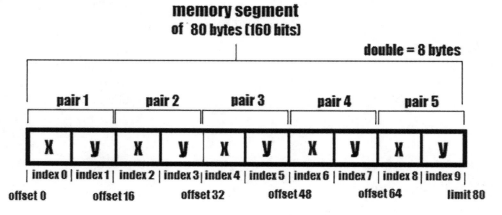

Figure 7.14: Memory segment to store (x, y) pairs

Based on this diagram, we can easily come up with the following snippet of code for setting the (x, y) pairs:

```
for (int i = 0; i < 5; i++) {
  segment.setAtIndex(
    ValueLayout.JAVA_DOUBLE, i * 2, Math.random());
  segment.setAtIndex(
    ValueLayout.JAVA_DOUBLE, i * 2 + 1, Math.random());
}
```

But another approach consists of using the StructLayout, which is more suitable for this scenario since it provides a wrapping structure around the data.

Introducing StructLayout

A StructLayout is a group layout. In this layout, the members (other memory layouts) are laid out one after the other exactly as in a C struct. This means that we can shape our C-like struct by laying out two ValueLayout.JAVA_DOUBLE as follows:

```
StructLayout struct = MemoryLayout.structLayout(
  ValueLayout.JAVA_DOUBLE.withName("x"),
  ValueLayout.JAVA_DOUBLE.withName("y"));
```

But we have 5 pairs of (x, y), so we need to nest this StructLayout in a SequenceLayout containing 5 StructLayout, as follows:

```
SequenceLayout struct
  = MemoryLayout.sequenceLayout(5,
      MemoryLayout.structLayout(
        ValueLayout.JAVA_DOUBLE.withName("x"),
        ValueLayout.JAVA_DOUBLE.withName("y")));
```

Next, as we already know from *Problem 152*, we need to define the proper layout paths via PathElement and get back the VarHandle. We need a VarHandle for x and one for y. Notice in the following code how we point them out via their names:

```
// VarHandle[varType=double,
// coord=[interface java.lang.foreign.MemorySegment, long]]
VarHandle xHandle = struct.varHandle(
  PathElement.sequenceElement(),
  PathElement.groupElement("x"));

// VarHandle[varType=double,
// coord=[interface java.lang.foreign.MemorySegment, long]]
VarHandle yHandle = struct.varHandle(
  PathElement.sequenceElement(),
  PathElement.groupElement("y"));
```

Finally, we can use VarHandle and the element count for setting the data, as follows:

```
try (Arena arena = Arena.ofConfined()) {

  MemorySegment segment = arena.allocate(struct);

  for (int i = 0; i < struct.elementCount(); i++) {
    xHandle.set(segment, i, Math.random());
    yHandle.set(segment, i, Math.random());
  }
  ...
```

Getting the data is straightforward:

```
  for (int i = 0; i < struct.elementCount(); i++) {
    System.out.printf("\nx = %.2f", xHandle.get(segment, i));
    System.out.printf("\ny = %.2f", yHandle.get(segment, i));
  }
}
```

Challenge yourself to implement this example via ValueLayout.JAVA_DOUBLE.
arrayElementVarHandle(int... shape).

154. Shaping C-like unions into memory segments

Let's consider the C-like union from the following figure (the members of a C union share the same
memory location (the member's largest data type dictates the size of the memory location), so only
one of the members has a value at any moment in time):

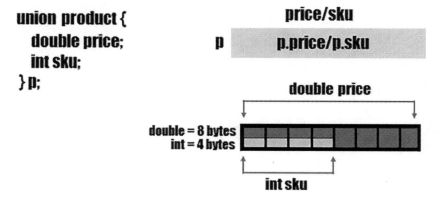

Figure 7.15: A C-like union

In *Figure 7.15*, we have a C-like union named product to shape two members, price (double) and sku
(int), while only one can have a value at any moment in time. We can shape a memory segment to fit
this model as follows (arena is an instance of Arena):

```
MemorySegment segment = arena.allocate(
  ValueLayout.JAVA_DOUBLE.byteSize(),
  ValueLayout.JAVA_DOUBLE.byteAlignment());
```

Because double needs 8 bytes and int needs only 4 bytes, we choose ValueLayout.JAVA_DOUBLE to shape the size of the memory segment. This way, the segment can accommodate a double and an int at the same offset.

Next, we can set the price or the sku and use it accordingly:

```
segment.setAtIndex(ValueLayout.JAVA_DOUBLE, 0, 500.99);
segment.setAtIndex(ValueLayout.JAVA_INT, 0, 101000);
```

When we set the sku (int), the value of price (double) became a *garbage value* and vice versa. For more details, check out the bundled code. Next, let's see an alternative to this implementation based on UnionLayout.

Introducing UnionLayout

A UnionLayout is a group layout. In this layout, the members (other memory layouts) are laid out at the same starting offset exactly as in a C union. This means that we can shape our C-like union by laying out the price (double) and the sku (int) members as follows:

```
UnionLayout union = MemoryLayout.unionLayout(
  ValueLayout.JAVA_DOUBLE.withName("price"),
  ValueLayout.JAVA_INT.withName("sku"));
```

Next, as we already know from *Problem 152*, we need to define the proper layout paths via PathElement and get back the VarHandle. We need a VarHandle for price and one for sku. Notice in the following code how we point them out via their names:

```
// VarHandle[varType=double,
// coord=[interface java.lang.foreign.MemorySegment]]
VarHandle pHandle = union.varHandle(
  PathElement.groupElement("price"));

// VarHandle[varType=double,
// coord=[interface java.lang.foreign.MemorySegment]]
VarHandle sHandle = union.varHandle(
  PathElement.groupElement("sku"));
```

Finally, we can use VarHandle to set price or sku:

```
try (Arena arena = Arena.ofConfined()) {

  MemorySegment segment = arena.allocate(union);
```

```
    pHandle.set(segment, 500.99);
    sHandle.set(segment, 101000);
}
```

When we set the `sku` (int), the value of `price` (double) became a *garbage value* and vice versa.

155. Introducing PaddingLayout

Data types are typically characterized by several properties: *size, alignment, stride, padding,* and *order* of bytes.

The padding layout (`java.lang.foreign.PaddingLayout`) allows us to specify the *padding*. In other words, `PaddingLayout` allows us to add at certain offsets some extra space that is usually ignored by the applications but is needed to align the member layouts of a memory segment.

For instance, let's consider the following two memory segments (the left-hand side is a memory segment without padding, while the right-hand side is a memory segment with two paddings of 4 bytes each).

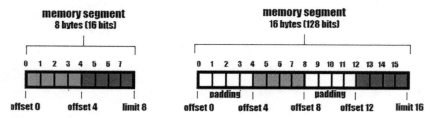

Figure 7.16: Memory segments with (right-hand side)/without (left-hand side) padding

In code lines, the padding-free memory segment can be shaped as follows:

```
StructLayout npStruct = MemoryLayout.structLayout(
    ValueLayout.JAVA_INT.withName("x"),
    ValueLayout.JAVA_INT.withName("y")
);
```

Since the size of `JAVA_INT` is 4 bytes, we can set *x* and *y* as follows:

```
VarHandle xpHandle = npStruct.varHandle(
    PathElement.groupElement("x"));
VarHandle ypHandle = npStruct.varHandle(
    PathElement.groupElement("y"));

try (Arena arena = Arena.ofConfined()) {

    MemorySegment segment = arena.allocate(npStruct);
```

```
    xnHandle.set(segment, 23); // offset 0
    ynHandle.set(segment, 54); // offset 4
}
```

This code writes the value 23 at offset 0, and 54 at offset 4. No surprises, right?

Next, let's code a memory segment with padding. For this, we call MemoryLayout.paddingLayout(long byteSize) as in the following snippet (since we have two interleaved paddings of 4 bytes, we have to interleave two calls of paddingLayout()):

```
StructLayout wpStruct = MemoryLayout.structLayout(
    MemoryLayout.paddingLayout(4), // 4 bytes
    ValueLayout.JAVA_INT.withName("x"),
    MemoryLayout.paddingLayout(4), // 4 bytes
    ValueLayout.JAVA_INT.withName("y")
);
```

Next, we write the two int values (23 and 54) again:

```
VarHandle xpHandle = wpStruct.varHandle(
    PathElement.groupElement("x"));
VarHandle ypHandle = wpStruct.varHandle(
    PathElement.groupElement("y"));

try (Arena arena = Arena.ofConfined()) {

    MemorySegment segment = arena.allocate(wpStruct);

    xpHandle.set(segment, 23); // offset 4
    ypHandle.set(segment, 54); // offset 12
}
```

This time, the padding zones are skipped, and 23 is written to offset 4, while 54 is written to offset 12. Reading *x* and *y* should be done from offset 4 and offset 12, respectively. From 0 to 3, and from 8 to 11, we have extra space added via paddingLayout() that is ignored by the application. Attempting to read an int from these zones results in values of 0 (default values).

These examples have nicely and smoothly introduced the *padding* notion but they are not that useful in real scenarios. Remember that we said earlier that padding is useful for aligning the members of a memory segment. In order to understand this, let's briefly hook a few more players.

Hooking size, alignment, stride, and padding

Before continuing to work with padding, we need to cover some notions that are closely related to each other and work hand in hand with padding.

Hooking size

By *size*, we mean the amount of memory (in bytes/bits) occupied by a memory layout (data type, C-like struct, C-like union, sequence layout, and so on). We know that a Java int consumes 4 bytes, a Java byte consumes 1 byte, a C-like struct consumes a number of bytes calculated as the sum of each property's size, a C-like union consumes a number of bytes equal to the bigger property's size, and so on.

We can easily query the size via byteSize()/bitSize(). Here are some examples:

```
long size = ValueLayout.JAVA_INT.byteSize();    // 4
long size = ValueLayout.JAVA_BYTE.byteSize();   // 1
long size = npStruct.byteSize();                // 8
long size = wpStruct.byteSize();                // 16
```

The npStruct and wpStruct were introduced earlier in this problem.

Hooking alignment

We know that each member layout starts in a memory segment at a specific address. We say that this address is *k*-byte-aligned if this address is a multiple of *k* (where *k* is any power of 2) or if this address is evenly divisible by *k*. Commonly, *k* is 1, 2, 4, or 8. Alignment is useful for sustaining CPU performance, which reads data in chunks of *k* bytes instead of reading byte by byte. If the CPU attempts to access a member layout that is not correctly aligned, then we'll get an IllegalArgumentException: *Misaligned access at address ...*.

In the case of basic data types (int, double, float, byte, char, and so on), the alignment value is equal to their size. For instance, an 8-bit (1-byte) Java byte has a size of 1 byte and needs to be aligned to 1 byte. A 32-bit (4 bytes) Java int has a size of 4 bytes and needs to be aligned to 4 bytes. In the case of a C-like struct/union, the alignment is the maximum alignment of all its member layouts.

We can easily query the alignment via byteAlignment()/bitAlignment(). Here are some examples:

```
long align = ValueLayout.JAVA_INT.byteAlignment();    // 4
long align = ValueLayout.JAVA_BYTE.byteAlignment();   // 1
long align = npStruct.byteAlignment();                // 4
long align = wpStruct.byteAlignment();                // 4
```

So, in a nutshell, a member layout should start with an address that must be at a multiple of its alignment. This applies to any kind of member layout (basic data type, C-like struct, C-like union, and so on).

Hooking stride

The minimum byte distance between two member layouts is called a *stride*. The stride can be greater than or equal to the size. When we don't face any alignment issues, the stride is equal to the size. Otherwise, the stride is computed by rounding up the size to the next multiple of the alignment. When the stride is greater than the size, it means that we also have some padding. If we have a C-like struct/union named foo, then the stride is the minimum byte distance between two foo objects.

Hooking padding

So, padding is the amount of extra space that we need to add in order to preserve a valid alignment of the member layouts.

Don't worry if you are a little bit confused about all these statements. We will clarify everything via a bunch of examples.

Adding implicit extra space (implicit padding) to validate alignment

Let's consider the following simple example:

```
MemorySegment segment = Arena.ofAuto().allocate(12);
segment.set(ValueLayout.JAVA_INT, 0, 1000);
segment.set(ValueLayout.JAVA_CHAR, 4, 'a');
```

We have a memory segment of 12 bytes and we have set an `int` of 4 bytes at offset 0 and a `char` of 2 bytes at offset 4 (immediately after the `int`). So, we still have 6 free bytes. Let's assume that we want to set one more `int` of 4 bytes after the `char`, a. What should the offset be? Our first thought may be that the proper offset is 6 since the `char` consumed 2 bytes:

```
segment.set(ValueLayout.JAVA_INT, 6, 2000);
```

But if we do this, then the result is `java.lang.IllegalArgumentException`: *Misaligned access at the address: ....* We have a misaligned member layout (the 2000 `int` value) because 6 is not evenly divisible by 4, which is the byte alignment of `int`. Check out the following figure:

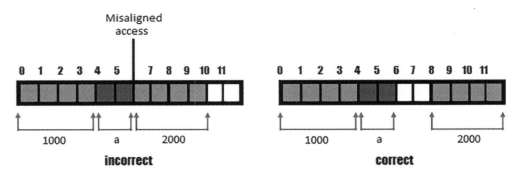

Figure 7.17: Fixing the misaligned issue

But what should we do? We know that the current offset is 6 and 6 is not evenly divisible by 4 (the `int` alignment). So, we are looking for the next offset that is evenly divisible by 4 and is the closest and greater than 6. Obviously, this is 8. So, before we set the 2000 `int` value, we need a padding of 2 bytes (16 bits). This padding will be automatically added if we simply specify the offset 8 instead of 6:

```
segment.set(ValueLayout.JAVA_INT, 8, 2000);
```

Since our memory segment has a size of 12 bytes, we fit this `int` exactly on bytes 8, 9, 10, and 11. A smaller size of the segment leads to an `IndexOutOfBoundsException`: *Out of bound access on segment MemorySegment*.

Adding explicit extra space (explicit padding) to validate alignment

Let's consider the following C-like struct (let's denote this as *Case 1*):

```
StructLayout product = MemoryLayout.structLayout(
  ValueLayout.JAVA_INT.withName("sku"),
  ValueLayout.JAVA_CHAR.withName("energy"),
  ValueLayout.JAVA_BYTE.withName("weight"));
```

The product size returned via `byteSize()` is 7 bytes (4 + 2 + 1). The product alignment returned via `byteAlignment()` is 4 (the greater alignment of 4, 2, and 1). The byte offset of each member layout returned by `byteOffset()` is as follows:

```
long boSku =product.byteOffset(         // 0
  PathElement.groupElement("sku"));
long boEnergy =product.byteOffset(      // 4
  PathElement.groupElement("energy"));
long boWeight =product.byteOffset(      // 6
  PathElement.groupElement("weight"));
```

If we represent this via a diagram, we obtain the following:

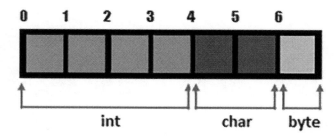

Figure 7.18: The representation of the struct

Everything looks fine, so we can go further. Now, let's use the same struct, but we arrange the member layouts as follows (let's denote this as *Case 2*):

```
StructLayout product = MemoryLayout.structLayout(
  ValueLayout.JAVA_CHAR.withName("energy"),
  ValueLayout.JAVA_INT.withName("sku"),
  ValueLayout.JAVA_BYTE.withName("weight"));
```

First, we place the energy (char) at offset 0. Since energy (char) consumes 2 bytes, it is followed by sku (int) at offset 2. Since sku (int) consumes 4 bytes, it is followed by weight (byte). But is this the correct logic? As you can see in the following figure (left-hand side), this logic is incorrect, because we have an invalid alignment error at offset 2 for the sku (int).

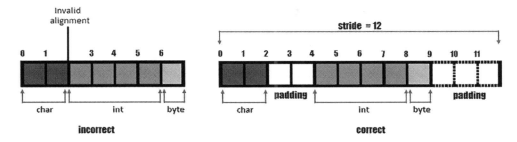

Figure 7.19: Incorrect/correct padding

The alignment of energy (char) is 2, so it can start only on 0, 2, 4, ... Since energy (char) is the first, we start with it on offset 0. Next, the alignment of sku (int) is 4, so it can start only on 0, 4, 8, ... That is why the start address of sku is at 4 and not at 2. Finally, the alignment of weight (byte) is 1, so it can go after sku (int) at offset 8.

So, by following the alignment rules, we conclude that the size of product is 9, not 7. At this point, we know that to align sku (int), we should add a padding of 2 bytes (16 bits) at offset 2, so let's do it:

```
StructLayout product = MemoryLayout.structLayout(
    ValueLayout.JAVA_CHAR.withName("energy"),
    MemoryLayout.paddingLayout(2),
    ValueLayout.JAVA_INT.withName("sku"),
    ValueLayout.JAVA_BYTE.withName("weight"));
```

Next, let's assume that we want to repeat this C-like struct 2 times (or *n* times). For this, we nest the struct in a sequence layout as follows (let's denote this as *Case 3*):

```
SequenceLayout product = MemoryLayout.sequenceLayout(
    2, MemoryLayout.structLayout(
    ValueLayout.JAVA_CHAR.withName("energy"),
    MemoryLayout.paddingLayout(2),
    ValueLayout.JAVA_INT.withName("sku"),
    ValueLayout.JAVA_BYTE.withName("weight")));
```

This time, the code fails with an exception as IllegalArgumentException: *Element layout size is not multiple of alignment*. What's happening now? Well, the first struct instance lies out from offset 0 to offset 8, and, conforming to our code, the second struct lies out from offset 9 to offset 18, as in the following figure (top diagram):

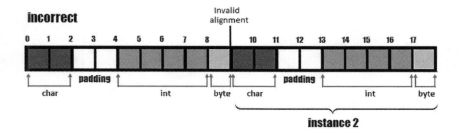

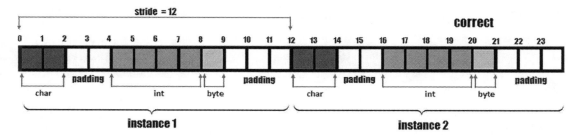

Figure 7.20: Calculating stride

But this is not correct, because the second instance of the struct (and the third, fourth, and so on) doesn't follow the alignment rules. The alignment of the struct is 4, so an instance of the struct should be at 0, 4, 8, 12, 16, ..., but not at 9. This means that we need to calculate the *stride*, which gives us the minimum byte distance between two member layouts – here, two instances of our struct.

We have that the size of the struct instance is 9 and its alignment is 4. So, we need to find the offset evenly divisible by 4 that is greater and closest to 9. This is 12. Since the *stride* is 12, it means that the second instance of the struct starts at offset 12. We need to add a padding of 3 (12-9) bytes:

```
SequenceLayout product = MemoryLayout.sequenceLayout(
  2, MemoryLayout.structLayout(
    ValueLayout.JAVA_CHAR.withName("energy"),
    MemoryLayout.paddingLayout(2),
    ValueLayout.JAVA_INT.withName("sku"),
    ValueLayout.JAVA_BYTE.withName("weight"),
    MemoryLayout.paddingLayout(3)));
```

Done! As you can see, the order of member layouts counts a lot. By being aware of the size, alignment, stride, and padding, we can optimize the memory allocation by simply arranging the member layouts in a proper order that requires 0 or minimum padding.

In the bundled code, you can find more examples of permutating the member layout of our struct.

156. Copying and slicing memory segments

Let's consider the following memory segment (arena is an instance of Arena):

```
MemorySegment srcSegment = arena.allocateArray(
    ValueLayout.JAVA_INT, 1, 2, 3, 4, -1, -1, -1,
                          52, 22, 33, -1, -1, -1, -1, -1, 4);
```

Next, let's see how we can copy the content of this segment.

Copying a segment

We can make a copy of this memory segment via copyFrom(MemorySegment src) as follows:

```
MemorySegment copySegment = srcSegment.copyFrom(srcSegment);
```

We can easily see if the data was copied as follows:

```
System.out.println("Data: " + Arrays.toString(
    copySegment.toArray(ValueLayout.JAVA_INT)));
```

This is a bulk operation that creates a full copy of the given memory segment.

Copying a part of the segment into another segment (1)

Let's suppose that we want to copy only a part of srcSegment into another segment (dstSegment). For instance, if we wanted to copy the last 8 elements ([22, 33, -1, -1, -1, -1, -1, 4]) from srcSegment to dstSegment, we'd start by allocating the dstSegment accordingly:

```
MemorySegment dstSegment
    = arena.allocateArray(ValueLayout.JAVA_INT, 8);
```

Next, we call the copy(MemorySegment srcSegment, long srcOffset, MemorySegment dstSegment, long dstOffset, long bytes) method as in the following figure:

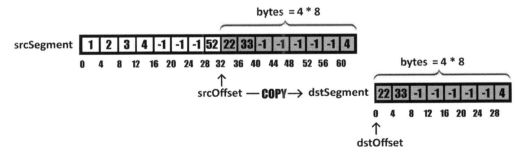

Figure 7.21: Copying a part of a segment into another segment (1)

So, we specify the source segment as srcSsegment, the source offset as 32 (skip the first 8 elements), the destination segment as dstSegment, the destination offset as 0, and the number of bytes to be copied as 32 (the last 8 elements are copied):

```
MemorySegment.copy(srcSegment, 32, dstSegment, 0, 32);
```

Practically, we copied half of the srcSegment to dstSegment.

Copying a segment into an on-heap array

Let's suppose that we want to copy only a part of srcSegment into an on-heap Java regular array (dstArray). For instance, if we wanted to copy the last 8 elements ([22, 33, -1, -1, -1, -1, -1, 4]) from srcSegment to dstArray, we'd start by creating the dstArray accordingly:

```
int[] dstArray = new int[8];
```

Next, we'd call copy(MemorySegment srcSegment, ValueLayout srcLayout, long srcOffset, Object dstArray, int dstIndex, int elementCount), as in the following figure:

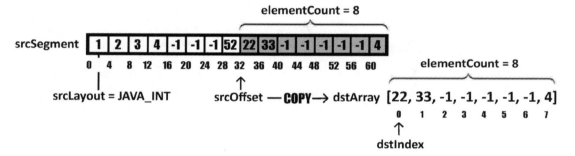

Figure 7.22: Copying a segment into an on-heap array

So, we specify the source segment as srcSegment, the source layout as JAVA_INT, the source offset as 32 (skip the first 8 elements), the destination array as dstArray, the destination array index as 0, and the number of elements to be copied as 8:

```
MemorySegment.copy(
    srcSegment, ValueLayout.JAVA_INT, 32, dstArray, 0, 8);
```

Practically, we copied half of the off-heap srcSegment to the on-heap dstArray.

Copying an on-heap array into a segment

Let's suppose that we want to copy an on-heap array (or a part of it) into a segment. The given on-heap array is srcArray:

```
int[] srcArray = new int[]{10, 44, 2, 6, 55, 65, 7, 89};
```

The destination segment can hold 16 integer values:

```
MemorySegment dstSegment
    = arena.allocateArray(ValueLayout.JAVA_INT, 16);
```

Next, we want to overwrite the last 8 elements from dstSegment with the elements from srcArray, while the first elements remain 0. For this, we call copy(Object srcArray, int srcIndex, MemorySegment dstSegment, ValueLayout dstLayout, long dstOffset, int elementCount), as in the following figure:

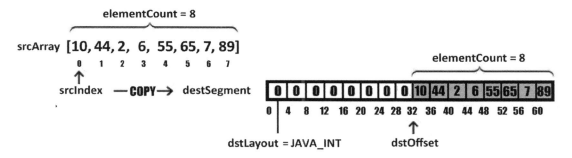

Figure 7.23: Copying an on-heap array into a segment

So, we specify the source array as srcArray, the source index as 0, the destination segment as dstSegment, the destination layout as JAVA_INT, the destination offset as 32 (skip the first 8 elements), and the number of elements to be copied as 8:

```
MemorySegment.copy(
    srcArray, 0, dstSegment, ValueLayout.JAVA_INT, 32, 8);
```

Practically, we copied the on-heap srcArray as the second half of the off-heap destSegment.

Copying a part of the segment into another segment (2)

Let's consider the srcSegment (1, 2, 3, 4, -1, -1, -1, 52, 22, 33, -1, -1, -1, -1, -1, 4) and the dstSegment (0, 0, 0, 0, 0, 0, 0, 0, 10, 44, 2, 6, 55, 65, 7, 89) from the previous sections. We want to copy the last 8 elements from srcSegment as the first 8 elements from dstSegment (22, 33, -1, -1, -1, -1, -1, 4, 10, 44, 2, 6, 55, 65, 7, 89). We know that this can be done via copy(MemorySegment srcSegment, long srcOffset, MemorySegment dstSegment, long dstOffset, long bytes), as follows:

```
MemorySegment.copy(srcSegment, 32, dstSegment, 0, 32);
```

Alternatively, we can use copy(MemorySegment srcSegment, ValueLayout srcElementLayout, long srcOffset, MemorySegment dstSegment, ValueLayout dstElementLayout, long dstOffset, long elementCount), as in the following figure:

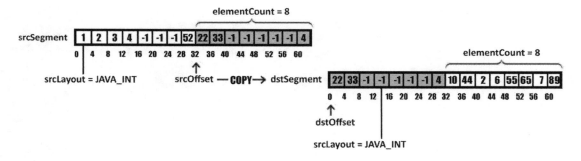

Figure 7.24: Copying a part of a segment into another segment (2)

So, we specify the source segment as `srcSegment`, the source layout as `JAVA_INT`, the source offset as 32 (skip the first 8 elements), the destination segment as `dstSegment`, the destination layout as `JAVA_INT`, the destination offset as 0, and the number of elements to be copied as 8:

```
MemorySegment.copy(srcSegment, ValueLayout.JAVA_INT,
    32, dstSegment, ValueLayout.JAVA_INT, 0, 8);
```

Feel free to test this method with different value layouts. Next, let's talk about slicing.

Slicing a segment

Next, let's suppose that we want to slice the segment containing (1, 2, 3, 4, -1, -1, -1, 52, 22, 33, -1, -1, -1, -1, -1, 4) into three separate `IntVector` instances the values that are not -1 without using the `copy()` methods. So, v1 should contain [1, 2, 3, 4], v2 should contain [52, 22, 33, 0], and v3 should contain [4, 0, 0, 0]. Since an int needs 4 bytes, and we have a maximum of 4 int values, we go for `SPECIES_128` (4 int values x 4 bytes = 16 bytes x 8 bits = 128 bits):

```
VectorSpecies<Integer> VS128 = IntVector.SPECIES_128;
```

Next, we need to slice the memory segment in order to eliminate the values of -1. This can be accomplished via the `asSlice(long offset)` and `asSlice(long offset, long newSize)` methods. The first argument represents the starting offset. The second argument represents the size of the new memory segment. The following figure helps us to clear this up:

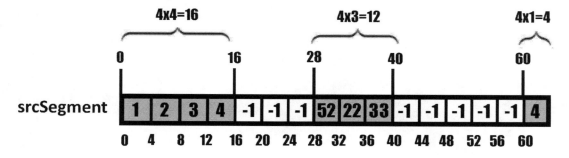

Figure 7.25: Slicing a memory segment

The first memory segment starts at offset 0 and ends at offset 16, so it contains 4 int values of 4 bytes (asSlice(0, 16)). The second memory segment starts at offset 28 and ends at offset 40, so it contains 3 int values of 4 bytes (asSlice(28, 12)). Finally, the third memory segment starts at offset 60 and ends at the end of the segment, so it contains a single int value of 4 bytes (asSlice(60) or asSlice(60, 4)). The resulting code is listed here:

```
IntVector v1, v2, v3;
try (Arena arena = Arena.ofConfined()) {
  MemorySegment srcSegment = arena.allocateArray(
    ValueLayout.JAVA_INT, 1, 2, 3, 4, -1, -1, -1, 52, 22, 33,
                          -1, -1, -1, -1, -1, 4);

  v1 = IntVector.fromMemorySegment(VS128,
    srcSegment.asSlice(0, 16), 0, ByteOrder.nativeOrder());

  v2 = IntVector.fromMemorySegment(VS128,
    srcSegment.asSlice(28, 12), 0, ByteOrder.nativeOrder(),
    VS128.indexInRange(0, 3));

  v3 = IntVector.fromMemorySegment(VS128,
    srcSegment.asSlice(60), 0, ByteOrder.nativeOrder(),
    VS128.indexInRange(0, 1));
}
```

Done! Of course, we can slice a memory segment in regular Java arrays as well. Here you go:

```
int[] jv1, jv2, jv3;
try (Arena arena = Arena.ofConfined()) {
  MemorySegment srcSegment = arena.allocateArray(
    ValueLayout.JAVA_INT, 1, 2, 3, 4, -1, -1, -1, 52, 22, 33,
                          -1, -1, -1, -1, -1, 4);

  jv1 = srcSegment
    .asSlice(0, 16).toArray(ValueLayout.JAVA_INT);
  jv2 = srcSegment
    .asSlice(28, 12).toArray(ValueLayout.JAVA_INT);
  jv3 = srcSegment
    .asSlice(60).toArray(ValueLayout.JAVA_INT);
}
```

The toArray() method returns a Java regular array (here, int[]) from the sliced memory segment.

Using asOverlappingSlice()

The `asOverlappingSlice(MemorySegment other)` method returns a slice of this segment that overlaps the given segment as an `Optional<MemorySegment>`. Consider the following segment (arena is an instance of `Arena`):

```
MemorySegment segment = arena.allocateArray(
  ValueLayout.JAVA_INT, new int[]{1, 2, 3, 4, 6, 8, 4, 5, 3});
```

And, we slice it at offset 12, so at value 4:

```
MemorySegment subsegment = segment.asSlice(12);
```

Finally, we call `asOverlappingSlice()` to see where the overlapping occurs:

```
int[] subarray = segment.asOverlappingSlice(subsegment)
  .orElse(MemorySegment.NULL).toArray(ValueLayout.JAVA_INT);
```

The resulting array is [4, 6, 8, 4, 5, 3].

Using segmentOffset()

The `segmentOffset(MemorySegment other)` returns the offset of the given segment (other) relative to this segment. Consider the following segment (arena is an instance of `Arena`):

```
MemorySegment segment = arena.allocateArray(
  ValueLayout.JAVA_INT, new int[]{1, 2, 3, 4, 6, 8, 4, 5, 3});
```

And, we slice it at offset 16, so at value 6:

```
MemorySegment subsegment = segment.asSlice(16);
```

Next, we call `segmentOffset()` to find out at what offset in segment we have subsegment:

```
// 16
long offset = segment.segmentOffset(subsegment);

// 6
segment.get(ValueLayout.JAVA_INT, offset)
```

You can practice all these examples in the bundled code. Challenge yourself to explore `MemorySegment.mismatch()` further.

157. Tackling the slicing allocator

Let's consider the following three Java regular `int` arrays:

```
int[] arr1 = new int[]{1, 2, 3, 4, 5, 6};
int[] arr2 = new int[]{7, 8, 9};
int[] arr3 = new int[]{10, 11, 12, 13, 14};
```

Next, we want to allocate a memory segment to each of these arrays. A straightforward approach relies on `Arena.allocateArray()` introduced in *Problem 150*:

```
try (Arena arena = Arena.ofConfined()) {
  MemorySegment segment1
    = arena.allocateArray(ValueLayout.JAVA_INT, arr1);
  MemorySegment segment2
    = arena.allocateArray(ValueLayout.JAVA_INT, arr2);
  MemorySegment segment3
    = arena.allocateArray(ValueLayout.JAVA_INT, arr3);
}
```

This approach allocates enough memory to accommodate each of the given arrays. But, sometimes, we want to allocate only a certain amount of memory. If this fixed amount is not enough, then we want to tackle the problem differently. For this, we can rely on a `java.lang.foreign.SegmentAllocator`. Of course, there are many other scenarios when `SegmentAllocator` is useful, but for now, let's tackle the following one.

Let's assume that we allow allocating a fixed size of $10 * 4 = 40$ bytes. This is a bulk amount of memory that should be sliced between our three arrays. First, we allocate these 40 bytes as follows:

```
try (Arena arena = Arena.ofConfined()) {
  SegmentAllocator allocator =
    SegmentAllocator.slicingAllocator(arena.allocate(10 * 4));
  ...
```

Next, we use the `allocator` to allocate a slice from these 40 bytes to each array. The first array (`arr1`) has 6 values, so the memory segment gets $6 * 4 = 24$ bytes:

```
  MemorySegment segment1 = allocator.allocateArray(
    ValueLayout.JAVA_INT, arr1);
  ...
```

The segment allocator has available $40 - 24 = 16$ more bytes. The second array (`arr2`) has 3 values, so the memory segment gets $3 * 4 = 12$ bytes:

```
  MemorySegment segment2 = allocator.allocateArray(
    ValueLayout.JAVA_INT, arr2);
  ...
```

The segment allocator has available $16 - 12 = 4$ more bytes. The third array (`arr3`) has 5 values, so it needs a memory segment of $5 * 4 = 20$ bytes, but only 4 are available. This causes an `IndexOutOfBoundsException` and gives us the control to handle this corner case:

```
  MemorySegment segment3 = allocator.allocateArray(
    ValueLayout.JAVA_INT, arr3);
} catch (IndexOutOfBoundsException e) {
  System.out.println(
```

```
      "There is not enough memory to fit all data");
      // handle exception
}
```

A possible approach to avoid this IndexOutOfBoundsException may consist of giving more memory to the segment allocator. In this case, we need to give it 16 more bytes, so we can express it as follows:

```
SegmentAllocator allocator = SegmentAllocator
  .slicingAllocator(arena.allocate(10 * 4 + 4 * 4));
```

Of course, you don't have to write 10 * 4 + 4 * 4. You can say 14 * 4, or just 56. Basically, our three arrays have 14 elements of 4 bytes each, and initially, we covered only 10 of them. Next, we increased the memory to cover the remaining 4 as well.

158. Introducing the slice handle

Let's suppose that we have the following nested model (10 sequences of 5 double values each):

```
SequenceLayout innerSeq
  = MemoryLayout.sequenceLayout(5, ValueLayout.JAVA_DOUBLE);
SequenceLayout outerSeq
  = MemoryLayout.sequenceLayout(10, innerSeq);
```

Next, we define a VarHandle via PathElement and we populate this model accordingly with some random data:

```
VarHandle handle = outerSeq.varHandle(
  PathElement.sequenceElement(),
  PathElement.sequenceElement());

try (Arena arena = Arena.ofConfined()) {

  MemorySegment segment = arena.allocate(outerSeq);

  for (int i = 0; i < outerSeq.elementCount(); i++) {
    for (int j = 0; j < innerSeq.elementCount(); j++) {
      handle.set(segment, i, j, Math.random());
    }
  }
}
```

OK, you should be familiar with this code, so nothing new so far. Next, we plan to extract from this model the third sequence from 10 containing 5 sequences of double values. We can accomplish this via the sliceHandle(PathElement... elements) method, which returns a java.lang.invoke. MethodHandle. This MethodHandle takes a memory segment and returns a slice of it corresponding to the selected memory layout. Here is the code for our scenario:

```
MethodHandle mHandle = outerSeq.sliceHandle(
  PathElement.sequenceElement());


System.out.println("\n The third sequence of 10: "
  + Arrays.toString(
    ((MemorySegment) mHandle.invoke(segment, 3))
      .toArray(ValueLayout.JAVA_DOUBLE)));
```

Done! Now, you know how to slice out a certain memory layout from the given memory segment.

159. Introducing layout flattening

Let's suppose that we have the following nested model (the exact same model as in *Problem 158*):

```
SequenceLayout innerSeq
  = MemoryLayout.sequenceLayout(5, ValueLayout.JAVA_DOUBLE);
SequenceLayout outerSeq
  = MemoryLayout.sequenceLayout(10, innerSeq);
```

Next, we define a VarHandle via PathElement and we populate this model accordingly with some random data in a memory segment named segment (you can see the code listed in *Problem 158*).

Our goal is to take this nested model and obtain a flat model. So, instead of having 10 sequences of 5 double values each, we want one sequence of 50 double values. This can be achieved via the flatten() method, as follows:

```
SequenceLayout flatten = outerSeq.flatten();


VarHandle fhandle = flatten.varHandle(
  PathElement.sequenceElement());


for (int i = 0; i < flatten.elementCount(); i++) {
  System.out.printf("\nx = %.2f", fhandle.get(segment, i));
}
```

Notice the PathElement, which traverses a single sequence. This is the sequence that resulted after the flatten operation. We can go further and allocate another memory segment for this sequence and set new data:

```
try (Arena arena = Arena.ofConfined()) {

  MemorySegment segment = arena.allocate(flatten);

  for (int i = 0; i < flatten.elementCount(); i++) {
    fhandle.set(segment, i, Math.random());
  }
}
```

Next, let's see how we can reshape a memory layout.

160. Introducing layout reshaping

Let's suppose that we have the following nested model (the exact same model as in *Problem 158*):

```
SequenceLayout innerSeq
  = MemoryLayout.sequenceLayout(5, ValueLayout.JAVA_DOUBLE);
SequenceLayout outerSeq
  = MemoryLayout.sequenceLayout(10, innerSeq);
```

Next, we define a `VarHandle` via `PathElement` and we populate this model accordingly with some random data (you can see the code listed in *Problem 158*).

Our goal is to reshape this model to look as follows:

```
SequenceLayout innerSeq
  = MemoryLayout.sequenceLayout(25, ValueLayout.JAVA_DOUBLE);
SequenceLayout outerSeq
  = MemoryLayout.sequenceLayout(2, innerSeq);
```

So, instead of having 10 sequences of 5 double values each, we want 25 sequences of 2 double values each. In order to accomplish this reshaping goal, we can rely on the `reshape(long... elementCounts)` method. This method takes the elements of this sequence layout and re-arranges them into a multi-dimensional sequence layout conforming to the given list of element counts per sequence. So, in our case, we do it as follows:

```
SequenceLayout reshaped = outerSeq.reshape(25, 2);
```

You can see the complete example in the bundled code.

161. Introducing the layout spreader

Let's suppose that we have the following nested model (the exact same model as in *Problem 158*):

```
SequenceLayout innerSeq
  = MemoryLayout.sequenceLayout(5, ValueLayout.JAVA_DOUBLE);
SequenceLayout outerSeq
  = MemoryLayout.sequenceLayout(10, innerSeq);
```

Next, we define a `VarHandle` via `PathElement` and we populate this model accordingly with some random data in a memory segment named `segment` (you can see the code listed in *Problem 158*).

Next, let's assume that we want to extract the third `double` value from the seventh sequence (count starts from 0). Among the approaches, we can rely on `sliceHandle()` introduced in *Problem 158,* as follows:

```
MethodHandle mHandle = outerSeq.sliceHandle(
  PathElement.sequenceElement(),
  PathElement.sequenceElement());
```

```
MemorySegment ms = (MemorySegment)
   mHandle.invokeExact(segment, 7L, 3L);


System.out.println(ms.get(ValueLayout.JAVA_DOUBLE, 0));
```

Another approach consists of using an *array-spreading* method handle. In other words, by calling the asSpreader(Class<?> arrayType, int arrayLength) method, we can obtain a *spreader-array* that contains the positional arguments that we want to pass over and has a length equal to the given arrayLength. Since we have two pass-over long arguments (7L and 3L), we need a long[] array of length 2:

```
MemorySegment ms = (MemorySegment) mHandle
   .asSpreader(Long[].class, 2)
   .invokeExact(segment, new Long[]{7L, 3L});
```

You may also be interested in asCollector(Class<?> arrayType, int arrayLength), which is basically the opposite of asSpreader(). You give a list of arguments and this method collects them in an *array-collecting*.

162. Introducing the memory segment view VarHandle

Let's consider the following simple memory segment for storing an int (arena is an instance of Arena):

```
MemorySegment segment = arena.allocate(ValueLayout.JAVA_INT);
```

We know that we can create a VarHandle via PathElement:

```
// VarHandle[varType=int,
// coord=[interface java.lang.foreign.MemorySegment]]
VarHandle handle = ValueLayout.JAVA_INT.varHandle();
```

Or, via arrayElementVarHandle():

```
// VarHandle[varType=int,
// coord=[interface java.lang.foreign.MemorySegment, long]]
VarHandle arrhandle
   = ValueLayout.JAVA_INT.arrayElementVarHandle();
```

The MethodHandles.memorySegmentViewVarHandle(ValueLayout layout) is another approach for creating a VarHandle that can be used to access a memory segment. The returned VarHandle perceives/views the content of the memory segment as a sequence of the given ValueLayout. In our case, the code looks as follows:

```
// VarHandle[varType=int,
// coord=[interface java.lang.foreign.MemorySegment, long]]
VarHandle viewhandle = MethodHandles
   .memorySegmentViewVarHandle(ValueLayout.JAVA_INT);
```

Next, we can rely on insertCoordinates(VarHandle target, int pos, Object... values) to specify the set of *bound coordinates* before the VarHandle is actually invoked. In other words, the returned VarHandle will expose fewer Coordinate Types (CTs) than the given target.

In our example, the target argument (invoked after inserting the set of *bound coordinates*) is viewhandle. The position of the first coordinate is 1, and we have a single *bound coordinate* representing the offset 0 of type long:

```
viewhandle = MethodHandles
  .insertCoordinates(viewhandle, 1, 0);
```

Now, when we call the popular VarHandle.set/get(Object...) on the returned VarHandler, the incoming coordinate values are automatically joined with the given *bound coordinate* values. The result is passed to the target VarHandle:

```
viewhandle.set(segment, 75);
System.out.println("Value: " + viewhandle.get(segment));
```

Done! Now, you know three ways to create a VarHandle for dereferencing a memory segment.

163. Streaming memory segments

Combining the Java Stream API with memory segments can be achieved via the elements(MemoryLayout elementLayout) method. This method gets an element layout and returns a Stream<MemorySegment>, which is a sequential stream over disjointed slices in this segment. The stream size matches the size of the specified layout.

Let's consider the following memory layout:

```
SequenceLayout xy = MemoryLayout
  .sequenceLayout(2, MemoryLayout.structLayout(
    ValueLayout.JAVA_INT.withName("x"),
    ValueLayout.JAVA_INT.withName("y")));
```

Next, we declare two VarHandle and set some data:

```
VarHandle xHandle = xy.varHandle(
  PathElement.sequenceElement(),
  PathElement.groupElement("x"));

VarHandle yHandle = xy.varHandle(
  PathElement.sequenceElement(),
  PathElement.groupElement("y"));

try (Arena arena = Arena.ofShared()) {
```

```
    MemorySegment segment = arena.allocate(xy);

    xHandle.set(segment, 0, 5);
    yHandle.set(segment, 0, 9);
    xHandle.set(segment, 1, 6);
    yHandle.set(segment, 1, 8);

    // stream operations
}
```

Let's assume that we want to sum up all data. For this, we can do the following:

```
int sum = segment.elements(xy)
    .map(t -> t.toArray(ValueLayout.JAVA_INT))
    .flatMapToInt(t -> Arrays.stream(t))
    .sum();
```

Or, we can simply pass the proper layout and even empower parallel processing:

```
int sum = segment.elements(ValueLayout.JAVA_INT)
    .parallel()
    .mapToInt(s -> s.get(ValueLayout.JAVA_INT, 0))
    .sum();
```

Both approaches return 28 = 5 + 9 + 6 + 8.

How about summing only the values from the first (*x*, *y*) pair? For this, we have to slice the layout corresponding to the first (*x*, *y*) pair via sliceHandle() – we introduced this method in *Problem 151*:

```
MethodHandle xyHandle
    = xy.sliceHandle(PathElement.sequenceElement());
```

Next, we slice the segment of the first (*x*, *y*) pair (if we replace 0 with 1, then we obtain the segment of the second (*x*, *y*) pair):

```
MemorySegment subsegment
    = (MemorySegment) xyHandle.invoke(segment, 0);
```

And, we use it to calculate the needed sum:

```
int sum = subsegment.elements(ValueLayout.JAVA_INT)
    .parallel()
    .mapToInt(s -> s.get(ValueLayout.JAVA_INT, 0))
    .sum();
```

The result is clear, 14 = 5 + 9.

How about summing y from the first pair with the second pair (x, y)? For this, we can slice the proper segment via `asSlice()` – we introduced this method in *Problem 156*:

```
var sum = segment.elements(xy)
  .parallel()
  .map(t -> t.asSlice(4).toArray(ValueLayout.JAVA_INT))
  .flatMapToInt(t -> Arrays.stream(t))
  .sum();
```

The `asSlice(4)` simply skips the first x since this is stored at offset 0 and consumes 4 bytes. From offset 4 to the end, we have the first y, and the second pair (x, y). So, the result is $23 = 9 + 6 + 8$.

Notice that, this time, we have used a shared arena (`Arena.ofShared()`). This is needed for parallel computations since the segment should be shared between multiple threads.

Done! Feel free to challenge yourself to solve more such scenarios.

164. Tackling mapped memory segments

We know that a computer has limited physical memory, referred to as RAM. Common sense, though, tells us that we cannot allocate a memory segment larger than the available RAM (this should lead to an out-of-memory error). But this is not quite true! Here is where *mapped memory segments* come into the discussion.

The mapped memory segment represents virtual memory and can be huge (gigabytes, terabytes, or whatever you may think of). This virtual memory is actually memory mapped by files or shortly *memory-mapped files* (a file can be from a regular file to any other kind of file descriptor).

Obviously, at any time, only a part of the virtual memory lives in the real memory. This is why we can allocate terabytes of virtual memory on a laptop with much less real RAM. Practically, a portion of missing mapped memory is loaded on demand in the real RAM. While loading, the process operating on this memory is temporarily suspended.

The goal of mapped memory files is to drastically reduce the I/O operations. The standard read/write operations rely on copying data into buffers, while mapped files put the file data directly into the process address space. This is much faster and sharable across processes.

In Java, we can set a mapped memory file via the `java.nio.channels.FileChannel` API, more precisely, via the `map(MapMode mode, long offset, long size, Arena arena)` method. Here is an example of setting a mapped memory file of 1 MB and writing/reading some text into it (feel free to try it on your machine for a file that is 1 GB (1,073,741,824 bytes) or larger:

```
try (FileChannel file = FileChannel.open(
  Path.of("readme.txt"), CREATE, READ, WRITE);
  Arena arena = Arena.ofConfined()) {

    MemorySegment segment
      = file.map(READ_WRITE, 0, 1048576, arena);
```

```
    // write the data
    segment.setUtf8String(0, "This is a readme file ...");
    segment.setUtf8String(1048576/2,
      "Here is the middle of the file ...");
    segment.setUtf8String(1048576-32,
      "Here is the end of the file ...");


    // read some data
    System.out.println(segment.getUtf8String(1048576/2));
}
```

When a file contains a significant number of empty bytes (so-called holes, \x00) it becomes a good candidate to become a *sparse* file. In a sparse file, these holes are no longer kept on the storage device, so they no longer consume physical memory. This is an attempt at using memory more efficiently and stops consuming physical memory with zero-byte blocks. Each operating system has its own way of handling sparse files, but generally speaking, the zero-byte blocks are simply reduced to some meaningful metadata useful for dynamically generating them. For more details and a useful diagram, consider this Wikipedia article (https://en.wikipedia.org/wiki/Sparse_file).

In Java, we can create a sparse file by adding the java.nio.file.StandardOpenOption.SPARSE option to the list of options next to CREATE_NEW:

```
try (FileChannel file = FileChannel.open(
  Path.of("sparse_readme.txt"),
    CREATE_NEW, SPARSE, READ, WRITE);
  Arena arena = Arena.ofConfined()) {

  MemorySegment segment
    = file.map(READ_WRITE, 0, 1048576, arena);

    // write the data
    segment.setUtf8String(0, "This is a readme file ...");
    segment.setUtf8String(1048576/2,
      "Here is the middle of the file ...");
    segment.setUtf8String(1048576-32,
      "Here is the end of the file ...");

    // read some data
    System.out.println(segment.getUtf8String(0));
}
```

Depending on your operating system (machine), you should use dedicated tools to inspect these files in detail and get a deeper insight into how they work.

If you find yourself using mapped memory files quite often, then you may prefer to extend the Arena interface and provide your own implementation starting from a simple skeleton, as follows:

```java
public class MappedArena implements Arena {

  private final String fileName;
  private final Arena shared;

  public MappedArena(String fileName) {

    this.fileName = fileName;
    this.shared = Arena.ofShared();
  }

  @Override
  public MemorySegment allocate(
    long byteSize, long byteAlignment) {

    try (FileChannel file = FileChannel.open(
      Path.of(fileName + System.currentTimeMillis() + ".txt"),
        CREATE_NEW, SPARSE, READ, WRITE)) {

      return file.map(
        READ_WRITE, 0, byteSize, shared);

    } catch (IOException e) {
      throw new RuntimeException(e);
    }
  }

  // more overridden methods
}
```

Using the MappedArena is straightforward:

```java
try (Arena arena = new MappedArena("readme")) {

  MemorySegment segment1 = arena.allocate(100);
  MemorySegment segment2 = arena.allocate(50);

  segment1.setUtf8String(0, "Hello");
  segment2.setUtf8String(0, "World");
```

```
    System.out.println(segment1.getUtf8String(0)
      + " " + segment2.getUtf8String(0));
  }
```

Of course, you can improve/modify this code to obtain other configurations. Maybe you want a confined arena (here, we have a shared arena), maybe you want to delete the files after the arena is closed (here, the files remain on disk, so you can inspect them), maybe you don't need sparse files (here, we use sparse files), maybe you prefer another file name (here, we concatenate the given name with System.currentTimeMillis() and the .txt extension), or maybe you need to take into account byte alignment.

165. Introducing the Foreign Linker API

The main goal of the Foreign Linker API is to provide a robust and easy-to-use API (no need to write C/C++ code) for sustaining interoperability between the Java code and C/C++ foreign functions of native shared libraries (in the future, other programming languages will be supported via this API).

The journey of calling foreign code starts with the java.lang.foreign.SymbolLookup functional interface. This interface represents the entry point and consists of looking up the address of a given symbol in a loaded native shared library. There are three ways of doing this, as follows:

Linker.defaultLookup() – as its name suggests, defaultLookup() represents a *default lookup* that scans and locates all the symbols of the commonly used native shared libraries depending on the current operating system:

```
  Linker linker = Linker.nativeLinker();
  SymbolLookup lookup = linker.defaultLookup();
```

SymbolLookup.loaderLookup() – represents a *loader lookup* that scans and locates all the symbols in all the native shared libraries loaded in the current class loader (via System.loadLibrary() and System.load() based on java.library.path):

```
  System.loadLibrary("fooLib"); // fooLib.dll is loaded here
  SymbolLookup lookup = SymbolLookup.loaderLookup();
```

SymbolLookup.libraryLookup(String name, Arena arena) – represents a *library lookup* capable of scanning and loading in the arena scope a native shared library with the given name. It also creates a symbol lookup for all symbols in that native shared library. Alternatively, we can specify a Path via SymbolLookup.libraryLookup(Path path, Arena arena):

```
  try (Arena arena = Arena.ofConfined()) {
    SymbolLookup lookup = SymbolLookup.libraryLookup(
      libName/libPath, arena);
  }
```

If this step is successfully accomplished, then we can choose the symbol(s) corresponding to the foreign function(s) that we want to call. Finding a foreign function can be done by its name via the SymbolLookup.find(String name) method.

If the pointed method exists among the located symbols, then find() returns a zero-length memory segment wrapped in an Optional (Optional<MemorySegment>). The *base address* of this segment points to the foreign function's entry point:

```
MemorySegment fooFunc = mathLookup.find("fooFunc").get();
```

So far, we have located the native shared library and found one of its methods (fooFunc). Next, we have to link Java code to this foreign function. This is accomplished via the Linker API, which is based on two concepts:

- *downcall* – call the native code from Java code
- *upcall* – call the Java code from the native code

These two concepts are materialized by the Linker interface. *downcall* is mapped in two methods with the following signatures:

```
MethodHandle downcallHandle(
    FunctionDescriptor function, Linker.Option... options)


default MethodHandle downcallHandle(MemorySegment symbol,
    FunctionDescriptor function, Linker.Option... options)
```

Typically, the default method is used via the MemorySegment obtained earlier via the find() method, a function descriptor that describes the signature of the foreign function, and an optional set of linker options. The returned MethodHandle is used later to invoke the foreign function via invoke(), invokeExact(), and so on. Via invoke() or invokeExact(), we pass arguments to the foreign function and access the returned result of running the foreign function (if any).

upcall is mapped by the following method:

```
MemorySegment upcallStub(MethodHandle target,
    FunctionDescriptor function, Arena arena)
```

Typically, the target argument refers to a Java method, the function argument describes the Java method signature, and the arena argument represents the arena associated with the returned MemorySegment. This MemorySegment is passed later as an argument of the Java code that invokes (invoke()/invokeExact()) a *downcall* method handle. As a consequence, this MemorySegment acts as a function pointer.

If we glue this knowledge together, then we can write a classical example of calling the getpid() method (on Windows 10, _getpid() – https://learn.microsoft.com/en-us/cpp/c-runtime-library/reference/getpid) as follows (consider reading the meaningful comments to get insight on each step):

```
// get the Linker of the underlying native platform
// (operating system + processor that runs the JVM)
Linker linker = Linker.nativeLinker();


// "_getpid" is part of the Universal C Runtime (UCRT) Library
```

```
SymbolLookup libLookup = linker.defaultLookup();

// find the "_getpid" foreign function
MemorySegment segmentGetpid = libLookup.find("_getpid").get();

// create a method handle for "_getpid"
MethodHandle func = linker.downcallHandle(segmentGetpid,
    FunctionDescriptor.of(ValueLayout.JAVA_INT));

// invoke the foreign function, "_getpid" and get the result
int result = (int) func.invokeExact();
System.out.println(result);
```

This code was tested on Windows 10. If you run a different operating system, then consider informing yourself about this foreign function to adjust the code accordingly.

166. Calling the sumTwoInt() foreign function

Do you remember the sumTwoInt() function? We have defined this C function in a native shared library named math.dll (check *Problems 144, 145*, and *146*). Let's assume that we have placed the math.dll library in the project folder under the lib/cpp path.

We can call this foreign function in almost the same manner as we've called _getpid(). Since math.dll is a user-defined library that is not commonly used, it cannot be loaded via defaultLookup(). The solution is to explicitly load the library from the lib/cpp path, as follows:

```
Linker linker = Linker.nativeLinker();
Path path = Paths.get("lib/cpp/math.dll");

try (Arena arena = Arena.ofConfined()) {

  SymbolLookup libLookup = SymbolLookup.libraryLookup(
    path, arena);
  ...
```

Next, we have to find in math.dll the foreign function by name. If your C compiler (for instance, G++) has applied the *mangling* (or *name decoration*) technique, then sumTwoInt will have been renamed in the library to something else (here, _Z9sumTwoIntii) and that name should be used:

```
MemorySegment segmentSumTwoInt
  = libLookup.find("_Z9sumTwoIntii").get();
  ...
```

Next, we define the MethodHandle for this *downcall*:

```
MethodHandle func = linker.downcallHandle(segmentSumTwoInt,
```

```
FunctionDescriptor.of(ValueLayout.JAVA_LONG,
  ValueLayout.JAVA_INT, ValueLayout.JAVA_INT));
...
```

Finally, we can invoke the foreign function and get the result:

```
long result = (long) func.invokeExact(3, 9);


System.out.println(result);
}
```

The result should be 12. Check out the complete code in the bundled code.

167. Calling the modf() foreign function

Let's consider that we want to call the modf() foreign function. This function is part of the C standard library with the following syntax (https://learn.microsoft.com/en-us/cpp/c-runtime-library/reference/modf-modff-modfl):

```
double modf(double x, double *intptr);
```

This method gets a double x and returns the signed fractional part of x. The intptr is a pointer argument used to point to the memory address where the integer part should be stored as a double value.

Since this method is part of UCRT, it can be found via defaultLookup():

```
Linker linker = Linker.nativeLinker();
SymbolLookup libLookup = linker.defaultLookup();

try (Arena arena = Arena.ofConfined()) {

  MemorySegment segmentModf = libLookup.find("modf").get();
  ...
```

Nothing new so far! Next, we need to define the proper MethodHandle. Because the second argument of modf() is a pointer, we need to specify a value layout of type ADDRESS:

```
MethodHandle func = linker.downcallHandle(segmentModf,
  FunctionDescriptor.of(ValueLayout.JAVA_DOUBLE,
    ValueLayout.JAVA_DOUBLE, ValueLayout.ADDRESS));
  ...
```

If we could invoke the foreign function at this point, we could collect the fractional part of the given x, but we cannot obtain the integer part. We have to create a memory segment and pass this memory segment to the foreign function at invocation time. The foreign function will write the integer part in this memory segment, which should be capable of storing a double value:

```
    MemorySegment segmentIntptr
      = arena.allocate(ValueLayout.JAVA_DOUBLE);

    double fractional
      = (double) func.invokeExact(x, segmentIntptr);
    ...
```

The fractional part is returned by the foreign key. The integer part is read from the memory segment at offset 0:

```
    System.out.println("Fractional part: " + fractional
      + " Integer part: " + segmentIntptr.get(
        ValueLayout.JAVA_DOUBLE, 0));
}
```

If x = 89.76655, then the output will be:

```
Fractional part: 0.7665499999999952 Integer part: 89.0
```

Challenge yourself to adapt this code to call `modff()` and `modfl()` foreign functions.

168. Calling the strcat() foreign function

The `strcat()` foreign function is part of the C standard library and has the following signature (https://learn.microsoft.com/en-us/cpp/c-runtime-library/reference/strcat-wcscat-mbscat):

```
char *strcat(char *strDestination, const char *strSource);
```

This function appends the `strSource` at the end of the `strDestination`. The function doesn't get these strings. It gets two pointers to these strings (so, two `ADDRESS`) and doesn't return a value, so we rely on `FunctionDescriptor.ofVoid()`, as follows:

```
Linker linker = Linker.nativeLinker();
SymbolLookup libLookup = linker.defaultLookup();

try (Arena arena = Arena.ofConfined()) {

  MemorySegment segmentStrcat
    = libLookup.find("strcat").get();

  MethodHandle func = linker.downcallHandle(
    segmentStrcat, FunctionDescriptor.ofVoid(
      ValueLayout.ADDRESS, ValueLayout.ADDRESS));

  ...
```

Since the arguments of strcat() are two pointers (ADDRESS), we have to create two memory segments and set the strings accordingly:

```
String strDestination = "Hello ";
String strSource = "World";

MemorySegment segmentStrSource
  = arena.allocate(strSource.length() + 1);
segmentStrSource.setUtf8String(0, strSource);

MemorySegment segmentStrDestination = arena.allocate(
  strSource.length() + 1 + strDestination.length() + 1);
segmentStrDestination.setUtf8String(0, strDestination);
...
```

Notice the size of segmentStrDestination. Since strcat() appends the source string (strSource) at the end of the destination string (strDestination), we have to prepare the size of segmentStrDestination to fit the source string as well, so its size is strSource.length() + 1 + strDestination.length() + 1. Next, we can invoke the foreign function as follows:

```
func.invokeExact(segmentStrDestination, segmentStrSource);
```

Finally, we read the result from segmentStrDestination:

```
// Hello World
System.out.println(segmentStrDestination.getUtf8String(0));
```

So, the World string was appended at the end of Hello.

169. Calling the bsearch() foreign function

The bsearch() foreign function is part of the C standard library and has the following signature (https://learn.microsoft.com/en-us/cpp/c-runtime-library/reference/bsearch):

```
void *bsearch(
  const void *key,
  const void *base,
  size_t num,
  size_t width,
  int ( __cdecl *compare ) (
    const void *key, const void *datum)
);
```

In a nutshell, this method gets pointers to a key, a sorted array (base), and a comparator. Its goal is to use the given comparator to perform a binary search of the given key in the given array. More precisely, bsearch() gets a pointer to the key, a pointer to the array, the number of elements in the array (num), the size of an element in bytes (width), and the comparator as a callback function.

The callback function gets a pointer to key and a pointer to the current element of the array to be compared with key. It returns the result of comparing these two elements.

The bsearch() function returns a pointer in the array pointing to the occurrence of the key. If the given key is not found, then bsearch() returns NULL.

We can start by coding the comparator callback function as a Java method:

```
static int comparator(MemorySegment i1, MemorySegment i2) {
  return Integer.compare(i1.get(ValueLayout.JAVA_INT, 0),
    i2.get(ValueLayout.JAVA_INT, 0));
}
```

The i1 memory segment is the pointer to key, and the i2 memory segment is the pointer to the current element of the array to be compared with key. This method will be called by the foreign function (native code calls Java code), so an *upcall stub* should be prepared. First, we need a method handle pointing to this comparator:

```
MethodHandle comparatorHandle = MethodHandles.lookup()
  .findStatic(Main.class, "comparator", MethodType.methodType(
    int.class, MemorySegment.class, MemorySegment.class));
```

Second, we create the *upcall stub*. For this, we need the Linker:

```
Linker linker = Linker.nativeLinker();
SymbolLookup libLookup = linker.defaultLookup();
```

And we are ready to use the confined arena:

```
try (Arena arena = Arena.ofConfined()) {

  MemorySegment comparatorFunc =
    linker.upcallStub(comparatorHandle,
      FunctionDescriptor.of(ValueLayout.JAVA_INT,
        ValueLayout.ADDRESS.withTargetLayout(
          MemoryLayout.sequenceLayout(ValueLayout.JAVA_INT)),
        ValueLayout.ADDRESS.withTargetLayout(
          MemoryLayout.sequenceLayout(ValueLayout.JAVA_INT))),
      arena);

  MemorySegment segmentBsearch
    = libLookup.find("bsearch").get();

  MethodHandle func = linker.downcallHandle(
    segmentBsearch, FunctionDescriptor.of(
      ValueLayout.ADDRESS, ValueLayout.ADDRESS,
```

```
      ValueLayout.ADDRESS, ValueLayout.JAVA_INT,
      ValueLayout.JAVA_LONG, ValueLayout.ADDRESS));
  ...
```

Here, we have used the `withTargetLayout()` method to create an *unbounded* address. The *unbounded* `ADDRESS` means addresses for which we don't know the size, so it is better to ensure that enough space will be available by setting them as *unbounded*. Practically, by creating a target sequence layout without an explicit size, we obtain a native memory segment with maximal size. Next, we find the `bsearch()` method and define its method handle.

Next, we prepare the `key` and the `array` arguments as `MemorySegment`:

```
int elem = 14;
int[] arr = new int[]{1, 3, 6, 8, 10, 12, 14, 16, 20, 22};

MemorySegment key = arena.allocate(
  ValueLayout.JAVA_INT, elem);
MemorySegment array
  = arena.allocateArray(ValueLayout.JAVA_INT, arr);
...
```

We have all the needed arguments, so we can invoke `bsearch()`:

```
MemorySegment result = (MemorySegment) func.invokeExact(
    key, array, 10, ValueLayout.JAVA_INT.byteSize(),
      comparatorFunc);
...
```

Keep in mind that `bsearch()` returns a pointer in the `array` pointing to the first occurrence of the `key`, or it returns `NULL` if the given `key` is not found in the given `array`. If `bsearch()` returned `NULL`, then the result should match `MemorySegment.NULL`, which is a zero-length native segment representing a `NULL` address:

```
if (result.equals(MemorySegment.NULL)) {
  System.out.println("Element " + elem
    + " not found in the given array "
    + Arrays.toString(arr));
} else {
  ...
```

Otherwise, we know that the result represents a pointer in the given `array`. So, we can rely on the `segmentOffset()` method (introduced in *Problem 149*) to find the offset of the result relative to `array`:

```
long offset = array.segmentOffset(result);
System.out.println("Element found in the given array at
  offset: " + offset);
System.out.println("Element value: "
```

```
        + array.get(ValueLayout.JAVA_INT, offset));
  }
}
```

For our key (14) and `array`, the returned offset is 24.

170. Introducing Jextract

Jextract (`https://github.com/openjdk/jextract`) is a very handy tool capable of consuming the headers of native libraries (`*.h` files) and producing low-level Java native bindings. Via this tool, we can save a lot of time since we can focus only on calling native code without caring about the mechanical steps of loading libraries, writing method handles, or *downcall* and *upcall stubs*.

Jextract is a command-line tool that can be downloaded from `https://jdk.java.net/jextract`. The main options of this tool are listed here:

*   `--source`: When we write `jextract --source`, we instruct Jextract to generate from the given header file the corresponding source files without classes. When this option is omitted, Jextract will generate classes.
*   `-- output path`: By default, the generated files are placed in the current folder. Via this option, we can point out the path where these files should be placed.
*   `-t <package>`: By default, Jextract uses the unnamed package name. Via this option, we can specify the package name for the generated classes.
*   `-I <dir>`: Specify one or more paths that should be appended to the existing search paths. The given order is respected during the search.
*   `--dump-includes <String>`: This option allows you to filter the symbols. First, use this option to extract all symbols in a file. Next, edit the file to keep only the needed symbols. Finally, pass this file to Jextract.

The complete list of options is available at `https://github.com/openjdk/jextract`.

171. Generating native binding for modf()

In *Problem 160*, we located, prepared, and called the `modf()` foreign function via the Foreign Linker API. Now, let's use Jextract to generate the native binding needed to call `modf()`.

For Windows, the `modf()` foreign function is described in the `math.h` header file. If you have installed MinGW (`https://sourceforge.net/projects/mingw-w64/`) for 64-bit, then this header file is available in the `mingw64\x86_64-w64-mingw32\include` folder. If we want to generate the native bindings for `math.h`, we can do it as follows:

```
C:\SBPBP\GitHub\Java-Coding-Problems-Second-Edition\Chapter07\P171_JextractAndModf>
    jextract --source --output src\main\java -t c.lib.math
  -I C:\MinGW64\mingw64\x86_64-w64-mingw32\include
    C:\MinGW64\mingw64\x86_64-w64-mingw32\include\math.h
```

Figure 7.26: Generating the native bindings from math.h

Or, as plain text:

```
C:\SBPBP\GitHub\Java-Coding-Problems-Second-Edition\Chapter07\P171_JextractAndModf>
  jextract --source --output src\main\java -t c.lib.math
  -I C:\MinGW64\mingw64\x86_64-w64-mingw32\include
  C:\MinGW64\mingw64\x86_64-w64-mingw32\include\math.h
```

So, we generated the source files (--sources) in the src\main\java subfolder of the current project (--output), in the package c.lib.math (-t). The math.h is loaded from mingw64\x86_64-w64-mingw32\include.

After running this command, you'll find in c.lib.math the native bindings for all the symbols found in math.h. Most probably, this is not what we want, since we're calling only the modf() foreign function. Filtering symbols is a two-step process. First, we generate a *dump* of all symbols, as follows:

```
C:\SBPBP\GitHub\Java-Coding-Problems-Second-Edition\Chapter07\P171_JextractAndModf>
  jextract --dump-includes includes.txt
  -I C:\MinGW64\mingw64\x86_64-w64-mingw32\include
  C:\MinGW64\mingw64\x86_64-w64-mingw32\include\math.h
```

Figure 7.27: Creating a dump file containing all symbols from math.h

Or, as plain text:

```
C:\SBPBP\GitHub\Java-Coding-Problems-Second-Edition\Chapter07\P171_JextractAndModf>
  jextract --dump-includes includes.txt
  -I C:\MinGW64\mingw64\x86_64-w64-mingw32\include
  C:\MinGW64\mingw64\x86_64-w64-mingw32\include\math.h
```

This command will write in the project root a file named includes.txt containing all symbols found in math.h. The second step consists of editing this file. For instance, we have kept only the symbol for modf(), as follows:

```
includes - Notepad
File  Edit  Format  View  Help
--include-function modf     # header: C:\MinGW64\mingw64\x86_64-w64-mingw32\include\math.h
```

Figure 7.28: Editing the includes.txt to keep only the needed symbols

Next, we pass the edited includes.txt to Jextract, as follows:

```
C:\SBPBP\GitHub\Java-Coding-Problems-Second-Edition\Chapter07\P171_JextractAndModf>
  jextract --source @includes.txt --output src\main\java -t c.lib.math
  -I C:\MinGW64\mingw64\x86_64-w64-mingw32\include
  C:\MinGW64\mingw64\x86_64-w64-mingw32\include\math.h
```

Figure 7.29: Run Jextract with the filtered includes.txt

Or, as plain text:

```
C:\SBPBP\GitHub\Java-Coding-Problems-Second-Edition\Chapter07\P171_JextractAndModf>
    jextract --source @includes.txt --output src\main\java -t c.lib.math
    -I C:\MinGW64\mingw64\x86_64-w64-mingw32\include
    C:\MinGW64\mingw64\x86_64-w64-mingw32\include\math.h
```

This time, in `c.lib.math`, you'll find the native bindings only for the `modf()` foreign function. Take your time to inspect each of these files and see how they interact at the code level. Since we generate only the sources, we have to compile the project to obtain the classes. If you prefer to generate the classes directly via Jextract, then you can use the following command (now, the sources will not be generated, only the classes):

```
C:\SBPBP\GitHub\Java-Coding-Problems-Second-Edition\Chapter07\P171_JextractAndModf>
    jextract @includes.txt --output target\classes -t c.lib.math
    -I C:\MinGW64\mingw64\x86_64-w64-mingw32\include
    C:\MinGW64\mingw64\x86_64-w64-mingw32\include\math.h
```

Figure 7.30: Generating the classes of native bindings

Or, as plain text:

```
C:\SBPBP\GitHub\Java-Coding-Problems-Second-Edition\Chapter07\P171_JextractAndModf>
    jextract @includes.txt --output target\classes -t c.lib.math
    -I C:\MinGW64\mingw64\x86_64-w64-mingw32\include
    C:\MinGW64\mingw64\x86_64-w64-mingw32\include\math.h
```

Next, we can use the generated bindings in a Java application to call the `modf()` function. The code is straightforward (we don't need to write the method handle and there is no need to explicitly use `invoke()`/`invokeExact()`):

```java
double x = 89.76655;

try (Arena arena = Arena.ofConfined()) {

  MemorySegment segmentIntptr
    = arena.allocate(ValueLayout.JAVA_DOUBLE);

  double fractional = modf(x, segmentIntptr);
  System.out.println("Fractional part: " + fractional
    + " Integer part: " + segmentIntptr.get(
      ValueLayout.JAVA_DOUBLE, 0));
}
```

The `modf()` function is imported from the `c.lib.math.math_h` package.

Summary

This chapter covered 28 problems. Most of them were focused on the new Foreign (Function) Memory APIs, or Project Panama. As you saw, this API is much more intuitive and powerful than the classical approaches of using JNI, JNA, and JNR. Moreover, the Jextract tool is very handy for generating native bindings from the headers of native shared libraries and saves us a lot of mechanical work.

Join our community on Discord

Join our community's Discord space for discussions with the author and other readers:

https://discord.gg/8mgytp5DGQ

8

Sealed and Hidden Classes

This chapter includes 13 problems covering sealed and hidden classes. The first 11 recipes will cover sealed classes, a very cool feature introduced in JDK 17 (JEP 409) to sustain *closed hierarchies*. The last two problems cover hidden classes, a JDK 15 (JEP 371) feature that allows frameworks to create and use runtime (dynamic) classes hidden in the JVM's internal linkages of bytecode, and to the explicit usage of class loaders.

You'll be skilled in both topics by the end of this chapter.

Problems

Use the following problems to test your programming prowess in manipulating sealed classes and hidden classes in Java. I strongly encourage you to give each problem a try before you turn to the solutions and download the example programs:

172. **Creating an electrical panel (hierarchy of classes):** Write the stub of a Java application that shapes an electrical panel. You can assume that the electrical panel is made of several types of electrical components (for instance, resistors, transistors, and so on), and electrical circuits (for instance, parallel circuits, series circuits, and so on).

173. **Closing the electrical panel before JDK 17:** Use the Java features (for instance, the final keyword and *package-private* hacks) to close this hierarchy (close to extension).

174. **Introducing JDK 17 sealed classes:** Provide a brief introduction to JDK 17 sealed classes. Exemplify how to write closed hierarchies in a single source file via sealed classes.

175. **Introducing the permits clause:** Explain and exemplify the role of the permits clause in sealed classes. Exemplify sealed classes in different source files (same package) and in different packages.

176. **Closing the electrical panel after JDK 17:** Use sealed classes to completely close the electrical panel hierarchy developed in problems 172 and 173.

177. **Combining sealed classes and records:** Exemplify the usage of Java records in combination with sealed classes.

178. **Hooking sealed classes and instanceof:** Write an application that highlights how sealed classes help the compiler to better handle the `instanceof` operator.

179. **Hooking sealed classes in switch:** Write an application that exemplifies how sealed classes help the compiler to sustain exhaustive switch expressions/statements.

180. **Reinterpreting the Visitor pattern via sealed classes and type pattern matching for switch:** Provide a quick sample of the traditional Visitor pattern implementation and transform it via sealed classes into simpler and more accessible code.

181. **Getting info about sealed classes (using reflection):** Explain and exemplify how we can access sealed classes via Java Reflection.

182. **Listing the top three benefits of sealed classes:** Provide what you think are the top three benefits of sealed classes with a few explanations and arguments.

183. **Briefly introducing hidden classes:** Provide a brief, crystal-clear, and meaningful explanation of hidden classes. List their main characteristics.

184. **Creating a hidden class:** Provide a regular example of creating and using a hidden class.

The following sections describe solutions to the preceding problems. Remember that there usually isn't a single correct way to solve a particular problem. Also, remember that the explanations shown here include only the most interesting and important details needed to solve the problems. Download the example solutions to see additional details and to experiment with the programs at https://github. com/PacktPublishing/Java-Coding-Problems-Second-Edition/tree/main/Chapter08.

172. Creating an electrical panel (hierarchy of classes)

Let's assume that we want to model in code lines an electrical panel. Of course, we are not electricians, so for our purposes, an electric panel means a box with some internal circuits made of electrical components and a breaker that turns on/off the electrical panel.

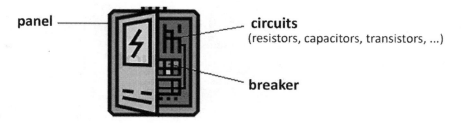

Figure 8.1: Electrical panel components

Everything in an electrical panel can be considered an electrical component, so we can start our code by defining an interface that must be implemented by everything in this panel:

```
public interface ElectricComponent {}
```

Before continuing, let's look at a diagram of the electric panel interfaces and classes that will help you to follow what comes after more easily:

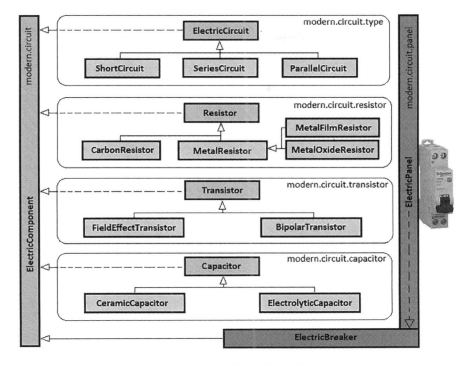

Figure 8.2: A model of the electrical panel

An electrical panel consists of more electrical circuits that interact (or do not interact) with each other. We can represent such a circuit via an abstract class as follows (this acts as a base class for its subclasses):

```
public abstract class ElectricCircuit
    implements ElectricComponent {


  public abstract void on();
  public abstract void off();
}
```

Let's assume that our electrical panel is made of three types of circuits. We have short circuits, series circuits, and parallel circuits. So, we can define the proper class for each type of circuit by extending the abstract ElectricCircuit (we'll show here only the ShortCircuit, while the ParallelCircuit and SeriesCircuit are available in the bundled code):

```
public class ShortCircuit extends ElectricCircuit {


  public ShortCircuit(ElectricComponent... comp) {}


  @Override
```

```
    public void on() {}

    @Override
    public void off() {}
}
```

Check out the constructor of the ShortCircuit class. It gets a varargs argument of the type ElectricComponent. This means that we can build a bigger circuit from smaller circuits and other components such as capacitors, transistors, resistors, and so on. Each such electrical component can be shaped via an abstract class. For instance, a capacitor is a base class that can be expressed as follows:

```
public abstract class Capacitor
    implements ElectricComponent {}
```

We need two types of capacitors (ceramic capacitors and electrolytic capacitors). A ceramic capacitor can be shaped as follows:

```
public class CeramicCapacitor extends Capacitor {}
```

Following the same logic, we can express other electrical components such as transistors (Transistor (abstract), BipolarTransistor, and FieldEffectTransistor) and resistors (Resistor (abstract), CarbonResistor, and MetalResistor, and its two subtypes, MetalFilmResistor and MetalOxideResistor).

We almost have all the electrical components required for building our panel. We just need the breaker, which is just another electrical component with the particularity that it exposes two methods for turning on/off the electrical panel:

```
public interface ElectricBreaker extends ElectricComponent {

    void switchOn();
    void switchOff();
}
```

And, finally, we can materialize the electrical panel as follows (we assume that we have three circuits, a central circuit, a peripheral circuit, and an auxiliary circuit):

```
public class ElectricPanel implements ElectricBreaker {

    private final ElectricCircuit centralCircuit;
    private final ElectricCircuit peripheralCircuit;
    private final ElectricCircuit auxiliaryCircuit;

    public ElectricPanel() {

        peripheralCircuit = new SeriesCircuit(
```

```
      new ElectrolyticCapacitor(),new ElectrolyticCapacitor(),
      new MetalFilmResistor(), new CarbonResistor());

    auxiliaryCircuit = new ShortCircuit(
      new CeramicCapacitor(), new ElectrolyticCapacitor(),
      new MetalResistor(), new FieldEffectTransistor(),
      new FieldEffectTransistor());

    centralCircuit = new ParallelCircuit(
      peripheralCircuit, auxiliaryCircuit,
      new CeramicCapacitor(), new BipolarTransistor(),
      new MetalOxideResistor());
  }

  @Override
  public void switchOn() {

    auxiliaryCircuit.off();
    peripheralCircuit.on();
    centralCircuit.on();
  }

  @Override
  public void switchOff() {

    auxiliaryCircuit.on();
    peripheralCircuit.off();
    centralCircuit.off();
  }
}
```

Done! Now, a client of our panel can operate it via the switchOn()/switchOff() methods:

```
ElectricPanel panel = new ElectricPanel();
panel.switchOn();
```

In the next problem, we will see how we can close this hierarchy of classes in order to increase encapsulation and avoid accidental/non-accidental extensions.

173. Closing the electrical panel before JDK 17

By its nature, an electrical panel is a closed unit of work. But our code from the previous problem is far from being a closed hierarchy. We can extend and implement almost any class/interface from inside or outside the hierarchy.

Using anything before JDK 17, closing a hierarchy of classes and interfaces can be done using several tools.

Applying the final modifier

For instance, we have the powerful final modifier. Once we declare a class as final, it cannot be extended, so it is completely closed to extension. Obviously, we cannot apply this technique consistently across a hierarchical model because it will lead to a non-hierarchical model.

If we scan our electrical panel model, then we can use the final modifier in several places. First, we eliminate interfaces (ElectricComponent and ElectricBreaker) since interfaces cannot be declared as final. Next, we can look at the ElectricCircuit class and its subclasses (ParallelCircuit, SeriesCircuit, and ShortCircuit). Obviously, since ElectricCircuit has subclasses, it cannot be final. However, its subclasses are modeling notions that shouldn't be extended, so they can be final. This is our first step in obtaining a closed hierarchical model:

```
public final class ParallelCircuit extends ElectricCircuit {}
public final class SeriesCircuit extends ElectricCircuit {}
public final class ShortCircuit extends ElectricCircuit {}
```

Other classes that model well-defined notions that shouldn't be extended are the classes that model capacitors, transistors, and resistors. So, the following classes can be final as well:

```
public final class CeramicCapacitor extends Capacitor {}
public final class ElectrolyticCapacitor extends Capacitor {}
public final class FieldEffectTransistor extends Transistor {}
public final class BipolarTransistor extends Transistor {}
public final class CarbonResistor extends Resistor {}
public final class MetalFilmResistor extends MetalResistor {}
public final class MetalOxideResistor extends MetalResistor {}
```

Finally, we have the ElectricPanel class. It doesn't make sense to derive something from an electrical panel, so this class can be final as well:

```
public final class ElectricPanel implements ElectricBreaker {}
```

So far, we managed to close some parts of the hierarchy. There are no other places where the final modifier can help us, so we can go further and try another technique.

Defining package-private constructors

Next, we can use the hack of defining *package-private* constructors (a constructor with no visible modifier). The classes having *package-private* constructors can be instantiated and extended only inside that package – from a readability point of view, this technique is far away from expressing its intentions. However, in complex designs, we can apply this technique sporadically since we cannot simply put everything in a single package. Nevertheless, it can be considered as a solution for increasing the hierarchical model closing level.

For instance, we can focus on our abstract classes. They cannot be instantiated (being abstract) but they can be extended from anywhere. However, some of them should be extended only in the package where they are defined. The ElectricCircuit class is abstract and it should be extended only by ParallelCircuit, SeriesCircuit, and ShortCircuit. These subclasses live in the same package as ElectricCircuit, so it makes sense to use this hack of declaring a *package-private* constructor:

```
public abstract class ElectricCircuit
    implements ElectricComponent {

  ElectricCircuit() {}

  ...

}
```

Now, the ElectricCircuit class is closed to any extension attempt coming from outside of its package. Of course, it is still open to extension attempts from inside of its package.

Declaring classes/interfaces as non-public

Going further, we can declare interfaces/classes as non-public (by skipping the public keyword from the class/interface definition, it becomes non-public and is set by default in the so-called *package-private* access mode). This way, those classes and interfaces are visible (can be used/extended) only inside their packages. We cannot apply this technique to the ElectricComponent interface. This interface has to be public because it is implemented by most of our classes. However, we can apply this technique to the ElectricBreaker interface, since this interface should be implemented only by the ElectricPanel class, which is in the same package as it:

```
interface ElectricBreaker extends ElectricComponent {}
```

Now, ElectricBreaker cannot be extended/implemented outside its package. Moreover, we can apply this technique to the abstract classes Transistor, Resistor, and Capacitor:

```
abstract class Capacitor implements ElectricComponent {}
abstract class Resistor implements ElectricComponent {}
abstract class Transistor implements ElectricComponent {}
```

Notice that we cannot apply this technique to the ElectricCircuit class. This class is abstract but it is used in the ElectricPanel class, so it cannot be non-public. However, it cannot be extended thanks to the *package-private* constructor added previously.

Throwing everything in a module

In addition, we can place the whole hierarchy inside a Java module and export/expose to our client only a small part of it. However, this practice will not affect the closing level from inside the module, so we will skip it (that is, we will not exemplify it).

At this moment almost the entire hierarchy is closed to extension/implementation. The exceptions are the `MetalResistor` class and the `ElectricComponent` interface, which can be extended/implemented from anywhere inside/outside the model, and the `ElectricCircuit`, `Capacitor`, `Transistor`, and `Resistor` classes, which can be extended from inside of their packages. By placing the model in a Java module, we can block these actions from outside the module, but they are still possible from inside the module.

Conclusion

From this point forward (prior to JDK 17), there are no more techniques, tricks, or hacks that we can apply. We can reconsider the model design, but this will be too costly and will basically mean redesigning the model entirely, which may affect the model structure and logic.

For the sake of discussion and in the context of redesigning, we may consider Java enums. Java enums give us a nice closed hierarchy and are transformed internally in regular Java classes. Nevertheless, using enums to design a closed model and shape arbitrary classes can be really weird, unwieldy, and inconvenient.

In conclusion, before JDK 17, we had the radical `final` modifier and some control at the package level via *package-private* access.

It is obvious that what's missing here is something in between, something to give us more granularity and control. Fortunately, JDK 17 can help us to achieve a 100% closed hierarchy via sealed classes. This is the topic of some of the next problems.

174. Introducing JDK 17 sealed classes

Among the cool features of JDK 17, we have JEP 409 (sealed classes). This JEP provides an explicit, intuitive, crystal-clear solution for nominating who will extend a class/interface or will implement an interface. In other words, sealed classes can control inheritance at a finer level. Sealed classes can affect classes, `abstract` classes, and interfaces and sustain the readability of the code – you have an easy and expressive solution to tell your colleagues who can extend/implement your code.

Figure 8.3: JDK 17, JEP 409

Via sealed classes, we have finer control over a hierarchy of classes. As you can see from the previous figure, sealed classes are the missing piece of the puzzle sitting between `final` and *package-private*. In other words, sealed classes provide a granularity that we cannot obtain via the `final` modifier and *package-private* access.

Important note

Sealed classes don't affect the semantics of the `final` and `abstract` keywords. They still act exactly as they have for years. A sealed class cannot be `final` and vice versa.

Let's consider the following class (`Truck.java`):

```
public class Truck {}
```

We know that, in principle, this class can be extended by any other class. But we have only three types of trucks: semi-trailer, tautliner, and refrigerated. So, only three classes should extend the `Truck` class. Any other extension should not be allowed. In order to achieve this goal, we seal the class `Truck` by adding in its declaration the `sealed` keyword, as follows:

```
public sealed class Truck {}
```

By adding the `sealed` keyword, the compiler will automatically scan for all the extensions of `Truck` predefined in `Truck.java`.

Next, we have to specify the subclasses of `Truck` (`SemiTrailer`, `Tautliner`, and `Refrigerated`).

Important note

A `sealed` class (`abstract` or not) must have at least a subclass (otherwise there is no point in declaring it `sealed`). A `sealed` interface must have at least a subinterface or an implementation (again, otherwise there is no point declaring it `sealed`). If we don't follow these rules, then the code will not compile.

If we declare the subclasses of `Truck` in the same source file (`Truck.java`), then we can do so as follows:

```
final class SemiTrailer extends Truck {}
final class Tautliner extends Truck {}
final class Refrigerated extends Truck {}
```

After checking this code, we have to push another important note.

Important note

A subclass of a `sealed` class must be declared `final`, `sealed`, or `non-sealed`. A subinterface of a `sealed` interface must be declared `sealed` or `non-sealed`. If the subclass (subinterface) of a `sealed` class (interface) is declared as `sealed`, then it must have its own subclasses (subinterfaces). The `non-sealed` keyword indicates that the subclass (subinterface) can be freely extended further with no restrictions (the hierarchy containing a `non-sealed` class/interface is not closed). And, a `final` subclass cannot be extended.

Since our subclasses (`SemiTrailer`, `Tautliner`, and `Refrigerated`) are declared `final`, they cannot be extended further. So, the `Truck` class can be extended only by `SemiTrailer`, `Tautliner`, and `Refrigerated`, and these classes are non-extendable.

In the case of interfaces, we do the same. For instance, a `sealed` interface looks like this:

```
public sealed interface Melon {}
```

By adding the `sealed` keyword, the compiler will automatically scan for all the implementations/extensions of `Melon` predefined in `Melon.java`. So, in the same source file (`Melon.java`), we declare the extensions and implementations of this interface:

```
non-sealed interface Pumpkin extends Melon {}

final class Gac implements Melon {}
final class Cantaloupe implements Melon {}
final class Hami implements Melon {}
```

The `Pumpkin` interface can be further freely implemented/extended since it is declared as `non-sealed`. The implementations/extensions of `Pumpkin` don't need to be declared `sealed`, `non-sealed`, or `final` (but we can still make this declaration).

Next, let's look at a more complex example. Let's name this model the *Fuel* model. Here, all classes and interfaces are placed in the same source file, `Fuel.java` (the `com.refinery.fuel` package). Take your time and analyze each class/interface to understand how `sealed`, `non-sealed`, and `final` work together in this hierarchal model:

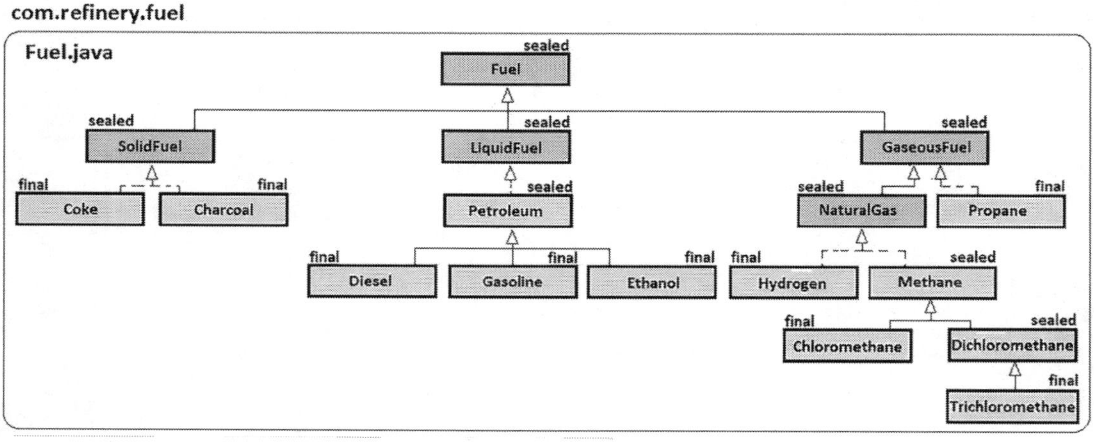

Figure 8.4: A hierarchical model using sealed, non-sealed, and final

In code lines, this model can be expressed as follows:

```
public sealed interface Fuel {}
```

```
sealed interface SolidFuel extends Fuel {}
sealed interface LiquidFuel extends Fuel {}
sealed interface GaseousFuel extends Fuel {}

final class Coke implements SolidFuel {}
final class Charcoal implements SolidFuel {}

sealed class Petroleum implements LiquidFuel {}
final class Diesel extends Petroleum {}
final class Gasoline extends Petroleum {}
final class Ethanol extends Petroleum {}

final class Propane implements GaseousFuel {}

sealed interface NaturalGas extends GaseousFuel {}

final class Hydrogen implements NaturalGas {}
sealed class Methane implements NaturalGas {}

final class Chloromethane extends Methane {}
sealed class Dichloromethane extends Methane {}

final class Trichloromethane extends Dichloromethane {}
```

Placing all the classes/interfaces in the same source file allows us to express closed hierarchical models like the previous one. However, placing all classes and interfaces in the same file is rarely a useful approach – maybe when the model contains a few small classes/interfaces.

In reality, we like to separate classes and interfaces into their own source files. It is more natural and intuitive to have each class/interface in its own source file. This way, we avoid large sources and it is much easier to follow the best practices of OOP. So, the goal of our next problem is to rewrite the *Fuel* hierarchical model by using a source file per class/interface.

175. Introducing the permits clause

In the previous problem, you saw how to write a closed hierarchical model in a single source file. Next, let's use the Fuel.java source file to rewrite this model by using separate sources and separate packages.

Working with sealed classes in separate sources (same package)

Let's consider the sealed Fuel interface from Fuel.java in package com.refinery.fuel:

```
public sealed interface Fuel {}    // Fuel.java
```

We know that this interface is extended by three other interfaces: `SolidFuel`, `LiquidFuel`, and `SolidFuel`. Let's define `SolidFuel` in the `SolidFuel.java` source (same package), as follows:

```
public sealed interface SolidFuel {} // SolidFuel.java
```

As you'll see, this code will not compile (it is like the compiler is asking: *hey, what's the point of a sealed interface without any implementation/extension?*). This time, we have to explicitly nominate the interfaces that can extend/implement the `Fuel` interface. For this, we use the `permits` keyword. Since `Fuel` is implemented by three interfaces, we just list their names via `permits` as follows:

```
public sealed interface Fuel
  permits SolidFuel, LiquidFuel, GaseousFuel {}
```

The list provided via `permits` is exhaustive. The `SolidFuel` is also a `sealed` interface, so it has to define its `permits` as well:

```
public sealed interface SolidFuel extends Fuel
  permits Coke, Charcoal {}
```

`LiquidFuel` and `GaseousFuel` work the same way as `SolidFuel`:

```
// LiquidFuel.java
public sealed interface LiquidFuel extends Fuel
  permits Petroleum {}

// GaseousFuel.java
public sealed interface GaseousFuel extends Fuel
  permits NaturalGas, Propane {}
```

The `Coke` (`Coke.java`) and `Charcoal` (`Charcoal.java`) are `final` implementations of `SolidFuel`, so they don't use the `permits` keyword:

```
public final class Coke implements SolidFuel {}
public final class Charcoal implements SolidFuel {}
```

The `Petroleum` class (`Petroleum.java`) is sealed and allows three extensions:

```
public sealed class Petroleum implements LiquidFuel
  permits Diesel, Gasoline, Ethanol {}
```

The `Diesel` (`Diesel.java`), `Gasoline` (`Gasoline.java`), and `Ethanol` (`Ethanol.java`) classes are `final`:

```
public final class Diesel extends Petroleum {}
public final class Gasoline extends Petroleum {}
public final class Ethanol extends Petroleum {}
```

The `NaturalGas` interface (`NaturalGas.java`) is a sealed extension of `GaseousFuel`, while `Propane` (`Propane.java`) is a `final` implementation of `GaseousFuel`:

```
public sealed interface NaturalGas extends GaseousFuel
  permits Hydrogen, Methane {}


public final class Propane implements GaseousFuel {}
```

As you can see, the NaturalGas interface permits two extensions. The Hydrogen class is a final extension, while Methane is a sealed class:

```
public final class Hydrogen implements NaturalGas {}
public sealed class Methane implements NaturalGas
  permits Chloromethane, Dichloromethane {}
```

The Chloromethane class is final, and Dichloromethane is sealed:

```
public final class Chloromethane extends Methane {}
public sealed class Dichloromethane extends Methane
  permits Trichloromethane {}
```

Finally, we have the Trichloromethane class. This is a final class:

```
public final class Trichloromethane extends Dichloromethane {}
```

Done! The hierarchical model is closed and complete. Any attempt to extend/implement any member of this hierarchy will lead to an exception. If we want to add a new extension/implementation to a sealed class/interface, then we have to add it to the permits list as well.

Working with sealed classes in separate packages

In the previous example, we expressed the classes/interfaces in separate sources but in the same package, com.refinery.fuel. Next, let's consider that we spread these classes and interfaces across different packages as in the following figure:

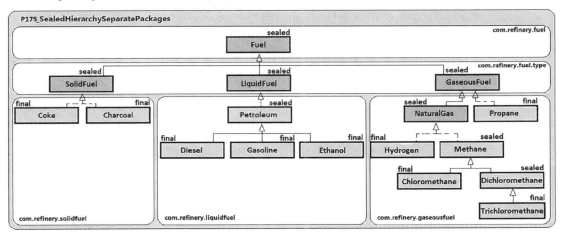

Figure 8.5: Sealed hierarchy in different packages

As long as the related `sealed` classes/interfaces live in the same package, we can use the JDK 9 *unnamed* special module (no explicit module). Otherwise, we have to use a *named* module. For instance, if we express our model as in *Figure 8.5*, then we have to add everything in a module via `module-info.java`:

```
module P175_SealedHierarchySeparatePackages {}
```

Without a *named* module, the code will not compile. In the bundled code, you can find both examples from this problem.

176. Closing the electrical panel after JDK 17

Do you remember our electrical panel model introduced earlier in *Problems 172* and *173*? In *Problem 173*, we closed this model as much as possible by using the Java capabilities available before JDK 17. Now, we can revisit that model (*Problem 173*) and close it completely via JDK 17 sealed classes.

We start with the `ElectricComponent` interface, which is declared as follows:

```
public interface ElectricComponent {}
```

At this moment, this interface is not closed. It can be extended/implemented from any other point of the application. But we can close it by transforming it into a `sealed` interface with the proper `permits` clause, as follows:

```
public sealed interface ElectricComponent
    permits ElectricCircuit, ElectricBreaker,
            Capacitor, Resistor, Transistor {}
```

Next, let's focus on the semi-closed `ElectricCircuit` class. This is an `abstract` class that uses a *package-private* constructor to block any extension from outside its package. However, it can still be extended from inside the package. We can close it completely by transforming it into a `sealed` class with the proper `permits` clause (the *package-private* constructor can be safely removed):

```
public sealed abstract class ElectricCircuit
    implements ElectricComponent
    permits ParallelCircuit, SeriesCircuit, ShortCircuit {}
```

The `ParallelCircuit`, `SeriesCircuit`, and `ShortCircuit` were declared as `final`, so they remain unchanged. We don't want to permit any extension of these classes.

Next, let's focus on the `Capacitor`, `Transistor`, and `Resistor` classes. These classes are also `abstract` and use *package-private* constructors to avoid any extension attempts coming from outside of their packages. So, we can remove these constructors and transform them into `sealed` classes exactly as we did with `ElectricCircuit`:

```
public sealed abstract class Capacitor
    implements ElectricComponent
    permits CeramicCapacitor, ElectrolyticCapacitor {}
```

```
public sealed abstract class Transistor
    implements ElectricComponent
    permits FieldEffectTransistor, BipolarTransistor {}

public sealed abstract class Resistor
    implements ElectricComponent
    permits MetalResistor, CarbonResistor {}
```

Check out the Resistor class. It permits only MetalResistor and CarbonResistor classes. Next, the MetalResistor class needs special attention. So far, this class is public and can be extended from any other point of the application:

```
public class MetalResistor extends Resistor {}
```

Closing this class can be done by sealing it as follows:

```
public sealed class MetalResistor extends Resistor
    permits MetalFilmResistor, MetalOxideResistor {}
```

The MetalFilmResistor and MetalOxideResistor classes are final and remain unchanged:

```
public final class MetalFilmResistor extends MetalResistor {}
public final class MetalOxideResistor extends MetalResistor {}
```

The same statement applies to the CeramicCapacitor, ElectrolyticCapacitor, BipolarTransistor, and FieldEffectTransistor classes.

Next, let's focus on the ElectricBreaker interface. This interface lives in the modern.circuit.panel package and was implemented only by ElectricPanel, so it was declared *package-private* (it cannot be extended/implemented from outside the package):

```
interface ElectricBreaker extends ElectricComponent {}
```

In order to completely close this interface, we transform it into a sealed interface, as follows:

```
public sealed interface ElectricBreaker
    extends ElectricComponent permits ElectricPanel {}
```

Notice that we added the public modifier as well. This is needed because ElectricBreaker must occur in the permits list of the ElectricComponent interface, so it has to be available outside its package.

Finally, the ElectricPanel remains unchanged (a final class implementing ElectricBreaker):

```
public final class ElectricPanel implements ElectricBreaker {}
```

Mission accomplished! The electric panel hierarchical model is completely closed to extension. We put everything in a *named* module (since we have sealed artifacts that interact across different packages) and we are done.

177. Combining sealed classes and records

As you know from *Chapter 4*, Java records are `final` classes that cannot be extended and cannot extend other classes. This means that records and `sealed` classes/interfaces can team up to obtain a closed hierarchy.

For instance, in the following figure, we can identify the classes that can be good candidates to become Java records in the *Fuel* model:

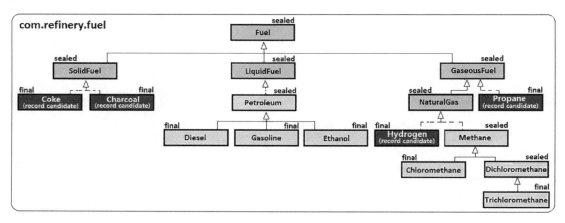

Figure 8.6: Identify classes that can become Java records

As you can see, we have four classes that can become Java records: `Coke`, `Charcoal`, `Hydrogen`, and `Propane`. Technically speaking, these classes can be Java records since they are `final` classes and don't extend other classes:

```
public record Coke() implements SolidFuel {}
public record Charcoal() implements SolidFuel {}
public record Hydrogen() implements NaturalGas {}
public record Propane() implements GaseousFuel {}
```

Of course, the technical aspect is important but it is not enough. In other words, you don't have to transform all classes into Java records just because it works and the code compiles. You also have to take into account the logic and the context of the application. Sometimes, a `final` class is all you need; otherwise, you may need an esoteric model made of a `sealed` interface with a few records and classes in the same source file (`A.java`):

```
public sealed interface A {

    record A1() implements A {}
    record A2() implements A {}
    final class B1 implements A {}
    non-sealed class B2 implements A {}

}
```

```
record A3() implements A {}
record A4() implements A {}
```

If you want to add the permits clause to A, then you can do it as follows:

```
public sealed interface A
  permits A.A1, A.A2, A.B1, A.B2, A3, A4 {…}
```

Done! Next, let's see how sealed classes can help the compiler to better handle instanceof checks.

178. Hooking sealed classes and instanceof

Sealed classes influence how the compiler understands the instanceof operator and, implicitly, how it performs internal cast and conversion operations.

Let's consider the following snippet of code:

```
public interface Quadrilateral {}
public class Triangle {}
```

So, we have here an interface (Quadrilateral) and a class that doesn't implement this interface. In this context, does the following code compile?

```
public static void drawTriangle(Triangle t) {

  if (t instanceof Quadrilateral) {
    System.out.println("This is not a triangle");
  } else {
    System.out.println("Drawing a triangle");
  }
}
```

We wrote if (t instanceof Quadrilateral) {…} but we know that Triangle doesn't implement Quadrilateral, so at first sight, we may think that the compiler will complain about this. But, actually, the code compiles because, at runtime, we may have a class Rectangle that extends Triangle and implements Quadrilateral:

```
public class Rectangle extends Triangle
  implements Quadrilateral {}
```

So, our instanceof makes sense and is perfectly legal. Next, let's close the Triangle class via the final keyword:

```
public final class Triangle {}
```

Since Triangle is final, Rectangle cannot extend it, but it can still implement Quadrilateral:

```
public class Rectangle implements Quadrilateral {}
```

This time, the `if (t instanceof Quadrilateral) {…}` code will not compile. The compiler knows that a `final` class cannot be extended, so a `Triangle` will never be a `Quadrilateral`.

So far, so good! Now, let's restore the `Triangle` class as a non-final class:

```
public class Triangle {}
```

And let's seal the `Quadrilateral` interface to permit only `Rectangle`:

```
public sealed interface Quadrilateral permits Rectangle {}
```

And, the `Rectangle` class is `final`, as follows (this time, it doesn't extend `Triangle`):

```
public final class Rectangle implements Quadrilateral {}
```

Again, the compiler will complain about this check, `if (t instanceof Quadrilateral) {…}`. It is obvious that `Triangle` cannot be an instance of `Quadrilateral` since `Quadrilateral` is sealed and permits only `Rectangle`, not `Triangle`. However, if we modify the `Rectangle` to extend `Triangle`, then the code compiles:

```
public final class Rectangle extends Triangle
  implements Quadrilateral {}
```

So, in conclusion, sealed classes can help the compiler to better understand `instanceof` checks and to signal us when it doesn't make sense.

179. Hooking sealed classes in switch

This is not the first time in this book that we've presented an example of sealed classes and `switch` expressions. In *Chapter 2, Problem 66*, we briefly introduced such an example via the `sealed Player` interface with the goal of covering completeness (type coverage) in pattern labels for `switch`.

If, at that time, you found this example confusing, I'm pretty sure that now it is clear. However, let's keep things fresh and see another example starting from this `abstract` base class:

```
public abstract class TextConverter {}
```

And, we have three converters available, as follows:

```
final public class Utf8 extends TextConverter {}
final public class Utf16 extends TextConverter {}
final public class Utf32 extends TextConverter {}
```

Now, we can write a `switch` expression to match these `TextConverter` instances, as follows:

```
public static String convert(
  TextConverter converter, String text) {

  return switch (converter) {
    case Utf8 c8 -> "Converting text to UTF-8: " + c8;
```

```
      case Utf16 c16 -> "Converting text to UTF-16: " + c16;
      case Utf32 c32 -> "Converting text to UTF-32: " + c32;


      case TextConverter tc -> "Converting text: " + tc;
      default -> "Unrecognized converter type";
   };
}
```

Check out the highlighted lines of code. After the three cases (case Utf8, case Utf16, and case Utf32), we must have one of the case TextConverter or the default case. In other words, after matching Utf8, Utf16, and Utf32, we must have a total type pattern (unconditional pattern) to match any other TextConverter or a default case, which typically means that we are facing an unknown converter.

If both the total type pattern and the default label are missing, then the code doesn't compile. The switch expression doesn't cover all the possible cases (input values), therefore it is not exhaustive. This is not allowed, since switch expressions and switch statements that use null and/or pattern labels should be exhaustive.

The compiler will consider our switch as non-exhaustive because we can freely extend the base class (TextConverter) with uncovered cases. An elegant solution is to seal the base class (TextConverter) as follows:

```
public sealed abstract class TextConverter
   permits Utf8, Utf16, Utf32 {}
```

And now the switch can be expressed as follows:

```
return switch (converter) {
   case Utf8 c8 -> "Converting text to UTF-8: " + c8;
   case Utf16 c16 -> "Converting text to UTF-16: " + c16;
   case Utf32 c32 -> "Converting text to UTF-32: " + c32;
};
```

This time, the compiler knows all the possible TextConverter types and sees that they are all covered in the switch. Since TextConverter is sealed, there are no surprises; no uncovered cases can occur. Nevertheless, if we later decide to add a new TextConverter (for instance, we add Utf7 by extending TextConverter and adding this extension in the permits clause), then the compiler will immediately complain that the switch is non-exhaustive, so we must take action and add the proper case for it.

At this moment, Utf8, Utf16, and Utf32 are declared as final, so they cannot be extended. Let's assume that Utf16 is modified to become non-sealed:

```
non-sealed public class Utf16 extends TextConverter {}
```

Now, we can extend Utf16 as follows:

```
public final class Utf16be extends Utf16 {}
public final class Utf16le extends Utf16 {}
```

Even if we added two subclasses to the `Utf16` class, our `switch` is still exhaustive because the case `Utf16` will cover `Utf16be` and `Utf16le` as well. Nevertheless, we can explicitly add cases for them, as long as we add these cases before case `Utf16`, as follows:

```
return switch (converter) {
  case Utf8 c8 -> "Converting text to UTF-8: " + c8;
  case Utf16be c16 -> "Converting text to UTF-16BE: " + c16;
  case Utf16le c16 -> "Converting text to UTF-16LE: " + c16;
  case Utf16 c16 -> "Converting text to UTF-16: " + c16;
  case Utf32 c32 -> "Converting text to UTF-32: " + c32;
};
```

We have to add case `Utf16be` and case `Utf16le` before case `Utf16` to avoid dominance errors (see *Chapter 2, Problem 65*).

Here is another example of combining sealed classes, pattern matching for switch, and Java records to compute the sum of nodes in a binary tree of integers:

```
sealed interface BinaryTree {

  record Leaf() implements BinaryTree {}
  record Node(int value, BinaryTree left, BinaryTree right)
    implements BinaryTree {}
}

static int sumNode(BinaryTree t) {

  return switch (t) {

    case Leaf nl -> 0;
    case Node nv -> nv.value() + sumNode(nv.left())
                                 + sumNode(nv.right());
  };
}
```

And here is an example of calling `sumNode()`:

```
BinaryTree leaf = new Leaf();
BinaryTree s1 = new Node(5, leaf, leaf);
BinaryTree s2 = new Node(10, leaf, leaf);
BinaryTree s = new Node(4, s1, s2);


int sum = sumNode(s);
```

In this example, the result is 19.

180. Reinterpreting the Visitor pattern via sealed classes and type pattern matching for switch

The Visitor pattern is part of the **Gang of Four (GoF)** design patterns and its goal is to define a new operation on certain classes without the need to modify those classes. You can find many excellent resources on this topic on the Internet, so for the classical implementation, we will provide here only the class diagram of our example, while the code is available on GitHub:

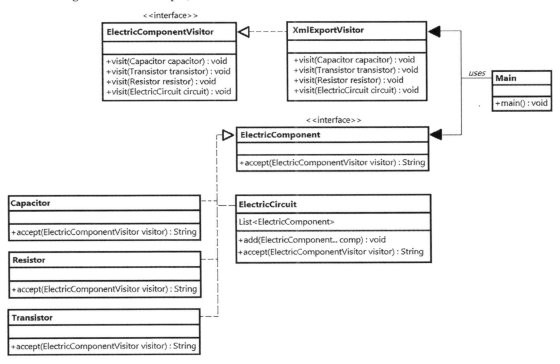

Figure 8.7: Visitor pattern class diagram (use case)

In a nutshell, we have a bunch of classes (`Capacitor`, `Transistor`, `Resistor`, and `ElectricCircuit`) that are used to create electrical circuits. Our operation is shaped in `XmlExportVisitor` (an implementation of `ElectricComponentVisitor`) and consists of printing an XML document containing the electrical circuit specifications and parameters.

Before continuing, consider getting familiar with the traditional implementation and output of this example available in the bundled code.

Next, let's assume that we want to transform this traditional implementation via sealed classes and type pattern matching for `switch`. The expected class diagram is simpler (has fewer classes) and it looks as follows:

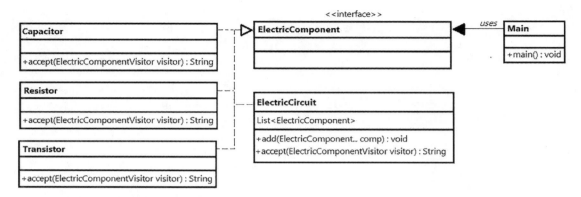

Figure 8.8: Visitor pattern reinterpreted via sealed classes and switch patterns

Let's start the transformation with the `ElectricComponent` interface. We know that this interface is implemented only by `Capacitor`, `Resistor`, `Transistor`, and `ElectricCircuit`. So, this interface is a good candidate to become `sealed`, as follows:

```
public sealed interface ElectricComponent
  permits Capacitor, Transistor, Resistor, ElectricCircuit {}
```

Notice that we deleted the `accept()` method from this interface. We no longer need this method. Next, the `Capacitor`, `Resistor`, `Transistor`, and `ElectricCircuit` become `final` classes and the `accept()` implementation is deleted as well.

Since we don't rely on the traditional Visitor pattern, we can safely remove its specific artifacts such as `ElectricComponentVisitor` and `XmlComponentVisitor`.

Pretty clean, right? We remained with a `sealed` interface and four `final` classes. Next, we can write a `switch` that visits each component of a circuit, as follows:

```
private static void export(ElectricComponent circuit) {

    StringBuilder sb = new StringBuilder();
    sb.append("<?xml version=\"1.0\" encoding=\"utf-8\"?>\n");

    export(sb, circuit);

    System.out.println(sb);
}
```

The `export(StringBuilder sb, ElectricComponent... comps)` is the effective visitor:

```
private static String export(StringBuilder sb,
        ElectricComponent... comps) {

  for (ElectricComponent comp : comps) {
```

```java
switch (comp) {
 case Capacitor c ->
  sb.append("""
      <capacitor>
        <maxImpedance>%s</maxImpedance>
        <dielectricResistance>%s</dielectricResistance>
        <coreTemperature>%s</coreTemperature>
      </capacitor>
    """.formatted(c.getMaxImpedance(),
                  c.getDielectricResistance(),
                  c.getCoreTemperature())).toString();
 case Transistor t ->
  sb.append("""
      <transistor>
        <length>%s</length>
        <width>%s</width>
        <threshholdVoltage>%s</threshholdVoltage>
      </transistor>
    """.formatted(t.getLength(), t.getWidth(),
                  t.getThreshholdVoltage())).toString();
 case Resistor r ->
  sb.append("""
      <resistor>
        <resistance>%s</resistance>
        <clazz>%s</clazz>
        <voltage>%s</voltage>
        <current>%s</current>
        <power>%s</power>
      </resistor>
    """.formatted(r.getResistance(), r.getClazz(),
                  r.getVoltage(), r.getCurrent(),
                  r.getPower())).toString();
 case ElectricCircuit ec ->
  sb.append("""
      <electric_circuit_%s>
      %s\
      </electric_circuit_%s>
    """.formatted(ec.getId(),
        export(new StringBuilder(),
          ec.getComps().toArray(ElectricComponent[]::new)),
          ec.getId())).indent(3)).toString();
```

```
    }
  }

  return sb.toString();
}
```

Mission accomplished! You can find the complete example in the bundled code.

181. Getting info about sealed classes (using reflection)

We can inspect `sealed` classes via two methods added as part of the Java Reflection API. First, we have `isSealed()`, which is a flag method useful to check if a class is or isn't `sealed`. Second, we have `getPermittedSubclasses()`, which returns an array containing the permitted classes. Based on these two methods, we can write the following helper to return the permitted classes of a `sealed` class:

```
public static List<Class> permittedClasses(Class clazz) {

  if (clazz != null && clazz.isSealed()) {
    return Arrays.asList(clazz.getPermittedSubclasses());
  }

  return Collections.emptyList();
}
```

We can easily test our helper via the `Fuel` model as follows:

```
Coke coke = new Coke();
Methane methane = new Methane();

// [interface com.refinery.fuel.SolidFuel,
//  interface com.refinery.fuel.LiquidFuel,
//  interface com.refinery.fuel.GaseousFuel]
System.out.println("Fuel subclasses: "
  + Inspector.permittedClasses(Fuel.class));

// [class com.refinery.fuel.Coke,
//  class com.refinery.fuel.Charcoal]
System.out.println("SolidFuel subclasses: "
  + Inspector.permittedClasses(SolidFuel.class));

// []
System.out.println("Coke subclasses: "
  + Inspector.permittedClasses(coke.getClass()));
```

```
// [class com.refinery.fuel.Chloromethane,
//   class com.refinery.fuel.Dichloromethane]
System.out.println("Methane subclasses: "
    + Inspector.permittedClasses(methane.getClass()));
```

I think you got the idea!

182. Listing the top three benefits of sealed classes

Maybe you have your own top three sealed class benefits that don't match the following list. That's OK, they are still benefits after all!

- **Sealed classes sustain better design and clearly expose their intentions:** Before using sealed classes, we have to rely only on the final keyword (which is expressive enough), and *package-private* classes/constructors. Obviously, *package-private* code requires some reading between the lines to understand its intention since it is not easy to spot a closed hierarchy modeled via this hack. On the other hand, sealed classes expose their intentions very clearly and expressively.

- **The compiler can rely on sealed classes to perform finer checks on our behalf:** Nobody can sneak a class into a hierarchy closed via sealed classes. Any such attempt is rejected via a clear and meaningful message. The compiler is guarding for us and acts as the first line of defense against any accidental/non-accidental attempt to use our closed hierarchies in an improper way.

- **Sealed classes help the compiler to provide better pattern matching:** You experimented with this benefit in *Problem 179*. The compiler can rely on sealed classes to determine if a switch is covering all the possible input values and therefore is exhaustive. And this is just the beginning of what sealed classes can do for pattern matching.

183. Briefly introducing hidden classes

Hidden classes were introduced in JDK 15 under JEP 371. Their main goal is to be used by frameworks as dynamically generated classes. They are runtime-generated classes with a short lifespan that are used by frameworks via reflection.

> **Important note**
>
> Hidden classes cannot be used directly by bytecode or other classes. They are not created via a class loader. Basically, a hidden class has the class loader of the lookup class.

Among other characteristics of hidden classes, we should consider that:

- They are not discoverable by the JVM internal linkage of bytecode or by the explicit usage of class loaders (they are invisible to methods such as Class.forName(), Lookup.findClass(), or ClassLoader.findLoadedClass()). They don't appear in stack traces.
- They extend **Access Control Nest** (ACN) with classes that cannot be discovered.

- Frameworks can define hidden classes, as many as needed, since they benefit from aggressive unloading. This way, a large number of hidden classes shouldn't have a negative impact on performance. They sustain efficiency and flexibility.
- They cannot be used as a field/return/parameter type. They cannot be superclasses.
- They can access their code directly without the presence of a class object.
- They can have `final` fields, and those fields cannot be modified regardless of their accessible flags.
- They deprecated the `misc.Unsafe::defineAnonymousClass`, which is a non-standard API. Starting with JDK 15, lambda expressions use hidden classes instead of anonymous classes.

Next, let's see how we can create and use a hidden class.

184. Creating a hidden class

Let's assume that our hidden class is named `InternalMath` and is as simple, as follows:

```
public class InternalMath {

  public long sum(int[] nr) {
    return IntStream.of(nr).sum();
  }
}
```

As we mentioned in the previous problem, hidden classes have the same class loader as the lookup class, which can be obtained via `MethodHandles.lookup()`, as follows:

```
MethodHandles.Lookup lookup = MethodHandles.lookup();
```

Next, we must know that `Lookup` contains a method named `defineHiddenClass(byte[] bytes, boolean initialize, ClassOption... options)`. The most important argument is represented by the array of bytes that contain the class data. The `initialize` argument is a flag specifying if the hidden class should be initialized or not, while the `options` argument can be `NESTMATE` (the created hidden class becomes a nestmate of the lookup class and has access to all the private members in the same nest) or `STRONG` (the created hidden class can be unloaded only if its defining loader is not reachable).

So, our goal is to obtain the array of bytes that contains the class data. For this, we rely on `getResourceAsStream()` and JDK 9's `readAllBytes()`, as follows:

```
Class<?> clazz = InternalMath.class;

String clazzPath = clazz.getName()
    .replace('.', '/') + ".class";
InputStream stream = clazz.getClassLoader()
    .getResourceAsStream(clazzPath);
byte[] clazzBytes = stream.readAllBytes();
```

Having `clazzBytes` in our hands, we can create the hidden class as follows:

```
Class<?> hiddenClass = lookup.defineHiddenClass(clazzBytes,
  true, ClassOption.NESTMATE).lookupClass();
```

Done! Next, we can use the hidden class from inside our framework, as follows:

```
Object obj = hiddenClass.getConstructor().newInstance();

Method method = obj.getClass()
    .getDeclaredMethod("sum", int[].class);

System.out.println(method.invoke(
    obj, new int[] {4, 1, 6, 7})); // 18
```

As you can see, we use the hidden class via reflection. The interesting part here is represented by the fact that we cannot cast the hidden class to `InternalMath`, so we use `Object obj = ....` So, this will not work:

```
InternalMath obj = (InternalMath) hiddenClass
    .getConstructor().newInstance();
```

However, we can define an interface implemented by the hidden class:

```
public interface Math {}
public class InternalMath implements Math {…}
```

And, now we can cast to `Math`:

```
Math obj = (Math) hiddenClass.getConstructor().newInstance();
```

Starting with JDK 16, the `Lookup` class was enriched with another method for defining a hidden class named `defineHiddenClassWithClassData(byte[] bytes, Object classData, boolean initialize, ClassOption... options)`. This method needs the class data obtained via `MethodHandles.classData(Lookup caller, String name, Class<T> type)` or `MethodHandles.classDataAt(Lookup caller, String name, Class<T> type, int index)`. Take your time to explore this further.

Summary

This chapter covered 13 problems. Most of them were focused on the sealed classes feature. The last two problems provided brief coverage of hidden classes.

Leave a review!

Enjoying this book? Help readers like you by leaving an Amazon review. Scan the QR code below for a 20% discount code.

Limited Offer

Functional Style Programming — Extending APIs

This chapter includes 24 problems covering a wide range of functional programming topics. We will start by introducing the JDK 16 `mapMulti()` operation, and continue with a handful of problems for working with predicates (`Predicate`), functions, and collectors.

If you don't have a background in functional programming in Java, then I strongly recommend you postpone this chapter until you have spent some time getting familiar with it. You could consider reading *Chapters 8* and *9* from *Java Coding Problems*, *First Edition*.

At the end of this chapter, you'll be deeply skilled in functional programming in Java.

Problems

Use the following problems to test your programming prowess in functional programming in Java. I strongly encourage you to give each problem a try before you turn to the solutions and download the example programs:

185. **Working with mapMulti()**: Explain and exemplify the JDK 16 `mapMulti()`. Provide a brief introduction, explain how it works in comparison with `flatMap()`, and point out when `mapMulti()` is a good fit.

186. **Streaming custom code to map**: Imagine a class that shapes some blog posts. Each post is identified by a unique integer ID, and the post has several properties, including its tags. The tags of each post are actually represented as a string of tags separated by a hashtag (#). Whenever we need the list of tags for a given post, we can call the `allTags()` helper method. Our goal is to write a stream pipeline that extracts from this list of tags a `Map<String, List<Integer>>` containing, for each tag (key), the list of posts (value).

187. **Exemplifying a method reference vs. a lambda**: Write a relevant snippet of code to highlight the difference in behavior between a method reference and the equivalent lambda expression.

188. **Hooking lambda laziness via Supplier/Consumer**: Write a Java program that highlights how `Supplier/Consumer` works. In this context, point out the lazy characteristic of lambdas.

189. **Refactoring code to add lambda laziness:** Provide a simple example of refactoring a piece of imperative code via functional code.

190. **Writing a Function<String, T> to parse data:** Imagine a given text (`test, a, 1, 4, 5, 0xf5, 0x5, 4.5d, 6, 5.6, 50000, 345, 4.0f, 6$3, 2$1.1, 5.5, 6.7, 8, a11, 3e+1, -11199, 55`). Write an application that exposes a `Function<String, T>` capable of parsing this text, and extract only doubles, integers, longs, and so on.

191. **Composing predicates in a Stream's filters:** Write several examples that highlight the usage of composite predicates in filters.

192. **Filtering nested collections with Streams:** Imagine that you have two nested collections. Provide several stream pipeline examples to filter data from the inner collection.

193. **Using BiPredicate:** Exemplify the usage of `BiPredicate`.

194. **Building a dynamic predicate for a custom model:** Write an application capable of dynamically generating predicates (`Predicate`) based on some simple inputs.

195. **Building a dynamic predicate from a custom map of conditions:** Consider having a map of conditions (the map's key is a field, and the map's value is the expected value for that field). In this context, write an application that dynamically generates the proper predicate.

196. **Logging in predicates:** Write a custom solution that allows us to log failures in predicates.

197. **Extending Stream with containsAll() and containsAny():** Provide a solution that extends the Java Stream API with two final operations named `containsAll()` and `containsAny()`.

198. **Extending Stream with removeAll() and retainAll():** Provide a solution that extends the Java Stream API with two final operations named `removeAll()` and `retainAll()`.

199. **Introducing stream comparators:** Provide a detailed covering (with examples) of using stream comparators.

200. **Sorting a map:** Write several snippets of code to highlight different use cases for sorting a map.

201. **Filtering a map:** Write several snippets of code to highlight different use cases for filtering a map.

202. **Creating a custom collector via Collector.of():** Write an arbitrarily chosen set of custom collectors via the `Collector.of()` API.

203. **Throwing checked exceptions from lambdas:** Provide a hack that allows us to throw checked exceptions from lambdas.

204. **Implementing distinctBy() for the Stream API:** Write a Java application that implements the `distinctBy()` stream intermediate operation. This is like the built-in `distinct()`, only it allows us to filter distinct elements by a given property/field.

205. **Writing a custom collector that takes/skips a given number of elements:** Provide a custom collector that allows us to collect only the first n elements. Moreover, provide a custom collector that skips the first n elements and collects the rest of them.

206. **Implementing a Function that takes five (or any other arbitrary number of) arguments:** Write and use a five-argument functional interface that represents a specialization of `java.util.function.Function`.

207. **Implementing a Consumer that takes five (or any other arbitrary number of) arguments:** Write and use a five-argument functional interface that represents a specialization of `java.util.function.Consumer`.

208. **Partially applying a Function**: Write an *n*-arity functional interface that represents a specialization of java.util.function.Function. Moreover, this interface should provide support (i.e., provide the necessary default methods) to apply only *n*-1, *n*-2, *n*-3,...,1 argument(s).

The following sections describe solutions to the preceding problems. Remember that there usually isn't a single correct way to solve a particular problem. Also, remember that the explanations shown here include only the most interesting and important details needed to solve the problems. Download the example solutions to see additional details and to experiment with the programs at https://github.com/PacktPublishing/Java-Coding-Problems-Second-Edition/tree/main/Chapter09.

185. Working with mapMulti()

Starting with JDK 16, the Stream API was enriched with a new intermediate operation, named mapMulti(). This operation is represented by the following default method in the Stream interface:

```
default <R> Stream<R> mapMulti (
  BiConsumer<? super T, ? super Consumer<R>> mapper)
```

Let's follow the learning-by-example approach and consider the next classical example, which uses a combination of filter() and map() to filter even integers and double their value:

```
List<Integer> integers = List.of(3, 2, 5, 6, 7, 8);

List<Integer> evenDoubledClassic = integers.stream()
  .filter(i -> i % 2 == 0)
  .map(i -> i * 2)
  .collect(toList());
```

The same result can be obtained via mapMulti() as follows:

```
List<Integer> evenDoubledMM = integers.stream()
  .<Integer>mapMulti((i, consumer) -> {
    if (i % 2 == 0) {
      consumer.accept(i * 2);
    }
  })
  .collect(toList());
```

So instead of using two intermediate operations, we used only one, mapMulti(). The filter() role was replaced by an if statement, and the map() role is accomplished in the accept() method. This time, we filtered the evens and doubled their values via mapper, which is a BiConsumer<? super T, ? super Consumer<R>>. This bi-function is applied to each integer (each stream element), and only the even integers are passed to the consumer. This consumer acts as a buffer that simply passes downstream (in the stream pipeline) the received elements. The mapper.accept(R r) can be called any number of times, which means that, for a given stream element, we can produce as many output elements as we need. In the previous example, we have a one-to-zero mapping (when i % 2 == 0 is evaluated as false) and a one-to-one mapping (when i % 2 == 0 is evaluated as true).

Important note

More precisely, `mapMulti()` gets an input stream of elements and outputs another stream containing zero, less, the same, or a larger number of elements that can be unaltered or replaced by other elements. This means that each element from the input stream can pass through a one-to-zero, one-to-one, or one-to-many mapping.

Have you noticed the `<Integer>mapMulti(…)` type-witness applied to the returned value? Without this type-witness, the code will not compile because the compiler cannot determine the proper type of R. This is the shortcoming of using `mapMulti()`, so we have to pay this price.

For primitive types (`double`, `long`, and `int`) we have `mapMultiToDouble()`, `mapMultiToLong()`, and `mapMultiToInt()`, which return `DoubleStream`, `LongStream`, and `IntStream`, respectively. For instance, if we plan to sum the even integers, then using `mapMultiToInt()` is a better choice than `mapMulti()`, since we can skip the type-witness and work only with a primitive `int`:

```
int evenDoubledAndSumMM = integers.stream()
  .mapMultiToInt((i, consumer) -> {
    if (i % 2 == 0) {
      consumer.accept(i * 2);
    }
  })
  .sum();
```

On the other hand, whenever you need a `Stream<T>` instead of `Double/Long/IntStream`, you still need to rely on `mapToObj()` or `boxed()`:

```
List<Integer> evenDoubledMM = integers.stream()
  .mapMultiToInt((i, consumer) -> {
    if (i % 2 == 0) {
      consumer.accept(i * 2);
    }
  })
  .mapToObj(i -> i) // or, .boxed()
  .collect(toList());
```

Once you get familiar with `mapMulti()`, you start to realize that it is pretty similar to the well-known `flatMap()`, which is useful to flatten a nested `Stream<Stream<R>>` model. Let's consider the following one-to-many relationship:

```
public class Author {

  private final String name;
  private final List<Book> books;
  ...
```

```
}

public class Book {

  private final String title;
  private final LocalDate published;
  ...
}
```

Each Author has a list of books. So a List<Author> (candidate to become Stream<Author>) will nest a List<Book> (candidate to become a nested Stream<Book>) for each Author. Moreover, we have the following simple model for mapping an author and a single book:

```
public class Bookshelf {

  private final String author;
  private final String book;
  ...
}
```

In functional programming, mapping this one-to-many model to the flat Bookshelf model is a classical scenario for using flatMap() as follows:

```
List<Bookshelf> bookshelfClassic = authors.stream()
  .flatMap(
    author -> author.getBooks()
                   .stream()
                   .map(book -> new Bookshelf(
                        author.getName(), book.getTitle())))
  ).collect(Collectors.toList());
```

The problem with flatMap() is that we need to create a new intermediate stream for each author (for a large number of authors, this can become a performance penalty), and only afterward we can apply the map() operation. With mapMulti(), we don't need these intermediate streams, and the mapping is straightforward:

```
List<Bookshelf> bookshelfMM = authors.stream()
  .<Bookshelf>mapMulti((author, consumer) -> {
    for (Book book : author.getBooks()) {
      consumer.accept(new Bookshelf(
        author.getName(), book.getTitle()));
    }
  })
  .collect(Collectors.toList());
```

This is a one-to-many mapping. For each author, the consumer buffers a number of `Bookshelf` instances equal to the number of author's books. These instances are flattened over the downstream and are finally collected in a `List<Bookshelf>` via the `toList()` collector.

And this route takes us to the following important note on `mapMulti()`.

Important note

The `mapMulti()` intermediate operation is useful when we have to replace just a few elements of the stream. This statement is formulated in the official documentation as follows: *"When replacing each stream element with a small (possibly zero) number of elements."*

Next, check out this example based on `flatMap()`:

```
List<Bookshelf> bookshelfGt2005Classic = authors.stream()
  .flatMap(
    author -> author.getBooks()
      .stream()
      .filter(book -> book.getPublished().getYear() > 2005)
      .map(book -> new Bookshelf(
        author.getName(), book.getTitle())))
  ).collect(Collectors.toList());
```

This example fits perfectly when using `mapMulti()`. An author has a relatively small number of books, and we apply a filter on them. So basically, we replace each stream element with a small (possibly zero) number of elements:

```
List<Bookshelf> bookshelfGt2005MM = authors.stream()
  .<Bookshelf>mapMulti((author, consumer) -> {
    for (Book book : author.getBooks()) {
      if (book.getPublished().getYear() > 2005) {
        consumer.accept(new Bookshelf(
          author.getName(), book.getTitle()));
      }
    }
  })
  .collect(Collectors.toList());
```

This is better than using `flatMap()`, since we reduce the number of intermediate operations (no more `filter()` calls), and we avoided intermediate streams. This is also more readable.

Another use case of `mapMulti()` is as follows.

Important note

The `mapMulti()` operation is also useful when the imperative approach is preferable against the stream approach. This statement is formulated in the official documentation as follows: *"When it is easier to use an imperative approach for generating result elements than it is to return them in the form of a* `Stream`.*"*

Imagine that we have added to the `Author` class the following method:

```
public void bookshelfGt2005(Consumer<Bookshelf> consumer) {

  for (Book book : this.getBooks()) {
    if (book.getPublished().getYear() > 2005) {
      consumer.accept(new Bookshelf(
        this.getName(), book.getTitle())));
    }
  }
}
```

Now, we get the `List<Bookshelf>` by simply using `mapMulti()`, as follows:

```
List<Bookshelf> bookshelfGt2005MM = authors.stream()
  .<Bookshelf>mapMulti(Author::bookshelfGt2005)
  .collect(Collectors.toList());
```

How cool is this?! In the next problem, we will use `mapMulti()` in another scenario.

186. Streaming custom code to map

Let's assume that we have the following legacy class:

```
public class Post {

  private final int id;
  private final String title;
  private final String tags;

  public Post(int id, String title, String tags) {
    this.id = id;
    this.title = title;
    this.tags = tags;
  }
  ...
```

```
    public static List<String> allTags(Post post) {

        return Arrays.asList(post.getTags().split("#"));
    }
}
```

So we have a class that shapes some blog posts. Each post has several properties, including its tags. The tags of each post are actually represented as a string of tags separated by hashtag (#). Whenever we need the list of tags for a given post, we can call the `allTags()` helper. For instance, here is a list of posts and their tags:

```
List<Post> posts = List.of(
    new Post(1, "Running jOOQ", "#database #sql #rdbms"),
    new Post(2, "I/O files in Java", "#io #storage #rdbms"),
    new Post(3, "Hibernate Course", "#jpa #database #rdbms"),
    new Post(4, "Hooking Java Sockets", "#io #network"),
    new Post(5, "Analysing JDBC transactions", "#jdbc #rdbms")
);
```

Our goal is to extract from this list a `Map<String, List<Integer>>`, containing, for each tag (key) the list of posts (value). For instance, for the tag #database, we have articles 1 and 3; for tag #rdbms, we have articles 1, 2, 3, and 5, and so on.

Accomplishing this task in functional programming can be done via `flatMap()` and `groupingBy()`. In a nutshell, `flatMap()` is useful for flattening a nested `Stream<Stream<R>>` model, while `groupingBy()` is a collector useful for grouping data in a map by some logic or property.

We need `flatMap()` because we have the `List<Post>` that, for each `Post`, nests via `allTags()` a `List<String>` (so if we simply call `stream()`, then we get back a `Stream<Stream<R>>`). After flattening, we wrap each tag in `Map.Entry<String, Integer>`. Finally, we group these entries by tags into a `Map`, as follows:

```
Map<String, List<Integer>> result = posts.stream()
    .flatMap(post -> Post.allTags(post).stream()
    .map(t -> entry(t, post.getId())))
    .collect(groupingBy(Entry::getKey,
                mapping(Entry::getValue, toList())));
```

However, based on the previous problem, we know that, starting with JDK 16, we can use `mapMulti()`. So, we can rewrite the previous snippet as follows:

```
Map<String, List<Integer>> resultMulti = posts.stream()
    .<Map.Entry<String, Integer>>mapMulti((post, consumer) -> {
        for (String tag : Post.allTags(post)) {
                consumer.accept(entry(tag, post.getId()));
        }
```

```
    })
    .collect(groupingBy(Entry::getKey,
            mapping(Entry::getValue, toList()))));
```

This time, we saved the `map()` intermediate operation and intermediate streams.

187. Exemplifying a method reference vs. a lamda

Have you ever written a lambda expression and your IDE advises you to replace it with a method reference? You probably have! And I'm sure that you preferred to follow the replacement because *names matter*, and method references are often more readable than lambdas. While this is a subjective matter, I'm pretty sure you'll agree that extracting long lambdas in methods and using/reusing them via method references is a generally accepted good practice.

However, beyond some esoteric JVM internal representations, do they behave the same? Is there any difference between a lambda and a method reference that may affect how the code behaves?

Well, let's assume that we have the following simple class:

```java
public class Printer {

  Printer() {
    System.out.println("Reset printer ...");
  }

  public static void printNoReset() {
    System.out.println(
      "Printing (no reset) ..." + Printer.class.hashCode());
  }

  public void printReset() {
    System.out.println("Printing (with reset) ..."
      + Printer.class.hashCode());
  }
}
```

If we assume that p1 is a method reference and p2 is the corresponding lambda, then we can perform the following calls:

```java
System.out.print("p1:");p1.run();
System.out.print("p1:");p1.run();
System.out.print("p2:");p2.run();
System.out.print("p2:");p2.run();
System.out.print("p1:");p1.run();
System.out.print("p2:");p2.run();
```

Next, let's see two scenarios of working with p1 and p2.

Scenario 1: Calling printReset()

In the first scenario, we call printReset() via p1 and p2, as follows:

```
Runnable p1 = new Printer()::printReset;
Runnable p2 = () -> new Printer().printReset();
```

If we run the code right now, then we get this output (the message generated by the Printer constructor):

```
Reset printer ...
```

This output is caused by the method reference, p1. The Printer constructor is invoked right away, even if we didn't call the run() method. Because p2 (the lambda) is lazy, the Printer constructor is not called until we call the run() method.

Going further, we fire the chain of run() calls for p1 and p2. The output will be:

```
p1:Printing (with reset) ...1159190947
p1:Printing (with reset) ...1159190947
p2:Reset printer ...
Printing (with reset) ...1159190947
p2:Reset printer ...
Printing (with reset) ...1159190947
p1:Printing (with reset) ...1159190947
p2:Reset printer ...
Printing (with reset) ...1159190947
```

If we analyze this output, we can see that the Printer constructor is called each time the lambda (p2. run()) is executed. On the other hand, for the method reference (p1.run()), the Printer constructor is not called. It was called a single time, at the p1 declaration. So p1 prints without resetting the printer.

Scenario 2: Calling static printNoReset()

Next, let's call the static method printNoReset():

```
Runnable p1 = Printer::printNoReset;
Runnable p2 = () -> Printer.printNoReset();
```

If we run the code right away, then nothing will happen (no output). Next, we fire up the run() calls, and we get this output:

```
p1:Printing (no reset) ...149928006
p1:Printing (no reset) ...149928006
p2:Printing (no reset) ...149928006
p2:Printing (no reset) ...149928006
p1:Printing (no reset) ...149928006
p2:Printing (no reset) ...149928006
```

The printNoReset() is a static method, so the Printer constructor is not invoked. We can interchangeably use p1 or p2 without having any difference in behavior. So, in this case, it is just a matter of preference.

Conclusion

When calling non-static methods, there is one main difference between a method reference and a lambda. A method reference calls the constructor immediately and only once (at method invocation (run()), the constructor is not called). On the other hand, lambdas are lazy. They call the constructor only at method invocation and at each such invocation (run()).

188. Hooking lambda laziness via Supplier/Consumer

The java.util.function.Supplier is a functional interface capable of supplying results via its get() method. The java.util.function.Consumer is another functional interface capable of consuming the argument given via its accept() method. It returns no result (void). Both of these functional interfaces are lazy, so it is not that easy to analyze and understand code that uses them, especially when a snippet of code uses both. Let's give it a try!

Consider the following simple class:

```
static class Counter {

    static int c;

    public static int count() {
        System.out.println("Incrementing c from "
            + c + " to " + (c + 1));
        return c++;
    }
}
```

And let's write the following Supplier and Consumer:

```
Supplier<Integer> supplier = () -> Counter.count();

Consumer<Integer> consumer = c -> {
    c = c + Counter.count();
    System.out.println("Consumer: " + c );
};
```

So, at this point, what is the value of Counter.c?

```
System.out.println("Counter: " + Counter.c); // 0
```

The correct answer is, Counter.c is 0. The supplier and the consumer are lazy, so none of the get() or accept() methods were called at their declarations. The Counter.count() was not invoked, so Counter.c was not incremented.

Here is a tricky one... how about now?

```
System.out.println("Supplier: " + supplier.get()); // 0
```

We know that by calling `supplier.get()`, we trigger the `Counter.count()` execution, and `Counter.c` should be incremented and become 1. However, the `supplier.get()` will return 0.

The explanation resides in the `count()` method at line `return  c++;`. When we write `c++`, we use the post-increment operation, so we use the current value of `c` in our statement (in this case, `return`), and afterward, we increment it by 1. This means that `supplier.get()` gets back the value of `c` as 0, while the incrementation takes place after this `return`, and `Counter.c` is now 1:

```
System.out.println("Counter: " + Counter.c); // 1
```

If we switch from post-increment (`c++`) to pre-increment (`++c`), then `supplier.get()` will get back the value of 1, which will be in sync with `Counter.c`. This happens because the incrementation takes place before the value is used in our statement (here, `return`).

OK, so far we know that `Counter.c` is equal to 1. Next, let's call the consumer and pass in the `Counter.c` value:

```
consumer.accept(Counter.c);
```

Via this call, we push the `Counter.c` (which is 1) in the following computation and display:

```
c -> {
  c = c + Counter.count();
  System.out.println("Consumer: " + c );
} // Consumer: 2
```

So `c = c + Counter.count()` can be seen as `Counter.c = Counter.c + Counter.count()`, which is equivalent to `1 = 1 + Counter.count()`, so `1 = 1 + 1`. The output will be `Consumer:  2`. This time, `Counter.c` is also 2 (remember the post-increment effect):

```
System.out.println("Counter: " + Counter.c); // 2
```

Next, let's invoke the supplier:

```
System.out.println("Supplier: " + supplier.get()); // 2
```

We know that `get()` will receive the current value of `c`, which is 2. Afterward, `Counter.c` becomes 3:

```
System.out.println("Counter: " + Counter.c); // 3
```

We can continue like this forever, but I think you've got an idea of how the `Supplier` and `Consumer` functional interfaces work.

189. Refactoring code to add lambda laziness

In this problem, let's have a refactoring session designed to transform a dysfunctional code into a functional one. We start from the following given code – a simple piece of class mapping information about application dependencies:

```java
public class ApplicationDependency {

  private final long id;
  private final String name;
  private String dependencies;

  public ApplicationDependency(long id, String name) {
    this.id = id;
    this.name = name;
  }

  public long getId() {
    return id;
  }

  public String getName() {
    return name;
  }

  public String getDependencies() {
    return dependencies;
  }

  private void downloadDependencies() {

    dependencies = "list of dependencies
      downloaded from repository " + Math.random();
  }
}
```

Why did we highlight the getDependencies() method? Because this is the point in the application where there is dysfunction. More precisely, the following class needs the dependencies of an application in order to process them accordingly:

```java
public class DependencyManager {

  private Map<Long,String> apps = new HashMap<>();

  public void processDependencies(ApplicationDependency appd){

    System.out.println();
    System.out.println("Processing app: " + appd.getName());
```

```
        System.out.println("Dependencies: "
          + appd.getDependencies());

        apps.put(appd.getId(), appd.getDependencies());
      }
    }
```

This class relies on the `ApplicationDependency.getDependecies()` method, which just returns `null` (the default value of the `dependencies` fields). The expected application's dependencies were not downloaded, since the `downloadDependecies()` method was not called. Most probably, a code reviewer will signal this issue and raise a ticket to fix it.

Fixing in imperative fashion

A possible fix will be as follows (in `ApplicationDependency`):

```java
public class ApplicationDependency {

  private String dependencies = downloadDependencies();
  ...

  public String getDependencies() {

    return dependencies;
  }
  ...

  private String downloadDependencies() {

    return "list of dependencies downloaded from repository "
      + Math.random();
  }
}
```

Calling `downloadDependencies()` at `dependencies` initialization will definitely fix the problem of loading the dependencies. When the `DependencyManager` calls `getDependencies()`, it will have access to the downloaded dependencies. However, is this a good approach? I mean, downloading the dependencies is a costly operation, and we do it every time an `ApplicationDependency` instance is created. If the `getDependencies()` method is never called, then this costly operation doesn't pay off the effort.

So a better approach would be to postpone the download of the application's dependencies until `getDependencies()` is actually called:

```java
public class ApplicationDependency {
  private String dependencies;
```

```
    ...

    public String getDependencies() {

      downloadDependencies();

      return dependencies;
    }
    ...

    private void downloadDependencies() {

      dependencies = "list of dependencies
        downloaded from repository " + Math.random();

    }
  }
```

This is better, but it is not the best approach! This time, the application's dependencies are downloaded every time the getDependencies() method is called. Fortunately, there is a quick fix for this. We just need to add a null check before performing the download:

```
public String getDependencies() {

  if (dependencies == null) {
    downloadDependencies();
  }

  return dependencies;
}
```

Done! Now, the application's dependencies are downloaded only at the first call of the getDependencies() method. This imperative solution works like a charm and passes the code review.

Fixing in functional fashion

How about providing this fix in a functional programming fashion? Practically, all we want is to lazy-download the application's dependencies. Since laziness is a specialty of functional programming, and we're now familiar with the Supplier (see the previous problem), we can start as follows:

```
public class ApplicationDependency {

  private final Supplier<String> dependencies
    = this::downloadDependencies;
  ...
```

```
public String getDependencies() {
  return dependencies.get();
}
...

private String downloadDependencies() {

  return "list of dependencies downloaded from repository "
    + Math.random();
  }
}
```

First, we defined a `Supplier` that calls the `downloadDependencies()` method. We know that the `Supplier` is lazy, so nothing happens until its `get()` method is explicitly called.

Second, we have modified `getDependencies()` to return `dependencies.get()`. So we delay the application's dependencies downloading until they are explicitly required.

Third, we modified the return type of the `downloadDependencies()` method from `void` to `String`. This is needed for the `Supplier.get()`.

This is a nice fix, but it has a serious shortcoming. We lost the caching! Now, the dependencies will be downloaded at every `getDependencies()` call.

We can avoid this issue via *memoization* (`https://en.wikipedia.org/wiki/Memoization`). This concept is also covered in detail in *Chapter 8* of *The Complete Coding Interview Guide in Java*. In a nutshell, memoization is a technique used to avoid duplicate work by caching results that can be reused later.

Memoization is a technique commonly applied in dynamic programming, but there are no restrictions or limitations. For instance, we can apply it in functional programming. In our particular case, we start by defining a functional interface that extends the `Supplier` interface (or, if you find it simpler, just use `Supplier` directly):

```
@FunctionalInterface
public interface FSupplier<R> extends Supplier<R> {}
```

Next, we provide an implementation of `FSupplier` that basically cashes the unseen results and serves, from the cache, the already seen ones:

```
public class Memoize {

  private final static Object UNDEFINED = new Object();

  public static <T> FSupplier<T> supplier(
    final Supplier<T> supplier) {
```

```
    AtomicReference cache = new AtomicReference<>(UNDEFINED);

    return () -> {

      Object value = cache.get();

      if (value == UNDEFINED) {

        synchronized (cache) {

          if (cache.get() == UNDEFINED) {

            System.out.println("Caching: " + supplier.get());
            value = supplier.get();
            cache.set(value);
          }
        }
      }

      return (T) value;
    };
  }
}
```

Finally, we replace our initial Supplier with FSupplier, as follows:

```
private final Supplier<String> dependencies
    = Memoize.supplier(this::downloadDependencies);
```

Done! Our functional approach takes advantage of Supplier's laziness and can cache the results.

190. Writing a Function<String, T> for parsing data

Let's assume that we have the following text:

```
String text = """
  test, a, 1, 4, 5, 0xf5, 0x5, 4.5d, 6, 5.6, 50000, 345,
  4.0f, 6$3, 2$1.1, 5.5, 6.7, 8, a11, 3e+1, -11199, 55
  """;
```

The goal is to find a solution that extracts from this text only the numbers. Depending on a given scenario, we may need only the integers, or only the doubles, and so on. Sometimes, we may need to perform some text replacements before extraction (for instance, we may want to replace the xf characters with a dot, 0xf5 = 0.5).

A possible solution to this problem is to write a method (let's name it `parseText()`) that takes as an argument a `Function<String, T>`. The `Function<String, T>` gives us the flexibility to shape any of the following:

```
List<Integer> integerValues
  = parseText(text, Integer::valueOf);
List<Double> doubleValues
  = parseText(text, Double::valueOf);
...
List<Double> moreDoubleValues
  = parseText(text, t -> Double.valueOf(t.replaceAll(
      "\\$", "").replaceAll("xf", ".").replaceAll("x", ".")));
```

The `parseText()` should perform several steps until it reaches the final result. Its signature can be as follows:

```
public static <T> List<T> parseText(
    String text, Function<String, T> func) {
  ...
}
```

First, we have to split the received text by the comma delimiter and extract the items in a `String[]`. This way, we have access to each item from the text.

Second, we can stream the `String[]` and filter any empty items.

Third, we can call the `Function.apply()` to apply the given function to each item (for instance, to apply `Double::valueOf`). This can be done via the intermediate operation `map()`. Since some items may be invalid numbers, we have to catch and ignore any `Exception` (it is bad practice to swallow an exception like this, but in this case, there is really nothing else to do). For any invalid number, we simply return `null`.

Fourth, we filter all `null` values. This means that the remaining stream contains only numbers that passed through `Function.apply()`.

Fifth, we collect the stream in a `List` and return it.

Putting these five steps together will result in the following code:

```
public static <T> List<T> parseText(
    String text, Function<String, T> func) {

  return Arrays.stream(text.split(",")) // step 1 and 2
    .filter(s -> !s.isEmpty())
    .map(s -> {
      try {
        return func.apply(s.trim());   // step 3
```

```
        } catch (Exception e) {}
        return null;
    })
    .filter(Objects::nonNull)              // step 4
    .collect(Collectors.toList());         // step 5
}
```

Done! You can use this example to solve a wide range of similar problems.

191. Composing predicates in a Stream's filters

A predicate (basically, a condition) can be modeled as a Boolean-valued function via the `java.util.function.Predicate` functional interface. Its functional method is named `test(T t)` and returns a `boolean`.

Applying predicates in a stream pipeline can be done via several stream intermediate operations, but we are interested here only in the `filter(Predicate p)` operation. For instance, let's consider the following class:

```
public class Car {

  private final String brand;
  private final String fuel;
  private final int horsepower;

  public Car(String brand, String fuel, int horsepower) {
    this.brand = brand;
    this.fuel = fuel;
    this.horsepower = horsepower;
  }

  // getters, equals(), hashCode(), toString()
}
```

If we have a `List<Car>` and we want to express a filter that produces all the cars that are Chevrolets, then we can start by defining the proper `Predicate`:

```
Predicate<Car> pChevrolets
    = car -> car.getBrand().equals("Chevrolet");
```

Next, we can use this `Predicate` in a stream pipeline, as follows:

```
List<Car> chevrolets = cars.stream()
    .filter(pChevrolets)
    .collect(Collectors.toList());
```

A `Predicate` can be negated in at least three ways. We can negate the condition via the logical not (!) operator:

```
Predicate<Car> pNotChevrolets
  = car -> !car.getBrand().equals("Chevrolet");
```

We can call the `Predicate.negate()` method:

```
Predicate<Car> pNotChevrolets = pChevrolets.negate();
```

Or we can call the `Predicate.not()` method:

```
Predicate<Car> pNotChevrolets = Predicate.not(pChevrolets);
```

No matter which of these three approaches you prefer, the following filter will produce all cars that are not Chevrolets:

```
List<Car> notChevrolets = cars.stream()
  .filter(pNotChevrolets)
  .collect(Collectors.toList());
```

In the previous examples, we applied a single predicate in a stream pipeline. However, we can apply multiple predicates as well. For instance, we may want to express a filter that produces all the cars that are not Chevrolets and have at least 150 horsepower. For the first part of this composite predicate, we can arbitrarily use pChevrolets.negate(), while, for the second part, we need the following `Predicate`:

```
Predicate<Car> pHorsepower
  = car -> car.getHorsepower() >= 150;
```

We can obtain a composite predicate by chaining the `filter()` calls, as follows:

```
List<Car> notChevrolets150 = cars.stream()
  .filter(pChevrolets.negate())
  .filter(pHorsepower)
  .collect(Collectors.toList());
```

It is shorter and more expressive to rely on `Predicate.and(Predicate<? super T> other)`, which applies the short-circuiting logical AND between two predicates. So the previous example is better expressed as follows:

```
List<Car> notChevrolets150 = cars.stream()
  .filter(pChevrolets.negate().and(pHorsepower))
  .collect(Collectors.toList());
```

If we need to apply the short-circuiting logical OR between two predicates, then relying on `Predicate.or(Predicate<? super T> other)` is the proper choice. For instance, if we want to express a filter that produces all Chevrolets or electric cars, then we can do it as follows:

```
Predicate<Car> pElectric
```

```
      = car -> car.getFuel().equals("electric");

  List<Car> chevroletsOrElectric = cars.stream()
    .filter(pChevrolets.or(pElectric))
    .collect(Collectors.toList());
```

If we are in a scenario that heavily relies on composite predicates, then we can start by creating two helpers that make our job easier:

```
@SuppressWarnings("unchecked")
public final class Predicates {

  private Predicates() {
    throw new AssertionError("Cannot be instantiated");
  }

  public static <T> Predicate<T> asOneAnd(
      Predicate<T>... predicates) {

    Predicate<T> theOneAnd = Stream.of(predicates)
      .reduce(p -> true, Predicate::and);

    return theOneAnd;
  }

  public static <T> Predicate<T> asOneOr(
      Predicate<T>... predicates) {

    Predicate<T> theOneOr = Stream.of(predicates)
      .reduce(p -> false, Predicate::or);

    return theOneOr;
  }
}
```

The goal of these helpers is to take several predicates and glue them into a single composite predicate, via the short-circuiting logical AND and OR.

Let's assume that we want to express a filter that applies the following three predicates via the short-circuiting logical AND:

```
Predicate<Car> pLexus = car -> car.getBrand().equals("Lexus");
Predicate<Car> pDiesel = car -> car.getFuel().equals("diesel");
Predicate<Car> p250 = car -> car.getHorsepower() > 250;
```

First, we join these predicates in a single one:

```
Predicate<Car> predicateAnd = Predicates
    .asOneAnd(pLexus, pDiesel, p250);
```

Afterward, we express the filter:

```
List<Car> lexusDiesel250And = cars.stream()
    .filter(predicateAnd)
    .collect(Collectors.toList());
```

How about expressing a filter that produces a stream containing all cars with horsepower between 100 and 200 or 300 and 400? The predicates are:

```
Predicate<Car> p100 = car -> car.getHorsepower() >= 100;
Predicate<Car> p200 = car -> car.getHorsepower() <= 200;


Predicate<Car> p300 = car -> car.getHorsepower() >= 300;
Predicate<Car> p400 = car -> car.getHorsepower() <= 400;
```

The composite predicate can be obtained as follows:

```
Predicate<Car> pCombo = Predicates.asOneOr(
    Predicates.asOneAnd(p100, p200),
    Predicates.asOneAnd(p300, p400)
);
```

Expressing the filter is straightforward:

```
List<Car> comboAndOr = cars.stream()
    .filter(pCombo)
    .collect(Collectors.toList());
```

You can find all these examples in the bundled code.

192. Filtering nested collections with Streams

This is a classical problem in interviews that usually starts from a model, as follows (we assume that the collection is a List):

```
public class Author {

    private final String name;
    private final List<Book> books;
    ...
}


public class Book {
```

```
    private final String title;
    private final LocalDate published;
    ...

}
```

Having List<Author> denoted as authors, write a stream pipeline that returns the List<Book> published in 2002. You already should recognize this as a typical problem for flatMap(), so without further details, we can write this:

```
List<Book> book2002fm = authors.stream()
  .flatMap(author -> author.getBooks().stream())
  .filter(book -> book.getPublished().getYear() == 2002)
  .collect(Collectors.toList());
```

From *Problem 185*, we know that wherever flatMap() is useful, we should also consider the JDK 16's mapMulti(). Before checking the following snippet of code, challenge yourself to rewrite the previous code via mapMulti():

```
List<Book> book2002mm = authors.stream()
  .<Book>mapMulti((author, consumer) -> {
    for (Book book : author.getBooks()) {
      if (book.getPublished().getYear() == 2002) {
        consumer.accept(book);
      }
    }
  })
  .collect(Collectors.toList());
```

OK, that's crystal clear! How about finding the List<Author> with books published in 2002? Of course, mapMulti() can help us again. All we have to do is to loop the books, and when we find a book published in 2002, we simply pass the author to the consumer instead of the book. Moreover, after passing the author to the consumer, we can break the loop for the current author and take the next one:

```
List<Author> author2002mm = authors.stream()
  .<Author>mapMulti((author, consumer) -> {
    for (Book book : author.getBooks()) {
      if (book.getPublished().getYear() == 2002) {
        consumer.accept(author);
        break;
      }
    }
  })
  .collect(Collectors.toList());
```

Another approach can rely on anyMatch() and a predicate that produces a stream of books published in 2002, as follows:

```
List<Author> authors2002am = authors.stream()
  .filter(
    author -> author.getBooks()
                    .stream()
                    .anyMatch(book -> book.getPublished()
                        .getYear() == 2002)
  )
  .collect(Collectors.toList());
```

Typically, we don't want to alter the given list, but if that is not an issue (or it is exactly what we want), then we can rely on removeIf() to accomplish the same result directly on the List<Author>:

```
authors.removeIf(author -> author.getBooks().stream()
  .noneMatch(book -> book.getPublished().getYear() == 2002));
```

Done! Now, you should have no issues if a problem like this comes up in your interviews.

193. Using BiPredicate

Let's consider the Car model and a List<Car> denoted as cars:

```
public class Car {

  private final String brand;
  private final String fuel;
  private final int horsepower;
  ...
}
```

Our goal is to see if the following Car is contained in cars:

```
Car car = new Car("Ford", "electric", 80);
```

We know that the List API exposes a method named contains(Object o). This method returns true if the given Object is present in the given List. So, we can easily write a Predicate, as follows:

```
Predicate<Car> predicate = cars::contains;
```

Next, we call the test() method, and we should get the expected result:

```
System.out.println(predicate.test(car)); // true
```

We can obtain the same result in a stream pipeline via filter(), anyMatch(), and so on. Here is via anyMatch():

```
System.out.println(
    cars.stream().anyMatch(p -> p.equals(car))
);
```

Alternatively, we can rely on `BiPredicate`. This is a functional interface representing a two-arity specialization of the well-known `Predicate`. Its `test(Object o1, Object o2)` method gets two arguments, so it is a perfect fit for our case:

```
BiPredicate<List<Car>, Car> biPredicate = List::contains;
```

We can perform the test as follows:

```
System.out.println(biPredicate.test(cars, car)); // true
```

In the next problem, you'll see a more practical example of using a `BiPredicate`.

194. Building a dynamic predicate for a custom model

Let's consider the `Car` model and a `List<Car>` denoted as cars:

```
public class Car {

    private final String brand;
    private final String fuel;
    private final int horsepower;
    ...
}
```

Also, let's assume that we need to dynamically produce a wide range of predicates that apply the operators <, >, <=, >=, !=, and == to the `horsepower` field. It will be cumbersome to hardcode such predicates, so we have to come up with a solution that can build, on the fly, any predicate that involves this field, and one of the comparison operators listed here.

There are a few approaches to accomplish this goal, and one of them is to use a Java enum. We have a fixed list of operators that can be coded as enum elements, as follows:

```
enum PredicateBuilder {

    GT((t, u) -> t > u),
    LT((t, u) -> t < u),
    GE((t, u) -> t >= u),
    LE((t, u) -> t <= u),
    EQ((t, u) -> t.intValue() == u.intValue()),
    NOT_EQ((t, u) -> t.intValue() != u.intValue());
    ...
```

In order to apply any of these (`t`, `u`) lambdas, we need a `BiPredicate` constructor (see *Problem 193*), as follows:

```
private final BiPredicate<Integer, Integer> predicate;

private PredicateBuilder(
    BiPredicate<Integer, Integer> predicate) {
  this.predicate = predicate;
}
...
```

Now that we can define a `BiPredicate`, we can write the method that contains the actual test and returns a `Predicate<T>`:

```
public <T> Predicate<T> toPredicate(
    Function<T, Integer> getter, int u) {
  return obj -> this.predicate.test(getter.apply(obj), u);
}
...
```

Finally, we have to provide here the `Function<T, Integer>`, which is the getter corresponding to `horsepower`. We can do this via Java Reflection, as follows:

```
public static <T> Function<T, Integer> getFieldByName(
    Class<T> cls, String field) {

  return object -> {
    try {
      Field f = cls.getDeclaredField(field);
      f.setAccessible(true);

      return (Integer) f.get(object);
    } catch (IllegalAccessException | IllegalArgumentException
            | NoSuchFieldException | SecurityException e) {
      throw new RuntimeException(e);
    }
  };
}
```

Of course, it can be any other class and integer field as well, not only the `Car` class and the `horsepower` field. Based on this code, we can dynamically create a predicate, as follows:

```
Predicate<Car> gtPredicate
  = PredicateBuilder.GT.toPredicate(
      PredicateBuilder.getFieldByName(
        Car.class, "horsepower"), 300);
```

Using this predicate is straightforward:

```
cars.stream()
    .filter(gtPredicate)
    .forEach(System.out::println);
```

You can use this problem as a source of inspiration to implement more types of dynamic predicates. For example, in the next problem, we use the same logic in another scenario.

195. Building a dynamic predicate from a custom map of conditions

Let's consider the Car model and a List<Car> denoted as cars:

```
public class Car {

    private final String brand;
    private final String fuel;
    private final int horsepower;

    ...
}
```

Also, let's assume that we receive a Map of conditions of type *field : value,* which could be used to build a dynamic Predicate. An example of such a Map is listed here:

```
Map<String, String> filtersMap = Map.of(
    "brand", "Chevrolet",
    "fuel", "diesel"
);
```

As you can see, we have a Map<String, String>, so we are interested in an equals() comparison. This is useful to start our development via the following Java enum (we follow the logic from *Problem 194*):

```
enum PredicateBuilder {

    EQUALS(String::equals);
    ...
```

Of course, we can add more operators, such as startsWith(), endsWith(), contains(), and so on. Next, based on the experience gained in *Problems 193* and *194*, we need to add a BiPredicate constructor, the toPredicate() method, and the Java Reflection code to fetch the getters corresponding to the given fields (here, brand and fuel):

```
    private final BiPredicate<String, String> predicate;

    private PredicateBuilder(
```

```
        BiPredicate<String, String> predicate) {
    this.predicate = predicate;
  }

  public <T> Predicate<T> toPredicate(
      Function<T, String> getter, String u) {
    return obj -> this.predicate.test(getter.apply(obj), u);
  }

  public static <T> Function<T, String>
      getFieldByName(Class<T> cls, String field) {
    return object -> {
      try {
        Field f = cls.getDeclaredField(field);
        f.setAccessible(true);

        return (String) f.get(object);
      } catch (
          IllegalAccessException | IllegalArgumentException
          | NoSuchFieldException | SecurityException e) {
        throw new RuntimeException(e);
      }
    };
  }
}
```

Next, we have to define a predicate for each map entry and chain them via the short-circuiting AND operator. This can be done in a loop, as follows:

```
Predicate<Car> filterPredicate = t -> true;
for(String key : filtersMap.keySet()) {
  filterPredicate
    = filterPredicate.and(PredicateBuilder.EQUALS
      .toPredicate(PredicateBuilder.getFieldByName(
        Car.class, key), filtersMap.get(key)));
}
```

Finally, we can use the resulting predicate to filter the cars:

```
cars.stream()
    .filter(filterPredicate)
    .forEach(System.out::println);
```

Done!

196. Logging in predicates

We already know that the `Predicate` functional interface relies on its `test()` method to perform the given check, and it returns a Boolean value. Let's suppose that we want to alter the `test()` method to log the failure cases (the cases that lead to the return of a `false` value).

A quick approach is to write a helper method that sneaks the logging part, as follows:

```
public final class Predicates {

  private static final Logger logger
    = LoggerFactory.getLogger(LogPredicate.class);

  private Predicates() {
    throw new AssertionError("Cannot be instantiated");
  }

  public static <T> Predicate<T> testAndLog(
      Predicate<? super T> predicate, String val) {

    return t -> {
      boolean result = predicate.test(t);

      if (!result) {
        logger.warn(predicate + " don't match '" + val + "'");
      }

      return result;
    };
  }
}
```

Another approach consists of extending the `Predicate` interface and providing a `default` method for testing and logging the failure cases, as follows:

```
@FunctionalInterface
public interface LogPredicate<T> extends Predicate<T> {

  Logger logger = LoggerFactory.getLogger(LogPredicate.class);

  default boolean testAndLog(T t, String val) {

    boolean result = this.test(t);
```

```
    if (!result) {
      logger.warn(t + " don't match '" + val + "'");
    }

    return result;
  }
}
```

You can practice these examples in the bundled code.

197. Extending Stream with containsAll() and containsAny()

Let's assume that we have the following code:

```
List<Car> cars = Arrays.asList(
  new Car("Dacia", "diesel", 100),
  new Car("Lexus", "gasoline", 300),
  ...
  new Car("Ford", "electric", 200)
);

Car car1 = new Car("Lexus", "diesel", 300);
Car car2 = new Car("Ford", "electric", 80);
Car car3 = new Car("Chevrolet", "electric", 150);

List<Car> cars123 = List.of(car1, car2, car3);
```

Next, in the context of a stream pipeline, we want to check if `cars` contains all/any of `car1`, `car2`, `car3`, or `cars123`.

The Stream API comes with a rich set of intermediate and final operations, but it doesn't have a built-in `containsAll()`/`containsAny()`. So, it is our mission to provide the following final operations:

```
boolean contains(T item);
boolean containsAll(T... items);
boolean containsAll(List<? extends T> items);
boolean containsAll(Stream<? extends T> items);
boolean containsAny(T... items);
boolean containsAny(List<? extends T> items);
boolean containsAny(Stream<? extends T> items);
```

We highlighted the methods that get a Stream argument, since these methods provide the main logic, while the rest of the methods just call these ones after converting their arguments to a Stream.

Exposing containsAll/Any() via a custom interface

The containsAll(Stream<? extends T> items) relies on a Set to accomplish its job, as follows (as a challenge, try to find an alternative implementation):

```
default boolean containsAll(Stream<? extends T> items) {

  Set<? extends T> set = toSet(items);

  if (set.isEmpty()) {
    return true;
  }

  return stream().filter(item -> set.remove(item))
                 .anyMatch(any -> set.isEmpty());
}
```

The containsAny(Stream<? extends T> items) method also relies on a Set:

```
default boolean containsAny(Stream<? extends T> items) {

  Set<? extends T> set = toSet(items);

  if (set.isEmpty()) {
    return false;
  }

  return stream().anyMatch(set::contains);
}
```

The toSet() method is just a helper that collects the Stream items into a Set:

```
static <T> Set<T> toSet(Stream<? extends T> stream) {

  return stream.collect(Collectors.toSet());
}
```

Next, let's sneak this code into its final place, which is a custom interface.

As you can see, the containsAll(Stream<? extends T> items) method and containsAny(Stream<? extends T> items) are declared as default, which means that they are part of an interface. Moreover, both of them call the stream() method, which is also part of this interface and hooks the regular Stream.

Basically, a quick approach for solving this problem (especially useful in interviews) consists of writing this custom interface (let's arbitrarily name it `Streams`) that has access to the original built-in `Stream` interface, as follows:

```java
@SuppressWarnings("unchecked")
public interface Streams<T> {

  Stream<T> stream();

  static <T> Streams<T> from(Stream<T> stream) {
    return () -> stream;
  }
  ...
```

Next, the interface exposes a set of `default` methods that represent the `containsAll()`/`containsAny()` flavors, as follows:

```java
default boolean contains(T item) {
  return stream().anyMatch(isEqual(item));
}

default boolean containsAll(T... items) {
  return containsAll(Stream.of(items));
}

default boolean containsAll(List<? extends T> items) {
  return containsAll(items.stream());
}

default boolean containsAll(Stream<? extends T> items) {
  ...
}

default boolean containsAny(T... items) {
  return containsAny(Stream.of(items));
}

default boolean containsAny(List<? extends T> items) {
  return containsAny(items.stream());
}

default boolean containsAny(Stream<? extends T> items) {
  ...
```

```
    }

    static <T> Set<T> toSet(Stream<? extends T> stream) {
        ...
    }
}
```

Done! Now, we can write different stream pipelines that use the brand-new `containsAll/Any()` operations. For instance, if we want to check if `cars` contains all items from `cars123`, we express the stream pipeline as follows:

```
boolean result = Streams.from(cars.stream())
    .containsAll(cars123);
```

Here are several more examples:

```
boolean result = Streams.from(cars.stream())
    .containsAll(car1, car2, car3);

boolean result = Streams.from(cars.stream())
    .containsAny(car1, car2, car3);
```

Involving more operations can be done as shown in the following example:

```
Car car4 = new Car("Mercedes", "electric", 200);

boolean result = Streams.from(cars.stream()
        .filter(car -> car.getBrand().equals("Mercedes"))
        .distinct()
        .dropWhile(car -> car.getFuel().equals("gasoline"))
    ).contains(car4);
```

A more expressive and complete solution to this problem consists of extending the `Stream` interface. Let's do it!

Exposing containsAll/Any() via an extension of Stream

The previous solution can be considered more like a hack. A more logical and realistic solution consists of extending the built-in Stream API and adding our `containsAll/Any()` methods as teammates next to the `Stream` operations. So the implementation starts as follows:

```
@SuppressWarnings("unchecked")
public interface Streams<T> extends Stream<T> {
    ...
}
```

Before implementing the `containsAll/Any()` methods, we need to handle some aspects resulting from extending the `Stream` interface. First, we need to override in `Streams` each of the `Stream` methods. Since the `Stream` interface has a lot of methods, we only list a few of them here:

```
@Override
public Streams<T> filter(Predicate<? super T> predicate);

@Override
public <R> Streams<R> map(
    Function<? super T, ? extends R> mapper);
...
@Override
public T reduce(T identity, BinaryOperator<T> accumulator);
...
@Override
default boolean isParallel() {
  return false;
}
...
@Override
default Streams<T> parallel() {
  throw new UnsupportedOperationException(
      "Not supported yet."); // or, return this
}

@Override
default Streams<T> unordered() {
  throw new UnsupportedOperationException(
      "Not supported yet."); // or, return this
}
...
@Override
default Streams<T> sequential() {
  return this;
}
```

Since `Streams` can handle only sequential streams (parallelism is not supported), we can implement the `isParallel()`, `parallel()`, `unordered()`, and `sequential()` methods as `default` methods directly in `Streams`.

Next, in order to use `Streams`, we need a `from(Stream s)` method that is capable of wrapping the given `Stream`, as follows:

```
static <T> Streams<T> from(Stream<? extends T> stream) {
```

```
  if (stream == null) {
    return from(Stream.empty());
  }

  if (stream instanceof Streams) {
    return (Streams<T>) stream;
  }

  return new StreamsWrapper<>(stream);
}
```

The `StreamsWrapper` is a class that wraps the current `Stream` into sequential `Streams`. The `StreamsWrapper` class implements `Streams`, so it has to override all the `Streams` methods and properly wrap the `Stream` into `Streams`. Because `Streams` has quite a lot of methods (as a consequence of extending `Stream`), we list here only a few of them (the rest are available in the bundled code):

```
@SuppressWarnings("unchecked")
public class StreamsWrapper<T> implements Streams<T> {

  private final Stream<? extends T> delegator;

  public StreamsWrapper(Stream<? extends T> delegator) {
    this.delegator = delegator.sequential();
  }

  @Override
  public Streams<T> filter(Predicate<? super T> predicate) {
    return Streams.from(delegator.filter(predicate));
  }

  @Override
  public <R> Streams<R> map(
      Function<? super T, ? extends R> mapper) {
    return Streams.from(delegator.map(mapper));
  }
  ...
  @Override
  public T reduce(T identity, BinaryOperator<T> accumulator) {
    return ((Stream<T>) delegator)
      .reduce(identity, accumulator);
  }
```

```
  ...
}
```

Finally, we add `Streams` to the `containsAll/Any()` methods, which are quite straightforward (since `Streams` extends `Stream`, we have access to all the `Stream` goodies without the need to write a `stream()` hack, as in the previous solution). First, we add the `containsAll()` methods:

```
default boolean contains(T item) {
  return anyMatch(isEqual(item));
}

default boolean containsAll(T... items) {
  return containsAll(Stream.of(items));
}

default boolean containsAll(List<? extends T> items) {
  return containsAll(items.stream());
}

default boolean containsAll(Stream<? extends T> items) {

  Set<? extends T> set = toSet(items);

  if (set.isEmpty()) {
    return true;
  }

  return filter(item -> set.remove(item))
    .anyMatch(any -> set.isEmpty());
}
```

Second, we add the `containsAny()` methods:

```
default boolean containsAny(T... items) {
  return containsAny(Stream.of(items));
}

default boolean containsAny(List<? extends T> items) {
  return containsAny(items.stream());
}

default boolean containsAny(Stream<? extends T> items) {

  Set<? extends T> set = toSet(items);
```

```
    if (set.isEmpty()) {
      return false;
    }

    return anyMatch(set::contains);
}
```

Finally, we add the toSet() method, which you already know:

```
static <T> Set<T> toSet(Stream<? extends T> stream) {

    return stream.collect(Collectors.toSet());
}
```

Mission accomplished! Now, let's write some examples:

```
boolean result = Streams.from(cars.stream())
    .filter(car -> car.getBrand().equals("Mercedes"))
    .contains(car1);

boolean result = Streams.from(cars.stream())
    .containsAll(cars123);

boolean result = Streams.from(cars123.stream())
    .containsAny(cars.stream());
```

You can find more examples in the bundled code.

198. Extending Stream with removeAll() and retainAll()

Before reading this problem, I strongly recommend that you read *Problem 197*.

In *Problem 197*, we extended the Stream API with two final operations named containsAll() and containsAny() via a custom interface. In both cases, the resulting interface was named Streams. In this problem, we follow the same logic to implement two intermediate operations, named removeAll() and retainAll(), with the following signatures:

```
Streams<T> remove(T item);
Streams<T> removeAll(T... items);
Streams<T> removeAll(List<? extends T> items);
Streams<T> removeAll(Stream<? extends T> items);
Streams<T> retainAll(T... items);
Streams<T> retainAll(List<? extends T> items);
Streams<T> retainAll(Stream<? extends T> items);
```

Since `removeAll()` and `retainAll()` are intermediate operations, they have to return `Stream`. More precisely, they have to return `Streams`, which is our implementation based on a custom interface or an interface that extends `Stream`.

Exposing removeAll()/retainAll() via a custom interface

The `removeAll(Stream<? extends T> items)` method relies on a `Set` to accomplish its job, as follows (as a challenge, try to find an alternative implementation):

```
default Streams<T> removeAll(Stream<? extends T> items) {

  Set<? extends T> set = toSet(items);

  if (set.isEmpty()) {
    return this;
  }

  return from(stream().filter(item -> !set.contains(item)));
}
```

The `retainAll(Stream<? extends T> items)` method also relies on a `Set`:

```
default Streams<T> retainAll(Stream<? extends T> items) {

  Set<? extends T> set = toSet(items);

  if (set.isEmpty()) {
    return from(Stream.empty());
  }

  return from(stream().filter(item -> set.contains(item)));
}
```

The `toSet()` method is just a helper that collects the `Stream` items into a `Set`:

```
static <T> Set<T> toSet(Stream<? extends T> stream) {

  return stream.collect(Collectors.toSet());
}
```

Next, we can sneak these `default` methods into a custom interface named `Streams`, exactly as we did in *Problem 197*:

```
@SuppressWarnings("unchecked")
public interface Streams<T> {
```

```
    Stream<T> stream();

    static <T> Streams<T> from(Stream<T> stream) {
      return () -> stream;
    }


    // removeAll()/retainAll() default methods and toSet()
}
```

There is a big problem with this implementation. The problem becomes obvious when we try to chain removeAll()/retainAll() in a stream pipeline next to other Stream operations. Because these two methods return Streams (not Stream), we cannot chain a Stream operation after them without first calling the Java built-in stream() before them. This is needed to switch from Streams to Stream. Here is an example (using cars, car1, car2, car3, and car123, as introduced in *Problem 197*):

```
Streams.from(cars.stream())
   .retainAll(cars123)
   .removeAll(car1, car3)
   .stream()
   .forEach(System.out::println);
```

The problem becomes even worse if we have to alternate between Streams and Stream multiple times. Check out this zombie:

```
Streams.from(Streams.from(cars.stream().distinct())
   .retainAll(car1, car2, car3)
   .stream()
   .filter(car -> car.getFuel().equals("electric")))
   .removeAll(car2)
   .stream()
   .forEach(System.out::println);
```

This hack is not a happy choice to enrich the Stream API with intermediate operations. However, it works quite well for terminal operations. So, the proper approach is to extend the Stream interface.

Exposing removeAll/retainAll() via an extension of Stream

We already know from *Problem 197* how to extend the Stream interface. The implementation of removeAll() is also straightforward:

```
@SuppressWarnings("unchecked")
public interface Streams<T> extends Stream<T> {

  default Streams<T> remove(T item) {
```

```
    return removeAll(item);
  }


  default Streams<T> removeAll(T... items) {
    return removeAll(Stream.of(items));
  }


  default Streams<T> removeAll(List<? extends T> items) {
    return removeAll(items.stream());
  }


  default Streams<T> removeAll(Stream<? extends T> items) {

    Set<? extends T> set = toSet(items);

    if (set.isEmpty()) {
      return this;
    }

    return filter(item -> !set.contains(item))
      .onClose(items::close);
  }
  ...
```

Then, retainAll() follows in the same manner:

```
  default Streams<T> retainAll(T... items) {
    return retainAll(Stream.of(items));
  }
  default Streams<T> retainAll(List<? extends T> items) {
    return retainAll(items.stream());
  }


  default Streams<T> retainAll(Stream<? extends T> items) {

    Set<? extends T> set = toSet(items);

    if (set.isEmpty()) {
      return from(Stream.empty());
    }

    return filter(item -> set.contains(item))
```

```
      .onClose(items::close);
   }
   ...
}
```

As you know from *Problem 197*, next, we have to override all the Stream methods to return Streams. While this part is available in the bundled code, here is an example of using removeAll()/retainAll():

```
Streams.from(cars.stream())
   .distinct()
   .retainAll(car1, car2, car3)
   .filter(car -> car.getFuel().equals("electric"))
   .removeAll(car2)
   .forEach(System.out::println);
```

As you can see, this time, the stream pipeline looks quite good. There is no need to perform switches between Streams and Stream via stream() calls. So, mission accomplished!

199. Introducing stream comparators

Let's assume that we have the following three lists (a list of numbers, a list of strings, and a list of Car objects):

```
List<Integer> nrs = new ArrayList<>();
List<String> strs = new ArrayList<>();
List<Car> cars = List.of(...);

public class Car {

   private final String brand;
   private final String fuel;
   private final int horsepower;

   ...
}
```

Next, we want to sort these lists in a stream pipeline.

Sorting via natural order

Sorting via natural order is very simple. All we have to do is to call the built-in intermediate operation, sorted():

```
nrs.stream()
   .sorted()
   .forEach(System.out::println);
```

```
strs.stream()
    .sorted()
    .forEach(System.out::println);
```

If nrs contains 1, 6, 3, 8, 2, 3, and 0, then sorted() will produce 0, 1, 2, 3, 3, 6, and 8. So, for numbers, the natural order is the ascending order by value.

If strs contains "book," "old," "new," "quiz," "around," and "tick," then sorted() will produce "around," "book," "new," "old," "quiz," and "tick". So, for strings, the natural order is the alphabetical order.

The same result can be obtained if we explicitly call Integer.compareTo() and String.compareTo() via sorted(Comparator<? super T> comparator):

```
nrs.stream()
    .sorted((n1, n2) -> n1.compareTo(n2))
    .forEach(System.out::println);

strs.stream()
    .sorted((s1, s2) -> s1.compareTo(s2))
    .forEach(System.out::println);
```

Alternatively, we can use the java.util.Comparator functional interface, as follows:

```
nrs.stream()
    .sorted(Comparator.naturalOrder())
    .forEach(System.out::println);

strs.stream()
    .sorted(Comparator.naturalOrder())
    .forEach(System.out::println);
```

All three approaches return the same result.

Reversing the natural order

Reversing the natural order can be done via Comparator.reverseOrder(), as follows:

```
nrs.stream()
    .sorted(Comparator.reverseOrder())
    .forEach(System.out::println);

strs.stream()
    .sorted(Comparator.reverseOrder())
    .forEach(System.out::println);
```

If nrs contains 1, 6, 3, 8, 2, 3, and 0, then sorted() will produce 8, 6, 3, 3, 2, 1, and 0. Reversing the natural order of numbers results in descending order by value.

If strs contains "book," "old," "new," "quiz," "around," and "tick," then sorted() will produce "tick," "quiz," "old," "new," "book," and "around." So for strings, reversing the natural order results in reversing the alphabetical order.

Sorting and nulls

If nrs/strs contains null values as well, then all the previous examples will throw a NullPointerException. However, java.util.Comparator exposes two methods that allow us to sort null values first (nullsFirst(Comparator<? super T> comparator)) or last (nullsLast(Comparator<? super T> comparator)). They can be used as shown in the following examples:

```
nrs.stream()
    .sorted(Comparator.nullsFirst(Comparator.naturalOrder()))
    .forEach(System.out::println);

nrs.stream()
    .sorted(Comparator.nullsLast(Comparator.naturalOrder()))
    .forEach(System.out::println);

nrs.stream()
    .sorted(Comparator.nullsFirst(Comparator.reverseOrder()))
    .forEach(System.out::println);
```

The third example sorts the null values first, followed by the numbers in reverse order.

Writing custom comparators

Sometimes, we need a custom comparator. For instance, if we want to sort strs ascending by the last character, then we can write a custom comparator, as follows:

```
strs.stream()
    .sorted((s1, s2) ->
        Character.compare(s1.charAt(s1.length() - 1),
                          s2.charAt(s2.length() - 1)))
    .forEach(System.out::println);
```

If strs contains "book," "old," "new," "quiz," "around," and "tick," then sorted() will produce "old," "around," "book," "tick," "new," and "quiz."

However, custom comparators are typically used to sort our models. For instance, if we need to sort the cars list, then we need to define a comparator. We cannot just say:

```
cars.stream()
    .sorted()
    .forEach(System.out::println);
```

This will not compile because there is no comparator for `Car` objects. An approach consists of implementing the `Comparable` interface and overriding the `compareTo(Car c)` method. For instance, if we want to sort `cars` ascending by `horsepower`, then we start by implementing `Comparable`, as follows:

```
public class Car implements Comparable<Car> {

  ...

  @Override
  public int compareTo(Car c) {

    return this.getHorsepower() > c.getHorsepower()
      ? 1 : this.getHorsepower() < c.getHorsepower() ? -1 : 0;
  }
}
```

Now, we can successfully write this:

```
cars.stream()
    .sorted()
    .forEach(System.out::println);
```

Alternatively, if we cannot alter the `Car` code, we can try to use one of the existing `Comparator` methods, which allow us to push a function that contains the sort key and returns a `Comparator` that automatically compares by that key. Since `horsepower` is an integer, we can use `comparingInt(ToIntFunction<? super T> keyExtractor)`, as follows:

```
cars.stream()
    .sorted(Comparator.comparingInt(Car::getHorsepower))
    .forEach(System.out::println);
```

Here it is in reverse order:

```
cars.stream()
    .sorted(Comparator.comparingInt(
            Car::getHorsepower).reversed())
    .forEach(System.out::println);
```

You may also be interested in `comparingLong(ToLongFunction)` and `comparingDouble(ToDoubleFunction)`.

`ToIntFunction`, `ToLongFunction`, and `ToDoubleFunction` are specializations of the `Function` method. In this context, we can say that `comparingInt()`, `comparingLong()`, and `comparingDouble()` are specializations of `comparing()`, which comes in two flavors: `comparing(Function<? super T,? extends U> keyExtractor)` and `comparing(Function<? super T,? extends U> keyExtractor, Comparator<? super U> keyComparator)`.

Here is an example of using the second flavor of comparing() to sort cars ascending by the fuel type (natural order), with null values placed at the end:

```
cars.stream()
    .sorted(Comparator.comparing(Car::getFuel,
            Comparator.nullsLast(Comparator.naturalOrder())))
    .forEach(System.out::println);
```

Also, here is another example of sorting cars ascending by the last character of the fuel type, with null values placed at the end:

```
cars.stream()
    .sorted(Comparator.comparing(Car::getFuel,
            Comparator.nullsLast((s1, s2) ->
                Character.compare(s1.charAt(s1.length() - 1),
                                  s2.charAt(s2.length() - 1)))))
    .forEach(System.out::println);
```

Usually, chaining multiple comparators in a functional expression leads to a less readable code. In such cases, you can sustain the readablility of your code by importing statics and assigning the comparators to variables which names starting with "by" as in the following example (the result of this code is the same as the result of the previous example, but is more readable):

```
import static java.util.Comparator.comparing;
import static java.util.Comparator.nullsLast;
...
Comparator<String> byCharAt = nullsLast(
   (s1, s2) -> Character.compare(s1.charAt(s1.length() - 1),
      s2.charAt(s2.length() - 1)));
Comparator<Car> byFuelAndCharAt = comparing(
  Car::getFuel, byCharAt);

cars.stream()
    .sorted(byFuelAndCharAt)
    .forEach(System.out::println);
```

Done! In the next problem, we will sort a map.

200. Sorting a map

Let's assume that we have the following map:

```
public class Car {
```

```
    private final String brand;
    private final String fuel;
    private final int horsepower;

    ...
}

Map<Integer, Car> cars = Map.of(
    1, new Car("Dacia", "diesel", 350),
    2, new Car("Lexus", "gasoline", 350),
    3, new Car("Chevrolet", "electric", 150),
    4, new Car("Mercedes", "gasoline", 150),
    5, new Car("Chevrolet", "diesel", 250),
    6, new Car("Ford", "electric", 80),
    7, new Car("Chevrolet", "diesel", 450),
    8, new Car("Mercedes", "electric", 200),
    9, new Car("Chevrolet", "gasoline", 350),
    10, new Car("Lexus", "diesel", 300)
);
```

Next, we want to sort this map into a List<String>, as follows:

- If the horsepower values are different, then sort in descending order by horsepower
- If the horsepower values are equal, then sort in ascending order by the map keys
- The result, List<String>, should contain items of type *key(horsepower)*

Under these statements, sorting the cars map will result in:

```
[7(450), 1(350), 2(350), 9(350), 10(300), 5(250),
8(200), 3(150), 4(150), 6(80)]
```

Obviously, this problem requires a custom comparator. Having two map entries (c1, c2), we elaborate the following logic:

1. Check if c2's horsepower is equal to c1's horsepower
2. If they are equal, then compare c1's key with c2's key
3. Otherwise, compare c2's horsepower with c1's horsepower
4. Collect the result into a List

In code lines, this can be expressed as follows:

```
List<String> result = cars.entrySet().stream()
    .sorted((c1, c2) -> c2.getValue().getHorsepower()
        == c1.getValue().getHorsepower()
      ? c1.getKey().compareTo(c2.getKey())
```

```
        : Integer.valueOf(c2.getValue().getHorsepower())
            .compareTo(c1.getValue().getHorsepower()))
    .map(c -> c.getKey() + "("
                            + c.getValue().getHorsepower() + ")")
    .toList();
```

Alternatively, if we rely on `Map.Entry.comparingByValue()`, `comparingByKey()`, and `java.util.Comparator`, then we can write it as follows:

```
List<String> result = cars.entrySet().stream()
    .sorted(Entry.<Integer, Car>comparingByValue(
            Comparator.comparingInt(
                Car::getHorsepower).reversed())
    .thenComparing(Entry.comparingByKey()))
    .map(c -> c.getKey() + "("
        + c.getValue().getHorsepower() + ")")
    .toList();
```

This approach is more readable and expressive.

201. Filtering a map

Let's consider the following map:

```
public class Car {

    private final String brand;
    private final String fuel;
    private final int horsepower;

    ...
}

Map<Integer, Car> cars = Map.of(
    1, new Car("Dacia", "diesel", 100),
    ...
    10, new Car("Lexus", "diesel", 300)
);
```

In order to stream a map, we can start from the `entrySet()` of the `Map`, `values()`, or `keyset()`, followed by a `stream()` call. For instance, if we want to express a pipeline as *Map -> Stream -> Filter -> String* that returns a `List<String>` containing all the electric brands, then we can rely on `entrySet()` as follows:

```
String electricBrands = cars.entrySet().stream()
    .filter(c -> "electric".equals(c.getValue().getFuel()))
    .map(c -> c.getValue().getBrand())
```

```
  .collect(Collectors.joining(", "));
```

However, as you can see, this stream pipeline doesn't use the map's keys. This means that we can better express it via `values()` instead of `entrySet()`, as follows:

```
String electricBrands = cars.values().stream()
  .filter(c -> "electric".equals(c.getFuel()))
  .map(c -> c.getBrand())
  .collect(Collectors.joining(", "));
```

This is more readable, and it clearly expresses its intention.

Here is another example that you should be able to follow without further details:

```
Car newCar = new Car("No name", "gasoline", 350);

String carsAsNewCar1 = cars.entrySet().stream()
 .filter(c -> (c.getValue().getFuel().equals(newCar.getFuel())
   && c.getValue().getHorsepower() == newCar.getHorsepower()))
 .map(map -> map.getValue().getBrand())
 .collect(Collectors.joining(", "));

String carsAsNewCar2 = cars.values().stream()
 .filter(c -> (c.getFuel().equals(newCar.getFuel())
   && c.getHorsepower() == newCar.getHorsepower()))
 .map(map -> map.getBrand())
 .collect(Collectors.joining(", "));
```

So, when the stream pipeline needs only the map's values, we can start from `values()`; when it needs only the keys, we can start from `keyset()`; and when it needs both (the values and the keys), we can start from `entrySet()`.

For instance, a stream pipeline expressed as *Map -> Stream -> Filter -> Map* that filters the top five cars by key and collects them into a resulting map needs the `entrySet()` starting point, as follows:

```
Map<Integer, Car> carsTop5a = cars.entrySet().stream()
  .filter(c -> c.getKey() <= 5)
  .collect(Collectors.toMap(
     Map.Entry::getKey, Map.Entry::getValue));
  //or, .collect(Collectors.toMap(
  //        c -> c.getKey(), c -> c.getValue()));
```

Here is an example that returns a `Map` of the top five cars with more than 100 horsepower:

```
Map<Integer, Car> hp100Top5a = cars.entrySet().stream()
  .filter(c -> c.getValue().getHorsepower() > 100)
  .sorted(Entry.comparingByValue(
```

```
          Comparator.comparingInt(Car::getHorsepower)))
   .collect(Collectors.toMap(
     Map.Entry::getKey, Map.Entry::getValue,
        (c1, c2) -> c2, LinkedHashMap::new));
  //or, .collect(Collectors.toMap(
  //      c -> c.getKey(), c -> c.getValue(),
  //      (c1, c2) -> c2, LinkedHashMap::new));
```

If we need to express such pipelines quite often, then we may prefer to write some helpers. Here is a set of four generic helpers for filtering and sorting a Map<K, V> by key:

```java
public final class Filters {

  private Filters() {
    throw new AssertionError("Cannot be instantiated");
  }

  public static <K, V> Map<K, V> byKey(
        Map<K, V> map, Predicate<K> predicate) {

  return map.entrySet()
    .stream()
    .filter(item -> predicate.test(item.getKey()))
    .collect(Collectors.toMap(
        Map.Entry::getKey, Map.Entry::getValue));
  }

  public static <K, V> Map<K, V> sortedByKey(
    Map<K, V> map, Predicate<K> predicate, Comparator<K> c) {

    return map.entrySet()
      .stream()
      .filter(item -> predicate.test(item.getKey()))
      .sorted(Map.Entry.comparingByKey(c))
      .collect(Collectors.toMap(
          Map.Entry::getKey, Map.Entry::getValue,
              (c1, c2) -> c2, LinkedHashMap::new));
  }
  ...
```

And a set for filtering and sorting a Map by value:

```java
  public static <K, V> Map<K, V> byValue(
```

```
          Map<K, V> map, Predicate<V> predicate) {

    return map.entrySet()
      .stream()
      .filter(item -> predicate.test(item.getValue()))
      .collect(Collectors.toMap(
        Map.Entry::getKey, Map.Entry::getValue));
  }

  public static <K, V> Map<K, V> sortedbyValue(Map<K, V> map,
      Predicate<V> predicate, Comparator<V> c) {

  return map.entrySet()
    .stream()
    .filter(item -> predicate.test(item.getValue()))
    .sorted(Map.Entry.comparingByValue(c))
    .collect(Collectors.toMap(
      Map.Entry::getKey, Map.Entry::getValue,
          (c1, c2) -> c2, LinkedHashMap::new));
  }
}
```

Now, our code has become much shorter. For instance, we can filter the top five cars by key and collect them into a resulting map, as follows:

```
Map<Integer, Car> carsTop5s
  = Filters.byKey(cars, c -> c <= 5);
```

Alternatively, we can filter the top five cars with more than 100 horsepower, as follows:

```
Map<Integer, Car> hp100Top5s
  = Filters.byValue(cars, c -> c.getHorsepower() > 100);

Map<Integer, Car> hp100Top5d
  = Filters.sortedbyValue(cars, c -> c.getHorsepower() > 100,
      Comparator.comparingInt(Car::getHorsepower));
```

Cool, right?! Feel free to extend Filters with more generic helpers to handle Map processing in stream pipelines.

202. Creating a custom collector via Collector.of()

Creating a custom collector is a topic that we covered in detail in *Chapter 9*, *Problem 193*, of *Java Coding Problem, First Edition*. More precisely, in that problem, you saw how to write a custom collector by implementing the java.util.stream.Collector interface.

Don't worry if you haven't read that book/problem; you can still follow this problem. First, we will create several custom collectors. This time, we will rely on two `Collector.of()` methods that have the following signatures:

```
static <T,R> Collector<T,R,R> of(
    Supplier<R> supplier,
    BiConsumer<R,T> accumulator,
    BinaryOperator<R> combiner,
    Collector.Characteristics... characteristics)

static <T,A,R> Collector<T,A,R> of(
    Supplier<A> supplier,
    BiConsumer<A,T> accumulator,
    BinaryOperator<A> combiner,
    Function<A,R> finisher,
    Collector.Characteristics... characteristics)
```

In this context, T, A, and R represent the following:

- T represents the type of elements from the Stream (elements that will be collected)
- A represents the type of object that was used during the collection process, known as the accumulator, which is used to accumulate the stream elements in a mutable result container
- R represents the type of the object after the collection process (the final result)

Moreover, a `Collector` is characterized by four functions and an enumeration. Here's a short note from *Java Coding Problems, First Edition*:

"These functions work together to accumulate entries into a mutable result container, and optionally perform a final transformation on the result. They are as follows:

- *Creating a new empty mutable result container (the supplier argument)*
- *Incorporating a new data element into the mutable result container (the accumulator argument)*
- *Combining two mutable result containers into one (the combiner argument)*
- *Performing an optional final transformation on the mutable result container to obtain the final result (the finisher argument)"*

In addition, we have the `Collector.Characteristics...` enumeration that defines the collector behavior. Possible values are UNORDERED (no order), CONCURRENT (more threads accumulate elements), and IDENTITY_FINISH (the finisher is the identity function, so no further transformation will take place).

In this context, let's try to fire up a few examples. But first, let's assume that we have the following model:

```
public interface Vehicle {}

public class Car implements Vehicle {

    private final String brand;
```

```java
    private final String fuel;
    private final int horsepower;

    ...
}


public class Submersible implements Vehicle {

    private final String type;
    private final double maxdepth;

    ...
}
```

Also, some data:

```java
Map<Integer, Car> cars = Map.of(
    1, new Car("Dacia", "diesel", 100),
    ...
    10, new Car("Lexus", "diesel", 300)
);
```

Next, let's make some collectors in a helper class named MyCollectors.

Writing a custom collector that collects into a TreeSet

In a custom collector that collects into a TreeSet and the supplier is TreeSet::new, the accumulator is TreeSet.add(), the combiner relies on TreeSet.addAll(), and the finisher is the identity function:

```java
public static <T>
    Collector<T, TreeSet<T>, TreeSet<T>> toTreeSet() {

    return Collector.of(TreeSet::new, TreeSet::add,
      (left, right) -> {
        left.addAll(right);

        return left;
    }, Collector.Characteristics.IDENTITY_FINISH);
}
```

In the following example, we use this collector to collect all electric brands in a TreeSet<String>:

```java
TreeSet<String> electricBrands = cars.values().stream()
    .filter(c -> "electric".equals(c.getFuel()))
    .map(c -> c.getBrand())
    .collect(MyCollectors.toTreeSet());
```

That was easy!

Writing a custom collector that collects into a LinkedHashSet

In a custom collector that collects into a LinkedHashSet where the supplier is LinkedHashSet::new, the accumulator is HashSet::add, the combiner relies on HashSet.addAll(), and the finisher is the identity function:

```
public static <T> Collector<T, LinkedHashSet<T>,
    LinkedHashSet<T>> toLinkedHashSet() {

  return Collector.of(LinkedHashSet::new, HashSet::add,
    (left, right) -> {
      left.addAll(right);

      return left;
    }, Collector.Characteristics.IDENTITY_FINISH);
}
```

In the following example, we use this collector to collect the sorted cars' horsepower:

```
LinkedHashSet<Integer> hpSorted = cars.values().stream()
  .map(c -> c.getHorsepower())
  .sorted()
  .collect(MyCollectors.toLinkedHashSet());
```

Done! The LinkedHashSet<Integer> contains the horsepower values in ascending order.

Writing a custom collector that excludes elements of another collector

The goal of this section is to provide a custom collector that takes, as arguments, a Predicate and a Collector. It applies the given predicate to elements to be collected, in order to exclude the failures from the given collector:

```
public static <T, A, R> Collector<T, A, R> exclude(
    Predicate<T> predicate, Collector<T, A, R> collector) {

  return Collector.of(
    collector.supplier(),
    (l, r) -> {
      if (predicate.negate().test(r)) {
        collector.accumulator().accept(l, r);
      }
    },
    collector.combiner(),
    collector.finisher(),
```

```
        collector.characteristics()
          .toArray(Collector.Characteristics[]::new)
    );
  }
```

The custom collector uses the supplier, combiner, finisher, and characteristics of the given collector. It only influences the accumulator of the given collector. Basically, it explicitly calls the accumulator of the given collector only for the elements that pass the given predicate.

For instance, if we want to obtain the sorted horsepower less than 200 via this custom collector, then we call it as follows (the predicate specifies what should be excluded):

```
LinkedHashSet<Integer> excludeHp200 = cars.values().stream()
  .map(c -> c.getHorsepower())
  .sorted()
  .collect(MyCollectors.exclude(c -> c > 200,
              MyCollectors.toLinkedHashSet()));
```

Here, we use two custom collectors, but we can easily replace the `toLinkedHashSet()` with a built-in collector as well. Challenge yourself to write the counterpart of this custom collector. Write a collector that includes the elements that pass the given predicate.

Writing a custom collector that collects elements by type

Let's suppose that we have the following `List<Vehicle>`:

```
Vehicle mazda = new Car("Mazda", "diesel", 155);
Vehicle ferrari = new Car("Ferrari", "gasoline", 500);

Vehicle hov = new Submersible("HOV", 3000);
Vehicle rov = new Submersible("ROV", 7000);

List<Vehicle> vehicles = List.of(mazda, hov, ferrari, rov);
```

Our goal is to collect only the cars or the submersibles, but not both. For this, we can write a custom collector that collects by type into the given supplier, as follows:

```
public static
  <T, A extends T, R extends Collection<A>> Collector<T, ?, R>
    toType(Class<A> type, Supplier<R> supplier) {

  return Collector.of(supplier,
      (R r, T t) -> {
        if (type.isInstance(t)) {
          r.add(type.cast(t));
        }
```

```
        },
        (R left, R right) -> {
            left.addAll(right);

            return left;
        },
        Collector.Characteristics.IDENTITY_FINISH
    );
}
```

Now, we can collect only the cars from `List<Vehicle>` into an `ArrayList`, as follows:

```
List<Car> onlyCars = vehicles.stream()
    .collect(MyCollectors.toType(
        Car.class, ArrayList::new));
```

Also, we can collect only the submersible into a `HashSet`, as follows:

```
Set<Submersible> onlySubmersible = vehicles.stream()
    .collect(MyCollectors.toType(
        Submersible.class, HashSet::new));
```

Finally, let's write a custom collector for a custom data structure.

Writing a custom collector for SplayTree

In *Chapter 5, Problem 127*, we implemented a SplayTree data structure. Now, let's write a custom collector capable of collecting elements into a SplayTree. Obviously, the supplier is `SplayTree::new`. Moreover, the accumulator is `SplayTree.insert()`, while the combiner is `SplayTree.insertAll()`:

```
public static
    Collector<Integer, SplayTree, SplayTree> toSplayTree() {

    return Collector.of(SplayTree::new, SplayTree::insert,
        (left, right) -> {
            left.insertAll(right);

            return left;
        },
        Collector.Characteristics.IDENTITY_FINISH);
}
```

Here is an example that collects the car's horsepower into a SplayTree:

```
SplayTree st = cars.values().stream()
    .map(c -> c.getHorsepower())
    .collect(MyCollectors.toSplayTree());
```

Done! Challenge yourself to implement a custom collector.

203. Throwing checked exceptions from lambdas

Let's suppose that we have the following lambda:

```
static void readFiles(List<Path> paths) {

  paths.forEach(p -> {
    try {
      readFile(p);
    } catch (IOException e) {
      ... // what can we throw here?
    }
  });
}
```

What can we throw in the catch block? Most of you will know the answer; we can throw an unchecked exception such as a RuntimeException:

```
static void readFiles(List<Path> paths) {

  paths.forEach(p -> {
    try {
      readFile(p);
    } catch (IOException e) {
      throw new RuntimeException(e);
    }
  });
}
```

Also, most people know that we cannot throw a checked exception such as an IOException. The following snippet of code will not compile:

```
static void readFiles(List<Path> paths) {

  paths.forEach(p -> {
    try {
      readFile(p);
    } catch (IOException e) {
      throw new IOException(e);
    }
  });
}
```

Can we change this rule? Can we come up with a hack that allows us to throw checked exceptions from lambdas? Short answer: sure we can!

Long answer: sure we can, *if* we simply hide the checked exception for the compiler, as follows:

```java
public final class Exceptions {

  private Exceptions() {
    throw new AssertionError("Cannot be instantiated");
  }

  public static void throwChecked(Throwable t) {
    Exceptions.<RuntimeException>throwIt(t);
  }

  @SuppressWarnings({"unchecked"})
  private static <X extends Throwable> void throwIt(
      Throwable t) throws X {
    throw (X) t;
  }
}
```

That's all there is to it! Now, we can throw any checked exception. Here, we throw an IOException:

```java
static void readFiles(List<Path> paths) throws IOException {

  paths.forEach(p -> {
    try {
      readFile(p);
    } catch (IOException e) {
      Exceptions.throwChecked(new IOException(
        "Some files are corrupted", e));
    }
  });
}
```

Also, we can catch it as follows:

```java
List<Path> paths = List.of(...);

try {
  readFiles(paths);
} catch (IOException e) {
  System.out.println(e + " \n " + e.getCause());
}
```

If a certain path was not found, then the reported error message will be:

```
java.io.IOException: Some files are corrupted
java.io.FileNotFoundException: ...
(The system cannot find the path specified)
```

Cool, right?!

204. Implementing distinctBy() for the Stream API

Let's suppose that we have the following model and data:

```java
public class Car {

  private final String brand;
  private final String fuel;
  private final int horsepower;

  ...
}

List<Car> cars = List.of(
  new Car("Chevrolet", "diesel", 350),
  ...
  new Car("Lexus", "diesel", 300)
);
```

We know that the Stream API contains the `distinct()` intermediate operation, which is capable of keeping only the distinct elements based on the `equals()` method:

```java
cars.stream()
    .distinct()
    .forEach(System.out::println);
```

While this code prints the distinct cars, we may want a `distinctBy()` intermediate operation that is capable of keeping only the distinct elements based on a given property/key. For instance, we may need all the cars distinct by brand. For this, we can rely on the `toMap()` collector and the identity function, as follows:

```java
cars.stream()
    .collect(Collectors.toMap(Car::getBrand,
            Function.identity(), (c1, c2) -> c1))
    .values()
    .forEach(System.out::println);
```

We can extract this idea into a helper method, as follows:

```java
public static <K, T> Collector<T, ?, Map<K, T>>
```

```
    distinctByKey(Function<? super T, ? extends K> function) {

    return Collectors.toMap(
      function, Function.identity(), (t1, t2) -> t1);
  }
```

Also, we can use it as shown here:

```
cars.stream()
  .collect(Streams.distinctByKey(Car::getBrand))
  .values()
  .forEach(System.out::println);
```

While this is a nice job that also works for null values, we can come up with other ideas that don't work for null values. For instance, we can rely on ConcurrentHashMap and putIfAbsent(), as follows (again, this doesn't work for null values):

```
public static <T> Predicate<T> distinctByKey(
    Function<? super T, ?> function) {

  Map<Object, Boolean> seen = new ConcurrentHashMap<>();

  return t -> seen.putIfAbsent(function.apply(t),
    Boolean.TRUE) == null;
}
```

Alternatively, we can optimize this approach a little bit and use a Set:

```
public static <T> Predicate<T> distinctByKey(
    Function<? super T, ?> function) {

  Set<Object> seen = ConcurrentHashMap.newKeySet();

  return t -> seen.add(function.apply(t));
}
```

We can use these two approaches, as shown in the following examples:

```
cars.stream()
    .filter(Streams.distinctByKey(Car::getBrand))
    .forEach(System.out::println);

cars.stream()
    .filter(Streams.distinctByKey(Car::getFuel))
    .forEach(System.out::println);
```

As a challenge, implement a `distinctByKeys()` operation using multiple keys.

205. Writing a custom collector that takes/skips a given number of elements

In *Problem 202*, we wrote a handful of custom collectors grouped in the `MyCollectors` class. Now, let's continue our journey, and let's try to add two more custom collectors here to take and/or keep a given number of elements from the current stream.

Let's assume the following model and data:

```java
public class Car {

  private final String brand;
  private final String fuel;
  private final int horsepower;

  ...
}

List<Car> cars = List.of(
  new Car("Chevrolet", "diesel", 350),
  ... // 10 more
  new Car("Lexus", "diesel", 300)
);
```

The Stream API provides an intermediate operation named `limit(long n)`, which can be used to truncate the stream to n elements. So, if this is exactly what we want, then we can use it out of the box. For instance, we can limit the resulting stream to the first five cars, as follows:

```java
List<Car> first5CarsLimit = cars.stream()
  .limit(5)
  .collect(Collectors.toList());
```

Moreover, the Stream API provides an intermediate operation named `skip(long n)`, which can be used to skip the first n elements in the stream pipeline. For instance, we can skip the first five cars, as follows:

```java
List<Car> last5CarsSkip = cars.stream()
  .skip(5)
  .collect(Collectors.toList());
```

However, there are cases when we need to compute different things and collect only the first/last five results. In such cases, a custom collector is welcome.

By relying on the `Collector.of()` method (as detailed in *Problem 202*), we can write a custom collector that keeps/collects the first n elements, as follows (just for fun, let's collect these *n* elements in an unmodifiable list):

```
public static <T> Collector<T, List<T>, List<T>>
   toUnmodifiableListKeep(int max) {

  return Collector.of(ArrayList::new,
    (list, value) -> {
       if (list.size() < max) {
         list.add(value);
       }
    },
    (left, right) -> {
       left.addAll(right);
       return left;
    },
    Collections::unmodifiableList);
}
```

So the supplier is `ArrayList::new`, the accumulator is `List.add()`, the combiner is `List.addAll()`, and the finalizer is `Collections::unmodifiableList`. Basically, the accumulator's job is to accumulate elements only until the given `max` is reached. From that point forward, nothing gets accumulated. This way, we can keep only the first five cars, as follows:

```
List<Car> first5Cars = cars.stream()
   .collect(MyCollectors.toUnmodifiableListKeep(5));
```

On the other hand, if we want to skip the first n elements and collect the rest, then we can try to accumulate `null` elements until we reach the given `index`. From this point forward, we accumulate the real elements. Finally, the finalizer removes the part of the list containing `null` values (from 0 to the given index) and returns an unmodifiable list from the remaining elements (from the given `index` to the end):

```
public static <T> Collector<T, List<T>, List<T>>
   toUnmodifiableListSkip(int index) {

  return Collector.of(ArrayList::new,
    (list, value) -> {
       if (list.size() >= index) {
         list.add(value);
       } else {
         list.add(null);
       }
    },
    (left, right) -> {
       left.addAll(right);

       return left;
```

```
    },
    list -> Collections.unmodifiableList(
      list.subList(index, list.size()))));
}
```

Alternatively, we can optimize this approach by using a supplier class that contains the resulting list and a counter. While the given index is not reached, we simply increase the counter. Once the given index is reached, we start to accumulate elements:

```
public static <T> Collector<T, ?, List<T>>
    toUnmodifiableListSkip(int index) {

  class Sublist {

    int index;
    List<T> list = new ArrayList<>();
  }

  return Collector.of(Sublist::new,
    (sublist, value) -> {
      if (sublist.index >= index) {
        sublist.list.add(value);
      } else {
        sublist.index++;
      }
    },
    (left, right) -> {
      left.list.addAll(right.list);
      left.index = left.index + right.index;

      return left;
    },
    sublist -> Collections.unmodifiableList(sublist.list));
}
```

Both of these approaches can be used, as shown in the following example:

```
List<Car> last5Cars = cars.stream()
  .collect(MyCollectors.toUnmodifiableListSkip(5));
```

Challenge yourself to implement a custom collector that collects in a given range.

206. Implementing a Function that takes five (or any other arbitrary number of) arguments

We know that Java already has java.util.function.Function and the specialization of it, java.util. function.BiFunction. The Function interface defines the method apply(T, t), while BiFunction has apply(T t, U u).

In this context, we can define a TriFunction, FourFunction, or (why not?) a FiveFunction functional interface, as follows (all of these are specializations of Function):

```
@FunctionalInterface
public interface FiveFunction <T1, T2, T3, T4, T5, R> {

    R apply(T1 t1, T2 t2, T3 t3, T4 t4, T5 t5);
}
```

As its name suggests, this functional interface takes five arguments.

Now, let's use it! Let's assume that we have the following model:

```
public class PL4 {

    private final double a;
    private final double b;
    private final double c;
    private final double d;
    private final double x;

    public PL4(double a, double b,
               double c, double d, double x) {
        this.a = a;
        this.b = b;
        this.c = c;
        this.d = d;
        this.x = x;
    }

    // getters

    public double compute() {
        return d + ((a - d) / (1 + (Math.pow(x / c, b))));
    }

    // equals(), hashCode(), toString()
}
```

The `compute()` method shapes a formula known as the Four-Parameter Logistic (4PL - https://www. myassays.com/four-parameter-logistic-regression.html). Without getting into irrelevant details, we pass, as inputs, four variables (a, b, c, and d) and, for different values of the x coordinate, we compute the y coordinate. The (x, y) pair of coordinates describes a curve (linear graphic).

We need a `PL4` instance for each x coordinate, and for each such instance, we call the `compute()` method. This means that we can use the `FiveFunction` interface in `Logistics` via the following helper:

```
public final class Logistics {
    ...
    public static <T1, T2, T3, T4, X, R> R create(
        T1 t1, T2 t2, T3 t3, T4 t4, X x,
        FiveFunction<T1, T2, T3, T4, X, R> f) {

        return f.apply(t1, t2, t3, t4, x);
    }
    ...
}
```

This acts as a factory for `PL4`:

```
PL4 pl4_1 = Logistics.create(
    4.19, -1.10, 12.65, 0.03, 40.3, PL4::new);
PL4 pl4_2 = Logistics.create(
    4.19, -1.10, 12.65, 0.03, 100.0, PL4::new);
...
PL4 pl4_8 = Logistics.create(
    4.19, -1.10, 12.65, 0.03, 1400.6, PL4::new);

System.out.println(pl4_1.compute());
System.out.println(pl4_2.compute());
...
System.out.println(pl4_8.compute());
```

However, if all we need is just the list of y coordinates, then we can write a helper method in `Logistics`, as follows:

```
public final class Logistics {
    ...
    public static <T1, T2, T3, T4, X, R> List<R> compute(
        T1 t1, T2 t2, T3 t3, T4 t4, List<X> allX,
        FiveFunction<T1, T2, T3, T4, X, R> f) {

        List<R> allY = new ArrayList<>();
```

```
    for (X x : allX) {
      allY.add(f.apply(t1, t2, t3, t4, x));
    }

    return allY;
  }
  ...
}
```

We can call this method as follows (here, we pass the 4PL formula, but it can be any other formula with five double parameters):

```
FiveFunction<Double, Double, Double, Double, Double, Double>
    pl4 = (a, b, c, d, x) -> d + ((a - d) /
                       (1 + (Math.pow(x / c, b)))));

List<Double> allX = List.of(40.3, 100.0, 250.2, 400.1,
                            600.6, 800.4, 1150.4, 1400.6);

List<Double> allY = Logistics.compute(4.19, -1.10, 12.65,
                            0.03, allX, pl4);
```

You can find the complete example in the bundled code.

207. Implementing a Consumer that takes five (or any other arbitrary number of) arguments

Before continuing with this problem, I strongly recommend that you read *Problem 206*.

Writing a custom Consumer that takes five arguments can be done as follows:

```
@FunctionalInterface
public interface FiveConsumer <T1, T2, T3, T4, T5> {

  void accept (T1 t1, T2 t2, T3 t3, T4 t4, T5 t5);
}
```

This is the five-arity specialization of the Java Consumer, just as the built-in BiConsumer is the two-arity specialization of the Java Consumer.

We can use FiveConsumer in conjunction with the PL4 formula, as follows (here, we compute y for x = 40.3):

```
FiveConsumer<Double, Double, Double, Double, Double>
  pl4c = (a, b, c, d, x) -> Logistics.pl4(a, b, c, d, x);
```

```
pl4c.accept(4.19, -1.10, 12.65, 0.03, 40.3);
```

The `Logistics.pl4()` is the method that contains the formula and displays the result:

```
public static void pl4(Double a, Double b,
                       Double c, Double d, Double x) {

  System.out.println(d + ((a - d) / (1
                     + (Math.pow(x / c, b)))));
}
```

Next, let's see how we can partially apply a `Function`.

208. Partially applying a Function

A `Function` that is partially applied is a `Function` that applies only a part of its arguments, returning another `Function`. For instance, here is a `TriFunction` (a functional function with three arguments) that contains the `apply()` method, next to two `default` methods that partially apply this function:

```
@FunctionalInterface
public interface TriFunction <T1, T2, T3, R> {

  R apply(T1 t1, T2 t2, T3 t3);

  default BiFunction<T2, T3, R> applyOnly(T1 t1) {
    return (t2, t3) -> apply(t1, t2, t3);
  }

  default Function<T3, R> applyOnly(T1 t1, T2 t2) {
    return (t3) -> apply(t1, t2, t3);
  }
}
```

As you can see, `applyOnly(T1 t1)` applies only the `t1` argument and returns a `BiFunction`. On the other hand, `applyOnly(T1 t1, T2 t2)` applies only `t1` and `t2`, returning a `Function`.

Let's see how we can use these methods. For instance, let's consider the formula $(a+b+c)^2 = a^2+b^2+c^2+2ab+2bc+2ca$, which can be shaped via the `TriFunction`, as follows:

```
TriFunction<Double, Double, Double, Double> abc2 = (a, b, c)
  -> Math.pow(a, 2) + Math.pow(b, 2) + Math.pow(c, 2)
     + 2.0*a*b + 2*b*c + 2*c*a;

System.out.println("abc2 (1): " + abc2.apply(1.0, 2.0, 1.0));
```

```
System.out.println("abc2 (2): " + abc2.apply(1.0, 2.0, 2.0));
System.out.println("abc2 (3): " + abc2.apply(1.0, 2.0, 3.0));
```

Here, we call apply(T1 t1, T2 t2, T3 t3) three times. As you can see, only the c term has a different value per call, while a and b are constantly equal with 1.0 and 2.0, respectively. This means that we can use apply(T1 t1, T2 t2) for a and b, and apply(T1 t1) for c, as follows:

```
Function<Double, Double> abc2Only1 = abc2.applyOnly(1.0, 2.0);

System.out.println("abc2Only1 (1): " + abc2Only1.apply(1.0));
System.out.println("abc2Only1 (2): " + abc2Only1.apply(2.0));
System.out.println("abc2Only1 (3): " + abc2Only1.apply(3.0));
```

If we assume that only a is constant (1.0) while b and c have different values per call, then we can use apply(T1 t1) for a and apply(T1 t1, T2 t2) for b and c, as follows:

```
BiFunction<Double, Double, Double> abc2Only2
    = abc2.applyOnly(1.0);

System.out.println("abc2Only2 (1): "
    + abc2Only2.apply(2.0, 3.0));
System.out.println("abc2Only2 (2): "
    + abc2Only2.apply(1.0, 2.0));
System.out.println("abc2Only2 (3): "
    + abc2Only2.apply(3.0, 2.0));
```

Mission accomplished!

Summary

This chapter covered 24 problems. Most of them focused on working with predicates, functions, and collectors, but we also covered the JDK 16 mapMulti() operation, refactoring imperative code to functional code, and much more.

Join our community on Discord

Join our community's Discord space for discussions with the author and other readers:

```
https://discord.gg/8mgytp5DGQ
```

10

Concurrency — Virtual Threads and Structured Concurrency

This chapter includes 16 problems that briefly introduce *virtual threads* and *structured concurrency*.

If you don't have a background in concurrency in Java, then I strongly recommend postponing this chapter until after you have read some good introductory coverage on the topic. For instance, you could try out *Chapters 10* and *11* from *Java Coding Problems, First Edition*.

Virtual threads are one of the most important and astonishing features added by Java in the last few years. They have a significant impact on how we will continue to write and understand concurrent code from this point forward. In this chapter, you'll learn, step by step, every single detail of this topic and the *structured concurrency* paradigm.

After this chapter, you'll be quite knowledgeable in working with virtual threads and structured concurrency.

Problems

Use the following problems to test your programming prowess in virtual threads and structured concurrency in Java. I strongly encourage you to give each problem a try before you turn to the solutions and download the example programs:

209. **Explaining concurrency vs. parallelism:** Provide a brief but meaningful explanation of concurrency vs. parallelism.

210. **Introducing structured concurrency:** Write an example highlighting the main issues of "unstructured" concurrency. Moreover, provide an introduction to the structured concurrency paradigm.

211. **Introducing virtual threads:** Explain and exemplify the main concepts of virtual threads.

212. **Using the ExecutorService for virtual threads:** Write several examples that highlight the *task-per-thread* model via ExecutorService and virtual threads.

213. **Explaining how virtual threads work:** Provide comprehensive coverage of how virtual threads work internally.

214. **Hooking virtual threads and sync code:** Explain and exemplify via a meaningful snippet of code how virtual threads and sync code work together.

215. **Exemplifying thread context switching:** Write several examples that show how *thread context switching* works for virtual threads.

216. **Introducing the ExecutorService invoke all/any for virtual threads – part 1:** Provide a brief introduction of `ExecutorService` invoke all/any for virtual threads.

217. **Introducing the ExecutorServiceinvoke all/any for virtual threads – part 2:** Re-write the example of "unstructured" concurrency from *Problem 210* via `ExecutorService` invoke all/any for virtual threads.

218. **Hooking task state:** Explain and exemplify the new `Future#state()` API.

219. **Combining new VirtualThreadPerTaskExecutor() and streams:** Write several examples that introduce how Java stream pipelines can be combined with the `newVirtualThreadPerTaskExecutor()` executor.

220. **Introducing a scope object (StructuredTaskScope):** Provide a brief introduction of structured concurrency via the `StructuredTaskScope` API.

221. **Introducing ShutdownOnSuccess:** Exemplify the `ShutdownOnSuccess` flavor of `StructuredTaskScope`.

222. **Introducing ShutdownOnFailure:** Exemplify the `ShutdownOnFailure` flavor of `StructuredTaskScope`.

223. **Combining StructuredTaskScope and streams:** Write several examples that introduce how Java stream pipelines can be combined with `StructuredTaskScope`.

224. **Observing and monitoring virtual threads:** Exemplify how we can use **JFR (Java Flight Recorder)**, **JMX (Java Management Extensions)**, and any other tool that you like, for observing and monitoring virtual threads.

The following sections describe solutions to the preceding problems. Remember that there usually isn't a single correct way to solve a particular problem. Also, remember that the explanations shown here include only the most interesting and important details needed to solve the problems. Download the example solutions to see additional details and to experiment with the programs at `https://github.com/PacktPublishing/Java-Coding-Problems-Second-Edition/tree/main/Chapter10`.

209. Explaining concurrency vs. parallelism

Before tackling the main topic of this chapter, *structured concurrency*, let's forget about *structure*, and let's keep only *concurrency*. Next, let's put *concurrency* against *parallelism*, since these two notions are often a source of confusion.

Both of them, concurrency and parallelism, use *tasks* as the main unit of work. However, the way that they handle these tasks makes them very different.

In the case of parallelism, a task is split into subtasks across multiple CPU cores. These subtasks are computed in parallel, and each of them represents a partial solution for the given task. By joining these partial solutions, we obtain the solution. Ideally, solving a task in parallel should result in less wall-clock time than in the case of solving the same task sequentially. In a nutshell, in parallelism, at least two threads run at the same time, which means that parallelism can solve a single task faster.

In the case of concurrency, we try to solve as many tasks as possible via several threads that compete with each other, progressing in a time-slicing fashion. This means that concurrency can complete multiple tasks faster. This is why concurrency is also referred to as virtual parallelism.

The following figure depicts parallelism vs. concurrency:

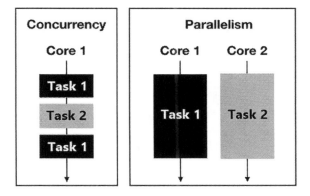

Figure 10.1: Concurrency vs. parallelism

In parallelism, tasks (subtasks) are part of the implemented solution/algorithm. We write the code, set/control the number of tasks, and use them in a context that has parallel computational capabilities. On the other hand, in concurrency, tasks are part of the problem.

Typically, we measure parallelism efficiency in *latency* (the amount of time needed to complete the task), while the efficiency of concurrency is measured in *throughput* (the number of tasks that we can solve).

Moreover, in parallelism, tasks control resource allocation (CPU time, I/O operations, and so on). On the other hand, in concurrency, multiple threads compete with each other to gain as many resources (I/O) as possible. They cannot control resource allocation.

In parallelism, threads operate on CPU cores in such a way that every core is busy. In concurrency, threads operate on tasks in such a way that, ideally, each thread has a separate task.

Commonly, when parallelism and concurrency are compared, somebody comes and says: *How about asynchronous methods?*

It is important to understand that *asynchrony* is a separate concept. Asynchrony is about the capability to accomplish non-blocking operations. For instance, an application sends an HTTP request, but it doesn't just wait for the response. It goes and solves something else (other tasks) while waiting for the response. We do asynchronous tasks every day. For instance, we start the washing machine and then go to clean other parts of the house. We don't just wait by the washing machine until it is finished.

210. Introducing structured concurrency

If you are as old as I am, then most probably you started programming with a language such as BASIC or a similar unstructured programming language. At that time, an application was just a sequence of lines that defined a sequential logic/behavior via a bunch of GOTO statements, driving the flow by jumping like a kangaroo back and forward between the code lines. Well, in Java, the building blocks of a typical concurrent code are so primitive that the code looks somewhat like unstructured programming because it is hard to follow and understand. Moreover, a thread dump of a concurrent task doesn't provide the needed answers.

Let's follow a snippet of Java concurrent code and stop every time we have a question (always check the code below the question). The task is to concurrently load three testers by ID and team them up in a testing team. First, let's list the server code (we will use this simple code to serve us in this problem and subsequent problems):

```java
public static String fetchTester(int id)
       throws IOException, InterruptedException {

  HttpClient client = HttpClient.newHttpClient();

  HttpRequest requestGet = HttpRequest.newBuilder()
    .GET()
    .uri(URI.create("https://reqres.in/api/users/" + id))
    .build();

  HttpResponse<String> responseGet = client.send(
    requestGet, HttpResponse.BodyHandlers.ofString());

  if (responseGet.statusCode() == 200) {
    return responseGet.body();
  }

  throw new UserNotFoundException("Code: "
    + responseGet.statusCode());
}
```

Next, the code that we are especially interested in starts as follows:

```java
private static final ExecutorService executor
  = Executors.newFixedThreadPool(2);

public static TestingTeam buildTestingTeam()
    throws InterruptedException {
  ...
```

First stop: As you can see, buildTestingTeam() throws an InterruptedException. So if the thread executing buildTestingTeam() gets interrupted, how can we easily interrupt the following threads?

```
Future<String> future1 = futureTester(1);
Future<String> future2 = futureTester(2);
Future<String> future3 = futureTester(3);

try {
    ...
```

Second stop: Here, we have three get() calls. So the current thread waits for other threads to complete. Can we easily observe those threads?

```
String tester1 = future1.get();
String tester2 = future2.get();
String tester3 = future3.get();

logger.info(tester1);
logger.info(tester2);
logger.info(tester3);

return new TestingTeam(tester1, tester2, tester3);

} catch (ExecutionException ex) {
    ...
```

Third stop: If an ExecutionException is caught, then we know that one of these three Future instances has failed. Can we easily cancel the remaining two, or will they just hang on there? future1 will probably fail while future2 and future3 will complete successfully, or maybe future2 will complete successfully while future3 will just run forever (a so-called *orphan* thread). This can lead to serious mismatches in the expected results, memory leaks, and so on:

```
    throw new RuntimeException(ex);
} finally {
    ...
```

Fourth stop: The next line of code is used to shut down the executor, but it is so easy to overlook. Is this the proper place to do this?

```
    shutdownExecutor(executor);
    }
}
```

Fifth stop: If you didn't spot the previous line of code, then it is legitimate to ask yourself how/where this executor got shut down:

```
public static Future<String> futureTester(int id) {

  return executor.submit(() -> fetchTester(id));
}
```

We skip the rest of the code, since you can find it in the bundled code.

Of course, we can implement code answers to each of these questions via error handling, task abandons and abortions, `ExecutorService`, and so on, but this means a lot of work for the developer. Writing failsafe solutions that carefully cover all possible scenarios across multiple tasks/subtasks while tracking their progress in a concurrent environment is not an easy job. That's not to mention how hard it is to understand and maintain the resulting code by another developer, or even the same developer after 1–2 years or even months.

It is time to add some structure to this code, so let's introduce *structured concurrency* (or Project Loom).

Structured concurrency relies on several pillars meant to bring lightweight concurrency to Java. The fundamental pillar or principle of structured concurrency is highlighted next.

Important note

The fundamental principle of structured concurrency is that when a task has to be solved concurrently, then all the threads needed to solve it are spun and rejoined in the same block of code. In other words, all these threads' lifetimes are bound to the block's lexical scope, so we have clear and explicit entry-exit points for each concurrent code block.

Based on this principle, the thread that initiates a concurrent context is the *parent-thread* or the *owner-thread*. All threads started by the parent-thread are *children-threads* or *forks*, so between them, these threads are siblings. Together, the parent-thread and the child-threads define a *parent-child hierarchy*.

Putting the structured concurrency principle into a diagram will show us the following:

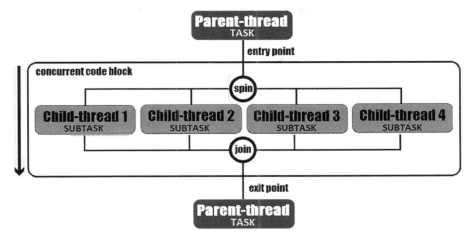

Figure 10.2: Parent-child hierarchy in structured concurrency

In the context of the parent-child hierarchy, we have support for error/exception handling with short-circuiting, cancellation propagation, and monitoring/observability:

- *Error/exception handling with short-circuiting*: If a child-thread fails, then all child-threads are canceled unless they are complete. For instance, if `futureTester(1)` fails, then `futureTester(2)` and `futureTester(3)` are automatically canceled.

- *Cancellation propagation*: If the parent-thread is interrupted until joining the child-threads is over, then these forks (the child-threads/subtasks) are canceled automatically. For instance, if the thread executing `buildTestingTeam()` gets interrupted, then its three forks are automatically canceled.

- *Monitoring/observability*: A thread dump reveals a crystal-clear image of the entire parent-child hierarchy, no matter how many levels have been spawned. Moreover, in structured concurrency, we take advantage of scheduling and the memory management of threads.

While these are purely concepts, writing code that respects and follows these concepts requires the proper API and the following awesome callout:

Figure 10.3: Don't reuse virtual threads

Cut this out and stick it somewhere so that you see it every day! So in structured concurrency, **don't reuse virtual threads**. I know what you are thinking: *hey dude, threads are expensive and limited, so we have to reuse them*. A quick hint: we are talking about *virtual threads* (massive throughput), not *classical threads*, but the virtual threads topic is covered in the next problem.

211. Introducing virtual threads

Java allows us to write multithreaded applications via the `java.lang.Thread` class. These are classical Java threads that are basically just thin wrappers of OS (kernel) threads. As you'll see, these classical Java threads are referred to as *platform threads*, and they have been available for quite a long time (since JDK 1.1, as the following diagram reveals):

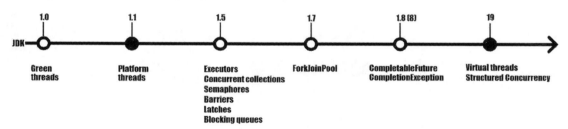

Figure 10.4: JDK multithreading evolution

Next, let's move on to JDK 19 virtual threads.

What's the problem with platform (OS) threads?

OS threads are expensive in every single way, or more specifically, they are costly in terms of time and space. Creating OS threads is, therefore, a costly operation that requires a lot of stack space (around 20 megabytes) to store their context, Java call stacks, and additional resources. Moreover, the OS thread scheduler is responsible for scheduling Java threads, which is another costly operation that requires moving around a significant amount of data. This is referred to as *thread context switching*.

In the following figure, you can see the one-to-one relationship between a Java thread and an OS thread:

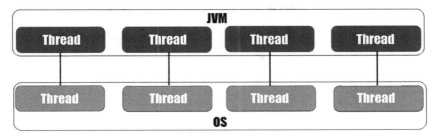

Figure 10.5: JVM to OS threads

For decades, our multithreaded applications have run in this context. All this time and experience taught us that we can create a limited number of Java threads (because of low throughput) and that we should reuse them wisely. The number of Java threads is a limiting factor that is usually exhausted before other resources, such as network connections, CPU, and so on. Java doesn't differentiate between threads that perform intensive computational tasks (i.e., threads that really exploit the CPU) or those that just wait for data (i.e., they just hang on the CPU).

Let's do a quick exercise. Let's assume that our machine has 8 GB of memory, and a single Java thread needs 20 MB. This means that we have room for around 400 Java threads (8 GB = 8,000 MB / 20 MB = 400 threads). Next, let's assume that these threads perform I/O operations over a network. Each I/O operation needs around 100 ms to complete, while the request preparation and response processing needs around 500 ns. So a thread works for 1,000 ns (0.001 ms) and then waits for 100 ms (100,000,000 ns) for the I/O operation to complete. This means that at 8 GB of memory, the 400 threads will use 0.4% of CPU availability (under 1%), which is very low. We can conclude that a thread is idle for 99.99% of the time.

Based on this exercise, it is quite obvious that Java threads become a bottleneck in throughput that doesn't allow us to solicit hardware at full capacity. Of course, we can sweeten the situation a little bit by using *thread pools* to minimize the costs, but it still does not solve the major issues of dealing with resources. You have to go for `CompletableFuture`, reactive programming (for instance, Spring `Mono` and `Flux`), and so on.

However, how many classical Java threads can we create? We can easily find out by running a simple snippet of code, as follows:

```
AtomicLong counterOSThreads = new AtomicLong();

while (true) {
  new Thread(() -> {
    long currentOSThreadNr
      = counterOSThreads.incrementAndGet();
    System.out.println("Thread: " + currentOSThreadNr);

    LockSupport.park();
```

```
      }).start();
  }
```

Alternatively, if we want to taste from the new concurrent API, we can call the new `Thread.ofPlatform()` method, as follows (`OfPlatform` is a `sealed` interface, introduced in JDK 19):

```
AtomicLong counterOSThreads = new AtomicLong();

while (true) {
  Thread.ofPlatform().start(() -> {
    long currentOSThreadNr
      = counterOSThreads.incrementAndGet();
    System.out.println("Thread: " + currentOSThreadNr);
    LockSupport.park();
  });
}
```

On my machine, I got an `OutOfMemoryError` after around 40,000 Java threads. Depending on your OS and hardware, this number may vary.

The `Thread.ofPlatform()` method was added in JDK 19 to easily distinguish between Java threads (i.e., classical Java threads as we have known them for decades – thin wrappers of OS threads) and the new kids in town, virtual threads.

What are virtual threads?

Virtual threads were introduced in JDK 19 as a preview (JEP 425), and they became a final feature in JDK 21 (JEP 444). Virtual threads run on top of platform threads in a one-to-many relationship, while the platform threads run on top of OS threads in a one-to-one relationship, as shown in the following figure:

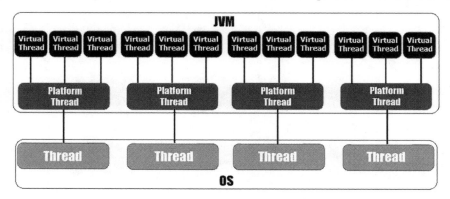

Figure 10.6: Virtual threads architecture

If we break this figure down into a few words, then we can say that JDK maps a large number of virtual threads to a small number of OS threads.

Before creating a virtual thread, let's see two important notes that will help us to quickly understand the fundamentals of virtual threads. First, let's have a quick note about a virtual thread's memory footprint:

Important note

Virtual threads are not wrappers of OS threads. They are lightweight Java entities (they have their own stack memory with a small footprint – only a few hundred bytes) that are cheap to create, block, and destroy (creating a virtual thread is around 1,000 times cheaper than creating a classical Java thread). There can be many of them at the same time (millions) so that they sustain a massive throughput. Virtual threads should not be reused (they are disposable) or pooled.

When we talk about virtual threads, there are more things that we should unlearn than things that we should learn. But where are virtual threads stored, and who's responsible for scheduling them accordingly?

Important note

Virtual threads are stored in the JVM heap (so they take advantage of Garbage Collector) instead of the OS stack. Moreover, virtual threads are scheduled by the JVM via a *work-stealing* ForkJoinPool scheduler. Practically, JVM schedules and orchestrates virtual threads to run on platform threads in such a way that a platform thread executes only one virtual thread at a time.

Next, let's create a virtual thread.

Creating a virtual thread

From the API perspective, a virtual thread is another flavor of java.lang.Thread. If we dig a little bit via getClass(), we can see that a virtual thread class is java.lang.VirtualThread, which is a final non-public class that extends the BaseVirtualThread class, which, in turn, is a sealed abstract class that extends java.lang.Thread:

```
final class VirtualThread extends BaseVirtualThread {…}


sealed abstract class BaseVirtualThread extends Thread
    permits VirtualThread, ThreadBuilders.BoundVirtualThread {…}
```

Let's consider that we have the following task (Runnable):

```
Runnable task = () -> logger.info(
    Thread.currentThread().toString());
```

Creating and starting a virtual thread

We can create and start a virtual thread for our task via the startVirtualThread(Runnable task) method, as follows:

```
Thread vThread = Thread.startVirtualThread(task);

// next you can set its name
vThread.setName("my_vThread");
```

The returned vThread is scheduled for execution by the JVM itself. But we can also create and start a virtual thread via Thread.ofVirtual(), which returns OfVirtual (the sealed interface introduced in JDK 19), as follows:

```
Thread vThread =Thread.ofVirtual().start(task);

// a named virtual thread
Thread.ofVirtual().name("my_vThread").start(task);
```

Now, vThread will solve our task.

Moreover, we have the Thread.Builder interface (and Thread.Builder.OfVirtual subinterface) that can be used to create a virtual thread, as follows:

```
Thread.Builder builder
    = Thread.ofVirtual().name("my_vThread");
Thread vThread = builder.start(task);
```

Here is another example of creating two virtual threads via Thread.Builder:

```
Thread.Builder builder
    = Thread.ofVirtual().name("vThread-", 1);

// name "vThread-1"
Thread vThread1 = builder.start(task);
vThread1.join();
logger.info(() -> vThread1.getName() + " terminated");

// name "vThread-2"
Thread vThread2 = builder.start(task);
vThread2.join();
logger.info(() -> vThread2.getName() + " terminated");
```

You can check out these examples further in the bundled code.

Waiting for a virtual task to terminate

The given `task` is executed by a virtual thread, while the main thread is not blocked. In order to wait for the virtual thread to terminate, we have to call one of the `join()` flavors. We have `join()` without arguments that waits indefinitely, and a few flavors that wait for a given time (for instance, `join(Duration duration)` and `join(long millis)`):

```
vThread.join();
```

These methods throw an `InterruptedException`, so you have to catch it and handle it (or just throw it). Now, because of `join()`, the main thread cannot terminate before the virtual thread. It has to wait until the virtual thread completes.

Creating an unstarted virtual thread

Creating an unstarted virtual thread can be done via `unstarted(Runnable task)`, as follows:

```
Thread vThread = Thread.ofVirtual().unstarted(task);
```

Or via `Thread.Builder` as follows:

```
Thread.Builder builder = Thread.ofVirtual();
Thread vThread = builder.unstarted(task);
```

This time, the thread is not scheduled for execution. It will be scheduled for execution only after we explicitly call the `start()` method:

```
vThread.start();
```

We can check if a thread is alive (i.e., it was started but not terminated) via the `isAlive()` method:

```
boolean isalive = vThread.isAlive();
```

The `unstarted()` method is available for platform threads as well (there is also the `Thread.Builder.OfPlatform` subinterface):

```
Thread pThread = Thread.ofPlatform().unstarted(task);
```

We can start pThread by calling the `start()` method.

Creating a ThreadFactory for virtual threads

You can create a `ThreadFactory` of virtual threads, as follows:

```
ThreadFactory tfVirtual = Thread.ofVirtual().factory();


ThreadFactory tfVirtual = Thread.ofVirtual()
    .name("vt-", 0).factory(); // 'vt-' name prefix, 0 counter
```

Or, via `Thread.Builder`, as follows:

```
Thread.Builder builder = Thread.ofVirtual().name("vt-", 0);
ThreadFactory tfVirtual = builder.factory();
```

And a `ThreadFactory` for platform threads, as follows (you can use `Thread.Builder` as well):

```
ThreadFactory tfPlatform = Thread.ofPlatform()
  .name("pt-", 0).factory(); // 'pt-' name prefix, 0 counter
```

Or a `ThreadFactory` that we can use to switch between virtual/platform threads, as follows:

```
static class SimpleThreadFactory implements ThreadFactory {

  @Override
  public Thread newThread(Runnable r) {
    // return new Thread(r);              // platform thread
    return Thread.ofVirtual().unstarted(r); // virtual thread
  }
}
```

Next, we can use any of these factories via the `ThreadFactory.newThread(Runnable task)`, as follows:

```
tfVirtual.newThread(task).start();
tfPlatform.newThread(task).start();

SimpleThreadFactory stf = new SimpleThreadFactory();
stf.newThread(task).start();
```

If the thread factory starts the created thread as well, then there is no need to explicitly call the `start()` method.

Checking a virtual thread's details

Moreover, we can check if a certain thread is a platform thread or a virtual thread via `isVirtual()`:

```
Thread vThread = Thread.ofVirtual()
  .name("my_vThread").unstarted(task);
Thread pThread1 = Thread.ofPlatform()
  .name("my_pThread").unstarted(task);
Thread pThread2 = new Thread(() -> {});

logger.info(() -> "Is vThread virtual ? "
  + vThread.isVirtual());  // true
logger.info(() -> "Is pThread1 virtual ? "
  + pThread1.isVirtual()); // false
logger.info(() -> "Is pThread2 virtual ? "
  + pThread2.isVirtual()); // false
```

Obviously, only vThread is a virtual thread.

A virtual thread always runs as a daemon thread. The isDaemon() method returns true, and trying to call setDaemon(false) will throw an exception.

The priority of a virtual thread is always NORM_PRIORITY (calling getPriority() always returns 5 – constant int for NORM_PRIORITY). Calling setPriority() with a different value has no effect.

A virtual thread cannot be part of a thread group because it already belongs to the *VirtualThreads* group. Calling getThreadGroup().getName() returns *VirtualThreads*.

A virtual thread has no permission with Security Manager (which is deprecated anyway).

Printing a thread (toString())

If we print a virtual thread (calling the toString() method), then the output will be something like the following:

```
VirtualThread[#22]/runnable@ForkJoinPool-1-worker-1
VirtualThread[#26,vt-0]/runnable@ForkJoinPool-1-worker-1
```

In a nutshell, this output can be interpreted as follows: VirtualThread[#22] indicates that this is a virtual thread that contains the thread identifier (#22) with no name (in the case of VirtualThread[#26,vt-0], the id is #26 and the name is vt-0). Then, we have the runnable text, which indicates the state of the virtual thread (runnable means that the virtual thread is running). Next, we have the *carrier thread* of the virtual thread, which is a platform thread; ForkJoinPool-1-worker-1 contains the platform thread name (worker-1) of the default ForkJoinPool (ForkJoinPool-1).

How many virtual threads we can start

Finally, let's run code that allows us to see how many virtual threads we can create and start:

```
AtomicLong counterOSThreads = new AtomicLong();

while (true) {
  Thread.startVirtualThread(() -> {
    long currentOSThreadNr
      = counterOSThreads.incrementAndGet();
    System.out.println("Virtual thread: "
      + currentOSThreadNr);

    LockSupport.park();
  });
}
```

On my machine, this code started to slow down after around 14,000,000 virtual threads. It continues to run slowly while memory becomes available (Garbage Collector is in action), but it didn't crash. So a massive throughput!

Backward compatibility

Virtual threads are compatible with:

- Synchronized blocks
- Thread-local variables
- `Thread` and `currentThread()`
- Thread interruption (`InterruptedException`)

Basically, virtual threads work out of the box once you update to at least JDK 19. They heavily sustain a clean, readable, and more structured code, being the bricks behind the structured concurrency paradigm.

Avoiding fake conclusions (potentially myths)

There are a few fake conclusions about virtual threads that we should consider as follow:

- *Virtual threads are faster than platform threads (WRONG!)*: There can be a lot of virtual threads, but they are not faster than classical (platform) threads. They don't boost in-memory computational capabilities (for that, we have parallel streams). Don't conclude that virtual threads do some magic that makes them faster or more optimal to solve a task. So virtual threads can seriously improve throughput (since millions of them can wait for jobs), but they cannot improve latency. However, virtual threads can be launched much faster than platform threads (a virtual thread has a creation time measured in μs and needs space in the order of kB).
- *Virtual threads should be pooled (WRONG!)*: Virtual threads should not be part of any thread pool and should never be pooled.
- *Virtual threads are expensive (WRONG!)*: Virtual threads are not for free (nothing is for free), but they are cheaper to create, block, and destroy than platform threads. A virtual thread is 1,000x cheaper than a platform thread.
- *Virtual threads can release a task (WRONG!)*: This is not true! A virtual thread takes a task and will return a result unless it gets interrupted. It cannot release the task.
- *Blocking a virtual thread blocks its carrier thread (WRONG!)*: Blocking a virtual thread doesn't block its carrier thread. The carrier thread can serve other virtual threads.

212. Using the ExecutorService for virtual threads

Virtual threads allow us to write more expressive and straightforward concurrent code. Thanks to the massive throughput obtained via virtual threads, we can easily adopt the *task-per-thread* model (for an HTTP server, this means a request per thread, for a database, this means a transaction per thread, and so on). In other words, we can assign a new virtual thread for each concurrent task.

Trying to use the *task-per-thread* model with platform threads will result in a throughput limited by the number of hardware cores – this is explained by Little's law (`https://en.wikipedia.org/wiki/Little%27s_law`), $L = \lambda W$, or throughput equals average concurrency multiplied by latency.

Whenever possible, it is recommended to avoid interacting with threads directly. JDK sustains this via the ExecutorService/Executor API. More precisely, we are used to submitting a task (Runnable/Callable) to an ExecutorService/Executor and working with the returned Future. This pattern is valid for virtual threads as well.

So we don't have to write ourselves all the plumbing code to adopt the *task-per-thread model* for virtual threads because, starting with JDK 19, this model is available via the Executors class. More precisely, it's via the newVirtualThreadPerTaskExecutor() method, which creates an ExecutorService capable of creating an unbounded number of virtual threads that follow the *task-per-thread* model. This ExecutorService exposes methods that allow us to give tasks such as the submit() (as you'll see next) and invokeAll/Any() (as you'll see later) methods, returning a Future containing an exception or a result.

 Important note

Starting with JDK 19, the ExecutorService extends the AutoCloseable interface. In other words, we can use ExecutorService in a try-with-resources pattern.

Consider the following simple Runnable and Callable:

```
Runnable taskr = () ->logger.info(
  Thread.currentThread().toString());

Callable<Boolean> taskc = () -> {
  logger.info(Thread.currentThread().toString());
  return true;
};
```

Executing the Runnable/Callable can be done as follows (here, we submit 15 tasks (NUMBER_OF_TASKS = 15)):

```
try (ExecutorService executor
      = Executors.newVirtualThreadPerTaskExecutor()) {

  for (int i = 0; i < NUMBER_OF_TASKS; i++) {

    executor.submit(taskr); // executing Runnable
    executor.submit(taskc); // executing Callable
  }
}
```

Of course, in the case of Runnable/Callable, we can capture a Future and act accordingly, via the blocking get() method or whatever we want to do:

```
Future<?> future = executor.submit(taskr);
Future<Boolean> future = executor.submit(taskc);
```

A possible output looks as follows:

```
VirtualThread[#28]/runnable@ForkJoinPool-1-worker-6
VirtualThread[#31]/runnable@ForkJoinPool-1-worker-5
VirtualThread[#29]/runnable@ForkJoinPool-1-worker-7
VirtualThread[#25]/runnable@ForkJoinPool-1-worker-3
VirtualThread[#24]/runnable@ForkJoinPool-1-worker-2
VirtualThread[#27]/runnable@ForkJoinPool-1-worker-5
VirtualThread[#26]/runnable@ForkJoinPool-1-worker-4
VirtualThread[#22]/runnable@ForkJoinPool-1-worker-1
VirtualThread[#36]/runnable@ForkJoinPool-1-worker-1
VirtualThread[#37]/runnable@ForkJoinPool-1-worker-2
VirtualThread[#35]/runnable@ForkJoinPool-1-worker-7
VirtualThread[#34]/runnable@ForkJoinPool-1-worker-4
VirtualThread[#32]/runnable@ForkJoinPool-1-worker-3
VirtualThread[#33]/runnable@ForkJoinPool-1-worker-2
VirtualThread[#30]/runnable@ForkJoinPool-1-worker-1
```

Check out the virtual threads' IDs. They range between #22 and #37 without repetition. Each task is executed by its own virtual thread.

The *task-per-thread* model is also available for classical threads via newThreadPerTaskExecutor(ThreadFactory threadFactory). Here is an example:

```
static class SimpleThreadFactory implements ThreadFactory {

  @Override
  public Thread newThread(Runnable r) {
    return new Thread(r);   // classic
    // return Thread.ofVirtual().unstarted(r); // virtual
  }
}

try (ExecutorService executor =
```

```
        Executors.newThreadPerTaskExecutor(
            new SimpleThreadFactory())) {

    for (int i = 0; i < NUMBER_OF_TASKS; i++) {

        executor.submit(taskr); // executing Runnable
        executor.submit(taskc); // executing Callable
    }
}
```

As you can see, `newThreadPerTaskExecutor()` can be used for classic or virtual threads. The number of created threads is unbounded. By simply modifying the thread factory, we can switch between virtual/classic threads.

A possible output looks as follows:

```
Thread[#75,Thread-15,5,main]
Thread[#77,Thread-17,5,main]
Thread[#76,Thread-16,5,main]
Thread[#83,Thread-23,5,main]
Thread[#82,Thread-22,5,main]
Thread[#80,Thread-20,5,main]
Thread[#81,Thread-21,5,main]
Thread[#79,Thread-19,5,main]
Thread[#78,Thread-18,5,main]
Thread[#89,Thread-29,5,main]
Thread[#88,Thread-28,5,main]
Thread[#87,Thread-27,5,main]
Thread[#86,Thread-26,5,main]
Thread[#85,Thread-25,5,main]
Thread[#84,Thread-24,5,main]
```

Check out the threads' IDs. They range between #75 and #89 without repetition. Each task is executed by its own thread.

213. Explaining how virtual threads work

Now that we know how to create and start a virtual thread, let's see how they actually work.

Let's start with a meaningful diagram:

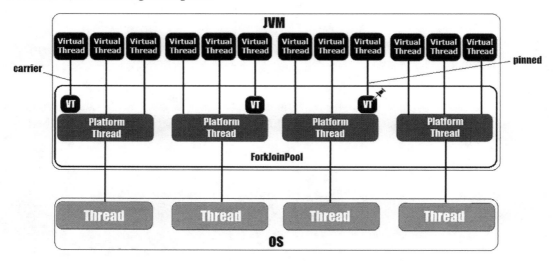

Figure 10.7: How virtual threads work

As you can see, *Figure 10.7* is similar to *Figure 10.6*, except that we have added a few more elements.

First of all, notice that the platform threads run under a ForkJoinPool umbrella. This is a **First-In-First-Out (FIFO)** dedicated fork/join pool, dedicated to scheduling and orchestrating the relationships between virtual threads and platform threads (detailed coverage of Java's fork/join framework is available in *Java Coding Problems, First Edition, Chapter 11*).

> **Important note**
>
> This dedicated ForkJoinPool is controlled by the JVM, and it acts as the virtual thread scheduler based on a FIFO queue. Its initial capacity (i.e., the number of threads) is equal to the number of available cores, and it can be increased to 256. The default virtual thread scheduler is implemented in the java.lang.VirtualThread class:
>
> ```
> private static ForkJoinPool createDefaultScheduler() {...}
> ```
>
> Do not confuse this ForkJoinPool with the one used for parallel streams (the Common Fork Join Pool - ForkJoinPool.commonPool()).

Between the virtual threads and the platform threads, there is a one-to-many association. Nevertheless, the JVM schedules virtual threads to run on platform threads in such a way that only one virtual thread runs on a platform thread at a time. When the JVM assigns a virtual thread to a platform thread, the so-called *stack chunk object* of the virtual thread is copied from the heap memory on the platform thread.

If the code running on a virtual thread encounters a blocking (I/O) operation that should be handled by the JVM, then the virtual thread is released by copying its *stack chunk object* back into the heap (this operation of copying the *stack chunk* between the heap memory and platform thread is the cost of blocking a virtual thread - this is much cheaper than blocking a platform thread). Meanwhile, the platform thread can run other virtual threads. When the blocking (I/O) of the released virtual thread is done, JVM reschedules the virtual thread for execution on a platform thread. This can be the same platform thread or another one.

Important note

The operation of assigning a virtual thread to a platform thread is called *mounting*. The operation of unassigning a virtual thread from the platform thread is called *unmounting*. The platform thread running the assigned virtual thread is called a *carrier thread*.

Let's see an example that reveals how the virtual threads are mounted:

```
private static final int NUMBER_OF_TASKS
  = Runtime.getRuntime().availableProcessors();

Runnable taskr = () ->
  logger.info(Thread.currentThread().toString());

try (ExecutorService executor
    = Executors.newVirtualThreadPerTaskExecutor()) {

  for (int i = 0; i < NUMBER_OF_TASKS + 1; i++) {
    executor.submit(taskr);
  }
}
```

In this snippet of code, we create a number of virtual threads equal to the number of available cores + 1. On my machine, I have 8 cores (so 8 *carriers*), and each of them carries a virtual thread. Since we have + 1, a *carrier* will work twice. The output reveals this scenario (check out the workers; here, worker-8 runs virtual threads #30 and #31):

```
VirtualThread[#25]/runnable@ForkJoinPool-1-worker-3
VirtualThread[#30]/runnable@ForkJoinPool-1-worker-8
VirtualThread[#28]/runnable@ForkJoinPool-1-worker-6
VirtualThread[#22]/runnable@ForkJoinPool-1-worker-1
VirtualThread[#24]/runnable@ForkJoinPool-1-worker-2
VirtualThread[#29]/runnable@ForkJoinPool-1-worker-7
VirtualThread[#26]/runnable@ForkJoinPool-1-worker-4
VirtualThread[#27]/runnable@ForkJoinPool-1-worker-5
VirtualThread[#31]/runnable@ForkJoinPool-1-worker-8
```

However, we can configure the `ForkJoinPool` via three system properties, as follows:

- `jdk.virtualThreadScheduler.parallelism` – the number of CPU cores
- `jdk.virtualThreadScheduler.maxPoolSize` – the maximum pool size (256)
- `jdk.virtualThreadScheduler.minRunnable` – the minimum number of running threads (half the pool size)

In a subsequent problem, we will use these properties to better shape *virtual thread context switching* (mounting/unmounting) details.

Capturing virtual threads

So far, we have learned that a virtual thread is mounted by the JVM to a platform thread, which becomes its carrier thread. Moreover, the carrier thread runs the virtual thread until it hits a blocking (I/O) operation. At that point, the virtual thread is unmounted from the carrier thread, and it will be rescheduled after the blocking (I/O) operation is done.

While this scenario is true for most of the blocking operations, resulting in unmounting the virtual threads and freeing the platform thread (and the underlying OS thread), there are a few exceptional cases when the virtual threads are not unmounted. There are two main causes for this behavior:

- Limitations on the OS (for instance, a significant number of filesystem operations)
- Limitations on the JDK (for instance, `Object.wait()`)

When the virtual thread cannot be unmounted from its carrier thread, it means that the carrier thread and the underlying OS thread are blocked. This may affect the scalability of the application, so if the platform threads pool allows it, the JVM can decide to add one more platform thread. So for a period of time, the number of platform threads may exceed the number of available cores.

Pinning virtual threads

There are also two other use cases when a virtual thread cannot be unmounted:

- When the virtual thread runs code inside a `synchronized` method/block
- When the virtual thread invokes a foreign function or native method (a topic covered in *Chapter 7*)

In this scenario, we say that the virtual thread is *pinned* to the carrier thread. This may affect the scalability of the application, but the JVM will not increase the number of platform threads. Instead of this, we should take action and refactor the `synchronized` blocks to ensure that the locking code is simple, clear, and short. Whenever possible, we should prefer `java.util.concurrent` locks instead of `synchronized` blocks. If we manage to avoid long and frequent locking periods, then we will not face any significant scalability issues. In future releases, the JDK team aims to eliminate the pinning inside `synchronized` blocks.

214. Hooking virtual threads and sync code

The goal of this problem is to highlight how virtual threads interact with synchronous code. For this, we use the built-in `java.util.concurrent.SynchronousQueue`. This is a built-in blocking queue that allows only one thread to operate at a time. More precisely, a thread that wants to insert an element in this queue is blocked until another thread attempts to remove an element from it, and vice versa. Basically, a thread cannot insert an element unless another thread attempts to remove an element.

Let's assume that a virtual thread attempts to insert an element into a `SynchronousQueue`, while a platform thread attempts to remove an element from this queue. In code lines, we have:

```
SynchronousQueue<Integer> queue = new SynchronousQueue<>();

Runnable task = () -> {
  logger.info(() -> Thread.currentThread().toString()
    + " sleeps for 5 seconds");
  try { Thread.sleep(Duration.ofSeconds(5)); }
    catch (InterruptedException ex) {}
  logger.info(() -> "Running "
    + Thread.currentThread().toString());

  queue.add(Integer.MAX_VALUE);
};

logger.info("Before running the task ...");

Thread vThread =Thread.ofVirtual().start(task);

logger.info(vThread.toString());
```

So the virtual thread (vThread) waits for 5 seconds before attempting to insert an element into the queue. However, it will not successfully insert an element until another thread attempts to remove an element from this queue:

```
logger.info(() -> Thread.currentThread().toString()
  + " can't take from the queue yet");

int max int = queue.take();

logger.info(() -> Thread.currentThread().toString()
  + "took from queue: " + maxint);

logger.info(vThread.toString());

logger.info("After running the task ...");
```

Here, the Thread.currentThread() refers to the main thread of the application, which is a platform thread not blocked by vThread. This thread successfully removes from the queue only if another thread attempts to insert (here, vThread):

The output of this code looks as follows:

```
[09:41:59] Before running the task ...

[09:42:00] VirtualThread[#22]/runnable

[09:42:00] Thread[#1,main,5,main]
           can't take from the queue yet

[09:42:00] VirtualThread[#22]/runnable@ForkJoinPool-1-worker-1
           sleeps for 5 seconds
[09:42:05] VirtualThread[#22]/runnable@ForkJoinPool-1-worker-1
           inserts in the queue

[09:42:05] Thread[#1,main,5,main]took from queue: 2147483647

[09:42:05] VirtualThread[#22]/terminated

[09:42:05] After running the task ...
```

The virtual thread started its execution (it is in a *runnable* state), but the main thread cannot remove an element from the queue until the virtual thread inserts an element, so it is blocked by the queue. take() operation:

```
[09:42:00] VirtualThread[#22]/runnable

[09:42:00] Thread[#1,main,5,main]
           can't take from the queue yet
```

Meanwhile, the virtual thread sleeps for 5 seconds (currently, the main thread has nothing to do), and afterward, it inserts an element:

```
[09:42:00] VirtualThread[#22]/runnable@ForkJoinPool-1-worker-1
           sleeps for 5 seconds
[09:42:05] VirtualThread[#22]/runnable@ForkJoinPool-1-worker-1
           inserts in the queue
```

The virtual thread has inserted an element into the queue, so the main thread can remove this element from it:

```
[09:42:05] Thread[#1,main,5,main]took from queue: 2147483647
```

The virtual thread is also terminated:

```
[09:42:05] VirtualThread[#22]/terminated
```

So virtual threads, platform threads, and synchronous code work as expected. In the bundled code, you can find an example where the virtual and platform threads switch places. So the platform thread attempts to insert elements, and the virtual thread attempts to remove them.

215. Exemplifying thread context switching

Remember that a virtual thread is mounted on a platform thread, and it is executed by that platform thread until a blocking operation occurs. At that point, the virtual thread is unmounted from the platform thread, and it will be rescheduled for execution by the JVM later on after the blocking operation is done. This means that, during its lifetime, a virtual thread can be mounted multiple times on a different or the same platform thread.

In this problem, let's write several snippets of code meant to capture and exemplify this behavior.

Example 1

In the first example, let's consider the following thread factory that we can use to easily switch between the platform and virtual threads:

```java
static class SimpleThreadFactory implements ThreadFactory {

  @Override
  public Thread newThread(Runnable r) {
  return new Thread(r);                        // classic thread
  // return Thread.ofVirtual().unstarted(r); // virtual thread
  }
}
```

Next, we try to execute the following task via 10 platform threads:

```java
public static void doSomething(int index) {

  logger.info(() -> index + " "
    + Thread.currentThread().toString());
  try { Thread.sleep(Duration.ofSeconds(3)); }
    catch (InterruptedException ex) {}
    logger.info(() -> index + " "
      + Thread.currentThread().toString());
}
```

Between the two logging lines, we have a blocking operation (`sleep()`). Next, we rely on `newThreadPerTaskExecutor()` to submit 10 tasks that should log their details, sleep for 3 seconds, and log again:

```
try (ExecutorService executor =
    Executors.newThreadPerTaskExecutor(
        new SimpleThreadFactory())) {

  for (int i = 0; i < MAX_THREADS; i++) {
    int index = i;
    executor.submit(() -> doSomething(index));
  }
}
```

Running this code with platform threads reveals the following side-to-side output:

```
[10:46:51]  5 Thread[#27,Thread-5,5,main]    [10:46:54]  7 Thread[#29,Thread-7,5,main]
[10:46:51]  1 Thread[#23,Thread-1,5,main]    [10:46:54]  0 Thread[#22,Thread-0,5,main]
[10:46:51]  9 Thread[#31,Thread-9,5,main]    [10:46:54]  8 Thread[#30,Thread-8,5,main]
[10:46:51]  4 Thread[#26,Thread-4,5,main]    [10:46:54]  6 Thread[#28,Thread-6,5,main]
[10:46:51]  7 Thread[#29,Thread-7,5,main]    [10:46:54]  4 Thread[#26,Thread-4,5,main]
[10:46:51]  0 Thread[#22,Thread-0,5,main]    [10:46:54]  9 Thread[#31,Thread-9,5,main]
[10:46:51]  6 Thread[#28,Thread-6,5,main]    [10:46:54]  1 Thread[#23,Thread-1,5,main]
[10:46:51]  8 Thread[#30,Thread-8,5,main]    [10:46:54]  5 Thread[#27,Thread-5,5,main]
[10:46:51]  3 Thread[#25,Thread-3,5,main]    [10:46:54]  3 Thread[#25,Thread-3,5,main]
[10:46:51]  2 Thread[#24,Thread-2,5,main]    [10:46:54]  2 Thread[#24,Thread-2,5,main]
        first logging              sleep              second logging
```

Figure 10.8: Using platform threads

By carefully inspecting this figure, we can see that there is a fixed association between these numbers. For instance, the task with ID 5 is executed by Thread-5, the task with ID 3 by Thread-3, and so on. After sleeping (i.e., a blocking operation), these numbers are unchanged. This means that while the tasks sleep, the threads just hang and wait there. They have no work to do.

Let's switch from platform threads to virtual threads and then run the code again:

```
@Override
public Thread newThread(Runnable r) {
  // return new Thread(r);     // classic thread
  return Thread.ofVirtual().unstarted(r); // virtual thread
}
```

Now, the output is resumed, as shown in the following figure:

```
[07:46:50]  4  [#27]/runnable@ForkJoinPool-1-worker-5      [07:46:53]  1  [#24]/runnable@ForkJoinPool-1-worker-1
[07:46:50]  3  [#26]/runnable@ForkJoinPool-1-worker-4      [07:46:53]  2  [#25]/runnable@ForkJoinPool-1-worker-4
[07:46:50]  1  [#24]/runnable@ForkJoinPool-1-worker-2      [07:46:53]  9  [#32]/runnable@ForkJoinPool-1-worker-7
[07:46:50]  2  [#25]/runnable@ForkJoinPool-1-worker-3      [07:46:53]  7  [#30]/runnable@ForkJoinPool-1-worker-5
[07:46:50]  0  [#22]/runnable@ForkJoinPool-1-worker-1      [07:46:53]  4  [#27]/runnable@ForkJoinPool-1-worker-8
[07:46:50]  7  [#30]/runnable@ForkJoinPool-1-worker-8      [07:46:53]  0  [#22]/runnable@ForkJoinPool-1-worker-2
[07:46:50]  9  [#32]/runnable@ForkJoinPool-1-worker-7      [07:46:53]  8  [#31]/runnable@ForkJoinPool-1-worker-3
[07:46:50]  8  [#31]/runnable@ForkJoinPool-1-worker-7      [07:46:53]  3  [#26]/runnable@ForkJoinPool-1-worker-6
[07:46:50]  6  [#29]/runnable@ForkJoinPool-1-worker-7      [07:46:53]  5  [#28]/runnable@ForkJoinPool-1-worker-4
[07:46:50]  5  [#28]/runnable@ForkJoinPool-1-worker-6      [07:46:53]  6  [#29]/runnable@ForkJoinPool-1-worker-1
           first logging                          sleep                    second logging
```

Figure 10.9: Using virtual threads

This time, we can see that things are more dynamic. For instance, the task with ID 5 is started by a virtual thread executed by worker-6, but it is finished by worker-4. The task with ID 3 is started by a virtual thread executed by worker-4, but it is finished by worker-6. This means that, while a task sleeps (a blocking operation), the corresponding virtual thread is unmounted, and its worker can serve other virtual threads. When the sleeping is over, the JVM schedules the virtual thread for execution and is mounted on another (it could also be the same) worker. This is also referred to as *thread context switching*.

Example 2

In this example, let's start by limiting the parallelism to 1 (which is like having a single core and a single virtual thread):

```
System.setProperty(
  "jdk.virtualThreadScheduler.maxPoolSize", "1");
System.setProperty(
  "jdk.virtualThreadScheduler.maxPoolSize", "1");
System.setProperty(
  "jdk.virtualThreadScheduler.maxPoolSize", "1");
```

Next, let's consider that we have a slow task (we call it slow because it sleeps for 5 seconds):

```
Runnable slowTask = () -> {
  logger.info(() -> Thread.currentThread().toString()
    + " | working on something");
  logger.info(() -> Thread.currentThread().toString()
    + " | break time (blocking)");
  try { Thread.sleep(Duration.ofSeconds(5)); }
    catch (InterruptedException ex) {} // blocking
  logger.info(() -> Thread.currentThread().toString()
    + " | work done");
};
```

And then, a fast task (similar to the slow task, but it sleeps for only 1 second):

```
Runnable fastTask = () -> {
  logger.info(() -> Thread.currentThread().toString()
    + " | working on something");
  logger.info(() -> Thread.currentThread().toString()
    + " | break time (blocking)");
  try { Thread.sleep(Duration.ofSeconds(1)); }
    catch (InterruptedException ex) {} // blocking
  logger.info(() -> Thread.currentThread().toString()
    + " | work done");
};
```

Next, we define two virtual threads to execute these two tasks, as follows:

```
Thread st = Thread.ofVirtual()
  .name("slow-", 0).start(slowTask);
Thread ft = Thread.ofVirtual()
  .name("fast-", 0).start(fastTask);

st.join();
ft.join();
```

If we run this code, then the output will be as follows:

```
[08:38:46] VirtualThread[#22,slow-0]/runnable
           @ForkJoinPool-1-worker-1 | working on something
[08:38:46] VirtualThread[#22,slow-0]/runnable
           @ForkJoinPool-1-worker-1 | break time (blocking)
[08:38:46] VirtualThread[#24,fast-0]/runnable
           @ForkJoinPool-1-worker-1 | working on something
[08:38:46] VirtualThread[#24,fast-0]/runnable
           @ForkJoinPool-1-worker-1 | break time (blocking)
[08:38:47] VirtualThread[#24,fast-0]/runnable
           @ForkJoinPool-1-worker-1 | work done
[08:38:51] VirtualThread[#22,slow-0]/runnable
           @ForkJoinPool-1-worker-1 | work done
```

If we analyze this output, we can see that the execution starts the slow task. The fast task cannot be executed, since worker-1 (the only available worker) is busy executing the slow task:

```
[08:38:46] VirtualThread[#22,slow-0]/runnable
           @ForkJoinPool-1-worker-1 | working on something
```

Worker-1 executes the slow task until this task hits the sleeping operation. Since this is a blocking operation, the corresponding virtual thread (#22) is unmounted from worker-1:

```
[08:38:46] VirtualThread[#22,slow-0]/runnable
           @ForkJoinPool-1-worker-1 | break time (blocking)
```

The JVM takes advantage of the fact that worker-1 is available and pushes for the execution of the fast task:

```
[08:38:46] VirtualThread[#24,fast-0]/runnable
           @ForkJoinPool-1-worker-1 | working on something
```

The fast task also hits a sleeping operation, and its virtual thread (#24) is unmounted:

```
[08:38:46] VirtualThread[#24,fast-0]/runnable
           @ForkJoinPool-1-worker-1 | break time (blocking)
```

However, the fast task sleeps for only 1 second, so its blocking operation is over before the slow task blocking operation, which is still sleeping. So the JVM can schedule the fast task for execution again, and worker-1 is ready to accept it:

```
[08:38:47] VirtualThread[#24,fast-0]/runnable
           @ForkJoinPool-1-worker-1 | work done
```

At this moment, the fast task is done, and worker-1 is free. But the slow task is still sleeping. After these 5 seconds, the JVM schedules the slow task for execution, and worker-1 is there to take it.

```
[08:38:51] VirtualThread[#22,slow-0]/runnable
           @ForkJoinPool-1-worker-1 | work done
```

Done!

Example 3

This example is just a slight modification of Example 2. This time, let's consider that the slow task contains a non-blocking operation that runs forever. In this case, this operation is simulated via an infinite loop:

```
Runnable slowTask = () -> {
  logger.info(() -> Thread.currentThread().toString()
    + " | working on something");
  logger.info(() -> Thread.currentThread().toString()
    + " | break time (non-blocking)");
  while(dummyTrue()) {} // non-blocking
  logger.info(() -> Thread.currentThread().toString()
    + " | work done");
};

static boolean dummyTrue() { return true; }
```

We have a single worker (`worker-1`), and the fast task is the same as in Example 2. If we run this code, the execution hangs on, as follows:

```
[09:02:45] VirtualThread[#22,slow-0]/runnable
           @ForkJoinPool-1-worker-1 | working on something
[09:02:45] VirtualThread[#22,slow-0]/runnable
           @ForkJoinPool-1-worker-1 | break time(non-blocking)
// hang on
```

The execution hangs on because the infinite loop is not seen as a blocking operation. In other words, the virtual thread of the slow task (#22) is never unmounted. Since there is a single worker, the JVM cannot push for the execution of the fast task.

If we increase the parallelism from 1 to 2, then the fast task will be successfully executed by `worker-2`, while `worker-1` (executing the slow task) will simply hang on to a partial execution. We can avoid such situations by relying on a timeout join, such as `join(Duration duration)`. This way, after the given timeout, the slow task will be automatically interrupted. So pay attention to such scenarios.

216. Introducing the ExecutorService invoke all/any for virtual threads – part 1

In this problem, we won't spend time on the basics and, instead, jump right into how to use `invokeAll()` and `invokeAny()`. If you need a primer on the `ExecutorService` API's `invokeAll()`/`invokeAny()` functions, then you could consider *Java Coding Problems*, *First Edition*, *Chapter 10*, *Problem 207*.

Working with invokeAll()

In a nutshell, `invokeAll()` executes a collection of tasks (`Callable`) and returns a `List<Future>` that holds the results/status of each task. The tasks can finish naturally or be forced by a given timeout. Each task can finish successfully or exceptionally. Upon return, all the tasks that have not been completed yet are automatically canceled. We can check out the status of each task via `Future.isDone()` and `Future.isCancelled()`:

```
<T> List<Future<T>> invokeAll(Collection<? extends
  Callable<T>> tasks) throws InterruptedException

<T> List<Future<T>> invokeAll(
  Collection<? extends Callable<T>> tasks, long timeout,
    TimeUnit unit) throws InterruptedException
```

Using `invokeAll()` with virtual threads via `newVirtualThreadPerTaskExecutor()` (or with `newThreadPerTaskExecutor()`) is straightforward. For instance, here we have a simple example of executing three `Callable` instances:

```
try (ExecutorService executor
    = Executors.newVirtualThreadPerTaskExecutor()) {
```

```
    List<Future<String>> futures = executor.invokeAll(
      List.of(() -> "pass01", () -> "pass02", () -> "pass03"));

    futures.forEach(f -> logger.info(() ->
      "State: " + f.state()));
}
```

Have you spotted the `f.state()` call? This API was introduced in JDK 19, and it computes the state of a future based on the well-known `get()`, `isDone()`, and `isCancelled()`. While we will detail this in a subsequent problem, currently, the output is as follows:

```
[10:17:41] State: SUCCESS
[10:17:41] State: SUCCESS
[10:17:41] State: SUCCESS
```

The three tasks have successfully completed.

Working with invokeAny()

In a nutshell, `invokeAny()` executes a collection of tasks (`Callable`) and strives to return a result corresponding to a task that has successfully terminated (before the given timeout, if any). All the tasks that have not been completed are automatically canceled:

```
<T> T invokeAny(Collection<? extends Callable<T>> tasks)
  throws InterruptedException, ExecutionException

<T> T invokeAny(Collection<? extends Callable<T>> tasks,
  long timeout, TimeUnit unit) throws InterruptedException,
    ExecutionException, TimeoutException
```

Using `invokeAny()` with virtual threads via `newVirtualThreadPerTaskExecutor()` is also straightforward (or with `newThreadPerTaskExecutor()`). For instance, here we have a simple example of executing three `Callable` instances when we are interested in a single result:

```
try (ExecutorService executor
    = Executors.newVirtualThreadPerTaskExecutor()) {

  String result = executor.invokeAny(
    List.of(() -> "pass01", () -> "pass02", () -> "pass03"));

  logger.info(result);
}
```

A possible output might be:

```
[10:29:33] pass02
```

This output corresponds to the second `Callable`.

In the next problem, we will come up with a more realistic example.

217. Introducing the ExecutorService invoke all/any for virtual threads — part 2

Earlier, in *Problem 210*, we wrote a piece of "unstructured" concurrency code to build a testing team of three testers, served by an external server.

Now, let's try to rewrite the `buildTestingTeam()` method via `invokeAll()`/`Any()` and `newVirtualTh readPerTaskExecutor()`. If we rely on `invokeAll()`, then the application will attempt to load three testers by ID, as follows:

```
public static TestingTeam buildTestingTeam()
      throws InterruptedException {

  try (ExecutorService executor
      = Executors.newVirtualThreadPerTaskExecutor()) {

    List<Future<String>> futures = executor.invokeAll(
      List.of(() -> fetchTester(1),
              () -> fetchTester(2),
              () -> fetchTester(3)));

    futures.forEach(f -> logger.info(() -> "State: "
      + f.state()));

    return new TestingTeam(futures.get(0).resultNow(),
      futures.get(1).resultNow(), futures.get(2).resultNow());
  }
}
```

We have three testers with IDs 1, 2, and 3. So the output will be:

```
[07:47:32] State: SUCCESS
[07:47:32] State: SUCCESS
[07:47:32] State: SUCCESS
```

In the next problem, we will see how we can make decisions based on task state.

If we can handle the testing phase even with a single tester, then we can rely on `invokeAny()`, as follows:

```java
public static TestingTeam buildTestingTeam()
        throws InterruptedException, ExecutionException {

  try (ExecutorService executor
    = Executors.newVirtualThreadPerTaskExecutor()) {

    String result = executor.invokeAny(
      List.of(() -> fetchTester(1),
              () -> fetchTester(2),
              () -> fetchTester(3)));

    logger.info(result);

    return new TestingTeam(result);
  }
}
```

This code will return a single result representing one of these three testers. If none of them is available, then we will get a `UserNotFoundException`.

218. Hooking task state

Starting with JDK 19, we can rely on `Future.state()`. This method computes the state of a `Future` based on the well-known `get()`, `isDone()`, and `isCancelled()`, returning a `Future.State` enum entry, as follows:

- `CANCELLED` – the task was canceled.
- `FAILED` – the task was completed exceptionally (with an exception).
- `RUNNING` – the task is still running (has not been completed).
- `SUCCESS` – the task was completed normally with a result (no exception).

In the following snippet of code, we analyze the state of loading the testing team members and act accordingly:

```java
public static TestingTeam buildTestingTeam()
        throws InterruptedException {

  List<String> testers = new ArrayList<>();

  try (ExecutorService executor
      = Executors.newVirtualThreadPerTaskExecutor()) {
```

```
List<Future<String>> futures = executor.invokeAll(
  List.of(() -> fetchTester(Integer.MAX_VALUE),
          () -> fetchTester(2),
          () -> fetchTester(Integer.MAX_VALUE)));


futures.forEach(f -> {

  logger.info(() -> "Analyzing " + f + " state ...");

  switch (f.state()) {
    case RUNNING -> throw new IllegalStateException(
      "Future is still in the running state ...");
    case SUCCESS -> {
      logger.info(() -> "Result: " + f.resultNow());
      testers.add(f.resultNow());
    }
    case FAILED ->
      logger.severe(() -> "Exception: "
        + f.exceptionNow().getMessage());
    case CANCELLED ->
      logger.info("Cancelled ?!?");
  }
});
}

return new TestingTeam(testers.toArray(String[]::new));
}
```

We know that when the execution reaches the switch block, the Future objects should be completely normal or exceptional. So if the current Future state is RUNNING, then this is a really weird situation (possibly a bug), and we throw an IllegalStateException. Next, if the Future state is SUCCESS (fetchTester(2)), then we have a result that can be obtained via resultNow(). This method was added in JDK 19, and it is useful when we know that we have a result. The resultNow() method returns immediately without waiting (as get()). If the state is FAILED (fetchTester(Integer.MAX_VALUE)), then we log the exception via exceptionNow(). This method was also added in JDK 19, and it returns immediately the underlying exception of a failed Future. Finally, if the Future was canceled, then there is nothing to do. We just report it in the log.

219. Combining newVirtualThreadPerTaskExecutor() and streams

Streams and newVirtualThreadPerTaskExecutor() is a handy combination. Here is an example that relies on IntStream to submit 10 simple tasks and collect the returned List of Future instances:

```
try (ExecutorService executor
        = Executors.newVirtualThreadPerTaskExecutor()) {

  List<Future<String>> futures = IntStream.range(0, 10)
    .mapToObj(i -> executor.submit(() -> {
      return Thread.currentThread().toString()
        + "(" + i + ")";
})).collect(toList());


  // here we have the following snippet of code
}
```

Next, we wait for each Future to complete by calling the get() method:

```
futures.forEach(f -> {
  try {
    logger.info(f.get());
  } catch (InterruptedException | ExecutionException ex) {
    // handle exception
  }
});
```

Moreover, using stream pipelines is quite useful in combination with invokeAll(). For instance, the following stream pipeline returns a List of results (it filters all Future instances that haven't completed successfully):

```
List<String> results = executor.invokeAll(
  List.of(() -> "pass01", () -> "pass02", () -> "pass03"))
  .stream()
  .filter(f -> f.state() == Future.State.SUCCESS)
  .<String>mapMulti((f, c) -> {
    c.accept((String) f.resultNow());
  }).collect(Collectors.toList());
```

Alternatively, we can write the following solution (without `mapMulti()`):

```
List<String> results = executor.invokeAll(
  List.of(() -> "pass01", () -> "pass02", () -> "pass03"))
  .stream()
  .filter(f -> f.state() == Future.State.SUCCESS)
  .map(f -> f.resultNow().toString())
  .toList();
```

Of course, if `List<Object>` is all you need, then you can go straight ahead via `Future::resultNow`, as follows:

```
List<Object> results = executor.invokeAll(
  List.of(() -> "pass01", () -> "pass02", () -> "pass03"))
  .stream()
  .filter(f -> f.state() == Future.State.SUCCESS)
  .map(Future::resultNow)
  .toList();
```

On the other hand, you may need to collect all the `Future` that has been completed exceptionally. This can be achieved via `exceptionNow()`, as follows (we intentionally sneaked into the given `List<Callable>` a `Callable` that will generate an `StringIndexOutOfBoundsException`, `() -> "pass02".substring(50)`):

```
List<Throwable> exceptions = executor.invokeAll(
  List.of(() -> "pass01",
          () -> "pass02".substring(50), () -> "pass03"))
  .stream()
  .filter(f -> f.state() == Future.State.FAILED)
  .<Throwable>mapMulti((f, c) -> {
    c.accept((Throwable) f.exceptionNow());
  }).collect(Collectors.toList());
```

If you don't prefer `mapMulti()`, then rely on the classical approach:

```
List<Throwable> exceptions = executor.invokeAll(
  List.of(() -> "pass01", () -> "pass02".substring(50),
          () -> "pass03"))
  .stream()
  .filter(f -> f.state() == Future.State.FAILED)
  .map(Future::exceptionNow)
  .toList();
```

You can find all these examples in the bundled code.

220. Introducing a scope object (StructuredTaskScope)

So far, we have covered a bunch of problems that use virtual threads directly or indirectly via an
ExecutorService. We already know that virtual threads are cheap to create and block and that an
application can run millions of them. We don't need to reuse them, pool them, or do any fancy stuff.
Use and throw is the proper and recommended way to deal with virtual threads. This means that virtual
threads are very useful for expressing and writing asynchronous code, which is commonly based on
a lot of threads that are capable of blocking/unblocking several times in a short period. On the other
hand, we know that OS threads are expensive to create, very expensive to block, and are not easy to
put into an asynchronous context.

Before virtual threads (so for many, many years), we had to manage the life cycle of OS threads via an
ExecutorService/Executor, and we could write asynchronous (or reactive) code via *callbacks* (you can
find detailed coverage of asynchronous programming in *Java Coding Problems, First Edition, Chapter 11*).

However, asynchronous/reactive code is hard to write/read, very hard to debug and profile, and almost
deadly hard to unit-test. Nobody wants to read and fix your asynchronous code! Moreover, once we
start to write an application via asynchronous callback, we tend to use this model for all tasks, even
for those that shouldn't be asynchronous. We can easily fall into this trap when we need to somehow
link asynchronous code/results to non-asynchronous code. And the easiest way to do it is to go only
for asynchronous code.

So is there a better way? Yes, there is! Structured concurrency is the answer. Structured concurrency
started as an *incubator* project and reached the *preview* stage in JDK 21 (JEP 453).

And, in this context, we should introduce StructuredTaskScope. A StructuredTaskScope is a virtual
thread launcher for Callable tasks that returns a Subtask. A subtask is an extension of the well-known
Supplier<T> functional interface represented by the StructuredTaskScope.Subtask<T> interface
and forked with StructuredTaskScope.fork(Callable task). It follows and works based on the
fundamental principle of structured concurrency (see *Problem 210*): "*When a task has to be solved concurrently, then all the threads needed to solve it are spun and rejoined in the same block of code. In other words,
all these threads' lifetimes are bound to the block's scope, so we have clear and explicit entry-exit points for
each concurrent code block.*" These threads are responsible for running subtasks (Subtask) of the given
task as a single unit of work.

Let's look at an example of fetching a single tester (with ID 1) from our web server via StructuredTaskScope:

```
public static TestingTeam buildTestingTeam()
        throws InterruptedException {

    try (StructuredTaskScope scope
        = new StructuredTaskScope<String>()) {

        Subtask<String> subtask
            = scope.fork(() -> fetchTester(1));
```

```
        logger.info(() -> "Waiting for " + subtask.toString()
          + " to finish ...\n");

        scope.join();

        String result = subtask.get();

        logger.info(result);

        return new TestingTeam(result);
    }
}
```

First, we create a `StructuredTaskScope` in a `try-with-resources` pattern. `StructuredTaskScope` implements `AutoCloseable`:

```
try (StructuredTaskScope scope
        = new StructuredTaskScope<String>()) {
    ...
}
```

The `scope` is a wrapper for the virtual threads' lifetimes. We use the `scope` to fork as many virtual threads (subtasks) as needed via the `fork(Callable task)` method. Here, we fork only one virtual thread and get back a `Subtask` (forking is a non-blocking operation):

```
Subtask<String> subtask = scope.fork(() -> fetchTester(1));
```

Next, we have to call the `join()` method (or `joinUntil(Instant deadline)`). This method waits for all threads (all `Subtask` instances) forked from this `scope` (or all threads that have been submitted to this `scope`) to complete, so it is a blocking operation. A scope should block only while it waits for its subtasks to complete, and this happens via `join()` or `joinUntil()`.

```
scope.join();
```

When the execution passes this line, we know that all threads (all forked `Subtask`) forked from this scope are complete, with a result or an exception (each subtask runs independently, so each of them can complete with a result or an exception). Here, we call the non-blocking `get()` method to get the result, but pay attention – calling `get()` for a task that did not complete will raise an exception as `IllegalStateException`(*"Owner did not join after forking subtask"*):

```
String result = subtask.get();
```

On the other hand, we can obtain the exception of a failed task via `exception()`. However, if we call `exception()` for a subtask (`Subtask`) that is completed with a result, then we will get back an exception as `IllegalStateException`(*"Subtask not completed or did not complete with exception"*).

So if you are not sure whether your task(s) completed with a result or an exception, it is better to call get() or exception() only after you test the state of the corresponding Subtask. A state of SUCCESS will safely allow you to call get(), while a state of FAILED will safely allow you to call exception(). So in our case, we may prefer it this way:

```
String result = "";
if (subtask.state().equals(Subtask.State.SUCCESS)) {
  result = subtask.get();
}
```

Besides Subtask.State.SUCCESS and Subtask.State.FAILED, we also have Subtask.State. UNAVAILABLE, which means that the subtask is not available (for instance, if the subtask is still running, then its state is UNAVAILABLE, but there could be another cause as well).

ExecutorService vs. StructuredTaskScope

The previous code looks like the code that we would write via a classical ExecutorService, but there are two big differences between these solutions. First of all, an ExecutorService holds the precious platform threads and allows us to pool them. On the other hand, a StructuredTaskScope is just a thin launcher for virtual threads that are cheap and shouldn't be pooled. So once we've done our job, a StructuredTaskScope can be destroyed and garbage-collected. Second, an ExecutorService holds a single queue for all the tasks, and the threads take from this queue whenever they have the chance to do so. A StructuredTaskScope relies on a fork/join pool, and each virtual thread has its own wait queue. However, a virtual thread can steal a task from another queue as well. This is known as the *work-stealing* pattern, and if you want to read more about it, we covered it in depth in *Java Coding Problem, First Edition, Chapter 11*.

221. Introducing ShutdownOnSuccess

In the previous problem, we introduced StructuredTaskScope and used it to solve a task via a single virtual thread (a single Subtask). Basically, we fetched the tester with ID 1 from our server (we had to wait until this one was available). Next, let's assume that we still need a single tester, but not mandatorily the one with ID 1. This time, it could be any of IDs 1, 2, or 3. We simply take the first one that is available from these three, and we cancel the other two requests.

Especially for such scenarios, we have an extension of StructuredTaskScope called StructuredTaskScope. ShutdownOnSuccess. This scope is capable of returning the result of the first task that completes successfully and interrupts the rest of the threads. It follows the "invoke any" model and can be used as follows:

```
public static TestingTeam buildTestingTeam()
      throws InterruptedException, ExecutionException {

  try (ShutdownOnSuccess scope
      = new StructuredTaskScope.ShutdownOnSuccess<String>()) {
```

```
    Subtask<String> subtask1
      = scope.fork(() -> fetchTester(1));
    Subtask<String> subtask2
      = scope.fork(() -> fetchTester(2));
    Subtask<String> subtask3
      = scope.fork(() -> fetchTester(3));

    scope.join();

    logger.info(() -> "Subtask-1 state: " + future1.state());
    logger.info(() -> "Subtask-2 state: " + future2.state());
    logger.info(() -> "Subtask-3 state: " + future3.state());

    String result = (String) scope.result();

    logger.info(result);

    return new TestingTeam(result);
  }
}
```

Here, we fork three subtasks (threads) that will compete with each other to complete. The first subtask (thread) that completes successfully wins and returns. The result() method returns this result (if none of the subtasks (threads) complete successfully, then it throws an ExecutionException).

If we check the state of these three Subtask, we can see that one succeeds while the other two are unavailable:

```
[09:01:50] Subtask-1 state: UNAVAILABLE
[09:01:50] Subtask-2 state: SUCCESS
[09:01:50] Subtask-3 state: UNAVAILABLE
```

Of course, you don't need the code that checks/prints the state of each Subtask. It was added here just to highlight how ShutdownOnSuccess works. You don't even need the explicit Subtask objects, since we don't call get() or anything else from this API. Basically, we can reduce the code to the following:

```
public static TestingTeam buildTestingTeam()
      throws InterruptedException, ExecutionException {

  try (ShutdownOnSuccess scope
      = new StructuredTaskScope.ShutdownOnSuccess<String>()) {

    scope.fork(() -> fetchTester(1));
    scope.fork(() -> fetchTester(2));
```

```
    scope.fork(() -> fetchTester(3));

    scope.join();

    return new TestingTeam((String) scope.result());
  }
}
```

Done! You just create the scope, fork your subtasks, call `join()`, and collect the result. So the scope is really business-focused.

A task that completes exceptionally under the `ShutdownOnSuccess` umbrella will never be chosen to produce a result. However, if all tasks complete exceptionally, then we will get an `ExecutionException` that wraps the exception (i.e., the cause) of the first completed task.

222. Introducing ShutdownOnFailure

As its name suggests, `StructuredTaskScope.ShutdownOnFailure` is capable of returning the exception of the first subtask that completes exceptionally and interrupts the rest of the subtasks (threads). For instance, we may want to fetch the testers with IDs 1, 2, and 3. Since we need exactly these three testers, we want to be informed if any of them are not available and, if so, cancel everything (i.e., the remaining threads). The code looks as follows:

```
public static TestingTeam buildTestingTeam()
        throws InterruptedException, ExecutionException {

  try (ShutdownOnFailure scope
      = new StructuredTaskScope.ShutdownOnFailure()) {

    Subtask<String> subtask1
      = scope.fork(() -> fetchTester(1));
    Subtask<String> subtask2
      = scope.fork(() -> fetchTester(2));
    Subtask<String> subtask3
      = scope.fork(() -> fetchTester(Integer.MAX_VALUE));

    scope.join();

    logger.info(() -> "Subtask-1 state: " + subtask1.state());
    logger.info(() -> "Subtask-2 state: " + subtask2.state());
    logger.info(() -> "Subtask-3 state: " + subtask3.state());

    Optional<Throwable> exception = scope.exception();
```

```
    if (exception.isEmpty()) {
      logger.info(() -> "Subtask-1 result:" + subtask1.get());
      logger.info(() -> "Subtask-2 result:" + subtask2.get());
      logger.info(() -> "Subtask-3 result:" + subtask3.get());

      return new TestingTeam(
        subtask1.get(), subtask2.get(), subtask3.get());
    } else {
      logger.info(() -> exception.get().getMessage());
      scope.throwIfFailed();
    }
  }

  return new TestingTeam();
}
```

In this example, we intentionally replaced ID 3 with `Integer.MAX_VALUE`. Since there is no tester with this ID, the server will throw `UserNotFoundException`. This means that the states of the subtasks will reveal that the third subtask has failed:

```
[16:41:15] Subtask-1 state: SUCCESS
[16:41:15] Subtask-2 state: SUCCESS
[16:41:15] Subtask-3 state: FAILED
```

Moreover, when we call the `exception()` method, we will get back an `Optional<Throwable>` containing this exception (if you're interested in reading more about this subject, in-depth coverage of the `Optional` feature is available in *Java Coding Problems, First Edition, Chapter 12*). If we decide to throw it, then we simply call the `throwIfFailed()` method, which wraps the original exception (the cause) in an `ExecutionException` and throws it. The message of the exception in our case will be:

```
Exception in thread "main"
java.util.concurrent.ExecutionException:
modern.challenge.UserNotFoundException: Code: 404
```

If we remove the guideline code, then we can compact the previous code, as follows:

```
public static TestingTeam buildTestingTeam()
      throws InterruptedException, ExecutionException {

  try (ShutdownOnFailure scope
     = new StructuredTaskScope.ShutdownOnFailure()) {

    Subtask<String> subtask1
      = scope.fork(() -> fetchTester(1));
    Subtask<String> subtask2
```

```
      = scope.fork(() -> fetchTester(2));
  Subtask<String> subtask3
    = scope.fork(() -> fetchTester(
      Integer.MAX_VALUE)); // this causes exception

  scope.join();
  scope.throwIfFailed();

  // because we have an exception the following
  // code will not be executed
  return new TestingTeam(
    subtask1.get(), subtask2.get(), subtask3.get());
  }
}
```

If no exception occurs, then `throwIfFailed()` doesn't do anything, and those three testers are available. The result of each `Subtask` is available via the non-blocking `Subtask.get()`.

A subtask that completes exceptionally under the `ShutdownOnFailure` umbrella will be chosen to produce an exception. However, if all subtasks complete normally, then we will not get any exceptions. On the other hand, if no subtasks were completed exceptionally but were canceled, then `ShutdownOnFailure` will throw `CancellationException`.

223. Combining StructuredTaskScope and streams

If you prefer functional programming, then you'll be happy to see that streams can be used with `StructuredTaskScope` as well. For instance, here we rewrite the application from *Problem 221*, using a stream pipeline to fork our tasks:

```
public static TestingTeam buildTestingTeam()
      throws InterruptedException, ExecutionException {

  try (ShutdownOnSuccess scope
      = new StructuredTaskScope.ShutdownOnSuccess<String>()) {

    Stream.of(1, 2, 3)
      .<Callable<String>>map(id -> () -> fetchTester(id))
      .forEach(scope::fork);

    scope.join();

    String result = (String) scope.result();

    logger.info(result);
```

```
        return new TestingTeam(result);
    }
}
```

Moreover, we can use stream pipelines to collect results and exceptions, as follows:

```
public static TestingTeam buildTestingTeam()
    throws InterruptedException, ExecutionException {

  try (ShutdownOnSuccess scope
   = new StructuredTaskScope.ShutdownOnSuccess<String>()) {

   List<Subtask> subtasks = Stream.of(Integer.MAX_VALUE, 2, 3)
     .<Callable<String>>map(id -> () -> fetchTester(id))
     .map(scope::fork)
     .toList();

   scope.join();

   List<Throwable> failed = subtasks.stream()
     .filter(f -> f.state() == Subtask.State.FAILED)
     .map(Subtask::exception)
     .toList();

   logger.info(failed.toString());

   TestingTeam result = subtasks.stream()
     .filter(f -> f.state() == Subtask.State.SUCCESS)
     .map(Subtask::get)
     .collect(collectingAndThen(toList(),
        list -> { return new TestingTeam(list.toArray(
           String[]::new)); }));

   logger.info(result.toString());

   return result;
   }
}
```

You can find these examples in the bundled code.

224. Observing and monitoring virtual threads

Observing and monitoring virtual threads can be done in several ways. First, we can use **Java Flight Recorder** (**JFR**) – we introduced this tool in *Chapter 6, Problem 143*.

Using JFR

Among its reach list of events, JFR can monitor and record the following events related to virtual threads:

- `jdk.VirtualThreadStart` – this event is recorded when a virtual thread starts (by default, it is disabled)
- `jdk.VirtualThreadEnd` – this event is recorded when a virtual thread ends (by default, it is disabled)
- `jdk.VirtualThreadPinned` – this event is recorded when a virtual thread is parked while pinned (by default, it is enabled with a threshold of 20 ms)
- `jdk.VirtualThreadSubmitFailed` – this event is recorded if a virtual thread cannot be started or unparked (by default, it is enabled)

You can find all the JFR events at `https://sap.github.io/SapMachine/jfrevents/`.

We start configuring JFR to monitor the virtual threads, by adding to the root folder of the application the following `vtEvent.jfc` file:

```xml
<?xml version="1.0" encoding="UTF-8"?>

<configuration version="2.0" description="test">
  <event name="jdk.VirtualThreadStart">
    <setting name="enabled">true</setting>
    <setting name="stackTrace">true</setting>
  </event>

  <event name="jdk.VirtualThreadEnd">
    <setting name="enabled">true</setting>
  </event>

  <event name="jdk.VirtualThreadPinned">
    <setting name="enabled">true</setting>
    <setting name="stackTrace">true</setting>
    <setting name="threshold">20 ms</setting>
  </event>

  <event name="jdk.VirtualThreadSubmitFailed">
    <setting name="enabled">true</setting>
    <setting name="stackTrace">true</setting>
```

```
    </event>
  </configuration>
```

Next, let's consider the following code (basically, this is the application from Problem 216):

```java
public static TestingTeam buildTestingTeam()
        throws InterruptedException, ExecutionException {

    try (ShutdownOnSuccess scope
        = new StructuredTaskScope.ShutdownOnSuccess<String>()) {

        Stream.of(1, 2, 3)
            .<Callable<String>>map(id -> () -> fetchTester(id))
            .forEach(scope::fork);

        scope.join();

        String result = (String) scope.result();

        logger.info(result);

        return new TestingTeam(result);
    }
}
```

Next, we use -XX:StartFlightRecording=filename=recording.jfr to instruct JFR to record output in a file named recording.jfr, and we continue with settings=vtEvent.jfc to highlight the configuration file listed previously.

So the final command is the one from this figure:

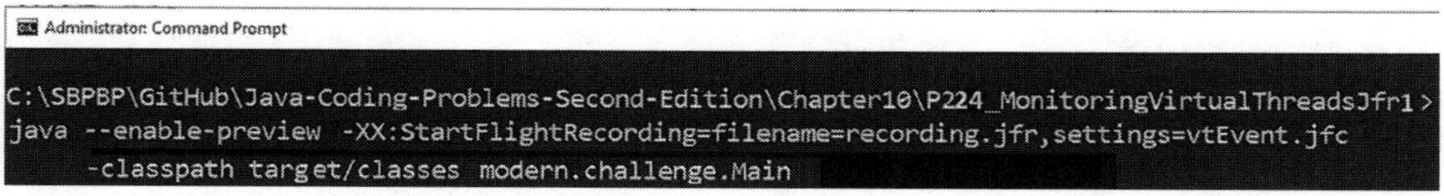

```
Administrator: Command Prompt
C:\SBPBP\GitHub\Java-Coding-Problems-Second-Edition\Chapter10\P224_MonitoringVirtualThreadsJfr1>
java --enable-preview -XX:StartFlightRecording=filename=recording.jfr,settings=vtEvent.jfc
    -classpath target/classes modern.challenge.Main
```

Figure 10.10: Running JFR

JFR has produced a file named recording.jfr. We can easily view the content of this file via the JFR CLI. The command (jfr print recording.jfr) will display the content of recording.jfr. The content is too large to be listed here (it contains three entries for jdk.VirtualThreadStart and three for jdk.VirtualThreadEnd), but here is the event specific to starting a virtual thread:

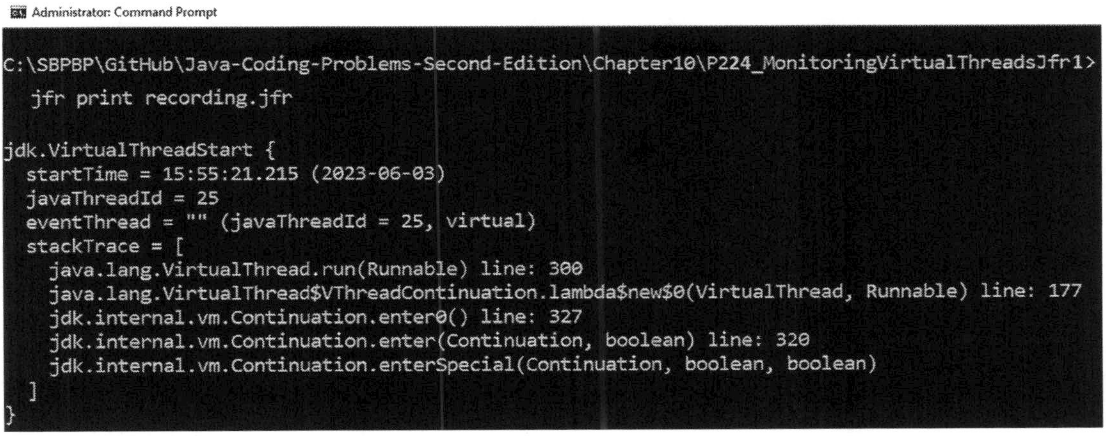

Figure 10.11: JFR event to start a virtual thread

And, in the next figure, you can see the event recorded to end this virtual thread:

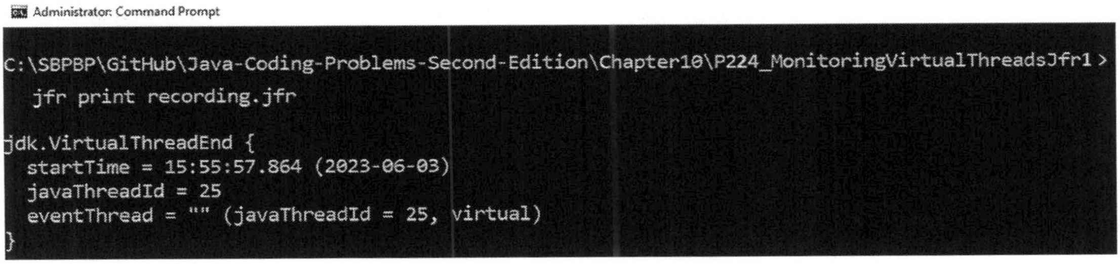

Figure 10.12: JFR event to end a virtual thread

Besides the JFR CLI, you can use more powerful tools to consume the virtual thread events, such as JDK Mission Control (`https://www.oracle.com/java/technologies/jdk-mission-control.html`) and the well-known Advanced Management Console (`https://www.oracle.com/java/technologies/advancedmanagementconsole.html`).

To get a stack trace for threads that block while pinned, we can set the system property, `jdk.tracePinnedThreads`. A complete (verbose) stack trace is available via `-Djdk.tracePinnedThreads=full`, or if all you need is a brief/short stack trace, then rely on `-Djdk.tracePinnedThreads=short`.

In our example, we can easily get a pinned virtual thread by marking the `fetchTester()` method as `synchronized` (remember that a virtual thread cannot be unmounted if it runs code inside a synchronized method/block):

```
public static synchronized String fetchTester(int id)
    throws IOException, InterruptedException {

  ...

}
```

In this context, JFR will record a pinned virtual thread, as shown in the following figure:

```
jdk.VirtualThreadPinned {
  startTime = 08:01:42.424 (2023-06-04)
  duration = 1.97 s
  eventThread = "" (javaThreadId = 28, virtual)
  stackTrace = [
    java.lang.VirtualThread.parkOnCarrierThread(boolean, long) line: 645
    java.lang.VirtualThread.parkNanos(long) line: 611
    java.lang.VirtualThread.doSleepNanos(long) line: 777
    java.lang.VirtualThread.sleepNanos(long) line: 750
    java.lang.Thread.sleep(Duration) line: 557
    ...
  ]
}
```

Figure 10.13: JFR event for a pinned virtual thread

If we run the application with `-Djdk.tracePinnedThreads=full`, then your IDE will print a detailed stack trace that starts as follows:

```
Thread[#26,ForkJoinPool-1-worker-1,5,CarrierThreads]     java.base/java.lang.
VirtualThread$VThreadContinuation.onPinned(VirtualThread.java:183)
...
```

You can see the complete output by executing the bundled code. Of course, you can get a thread dump and analyze it via several other tools. You may prefer any of `jstack`, **Java Mission Control** (**JMC**), `jvisualvm`, or `jcmd`. For instance, we can obtain a thread dump in plain text or the JSON format via `jcmd`, as follows:

```
jcmd <PID> Thread.dump_to_file -format=text <file>
jcmd <PID> Thread.dump_to_file -format=json <file>
```

Next, let's play with `jconsole` (JMX) to quickly analyze the performance of virtual threads.

Using Java Management Extensions (JMX)

Until JDK 20 (inclusive), JMX provided support for monitoring only the platform and threads. However, we can still use JMX to observe the performance brought by virtual threads in comparison with platform threads.

For instance, we can use JMX to monitor platform threads at 500 ms each, via the following snippet of code:

```
ScheduledExecutorService scheduledExecutor
        = Executors.newScheduledThreadPool(1);

scheduledExecutor.scheduleAtFixedRate(() -> {
  ThreadMXBean threadBean
    = ManagementFactory.getThreadMXBean();
  ThreadInfo[] threadInfo
    = threadBean.dumpAllThreads(false, false);

  logger.info(() -> "Platform threads: " + threadInfo.length);
}, 500, 500, TimeUnit.MILLISECONDS);
```

We rely on this code in the following three scenarios.

Running 10,000 tasks via the cached thread pool executor

Next, let's add a snippet of code that runs 10,000 tasks via newCachedThreadPool() and platform threads. We also measure the time elapsed to execute these tasks:

```
long start = System.currentTimeMillis();

try (ExecutorService executorCached
     = Executors.newCachedThreadPool()) {

  IntStream.range(0, 10_000).forEach(i -> {
    executorCached.submit(() -> {
      Thread.sleep(Duration.ofSeconds(1));
      logger.info(() -> "Task: " + i);
      return i;
    });
  });
}

logger.info(() -> "Time (ms): "
    + (System.currentTimeMillis() - start));
```

On my machine, it took 8,147 ms (8 seconds) to run these 10,000 tasks, using at peak 7,729 platform threads. The following screenshot from jconsole (JMX) reveals this information:

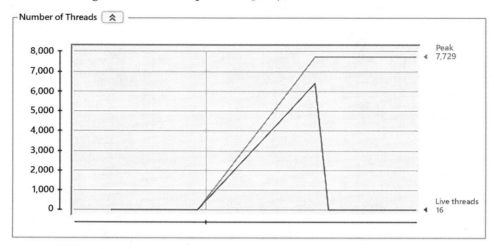

Figure 10.14: Running 10,000 tasks via the cached thread pool executor

Next, let's repeat this test via a fixed thread pool.

Running 10,000 tasks via the fixed thread pool executor

Depending on your machine, the previous test may finish successfully, or it may result in an OutOfMemoryError. We can avoid this unpleasant scenario by using a fixed thread pool. For instance, let's limit the number of platform threads to 200 via the following snippet of code:

```java
long start = System.currentTimeMillis();

try (ExecutorService executorFixed
    = Executors.newFixedThreadPool(200)) {

  IntStream.range(0, 10_000).forEach(i -> {
    executorFixed.submit(() -> {
      Thread.sleep(Duration.ofSeconds(1));
      logger.info(() -> "Task: " + i);
      return i;
    });
  });
}

logger.info(() -> "Time (ms): "
  + (System.currentTimeMillis() - start));
```

On my machine, it took 50,190 ms (50 seconds) to run these 10,000 tasks, using at peak 216 platform threads. The following screenshot from JMX reveals this information:

Figure 10.15: Running 10,000 tasks via the fixed thread pool executor

Obviously, a smaller number of platform threads is reflected in performance. If we put 216 workers to do the job of 7,729 workers, of course, it will take longer. Next, let's see how virtual threads will handle this challenge.

Running 10,000 tasks via the virtual thread per task executor

This time, let's see how the newVirtualThreadPerTaskExecutor() can handle these 10,000 tasks. The code is straightforward:

```
long start = System.currentTimeMillis();

try (ExecutorService executorVirtual
        = Executors.newVirtualThreadPerTaskExecutor()) {

  IntStream.range(0, 10_000).forEach(i -> {
    executorVirtual.submit(() -> {
      Thread.sleep(Duration.ofSeconds(1));
      logger.info(() -> "Task: " + i);
      return i;
    });
  });
}

logger.info(() -> "Time (ms): "
    + (System.currentTimeMillis() - start));
```

On my machine, it took 3,519 ms (3.5 seconds) to run these 10,000 tasks, using at peak 25 platform threads. The following screenshot from JMX reveals this information:

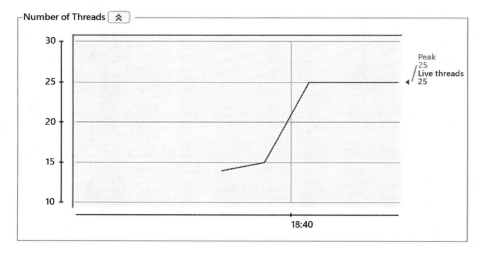

Figure 10.16: Running 10000 tasks via the virtual thread per task executor

Wow! How cool is this?! The resulting time is far and away the best in comparison with the previous tests, and it uses fewer resources (only 25 platform threads). So virtual threads really rock!

I also strongly recommend you check out the following benchmark: https://github.com/colincachia/loom-benchmark/tree/main.

Starting with JDK 21, JMX's `HotSpotDiagnosticMXBean` was enriched with the `dumpThreads(String outputFile, ThreadDumpFormat format)` method. This method outputs a thread dump to the given file (`outputFile`) in the given format (`format`). The thread dump will contain all platform threads, but it may also contain some or all virtual threads.

In the following code, we attempt to obtain a thread dump for all subtasks (threads) of a `StructuredTaskScope`:

```
try (ShutdownOnSuccess scope
  = new StructuredTaskScope.ShutdownOnSuccess<String>()) {

    Stream.of(1, 2, 3)
            .<Callable<String>>map(id -> () -> fetchTester(id))
            .forEach(scope::fork);

    HotSpotDiagnosticMXBean mBean = ManagementFactory
      .getPlatformMXBean(HotSpotDiagnosticMXBean.class);
    mBean.dumpThreads(Path.of("dumpThreads.json")
      .toAbsolutePath().toString(),
    HotSpotDiagnosticMXBean.ThreadDumpFormat.JSON);
```

```
    scope.join();

    String result = (String) scope.result();

    logger.info(result);
}
```

The output file is named threadDump.json, and you can find it in the root folder of the application. The part of the output that we are interested in is partially listed here:

```
...
{
  "container": "java.util.concurrent
              .StructuredTaskScope$ShutdownOnSuccess@6d311334",
  "parent": "<root>",
  "owner": "1",
  "threads": [
    {
    "tid": "22"
    "name": "",
    "stack": [
      ...
      "java.base\/java.lang.VirtualThread
        .run(VirtualThread.java:311)"
      ]
    },
    {
    "tid": "24",
    "name": "",
    "stack": [
      ...
      "java.base\/java.lang.VirtualThread
        .run(VirtualThread.java:311)"
      ]
    },
    {
    "tid": "25",
    "name": "",
    "stack": [
      ...
      "java.base\/java.lang.VirtualThread
```

```
            .run(VirtualThread.java:311)"
        ]
      }
    ],
    "threadCount": "3"
  }
  ...
```

As you can see, we have three virtual threads (#22, #24, and #25) that run subtasks of our scope. In the bundled code, you can find the complete output.

Summary

This chapter covered 16 introductory problems about virtual threads and structured concurrency. You can see this chapter as preparation for the next one, which will cover more detailed aspects of these two topics.

Join our community on Discord

Join our community's Discord space for discussions with the author and other readers:

```
https://discord.gg/8mgytp5DGQ
```

11

Concurrency – Virtual Threads and Structured Concurrency: Diving Deeper

This chapter includes 18 problems meant to dive deep into how *virtual threads* and *structured concurrency* work and how they should be used in your applications.

If you don't have a background in concurrency in Java then I strongly recommend postponing this chapter until you read some good introductory coverage on this topic. For instance, you could try out *Chapter 10* and *Chapter 11* from *Java Coding Problems, First Edition*.

We start this chapter by explaining how virtual threads work internally. This will be helpful to help you better understand the subsequent problems about extending and assembling StructuredTaskScope, hooking ThreadLocal and virtual threads, avoiding *pinning*, solving *producer-consumer* problems, implementing an HTTP web server, and so on.

By the end of this chapter, you'll have comprehensive and crystal-clear knowledge about working with *virtual threads* and *structured concurrency*.

Problems

Use the following problems to test your advanced programming prowess in virtual threads and structured concurrency in Java. I strongly encourage you to give each problem a try before you turn to the solutions and download the example programs:

225. **Tackling continuations:** Provide a detailed explanation of what *continuations* are and how they work in the context of virtual threads.

226. **Tracing virtual thread states and transitions:** Build a meaningful diagram of virtual thread states and transitions and explain it.

227. **Extending StructuredTaskScope:** Explain and demonstrate the steps for extending the `StructuredTaskScope`. Explain why we cannot extend `ShutdownOnSuccess` and `ShutdownOnFailure`.

228. **Assembling StructuredTaskScope:** Write a Java application that assembles (nests) multiple `StructuredTaskScope` instances.

229. **Assembling StructuredTaskScope with timeout:** Modify the application developed in *Problem 228* to add a timeout/deadline to the forked tasks.

230. **Hooking ThreadLocal and virtual threads:** Demonstrate the use of `ThreadLocal` and virtual threads.

231. **Hooking ScopedValue and virtual threads:** Provide a comprehensive introduction with examples of the `ScopedValue` API.

232. **Using ScopedValue and executor services:** Write a snippet of code that emphasizes the usage of the `ScopedValue` API in the context of executor services.

233. **Chaining and rebinding scoped values:** Provide a few snippets of code that show how scoped values can be chained and rebound.

234. **Using ScopedValue and StructuredTaskScope:** Write a Java application that highlights the usage of `ScopedValue` and `StructuredTaskScope`. Explain in your code where every `ScopedValue` is bound and not bound.

235. **Using Semaphore instead of Executor:** In the context of virtual threads, explain the benefits and exemplify the usage of `Semaphore` instead of an executor (for instance, instead of `newFixedThreadPool()`).

236. **Avoiding pinning via locking:** Explain and exemplify how we can avoid pinned virtual threads by refactoring `synchronized` code via `ReentrantLock`.

237. **Solving the producer-consumer problem via virtual threads:** Write a program that simulates, via the producer-consumer pattern, an assembly line for checking and packing up bulbs using multiple workers (virtual threads).

238. **Solving the producer-consumer problem via virtual threads (fixed via Semaphore):** Adapt the application developed in *Problem 237* to use `Semaphore` instead of executor services.

239. **Solving the producer-consumer problem via virtual threads (increase/decrease consumers):** Write a program that simulates an assembly line for checking and packing up bulbs using workers as needed (e.g., adapt the number of packers (increase or decrease them) to ingest the incoming flux produced by the checker). Use virtual threads and `Semaphore`.

240. **Implementing an HTTP web server on top of virtual threads:** Rely on Java `HttpServer` to write a simple HTTP web server implementation capable of supporting platform threads, virtual threads, and locking (for simulating a database connection pool).

241. **Hooking CompletableFuture and virtual threads:** Demonstrate the usage of `CompletableFuture` and virtual threads to solve asynchronous tasks.

242. **Signaling virtual threads via wait() and notify():** Write several examples that use `wait()` and `notify()` to coordinate access to resources (objects) via virtual threads. Demonstrate the good signal and missed signal scenarios.

The following sections describe solutions to the preceding problems. Remember that there usually isn't a single correct way to solve a particular problem. Also, remember that the explanations shown here include only the most interesting and important details needed to solve the problems. Download the example solutions to see additional details and to experiment with the programs at https://github.com/PacktPublishing/Java-Coding-Problems-Second-Edition/tree/main/Chapter11.

225. Tackling continuations

The concept that sits behind virtual threads is known as *delimited continuations* or simply *continuations*. This concept is used internally by the JVM in the following piece of code:

```
List<Thread> vtThreads = IntStream.range(0, 5)
  .mapToObj(i -> Thread.ofVirtual().unstarted(() -> {

    if (i == 0) {
      logger.info(Thread.currentThread().toString());
    }

    try { Thread.sleep(1000); }
      catch (InterruptedException ex) {}

    if (i == 0) {
      logger.info(Thread.currentThread().toString());
    }
})).toList();

vtThreads.forEach(Thread::start);
vtThreads.forEach(thread -> {
  try { thread.join(); } catch (InterruptedException ex) {}
});
```

In this code, we create and start five virtual threads but we only log information about one thread (thread #22 – of course, the id value may vary among executions). So, the output will be as follows:

```
VirtualThread[#22]/runnable@ForkJoinPool-1-worker-1
VirtualThread[#22]/runnable@ForkJoinPool-1-worker-4
```

Thread #22 has started running on *worker-1*, but after the blocking operation (sleep(1000)), it continues to run on *worker-4*. Behind this *thread context switching*, we have the so-called *continuations*.

Basically, the behavior of *continuations* can easily be explained via a popular debugger use case. When we debug the code, we set a breakpoint and run the code. When the flow hits this breakpoint, the execution freezes and we can inspect the current status of the application. Later on, when we've done the inspection, we continue running the code from this breakpoint forward. The debugger knows how to resume the execution from where it was left off (frozen). So, the execution continues until it hits the end of the application or until another breakpoint is encountered.

Briefly, virtual threads follow the same behavior. A virtual thread is mounted on a platform thread (*worker-x*) and starts running. When the execution hits a blocking operation (for instance, a `sleep()` call), then the virtual thread is unmounted from its worker. Later on, after the blocking operation ends, the thread execution is resumed by scheduling and mounting it on a platform thread (same worker, *worker-x*, or another *worker-y*).

Introducing continuations

Going deeper, we have to introduce *subroutines* and *coroutines*. Subroutines are functions that can be called and get back a response, while coroutines are *cooperating subroutines* that run at the same time and talk to each other like in a human conversation. Exactly like how two people talk to each other, coroutines set up a conversational state via two subroutines that are talking to each other. Via this paradigm, an application can perform some tasks, do nothing for a while, and then perform more tasks later.

But, how can coroutines remember the data involved in the conversations? The short answer is *continuations*. Continuations are data structures capable of carrying data (the conversational state) between coroutines. They can resume processing from where it was left off.

Virtual threads take advantage of continuations by being capable of doing some work, then unmounting, and, later on, resuming from where they left off.

Project Loom provides the API for working with continuations as an internal API, so it is not meant to be used directly in applications (we shouldn't try to use this low-level API unless our goal is to write some higher-level API (libraries) on top of it). However, this API relies on two main classes and three methods. As classes, we have the `ContinuationScope`, which is the scope for handling nested `Continuation` instances. As methods, we have:

- `run()` – run a continuation from where it was left off
- `yield()` – freeze (suspend) the continuation at this point and give control to the continuation's caller (`run()` will be able to resume the execution from here)
- `isDone()` – test if the current continuation is complete

So, under a `ContinuationScope` umbrella, we can have multiple nested continuations that set up a conversational state via `run()`, `yield()`, and `isDone()`. For virtual threads, there is a single `ContinuationScope` named `VTHREAD_SCOPE`.

Here is a snippet of code that explains this statement:

```
ContinuationScope cscope = new ContinuationScope("cscope");

Continuation continuation = new Continuation(cscope, () ->
    logger.info("Continuation is running ...");
});

continuation.run();
```

Since we call `continuation.run()`, this code will output:

```
Continuation is running ...
```

This is quite straightforward. Next, let's suspend the continuation via `yield()`:

```
Continuation continuation = new Continuation(cscope, () ->
    logger.info("Continuation is running ...");
    Continuation.yield(cscope);
    logger.info("Continuation keeps running ...");
});

continuation.run();
```

At the moment, the output is the same:

```
Continuation is running ...
```

Practically, when we call the `yield()` method, the continuation is suspended and control is given to the caller. We can easily see this by adding some logs after calling the `run()` method as follows:

```
continuation.run();
logger.info("The continuation was suspended ...");
```

Now, the output will be:

```
Continuation is running ...
The continuation was suspended ...
```

As you can see, the `logger.info("Continuation keeps running ...");` code line was not executed. The `yield()` method has frozen the execution before this line and returned the control to the caller. In order to resume the continuation from where it was left off, we have to call `run()` again:

```
continuation.run();
logger.info("The continuation was suspended ...");
continuation.run();
logger.info("The continuation is done ...");
```

This time, the output will be as follows (you can check if the continuation is done via `isDone()`):

```
Continuation is running ...
The continuation was suspended ...
Continuation keeps running ...
The continuation is done ...
```

As you can see, when we call `run()` again, the execution is resumed from where it was left off, not from the beginning. This is how continuations work.

Continuations and virtual threads

Now, let's see how virtual threads and sleep() work via continuations in our example. Our virtual thread (#22) starts its journey by logging a simple message. Afterward, it hits the Thread.sleep(1000); code line, as in the following diagram:

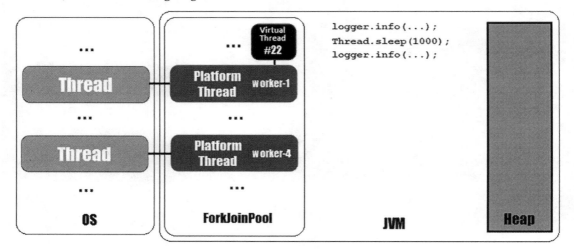

Figure 11.1: The virtual thread #22 running on worker-1

If we check the JDK 21 source code, we can easily highlight the following snippet of code from the sleep() method in the Thread class:

```
// this is the JDK 21 code

public static void sleep(long millis)
    throws InterruptedException {
  ...
  long nanos = MILLISECONDS.toNanos(millis);
  ...
  if (currentThread() instanceofVirtualThread vthread) {
    vthread.sleepNanos(nanos);
  }
  ...
}
```

So, if the thread that has called sleep() is a virtual thread, then the code simply calls the internal sleepNanos() method from the VirtualThread class. The relevant code that we are interested in is the following:

```
// this is the JDK 21 code
```

```
void sleepNanos(long nanos) throws InterruptedException {
  ...
  if (nanos == 0) {
    tryYield();
  } else {
    // park for the sleep time
    try {
      ...
      parkNanos(remainingNanos);
      ...
    } finally {
      // may have been unparked while sleeping
      setParkPermit(true);
    }
  }
}
```

So, here the code can call the tryYield() method (if nanos is 0) or the parkNanos() method. If tryYield() is called, then the thread state is set as YIELDING. On the other hand, if parkNanos() is called, then the thread state is set as PARKING. In both cases (via tryYield() or parkNanos()), the execution hits the yieldContinuation(), which is the climax of our journey:

```
// this is the JDK 21 code

private boolean yieldContinuation() {
  // unmount
  notifyJvmtiUnmount(/*hide*/true);
  unmount();
  try {
    return Continuation.yield(VTHREAD_SCOPE);
  } finally {
    // re-mount
    mount();
    notifyJvmtiMount(/*hide*/false);
  }
}
```

As you can see, here the virtual thread is unmounted, and `yield()` is called. So, the virtual thread stack is copied into the heap and the thread is unmounted from the carrier thread (it becomes PARKED). We can see this via the following diagram:

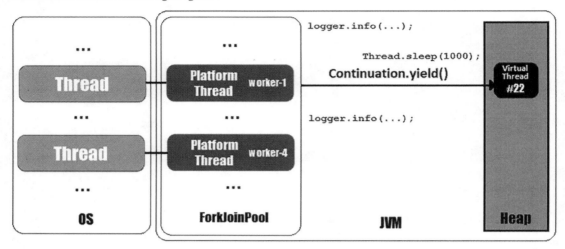

Figure 11.2: The virtual thread #22 is unmounted and moved to the heap

This scenario takes place for any blocking operation, not just for `sleep()`. Once virtual thread #22 is uncounted, *worker-1* is ready to serve another virtual thread or do some other processing.

After the blocking operation finishes (here, `sleep(1000)`), the `private` method `runContinuation()` from the `VirtualThread` class is called and the execution of #22 is resumed. As you can see in the following diagram, #22 is mounted now on *worker-4* since *worker-1* is not available (it has to execute some hypothetical virtual thread, #41).

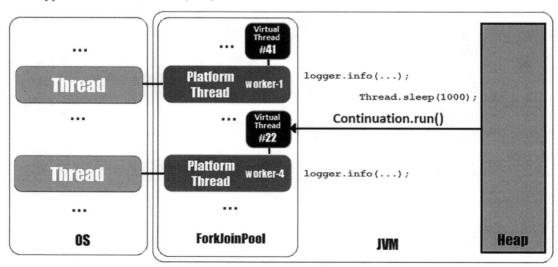

Figure 11.3: The execution of virtual thread #22 is resumed on worker-4

The execution continues with the second logging instruction and terminates. This is how continuations and virtual threads work internally to sustain a massive throughput.

226. Tracing virtual thread states and transitions

As you know, a thread can be in one of the following states: NEW, RUNNABLE, BLOCKED, WAITING, TIMED_WAITING, or TERMINATED. These states are elements of the State enum and are exposed via the Thread.currentThread().getState() call. These states are valid for platform threads and for virtual threads as well and we can use them in our applications. (If you're unfamiliar with this, you can find more details about it in *Java Coding Problems, First Edition, Chapter 10, Problem 199.*)

However, internally speaking, a virtual thread works on a state transition model, as shown in the following figure:

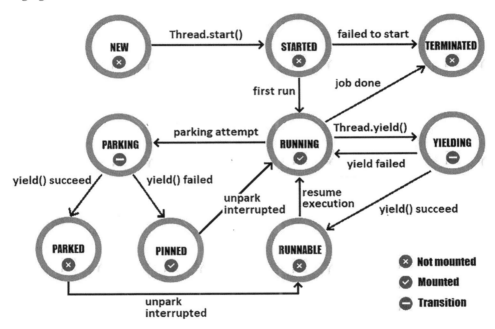

Figure 11.4: Virtual thread state transitions

These states are declared in the VirtualThread class as private static final int. So, they are not public. However, they are essential for understanding the lifecycle of a virtual thread, so let's briefly attempt to trace a virtual thread's states during its lifetime.

NEW

When a virtual thread is created (for instance, via the unstarted() method), it is in the NEW state. In this state, the thread is not mounted and not even started. However, at that moment, JVM calls the constructor of the VirtualThread listed here:

```
// this is the JDK 21 code
```

```java
VirtualThread(Executor scheduler, String name,
    int characteristics, Runnable task) {

  super(name, characteristics, /*bound*/ false);
  Objects.requireNonNull(task);

  // choose scheduler if not specified
  if (scheduler == null) {
    Thread parent = Thread.currentThread();
    if (parent instanceofVirtualThread vparent) {
      scheduler = vparent.scheduler;
    } else {
      scheduler = DEFAULT_SCHEDULER;
    }
  }

  this.scheduler = scheduler;
  this.cont = new VThreadContinuation(this, task);
  this.runContinuation = this::runContinuation;
}
```

So, this constructor is responsible for choosing the scheduler to create a Continuation (which is a VThreadContinuation object that stores the information of what has to be run as a task) and prepare the runContinuation private field, which is a Runnable used to run the Continuation when the virtual thread is started.

STARTED

A virtual thread passes from NEW to STARTED when we call the start() method:

```java
// this is the JDK 21 code

@Override
void start(ThreadContainer container) {
  if (!compareAndSetState(NEW, STARTED)) {
    throw new IllegalThreadStateException("Already started");
  }
  ...
  // start thread
  boolean started = false;
  ...
  try {
```

```
  ...
  // submit task to run thread
  submitRunContinuation();
  started = true;
} finally {
  if (!started) {
    setState(TERMINATED);
    ...
  }
}
}
```

Moreover, at the moment, the runContinuation runnable is scheduled on the virtual thread scheduler via submitRunContinuation().

RUNNING

The runContinuation runnable moves the virtual thread state from STARTED to RUNNING and calls cont. run(). The virtual thread is mounted (it could be for the first time or just a subsequent mounting that resumes the execution from where it was left off) on a platform thread and starts running:

```
// this is the JDK 21 code

private void runContinuation() {

  ...

  // set state to RUNNING
  int initialState = state();
  if (initialState == STARTED
        && compareAndSetState(STARTED, RUNNING)) {
    // first run
  } else if (initialState == RUNNABLE
        && compareAndSetState(RUNNABLE, RUNNING)) {
    // consume parking permit
    setParkPermit(false);
  } else {
    // not runnable
    return;
  }

  // notify JVMTI before mount
  notifyJvmtiMount(/*hide*/true);
```

```
try {
  cont.run();
} finally {
  if (cont.isDone()) {
    afterTerminate();
  } else {
    afterYield();
  }
}
}
```

From this point forward, the virtual thread state can be moved to TERMINATED (the execution is done), PARKING (a blocking operation has been encountered), or YIELDING (the effect of calling Thread. yield()).

PARKING

The virtual thread is running until its job is done or it reaches a blocking operation. At this moment, the virtual thread should be unmounted from the platform thread (should be parked). In order to accomplish this, the JVM moves the virtual thread state from RUNNING to PARKING via the park() method. This is a transitional state to PARKED (park on the heap) or PINNED (park on its carrier thread).

PARKED/PINNED

Further, the yieldContinuation() is called from park() and the result of unmounting the virtual thread is signaled via the flag returned by Continuation.yield(VTHREAD_SCOPE). In other words, if the unmounting operation is a success, then the virtual thread state is moved from PARKING to PARKED (the virtual thread was successfully parked on the heap). Otherwise, if the unmounting operation fails, then the parkOnCarrierThread() method is called and the virtual thread state is moved to PINNED (the virtual thread is parked on the carrier thread). A PINNED virtual thread is moved to the RUNNING state when the execution can be resumed (since it was parked on its carrier thread). On the other hand, a PARKED virtual thread is moved to the RUNNABLE state when it is unparked (or interrupted). In this case, the virtual thread (which is not mounted) is mounted and the execution continues from where it was left by moving the state from RUNNABLE to RUNNING.

YIELDING

A virtual thread state is moved from RUNNING to YIELDING when a Thread.yield() call is encountered (for instance, this happens when we call Thread.yield() or Thread.sleep(0)). If the yield fails, then the virtual thread state is moved back to RUNNING. Otherwise, it is moved to RUNNABLE.

RUNNABLE

A virtual thread is in the RUNNABLE state when it is not mounted but it wants to resume its execution. It comes into this state from the PARKED or YIELDING states. At this moment, the virtual thread state is moved from RUNNABLE to RUNNING and the execution continues from where it was left off (this happens in runContinuation()).

TERMINATED

Now, the circle is closed. The virtual thread finishes its execution and gets into the TERMINATED state. Moreover, a virtual thread that couldn't be started is also moved to this state.

227. Extending StructuredTaskScope

We cannot extend StructuredTaskScope.ShutdownOnSuccess (*Chapter 10*, *Problem 221*) or ShutdownOnFailure (*Chapter 10*, *Problem 222*) since these are final classes. But, we can extend StructuredTaskScope and provide a custom behavior via its handleComplete() method.

Let's assume that we want to travel from our current location to a certain destination in our town:

```
String loc = "124 NW Bobcat L, St. Robert"; // from user
String dest = "129 West 81st Street";       // from user
```

On our phone, we have an application that can query a ridesharing service and the public transport service. The ridesharing service can simultaneously query multiple ridesharing servers to find the cheapest offer. On the other hand, the public transport service can simultaneously query the public transport servers to find the offer that leaves the earliest, no matter whether it is by bus, train, tram, or subway. In a diagram, we can represent these statements as follows:

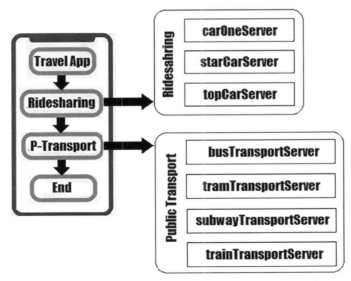

Figure 11.5: Querying ridesharing and public transport services

Both services are implemented via a `StructuredTaskScope`, but the one that queries the public transport servers uses a custom `StructuredTaskScope`, while the one that queries the ridesharing servers uses a classical `StructuredTaskScope`.

Since we are already familiar with the classical `StructuredTaskScope`, let's quickly cover the ridesharing service. An offer received from this service is shaped as a record:

```
public record RidesharingOffer(String company, Duration
   minutesToYou, Duration minutesToDest, double price) {}
```

The core of our code starts by forking a task for each of the three ridesharing servers:

```
public static RidesharingOffer
    fetchRidesharingOffers(String loc, String dest)
        throws InterruptedException {

  try (StructuredTaskScope scope
    = new StructuredTaskScope<RidesharingOffer>()) {

    Subtask<RidesharingOffer> carOneOffer
     = scope.fork(() -> Ridesharing.carOneServer(loc, dest));
    Subtask<RidesharingOffer> starCarOffer
     = scope.fork(() -> Ridesharing.starCarServer(loc, dest));
    Subtask<RidesharingOffer> topCarOffer
     = scope.fork(() -> Ridesharing.topCarServer(loc, dest));

    scope.join();
    ...
```

After `scope.join()` finishes, we know that all subtasks have been finished successfully or exceptionally. We filter the results to extract the cheapest offer. If no offer is available, then we collect all exceptions and wrap them in a custom `RidesharingException`. Writing this as a functional programming snippet of code can be done as follows:

```
RidesharingOffer offer
 = Stream.of(carOneOffer, starCarOffer, topCarOffer)
 .filter(s -> s.state() == Subtask.State.SUCCESS)
 .<RidesharingOffer>mapMulti((s, c) -> {
    c.accept((RidesharingOffer) s.get());
 })
 .min(Comparator.comparingDouble(RidesharingOffer::price))
 .orElseThrow(() -> {
    RidesharingException exceptionWrapper
     = new RidesharingException("Ridesharing exception");
    Stream.of(carOneOffer, starCarOffer, topCarOffer)
```

```
            .filter(s -> s.state() == Subtask.State.FAILED)
            .<Throwable>mapMulti((s, c) -> {
                c.accept(s.exception());
            }).forEach(exceptionWrapper::addSuppressed);
        throw exceptionWrapper;
    });
    ...
```

Finally, we return the offer:

```
    return offer;
}
```

A possible output will be:

```
RidesharingOffer[company=TopCar, minutesToYou=PT9M, minutesToDest=PT16M,
price=7.62]
```

Next, let's focus on the public transport service. This service queries the public transport servers via a custom StructuredTaskScope. A public transport offer is wrapped in the following record:

```
public record PublicTransportOffer(String transport,
    String station, LocalTime goTime) {}
```

The custom StructuredTaskScope is named PublicTransportScope and its goal is to analyze each subtask (Subtask) and to fetch the best offer. Extending the StructuredTaskScope is straightforward:

```
public class PublicTransportScope
    extends StructuredTaskScope<List<PublicTransportOffer>> {
    ...
```

A public transport server returns a List<PublicTransportOffer>. For instance, there can be three trains, or five buses in a day that cover our route. We will get them all on a separate list.

When we extend StructuredTaskScope, we have to override a single method named handleComplete(). This method is automatically invoked for each Subtask that completes successfully or exceptionally. It is our job to collect and store the results for analysis later. To collect the results, we need a collection for valid results and a collection for exceptional results. These should be thread-safe collections since multiple Subtask instances may complete (almost) at the same time, which leads to race conditions. For instance, we can use CopyOnWriteArrayList:

```
    private final List<List<PublicTransportOffer>> results
        = new CopyOnWriteArrayList<>();
    private final List<Throwable> exceptions
        = new CopyOnWriteArrayList<>();
    ...
```

Next, we override `handleComplete()`, and based on the `Subtask` state, we collect the results accordingly:

```
@Override
protected void handleComplete(
    Subtask<? extends List<PublicTransportOffer>> subtask) {

    switch (subtask.state()) {
      case SUCCESS ->
        results.add(subtask.get());
      case FAILED ->
        exceptions.add(subtask.exception());
      case UNAVAILABLE ->
        throw new IllegalStateException(
          "Subtask may still running ...");
    }
  }
}
...
```

When we reach this point, we have collected all successful and exceptional results. It is time to analyze this data and recommend the best offer. We consider that the best offer is the offer that leaves the earliest no matter whether it is by bus, train, tram, or subway. So, we just have to find the best `goTime`:

```
public PublicTransportOffer recommendedPublicTransport() {

    super.ensureOwnerAndJoined();

    return results.stream()
      .flatMap(t -> t.stream())
      .min(Comparator.comparing(PublicTransportOffer::goTime))
      .orElseThrow(this::wrappingExceptions);
}
...
```

If we cannot find any valid offer, then we collect the exceptions and wrap them in a custom `PublicTransportException` via the following helper:

```
private PublicTransportException wrappingExceptions() {

    super.ensureOwnerAndJoined();

    PublicTransportException exceptionWrapper = new
      PublicTransportException("Public transport exception");
    exceptions.forEach(exceptionWrapper::addSuppressed);
```

```
      return exceptionWrapper;
   }
}
```

Notice that both of these methods are calling the ensureOwnerAndJoined() method. This built-in method guarantees that the current thread is the owner of this task scope (otherwise, it throws WrongThreadException) and that it joined after forking subtasks via join()/joinUntil() (otherwise, it throws an IllegalStateException).

Important note

As a rule of thumb it is good practice to rely on the ensureOwnerAndJoined() check on every StructuredTaskScope that needs to be called by the main task.

Done! Our custom StructuredTaskScope is ready. Next, we can use it by forking our tasks and calling the recommendedPublicTransport() method:

```
public static PublicTransportOffer
    fetchPublicTransportOffers(String loc, String dest)
        throws InterruptedException {

   try (PublicTransportScope scope
                 = new PublicTransportScope()) {

      scope.fork(() -> PublicTransport
         .busTransportServer(loc, dest));
      scope.fork(() -> PublicTransport
         .subwayTransportServer(loc, dest));
      scope.fork(() -> PublicTransport
         .trainTransportServer(loc, dest));
      scope.fork(() -> PublicTransport
         .tramTransportServer(loc, dest));

      scope.join();

      PublicTransportOffer offer
         = scope.recommendedPublicTransport();

      logger.info(offer.toString());

      return offer;
```

```
    }
}
```

A possible output looks like this:

```
PublicTransportOffer[transport=Tram, station=Tram_station_0, goTime=10:26:39]
```

Finally, we can call both services (ridesharing and public transport) as follows:

```
RidesharingOffer roffer
    = fetchRidesharingOffers(loc, dest);
PublicTransportOffer ptoffer
    = fetchPublicTransportOffers(loc, dest);
```

So far, these two services run sequentially. In the next problem, we will run these two services concurrently by introducing another custom StructuredTaskScope. Until then, you can challenge yourself to write a custom StructuredTaskScope for the ridesharing service as well.

228. Assembling StructuredTaskScope

In the previous problem (*Problem 227*), we developed an application containing a ridesharing service and a public transport service. In both services, we used StructuredTaskScope to concurrently query the proper servers. However, only the servers were called concurrently while these two services were executed sequentially – first, we run the ridesharing service (which queries concurrently three servers), and after we have a result from this service, we run the public transport service (which queries concurrently four servers).

Going further, we want to assemble these two services into a third service capable of running them concurrently as in the following diagram:

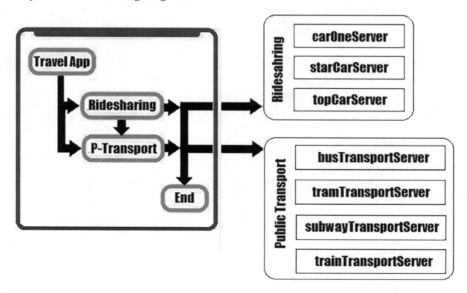

Figure 11.6: Running the ridesharing and public transport services concurrently

We start by assembling the `RidesharingOffer` and `PublicTransportOffer` into a record named `TravelOffer`:

```
public record TravelOffer(RidesharingOffer ridesharingOffer,
  PublicTransportOffer publicTransportOffer) {}
```

Next, we write a custom `StructuredTaskScope` that forks the two `Callable` objects created in *Problem 227*. One `Callable` represents the ridesharing services (already implemented in *Problem 227* via a classic `StructuredTaskScope`), and the second `Callable` represents the public transport services (already implemented in *Problem 227* via the custom `PublicTransportScope`). We can name this `StructuredTaskScope` as `TravelScope`:

```
public class TravelScope extends StructuredTaskScope<Travel> {
  ...
```

The `StructuredTaskScope` is parametrized – notice the `StructuredTaskScope<Travel>`. Since we have to fork different types of `Callable` instances, it would be handy to rely on `Object` and write `StructuredTaskScope<Object>`. But this will not be very expressive and neat. We better define an interface that narrows down the `Object` domain and that is implemented by our `Callable` instance's results as follows (*sealed interfaces* were covered in detail in *Chapter 8*):

```
public sealed interface Travel
  permits RidesharingOffer, PublicTransportOffer {}

public record RidesharingOffer(String company,
  Duration minutesToYou, Duration minutesToDest, double price)
    implements Travel {}

public record PublicTransportOffer(String transport,
  String station, LocalTime goTime) implements Travel {}
```

Getting back to `TravelScope`, we have to override the `handleComplete()` method to handle each completed `Subtask`. We know that the ridesharing service can return a valid result as a `RidesharingOffer` or an exceptional result as a `RidesharingException`. Moreover, the public transport service can return a valid result as `PublicTransportOffer` or an exceptional result as a `PublicTransportException`. We have to store these results in order to analyze them later when we create the `TravelOffer` answer. So, we define the following variables to cover all possible cases:

```
private volatile RidesharingOffer ridesharingOffer;
private volatile PublicTransportOffer publicTransportOffer;
private volatile RidesharingException ridesharingException;
private volatile PublicTransportException
  publicTransportException;
...
```

Next, we override the handleComplete() and, exactly as in the case of PublicTransportScope, we rely on a simple switch to collect the results (for the SUCCESS and FAILED states, we need a nested switch to distinguish between the offer/exception received from the ridesharing service and the offer/ exception received from the public transport service):

```java
@Override
protected void handleComplete(
    Subtask<? extends Travel> subtask) {

  switch (subtask.state()) {
    case SUCCESS -> {
      switch (subtask.get()) {
        case RidesharingOffer ro ->
          this.ridesharingOffer = ro;
          case PublicTransportOffer pto ->
          this.publicTransportOffer = pto;
      }
    }
    case FAILED -> {
      switch (subtask.exception()) {
        case RidesharingException re ->
          this.ridesharingException = re;
        case PublicTransportException pte ->
          this.publicTransportException = pte;
        case Throwable t ->
          throw new RuntimeException(t);
      }
    }
    case UNAVAILABLE ->
      throw new IllegalStateException(
        "Subtask may still running ...");
  }
}
...
```

Finally, we analyze these results and create the proper TravelOffer. One way to accomplish this is as follows (feel free to think of a cooler/smarter implementation):

```java
public TravelOffer recommendedTravelOffer() {

  super.ensureOwnerAndJoined();
```

```
      return new TravelOffer(
         ridesharingOffer, publicTransportOffer);
   }
}
```

Our TravelScope is ready to be used. All we need to do is to fork our two services to be executed concurrently and call the recommendedTravelOffer() method to get the best offer:

```
public static TravelOffer fetchTravelOffers(
    String loc, String dest)
        throws InterruptedException {

  try (TravelScope scope = new TravelScope()) {

    scope.fork(() -> fetchRidesharingOffers(loc, dest));
    scope.fork(() -> fetchPublicTransportOffers(loc, dest));

    scope.join();

    return scope.recommendedTravelOffer();
  }
}
```

Now, instead of sequentially calling fetchRidesharingOffers() and fetchPublicTransportOffers(), we simply call fetchTravelOffers():

```
TravelOffer toffer = fetchTravelOffers(loc, dest);
```

A possible output would be:

```
TravelOffer[
    ridesharingOffer=RidesharingOffer[company=CarOne,
    minutesToYou=PT5M, minutesToDest=PT5M, price=3.0],

    publicTransportOffer=PublicTransportOffer[transport=Train,
    station=Train_station_0, goTime=11:59:10]
]
```

Mission accomplished! Now you know how to write custom StructuredTaskScope instances and how to assemble/nest them to shape complex concurrent models.

229. Assembling StructuredTaskScope instances with timeout

Let's continue our journey from *Problem 228* by assuming that the ridesharing service should be implemented with a timeout/deadline. In other words, if any of the ridesharing servers don't answer in 10 milliseconds, then we abort the request and report the thrown `TimeoutException` via a meaningful message to the user.

This means that instead of `scope.join()`, which waits indefinitely, we should use `joinUntil(Instant deadline)`, which waits only for the given `deadline` before throwing a `TimeoutException`. So, the `fetchRidesharingOffers()` method should be modified as follows:

```
public static RidesharingOffer fetchRidesharingOffers(
    String loc, String dest)
      throws InterruptedException, TimeoutException {

  try (StructuredTaskScope scope
    = new StructuredTaskScope<RidesharingOffer>()) {

    ...

    scope.joinUntil(Instant.now().plusMillis(10));
    ...

  }
}
```

By simply simulating a delay bigger than 10 milliseconds in any of the ridesharing servers, we help this `joinUntil()` to fail with a `TimeoutException`:

```
public final class Ridesharing {

  public static RidesharingOffer carOneServer(
    String loc, String dest) throws InterruptedException {

    ...

    Thread.sleep(100); // simulating a delay
    ...

  }
  ...
}
```

In order to capture this `TimeoutException` and replace it with a friendly message for the end user, we have to adapt the `TravelScope` class. First, we define a variable to store the potential `TimeoutException`. Second, we adapt the `case FAILED` to populate this variable accordingly:

```
public class TravelScope extends StructuredTaskScope<Travel> {
```

```
...
private volatile TimeoutException timeoutException;

@Override
protected void handleComplete(Subtask<? extends Travel> subtask) {

  switch (subtask.state()) {
    ...
    case FAILED -> {
      switch (subtask.exception()) {
        ...
        case TimeoutException te ->
            this.timeoutException = te;
        ...
      }
    }
    ...
  }
}
... // the recommendedTravelOffer() method from below
}
```

Third, we modify the recommendedTravelOffer() method to return a friendly message if timeoutException is not null:

```
public TravelOffer recommendedTravelOffer() {

  super.ensureOwnerAndJoined();

  if (timeoutException != null) {
    logger.warning("Some of the called services
                    did not respond in time");
  }

  return new TravelOffer(
    ridesharingOffer, publicTransportOffer);
}
```

If the ridesharing service timeouts and the public transport service provides an offer, then the output should be something like this:

```
[14:53:34] [WARNING] Some of the called services
                    did not respond in time
```

```
[14:53:35] [INFO] TravelOffer[ridesharingOffer=null,
publicTransportOffer=PublicTransportOffer[transport=Bus, station=Bus_station_2,
goTime=15:02:34]]
```

Done! Check out the bundled code to practice this example. Challenge yourself to add a timeout/deadline for the public transport service as well.

230. Hooking ThreadLocal and virtual threads

In a nutshell, ThreadLocal was introduced in JDK 1.2 (in 1998) as a solution to provide dedicated memory for each thread in order to share information with untrusted code (maybe some of your code has been written externally as third-party components) or between different components (that may run in multiple threads) of your application. Basically, if you are in such a scenario, then you don't want to (or you cannot) share information via method arguments. If you need a more in-depth introduction to the ThreadLocal API, then consider *Java Coding Problems, First Edition, Chapter 11, Problem 220*.

A thread-local variable is of type ThreadLocal and relies on set() to set a value and on get() to get a value. In *Java Coding Problems, First Edition,* it was said that: *"If thread* A *stores the* x *value and thread* B *stores the* y *value in the same instance of* ThreadLocal, *then later on, thread* A *retrieves the* x *value and thread* B *retrieves the* y *value. So, we can say that the* x *value is local to thread* A, *while the* y *value is local to thread* B." Each thread that calls get() or set() has its own copy of the ThreadLocal variable.

Important note

Internally, ThreadLocal manages a map (ThreadLocalMap). The keys of the map are the threads, and the values are those values given via the set() method. ThreadLocal variables fit well for implementing the *one thread per request* model (for instance, one thread per HTTP request) since they allow us to easily manage the lifecycle of a request.

Typically, a thread-local variable is global and static and it can be declared and initialized as follows:

```
private static final ThreadLocal<StringBuilder> threadLocal
    = ThreadLocal.<StringBuilder>withInitial(() -> {
        return new StringBuilder("Nothing here ...");
});
```

A thread-local variable should be reachable in the code from where it is needed (sometimes from everywhere in the code). Basically, the current thread and all the threads spawned by this thread should have access to the thread-local variables. In our case, it is reachable from everywhere in the current class. Next, let's consider the following Runnable:

```
Runnable task = () -> {

    threadLocal.set(
        new StringBuilder(Thread.currentThread().toString()));
```

```
    logger.info(() -> " before sleep -> "
      + Thread.currentThread().toString()
        + " [" + threadLocal.get() + "]");

    try {
      Thread.sleep(Duration.ofSeconds(new Random().nextInt(5)));
    } catch (InterruptedException ex) {}

    logger.info(() -> " after sleep -> "
      + Thread.currentThread().toString()
        + " [" + threadLocal.get() + "]");

    threadLocal.remove();
};
```

Here, we set a thread-local value representing information about the current thread, we get and log that value, we sleep for a random number of seconds (between 0 and 5), and we log that value again.

Next, let's execute 10 tasks via a classical fixed thread pool (platform threads):

```
try (ExecutorService executor
        = Executors.newFixedThreadPool(10)) {

  for (int i = 0; i < 10; i++) {

    executor.submit(task);
  }
}
```

A snippet of the output may look as follows:

```
[16:14:05] before sleep -> Thread[#24,pool-1-thread-3,5,main] [Thread[#24,pool-
1-thread-3,5,main]]
[16:14:05] before sleep -> Thread[#31,pool-1-thread-10,5,main]
[Thread[#31,pool-1-thread-10,5,main]]
[16:14:05] before sleep -> Thread[#22,pool-1-thread-1,5,main] [Thread[#22,pool-
1-thread-1,5,main]]
...
[16:14:06] after sleep -> Thread[#24,pool-1-thread-3,5,main] [Thread[#24,pool-
1-thread-3,5,main]]
[16:14:07] after sleep -> Thread[#31,pool-1-thread-10,5,main] [Thread[#31,pool-
1-thread-10,5,main]]
```

```
[16:14:09] after sleep -> Thread[#22,pool-1-thread-1,5,main] [Thread[#22,pool-
1-thread-1,5,main]]
...
```

We can easily see that each of threads #24, #31, and #22 sets information about themselves, and this information is available after sleeping. For instance, thread #22 sets the value [Thread[#22,pool-1-thread-1,5,main]], and this value is exactly what it gets after sleeping for 4 seconds.

Now, let's switch to virtual threads:

```
try (ExecutorService executor
    = Executors.newVirtualThreadPerTaskExecutor()) {

  for (int i = 0; i < 10; i++) {

    executor.submit(task);
  }
}
```

The output will be:

```
[16:24:24] before sleep ->VirtualThread[#25]/runnable@ForkJoinPool-1-worker-3
[VirtualThread[#25]/runnable@ForkJoinPool-1-worker-3]
[16:24:24] before sleep ->VirtualThread[#27]/runnable@ForkJoinPool-1-worker-5
[VirtualThread[#27]/runnable@ForkJoinPool-1-worker-5]
[16:24:24] before sleep ->VirtualThread[#28]/runnable@ForkJoinPool-1-worker-6
[VirtualThread[#28]/runnable@ForkJoinPool-1-worker-6]
...
[16:24:24] after sleep ->VirtualThread[#28]/runnable@ForkJoinPool-1-worker-3
[VirtualThread[#28]/runnable@ForkJoinPool-1-worker-6]
[16:24:27] after sleep ->VirtualThread[#25]/runnable@ForkJoinPool-1-worker-4
[VirtualThread[#25]/runnable@ForkJoinPool-1-worker-3]
[16:24:27] after sleep ->VirtualThread[#27]/runnable@ForkJoinPool-1-worker-8
[VirtualThread[#27]/runnable@ForkJoinPool-1-worker-5]
...
```

We can easily see that each of threads #25, #27, and #28 sets information about themselves and this information is available after the sleeping period. For instance, thread #25 sets the value [VirtualThread[#25]/runnable@ForkJoinPool-1-worker-3], and this value is exactly what it gets after sleeping for 3 seconds.

However, when we get this information, thread #25 is executed on *worker-4*, not on *worker-3*, as the information reveals. Practically, thread #25 has been executed on *worker-3* when the information was set, and it has been executed on *worker-4* when the information (which remains unchanged) was get.

This is perfectly normal since the thread was unmounted from *worker-3* when the execution hit the `Thread.sleep()` blocking operation. After sleeping, it was mounted on *worker-4*. However, the information was not altered, so virtual threads and `ThreadLocal` work together as expected. In other words, the mounting-unmounting cycles of a virtual thread don't affect how `ThreadLocal` works. `ThreadLocal` variables are fully supported by virtual threads.

231. Hooking ScopedValue and virtual threads

The `ScopedValue` API was added to handle the shortcomings of `ThreadLocal`. But what are the shortcomings of `ThreadLocal`?

Thread-local variables' shortcomings

First of all, it is hard to say and track who's mutating a thread-local variable. This is a shortcoming of the API design. Basically, a `ThreadLocal` variable is globally available (at the application level or at a lower level), so it is hard to say from where it is mutated. Imagine that it is your responsibility to read, understand, and debug an application that uses several thread-local variables. How will you manage to follow the code logic and how will you know, at any given time, what values are stored by these thread-local variables? It would be a nightmare to track these variables from class to class and to signal when they mutated.

Second, thread-local variables may live forever or longer than they should. How is this possible? Thread-local variables will live as long as the platform threads that use them will live, or even longer. It is true that we can remove a thread-local variable from the internal map by explicitly calling `remove()`. But, if we forget to call `remove()`, then we just open the gate for memory leaks (we just hope that the garbage collector will collect this data at some point). Never forget to call `remove()` when you are done with a thread-local variable used by a platform thread! On the other hand, if you are using thread-local variables with virtual threads, then there is no need to call `remove()` because the thread-local variable is removed once the virtual thread dies.

Third, thread-local variables are prone to being duplicated. When we create a new thread (child thread) from the current thread (parent thread), the child thread copies all thread-local variables of the parent thread. So, if we spawn multiple threads from the current thread that has a significant number of thread-local variables, then we will duplicate a significant number of these variables. This is true for platform threads and for virtual threads. Since thread-local variables are not immutable, we cannot simply share the reference between threads. We have to copy them. Of course, this cannot be good for the application since it will negatively impact the memory footprint of these variables (imagine a million virtual threads having copies of thread-local variables).

Introducing scoped values

Starting with JDK 20 (JEP 429) we have an alternative to thread-local variables called *scoped values*. This is meant to work with virtual threads and to overcome the shortcomings of thread-local variables. In JDK 20, this feature is in the incubator phase, and in JDK 21 (JEP 446) it is in the preview phase, so don't forget to run the code using the `–code-preview` VM option.

Scoped values allow us to share immutable information (no need to copy) across the application's components and have a limited lifetime (no risk of memory leaks).

As you'll see, the ScopedValue API is very neat and easy to use. To create a ScopedValue, we just call a factory method named newInstance() as follows:

```
ScopedValue<String> SCOPED_VALUE = ScopedValue.newInstance();
```

Here, we've created a ScopedValue (not bound) that is capable of carrying a value of type String (of course, it could be anything else). You can declare it locally, globally, or however you need it to be declared depending on the place(s) that it should be accessible from. However, the value mapped to a ScopedValue is available for the current thread and all threads spawned by the current thread (so far, this is like ThreadLocal) but it is restricted to a method call. We will clarify this shortly.

> **Important note**
>
> A ScopedValue is considered bound if a value is mapped to it. Otherwise, the ScopedValue is considered not bound. We can check if a ScopedValue is bound via the isBound() flag method. This is an important check because if we attempt to get a value of a ScopedValue that is not bound, then we will get back NoSuchElementException. Besides isBound(), we also have orElse() and orElseThrow(). Using orElse(), we can set a default value for a ScopedValue that is not bound, while via orElseThrow(), we can throw a default exception.

A value can be mapped to a ScopedValue (so, the ScopedValue becomes bound to a value) via the where() method. The syntax of this method is listed here:

```
public static <T> Carrier where(ScopedValue<T> key, T value)
```

Or, via the runWhere() and callWhere() methods:

```
public static <T> void runWhere(
  ScopedValue<T> key, T value, Runnable op)

public static <T,R> R callWhere(
  ScopedValue<T> key, T value, Callable<? extends R> op)
    throws Exception
```

These three methods have in common the key and value parameters. The key represents the ScopedValue key (for instance, SCOPED_VALUE), while the value is the value mapped to this key. Whereas the where() method just creates a ScopedValue bound to a value, the runWhere() method can create a ScopedValue bound to a value and calls a Runnable operation (op) in the current thread, while callWhere() calls a Callable operation (op) in the current thread. If you prefer to rely only on the where() method, then simply rely on the following syntaxes:

```
ScopedValue.where(key, value).run(op); // like runWhere()
ScopedValue.where(key, value).call(op); // like callWhere()
```

So, chaining where().run() acts as runWhere(), while where().call() acts as callWhere(). The advantage of using where() suffixed with run()/call() consists of the fact that we can write ScopedValue.where(key1, value1).where(key2, value2), ...run()/call() to obtain multiple ScopedValue instances bound to their values.

> **Important note**
>
> A ScopedValue has no set() method. Once we map a value to a ScopedValue, we cannot change it (it is immutable). This means that the JVM doesn't need to copy values around (remember that this is a shortcoming specific to ThreadLocal).

The value is mapped to this key only for a method (Runnable or Callable) call. For instance, let's assume the following Runnable:

```
Runnable taskr = () -> {
  logger.info(Thread.currentThread().toString());
  logger.info(() -> SCOPED_VALUE.isBound() ?
    SCOPED_VALUE.get() : "Not bound");
};
```

Via the isBound() method, we can check if a ScopedValue is bound (if it has a value). If a value is present, then we can successfully access it via the get() method. Calling get() for a ScopedValue that is not bound will result in a NoSuchElementException exception. For instance, if we run this task now:

```
taskr.run();
```

Then, the output will be:

```
Thread[#1,main,5,main]
Not bound
```

This is normal since we didn't map any values to SCOPED_VALUE.

Next, we can use the where() method to map a value to SCOPED_VALUE and share this value with the previous Runnable:

```
Carrier cr = ScopedValue.where(SCOPED_VALUE, "Kaboooom!");
cr.run(taskr);
```

The Carrier object is an immutable and thread-safe accumulator of key-value mappings that can be shared with a Runnable/Callable. By calling cr.run(taskr), we share the value Kaboooom! with the Runnable, so the output will be:

```
Thread[#1,main,5,main]
Kaboooom!
```

But we can write this example more compactly as follows:

```
ScopedValue.where(SCOPED_VALUE, "Kaboooom!").run(taskr);
```

Or, by using runWhere():

```
ScopedValue.runWhere(SCOPED_VALUE, "Kaboooom!", taskr);
```

Calling taskr.run() will output Not bound again. This is happening because the ScopedValue is bound only for a method call. *Figure 11.7* highlights this via a more expressive example.

```
public static void sayHelloTL() {                    public static void sayHelloSV() {

  logger.info(Thread.currentThread().toString());       logger.info(Thread.currentThread().toString());
  logger.info(() -> "Hello " + threadLocal.get());       logger.info(() -> "Hello " + SCOPED_VALUE.orElse("you"));
}                                                    }

public static void sayGoodByeTL() {                  public static void sayGoodByeSV() {

  logger.info(Thread.currentThread().toString());       logger.info(Thread.currentThread().toString());
  logger.info(() -> "Good bye " + threadLocal.get());    logger.info(() -> "Good bye " + SCOPED_VALUE.orElse("you"));
}                                                    }

threadLocal.set("Mike");                             ScopedValue.where(SCOPED_VALUE, "Mike").run(() -> sayHelloSV());
sayHelloTL();                                        sayGoodByeSV();
sayGoodByeTL();

-------------------------                             -----------------------
Hello Mike                                           Hello Mike
Good bye Mike                                        Good bye you
```

ThreadLocal   **ScopedValue**

Figure 11.7: ThreadLocal vs. ScopedValue

As you can see from this figure (left-hand side), once the thread local sets the value, Mike, this value is available in sayHelloTL() and in sayGoodByeTL(). The value is bound to this thread. On the other hand (right-hand side), the value Mike is mapped to a ScopedValue, but this value is available only in sayHelloSV(). This is happening because we bound the SCOPED_VALUE only to the sayHelloSV() method call. When the execution leaves the sayHelloSV(), the SCOPED_VALUE is not bound, and the value Mike is not available anymore. If sayGoodByeSV() was called from sayHelloSV(), then the value Mike would have been available. Or, if we call sayGoodByeSV() as follows, then the value Mike is available:

```
ScopedValue.where(SCOPED_VALUE, "Mike").run(
  () -> sayGoodByeSV());
```

ScopedValue works with Callable as well, but we have to replace run() with call(). For instance, let's assume the following pretty dummy Callable:

```
Callable<Boolean> taskc = () -> {
  logger.info(Thread.currentThread().toString());
  logger.info(() -> SCOPED_VALUE.isBound() ?
    SCOPED_VALUE.get() : "Not bound");
  return true;
};
```

And the following sequence of calls:

```
taskc.call();


ScopedValue.where(SCOPED_VALUE, "Kaboooom-1!").call(taskc);


ScopedValue.callWhere(SCOPED_VALUE, "Kaboooom-2!", taskc);


Carrier cc = ScopedValue.where(SCOPED_VALUE, "Kaboooom-3!");
cc.call(taskc);


taskc.call();
```

Can you intuit the output? It should be Not bound, Kaboooom-1!, Kaboooom-2!, Kaboooom-3!, and Not bound again:

```
Thread[#1,main,5,main]
Not bound
Thread[#1,main,5,main]
Kaboooom-1!
Thread[#1,main,5,main]
Kaboooom-2!
Thread[#1,main,5,main]
Kaboooom-3!
Thread[#1,main,5,main]
Not bound
```

So, let me emphasize this once again. A ScopedValue is bound (it has a value) during a method call's lifetime. The isBound() will return false outside this method.

> **Important note**
>
> As you can see in this example, a ScopedValue can have different values in the same thread. Here, the same Callable was executed five times in the same thread.

Setting a ScopedValue from a certain thread (other than the main thread) can be done quite easily. For instance, we can set a ScopedValue from a platform thread as follows:

```
Thread tpr = new Thread(() ->
  ScopedValue.where(SCOPED_VALUE, "Kaboooom-r!").run(taskr));


Thread tpc = new Thread(() -> {
 try {
  ScopedValue.where(SCOPED_VALUE, "Kaboooom-c!").call(taskc);
```

```
  } catch (Exception ex) { /* handle exception */ }
});
```

Or, via the ofPlatform() method as follows:

```
Thread tpr = Thread.ofPlatform().unstarted(
  () -> ScopedValue.where(SCOPED_VALUE, "Kaboooom-r!")
  .run(taskr));

Thread tpc = Thread.ofPlatform().unstarted(()-> {
  try {
    ScopedValue.where(SCOPED_VALUE, "Kaboooom-c!").call(taskc);
  } catch (Exception ex) { /* handle exception */ }
});
```

Mapping a ScopedValue from a certain virtual thread can be done as follows:

```
Thread tvr = Thread.ofVirtual().unstarted(
  () -> ScopedValue.where(SCOPED_VALUE, "Kaboooom-r!")
  .run(taskr));

Thread tvc = Thread.ofVirtual().unstarted(() -> {
  try {
    ScopedValue.where(SCOPED_VALUE, "Kaboooom-c!").call(taskc);
  } catch (Exception ex) { /* handle exception */ }
});
```

Here, we have two threads, and each of them maps a different value to SCOPED_VALUE:

```
Thread tpcx = new Thread(() ->
  ScopedValue.where(SCOPED_VALUE, "Kaboooom-tpcx!")
    .run(taskr));

Thread tpcy = new Thread(() ->
  ScopedValue.where(SCOPED_VALUE, "Kaboooom-tpcy!")
    .run(taskr));
```

So, the first thread (tpcx) maps the value Kaboooom-tpcx!, while the second thread (tpcy) maps the value Kaboooom-tpcy!. When taskr is executed by tpcx, the mapped value will be Kaboooom-tpcx!, while when taskr is executed by tpcy, the mapped value will be Kaboooom-tpcy!.

Here is an example where tpca maps the value Kaboooom-tpca!, and tpcb doesn't map any value:

```
Thread tpca = new Thread(() ->
  ScopedValue.where(SCOPED_VALUE, "Kaboooom-tpca!")
    .run(taskr));
Thread tpcb = new Thread(taskr);
```

Make sure to not conclude from this that a ScopedValue is bound to a particular thread. The following note should clarify this aspect.

> **Important note**
>
> A ScopedValue is bound to a particular method call not to a particular thread (as in the case of ThreadLocal). In other words, a method can get a value of a ScopedValue if the code that calls it has mapped it. Data/values are passed in one way only: from *caller* to *callee*. Otherwise, ScopedValue is not bound and cannot be bounded and used in the current context of the method. As in the case of ThreadLocal, a ScopedValue is passed (and available) to all threads spawned by the task executed in the context of the current ScopedValue.

Besides the isBound() method, a ScopedValue also has orElse() and orElseThrow(). Via orElse(), we can specify an alternative/default value when the ScopedValue is not bound, while via orElseThrow(), we can throw a default exception. Here is an example of two Runnable objects that use these methods:

```
Runnable taskr1 = () -> {
  logger.info(Thread.currentThread().toString());
  logger.info(() -> SCOPED_VALUE.orElse("Not bound"));
};


Runnable taskr2 = () -> {
  logger.info(Thread.currentThread().toString());
  logger.info(() -> SCOPED_VALUE.orElseThrow(() ->
    new RuntimeException("Not bound")));
};
```

Of course, we can use these methods outside of Runnable/Callable as well. Here is an example:

```
Runnable taskr = () -> {
  logger.info(Thread.currentThread().toString());
  logger.info(() -> SCOPED_VALUE.get());
};


Thread.ofVirtual().start(() -> ScopedValue.runWhere(
  SCOPED_VALUE, SCOPED_VALUE.orElse("Kaboooom"), taskr))
    .join();


Thread.ofVirtual().start(() -> ScopedValue.runWhere(
  SCOPED_VALUE, SCOPED_VALUE.orElseThrow(() ->
    new RuntimeException("Not bound")), taskr)).join();
```

In the first virtual thread, we rely on orElse() to map the value of SCOPED_VALUE, so the SCOPED_VALUE.get() from taskr will return the Kaboo000m value. In the second virtual thread, we rely on orElseThrow(), so taskr will not be executed since the RuntimeException will be thrown.

In the next problems, we will tackle more aspects of scoped values.

232. Using ScopedValue and executor services

In *Problem 230*, we wrote an application that combines ThreadLocal and executor services (we have used newVirtualThreadPerTaskExecutor() and newFixedThreadPool()).

In this problem, we re-write the code from *Problem 230* in order to use ScopedValue. First, we have the following Runnable:

```
Runnable task = () -> {

  logger.info(() -> Thread.currentThread().toString()
    + " | before sleep | " + (SCOPED_VALUE.isBound()
    ? SCOPED_VALUE.get() : "Not bound"));

  try {
    Thread.sleep(Duration.ofSeconds(new Random().nextInt(5)));
  } catch (InterruptedException ex) {}

  logger.info(() -> Thread.currentThread().toString()
    + " | after sleep | " + (SCOPED_VALUE.isBound()
    ? SCOPED_VALUE.get() : "Not bound"));
};
```

This code is straightforward. We retrieve the value mapped to SCOPED_VALUE, we sleep from a random number of seconds (between 0 and 5), and we retrieve the value mapped to SCOPED_VALUE again. Next, let's run this code via newFixedThreadPool():

```
try (ExecutorService executor
    = Executors.newFixedThreadPool(10)) {

  for (int i = 0; i < 10; i++) {
    int copy_i = i;
    executor.submit(() -> ScopedValue.where(
      SCOPED_VALUE, "Kabooooom-" + copy_i).run(task));
  }
}
```

So, we have 10 platform threads and 10 tasks. Each thread maps the value Kabooooom-I to SCOPED_VALUE and calls the Runnable. A possible output would be:

```
Thread[#30,pool-1-thread-9,5,main] | before sleep | Kaboooom-8
Thread[#24,pool-1-thread-3,5,main] | before sleep | Kaboooom-2
Thread[#27,pool-1-thread-6,5,main] | before sleep | Kaboooom-5
...
Thread[#30,pool-1-thread-9,5,main] | after sleep | Kaboooom-8
Thread[#27,pool-1-thread-6,5,main] | after sleep | Kaboooom-5
Thread[#24,pool-1-thread-3,5,main] | after sleep | Kaboooom-2
...
```

Let's arbitrarily check out thread #27. Before sleeping, this thread sees the scoped value, `Kabooom-2`. After sleeping, thread #27 sees the same value, `Kabooom-2`. Each platform thread sees the scoped value that was mapped when the thread was created and the task was submitted. So, we have the same behavior as in the case of using `ThreadLocal`.

Next, let's switch to `newVirtualThreadPerTaskExecutor()`:

```
try (ExecutorService executor
    = Executors.newVirtualThreadPerTaskExecutor()) {
  ...
}
```

Now, a possible output would be:

```
VirtualThread[#22]/runnable@ForkJoinPool-1-worker-1
  | before sleep | Kaboooom-0
VirtualThread[#25]/runnable@ForkJoinPool-1-worker-3
  | before sleep | Kaboooom-2
VirtualThread[#27]/runnable@ForkJoinPool-1-worker-5
  | before sleep | Kaboooom-4
...
VirtualThread[#22]/runnable@ForkJoinPool-1-worker-1
| after sleep | Kaboooom-0
VirtualThread[#25]/runnable@ForkJoinPool-1-worker-1
| after sleep | Kaboooom-2
VirtualThread[#27]/runnable@ForkJoinPool-1-worker-7
  | after sleep | Kaboooom-4
...
```

Again, we can conclude that each virtual thread sees the scoped value that was mapped when the thread was created and the task was submitted. The only difference is that virtual threads are running on different workers before and after sleeping.

So, we can rely on `ScopedValue` instead of `ThreadLocal` and take advantage of all the goodies (see *Problem 231*) brought by this API in comparison to `ThreadLocal`.

233. Chaining and rebinding scoped values

In this problem, you'll see how to *chain* and *rebind* scoped values. These are very handy operations that you'll love to use.

Changing scoped values

Let's assume that we have three ScopedValue instances, as follows:

```
private static final ScopedValue<String> SCOPED_VALUE_1
  = ScopedValue.newInstance();
private static final ScopedValue<String> SCOPED_VALUE_2
  = ScopedValue.newInstance();
private static final ScopedValue<String> SCOPED_VALUE_3
  = ScopedValue.newInstance();
```

We also have a Runnable that uses all three ScopedValue instances:

```
Runnable task = () -> {
  logger.info(Thread.currentThread().toString());
  logger.info(() -> SCOPED_VALUE_1.isBound()
    ? SCOPED_VALUE_1.get() : "Not bound");
  logger.info(() -> SCOPED_VALUE_2.isBound()
    ? SCOPED_VALUE_2.get() : "Not bound");
  logger.info(() -> SCOPED_VALUE_3.isBound()
    ? SCOPED_VALUE_3.get() : "Not bound");
};
```

We can map the values to these three ScopedValue instances by simply chaining the where() calls. This is a very convenient way to set up multiple scoped values:

```
ScopedValue.where(SCOPED_VALUE_1, "Kaboooom - 1")
          .where(SCOPED_VALUE_2, "Kaboooom - 2")
          .where(SCOPED_VALUE_3, "Kaboooom - 3")
          .run(task);
```

That's all! Quite simple!

Rebinding scoped values

Let's imagine that we have two Runnable objects, taskA, and taskB. We start with taskB, which is straightforward:

```
Runnable taskB = () -> {
  logger.info(() -> "taskB:"
    + Thread.currentThread().toString());
  logger.info(() -> SCOPED_VALUE_1.isBound()
```

```
        ? SCOPED_VALUE_1.get() : "Not bound");
    logger.info(() -> SCOPED_VALUE_2.isBound()
        ? SCOPED_VALUE_2.get() : "Not bound");
    logger.info(() -> SCOPED_VALUE_3.isBound()
        ? SCOPED_VALUE_3.get() : "Not bound");
};
```

So, taskB simply logs three ScopedValue instances. Next, taskA needs only SCOPED_VALUE_1, but it also has to call taskB. So, taskA should map the proper values for SCOPED_VALUE_2 and SCOPED_VALUE_3. How about SCOPED_VALUE_1? Well, taskA doesn't want to pass the current value of SCOPED_VALUE_1 to taskB, so it must rebind this scoped value as follows:

```
Runnable taskA = () -> {
    logger.info(() -> "taskA: "
        + Thread.currentThread().toString());
    logger.info(() -> SCOPED_VALUE_1.isBound()
        ? SCOPED_VALUE_1.get() : "Not bound");
    ScopedValue.where(SCOPED_VALUE_1, "No kaboooom") // rebind
              .where(SCOPED_VALUE_2, "Kaboooom - 2")
              .where(SCOPED_VALUE_3, "Kaboooom - 3")
              .run(taskB);
    logger.info(() -> SCOPED_VALUE_1.isBound()
        ? SCOPED_VALUE_1.get() : "Not bound");
    logger.info(() -> SCOPED_VALUE_2.isBound()
        ? SCOPED_VALUE_2.get() : "Not bound");
    logger.info(() -> SCOPED_VALUE_3.isBound()
        ? SCOPED_VALUE_3.get() : "Not bound");
};
```

Calling taskA maps a value only to SCOPED_VALUE_1:

```
ScopedValue.where(SCOPED_VALUE_1, "Kaboooom - 1").run(taskA);
```

The output will be as follows (the comments have been manually added; they are not part of the output):

```
taskA: Thread[#1,main,5,main]
Kaboooom - 1
taskB: Thread[#1,main,5,main]
No kaboooom                        // this is the rebinded value
Kaboooom - 2
Kaboooom - 3
Kaboooom- 1                        // back in taskA
Not bound
Not bound
```

So, taskA sees the value Kabooom-1 for SCOPED_VALUE_1, but it doesn't pass this value to taskB. It rebinds this scoped value to No kaboooom. This is the value that lands in taskB next to Kaboooom -2 and Kaboooom -3, which has been mapped for SCOPED_VALUE_2 and SCOPED_VALUE_3. This technique is useful if you don't want to allow a certain scoped value to go beyond your goals or if you just need another value. Once the execution gets back in taskA, the SCOPED_VALUE_1 is restored to Kaboooom - 1, so the initial value is not lost and is available in taskA. On the other hand, SCOPED_VALUE_2 and SCOPED_VALUE_3 are not bound. They have been bound only for the execution of taskB. How cool is that?!

234. Using ScopedValue and StructuredTaskScope

In this problem, we will reiterate the application developed in *Problems 227* and *228*, and we will enrich it with a few ScopedValue variables for implementing new features. I'll consider that you are already familiar with that application.

The ScopedValue that we plan to add are listed here (these are added in the main class because we want them to be accessible at the application level):

```
public static final ScopedValue<String> USER
  = ScopedValue.newInstance();
public static final ScopedValue<String> LOC
  = ScopedValue.newInstance();
public static final ScopedValue<String> DEST
  = ScopedValue.newInstance();
public static final ScopedValue<Double> CAR_ONE_DISCOUNT
  = ScopedValue.newInstance();
public static final ScopedValue<Boolean>
  PUBLIC_TRANSPORT_TICKET = ScopedValue.newInstance();
```

First, let's focus on the fetchTravelOffers() method, which is the point from where we fork our two tasks, fetchRidesharingOffers() and fetchPublicTransportOffers(). The code that calls fetchTravelOffers() gets modified as follows:

```
TravelOffer offer;
if (user != null && !user.isBlank()) { // is user logged in ?
  offer = ScopedValue.where(USER, user)
    .call(() -> fetchTravelOffers(loc, dest));
} else {
  offer = fetchTravelOffers(loc, dest);
}
```

So, our travel page needs the user credentials (for simplicity, only the username). If the user is logged in, then we should have a valid username and we can share it with fetchTravelOffers() via the USER scoped value. If the user is not logged in, then USER remains unbound. The fetchTravelOffers() gets modified as follows:

```
public static TravelOffer fetchTravelOffers(
    String loc, String dest) throws Exception {

  return ScopedValue
    .where(LOC, loc)
    .where(DEST, dest)
    .call(() -> {
      try (TravelScope scope = new TravelScope()) {

        if (USER.isBound()) {
          scope.fork(() -> fetchRidesharingOffers());
        } else {
          logger.warning("Ridesharing services can be
                        accessed only by login users");
        }
        scope.fork(() ->
          ScopedValue.where(PUBLIC_TRANSPORT_TICKET, true)
            .call(Main::fetchPublicTransportOffers));

        scope.join();

        return scope.recommendedTravelOffer();
      }
    });
}
```

There are a lot of things happening in this code, so let's take it one by one.

The ridesharing service is accessible only for logged-in users, so we call it only if USER is bound. Otherwise, we log a message for the user:

```
if (USER.isBound()) {
  scope.fork(() -> fetchRidesharingOffers());
} else {
  logger.warning("Ridesharing services can be
                accessed only by login users");
```

On the other hand, the public transport service doesn't require the user to be logged in. However, in order to use public transport we need a special ticket. We have such a ticket and we share it with the public transport service via the PUBLIC_TRANSPORT_TICKET scoped value:

```
scope.fork(() ->
  ScopedValue.where(PUBLIC_TRANSPORT_TICKET, true)
    .call(Main::fetchPublicTransportOffers));
```

The `PUBLIC_TRANSPORT_TICKET` scoped value will be accessible only from the public transport service (only from `fetchPublicTransportOffers()` and other methods called from this one).

Next, the ridesharing and public transport services need our location and destination. This information is collected from the user/client and passed as arguments in `fetchTravelOffers()`. Thereafter, we map this information to `LOC` and `DEST` scoped values:

```
return ScopedValue
  .where(LOC, loc)
  .where(DEST, dest)
  .call(() -> {
    ...
  });
```

Now, `LOC` and `DEST` are bound and are accessible only from ridesharing and public transport services. They will be shared with all threads forked from these services.

Next, let's check out the ridesharing service, `fetchRidesharingOffers()`. This service checks if the user is logged in and logs a meaningful message:

```
public static RidesharingOffer fetchRidesharingOffers()
    throws InterruptedException, Exception {

  logger.info(() -> "Ridesharing: Processing request for "
    + USER.orElseThrow(() -> new RuntimeException(
      "Ridesharing: User not login")));
  ...
}
```

One of the ridesharing companies (`CarOne`) provides a random discount to its clients. We have a discount of 0.5 that we can map to `CAR_ONE_DISCOUNT` scoped value:

```
Subtask<RidesharingOffer> carOneOffer
  = scope.fork(() -> ScopedValue.where(CAR_ONE_DISCOUNT, 0.5)
    .call(Ridesharing::carOneServer));
```

If we visit the scoped values status in the context of `fetchRidesharingOffers()`, then we can say that the `USER` scoped value was bound at the application level, so it should be available everywhere in the application. The `LOC` and `DEST` scoped values have been bound in `fetchTravelOffers()`, so they are also available in `fetchRidesharingOffers()`. On the other hand, `PUBLIC_TRANSPORT_TICKET` is not available (not bound) in `fetchRidesharingOffers()`.

Next, let's focus on the public transport service, `fetchPublicTransportOffers()`. This service doesn't require the user to be logged in, but it can use this information to log a friendly message as follows:

```
public static PublicTransportOffer
    fetchPublicTransportOffers() throws InterruptedException {
```

```
    logger.info(() -> "Public Transport: Processing
      request for " + USER.orElse("anonymous"));
    ...
}
```

If we briefly review the current status of the scoped values in the context of fetchPublicTransportOffers(), then we can say that the USER scoped value was bound at the application level, so it should be available everywhere in the application. The LOC and DEST scoped values have been bound in fetchTravelOffers(), so they are also available in fetchPublicTransportOffers(). On the other hand, PUBLIC_TRANSPORT_TICKET and CAR_ONE_DISCOUNT are not available (not bound) in fetchPublicTransportOffers().

At this point, we have used all five scoped values. We continue to track them in the Ridesharing class, which simulates the ridesharing servers. In this class, we have access to USER, DEST, and LOC scoped values. Moreover, only in carOneServer() do we have access to CAR_ONE_DISCOUNT:

```
public static RidesharingOffer carOneServer() {
    ...
    if (CAR_ONE_DISCOUNT.isBound()) {
      logger.info(() -> "Congrats " + USER.get()
        + "! You have a discount of "
        + CAR_ONE_DISCOUNT.orElse(0.0));
      price = price - CAR_ONE_DISCOUNT.orElse(0.0);
    }
    ...
    throw new RidesharingException(
      "No drivers are available at CarOne for route: "
        + LOC.get() + " -> " + DEST.get());
}
```

So, if we have a discount (and we have one), the server of CarOne will apply it. If no drivers are available for our route, then the server will throw a meaningful exception. This exception is thrown from topCarServer() and starCarServer() as well. These are the servers of TopCar company and the StarCar company respectively.

Ok, so far so good! Next, let's check out the PublicTransport class, which simulates the public transport servers. In this class, we have access to USER, DEST, LOC, and PUBLIC_TRANSPORT_TICKET scoped values. We arbitrarily choose one of the servers (all of them use the same core code) and list here the code that we are interested in:

```
public static List<PublicTransportOffer>
      tramTransportServer() {

  List<PublicTransportOffer> listOfOffers = new ArrayList<>();
```

```
    Random rnd = new Random();
    boolean makeAnOffer = rnd.nextBoolean();

    if (makeAnOffer && PUBLIC_TRANSPORT_TICKET.isBound()
      && PUBLIC_TRANSPORT_TICKET.get()) {
      ...
    }

    if (listOfOffers.isEmpty()) {
      throw new RidesharingException(
        "No public tram-transport is available for route: "
        + LOC.get() + " -> " + DEST.get());
    }

    return listOfOffers;
}
```

As you can see, the public transport services can make an offer only if we have a special ticket that is verified via the PUBLIC_TRANSPORT_TICKET scoped value. If no public tram transport is available for our route, then the server throws an exception that uses the LOC and DEST scoped values to build a meaningful message.

Done! Using ScopedValue with StructuredTaskScope allows us to design complex concurrent models.

235. Using Semaphore instead of Executor

Let's say that we have the following task (Runnable):

```
Runnable task = () -> {
  try {
    Thread.sleep(5000);
  } catch (InterruptedException ex) { /* handle exception */ }
  logger.info(Thread.currentThread().toString());
};
```

And we plan to execute this task 15 times by 3 threads:

```
private static final int NUMBER_OF_TASKS = 15;
private static final int NUMBER_OF_THREADS = 3;
```

We can easily solve this problem via Executors.newFixedThreadPool() and platform threads:

```
// using cached platform threads
try (ExecutorService executor =
  Executors.newFixedThreadPool(NUMBER_OF_THREADS)) {
```

```
    for (int i = 0; i < NUMBER_OF_TASKS; i++) {

        executor.submit(task);
    }
}
```

A snippet of the possible output:

```
Thread[#24,pool-1-thread-3,5,main]
Thread[#22,pool-1-thread-1,5,main]
Thread[#23,pool-1-thread-2,5,main]
Thread[#22,pool-1-thread-1,5,main]
Thread[#24,pool-1-thread-3,5,main]
Thread[#23,pool-1-thread-2,5,main]
...
```

As you can see, the application has only three platform threads (#22, #23, and #24).

But, we already know that platform threads are expensive and it will be better to rely on virtual threads. The problem is that we cannot simply replace this fixed thread pool with newVirtualThreadPerTas kExecutor() because we can't control the number of threads. While we want to use only 3 threads, the virtual thread executor will allocate a virtual thread per task, so we will end up with 15 threads.

In order to control the number of virtual threads, we can rely on Semaphore (if you want more details about this topic you can check out *Java Coding Problems, First Edition, Chapter 10, Problem 211*). First, we declare a Semaphore with NUMBER_OF_THREADS permits:

```
Semaphore semaphore = new Semaphore(NUMBER_OF_THREADS);
```

Next, we rely on semaphore.acquire() and semaphore.release() to control the access to these permits and execute NUMBER_OF_TASKS tasks as follows:

```
Thread vt = Thread.currentThread();
for (int i = 0; i < NUMBER_OF_TASKS; i++) {

    vt = Thread.ofVirtual().start(() -> {
        try {
            semaphore.acquire();
        } catch (InterruptedException ex) { /* handle it */ }
            try {
                task.run();
            } finally {
                semaphore.release();
            }
    });
```

```
    }

    vt.join();
```

A snippet of the possible output:

```
VirtualThread[#27]/runnable@ForkJoinPool-1-worker-2
VirtualThread[#33]/runnable@ForkJoinPool-1-worker-8
VirtualThread[#28]/runnable@ForkJoinPool-1-worker-3


VirtualThread[#30]/runnable@ForkJoinPool-1-worker-3
VirtualThread[#25]/runnable@ForkJoinPool-1-worker-8
VirtualThread[#31]/runnable@ForkJoinPool-1-worker-4
...
```

Here, we have six virtual threads (#27, #33, #28, #30, #25, and #31), not three. The idea is that the Semaphore allows only three virtual threads to be created and to run concurrently at a time. You can probe this statement by running the code by yourself. After the first three virtual threads are created, they will sleep for 5 seconds. But because virtual threads are cheap, they do not go back into a thread pool, so they are not reused. It is much cheaper to create another three to use and throw. The idea is that there will not be more than three at a time.

236. Avoiding pinning via locking

Remember from *Chapter 10*, *Problem 213*, that a virtual thread is pinned (not unmounted from its carrier thread) when the execution goes through a synchronized block of code. For instance, the following Runnable will cause virtual threads to be pinned:

```java
Runnable task1 = () -> {
  synchronized (Main.class) {
    try {
      Thread.sleep(1000);
    } catch (InterruptedException ex) { /* handle it */ }
    logger.info(() -> "Task-1 | "
      + Thread.currentThread().toString());
  }
};
```

The synchronized block contains a blocking operation (sleep()), but the virtual thread that hits this point of execution is not unmounted. It is pinned on its carrier thread. Let's try to capture this behavior via the following executor:

```java
private static final int NUMBER_OF_TASKS = 25;
```

```
try (ExecutorService executor
      = Executors.newVirtualThreadPerTaskExecutor()) {

  for (int i = 0; i < NUMBER_OF_TASKS; i++) {

    executor.submit(task1);
  }
}
```

A possible output would look as follows:

```
Task-1 | VirtualThread[#22]/runnable@ForkJoinPool-1-worker-1
Task-1 | VirtualThread[#30]/runnable@ForkJoinPool-1-worker-8
Task-1 | VirtualThread[#29]/runnable@ForkJoinPool-1-worker-7
Task-1 | VirtualThread[#28]/runnable@ForkJoinPool-1-worker-6
Task-1 | VirtualThread[#27]/runnable@ForkJoinPool-1-worker-5
Task-1 | VirtualThread[#26]/runnable@ForkJoinPool-1-worker-4
Task-1 | VirtualThread[#25]/runnable@ForkJoinPool-1-worker-3
Task-1 | VirtualThread[#24]/runnable@ForkJoinPool-1-worker-2
Task-1 | VirtualThread[#37]/runnable@ForkJoinPool-1-worker-3
Task-1 | VirtualThread[#36]/runnable@ForkJoinPool-1-worker-4
Task-1 | VirtualThread[#35]/runnable@ForkJoinPool-1-worker-5
Task-1 | VirtualThread[#34]/runnable@ForkJoinPool-1-worker-6
...
```

Check out the workers! Because the virtual threads are pinned on their carriers, the application uses all the available workers (eight on my machine). The workers are not accessible during that sleep(1000), so they are not available to execute other tasks. In other words, a carrier thread is available only after the virtual thread finishes its execution.

But, we can avoid this situation by re-writing the application via ReentrantLock instead of synchronized. If you want more details about ReentrantLock, then you can check out *Java Coding Problems*, *First Edition*, *Chapter 11*, *Problems 222* and *223*. So, considering that you are familiar with ReentrantLock, we can come up with the following non-pinned solution:

```
Lock lock = new ReentrantLock();
Runnable task2 = () -> {
  lock.lock();
  try {
    Thread.sleep(1000);
    logger.info(() -> "Task-2 | "
      + Thread.currentThread().toString());
  } catch (InterruptedException ex) { /* handle it */
```

```
    } finally {
      lock.unlock();
    }
  };
```

We execute this code via the same `newVirtualThreadPerTaskExecutor()`:

```
executor.submit(task2);
```

Let's analyze a snippet of a possible output:

```
Task-2 | VirtualThread[#22]/runnable@ForkJoinPool-1-worker-1
Task-2 | VirtualThread[#24]/runnable@ForkJoinPool-1-worker-1
Task-2 | VirtualThread[#25]/runnable@ForkJoinPool-1-worker-5
Task-2 | VirtualThread[#26]/runnable@ForkJoinPool-1-worker-1
Task-2 | VirtualThread[#27]/runnable@ForkJoinPool-1-worker-3
Task-2 | VirtualThread[#28]/runnable@ForkJoinPool-1-worker-1
Task-2 | VirtualThread[#29]/runnable@ForkJoinPool-1-worker-3
Task-2 | VirtualThread[#30]/runnable@ForkJoinPool-1-worker-1
Task-2 | VirtualThread[#31]/runnable@ForkJoinPool-1-worker-3
Task-2 | VirtualThread[#33]/runnable@ForkJoinPool-1-worker-1
Task-2 | VirtualThread[#32]/runnable@ForkJoinPool-1-worker-5
Task-2 | VirtualThread[#34]/runnable@ForkJoinPool-1-worker-1
...
```

This time, we can see that only three workers are used, *worker-1*, *3*, and *5*. Because the virtual threads are not pinned, they can free up their carrier threads. This way, the platform threads can be reused and we save the rest of the resources for other tasks. If pinning is intensive, then it will affect the scalability of the application, so it is recommended to revisit your `synchronized` code and, whenever achievable, replace it with `ReentrantLock`.

237. Solving the producer-consumer problem via virtual threads

Let's assume that we want to write a program simulating an assembly line (or a conveyor) for checking and packing bulbs using two workers. By checking, we mean that the worker tests if the bulb lights up or not. By packing, we mean that the worker takes the verified build and puts it in a box.

Next, let's assume a fixed number of producers (3), and a fixed number of consumers (2); let's represent it via the following diagram:

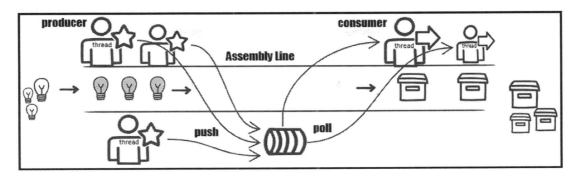

Figure 11.8: The producer-consumer problem with a fixed number of workers

We can implement this scenario via the well-known Executors.newFixedThreadPool(PRODUCERS),
Executors.newFixedThreadPool(CONSUMERS), and ConcurrentLinkedQueue as the temporary storage
for checked bulbs, as you can see at https://github.com/PacktPublishing/Java-Coding-Problems/
tree/master/Chapter10/P203_ThreadPoolFixed_ConcurrentLinkedQueue.

Let's consider this code as legacy and let's refactor it via virtual threads. All we have to do is to replace
Executors.newFixedThreadPool() (executor used for producers and consumers) with newVirtualT
hreadPerTaskExecutor() as follows:

```
private static ExecutorService producerService;
private static ExecutorService consumerService;
...
producerService = Executors.newVirtualThreadPerTaskExecutor();
for (int i = 0; i < PRODUCERS; i++) {
  producerService.execute(producer);
}


consumerService = Executors.newVirtualThreadPerTaskExecutor();
for (int i = 0; i < CONSUMERS; i++) {
  consumerService.execute(consumer);
}
```

That's all! Isn't it astonishing how easily we refactor this code to move from platform threads to virtual
threads? The possible output is listed here:

```
Checked: bulb-106 by producer: VirtualThread[#24]/runnable@ForkJoinPool-1-
worker-2
Checked: bulb-58 by producer: VirtualThread[#25]/runnable@ForkJoinPool-1-
worker-2
Packed: bulb-106 by consumer: VirtualThread[#26]/runnable@ForkJoinPool-1-
worker-2
```

```
Packed: bulb-58 by consumer: VirtualThread[#27]/runnable@ForkJoinPool-1-
worker-5
...
```

Of course, you'll find the complete code on GitHub. Take your time to get familiar with it especially if you didn't read the first edition of this book. We will rely on this code in the following two problems as well.

238. Solving the producer-consumer problem via virtual threads (fixed via Semaphore)

In the previous problem, we implemented the producer-consumer problem via a fixed number of producers (three virtual threads) and consumers (two virtual threads). Moreover, since our application works as an assembly line, we can say that the number of tasks is boundless. Practically, the producers and consumers work without breaks until the assembly line is stopped. This means the virtual threads assigned by the executor as producers and consumers remain exactly the same between a start-stop lifecycle of the assembly line.

Next, let's assume that we want to use Semaphore objects instead of newVirtualThreadPerTaskExecu tor() to obtain the exact same behavior.

Based on *Problem 235*, we can implement the fixed number of producers as follows:

```
private final static Semaphore producerService
    = new Semaphore(PRODUCERS);
...
for (int i = 0; i < PRODUCERS; i++) {

  Thread.ofVirtual().start(() -> {
    try {
      producerService.acquire();
    } catch (InterruptedException ex) {  /* handle it */ }
    try {
      producer.run();
    } finally {
      producerService.release();
    }
  });
}
```

And the fixed number of consumers is shaped as follows:

```
private final static Semaphore consumerService
    = new Semaphore(CONSUMERS);
...
```

```
  for (int i = 0; i < CONSUMERS; i++) {


    Thread.ofVirtual().start(() -> {
      try {
        consumerService.acquire();
      } catch (InterruptedException ex) { /* handle it */ }
      try {
        consumer.run();
      } finally {
        consumerService.release();
      }
    });
  }
```

In the next problem, we will complicate things a little bit.

239. Solving the producer-consumer problem via virtual threads (increase/decrease consumers)

Let's continue our producer-consumer problem with another scenario that starts with three producers and two consumers:

```
  private static final int PRODUCERS = 3;
  private static final int CONSUMERS = 2;
```

Let's assume that each producer checks a bulb in no more than one second. However, a consumer (packer) needs a maximum of 10 seconds to pack a bulb. The producer and consumer times can be shaped as follows:

```
  private static final int MAX_PROD_TIME_MS = 1 * 1000;
  private static final int MAX_CONS_TIME_MS = 10 * 1000;
```

Obviously, in these conditions, the consumers cannot face the incoming flux. The queue (here, LinkedBlockingQueue) used for storing bulbs until they are packed will continuously increase. The producers will push into this queue much faster than the consumers can poll.

Since we have only two consumers, we have to increase their number to be able to handle and stabilize the queue's load. But, after a while, the producers will get tired and will need more time to check each bulb. If the producers slow down the production rate, the number of consumers should be decreased as well since many of them will just sit there. Later on, the producers may speed up again, and so on.

This kind of problem can be solved via newCachedThreadPool() and platform threads. If you are not familiar with this topic then you can find more details in *Java Coding Problems, First Edition, Chapter 10, Problem 204*.

How about solving it via virtual threads? We can start the producers and consumers via two `Semaphore` objects exactly as we did in *Problem 238*. Next, we need to monitor the queue size and act accordingly. Let's assume that we should take action only if the queue size is greater than five bulbs:

```
private static final int MAX_QUEUE_SIZE_ALLOWED = 5;
```

Moreover, let's assume that we can increase the number of consumers up to 50:

```
private static final int MAX_NUMBER_OF_CONSUMERS = 50;
```

We want to monitor the queue every 3 seconds with an initial delay of 5 seconds, so we can rely on a `ScheduledExecutorService`:

```
private static ScheduledExecutorService monitorService;
```

The `monitorQueueSize()` method is responsible for initializing the `monitorService` and calling `addNewConsumer()`, `removeConsumer()`, and log the status as follows:

```
private static final int
  MONITOR_QUEUE_INITIAL_DELAY_MS = 5000;
private static final int MONITOR_QUEUE_RATE_MS = 3000;

private static final AtomicInteger nrOfConsumers
  = new AtomicInteger(CONSUMERS);
...
private static void monitorQueueSize() {

  monitorService = Executors
    .newSingleThreadScheduledExecutor();

  monitorService.scheduleAtFixedRate(() -> {

    if (queue.size() > MAX_QUEUE_SIZE_ALLOWED
      && nrOfConsumers.get() < MAX_NUMBER_OF_CONSUMERS) {

      addNewConsumer();
    } else {
      if (nrOfConsumers.get() > CONSUMERS) {
      removeConsumer();
      }
    }

  logger.warning(() -> "### Bulbs in queue: " + queue.size()
    + " | Consumers waiting: "
      + consumerService.getQueueLength()
```

```
          + " | Consumer available permits: "
            + consumerService.availablePermits()
          + " | Running consumers: " + nrOfConsumers.get());
    }, MONITOR_QUEUE_INITIAL_DELAY_MS,
        MONITOR_QUEUE_RATE_MS, TimeUnit.MILLISECONDS);
}
```

So, if the queue size is above MAX_QUEUE_SIZE_ALLOWED and the number of consumers is under MAX_NUMBER_OF_CONSUMERS, then we should add a new consumer. This can be done by releasing a new permit for the Semaphore that handles the consumers. Releasing a permit when the number of current permits is zero will simply add a new permit, so a new virtual thread can acquire this permit and become a new consumer:

```
private static void addNewConsumer() {

    logger.warning("### Adding a new consumer ...");

    if (consumerService.availablePermits() == 0) {
      consumerService.release();
    }

    Thread.ofVirtual().start(() -> {
      try {
        consumerService.acquire();
      } catch (InterruptedException ex) { /* handle it */ }
      try {
        consumer.run();
      } finally {
        consumerService.release();
      }
    });

    nrOfConsumers.incrementAndGet();
}
```

Most likely, when the producers slow down the production rate, there will be too many consumers that just hand on. In such cases, we have to interrupt virtual threads until we manage to balance the work between producers and consumers. The removeConsumer() method is responsible for signaling that a consumer must be interrupted, and for this, it sets an AtomicBoolean to true:

```
private static final AtomicBoolean
    removeConsumer = new AtomicBoolean();
...
```

```
private static void removeConsumer() {

  logger.warning("### Removing a consumer ...");

  removeConsumer.set(true);
}
```

The Consumer checks this flag at each run and when it is true, it will simply interrupt the currently running virtual thread:

```
private static class Consumer implements Runnable {

  @Override
  public void run() {
    while (runningConsumer) {
      ...
      if (removeConsumer.get()) {

        nrOfConsumers.decrementAndGet();
        removeConsumer.set(false);
        Thread.currentThread().interrupt();
      }
    }
  }
}
```

In order to simulate the decrease in the production rate for producers, we can rely on ScheduledExecutorService as follows:

```
private static int extraProdTime;
private static final int EXTRA_TIME_MS = 4 * 1000;
private static final int SLOW_DOWN_PRODUCER_MS = 150 * 1000;

private static ScheduledExecutorService slowdownerService;
...
private static void slowdownProducer() {

  slowdownerService = Executors
    .newSingleThreadScheduledExecutor();

  slowdownerService.schedule(() -> {
    logger.warning("### Slow down the producers ...");
```

```
      extraProdTime = EXTRA_TIME_MS;
   }, SLOW_DOWN_PRODUCER_MS, TimeUnit.MILLISECONDS);
}
```

So, we start the assembly line and the producers will check bulbs at a very high rate. After 2.5 minutes, we decrease this rate by adding an extra time of 4 seconds for each producer via the `extraProdTime` variable. Initially, this is 0, but after 2.5 minutes it becomes 4000. Since it is part of the production time it will slow down the producer by 4 seconds:

```
Thread.sleep(rnd.nextInt(MAX_PROD_TIME_MS) + extraProdTime);
```

Let's try to trace a run of our assembly line to see how it works. So, we start the assembly line and, pretty soon, we notice that the number of bulbs in the queue (27) is greater than 5 and the application started to add consumers:

```
...
[14:20:41] [INFO] Checked: bulb-304 by producer: VirtualThread[#22]/runnable@
ForkJoinPool-1-worker-1
[14:20:42] [INFO] Checked: bulb-814 by producer: VirtualThread[#24]/runnable@
ForkJoinPool-1-worker-1
[14:20:42] [INFO] Checked: bulb-155 by producer: VirtualThread[#22]/runnable@
ForkJoinPool-1-worker-1
[14:20:42] [WARNING] ### Adding a new consumer ...
[14:20:42] [INFO] Checked: bulb-893 by producer: VirtualThread[#25]/runnable@
ForkJoinPool-1-worker-1
[14:20:42] [WARNING] ### Bulbs in queue: 27 | Consumers waiting: 0 | Consumer
available permits: 0 | Running consumers: 3
...
```

The application continues to add consumers while the number of unprocessed bulbs keeps growing (here we have 237 bulbs in the queue and 32 consumers):

```
...
[14:22:09] [INFO] Checked: bulb-388 by producer: VirtualThread[#25]/runnable@
ForkJoinPool-1-worker-1
[14:22:09] [INFO] Packed: bulb-501 by consumer: VirtualThread[#43]/runnable@
ForkJoinPool-1-worker-1
[14:22:09] [INFO] Packed: bulb-768 by consumer: VirtualThread[#27]/runnable@
ForkJoinPool-1-worker-3
[14:22:09] [WARNING] ### Adding a new consumer ...
[14:22:09] [WARNING] ### Bulbs in queue: 237 | Consumers waiting: 0 | Consumer
available permits: 1 | Running consumers: 32
...
```

When the application reaches around 37 consumers, the queue size enters a descending trend. Here you can see two consecutive logs of queue status (meanwhile, the application is still adding more consumers – it does this until the queue.size() is less than 5):

```
...
[14:22:24] [WARNING] ### Adding a new consumer ...
[14:22:24] [WARNING] ### Bulbs in queue: 214 | Consumers waiting: 0 | Consumer
available permits: 1 | Running consumers: 37
...
[14:22:27] [WARNING] ### Adding a new consumer ...
[14:22:27] [WARNING] ### Bulbs in queue: 203 | Consumers waiting: 0 | Consumer
available permits: 1 | Running consumers: 38
...
```

The queue size continues to decrease and the number of consumers reaches the maximum of 50. At some point, the queue is depleted. The number of customers is much higher than needed so they are removed one by one. Here is the moment when the last consumer (consumer #50 was removed):

```
...
[14:23:15] [INFO] Packed: bulb-180 by consumer: VirtualThread[#46]/runnable@
ForkJoinPool-1-worker-3
[14:23:15] [INFO] Packed: bulb-261 by consumer: VirtualThread[#67]/runnable@
ForkJoinPool-1-worker-3
[14:23:15] [WARNING] ### Removing a consumer ...
[14:23:15] [WARNING] ### Bulbs in queue: 0 | Consumers waiting: 0 | Consumer
available permits: 1 | Running consumers: 49
...
```

While the application continues to calibrate itself by removing consumers, the producers slow down:

```
...
[14:23:07] [WARNING] ### Slow down the producers ...
...
```

Since the producers have slowed down, the number of consumers continues to decrease and the queue load can be processed by two consumers:

```
...
[14:28:24] [WARNING] ### Bulbs in queue: 3 | Consumers waiting: 0 | Consumer
available permits: 48 | Running consumers: 2
[14:28:26] [INFO] Checked: bulb-812 by producer: VirtualThread[#25]/runnable@
ForkJoinPool-1-worker-3
[14:28:26] [INFO] Packed: bulb-207 by consumer: VirtualThread[#102]/runnable@
ForkJoinPool-1-worker-3
...
```

```
[14:28:27] [WARNING] ### Bulbs in queue: 4 | Consumers waiting: 0 | Consumer
available permits: 48 | Running consumers: 2
[14:28:28] [INFO] Checked: bulb-259 by producer: VirtualThread[#24]/runnable@
ForkJoinPool-1-worker-3
...
[14:28:30] [WARNING] ### Bulbs in queue: 3 | Consumers waiting: 0 | Consumer
available permits: 48 | Running consumers: 2
...
```

At this point, the assembly line is calibrated. If the producers increase their production rate again then the application is ready to respond. As you can see, the consumer's Semaphore has 48 permits available, so we shouldn't create them again. If you want to remove the permit corresponding to an interrupted consumer then you have to extend the Semaphore class and override the protected method reducePermits(). The number of permits is just a counter; so, in this scenario, removing permits is not really necessary.

240. Implementing an HTTP web server on top of virtual threads

Implementing a simple HTTP web server in Java is quite easy since we already have an API ready to guide and serve our goals. We start from the HttpServer class (this class is present in the com.sun. net.httpserver package), which allows us to achieve our goal straightforwardly in a few steps.

Before jumping into the code, let's quickly mention that our web server will allow us to choose between platform and virtual threads and between non-locking or locking (for instance, to simulate access to a database). We will make these choices via two boolean parameters of our startWebServer(boolean virtual, boolean withLock) method, named virtual and withLock, respectively. So, we will have four possible configurations.

First, we create an HttpServer via the create() method. At this point, we also set up the port of our web server:

```
private static final int MAX_NR_OF_THREADS = 200;
private static final int WEBSERVER_PORT = 8001;

private static void startWebServer(
    boolean virtual, boolean withLock) throws IOException {

  HttpServer httpServer = HttpServer
    .create(new InetSocketAddress(WEBSERVER_PORT), 0);
  ...
```

Next, we create the web server context by specifying the access page and the handler that will deal with the HTTP requests (the WebServerHandler is implemented later):

```
    httpServer.createContext("/webserver",
```

```
        new WebServerHandler(withLock));
    ...
```

Next, we can choose the executor service (override the default one) that will orchestrate the threads of our web server. This can be done via the setExecutor() method. Since we can choose between platform threads (we arbitrarily chose to have 200 such threads) and virtual threads, we have to cover both cases as follows:

```
if (virtual) {
  httpServer.setExecutor(
    Executors.newVirtualThreadPerTaskExecutor());
} else {
  httpServer.setExecutor(
    Executors.newFixedThreadPool(MAX_NR_OF_THREADS));
}
...
```

Finally, we call the start() method to start the web server, and we log this accordingly:

```
httpServer.start();

logger.info(() -> " Server started on port "
  + WEBSERVER_PORT);
}
```

Next, we focus on the WebServerHandler class, which implements the com.sun.net.httpserver. HttpHandler interface and is responsible for handling the incoming HTTP requests. We simulate an HTTP request processing by sleeping 200 milliseconds and create a simple String response via a Callable named task:

```
public class WebServerHandler implements HttpHandler {

  private final static Logger logger
    = Logger.getLogger(WebServerHandler.class.getName());

  private final static int PERMITS = 20;
  private final static Semaphore semaphore
    = new Semaphore(PERMITS);

  private final static AtomicLong
    requestId = new AtomicLong();

  private static final Callable<String> task = () -> {

    String response = null;
```

```
  try {
    Thread.sleep(200);
    response = "Request id_" + requestId.incrementAndGet();
  } catch (InterruptedException e) {
    throw new RuntimeException(e);
  }

  return response;
};


private final boolean withLock;

public WebServerHandler(boolean withLock) {
  this.withLock = withLock;
}
...
```

When the WebServerHandler is initiated, we also set up the withLock value. If this value is true, then our implementation will rely on a Semaphore with 20 permits to limit the access of the platform threads (200) or of the unbounded number of virtual threads. This Semaphore simulates an external resource, such as a database that relies on a connection pool of 20 connections.

The HTTP requests (we focus only on GET) are handled in the overridden handle(HttpExchange exchange) method as follows:

```
@Override
public void handle(HttpExchange exchange)
    throws IOException {

  String response = null;

  if (withLock) {
    try {
      semaphore.acquire();
    } catch (InterruptedException e) {
      throw new RuntimeException(e); }
    try {
      response = task.call();
    } catch (Exception e) {
      throw new RuntimeException(e);
    } finally {
      semaphore.release();
```

```
      }
    } else {
      try {
        response = task.call();
      } catch (Exception e) {
        throw new RuntimeException(e); }
      }

      logger.log(Level.INFO, "{0} | {1}",
        new Object[]{response, Thread.currentThread()}
  });
  ...
```

Once the HTTP GET request is processed, we have to prepare the response for our client and send it. This job is done via the HttpExchange object as follows:

```
    exchange.sendResponseHeaders(
      200, response == null ? 0 : response.length());

    try (OutputStream os = exchange.getResponseBody()) {
      os.write(response == null ? new byte[0]
        : response.getBytes());
    }
  }
}
```

Done! Our HTTP web server is ready to rock and roll.

If we start the web server via startWebServer(false, false), then we will get a web server that has 200 platform threads ready to serve in a non-locking context. If we set the first argument to true, then we switch to an unbounded number of virtual threads. In the following figure, you can see the heap usage in these two scenarios for 400 requests ramped up in 2 seconds via a JMeter test:

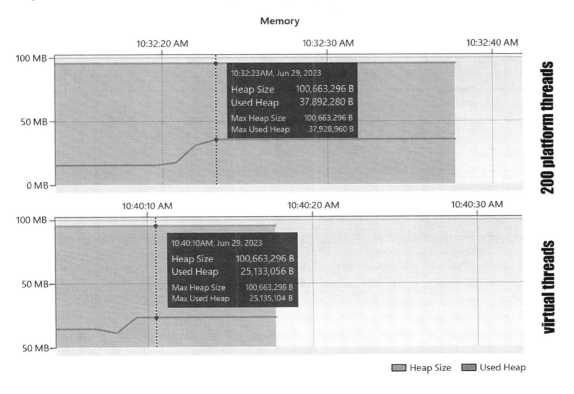

Figure 11.9: Memory usage (lock free)

As you can see, virtual threads used less heap memory than platform threads being more efficient.

If we add locking into the equation (we set the second argument of startWebServer() to true), then a possible profile of heap memory looks as in the following figure:

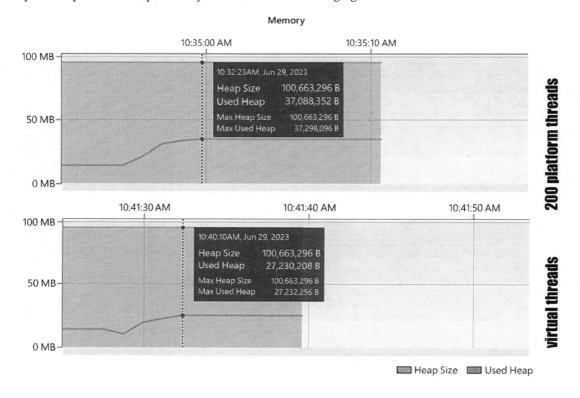

Figure 11.10: Memory usage (using locking)

As you can see, even with locking, the virtual threads are still using less memory than platform threads. In *Chapter 13*, we will dive deeper into creating web servers via the JDK API, including the new features brought by JDK 18.

241. Hooking CompletableFuture and virtual threads

CompletableFuture is one of the main asynchronous programming APIs in Java (if you need deep coverage of this topic, then you could consider checking out *Java Coding Problems, First Edition, Chapter 11*).

In order to use CompletableFuture with virtual threads, we just have to use the proper executor for virtual threads:

```
private static final ExecutorService executor
    = Executors.newVirtualThreadPerTaskExecutor();
```

Next, we use this executor to fetch three application testers in asynchronous mode via `CompletableFuture`:

```java
public static CompletableFuture<String> fetchTester1() {

  return CompletableFuture.supplyAsync(() -> {

  String tester1 = null;
  try {
    logger.info(Thread.currentThread().toString());
    tester1 = fetchTester(1);
  } catch (IOException | InterruptedException ex)
    { /* handle exceptions */ }

  return tester1;

  }, executor);
}

public static CompletableFuture<String> fetchTester2() { … }
public static CompletableFuture<String> fetchTester3() { … }
```

Next, we are interested in returning a `TestingTeam` only after all three of these `CompletableFuture` instances have completed. For this, we rely on `allOf()` as follows:

```java
public static TestingTeam buildTestingTeam()
        throws InterruptedException, ExecutionException {

  CompletableFuture<String> cfTester1 = fetchTester1();
  CompletableFuture<String> cfTester2 = fetchTester2();
  CompletableFuture<String> cfTester3 = fetchTester3();

  CompletableFuture<Void> fetchTesters
    = CompletableFuture.allOf(
      cfTester1, cfTester2, cfTester3);

  fetchTesters.get();

  TestingTeam team = new TestingTeam(cfTester1.resultNow(),
    cfTester2.resultNow(), cfTester3.resultNow());

  return team;
}
```

If we run this code, then the output reveals the usage of three virtual threads in asynchronous mode:

```
[12:04:32] VirtualThread[#22]/runnable@ForkJoinPool-1-worker-1
[12:04:32] VirtualThread[#24]/runnable@ForkJoinPool-1-worker-2
[12:04:32] VirtualThread[#26]/runnable@ForkJoinPool-1-worker-3
```

Done! Employing virtual threads for `CompletableFuture` is quite easy.

242. Signaling virtual threads via wait() and notify()

The `wait()`, `notify()`, and `notifyAll()` are three methods defined in the `Object` class that allow multiple threads to communicate with each other and coordinate their access to resources without issues.

The `wait()` method must be called only by the thread that owns the object's *monitor* to force this thread to wait indefinitely until another thread calls `notify()` or `notifyAll()` on the same object. In other words, the `wait()` method must be called in a `synchronized` context (instance, block, or static method).

Here is a virtual thread calling the `wait()` method:

```
Object object = new Object();

Thread wThread = Thread.ofVirtual().unstarted(() -> {
  synchronized (object) {
    try {
      logger.info("Before calling wait()");
      logger.info(() -> Thread.currentThread() + " | "
        + Thread.currentThread().getState());
      object.wait();
      logger.info("After calling notify()");
      logger.info(() -> Thread.currentThread() + " | "
        + Thread.currentThread().getState());
    } catch (InterruptedException e) {}
  }
});
```

And here is another virtual thread that wakes up the previous one via the `notify()` call:

```
Thread nThread = Thread.ofVirtual().unstarted(() -> {
  synchronized (object) {
    logger.info(() -> Thread.currentThread()
      + " calls notify()");
    object.notify();
  }
});
```

At this point, nothing has happened, since wThread and nThread are not started. We start wThread and we give it 1 second to do it:

```
wThread.start();
Thread.sleep(1000); // give time to 'wThread' to start
logger.info("'wThread' current status");
logger.info(() -> wThread + " | " + wThread.getState());
```

Next, we start nThread and give it 1 second to do it:

```
nThread.start();
Thread.sleep(1000); // give time to 'nThread' to start
```

Finally, we log the state of wThread:

```
logger.info("After executing 'wThread'");
logger.info(() -> wThread + " | " + wThread.getState());
```

Running this code reveals the following output:

```
[14:25:06] Before calling wait()
[14:25:06] VirtualThread[#22]
           /runnable@ForkJoinPool-1-worker-1 | RUNNABLE
[14:25:07] 'wThread' current status
[14:25:07] VirtualThread[#22]
           /waiting@ForkJoinPool-1-worker-1 | WAITING
[14:25:07] VirtualThread[#23]
           /runnable@ForkJoinPool-1-worker-3 calls notify()
[14:25:07] After calling notify()
[14:25:07] VirtualThread[#22]
           /runnable@ForkJoinPool-1-worker-1 | RUNNABLE
[14:25:08] After executing 'wThread'
[14:25:08] VirtualThread[#22]/terminated | TERMINATED
```

The virtual thread #22 is our wThread. Initially (before calling wait()), it is in the RUNNABLE state, so the thread is in execution on the JVM. After wait() is called, the state of this thread is set to WAITING, so thread #22 is waiting indefinitely for another thread to wake it up. This is the moment when the virtual thread #23 (nThread) calls the notify() method on the same object. After calling the notify() method, thread #22 wakes up, and its state is RUNNABLE again. After finishing its execution, the wThread state is TERMINATED.

Well, this scenario is the happy path or a *good signal*. Let's check out the following scenario based on the same wThread and nThread:

```
nThread.start();
Thread.sleep(1000); // give time to 'nThread' to start
```

```
wThread.start();
Thread.sleep(1000); // give time to 'wThread' to start
logger.info("'wThread' current status");
logger.info(() -> wThread + " | " + wThread.getState());


wThread.join(); // waits indefinitely - notify() was missed
```

The output will be (#22 is wThread and #23 is nThread):

```
[14:38:25] VirtualThread[#23]
           /runnable@ForkJoinPool-1-worker-1 calls notify()
[14:38:26] Before calling wait()
[14:38:26] VirtualThread[#22]
           /runnable@ForkJoinPool-1-worker-1 | RUNNABLE
[14:38:27] 'wThread' current status
[14:38:27] VirtualThread[#22]
           /waiting@ForkJoinPool-1-worker-1 | WAITING
```

This time, nThread starts first and calls notify(). This is just a shot in the dark since wThread is not in the WAITING state. Later on, wThread calls wait() and waits indefinitely to be woken up by nThread. But this will never happen since notify() was already triggered, so wThread is blocked forever. In short, this is called a *missed signal*.

When we develop concurrent applications that involve wait(), notify(), and notifyAll(), we have to ensure that the application complexity will not hide such *missed signals*. We can avoid *missed signals* by simply counting the number of wait() and notify() calls and acting accordingly. For instance, let's move this logic in the object that should be signaled, and let's call it SignaledObject. First, we have the callWait() method, which uses the counter as follows:

```
public class SignaledObject {

  private static final Logger logger
    = Logger.getLogger(SignaledObject.class.getName());

  private int counter;

  public void callWait() throws InterruptedException {

    synchronized (this) {

      counter = counter - 1;

      if (counter >= 0) {
```

```
        logger.info(() -> Thread.currentThread()
          + " | Missed signals: " + counter
          + " | 'wait() will not be called'");
        return;
      }

      logger.info("Before calling wait()");
      logger.info(() -> Thread.currentThread() + " | "
        + Thread.currentThread().getState());
      wait();
      logger.info("After calling notify()");
      logger.info(() -> Thread.currentThread() + " | "
        + Thread.currentThread().getState());
    }
  }
  ...
```

If no signal was missed, then the counter variable should be 0. Otherwise, we have at least one *missed signal* (notify() call) so there is no reason to wait. We return immediately, without calling wait(), since this may lead to a deadly trap.

On the other hand, callNotify() increases the counter at each call as follows:

```
public void callNotify() {

  synchronized (this) {

    counter = counter + 1;

    logger.info(() -> "Signal counter: " + counter);

    notify();
  }
}
```

If we run the happy path (*good signal*) scenario, then the output will be as follows:

```
[14:50:32] Before calling wait()
[14:50:32] VirtualThread[#22]
          /runnable@ForkJoinPool-1-worker-1 | RUNNABLE
[14:50:33] 'wThread' current status
[14:50:33] VirtualThread[#22]
          /waiting@ForkJoinPool-1-worker-1 | WAITING
```

```
[14:50:33] Signal counter: 0
[14:50:33] After calling notify()
[14:50:33] VirtualThread[#22]
           /runnable@ForkJoinPool-1-worker-1 | RUNNABLE
[14:50:34] After executing 'wThread'
[14:50:34] VirtualThread[#22]/terminated | TERMINATED
```

Everything works as expected since `counter` is 0. If we try out the missed signal scenario, then we have the following output:

```
[14:52:24] Signal counter: 1
[14:52:25] VirtualThread[#22]/runnable@ForkJoinPool-1-worker-1
           | Missed signals: 0 | 'wait() will not be called'
[14:52:26] 'wThread' current status
[14:52:26] VirtualThread[#22]/terminated | TERMINATED
```

As you can see, we avoided the indefinite blocking by not calling `wait()`. We managed to elegantly handle the *missed signal*. Cool, right!?

Summary

This chapter covered 18 advanced problems about virtual threads and structured concurrency. You can see this chapter as a masterclass designed to help you speed up your learning and get ready for production with strong confidence in your knowledge. With that covered, you have now finished the chapter and the book.

Join our community on Discord

Join our community's Discord space for discussions with the author and other readers:

`https://discord.gg/8mgytp5DGQ`

12

Garbage Collectors and Dynamic CDS Archives

This chapter includes 15 problems covering garbage collectors and **Application Class Data Sharing (AppCDS)**.

By the end of this chapter, you'll have a profound understanding of how a **garbage collector (GC)** works and how you can tune it for maximum performance. Moreover, you'll have a good understanding of how AppCDS can boost your application startup.

Problems

Use the following problems to test your advanced programming prowess in garbage collectors and application class data sharing in Java. I strongly encourage you to give each problem a try before you turn to the solutions and download the example programs:

243. **Hooking the garbage collector goal:** Introduce Java garbage collectors quickly. Highlight the main objectives (advantages) and disadvantages of a garbage collector.

244. **Handling the garbage collector stages:** List and briefly describe the most common stages of a garbage collector.

245. **Covering some garbage collector terminology:** A garbage collector has specific terminology. Provide here the main terms used in conjunction with garbage collectors.

246. **Tracing the generational GC process:** Exemplify and explain a hypothetical scenario containing several consecutive runs of a generational garbage collector.

247. **Choosing the correct garbage collector:** List and explain the three main factors that should be considered for choosing the correct garbage collector.

248. **Categorizing garbage collectors:** Highlight the main categories of garbage collector across JDK's evolution.

249. **Introducing G1:** Provide a brief introduction to the G1 GC, including its design principles.

250. **Tackling G1 throughput improvements:** List the main improvements of G1 GC throughput across JDK versions.

251. **Tackling G1 latency improvements:** List the main improvements of G1 GC latency across JDK versions.

252. **Tackling G1 footprint improvements:** List the main improvements of the G1 GC footprint across JDK versions.

253. **Introducing ZGC:** Provide a brief introduction to the Z Garbage Collector.

254. **Monitoring garbage collectors:** Explain and exemplify at least one tool for monitoring garbage collectors.

255. **Logging garbage collectors:** Provide the steps needed to log the garbage collector activity. Moreover, highlight some tools capable of analyzing and plotting the logged data.

256. **Tuning garbage collectors:** Explain how to tune garbage collectors, including G1 and ZGC.

257. **Introducing Application Class Data Sharing (AppCDS, or Java's Startup Booster):** Give a quick and practical guide to using CDS and AppCDS in JDK 10/11, 13, and 19.

The following sections describe solutions to the preceding problems. Remember that there usually isn't a single correct way to solve a particular problem. Also, remember that the explanations shown here include only the most interesting and important details needed to solve the problems. Download the example solutions to see additional details and experiment with the programs at `https://github.com/PacktPublishing/Java-Coding-Problems-Second-Edition/tree/main/Chapter12`.

243. Hooking the garbage collector goal

Every programming language has to manage memory usage. Some programming languages delegate this task to programmers, while others leverage different mechanisms to partially control how memory is used. Java programmers can focus 100% on the functionalities of the application and let the *garbage collector* manage how memory is used.

The name *garbage collector* suggests an entity capable of finding and collecting garbage from memory. Actually, a garbage collector is a very complex process representing the climax of Java memory management that is capable of tracking every object from the heap and identifying and removing the ones that are not used/referenced by the application. The main advantages of a garbage collector include:

- The Java programmer doesn't need to manually handle the allocation/deallocation of memory.
- The Java programmer doesn't need to deal with *dangling* and *wild pointers* (`https://en.wikipedia.org/wiki/Dangling_pointer`).
- In a wide range of scenarios, a garbage collector prevents *memory leaks* (`https://en.wikipedia.org/wiki/Memory_leak`). However, this issue is not 100% covered.

While these advantages are major, there are a few disadvantages as well:

- A garbage collector itself is a resource that needs CPU power to work. We're talking about CPU power that is in addition to the CPU power needed by the application. More garbage collector activity requires more CPU power.

- The programmer cannot control the garbage collector scheduler. This may cause performance issues at peaks or when the application deals with intensive computations.
- Some garbage collectors cause long and unpredictable pauses of the application.
- Learning and tuning the correct garbage collector can be really cumbersome.

In the next problems, we'll go deeper into this topic.

244. Handling the garbage collector stages

During its work, GC passes through different stages or steps. It can pass through one or more of the following stages:

- *Mark* – In this stage, the GC identifies and marks (or paints) all pieces of memory (blocks) that are used (have references) and not used (have no references). The marked (painted) blocks are called *live objects*, while the rest are called *non-live objects*. *Imagine that you go to the pantry and identify all the fresh fruits and vegetables and separate them from the spoiled ones.*
- *Sweep* – In this stage, the GC removes all *non-live objects* from memory. *Next, you take all the spoiled fruits and vegetables out of the pantry and throw them away.*
- *Compact* – In this stage, the GC attempts to group the *live objects* closer together – in other words, it arranges the live objects at the start of the heap in a continuous sequence of memory blocks. So, compacting involves *defragmentation* and *relocation* of the *live objects*. The goal of compaction is to obtain large memory blocks that are free and ready to serve other objects. *Next, we go to the pantry and stack all the fruits and vegetables in crates so that we get as much free space as possible. We will use this space for other fruits and vegetables that we are going to buy.*
- *Copy* – This is another stage dedicated to organizing memory. It is an alternative to the *mark* stage. In this stage, the GC moves the *live objects* into a so-called *ToSpace*. The rest of the objects are considered *non-live* and remain in the so-called *FromSpace*.

Typically, a GC follows one of these three scenarios:

- Mark -> Sweep -> Compact
- Copy
- Mark -> Compact

Next, let's cover some GC terminology.

245. Covering some garbage collector terminology

Garbage collection has its own terminology that it is essential to know in order to better understand how it works. Some of these terms are presented here; we start with *epoch*, *single pass*, and *multiple passes*.

Epoch

A GC works in cycles. A complete cycle of a GC is known as an *epoch*.

Single and multiple passes

A GC can handle its internal steps in a single pass (*single-pass*) or multiple passes (*multi-pass*). In the case of *single-pass*, the GC groups multiple steps and handles them in a single run. On the other hand, in the case of *multi-pass*, the GC handles multiple steps in a sequence of several passes.

Serial and parallel

A GC is considered *serial* if it uses a single thread. On the other hand, a GC is considered *parallel* if it uses multiple threads.

Stop-the-World (STW) and concurrent

A GC is of the type *Stop-the-World* (STW) if it has to stop (temporarily suspend) the application execution in order to carry out its cycle. On the other hand, a GC is *concurrent* if it is capable of running at the same time as the application without affecting its execution.

Live set

A GC *live set* represents all the *live objects* of the current application. If there is no memory leak (or other issues), then the *live set* should have a constant load factor and a relatively constant size. During application execution, objects are added/removed from the heap and from the *live set* respectively.

Allocation rate

Java allows us to set the size of the heap memory via the –Xmx options. This size should not exceed the memory available on your machine (server) and should be big enough to serve the *live set*. This can be achieved by taking into account the *allocation rate*, which is expressed as the amount of memory (for instance, MB) allocated per unit of time (for instance, seconds).

> **Important note**
>
> As a rule of thumb, try to set the heap size as 2.5 to 5 times the average size of the *live set*.

In other words, when many objects are created, there will be many cleanups as well. This means that the GC will run at a high frequency and will need a higher *allocation rate*.

NUMA

NUMA is the acronym for non-uniform memory access. A processor has its own memory (called local memory) but it can also access the memory of other processors. Access to its local memory is faster than access to non-local memory. Basically, NUMA is a memory architecture that attempts to optimize access to local memory.

Region-based

A *region-based* GC divides the heap into smaller (eventually equal) regions/chunks of memory (for instance, G1 and ZGC are *region-based* GCs). Each such region can be allocated for different purposes.

Generational garbage collection

Generational garbage collection is an algorithm that excels in handling short-living objects. A GC that implements this algorithm is called a *generational GC*.

This algorithm distinguishes between *young* and *old* objects and keeps them separate. The *young* objects are kept in an area called the *Young* generation or *Nursery* space, while the *old* objects are kept in an area called the *Old* generation or *Tenured* space. The following figure highlights the transitions of objects through the *Young* and *Old* generations:

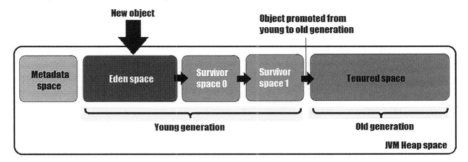

Figure 12.1: The transitions of objects through Young and Old generations

As you can see, the *Young* generation is divided into two regions/spaces, named the *Eden* region or *Eden* space and the *Survivor* region or *Survivor* space. Initially, the *Young* generation is empty.

Objects that are newly created are placed in the *Eden* space by default. However, there is an exception for extremely large objects, called *humongous objects*, that exceed 50% of the region's size. These objects are placed directly into the *Old* generation area, which may cause performance issues due to the increased occurrence of *major/full* GC events. It is important to note that GCs can trigger different types of events:

- *MinorGC* – This event occurs in the *Young* generation when the *Eden* space becomes full. Its purpose is to collect *non-live* objects and promote the remaining ones into the *Survivor* space. This event is the most commonly triggered by a GC.
- *MajorGC* – This event occurs in the *Old* generation and is responsible for collecting garbage from this area.
- *MixedGC* – This is a *MinorGC* event followed by reclaiming the *Old* generation.
- *FullGC* – Clean up the *Young* and *Old* generations and perform compacting of the *Old* generation (we can programmatically force a *FullGC* via System.gc() or Runtime.getRunTime().gc()).

Next, let's return to the topic of the *Young* generation. During the *epoch* (a GC complete cycle), the objects that survive (have not been garbage collected) are promoted into the *Survivor* space (the GC algorithm chooses between *Survivor space 0* (known as *S0* or *FromSpace*) or *1* (known as *S1* or *ToSpace*)). The objects that don't fit into the *Survivor* space (if any) will be moved into the *Tenured* space – this is known as *premature promotion*. Usually, the GC handles the *Eden* space pretty quickly via the *MinorGC* events. Using local variables with short-living methods encourages the usage of *Eden* space and sustains the GC's performance.

Objects that are considered old enough (they have survived during multiple epochs) are eventually promoted into the *Old* generation. This is an area typically (but not mandatorily) larger than the *Young* generation. Some GCs use a fixed delimitation between these areas (for instance, the **Concurrent Mark Sweep** (**CMS**) GC) while others use an elastic boundary between these areas (for instance, the G1 GC). The *Old* generation area takes a relatively long time to be garbage collected and has a lower frequency than the *Young* generation.

As you can see in *Figure 12.1*, the heap also contains an area named the *Metadata* space. Before JDK 8, this area was named *PermGenSpace* or *Permanent* generation. This area is used to store classes and methods. This area is specially designed to grow beyond the heap size into the native memory (if the size of this area goes beyond the physical memory, the operating system will use virtual memory – but be aware that moving data between physical and virtual memory is a costly operation that will affect the application performance). Via *Metadata* space, JVM avoids out-of-memory errors. However, this area can be garbage collected in order to remove unused classes/methods. In this context, there are a few flags that can help us to tune it, but we will cover these flags in *Problem 256*.

246. Tracing the generational GC process

In this problem, let's start from an arbitrary initial state of a generational GC and follow a few hypothetical epochs (generally, all generational GC works more or less as you'll see in this problem). We start with the following diagram:

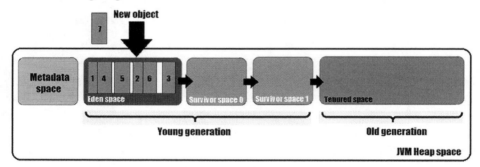

Figure 12.2: GC initial state

At its initial state, the GC has an almost full *Eden* space (it stores objects 1, 4, 5, 2, 6, and 3, and some free space – represented by those white gaps between objects) and empty *Survivor* and *Tenured* spaces. Moreover, object 7 should be added in the *Eden* space but there is not enough memory for it. When the *Eden* space cannot accommodate more objects, the GC triggers a *MinorGC* event. First, the *non-live objects* are identified. Here (as you can see in the following diagram), we have three objects (5, 2, and 3) that should be collected as garbage:

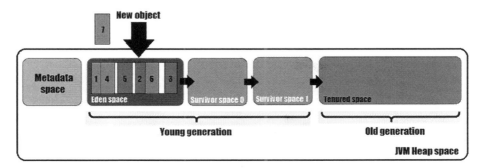

Figure 12.3: Identify the non-live objects from the Eden space

These three objects are collected as garbage, so they are removed from the heap. Next, the *live objects* (1, 4, and 6) are moved into *Survivor space 0*. Finally, the new object (7) is added into the *Eden* space, as in the following figure:

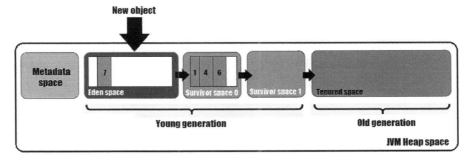

Figure 12.4: Removing objects from memory (5, 2, and 3), moving objects to Survivor space 0 (1, 4, and 6), and adding object 7 into the Eden space

Here, an *epoch* (complete GC cycle) has ended.

Later on, more objects are added into the *Eden* space until it is almost full again:

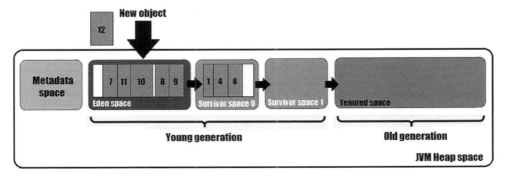

Figure 12.5: The Eden space is almost full again

Adding the new object (12) requires a *Minor GC* event. Again, the *non-living objects* are identified as follows:

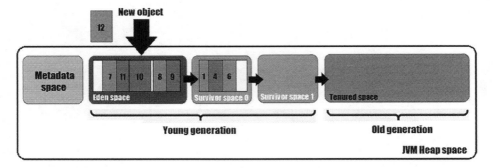

Figure 12.6: There are non-live objects in the Eden and Survivor 0 spaces

There are four objects that should be collected as garbage. In the *Eden* space, there are three objects (11, 10, and 9), and in *Survivor space 0*, there is one object (4). All four of these objects are removed from the heap. The *live objects* from *Survivor space 0* (1 and 6) are moved to *Survivor space 1*. The *live objects* from the *Eden* space (7 and 8) are also moved into *Survivor space 1*. At any moment in time, one of the *Survivor* spaces is empty. Finally, the new object (12) is added to *Eden* space, as in the following figure:

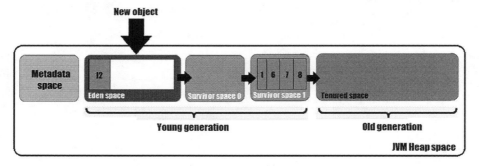

Figure 12.7: At the end of another epoch

Here, another epoch has ended.

Next, objects 13, 14, 15, and 16 are added to the *Eden* space, which is almost full again:

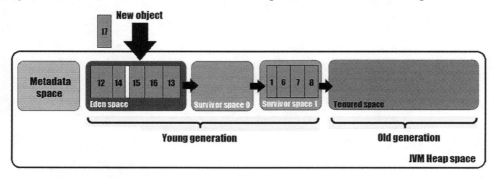

Figure 12.8: There is no memory available for object 17

Being almost full, the *Eden* space cannot accommodate the new object, 17. A new *Minor GC* event is triggered and objects 12, 15, 16, 13, 6, and 8 are identified as *non-live objects*:

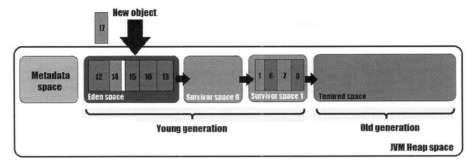

Figure 12.9: There are several non-live objects in different spaces

These objects (12, 15, 16, 13, 6, and 8) are removed from the heap. Next, object 14 is moved from the *Eden* space to *Survivor space 0*. Afterward, objects 1 and 7 (from *Survivor space 1*) are moved into *Survivor space 0*. Finally, the new object 17 is moved into the *Eden* space, as in the following figure:

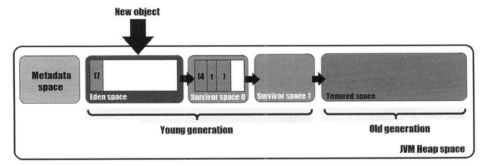

Figure 12.10: The new object (17) is added to the Eden space

Here, another *epoch* has ended.

We repeat the scenario and fill up the *Eden* space again. We stop when object 22 should be added into the *Eden* space:

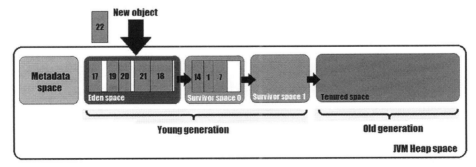

Figure 12.11: Trying to add in Eden space object 22

As we already know, the GC marks all the *non-live objects* (here, 17, 21, 18, and 7):

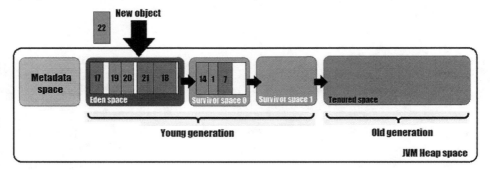

Figure 12.12: Marking the non-live objects

This time, the GC promotes object 1 (when it is considered old enough) from the *Young* generation to the *Old* generation. Next, the objects from the *Eden* space (19 and 20) and the objects from *Survivor space 0* (14) are moved into *Survivor space 1*. The result is sketched in the next figure:

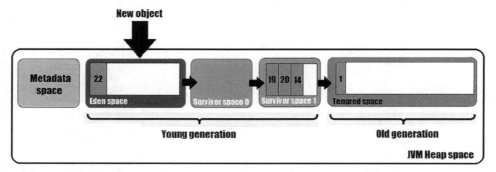

Figure 12.13: We have the first object promoted to Old generation

At the end of this *epoch*, we finally have an object (1) in *Tenured* space. Continuing to run *epoch* after *epoch* will eventually fill up the *Tenured* space, which will not be able to accommodate more objects. In other words, the *Minor GC* events (which are *stop-the-world* events) will reclaim the memory of the *Young* generation until the *Old* generation is full. When that happens, a *Mixed GC* or even *Full GC* event will be triggered (the *Full GC* is also an STW event and will handle the *Metadata* space as well).

In a nutshell, this is how a GC works. Of course, there are many other internal/external factors that may influence the GC's decisions.

247. Choosing the correct garbage collector

As you'll see in the next problem, Java allows us to choose between several garbage collectors. There is no silver bullet, so choosing the correct garbage collector for your particular application is an important decision that should be made based on three factors: *throughput, latency,* and *footprint*.

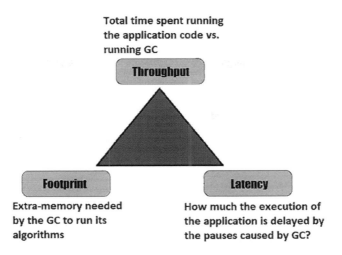

Figure 12.14: The factors that affect the choice of GC

Throughput represents the total time spent running the application code vs. running the GC. For instance, your application may run 97% of the total time, so you have a throughput of 97%. The remaining 3% is the time spent running the GC.

Latency measures how much the execution of the application is delayed by pauses caused by the GC. This is important because latency can affect the application's responsiveness. These pauses may lead, at the interactivity level, to an unpleasant experience for the end users.

Footprint represents the extra memory needed by the GC to run its algorithms. This is the memory needed in addition to the memory used by the application itself.

Choosing the proper GC based on these three factors is a very subjective decision. You may need a massive throughput while you can bear latencies, or you may not be able to afford latencies because you have high interactivity with the end users, or your scalability is in direct correlation with limited physical memory, so you are really interested in the footprint factor. As you'll see in the next problem, each GC type has its own advantages and disadvantages in the context of these three factors.

248. Categorizing garbage collectors

Garbage collectors have evolved exactly as Java itself has evolved. Today (JDK 21), we distinguish between several GC types, as follows:

- Serial garbage collector
- Parallel garbage collector
- Garbage-First (G1) collector
- Z Garbage Collector (ZGC)
- Shenandoah Garbage Collector (not generational)
- Concurrent Mark Sweep (CMS) collector (deprecated)

Let's tackle the main aspects of each GC type.

Serial garbage collector

The serial garbage collector is an STW single-threaded generational collector. Before running its own algorithms, this GC freezes/pauses all the application threads. This means that this GC is not suitable for multi-threaded applications such as server-side components. However, being focused on a very small footprint (useful for small heaps), this collector is a good fit for single-threaded applications (and single-processor machines) that can easily accommodate and tolerate a significant latency (for instance, batch jobs or bulk processing).

Parallel garbage collector

The parallel garbage collector is an STW multi-threaded generational collector. Before running its own algorithms, this GC freezes/pauses all the application threads, but it speeds up the garbage collection by using multiple threads. In other words, this GC can take advantage of multi-processor machines and can be a good fit for multi-threaded applications that use medium/large datasets. This GC is focused on throughput rather than latency and comes with pauses of 1 second or more. So, if you are in a multi-threaded context that can afford pauses of 1 second or more, then this GC is the right choice.

Garbage-First (G1) collector

The Garbage-First (G1) collector is an STW multi-threaded, region-based, generational collector focused on balanced performance. This GC was introduced in JDK 7 update 4 as a default (since JDK 9) solution that sustains high throughput and low latency (a few hundred milliseconds). The price to pay for this performance is a more frequent rate of epochs. The GC will run more often, so be prepared to provide a CPU ready to accommodate more cycles than other GCs. This GC was designed for server-style applications that are executed on multi-processor machines with massive memory (large heap size). Also known as a *mostly concurrent* collector, G1 performs heavily next to the application using equally sized spaces/regions (from 1 to 32 MB). So, if you can afford a large heap size and need low latency, then G1 is the proper choice. We will talk in detail about G1 in subsequent problems.

Z Garbage Collector (ZGC)

Z Garbage Collector (ZGC) was introduced for production starting with JDK 15 as a low-latency GC that can handle large heap sizes (terabytes). Like G1, ZGC works concurrently but it guarantees to not stop the application threads for more than a few milliseconds (the documentation even states that ZGC can perform with sub-millisecond max pause times). We will cover it in detail in subsequent problems.

Shenandoah Garbage Collector

Shenandoah Garbage Collector was introduced in JDK 12 (and became more reliable in JDK 17) as a very low-latency, highly responsive GC (sub-millisecond pauses). It performs its job (including compaction) concurrently with the application. Shenandoah pauses are extremely short and independent of the heap size. Garbage collecting a 1 GB heap or a 300 GB heap should produce similar pauses.

Concurrent Mark Sweep (CMS) collector (deprecated)

CMS is a *mostly concurrent* collector deprecated by G1. Since it is deprecated, I will not talk about it further.

249. Introducing G1

The G1 Garbage Collector is probably the most mature, maintained, and improved GC in Java. It was introduced in JDK 7 update 4, and from JDK 9, it became the default GC. This GC sustains high throughput and low latency (a few hundred milliseconds), being known for its balanced performance.

Internally, G1 splits the heap into equally small chunks (max size of 32 MB), which are independent of each other and can be allocated dynamically to *Eden*, *Survivor*, or *Tenured* spaces. Each such chunk is called the G1 *heap region*. So, G1 is a region-based GC.

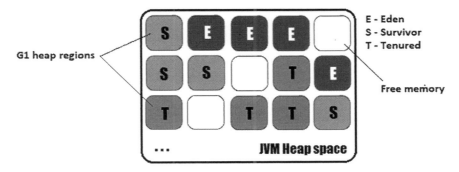

Figure 12.15: G1 splits the memory heap into equal small chunks

This architecture has a significant number of advantages. Probably, the most important one is represented by the fact that the *Old* generation can be cleaned up efficiently by cleaning it up in parts that sustain low latency.

For a heap size smaller than 4 GB, G1 will create regions of 1 MB. For heaps between 4 and 8 GB, G1 will create regions of 2 MB, and so on, up to 32 MB for a heap of 64 GB or larger. Basically, the JVM sets a number of regions that have a power of 2 and between 1 and 32 MB (typically, during the application start, the JVM sets up around 2,000+ regions).

Design principles

G1 was designed on a set of principles, as follows:

- Balanced performance – Designed to balance throughput and low latency to sustain performance.

- Generational – Dynamically split the heap into the *Young* and *Old* generations and focus on the *Young* generation, since in this region there is more garbage (most objects die in the *Young* generation region). The idea that most objects are short-lived is also known as the *generational hypothesis*.

- Incremental collecting of *Old* generation – G1 eventually moves objects from the *Young* to the *Old* generation and leaves them there to die slowly and collects them incrementally.

- Mostly concurrent – G1 strives to perform heavy tasks next to the application (concurrently) with low and predictable pauses.

Thanks to these design principles, G1 has deprecated the CMS collector.

250. Tackling G1 throughput improvements

G1 has made major progress from JDK 8 to JDK 20. Some of these improvements have been reflected in throughput. Of course, this throughput improvement is dependent on a lot of factors (application, machine, tuning, and so on) but you may expect at least 10% higher throughput in JDK 18/20 than in JDK 8.

In order to increase throughput, G1 has passed through several changes, as follows.

Delaying the start of the Old generation

Starting with JDK 9, G1 is heavily focused on collecting garbage from the *Young* generation while delaying the start (initialization, resource allocation, and so on) of the *Old* generation to the last moment (it anticipates when the *Old* generation should be started).

Focusing on easy pickings

By easy pickings, we mean objects that are short-lived (for instance, temporary buffers), occupy a significant amount of heap, and can be collected easily at low cost with important benefits. Starting with JDK 9, G1 is highly focused on easy pickings.

Improving NUMA-aware memory allocation

NUMA stands for non-uniform memory access and it was described in *Problem 245*. G1 takes advantage of NUMA from JDK 14 and it is continuously improved. If NUMA is enabled, then JVM requires the OS to place G1 heap regions on NUMA nodes. At the end of this process, the whole heap should be located evenly across the NUMA nodes that are active.

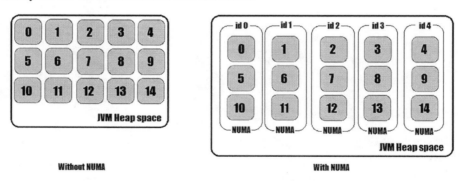

Figure 12.16: Heap memory without and with NUMA

The relationship between G1 heap regions and memory pages (operating system pages – https:// en.wikipedia.org/wiki/Page_(computer_memory)) falls into one of these two cases:

- If the size of a G1 heap region is greater than or equal to the size of a memory page, then a G1 heap region will consist of multiple memory pages (*Figure 12.17*, left-hand side).
- If the size of a G1 heap region is smaller than or equal to the size of a memory page, then a memory page will consist of multiple G1 heap regions (*Figure 12.17*, right-hand side).

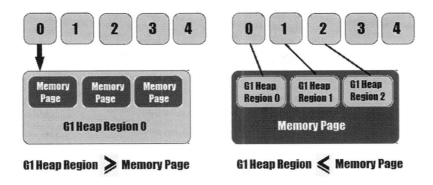

Figure 12.17: G1 heap region and memory page relationship

Without NUMA, the G1 GC allocates memory to threads from a single common memory allocator. With NUMA, there is a memory allocator per NUMA node, and memory is allocated to threads based on these NUMA nodes.

Improving NUMA allocation awareness is a continuous goal of G1.

Parallelized full-heap collections

Among other not-so-common optimizations, we have the parallelization of full-heap collection. This was added in JDK 10 as a solution to make full-heap collections as fast as possible.

Other improvements

Tons of small improvements have been added to JVM itself, and their effects are reflected in GC performance as well. This means that by simply updating to the latest JDK, our GC will perform better. You'll notice an improvement of at least 10% between JDK 8 and JDK 20.

251. Tackling G1 latency improvements

G1 GC latency has also recorded some improvements from JDK 8 to JDK 20 (which are obviously reflected in G1 GC throughput as well).

In order to decrease latency, G1 has passed through several changes, as follows.

Merge parallel phases into a larger one

Starting with JDK 8, many aspects of G1 have been parallelized. In other words, at any moment in time, we may have in execution multiple parallel phases. Starting with JDK 9, these parallel phases can be merged into a single larger one. In practice, this means less synchronization and less time spent creating/destroying threads. As a result, this improvement speeds up the parallelization processing, leading to less latency.

Reduction of metadata

Reduction of metadata was added in JDK 11. Practically, G1 attempts to manage less metadata by reducing its amount as much as possible. Less data to manage means better latency. Of course, this means a smaller footprint as well.

Better work balancing

Work balancing was improved starting with JDK 11. In a nutshell, this means that threads that have finished their current work can steal work from other threads. In practice, this means that the tasks are done faster since all threads are working (on their own work or on stolen work) and none of them are just hanging on. So, smarter algorithms have been developed to orchestrate and keep threads busy in order to finish the tasks faster and decrease latency. However, reducing the overhead of stealing work is still a subject of improvement.

Better parallelization

Better parallelization is available starting with JDK 14. In practice, G1 removes all duplicates from potential areas with references. Afterward, it applies parallelization instead of brute force.

Better reference scanning

In order to sustain better parallelization, JDK 15 has also improved the reference scanning in the collected areas. JDK 14 knows how to remove duplicates and parallelize the data processing, while JDK 15 knows how to scan references more optimally. Their effects are combined into decreasing latency.

Other improvements

A lot of time has been spent improving so-called uncommon situations. For instance, special attention has been focused on *evacuation failures* (the attempt of moving the *live objects* between two memory areas and compacting them is known as *evacuation fashion*, and when moving objects around leads to out-of-memory issues, then we have an *evacuation failure*). This corner case has been seriously improved in order to handle such scenarios faster than before (before JDK 17).

252. Tackling G1 footprint improvements

Between JDK 8 and JDK 20, the G1 footprint has been improved by focusing on efficient metadata and freeing the memory as quickly as possible.

In order to optimize its footprint, G1 has passed through several changes, as follows.

Maintain only the needed metadata

In order to maintain only the needed metadata, JDK 11 is capable of concurrently (re)creating the needed data and freeing it as fast as possible. In JDK 17, the focus on the needed metadata has been reiterated and only the absolutely required data is kept around. Moreover, JDK 18 comes up with a denser representation of data. All these improvements are reflected in a smaller footprint.

Release memory

Starting with JDK 17, the G1 GC is capable of concurrently releasing memory (giving it back to the OS). This means that memory can be optimally reused and is available to serve other tasks.

253. Introducing ZGC

Z Garbage Collector (ZGC) was introduced for the first time (as an experimental feature) in JDK 11. It was promoted to the production stage (production ready) in JDK 15 under JEP 377. It continues to be improved as we speak – in JDK 21, ZGC sustains application performance by maintaining separate generations for young and old objects. Basically, this minimizes allocation stalls and heap memory overhead. Moreover, JDK 21 (JEP 439) has promoted ZGC's status from Targeted to Completed.

ZGC is concurrent (works at the same time as the application based on low-level concurrency primitives such as *load barriers* and *colored pointers*), tracing (traversing the object graph to identify *live* and *non-live* objects), and compacting (fight against fragmentation). It is also NUMA-aware and region-based.

ZGC was specially designed as a low-latency, highly scalable GC capable of handling from small (a few megabytes; the documentation states 8 MB) to massive heaps (terabytes; the documentation states 16 TB) with pauses (pulse times) of a maximum of a few milliseconds (the documentation states sub-millisecond max pause times).

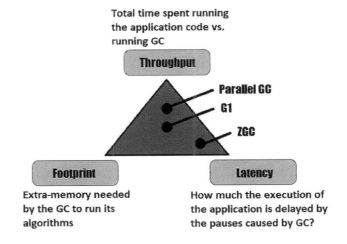

Figure 12.18: ZGC is focused on low latency

It is very important to say that pauses don't increase with the heap size (pulse times are O(1), so they execute in constant time).

The shortcoming (trade-off) of ZGC relies on throughput. In other words, ZGC throughput is slightly reduced (a few percent, for instance from 0% to 10% in some cases) in comparison with G1 throughput.

Starting with JDK 16, ZGC takes advantage of a concurrent thread stack, and starting with JDK 18, it supports string de-duplication. These are just two of the major improvements next to many other improvements.

ZGC is auto-tuned. In other words, as you'll see in *Problem 256*, ZGC has just a few options that we can tune while most of the tuning is automatic.

ZGC is concurrent

G1 and ZGC are both concurrent, but they don't follow the same path. ZGC strives to collect as much garbage as possible in a concurrent fashion. For this, ZGC relies on three main lightweight (very short, sub-millisecond) pauses and three concurrent phases, as in the following figure:

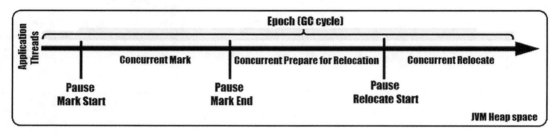

Figure 12.19: ZGC concurrency

Each of the three phases is signaled by a synchronization point (pause):

- *Pause Mark Start* – This pause signals that the *Concurrent Mark* phase follows. During this synchronization point, ZGC prepares the current state for executing the *Concurrent Mark* phase. This is a lightweight pause that performs some settings on *colored pointers* and resets a few flags and counters. Next, the *Concurrent Mark* phase runs concurrently and marks the objects from the heap.

- *Pause Mark End* – This pause signals the end of the *Concurrent Mark* phase. It also pauses before executing the *Concurrent Prepare for Relocation* phase. This phase is responsible for locating all the *live* objects from sparsely populated regions and marks them as candidates to be moved/ evacuated to other regions. Moreover, during this phase, ZGC deallocates regions that don't contain *live* objects.

- *Pause Relocate Start* – This pause signals that the *Concurrent Relocate* phase follows. During this phase, the objects marked as evacuation candidates in the previous phase are effectively moved (copied) from the current region to the new region. Their references are also restored, being deallocated from the current region and reallocated to the new region.

ZGC and colored pointers

ZGC runs next to the application and manipulates (moves around) the objects used by that application. This may lead to unexpected errors (for instance, the application may attempt to use out-of-date references) that cause the application to act weirdly or even crash. In order to prevent such scenarios, ZGC relies on two low-level concurrency primitives known as *colored pointer* and *load barriers*.

A *colored pointer* is a 64-bit pointer. This pointer is used by ZGC with a 44-bit object address capable of handling up to 16 terabytes.

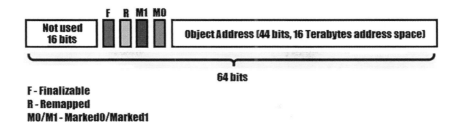

Figure 12.20: Colored pointer

A *colored pointer* reserves 20 bits for storing metadata about this pointer. The most important metadata is:

- *Finalizable* – 1 bit that indicates if an object is reachable (*live* object)
- *Remapped* – 1 bit that indicates if an object doesn't point into a relocation set
- *Marked0/Marked1* – 2 bits that indicate if an object is or is not marked

As well as colored pointers, ZGC needs load barriers.

ZGC and load barriers

Load barriers are portions of code injected by the compiler to handle *colored pointers*. While the application is not aware of *colored pointers*, ZGC needs to interpret and work with them, and this is exactly the job of *load barriers*. For instance, let's assume that we have, in the application, the following snippet of code (I've intentionally added the line numbers manually):

```
1: Manager manager = company.manager;
2: Manager cManager = manager;
3: manager.attendMeeting();
4: int employeeNr = company.size;
```

The compiler analyzes the code to decide where to inject a *load barrier*. The conclusion is that the only place where a *load barrier* should be injected is between lines 1 and 2 because that is the only place where an object is loaded from the heap. In line 2, there is no need for a *load barrier* since there is a copy of the memory reference. In line 3, there is also no need for a *load barrier* since there is a method reference. Finally, in line 4, there is no need for a *load barrier* since there is no object reference. So, ZGC sees this code as follows:

```
1: Manager manager = company.manager;
<load barrier injected at this point>
2: Manager cManager = manager;      // copying reference
3: manager.attendMeeting();         // method reference
4: int employeeNr = company.size; // no object reference
```

The purpose of the *load barrier* is to ensure that the pointers are valid (shown by having a good color). If a bad color is encountered, then the *load barrier* tries to heal it (update the pointer, relocate the object reference, and so on).

ZGC is region-based

ZGC is a *region-based* GC, so it divides the heap into smaller regions/chunks that are allocated to the *Young* or *Old* generation, as in the following figure:

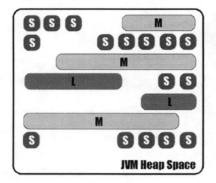

Figure 12.21: ZGC heap regions

Exactly like G1, ZGC is a *region-based* GC. Nevertheless, ZGC is more powerful than G1 and has the capability to dynamically increase/decrease the number of active regions during runtime. Moreover, ZGC can rely on regions of three sizes, as follows:

- Small region – These regions are 2 MB.
- Medium region – These regions can be from 4 MB to 32 MB. They are dynamically sized.
- Large region – These are regions reserved for *humongous* objects. These are tightly fitted regions that can be smaller or larger than a medium region.

So, at a glance, ZGC is a concurrent GC with constant pause times (sub-millisecond), working in parallel mode, and capable of fighting against fragmentation via compacting. Moreover, it is region-based, NUMA-aware, capable of auto-tuning, and relies on *colored pointers* and *load barriers*.

254. Monitoring garbage collectors

Monitoring the activity and evolution in the timeline of your GC is a major aspect in order to identify potential performance issues. For instance, you may be interested in monitoring pause times, identifying the frequency and types of GC events, what spaces are filled up by the triggered GC events, and so on. The main goal is to collect as much information as possible that can be helpful in troubleshooting performance issues related to heap memory and GC evolution.

Any modern IDE provides profilers that contain (among other related things) information and real-time graphs about the GC *epochs*/cycles. For instance, the following figure is from the NetBeans IDE, which displays the GC evolution (heap status) as an item of the toolbar (by simply clicking on that area, you can force the GC to perform garbage collection):

Figure 12.22: NetBeans display GC evolution on the toolbar

Of course, a more detailed view is available via the NetBeans profiler:

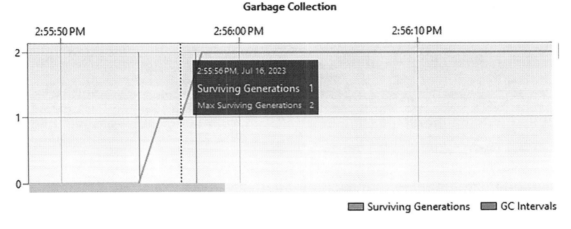

Figure 12.23: NetBeans profiler for GC

Among other tools that can be used to monitor your GC are the *jstat* command-line utility (jstat -gc $JAVA_PID) and *JConsole* (Java Monitoring and Management Console).

The following figure is a screenshot from *JConsole*:

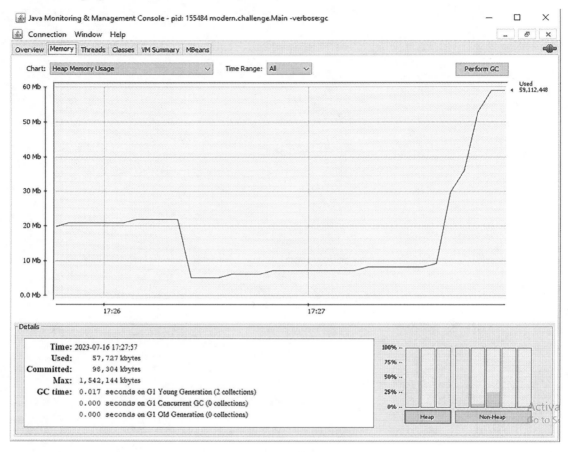

Figure 12.24: Monitoring the GC via JConsole

You may also be interested in **visualgc** (**Visual Garbage Collection Monitoring Tool**) from Oracle, **JDK VisualGC** (IntelliJ IDE plugin), and **Memory Analyzer** (**MAT**) from Eclipse.

255. Logging garbage collectors

Analyzing the GC logs is another approach that can be useful for finding memory issues. Since GC logs don't add a significant overhead, they can be enabled in production for debugging purposes. Really, GC logs have an insignificant overhead, so you should definitely use them!

Let's consider some simple Java code that adds and removes from `List<String>`. Adding and removing the code requires a full GC via `System.gc()`:

```
private static final List<String> strings = new ArrayList<>();
...
logger.info("Application started ...");
```

```java
String string = "prefixedString_";

// Add in heap 5 millions String instances
for (int i = 0; i < 5_000_000; i++) {
  String newString = string + i;
  strings.add(newString);
}

logger.info(() -> "List size: " + strings.size());

// Force GC execution
System.gc();

// Remove 10_000 out of 5 millions
for (int i = 0; i < 10_000; i++) {
  String newString = string + i;
  strings.remove(newString);
}

logger.info(() -> "List size: " + strings.size());
logger.info("Application done ...");
```

Next, we want to run this simple application and log the GC activity.

Before JDK 9, we can obtain a quick and verbose log of GC via the -verbose:gc option:

```
java … -verbose:gc
```

A possible output will look as follows:

```
[0.319s][info][gc] Using G1
[17:03:47] [INFO] Application started ...
[0.917s][info][gc] GC(0) Pause Young (Normal)
        (G1 Evacuation Pause) 27M->24M(96M) 34.391ms
[0.948s][info][gc] GC(1) Pause Young (Normal)
        (G1 Evacuation Pause) 40M->40M(96M) 21.300ms
[0.986s][info][gc] GC(2) Pause Young (Normal)
        (G1 Evacuation Pause) 60M->60M(96M) 24.085ms
[0.997s][info][gc] GC(3) Pause Young (Concurrent Start)
        (G1 Humongous Allocation) 63M->64M(96M) 8.072ms
[0.997s][info][gc] GC(4) Concurrent Mark Cycle
[1.030s][info][gc] GC(5) Pause Young (Normal)
        (G1 Evacuation Pause) 78M->78M(288M) 17.036ms
[1.059s][info][gc] GC(4) Pause Remark 101M->94M(288M) 0.867ms
```

```
[1.083s][info][gc] GC(4) Pause Cleanup 109M->109M(288M) 0.14ms
[1.085s][info][gc] GC(4) Concurrent Mark Cycle 87.261ms
[1.125s][info][gc] GC(6) Pause Young (Prepare Mixed)
          (G1 Evacuation Pause) 116M->118M(288M) 32.640ms
[1.220s][info][gc] GC(7) Pause Young (Mixed)
          (G1 Evacuation Pause) 181M->181M(288M) 42.497ms
[1.257s][info][gc] GC(8) Pause Young (Concurrent Start)
          (G1 Humongous Allocation) 200M->201M(288M) 23.297ms
[1.257s][info][gc] GC(9) Concurrent Mark Cycle
[1.316s][info][gc] GC(10) Pause Young (Normal)
          (G1 Evacuation Pause) 243M->244M(288M) 24.492ms
[1.345s][info][gc] GC(11) Pause Young (Normal)
          (G1 Evacuation Pause) 256M->258M(776M) 12.445ms
[1.400s][info][gc] GC(9) Pause Remark 290M->274M(776M) 0.732ms
[1.461s][info][gc] GC(9) Pause Cleanup 335M->335M(776M) 0.25ms
[1.466s][info][gc] GC(9) Concurrent Mark Cycle 209.289ms
[1.531s][info][gc] GC(12) Pause Young (Prepare Mixed)
          (G1 Evacuation Pause) 344M->345M(776M) 54.939ms
[17:03:48] [INFO] List size: 5000000
[1.830s][info][gc] GC(13) Pause Full (System.gc())
          368M->330M(776M) 277.793ms
[17:04:15] [INFO] List size: 4990000
[17:04:15] [INFO] Application done ...
```

This is the simplest GC log. For more details, we can add the `-XX:+PrintGCDetails` option:

```
java … -XX:+PrintGCDetails -verbose:gc
```

Moreover, we can attach a few options for obtaining information about tenuring distribution (`-XX:+PrintTenuringDistribution`), garbage collector time stamps (`-XX:+PrintGCTimeStamps`), the class histogram (`-XX:+PrintClassHistogram`), and the application stopped time (`-XX:+PrintGCApplicationStoppedTime`).

In this context, GC logs are available on the console (stdout) using the info level. You can easily redirect the GC logs to a file via the `-Xloggc` option:

```
java … -verbose:gc -Xloggc:gclog.txt
```

Actually, `-Xloggc` is deprecated and you should use it only if you are using a JDK earlier than version 9. Starting with JDK 9 (JEP 158 – https://openjdk.org/jeps/158), we have a *unified logging system* for all JVM components.

So, starting with JDK 9, we have a unified logging system via the `–Xlog` option. The equivalent of `-XX:+PrintGCDetails -verbose:gc` is `-Xlog:gc*`. If we want to redirect GC logs to a file using the debug level, then we can do it as follows:

```
java … -Xlog:gc*=debug:file=gclog.txt
```

The gclog.txt will be saved in the application root folder. If you remove the * character, then you'll get a less verbose GC log.

Logging only NUMA logs is available via -Xlog:numa*={log level}.

Having the GC log is half of the problem. The other half consists of interpreting this log. As you can see, this is not that easy. Fortunately, you don't have to bother reading the log files because we have tools capable of parsing, analyzing, and providing detailed reports from GC logs.

One of these tools is Universal GC Log Analyzer (https://gceasy.io/). Using the free version, we can upload our gclog.txt file and get a detailed report. For instance, in the following figure, we can see how memory was allocated for our application.

Generation	Allocated	Peak
Young Generation	119 mb	81 mb
Old Generation	657 mb	285 mb
Humongous	n/a	51 mb
Meta Space	1.12 mb	950 kb
Young + Old + Meta space	777.12 mb	369.93 mb

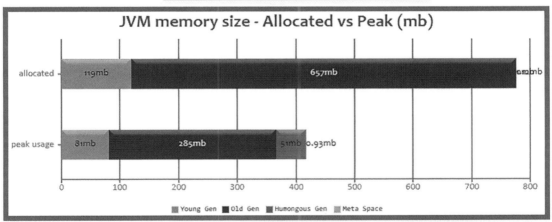

Figure 12.25: A screenshot from Universal GC Log Analyzer (GCEasy) report

This figure is just a very small part of the report. Try it yourself to see the full report. Other similar tools that you may like to try are GCViewer, GCPlot, IBM Garbage Collection and Memory Visualizer, garbagecat, SolarWinds Loggly, Sematext Logs, **Java Flight Recorder** (JFR), jvm-gc-logs-analyzer, and so on.

256. Tuning garbage collectors

Garbage collectors are complex machinery whose performances are highly related to their settings (startup parameters) in the context of the current JVM, current application, and hardware. Since the GC consumes and shares resources (memory, CPU time, and so on) with our application, it is essential to tune it to work as efficiently as possible. If the GC is not efficient, then we may face significant pause times that will negatively impact the application run.

In this problem, we will cover the main tuning options available for the serial GC, parallel GC, G1 GC, and ZGC.

How to tune

Before attempting to tune the GC, ensure that it is really causing trouble. By inspecting and correlating the charts and logs, you can identify such troubles and decide where you should act (what parameters should be tuned). Check out the usage of the heap memory and how objects fill up the *Eden*, *Survivor*, and *Tenured* spaces.

Typically, a healthy GC produces a heap usage graph known as *shark teeth*, as in the following figure:

Figure 12.26: Healthy heap usage

Moreover, check out the 90th and 99th percentiles along with the average GC time. This information can give you a hint about whether more memory is needed or if it is cleared properly.

Once you identify the GC troubles, try to tackle them one by one. Don't rush to change several parameters at once because it will be hard to manage and analyze their combined effect. Try to modify one of them and experiment to see what's happening and what the results are. If you see some benefits, then go for the next one and experiment again. Observe if the combined effect has been improved or not. Otherwise, maybe it is better to restore this one to its default value before going for the next one.

Tuning the serial garbage collector

The serial garbage collector can be enabled via -XX:+UseSerialGC.

Since this is a single-threaded GC, there is not much to tune. However, you may adjust the heap size via –Xmx and –Xms (for instance, a heap size of 3 GB can be set via –Xmx3g and –Xms3g) and the *Young* generation size via the –Xmn option. Nevertheless, these options work with all types of GC for setting the heap size.

Tunning the parallel garbage collector

The parallel garbage collector can be enabled via -XX:+UseParallelGC.

This GC is multi-threaded and we can control the number of threads used for cleaning tasks via the -XX:ParallelGCThreads option (for instance, setting six threads can be done with -XX:ParallelGCThreads=6).

Keep in mind that a higher number of threads results in a higher fragmentation of the heap reserved for the *Tenured* space. Each thread that participates in a *Minor* GC event will reserve some space in the *Tenured* space for its promotions goals. This will lead to serious fragmentation of the *Tenured* space. Fixing this issue requires reducing the number of threads and increasing the size of the *Old* generation.

The maximum pause time can be controlled via the `-XX:MaxGCPauseMillis` option (for instance, `-XX:MaxGCPauseMillis=150`, which will ensure maximum pause times of 150 milliseconds between two consecutive runs/events of GC). However, be aware that bigger pause times will allow more garbage to hit the heap. This means that the next run of the GC will be more expensive. On the other hand, a small pause time will instruct the GC to run more frequently, and this may cause the application to spend too much time on garbage collection.

Next, the maximum throughput that we want to achieve can be set via the `-XX:GCTimeRatio` option. This option is evaluated as the ratio between the time spent inside vs. outside the GC. It is a percentage computed as $1/(1 + n)$. In other words, `-XX:GCTimeRatio` specifies the amount of time dedicated to garbage collection in a $1/(1+n)$ ratio.

For instance, if we set this option as `-XX:GCTimeRatio=14`, then we target a goal of 1/15. This means that 6% of the total time should be spent in garbage collection (by default, this option is set to 99, or 1% of time is spent on garbage collection).

If you get an `OutOfMemoryError`, then most probably, this is caused by too much time spent on garbage collection. For instance, if more than 98% of the time is spent recovering less than 2% of the heap, then you'll see such an error. In other words, GC has spent a lot of time cleaning a small part of the heap. This may indicate memory leaks or a heap that is too small. Nevertheless, if you can live with this error, then you can suppress it via the `-XX:-UseGCOverheadLimit` option.

We can also control the size of the *Young*/*Old* generation. You can control the growth of the *Young* generation via `-XX:YoungGenerationSizeIncrement`, and the growth of the *Old* generation via `-XX:Te nuredGenerationSizeIncrement`. The values of these options are percentages (by default, the growth percentage is 20% and the shrinking percentage is 5%). Moreover, you can control the shrinking percentage by simply setting the `-XX:AdaptiveSizeDecrementScaleFactor` option. The shrinking of the *Young* generation is automatically computed via `-XX:YoungGenerationSizeIncrement/-XX:Ada ptiveSizeDecrementScaleFactor`.

Tuning the G1 garbage collector

The G1 garbage collector can be enabled via `-XX:+UseG1GC`.

By default, G1 takes care of the *Young* generation. Basically, it cleans the *Young* generation and promotes the reachable objects to the *Old* generation until it hits a threshold of 45%. This default value can be altered via `-XX:InitiatingHeapOccupancyPercent`.

When tuning the G1 collector, we can target throughput, latency, or footprint. When tuning for latency, we have to focus on low pause times. This can be achieved by setting the –Xmx and –Xms options at the same value (to avoid heap resizing). Moreover, we can rely on the `-XX:+AlwaysPreTouch` and `-XX:+UseLargePages` flag options to load the (large) memory pages at the start of the application.

If latency is affected by the *Young* generation size, then it is a good idea to decrease its size via -XX:G1NewSizePercent and -XX:G1MaxNewSizePercent. On the other hand, if the *Mixed* GC events affect latency, then we should focus on spreading the *Tenured* space across more collections via the -XX:G1MixedGCCountTarget flag option. In addition, we may want to focus on -XX:G1HeapWastePercent (stop earlier the *Tenured* space cleanup) and -XX:G1MixedGCLiveThresholdPercent (the *Tenured* space becomes part of a mixed collection only when this threshold is exceeded (defaults to 65)). You may also be interested in -XX:G1RSetUpdatingPauseTimePercent, -XX:-ReduceInitialCardMarks, and -XX:G1RSetRegionEntries (for details, see the G1 documentation).

When tuning for throughput (applications that manipulate a lot of data need a GC capable of cleaning as much garbage as possible), we have to focus on the -XX:MaxGCPauseMillis option. When this option has a low effect, then you should focus on -XX:G1NewSizePercent and -XX:G1MaxNewSizePercent. Basically, G1 strives to bound the *Young* generation size between the values of -XX:G1NewSizePercent (default is 5) and -XX:G1MaxNewSizePercent (default is 60). By juggling these three options, we can relax the GC and give it more time and space to process a lot of garbage. In addition, throughput can be sustained via the -XX:G1RSetUpdatingPauseTimePercent option.

By increasing the value of this option, we decrease the time spent in concurrent parts while performing more work when pausing the application's threads. In addition, as in the case of tuning for latency, we may want to avoid heap resizing (set –Xmx and –Xms at the same value) and turn on the -XX:+AlwaysPreTouch and -XX:+UseLargePages flag options.

Tuning for footprint may be influenced by setting the -XX:GCTimeRatio. This defaults to 12 (8%) but we can increase it to force the GC to spend more time in garbage collection. As a result, more heap memory will be free, but this is not a general rule. It is recommended to experiment and see how it really works. Moreover, since JDK 8 (update 20), we can set up the -XX:+UseStringDeduplication flag option. Practically, if this option is enabled, then G1 locates duplicate strings and holds a single reference to one string while cleaning up the duplicates. This should result in a more efficient and optimal usage of the heap memory. You also may want to consult the documentation for -XX:+Print StringDeduplicationStatistics and -XX:StringDeduplicationAgeThreshold=n.

As you already know, G1 splits the heap into small regions up to 32 MB. In practice, this may lead to performance degradation, especially for large objects on very large heaps. But, starting with JDK 18, the maximum region size was set up to 512 MB. Whenever you need, you can control the maximum region size via the -XX:G1HeapRegionSize.

Tuning Z Garbage Collector

Z Garbage Collector can be enabled via -XX:+UseZGC (before JDK 15, you may also need -XX:+Unloc kExperimentalVMOptions).

One of the most important settings of this GC is –Xmx to set up the maximum heap size. Next to this one, we have -XX:ConcGCThreads=n, where n is the number of threads used by ZGC. However, ZGC is fully capable of dynamically determining the optimal value for this option, so think twice before modifying it.

Tuning Metaspace (Metadata space)

If your focus is on tuning Metaspace, then you'll be interested in the following options:

- `-XX:MetaspaceSize` – Set the initial size of Metaspace
- `-XX:MaxMetaspaceSize` – Set the maximum size of Metaspace
- `-XX:MinMetaspaceFreeRatio` – Set the class metadata capacity that should be free after running the GC (this is the minimum value as a percentage)
- `-XX:MaxMetaspaceFreeRatio` – Set the class metadata capacity that should be free after running the GC (this is the maximum value as a percentage)

Controlling the size and behavior of the Metaspace can also be part of tuning your GC. Again, experimenting and comparing the results is the main rule of thumb that can lead you to a successful and optimal GC.

257. Introducing Application Class Data Sharing (AppCDS, or Java's Startup Booster)

Launching a Java application is a multi-step process. Before executing the bytecode of a class, the JVM has to perform at least the following steps for a given class name:

1. Look up the class on disk (JVM has to scan the disk and find the given class name).
2. Load the class (JVM opens the file and loads its content).
3. Check the bytecode (JVM verifies the integrity of the content).
4. Pull the bytecode internally (JVM transfers the code into an internal data structure).

Obviously, these steps are not cost-free. Loading hundreds/thousands of classes will have a significant overhead on launching time and memory footprint. Typically, an application's JAR remains unchanged for a long time, but JVM performs the previous steps and obtains the same result every time we launch the application.

Improving/accelerating the startup performance and even reducing the memory footprint are the main goals of Application Class Data Sharing (AppCDS). In a nutshell, AppCDS was initially popularized in JDK 10 (2018), and it was simplified in JDK 13 and JDK 19. The idea of AppCDS is to perform the previous steps once and dump the result into an archive. This archive can be reused for subsequent launches and even shared across multiple JVM instances running on the same host. The bigger the application is, the bigger the startup benefits are.

Putting these ideas into practice requires the following three steps:

1. Create the list of classes that should be shared between the application instances.
2. Archive this list of classes in an archive suitable for memory mapping.
3. Give the resulting archive to every application startup (every application instance).

Depending on the JDK used, you may have to manually follow these steps or only a part of them. The AppCDS algorithm is constantly improved, so its use depends on your JDK, as follows:

- In JDK 10/11, you have to follow the previous three steps. However, if you want to share only the JDK classes (not the application classes), then you can skip step 1. JDK has already prepared the list of classes that should be shared in $JAVA_HOME\lib\classlist (there are around 1,200 classes).

- In JDK 12+, you can skip steps 1 and 2 because an archive of JDK classes is already available. However, if you want to share the application classes as well, then you need to follow all three steps.

- In JDK 13+, we can take advantage of dynamic CDS archives. Practically, JVM collects the classes to be added into the archive at application runtime. Steps 1 and 2 are merged automatically.

- In JDK 19+, we can take advantage of the autogenerated shared archive. The CDS archive is built and used in a single command.

Tackling a JDK class data archive

Tackling a JDK class data archive means that we will create a reusable archive containing only JDK classes, not the classes of our application.

JDK 10/JDK 11

In JDK 10/11, we can use the already existent $JAVA_HOME/lib/classlist. This is a file that contains the list of JDK classes, and you can easily inspect it with a text editor. Having the class list, we can create the proper CDS archive via the -Xshare:dump option, as follows:

```
java … -Xshare:dump
```

The resulting archive will be stored in $JAVA_HOME\bin\server\classes.jsa (this is the default location and you may need to run this command as an administrator to avoid a permission denied restriction).

Next, we can use this archive via -Xshare:on, as follows (if you run under JDK 11, then --enable-preview is also needed, but I'll skip it here):

```
java … -Xshare:on
```

We can use the unified logging system to track CDS work via -Xlog, as follows:

```
java … -Xshare:on -Xlog:class+load:file=cds.log
```

In the output, we can see that a shared object is marked with a significant message, as follows (objects that are not shared don't contain the "*shared objects file*" text):

```
[6.376s][info][class,load] java.lang.Object source: shared objects file
```

By default, JVM scans for archives in the default location. But, if we move the archive to another location (for instance, in the application root folder), then we have to indicate this location via -XX:SharedArchiveFile, as follows:

```
java … -Xshare:on -XX:SharedArchiveFile=./classes.jsa
        -Xlog:class+load:file=cds.log
```

Actually, the default value of –Xshare is auto. This means that if an archive is found, then it is used automatically. So, if you omit –Xshare:on, then JVM relies on –Xshare:auto, which has the same effect. If you want to shut down CDS support, then use –Xshare:off.

JDK 12+

JDK 12+ comes with an already prepared archive for JDK classes, so there is no need to create one (no need to use –Xshare:dump). JVM will use it automatically thanks to –Xshare:auto or via the explicit –Xshare:on:

```
java … -Xshare:on -Xlog:class+load:file=cds.log
```

Of course, if you have a different location than the default one ($JAVA_HOME\bin\server\classes.jsa), then use -XX:SharedArchiveFile.

Tackling application class data archive

Besides the JDK classes, we may want to share our application classes as well. This can be done in several steps depending on the JDK.

Before JDK 13

Before JDK 13, we need to create the list of classes that we want to share. We can do it manually or via the -XX:DumpLoadedClassList option, as follows (I'll skip it here, but you'll need --enable-preview as well):

```
java ... -XX:DumpLoadedClassList=classes.lst
```

The generated classes.lst contains all classes (classes used by the JDK + your application classes) that will be shared. Next, we can obtain the archive, as follows:

```
java … -Xshare:dump -XX:SharedClassListFile=classes.lst
          -XX:SharedArchiveFile=appcds.jsa --class-path app.jar
```

Consider the following important note.

> **Important note**
>
> Notice that CDS (AppCDS) can archive classes from JAR files only. Don't use classpaths with wildcards or exploded paths such as target/classes. Replace app.jar with your JAR.

The archive (appcds.jsa) is stored in the application root folder, not in $JAVA_HOME.

Finally, we can share the archive and get some logs, as follows:

```
java … -Xshare:on -XX:SharedArchiveFile=./appcds.jsa
          -Xlog:class+load:file=cds.log
```

Done!

JDK 13+

Starting with JDK 13, we can take advantage of *dynamic application class-data sharing*. In other words, we can obtain the archive when JVM exits via the `-XX:ArchiveClassesAtExit` option, as follows:

```
java ... -XX:ArchiveClassesAtExit=appcds.jsa -jar app.jar
```

Replace `app.jar` with your JAR. Use the generated archive as usual via `-Xshare:on` and `-XX:SharedArchiveFile`.

JDK 19+

Starting with JDK 19, we can rely on autogenerated archives. This is possible in a single command, as follows:

```
java … -XX:+AutoCreateSharedArchive
-XX:SharedArchiveFile=appcds.jsa –jar app.jar
```

This time, JVM checks if an archive exists at the path given via `-XX:SharedArchiveFile`. If such an archive exists, then JVM loads and uses it; otherwise, at exit, JVM will generate an archive at that location. Moreover, JVM checks the JDK version used for creating the archive. If the current JDK version (the JVM JDK version) and the archive JDK are not the same, then JVM will overwrite the existing archive.

You may also be interested in the following article: `https://spring.io/blog/2023/12/04/cds-with-spring-framework-6-1`.

Summary

This chapter covered 15 problems with garbage collectors and AppCDS. Even if these problems have been mostly theoretical, they still represent major topics that can boost your application performance at runtime (in the GC case) and startup (in the AppCDS case).

Join our community on Discord

Join our community's Discord space for discussions with the author and other readers:

`https://discord.gg/8mgytp5DGQ`

13

Socket API and Simple Web Server

This chapter includes 11 problems covering the Socket API and 8 problems covering JDK 18 **Simple Web Server (SWS)**. In the first 11 problems we will discuss implementing socket-based applications such as blocking/non-blocking server/client applications, datagram-based applications, and multicast applications. In the second part of this chapter, we discuss SWS as a command-line tool and a suite of API points.

At the end of this chapter, you'll know how to write applications via the Socket API and how to use SWS for testing, debugging, and prototyping tasks.

Problems

Use the following problems to test your advanced programming prowess in Socket API and SWS. I strongly encourage you to give each problem a try before you turn to the solutions and download the example programs:

258. **Introducing socket basics:** Provide a brief but meaningful introduction to socket basics and related context (TCP, UDP, IP, etc.).

259. **Introducing TCP server/client applications:** Introduce the knowledge needed for writing a blocking/non-blocking TCP server/client application.

260. **Introducing the Java Socket API:** Highlight the main Socket API (NIO.2) needed for writing socket-based applications in Java.

261. **Writing a blocking TCP server/client application:** Provide a detailed example (theory and code) of a blocking TCP server/client application.

262. **Writing a non-blocking TCP server/client application:** Provide a detailed example (theory and code) of a non-blocking TCP server/client application.

263. **Writing UDP server/client applications:** Write a UDP server/client application including a connectionless client and a connected client.

264. **Introducing multicasting:** Explain in simple terms the meaning of multicast.

265. **Exploring network interfaces:** Write a snippet of code that displays details about the network interfaces available on your machine.

266. **Writing a UDP multicast server/client application:** Explain and exemplify the implementation of a UDP multicast-based application.

267. **Adding Key Encapsulation Mechanism (KEM) to a TCP server/client application:** Explain and exemplify the usage of JDK 21 KEM for encrypting/decrypting the communication in a TCP server/client application.

268. **Reimplementing the legacy Socket API:** Provide a quick overview of the Socket API evolution among JDK releases.

269. **Quick overview of SWS:** Provide a brief introduction to the JDK 18 SWS. Explain how it works and what its key abstractions are.

270. **Exploring the SWS command-line tool:** Provide a step-by-step guide for starting, using, and stopping SWS via the command line.

271. **Introducing the com.sun.net.httpserver API:** Describe the pillars of the SWS API.

272. **Adapting request/exchange:** Provide a few snippets of code that adapt the SWS request/exchange for custom scenarios.

273. **Complementing a conditional HttpHandler with another handler:** Write an example that shows how to conditionally choose between two `HttpHandler` instances.

274. **Implementing SWS for an in-memory file system:** Write an SWS implementation that serves resources from an in-memory file system (for instance, the Google Jimfs in-memory file system or other similar solutions).

275. **Implementing SWS for a zip file system:** Write an SWS implementation that serves resources from a ZIP archive.

276. **Implementing SWS for a Java runtime directory:** Write an SWS implementation that serves resources from a Java runtime directory (JEP 220).

The following sections describe solutions to the preceding problems. Remember that there usually isn't a single correct way to solve a particular problem. Also, remember that the explanations shown here include only the most interesting and important details needed to solve the problems. Download the example solutions to see additional details and to experiment with the programs at `https://github.com/PacktPublishing/Java-Coding-Problems-Second-Edition/tree/main/Chapter13`.

258. Introducing socket basics

The socket notion was introduced in the '80s. This notion was introduced on **Berkeley Software Distribution (BSD)** (a Unix flavor) as a solution for network communication between processes via **Internet Protocol (IP)**. Java introduced its first cross-platform API for sockets in 1996 (JDK 1.0). As you'll see soon, with just a few notions such as network interface, IP address and port, a Java developer can write applications that communicate via sockets.

At the IP level, data travels from source to destination in chunks (*packets*) of data. Each packet is seen as an individual entity and there is no guarantee that all packets sent from a source will hit the destination. Nevertheless, on top of IP, we have other protocols that are more popular such as **Transmission Control Protocol** (**TCP**) and **User Datagram Protocol** (**UDP**). Moreover, on top of these protocols, we have the well-known HTTP, DNS, Telnet, and so on. Machine communication via sockets works on IP, so Java applications that use the Socket API can communicate with other socket-based applications (servers) based on their predefined protocol.

Every machine connected to the Internet is represented by a number or numerical label, which is commonly named the *IP address* of that machine. As Java developers, we should know that there are categories of IP addresses:

- IPv4 – IP addresses represented on 32 bits (for instance, 89.165.254.108)
- IPv6 – IP addresses represented on 128 bits (for instance, 2001:db8:3333:4444:5555:6666: 7777:8888)

In addition, IP addresses are split into classes A, B, C, D, and E. For instance, class D of IP addresses ranges from 224.0.0.0 to 239.255.255.255 and is reserved for multicasting applications. And, of course, the 127.0.0.1 is a special IP reserved for *localhost*.

Now, speaking about ports, you should know that Java represents them as integers in the range 0-65535. Some of the ports are famous and commonly associated with a certain type of server – for instance, port 80 is associated with an HTTP server, port 23 with a Telnet server, port 21 with an FTP server, and so on.

While these notions have books that go deep into detail dedicated to them, we have enough information here to start writing server/client applications that rely on sockets. Practically, in such a server/client application, we have a server that runs on a host (a remote or localhost identified via an IP address and a port). While running, the server listens for incoming clients on a certain port. A client can locate the server via these two coordinates: the server IP address and the port. A client needs to present to the server a local port (automatically assigned by the kernel or explicitly set by us) that is used by the server to locate the client. A socket (client socket) is associated or bound to this local port and is used for communicating with the server. Upon acceptance, the server gets a socket (server socket) as well that is bound to a new local port (not the server port used for listening for incoming clients). Now, bidirectional communication can take place via these two sockets (endpoints).

259. Introducing TCP server/client applications

We don't need to be TCP experts in order to write a Java server/client TCP-based application. While this topic (TCP) is detailed (very well-documented) in dedicated books and articles, let's have a brief overview of TCP principles.

TCP's goal is to provide a point-to-point communication mechanism between two endpoints. Once the connection between these two endpoints is established (via sockets) it remains open during the communication until one of the sides closes it (usually, the client). In other words, two processes that are on different machines or the same machine can communicate with each other as in a telephone connection. In the following figure, you can see a classical server-client session based on sockets:

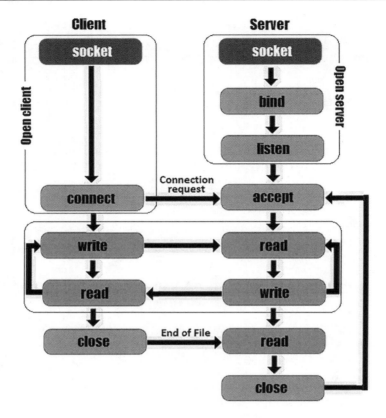

Figure 13.1: Server/client session based on sockets (TCP)

A server/client TCP connection is represented by certain coordinates as follows:

- The server side is represented by its IP address and port
- The client side is represented by its IP address and port
- The server and client communicate via a protocol (UDP, TCP/IP, etc.)

As you can see in *Figure 13.1*, the server's socket is bound and it listens for clients' requests (the server can communicate with many clients at the same time). The client's socket is bound and is ready to request a connection to the server. Once the connection is accepted, they can bidirectionally communicate (complete read/write operations) until the client closes the connection. The client can connect again later.

TCP (in contrast to UDP) is specialized in handling data packets being able to break data into packets, buffer data, and track-resend the lost or out-of-order data packets. Moreover, TCP is capable of controlling the speed of sending data in order to accommodate the processing capabilities of the receiver. TCP can send data as I/O streams of data or as byte arrays.

Blocking vs. non-blocking mechanisms

A Java TCP-based server/client application can be *blocking* or *non-blocking*. In a blocking application, a given thread is blocked until the I/O is completely received. So, the thread cannot do anything else until the I/O is ready to be processed – it will just hang on. On the other hand, in a non-blocking application, the I/O requests are queued and the thread is free to do other tasks. The queued requests will be processed later by the kernel.

From the Java implementation perspective, writing blocking applications is much easier than writing non-blocking applications. However, non-blocking applications are more performant and sustain scalability. NIO.2 supports both and we will implement both as well, but after a brief introduction to the Java Socket API.

260. Introducing the Java Socket API

Java Socket API support in Java has constantly evolved from JDK 1.0 to JDK 7. Starting with JDK 7 and NIO.2, sockets support has been seriously improved with a new API (new classes and interfaces) for easily writing complex TCP/UDP-based applications. For instance, the NetworkChannel interface was introduced as a common implementation point for all network channel classes. Any class that implements NetworkChannel has access to common methods useful for handling channels to network sockets. Such classes are SocketChannel, ServerSocketChannel, and DatagramChannel. These classes take advantage of methods for handling local addresses and for configuring socket options via SocketOption<T> (interface) and StandardSocketOptions (class). Moreover, this API exposes methods for accessing remote addresses, checking connection status, and shutting down sockets.

One of the most important subinterfaces of NetworkChannel is MulticastChannel. This interface is implemented only by DatagramChannel and it knows how to map a network channel that is capable of providing IP multicasting. Anybody can get a membership key (like a token) that can be used to join a multicast group and become a member. The membership key is useful for customizing your presence in the multicast group (for instance, block or unblock datagrams based on their sender addresses).

Introducing NetworkChannel

NetworkChannel provides methods that are common to all sockets, so NetworkChannel is a pillar of the Socket API. One of the most important methods exposed by NetworkChannel is bind(). As its name suggests, this method binds a socket channel to a local address (or in short, a socket is associated with a local address). More precisely, a socket is bound to a local address via an instance of InetSocketAddress – this class extends the SocketAddress (abstract class) and it maps a socket address as a hostname (IP)-port pair. The bind() method returns the bound socket channel (server socket channel, datagram socket channel, and so on). The returned channel was explicitly/manually bound to the given host port or automatically (if no host port is given):

```
NetworkChannel bind(SocketAddress local) throws IOException
```

The bound local address can be obtained via `getLocalAddress()`:

```
SocketAddress getLocalAddress() throws IOException
```

If no address is present then this method returns `null`.

Tackling socket options

A socket has several options represented via the `SocketOption<T>` interface. NIO.2 provides an implementation of `SocketChannel<T>` as a set of standard options via `StandardSocketOptions` as follows:

- `IP_MULTICAST_IF`: Via this option, we set the `NetworkInterface` used by a bounded datagram-oriented socket (or simply, datagram socket) for multicast datagrams. We can set this option explicitly or allow the **operating system (OS)** to choose one (if any is available) by leaving this option as default (`null`).

- `IP_MULTICAST_LOOP`: This is a flag option (defaults to `true`) that can be set for a bounded datagram socket to control the *loopback* (`true` means that the sent data should be looped back to your host) of multicast datagrams.

- `IP_MULTICAST_TTL`: This option applies to a bounded datagram socket. It is known as **time-to-live (TTL)** and is useful for setting the scope of multicast datagrams (setting the TTL for the multicast packets). By default, the value of this option is 1, which means that multicast datagrams are not sent beyond the local network. The value of this option ranges between 0 and 255.

- `IP_TOS`: Via this option, we set the value of the **type-of-service (ToS)** octet in IP packets for IPv4. It can be set anytime for a bounded datagram socket and its default value is 0. Further information on the ToS octet can be found in RFC 2474 and RFC 1349 (the interpretation of the ToS octet is network-specific).

- `SO_BROADCAST`: This is a flag option that applies to a bounded datagram socket sending data to IPv4 broadcast addresses (defaults to `false`). When it is `true`, this option allows the transmission of broadcast datagrams.

- `SO_KEEPALIVE`: This is a flag option (defaults to `false`) that applies to a bounded socket for indicating if the connection should be kept alive by the OS or not.

- `SO_LINGER`: This option defines the so-called *linger interval* as an integer (timeout in seconds). The linger interval is specific to sockets that work in blocking mode only and it represents the timeout applied to the `close()` method. In other words, when the `close()` method is called on a socket, its execution will be blocked for this timeout (linger interval) while the OS attempts to transmit the unsent data (if it is possible). This option can be set at any time (by default, it has a negative value that is interpreted as disabled) and the maximum timeout is OS-specific.

- `SO_RCVBUF`: This option is a positive integer that can be set before the socket is bound/connected (defaults to an OS-dependent value). You need this option if you want to set the size of the networking input buffer (in bytes).

- `SO_SNDBUF`: This option is a positive integer that can be set before the socket is bound/connected (defaults to an OS-dependent value). You need this option if you want to set the size of the networking output buffer (in bytes).

- SO_REUSEADDR: Via this integer option, we can indicate if an address can be reused or not. For datagram multicasting (datagram sockets), this means that multiple programs can use (can be bound to) the same address. In the case of stream-oriented sockets (or simply, stream sockets), an address can be reused only if the previous connection is in the TIME_WAIT state (the socket is about to be closed by the OS but it still waits for the client side to send possible late communications). The default value for this option is OS-dependent and it should be set before the socket is bound/connected.

- SO_REUSEPORT: Via this integer option (available from JDK 9), we can indicate if a port can be reused or not. For datagram multicasting (datagram sockets) and stream sockets, this means that multiple sockets can use (can be bound to) the same port and address. The SO_REUSEPORT should be set before connecting/binding the socket; otherwise, the OS will deliver its default value for it.

- TCP_NODELAY: This flag option (defaults to false) is used for enabling/disabling Nagle's algorithm (http://en.wikipedia.org/wiki/Nagle%27s_algorithm). It can be set at any time.

Setting an option can be done via NetworkChannel.getOption() while getting an option can be done via NetworkChannel.setOption():

```
<T> T getOption(SocketOption<T> op_name) throws IOException
<T> NetworkChannel setOption(SocketOption<T> op_name, T op_value)
   throws IOException
```

Moreover, via NetworkChannel, we can obtain the options supported by a specific network socket via supportedOptions():

```
Set<SocketOption<?>> supportedOptions()
```

Having this information in your hands, it is time to start writing out our first client/server socket-based application.

261. Writing a blocking TCP server/client application

In this problem, we will write a blocking TCP server/client application. More precisely, let's start with a single-thread blocking TCP echo server.

Writing a single-thread blocking TCP echo server

In order to write a single-thread blocking TCP echo server, we will follow these steps:

1. Create a new server socket channel
2. Configure the blocking mechanism
3. Set the server socket channel options
4. Bind the server socket channel
5. Accept connections
6. Transmit data over a connection
7. Close the channel

So, let's start with the first step.

Creating a new server socket channel

Creating and opening a new server socket channel (stream-oriented listening socket) can be done via the thread-safe `java.nio.channels.ServerSocketChannel` API as follows:

```
ServerSocketChannel serverSC = ServerSocketChannel.open();
```

The resulting server socket channel is not bound/connected. However, it is open, and this can be verified via the `isOpen()` method:

```
if (serverSC.isOpen()) {
  ...
}
```

Next, let's configure the blocking mechanism.

Configuring the blocking mechanism

Once the server socket channel has been successfully opened, we can decide on the blocking mechanism. This can be done via the `configureBlocking()` method, which gets a boolean argument (`true` means a blocking server socket channel):

```
serverSC.configureBlocking(true);
```

A special type of channel (covered in subsequent problems) is `SelectableChannel`. Such a channel is returned by the `configureBlocking()` method (inherited from `AbstractSelectableChannel`) and is useful for achieving *multiplexing* via the `Selector` API. But, as I said, this is covered later.

Setting server socket channel options

Since all options have default values, we can go with them out of the box or explicitly set only the ones that we need. For instance, let's set the `SO_RCVBUF` and `SO_REUSEADDR` as follows:

```
serverSC.setOption(StandardSocketOptions.SO_RCVBUF, 4 * 1024);
serverSC.setOption(StandardSocketOptions.SO_REUSEADDR, true);
```

The options supported for a server socket channel are available via `supportedOptions()`:

```
Set<SocketOption<?>> options = serverSC.supportedOptions();

for (SocketOption<?> option : options)  {
  System.out.println(option);
}
```

As you can see, you can simply print the supported options on the console.

Binding the server socket channel

Binding the server socket channel to a local address is a very important step. We accomplish this via the bind() method – for instance, let's bind our serverSC to localhost (127.0.0.1) and to the arbitrarily chosen port, 4444:

```
private static final int SERVER_PORT = 4444;
private static final String SERVER_IP = "127.0.0.1";
...
serverSC.bind(new InetSocketAddress(SERVER_IP, SERVER_PORT));
```

If we omit the IP address and use the InetSocketAddress constructor that takes only the port argument then Java will rely on the *wildcard* IP address. This address is a special local IP dedicated for bind operations only and typically it is interpreted as *any*:

```
serverSC.bind(new InetSocketAddress(SERVER_PORT));
```

However, when you decide to use the wildcard IP address keep in mind the following note.

Important note

Pay attention that IP wildcard addresses may lead to undesirable complications in the presence of multiple network interfaces with separate IP addresses. If you are not prepared to handle such complications, then it is better to bind the socket to a specific network address, rather than to the IP wildcard.

If we need to specify the socket address (local_addr) and the number of pending connections (pending_c), then we should rely on the following bind():

```
public abstract ServerSocketChannel bind(
  SocketAddress local_addr,int pending_c) throws IOException
```

Getting the bound local address (SocketAddress) can be done via getLocalAddress(). This method returns null if the socket has not been bound yet.

Accepting connections

So far, the server socket channel is open and bound. We are ready to accept the incoming clients. Since we set up the blocking mode, the application will be blocked until a connection is established (a client connection request is accepted) or an I/O error occurs.

Accepting connections can be done via the accept() method as follows:

```
SocketChannel acceptSC = serverSC.accept();
```

This method returns a SocketChannel representing the client socket channel (or simply, the socket channel associated with the new connection). The returned SocketChannel is a selectable channel for stream sockets.

Important note

If we call the `accept()` method for a server socket channel that it was not bound to yet, then we will get back a `NotYetBoundException` exception.

The remote address (`SocketAddress`) to which this channel's socket is connected is available via the `getRemoteAddress()` method:

```
System.out.println("New connection: "
  + acceptSC.getRemoteAddress());
```

Next, let's see how we can transmit data over this connection.

Transmitting data over a connection

At this point, the two-way connection between the server and client is established and they can start transmitting data to each other. Each part can send/receive data packets mapped using the Java I/O streams or byte arrays. Implementing the communication protocol and choosing the proper API is quite flexible. For instance, we can rely on `ByteBuffer` to implement our echo server:

```
ByteBuffer tBuffer = ByteBuffer.allocateDirect(1024);
...
while (acceptSC.read(tBuffer) != -1) {

  tBuffer.flip();

  acceptSC.write(tBuffer);

  if (tBuffer.hasRemaining()) {
    tBuffer.compact();
  } else {
    tBuffer.clear();
  }
}
```

To support data transmission via `ByteBuffer`, `SocketChannel` exposes a set of `read()`/`write()` methods as follows:

- Read from a channel into the given buffer and return the number of bytes read (`-1` if the end of stream has been reached):

  ```
  public abstract int read(ByteBuffer dest_buffer)
    throws IOException

  public final long read(ByteBuffer[] dests_buffers)
  ```

```
        throws IOException


    public abstract long read(ByteBuffer[] dests_buffers,
      int buffer_offset, int buffer_length) throws IOException
```

- Write the bytes of a buffer into a channel and return the number of written bytes:

```
    public abstract int write(ByteBuffer source_buffer)
     throws IOException


    public final long write(ByteBuffer[] source_buffers)
     throws IOException


    public abstract long write(ByteBuffer[] source_buffers,
       int buffer_offset, int buffer_length) throws IOException
```

If you prefer using the Java I/O API instead of manipulating multiple instances of ByteBuffer, then go for it:

```
InputStream in = acceptSC.socket().getInputStream();
OutputStream out = acceptSC.socket().getOutputStream();
```

Or, like this:

```
BufferedReader in = new BufferedReader(
  new InputStreamReader(acceptSC.getInputStream()));
PrintWriter out = new PrintWriter(
  acceptSC.getOutputStream(), true);
```

When I/O streams are involved, we have to talk about shutting down a connection for I/O as well. Without closing the channel, a connection for I/O can be shut down via shutdownInput() and shutdownOutput(). The shutdownInput() method shuts down the connection for reading, while the shutdownOutput() method shuts down the connection for writing. Attempting to read from a closed reading connection (end of stream) will result in -1. On the other hand, attempting to write on a closed writing connection will result in a ClosedChannelException exception:

```
// connection will be shut down for reading
acceptSC.shutdownInput();


// connection will be shut down for writing
acceptSC.shutdownOutput();
```

On the other hand, if all you need is to check if a connection for I/O is open or not, this can be done via the following code:

```
boolean inputdown = acceptSC.socket().isInputShutdown();
boolean outputdown = acceptSC.socket().isOutputShutdown();
```

These checks are useful before attempting to perform read/write operations via this connection for I/O.

Closing the channel

Closing a channel can be done via the close() method. If we want to close a certain client socket channel, then we rely on SocketChannel.close() – this will not close the server (stop it listening for incoming clients). On the other hand, if we want to close the server to stop it listening for incoming clients, then simply call ServerSocketChannel.close() as follows:

```
acceptSC.close(); // close a specific client
serverSC.close(); // close the server itself
```

Typically, you'll close these resources in a *try-with-resources* block.

Putting it all together into the echo server

The source code of our echo server can be obtained by chaining the previous snippets of code and adding some gluing code and comments:

```
public class Main {

  private static final int SERVER_PORT = 4444;
  private static final String SERVER_IP = "127.0.0.1";

  public static void main(String[] args) {

    ByteBuffer tBuffer = ByteBuffer.allocateDirect(1024);

    // open a brand new server socket channel
    try (ServerSocketChannel serverSC
            = ServerSocketChannel.open()) {

      // server socket channel was created
      if (serverSC.isOpen()) {

        // configure the blocking mode
        serverSC.configureBlocking(true);

        // optionally, configure the server side options
        serverSC.setOption(
          StandardSocketOptions.SO_RCVBUF, 4 * 1024);
        serverSC.setOption(
          StandardSocketOptions.SO_REUSEADDR, true);

        // bind the server socket channel to local address
```

```
            serverSC.bind(new InetSocketAddress(
              SERVER_IP, SERVER_PORT));

            // waiting for clients
            System.out.println("Waiting for clients ...");

            // ready to accept incoming connections
            while (true) {
              try (SocketChannel acceptSC = serverSC.accept()) {
                System.out.println("New connection: "
                  + acceptSC.getRemoteAddress());

                // sending data
                while (acceptSC.read(tBuffer) != -1) {

                  tBuffer.flip();

                  acceptSC.write(tBuffer);

                  if (tBuffer.hasRemaining()) {
                    tBuffer.compact();
                  } else {
                    tBuffer.clear();
                  }
                }
              } catch (IOException ex) {
                // handle exception
              }
            }
          } else {
            System.out.println(
              "Server socket channel unavailable!");
          }
        } catch (IOException ex) {
          System.err.println(ex);
          // handle exception
        }
      }
    }
```

Next, let's focus on developing a client for our echo server.

Writing a single-thread blocking TCP client

Before writing a client, we have to define how it works. For instance, our client connects to the server and sends the *Hey!* text. Afterward, it continues sending random integers in the range 0-100 until the number 50 is generated and sent. Once 50 are sent, the client will close the channel. The server will simply echo each message received from the client. Now, based on this scenario, we can develop a client by following these steps:

1. Create a new (client) socket channel
2. Configure the blocking mechanism
3. Connect the client socket channel
4. Transmit data over a connection
5. Close the channel

Let's tackle the first step.

Creating a new (client) socket channel

Creating and opening a new client socket channel (stream-oriented connecting socket) can be done via the thread-safe `java.nio.channels.SocketChannel` API as follows:

```
SocketChannel clientSC = SocketChannel.open();
```

The resulting client socket channel is not connected. However, it is open, and this can be verified via the `isOpen()` method:

```
if (clientSC.isOpen()) {
    ...
}
```

However, a client socket channel can be opened and connected in a single step via the `open(SocketAddress)` flavor. Next, let's configure the blocking mechanism.

Configuring the blocking mechanism

Once the client socket channel has been successfully opened, we can decide on the blocking mechanism. This can be done via the `configureBlocking()` method, which gets a boolean argument (`true` means a blocking client socket channel):

```
clientSC.configureBlocking(true);
```

Next, we set a few options for this client socket channel.

Setting client socket channel options

The following options are specific to a client socket channel: `IP_TOS`, `SO_RCVBUF`, `SO_LINGER`, `SO_OOBINLINE`, `SO_REUSEADDR`, `TCP_NODELAY`, `SO_KEEPALIVE`, and `SO_SNDBUF`. These options come with default values but they can be explicitly set as in this example:

```
clientSC.setOption(
```

```
      StandardSocketOptions.SO_RCVBUF, 131072); // 128 * 1024
  clientSC.setOption(
      StandardSocketOptions.SO_SNDBUF, 131072); // 128 * 1024
  clientSC.setOption(
      StandardSocketOptions.SO_KEEPALIVE, true);
  clientSC.setOption(
      StandardSocketOptions.SO_LINGER, 5);
```

A client socket channel reveals the supported options via `supportedOptions()`:

```
Set<SocketOption<?>> options = clientSC.supportedOptions();

for (SocketOption<?> option : options) {
  System.out.println(option);
}
```

As you can see, you can simply print the supported options to the console.

Connecting the client socket channel

After opening the client socket channel, we have to connect it to the server that listens for incoming clients on `127.0.0.1` and port `4444`. This can be done via the `connect()` method as follows:

```
private final int SERVER_PORT = 4444;
private final String SERVER_IP = "127.0.0.1";
...
clientSC.connect(
  new InetSocketAddress(SERVER_IP, SERVER_PORT));
```

Since this is a blocking client, the application blocks until a connection to this remote address is established or an I/O error occurs.

Until transmitting data (sending/receiving data packets), you should ensure that the connection is available via `isConnected()` as follows:

```
if (clientSC.isConnected()) {
  ...
}
```

Moreover, keep in mind the following note:

Important note

In our simple example, the server and the client run on the same machine (`localhost`/`127.0.0.1`). However, in reality, you should avoid hard-coding IP addresses and use the server hostname in place of its IP address. Since IP addresses can be changed and/or dynamically assigned via services such as DHCP, you should rely on hostnames (eventually configured via DNS).

Next, let's see how we can send and receive data to/from the server.

Transmitting data over a connection

First, we send the text *Hey!*. Afterward, we send integers between 0 and 100 until the integer 50 is generated. At the API level, we rely on `ByteBuffer/CharBuffer` as follows:

```
ByteBuffer tBuffer = ByteBuffer.allocateDirect(1024);


ByteBuffer hBuffer = ByteBuffer.wrap("Hey !".getBytes());
ByteBuffer rBuffer;
CharBuffer cBuffer;
Charset charset = Charset.defaultCharset();
CharsetDecoder chdecoder = charset.newDecoder();
...
clientSC.write(hBuffer);

while (clientSC.read(tBuffer) != -1) {

  tBuffer.flip();

  cBuffer = chdecoder.decode(tBuffer);

  System.out.println(cBuffer.toString());

  if (tBuffer.hasRemaining()) {
    tBuffer.compact();
  } else {
    tBuffer.clear();
  }

  int r = new Random().nextInt(100);
  if (r == 50) {
    System.out.println(
      "Number 50 is here so the channel will be closed");
    break;
  } else {
    rBuffer = ByteBuffer.wrap(
      "Random number:".concat(String.valueOf(r)).getBytes());
    clientSC.write(rBuffer);
  }
}
```

As you can see, we use `ByteBuffer` for sending/receiving data and `CharBuffer` for decoding the data received from the server.

Closing the channel

Disconnecting the client from the server (closing the client socket channel) can be done via the `close()` method as follows:

```
clientSC.close();
```

Typically, you'll close these resources in a *try-with-resources* block.

Putting it all together into the client

The source code of our client can be obtained by chaining the previous snippets of code and adding some gluing code and comments:

```java
public class Main {

  private static final int SERVER_PORT = 4444;
  private static final String SERVER_IP = "127.0.0.1";

  public static void main(String[] args) {

    ByteBuffer tBuffer = ByteBuffer.allocateDirect(1024);

    ByteBuffer hBuffer = ByteBuffer.wrap("Hey !".getBytes());
    ByteBuffer rBuffer;
    CharBuffer cBuffer;
    Charset charset = Charset.defaultCharset();
    CharsetDecoder chdecoder = charset.newDecoder();

    // create a brand new client socket channel
    try (SocketChannel clientSC = SocketChannel.open()) {

      // client socket channel was created
      if (clientSC.isOpen()) {

        // configure the blocking mode
        clientSC.configureBlocking(true);

        // optionally, configure the client side options
        clientSC.setOption(
          StandardSocketOptions.SO_RCVBUF, 128 * 1024);
        clientSC.setOption(
```

```
        StandardSocketOptions.SO_SNDBUF, 128 * 1024);
clientSC.setOption(
  StandardSocketOptions.SO_KEEPALIVE, true);
clientSC.setOption(
  StandardSocketOptions.SO_LINGER, 5);


// connect this channel's socket to the proper address
clientSC.connect(
  new InetSocketAddress(SERVER_IP, SERVER_PORT));


// check the connection availability
  if (clientSC.isConnected()) {

    // sending data
    clientSC.write(hBuffer);

    while (clientSC.read(tBuffer) != -1) {

      tBuffer.flip();

      cBuffer = chdecoder.decode(tBuffer);

      System.out.println(cBuffer.toString());

      if (tBuffer.hasRemaining()) {
        tBuffer.compact();
      } else {
        tBuffer.clear();
      }

      int r = new Random().nextInt(100);
      if (r == 50) {
        System.out.println(
          "Number 50 is here so the channel
          will be closed");
        break;
      } else {
        rBuffer = ByteBuffer.wrap(
          "Random number:".concat(
            String.valueOf(r)).getBytes());
        clientSC.write(rBuffer);
```

```
              }
           }
         } else {
           System.out.println("Connection unavailable!");
         }
       } else {
         System.out.println(
           "Client socket channel unavailable!");
       }
     } catch (IOException ex) {
       System.err.println(ex);
       // handle exception
     }
   }
 }
}
```

Finally, let's test our server/client application.

Testing the blocking echo application

First, start the server application. Second, start the client application and check out the console output:

```
Hey !
Random number:17
Random number:31
Random number:53
...
Random number:7
Number 50 is here so the channel will be closed
```

You can even start a few clients at the same time to see how it works. The server will display the remote address of each client.

262. Writing a non-blocking TCP server/client application

In this problem, we will write a non-blocking TCP server/client application.

A non-blocking socket (or a socket in non-blocking mode) allows us to perform I/O operations on socket channels without blocking the processes that are using it. The major steps of a non-blocking application are exactly the same as for a blocking application. The server is opened and bound to a local address ready to handle incoming clients. A client is opened and connected to the server. From this point forward, the server and the client can exchange data packets in a non-blocking fashion.

When we refer to exchanging data in a non-blocking fashion, we refer to the pillar of non-blocking technology, which is the `java.nio.channels.Selector` class. The role of the `Selector` is to orchestrate data transfer across multiple available socket channels. Basically, a `Selector` can monitor every single recorded socket channel and detect the channels that are available for data transfer in order to handle the clients' requests. In addition, a `Selector` is capable of handling multiple sockets' I/O operations via a single thread. This is possible via a concept known as *multiplexing*. So, instead of having a thread per socket connection, *multiplexing* allows the usage of a single thread for multiple socket connections. The `Selector` is known and referred to as the *multiplexor* of a `SelectableChannel` that is registered via the `register()` method of `SocketChannel` or `ServerSocketChannel` (subclasses of `SelectableChannel`). The `Selector` and the `SelectableChannel` are deregistered/deallocated together.

Using the SelectionKey class

It is time to take a step further and introduce the `SelectionKey` class. A channel is registered with a `Selector` via an instance of `java.nio.channels.SelectionKey` and all the `SelectionKey` instances are known as selection keys. A selection key acts as a helper for the selector being used to sort the requests of a client. Practically, a selection key carries information (metadata) about a single client subrequest such as the type of subrequest (connect, write, read, and so on) and information needed to uniquely identify the client.

During the registration of a `SelectableChannel` with a `Selector`, we point out the set of operations for which the key's channel will be monitored by this selector – this is known as the *interest set*. When an operation becomes eligible to be performed, it becomes part of the so-called *ready set* (this set is initialized with 0 when the key is created). So, a selection key handles two operation sets (*interest set* and *ready set*) represented as integer values. Each bit of an operation set represents a category of selectable operations that are supported by the key's channel. A key can be of one of the following types:

- `SelectionKey.OP_ACCEPT` (*acceptable*): Bit for marking socket-accept operations
- `SelectionKey.OP_CONNECT` (*connectable*): Bit for marking socket-connect operations
- `SelectionKey.OP_READ` (*readable*): Bit for marking read operations
- `SelectionKey.OP_WRITE` (*writable*): Bit for marking write operations

A selector must handle three sets of selection keys as follows:

- *key-set*: Contains all the keys of the currently registered channel.
- *selected-key*: Every key that is ready for at least one of the operations from the key's *interest set* is part of the *selected-key*.
- *canceled-key*: This contains all the keys that have been canceled but still have registered channels.

Important note

When a selector is created, these three sets are empty. Pay attention that the `Selector` instances are thread-safe, but their key sets however are not.

When some action takes place, the selector wakes up. It starts creating the SelectionKey, where each such key contains information about the current request.

The selector waits for the recorded events (for instance, incoming connection requests) in an infinite loop. Commonly, the first line of this loop is Selector.select(). This is a blocking call that takes place until the Selector.wakeup() method is called, at least one channel is selectable, or the current thread gets interrupted. There is also a select(long timeout) method that works as select() but with a timeout. In addition, we have selectNow(), which is non-blocking – if there are no selectable channels, then selectNow() returns 0 immediately.

Let's assume that the selector waits for a connection attempt. When a client attempts to connect, the server checks the type of each key created by the selector. If the type is OP_ACCEPT (acceptable key) then the SelectionKey.isAcceptable() method takes action. When this method returns true the server locates the client socket channel via the accept() methods. In addition, it sets this socket channel as non-blocking and registers it to the selector as eligible for OP_READ and/or OP_WRITE operations. While processing the keys created by the selector the server removes them from the list (an Iterator over these keys) in order to prevent the re-evaluation of the same key.

So far, the client socket channel is registered to the selector for read/write operations. Now, if the client sends (writes to the channel) some data on the socket channel then the selector will inform the server side that it should/can read that data (in this scenario, the SelectionKey.isReadable() method, returns true). On the other hand, when the client receives (reads) some data from the server, the SelectionKey.isWritable() method returns true.

The following diagram highlights the selector-based non-blocking flow:

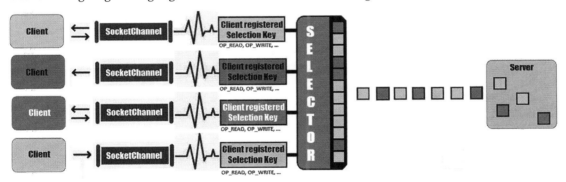

Figure 13.2: The selector-based non-blocking flow

Important note

In non-blocking mode, we may face the so-called *partial read/write*. This means that an I/O operation has partially transferred (read or written) some data (fewer bytes) or no data at all (0 bytes).

Next, let's briefly cover the Selector methods.

Using the Selector methods

Before coding a non-blocking TCP server/client application, we have to know a few built-in methods that sustain our goal:

- `Selector.open()`: This creates and opens a new selector.
- `Selector.select()`: This is a blocking operation that selects a set of keys.
- `Selector.select(long t)`: This works exactly as `select()`, but with a timeout specified in milliseconds. If there is nothing to select during t, then this method returns 0.
- `Selector.selectNow()`: This is a non-blocking version of `select()`. If there is nothing to select, then this method returns 0.
- `Selector.keys()`: This returns `Set<SelectionKey>` (selector's key set).
- `Selector.selectedKeys()`: This returns `Set<SelectionKey>` (selector's selected key set).
- `Selector.wakeup()`: The first selection operation (which has not yet returned) will return immediately.
- `SelectionKey.isReadable()`: This checks if this key's channel is ready for reading.
- `SelectionKey.isWritable()`: This checks if this key's channel is ready for writing.
- `SelectionKey.isValid()`: This checks this key's validity. An invalid key is canceled, its selector is closed, or its channel is closed.
- `SelectionKey.isAcceptable()`: If this method returns `true`, then a new socket connection will be accepted by this key's channel.
- `SelectionKey.isConnectable()`: This checks if this key's channel has successfully finished or failed to finish its current socket connection operation.
- `SelectionKey.interestOps()`: This returns this key's *interest set*.
- `SelectionKey.interestOps(t)`: This sets this key's *interest set* to t.
- `SelectionKey.readyOps()`: This returns this key's *ready-operation set*.
- `SelectionKey.cancel()`: This cancels the registration of this key's channel with its selector.

Registering a channel with a given selector can be done via the `register()` method of `ServerSocketChannel` and `SocketChannel`:

```
public final SelectionKeyregister(
    Selector s, int p, Object a) throws ClosedChannelException
```

The s argument is the given selector. The p argument is the *interest set* for the selection key, and the a argument is the attachment for the selection key (may be `null`).

Writing the non-blocking server

Based on the previous information, we can write the following non-blocking echo server (the code may look a little bit large, but it is sprinkled with helpful comments):

```
public class Main {
```

```
    private static final int SERVER_PORT = 4444;

    private final Map<SocketChannel, List<byte[]>>
      registerTrack = new HashMap<>();
    private final ByteBuffer tBuffer
      = ByteBuffer.allocate(2 * 1024);

    private void startEchoServer() {

      // call the open() method for Selector/ServerSocketChannel
      try (Selector selector = Selector.open();
        ServerSocketChannel serverSC
          = ServerSocketChannel.open()) {

        // ServerSocketChannel and Selector successfully opened
        if ((serverSC.isOpen()) && (selector.isOpen())) {

          // configure non-blocking mode
          serverSC.configureBlocking(false);

          // optionally, configure the client side options
          serverSC.setOption(
            StandardSocketOptions.SO_RCVBUF, 256 * 1024);
          serverSC.setOption(
            StandardSocketOptions.SO_REUSEADDR, true);

          // bind the server socket channel to the port
          serverSC.bind(new InetSocketAddress(SERVER_PORT));

          // register this channel with the selector
          serverSC.register(selector, SelectionKey.OP_ACCEPT);

          // waiting for clients
          System.out.println("Waiting for clients ...");
          ...
```

Next, we have the infinite loop of the `Selector`:

```
          while (true) {
            // waiting for events
            selector.select();
```

```
        // the selected keys have something to be processed
        Iterator itkeys =selector.selectedKeys().iterator();

        while (itkeys.hasNext()) {
          SelectionKey selkey
            = (SelectionKey) itkeys.next();

           // avoid processing the same key twice
          itkeys.remove();

          if (!selkey.isValid()) {
            continue;
          }

          if (selkey.isAcceptable()) {
            acceptOperation(selkey, selector);
          } else if (selkey.isReadable()) {
            this.readOperation(selkey);
          } else if (selkey.isWritable()) {
            this.writeOperation(selkey);
          }
        }
      }
    } else {
      System.out.println(
        "Cannot open the selector/channel");
    }
  } catch (IOException ex) {
    System.err.println(ex);
    // handle exception
  }
}
...
```

Further, we have a set of helpers responsible for accepting connections and performing read/write operations. First, we have the acceptOperation() helper:

```
// isAcceptable = true
private void acceptOperation(SelectionKey selkey,
    Selector selector) throws IOException {
```

```
    ServerSocketChannel serverSC
      = (ServerSocketChannel) selkey.channel();
    SocketChannel acceptSC = serverSC.accept();
    acceptSC.configureBlocking(false);

    System.out.println("New connection: "
      + acceptSC.getRemoteAddress());

    // send an welcome message
    acceptSC.write(ByteBuffer.wrap(
      "Hey !\n".getBytes("UTF-8")));

    // register the channel with selector to support more I/O
    registerTrack.put(acceptSC, new ArrayList<>());
    acceptSC.register(selector, SelectionKey.OP_READ);
  }
  ...
```

The helpers for read/write operations are:

```
// isReadable = true
  private void readOperation(SelectionKey selkey) {

    try {
      SocketChannel socketC
        = (SocketChannel) selkey.channel();

      tBuffer.clear();

      int byteRead = -1;
      try {
        byteRead = socketC.read(tBuffer);
      } catch (IOException e) {
        System.err.println("Read error!");
        // handle exception
      }

      if (byteRead == -1) {
        this.registerTrack.remove(socketC);

        System.out.println("Connection was closed by: "
```

```
          + socketC.getRemoteAddress());

      socketC.close();
      selkey.cancel();

      return;
    }

    byte[] byteData = new byte[byteRead];
    System.arraycopy(
      tBuffer.array(), 0, byteData, 0, byteRead);
    System.out.println(new String(byteData, "UTF-8")
      + " from " + socketC.getRemoteAddress());

    // send the bytes back to client
    doEchoTask(selkey, byteData);
  } catch (IOException ex) {
    System.err.println(ex);
    // handle exception
  }
}

// isWritable = true
private void writeOperation(SelectionKey selkey)
      throws IOException {

  SocketChannel socketC = (SocketChannel) selkey.channel();

  List<byte[]> channelByteData = registerTrack.get(socketC);
  Iterator<byte[]> iter = channelByteData.iterator();

  while (iter.hasNext()) {
    byte[] itb = iter.next();
    iter.remove();
    socketC.write(ByteBuffer.wrap(itb));
  }

  selkey.interestOps(SelectionKey.OP_READ);
}

private void doEchoTask(
```

```
        SelectionKey selkey, byte[] dataByte) {

    SocketChannel socketC = (SocketChannel) selkey.channel();
    List<byte[]> channelByteData = registerTrack.get(socketC);
    channelByteData.add(dataByte);

    selkey.interestOps(SelectionKey.OP_WRITE);
}
...
```

Finally, we have to call the startEchoServer():

```
public static void main(String[] args) {

    Main main = new Main();
    main.startEchoServer();
}
}
```

Next, let's focus on writing the client for our non-blocking echo server.

Writing the non-blocking client

The main structure of the non-blocking client is the same as the structure of the non-blocking server. However, there are a few things that are not the same and they deserve a brief overview as follows:

- The client socket channel must be registered with the SelectionKey.OP_CONNECT operation. This is needed because the client must be informed by the selector when the non-blocking server accepts its connection request.

- While the server side may wait for incoming clients infinitely, a client cannot attempt to connect in the same way. In other words, a client will rely on Selector.select(long timeout). A timeout that ranges from 500 to 1,000 ms should do the job.

- The client is also responsible for checking if the key is connectable via SelectionKey. isConnectable(). If this method returns true, then the client joins the isConnectionPending() and finishConnect() APIs in a conditional statement. This construction is needed for closing any pending connections. Practically, the isConnectionPending() method tells us if there is any connection operation in progress on the current client channel, while the finishConnect() method will finish the process of connecting a socket channel.

Now, we are ready to list the client code, which follows the same scenario as in the previous problem (we send the *Hey!* text followed by random integers ranging from 0 to 100 until the number 50 is generated):

```
public class Main {

    private static final int SERVER_PORT = 4444;
    private static final String SERVER_IP = "127.0.0.1";
```

```java
private static final int TIMEOUT_SELECTOR = 1_000;

public static void main(String[] args)
    throws InterruptedException {

  ByteBuffer tBuffer = ByteBuffer.allocateDirect(2 * 1024);
  ByteBuffer rBuffer;
  CharBuffer cBuffer;

  Charset charset = Charset.defaultCharset();
  CharsetDecoder chdecoder = charset.newDecoder();

  // call the open() for ServerSocketChannel and Selector
  try (Selector selector = Selector.open();
    SocketChannel clientSC = SocketChannel.open()) {

    // ServerSocketChannel and Selector successfully opened
    if ((clientSC.isOpen()) && (selector.isOpen())) {

      // configure non-blocking mode
      clientSC.configureBlocking(false);

      // optionally, configure the client side options
      clientSC.setOption(
        StandardSocketOptions.SO_RCVBUF, 128 * 1024);
      clientSC.setOption(
        StandardSocketOptions.SO_SNDBUF, 128 * 1024);
      clientSC.setOption(
        StandardSocketOptions.SO_KEEPALIVE, true);

      // register this channel with the selector
      clientSC.register(selector, SelectionKey.OP_CONNECT);

      // connecting to the remote host
      clientSC.connect(new java.net.InetSocketAddress(
        SERVER_IP, SERVER_PORT));

      System.out.println("Local host: "
        + clientSC.getLocalAddress());
      ...
```

Next, we are ready to wait to connect to the server:

```
// waiting for the connection
while (selector.select(TIMEOUT_SELECTOR) > 0) {

  // get the keys
  Set selkeys = selector.selectedKeys();
  Iterator iter = selkeys.iterator();

  // traverse and process the keys
  while (iter.hasNext()) {
    SelectionKey selkey = (SelectionKey) iter.next();

    // remove the current key
    iter.remove();

    // get the key's socket channel
    try (SocketChannel keySC
        = (SocketChannel) selkey.channel()) {

      // attempt a connection
      if (selkey.isConnectable()) {

        // connection successfully achieved
        System.out.println(
          "Connection successfully achieved!");

        // pending connections will be closed
        if (keySC.isConnectionPending()) {
          keySC.finishConnect();
        }
        ...
```

Once the client is connected, it can read/write data from/to the server side:

```
// read/write from/to server
while (keySC.read(tBuffer) != -1) {

    tBuffer.flip();

    cBuffer = chdecoder.decode(tBuffer);

    System.out.println(cBuffer.toString());
```

```
                              if (tBuffer.hasRemaining()) {
                                tBuffer.compact();
                              } else {
                                tBuffer.clear();
                              }

                              int r = new Random().nextInt(100);
                              if (r == 50) {
                                System.out.println(
                                  "Number 50 is here so
                                    the channel will be closed");
                                break;
                              } else {
                                rBuffer = ByteBuffer.wrap(
                                  "Random number:".concat(
                                    String.valueOf(r).concat(" "))
                                    .getBytes("UTF-8"));
                                keySC.write(rBuffer);
                              }
                            }
                          }
                        }
                      } catch (IOException ex) {
                        System.err.println(ex);
                        // handle exception
                      }
                    }
                  }
                } else {
                  System.out.println(
                    "Cannot open the selector/channel");
                }
              } catch (IOException ex) {
                System.err.println(ex);
                // handle exception
              }
            }
          }
```

Finally, let's test our non-blocking application.

Testing the non-blocking echo application

First, start the server side. Afterward, start a few clients and check each console output:

```
Output ×    Main.java ×    Main.java ×

Run (P262_NonBlockingEchoServer) ×    Run (P262_NonBlockingEchoClient) ×    Run (P262_NonBlockingEchoClient) ×    Run (P262_NonBlockingEchoClient) ×

Waiting for clients ...
New connection: /127.0.0.1:58992
New connection: /127.0.0.1:58993
New connection: /127.0.0.1:58994
Random number:84   from /127.0.0.1:58992
Random number:13   from /127.0.0.1:58994
Random number:0    from /127.0.0.1:58992
Random number:16   from /127.0.0.1:58993
Random number:19   from /127.0.0.1:58994
Random number:58   from /127.0.0.1:58994
Random number:66   from /127.0.0.1:58992
Random number:11   from /127.0.0.1:58994
Random number:90   from /127.0.0.1:58993
Random number:9    from /127.0.0.1:58993
Random number:53   from /127.0.0.1:58992
Random number:21   from /127.0.0.1:58994
Random number:28   from /127.0.0.1:58993
Random number:24   from /127.0.0.1:58993
Random number:46   from /127.0.0.1:58994
Random number:51   from /127.0.0.1:58993
...
```

Figure 13.3: A possible output of our non-blocking server

Keep in mind that this is not a multithreading application. It is just a single-threaded application that relies on the *multiplexing* technique.

263. Writing UDP server/client applications

UDP is a protocol built on top of IP. Via UDP, we can send data packets of at most 65,507 bytes (that is, 65,535-byte IP packet size – plus the minimum IP header of 20 bytes – plus the 8-byte UDP header = 65,507 bytes total). In UDP, data packets are seen as individual entities. In other words, no packet is aware of others. Data packets may arrive in any order or may not arrive at all. The sender will not be informed about the lost packets, so it will not know what to resend. Moreover, data packets may arrive too fast or too slow, so processing them may be a real challenge.

While TCP is famous for high-reliability data transmissions, UDP is famous for low-overhead transmissions. So, UDP is more like sending a letter (remember that TCP is like a phone call). You write on the envelope the address of the receiver (here, the remote IP and port) and your address (here, local IP and port) and send it (here, over the wires). You don't know if the letter will ever arrive at the receiver (here, the sender cannot trace the routes of the packets) and if you send more letters you cannot control the order of their arrival (here, an old packet can arrive after a more recent packet). In this context, UDP fits well if all you care about is speed. So, if you can afford losing packets and the order of receiving them is not important then UDP might be the right choice. For instance, an application that should send the state of a sensor every n milliseconds may take advantage of the UDP protocol.

Writing a single-thread blocking UDP echo server

In order to write a single-thread blocking UDP echo server, we will follow these steps:

1. Create a server datagram-oriented socket channel
2. Set datagram-oriented socket channel options
3. Bind the server datagram-oriented socket channel
4. Transmit data packets
5. Close the channel

Let's start with the first step.

Creating a server datagram-oriented socket channel

The climax of a server/client UDP application is represented by a thread-safe selectable channel dedicated to working with datagram-oriented sockets (or simply, datagram sockets). In API terms, this is referred to as java.nio.channels.DatagramChannel.

Such a channel can be obtained via DatagramChannel.open(), which gets a single parameter of the type java.net.ProtocolFamily. The protocol family implementation (java.net.StandardProtocolFamily) has two possible values:

* StandardProtocolFamily.INET: IP version 4 (IPv4)
* StandardProtocolFamily.INET6: IP version 6 (IPv6)

Next, we focus on the datagram socket for IPv4, so we call the open() method as follows:

```
DatagramChannel dchannel
  = DatagramChannel.open(StandardProtocolFamily.INET);
```

If you don't care about the protocol family, then you can call the open() method without arguments. In that case, the protocol family is platform-dependent.

Before going further, we can check if a datagram socket is open via the isOpen() flag method:

```
if (dchannel.isOpen()) {
  ...
}
```

A client datagram socket can be opened in the same manner as a server datagram socket.

Setting datagram-oriented socket channel options

The options supported by a datagram socket channel are SO_BROADCAST, IP_TOS, IP_MULTICAST_LOOP, IP_MULTICAST_TTL,SO_SNDBUF, SO_REUSEADDR, IP_MULTICAST_IF, and SO_RCVBUF. Here are some examples of setting a few of them:

```
dchannel.setOption(StandardSocketOptions.SO_RCVBUF, 4 * 1024);
dchannel.setOption(StandardSocketOptions.SO_SNDBUF, 4 * 1024);
```

The supported options are available via `supportedOptions()`:

```
Set<SocketOption<?>> options = dchannel.supportedOptions();

for(SocketOption<?> option : options) {
  System.out.println(option);
}
```

Next, let's bind the server datagram socket.

Binding the server datagram-oriented socket channel

Before listening for connections, the server datagram socket channel should be bound to a local address via the `bind()` method. Here, we have *localhost* (`127.0.0.1`) and the arbitrarily chosen port `4444`:

```
private static final int SERVER_PORT = 4444;
private static final String SERVER_IP = "127.0.0.1";
...
dchannel.bind(new InetSocketAddress(SERVER_IP, SERVER_PORT));

// or, if you prefer the wildcard address
dchannel.bind(new InetSocketAddress(SERVER_PORT));
```

If we go for `bind(null)`, then the local address will be automatically assigned. We can discover the local address via the `getLocalAddress()` method.

Transmitting data packets

The datagram-based echo server is almost ready. We can start sending and receiving packets in a connectionless fashion (UDP is a connectionless network protocol). This can be done via `send()` and `receive()` methods. The `send()` method gets the data to be sent as a `ByteBuffer` and the remote address and returns the number of bytes sent. The official documentation gives us the best explanation of how it works:

If this channel is in non-blocking mode and there is sufficient room in the underlying output buffer, or if this channel is in blocking mode and sufficient room becomes available, then the remaining bytes in the given buffer are transmitted as a single datagram to the given target address. This method may be invoked at any time. If another thread has already initiated a write operation upon this channel, however, then an invocation of this method will block until the first operation is complete. If this channel's socket is not bound then this method will first cause the socket to be bound to an address that is assigned automatically, as if by invoking the bind() method with a parameter of null.

On the other hand, the `receive()` method gets the `ByteBuffer` where you are expecting to find the received datagram. The datagram's source address is the return of this method and it can be used to send back an answer packet (if this method returns `null`, it means that the channel is in non-blocking mode and no datagram is immediately available). Again, the official documentation gives us the best explanation of how this method will act:

If a datagram is immediately available, or if this channel is in blocking mode and one eventually becomes available, then the datagram is copied into the given byte buffer and its source address is returned. If this channel is in non-blocking mode and a datagram is not immediately available then this method immediately returns null. This method may be invoked at any time. If another thread has already initiated a read operation upon this channel, however, then an invocation of this method will block until the first operation is complete. If this channel's socket is not bound then this method will first cause the socket to be bound to an address that is assigned automatically, as if by invoking the bind() method with a parameter of null.

The remote address can be discovered via `getRemoteAddress()`.

Our blocking echo server listens for packets in an infinite loop. When a packet is available (has arrived on the server), we extract from it the data and the address of the sender (the remote address). We use this address to send back the same data (to echo):

```
private static final int MAX_SIZE_OF_PACKET = 65507;
...
ByteBuffer echoBuffer
  = ByteBuffer.allocateDirect(MAX_SIZE_OF_PACKET);
...
while (true) {
  SocketAddress clientSocketAddress
    = dchannel.receive(echoBuffer);

  echoBuffer.flip();

  System.out.println("Received " + echoBuffer.limit()
    + " bytes from " + clientSocketAddress.toString()
    + "! Echo ...");

  dchannel.send(echoBuffer, clientSocketAddress);

  echoBuffer.clear();
}
```

Closing the channel

Disconnecting the datagram socket channel can be done via the `close()` method as follows:

```
dchannel.close();
```

Typically, you'll close these resources in a *try-with-resources* block.

Putting it all together into the client

The source code of our server can be obtained by chaining the previous snippets of code and adding some gluing code and comments:

```java
public class Main {

  private static final int SERVER_PORT = 4444;
  private static final String SERVER_IP = "127.0.0.1";
  private static final int MAX_SIZE_OF_PACKET = 65507;

  public static void main(String[] args) {

    ByteBuffer echoBuffer
      = ByteBuffer.allocateDirect(MAX_SIZE_OF_PACKET);

    // create a datagram channel
    try (DatagramChannel dchannel
      = DatagramChannel.open(StandardProtocolFamily.INET)) {

      // if the channel was successfully opened
      if (dchannel.isOpen()) {

        System.out.println("The echo server is ready!");

        // optionally, configure the server side options
        dchannel.setOption(
          StandardSocketOptions.SO_RCVBUF, 4 * 1024);
        dchannel.setOption(
          StandardSocketOptions.SO_SNDBUF, 4 * 1024);

        // bind the channel to local address
        dchannel.bind(new InetSocketAddress(
          SERVER_IP, SERVER_PORT));

        System.out.println("Echo server available at: "
          + dchannel.getLocalAddress());
        System.out.println("Ready to echo ...");

        // sending data packets
        while (true) {
```

```
              SocketAddress clientSocketAddress
                = dchannel.receive(echoBuffer);

              echoBuffer.flip();

              System.out.println("Received " + echoBuffer.limit()
                + " bytes from " + clientSocketAddress.toString()
                + "! Echo ...");

              dchannel.send(echoBuffer, clientSocketAddress);

              echoBuffer.clear();
            }
          } else {
            System.out.println("The channel is unavailable!");
          }
        } catch (SecurityException | IOException ex) {
          System.err.println(ex);
          // handle exception
        }
      }
    }
  }
```

Next, let's focus on writing a client for the echo server.

Writing a connectionless UDP client

In implementation terms, writing a connectionless UDP client is almost the same as writing the server side. We create a `DatagramChannel`, set the needed options, and we are ready to go (ready to send/receive data packets). Notice that a datagram client doesn't need to be bound (but it can be) to a local address because the server can extract the IP/port pair from each data packet – the server knows where the client lives. However, if the server was bound via `bind(null)` (so, automatically bound) then the client should know the assigned server IP/port pair (server address). Of course, the reverse is also true: if the server is the first one sending a data packet (in this case, the client should be bound).

In our case, the client is aware that the echo server listens on `127.0.0.1/4444`, so it can send the first data packet via the following code:

```java
public class Main {

  private static final int SERVER_PORT = 4444;
  private static final String SERVER_IP = "127.0.0.1";
  private static final int MAX_SIZE_OF_PACKET = 65507;
```

```
public static void main(String[] args)
      throws InterruptedException {

  CharBuffer cBuffer;
  Charset charset = Charset.defaultCharset();
  CharsetDecoder chdecoder = charset.newDecoder();
  ByteBuffer bufferToEcho = ByteBuffer.wrap(
    "Echo: I'm a great server!".getBytes());
  ByteBuffer echoedBuffer
    = ByteBuffer.allocateDirect(MAX_SIZE_OF_PACKET);

  // create a datagram channel
  try (DatagramChannel dchannel
    = DatagramChannel.open(StandardProtocolFamily.INET)) {

    // if the channel was successfully opened
    if (dchannel.isOpen()) {

      // optionally, configure the client side options
      dchannel.setOption(
        StandardSocketOptions.SO_RCVBUF, 4 * 1024);
      dchannel.setOption(
        StandardSocketOptions.SO_SNDBUF, 4 * 1024);

      // sending data packets
      int sentBytes = dchannel.send(bufferToEcho,
        new InetSocketAddress(SERVER_IP, SERVER_PORT));

      System.out.println("Sent " + sentBytes
        + " bytes to the server");

      dchannel.receive(echoedBuffer);

      // hack to wait for the server to echo
      Thread.sleep(5000);

      echoedBuffer.flip();

      cBuffer = chdecoder.decode(echoedBuffer);
      System.out.println(cBuffer.toString());
```

```
            echoedBuffer.clear();

        } else {
          System.out.println("Cannot open the channel");
        }
      } catch (SecurityException | IOException ex) {
        System.err.println(ex);
        // handle exception
      }
    }
  }
}
```

Finally, let's test our blocking server/client datagram-based application.

Testing the UDP connectionless echo application

For testing our application, we start the server, which will output these messages:

```
The echo server is ready!
Echo server available at: /127.0.0.1:4444
Ready to echo ...
```

Next, we start the client, which sends the text *Echo: I'm a great server!* to the server. The client will output the following:

```
Sent 25 bytes to the server
```

The server will receive this datagram and send it back:

```
Received 25 bytes from /127.0.0.1:59111! Echo ...
```

The client will wait for the server to echo for 5 seconds (arbitrarily chosen timeout). Since the server will echo the received datagram, the client will get it back and print it to the console:

```
Echo: I'm a great server!
```

At this moment, the client is stopped and the server continues to wait for incoming datagrams. So, don't forget to manually stop the server.

Writing a connected UDP client

Besides the connectionless `send()` and `receive()` methods, the Java API also supports the `read()` and `write()` methods. These methods work only for a connected UDP client and are based on `ByteBuffer` for holding the read/write data. A connected UDP client (in contrast with a connectionless one) relies on a socket channel that allows interactions (sending/receiving datagrams) only with the given remote peer address. The client datagram socket remains connected. It must be explicitly closed.

Connecting a UDP client is accomplished via the `connect()` method, which takes as arguments the server-side remote address:

```
private static final int SERVER_PORT = 4444;
private static final String SERVER_IP = "127.0.0.1";
...
dchannel.connect(new InetSocketAddress(
  SERVER_IP, SERVER_PORT));
```

Since UDP is a connectionless protocol, the connect() method doesn't exchange any data packets with the server across the network. The method returns immediately without actually blocking the application. Mainly, the connect() method can be called at any time since it doesn't affect the currently processed read/write operations. Its goal is to bind this socket channel (if it is not) to an automatically assigned address (it's like calling bind(null)).

The connection status can be obtained via isConnected():

```
if (dchannel.isConnected()) {
  ...
}
```

In this context, writing a UDP-connected client for our UDP echo server can be done as follows:

```
public class Main {

  private static final int SERVER_PORT = 4444;
  private static final String SERVER_IP = "127.0.0.1";
  private static final int MAX_SIZE_OF_PACKET = 65507;

  public static void main(String[] args) {

    CharBuffer cBuffer;
    Charset charset = Charset.defaultCharset();
    CharsetDecoder chdecoder = charset.newDecoder();
    ByteBuffer bufferToEcho = ByteBuffer.wrap(
      "Echo: I'm a great server!".getBytes());
    ByteBuffer echoedBuffer
      = ByteBuffer.allocateDirect(MAX_SIZE_OF_PACKET);

    // create a datagram channel
    try (DatagramChannel dchannel
        = DatagramChannel.open(StandardProtocolFamily.INET)) {

      // optionally, configure the client side options
      dchannel.setOption(
        StandardSocketOptions.SO_RCVBUF, 4 * 1024);
      dchannel.setOption(
```

```java
    StandardSocketOptions.SO_SNDBUF, 4 * 1024);

  // if the channel was successfully opened
  if (dchannel.isOpen()) {

    // connect to server (remote address)
    dchannel.connect(new InetSocketAddress(
      SERVER_IP, SERVER_PORT));

    // if the channel was successfully connected
    if (dchannel.isConnected()) {

      // sending data packets
      int sentBytes = dchannel.write(bufferToEcho);
      System.out.println("Sent " + sentBytes
        + " bytes to the server");

      dchannel.read(echoedBuffer);

      echoedBuffer.flip();

      cBuffer = chdecoder.decode(echoedBuffer);
      System.out.println(cBuffer.toString());

      echoedBuffer.clear();

    } else {
      System.out.println("Cannot connect the channel");
    }
  } else {
    System.out.println("Cannot open the channel");
  }
} catch (SecurityException | IOException ex) {
  System.err.println(ex);
  // handle exception
}
  }
}
```

Testing this client is straightforward. First, start the server. Second, start the client and check out the console output.

264. Introducing multicasting

Multicasting is like a flavor of internet broadcasting. We know that a TV station can broadcast (share) its signal from the source to all its subscribers or to everybody in a certain area. The exceptions are represented by the people who don't have the proper receiver (equipment) or aren't interested in this TV station.

From a computer perspective, the TV station can be considered a source that sends datagrams to a group of listeners/subscribers or simply destination hosts. While point-to-point communication is possible via the *unicast transport service*, in multicasting (sending datagrams from a source to multiple destinations in a single call) we have the *multicast transport service*. In the case of the *unicast transport service*, sending the same data to multiple points is possible via the so-called *replicated unicast* (practically each point receives a copy of the data).

In multicasting terms, the receivers of multicasted datagrams are known as a *group*. This group is uniquely identified by an IP of class D (224.0.0.0-239.255.255.255). A new client can listen and receive the multicasted datagrams only after it gets connected to the group via the corresponding IP address. There are multiple domains where multicasting is useful such as data-sharing management, conferencing, email groups, advertising, and so on.

Java (NIO.2) shapes multicasting via the `MulticastChannel` interface (a subinterface of `NetworkChannel`), which has a single implementation named `DatagramChannel`. This interface exposes two `join()` methods as follows:

```
MembershipKey join(InetAddress g, NetworkInterface i)
    throws IOException

MembershipKey join(InetAddress g, NetworkInterface i,
    InetAddress s) throws IOException
```

A client who wants to join a multicast group must call one of these `join()` methods. The first `join()` method requires the IP address of the multicasting group and a network interface capable of performing multicasting. The second `join()` method has an additional argument (`InetAddress s`) for indicating a source address from which group members can begin receiving datagrams. Since membership is *cumulative*, we can use multiple sources with the same group and network interface.

If a client manages to join a multicasting group, then it gets back a `MembershipKey` instance, which acts as a token, useful for performing different actions in that group.

 Important note

A multicast channel can join multiple groups. Moreover, a multicast channel can join the same group on more than one network interface.

Leaving a multicast group can be done at any moment via the `close()` method.

A brief overview of MembershipKey

The most common actions that can be performed by a client of a multicast group via the MembershipKey instance are as follows:

- **Block/unblock:** By calling the block() method with a source address, we can block datagrams sent from that source. On the other hand, we can unblock a source via the unblock() method.
- **Get group:** The group() method returns the source address (InetAddress) of the group where the current membership key was created.
- **Get channel:** The channel() method returns the channel (MulticastChannel) of the group where the current membership key was created.
- **Get source address:** For a source-specific membership key (receive datagrams only from that source), the sourceAddress() method returns the source address (InetAddress).
- **Get network interface:** The network interface of this membership key (NetworkInterface) is available via networkInterface().
- **Check validity:** If a membership key is valid, then the isValid() method returns true.
- **Drop:** Dropping membership (no longer receiving datagrams from this group) can be done via the drop() method. Typically, a membership key becomes valid after creation and remains like this until the drop() method is called or the channel is closed.

Next, let's talk about network interfaces.

265. Exploring network interfaces

In Java, a network interface is represented by the NetworkInterface API. Basically, a network interface is identified by a name and a list of IPs that are assigned to it. Via this information, we can associate a network interface with different network tasks such as a multicast group.

The following snippet of code lists all network interfaces that are available on your machine:

```
public class Main {

  public static void main(String[] args)
          throws SocketException {

    Enumeration allNetworkInterfaces
      = NetworkInterface.getNetworkInterfaces();

    while (allNetworkInterfaces.hasMoreElements()) {

      NetworkInterface ni = (NetworkInterface)
        allNetworkInterfaces.nextElement();
      System.out.println("\nDisplay Name: "
        + ni.getDisplayName());
```

```
        System.out.println(ni.getDisplayName()
          + " is up and running ? " + ni.isUp());
        System.out.println(ni.getDisplayName()
          + " is multicast capable ? "
          + ni.supportsMulticast());
        System.out.println(ni.getDisplayName() + " name: "
          + ni.getName());
        System.out.println(ni.getDisplayName()
          + " is virtual ? " + ni.isVirtual());

        Enumeration ips = ni.getInetAddresses();
        if (!ips.hasMoreElements()) {
          System.out.println("IP addresses: none");
        } else {
          System.out.println("IP addresses:");
          while (ips.hasMoreElements()) {
            InetAddress ip = (InetAddress) ips.nextElement();
            System.out.println("IP: " + ip);
          }
        }
      }
    }
}
```

For each network interface, we print at the console the display name (this is just a human-readable text that describes the network interface) and the name (this is useful to identify the network interface by name). In addition, we check if the network interface is virtual (if it is practically a subinterface), supports multicast, and is up and running. Running this application on my machine has returned multiple network interfaces, and in the following figure, there is a screenshot that shows a network interface that supports multicast (ethernet_32775):

```
Display Name: Hyper-V Virtual Ethernet Adapter
Hyper-V Virtual Ethernet Adapter is up and running ? true
Hyper-V Virtual Ethernet Adapter is multicast capable ? true
Hyper-V Virtual Ethernet Adapter name: ethernet_32775
Hyper-V Virtual Ethernet Adapter is virtual ? false
IP addresses:
IP: /fe80:0:0:0:4599:d8a1:418c:2427%ethernet_32775
IP: /172.18.64.1
```

Figure 13.4: A multicast network interface

Next, let's see how we can use ethernet_32775 to write a server/client multicast application.

266. Writing a UDP multicast server/client application

In *Problem 263*, we developed a UDP server/client application. So, based on that experience, we can go further and highlight the main aspects that can transform a classical UDP-based application into a multicast one.

For instance, let's assume that we want to write a multicast server that sends to the group (to all members interested in receiving datagrams from this server) a datagram that encapsulates the current date-time on the server. This datagram is sent every 10 seconds.

Writing a UDP multicast server

Writing a UDP multicast server starts with a new `DatagramChannel` instance obtained via the `open()` method. Next, we set the `IP_MULTICAST_IF` option (used to indicate the multicast network interface) and the `SO_REUSEADDR` option (used to allow multiple members to bind to the same address – this should be done before binding the socket):

```
private static final String
  MULTICAST_NI_NAME = "ethernet_32775";
...
NetworkInterface mni
  = NetworkInterface.getByName(MULTICAST_NI_NAME);

dchannel.setOption(
  StandardSocketOptions.IP_MULTICAST_IF, mni);
dchannel.setOption(
  StandardSocketOptions.SO_REUSEADDR, true);
...
```

Next, we call the `bind()` method to bind the channel's socket to the local address:

```
private static final int SERVER_PORT = 4444;
...
dchannel.bind(new InetSocketAddress(SERVER_PORT));
```

Finally, we need the code for transmitting the datagram containing the date-time of the server. We have arbitrarily chosen `225.4.5.6` as the IP address of the multicast group. Gluing everything together results in the following server code:

```
public class Main {

  private static final int SERVER_PORT = 4444;
  private static final String MULTICAST_GROUP = "225.4.5.6";
  private static final String MULTICAST_NI_NAME
    = "ethernet_32775";
```

```java
public static void main(String[] args) {

  ByteBufferd tBuffer;

  // create a channel
  try (DatagramChannel dchannel
    = DatagramChannel.open(StandardProtocolFamily.INET)) {

    // if the channel was successfully opened
    if (dchannel.isOpen()) {

      // get the multicast network interface
      NetworkInterface mni
        = NetworkInterface.getByName(MULTICAST_NI_NAME);

      // optionally, configure the server side options
      dchannel.setOption(
        StandardSocketOptions.IP_MULTICAST_IF, mni);
      dchannel.setOption(
        StandardSocketOptions.SO_REUSEADDR, true);

      // bind the channel to local address
      dchannel.bind(new InetSocketAddress(SERVER_PORT));
      System.out.println(
        "Server is ready...sending date-time info soon...");

      // sending datagrams
      while (true) {

        // sleep for 10000 ms (10 seconds)
        try {
          Thread.sleep(10000);
        } catch (InterruptedException ex) {}

        System.out.println("Sending date-time ...");

        dtBuffer = ByteBuffer.wrap(
          new Date().toString().getBytes());
        dchannel.send(dtBuffer, new InetSocketAddress(
          InetAddress.getByName(MULTICAST_GROUP),
```

```
                    SERVER_PORT));
                dtBuffer.flip();
            }
        } else {
          System.out.println("The channel is unavailable!");
        }
      } catch (IOException ex) {
        System.err.println(ex);
      }
    }
  }
}
```

Next, let's write a client interested in receiving datagrams from this server.

Writing a UDP multicast client

Writing a UDP multicast client is not very different from writing a multicast server. However, there are some differences – for instance, we may want to check via isMulticastAddress() if the remote address (the address from where we receive datagrams) is a multicast address. Next, a client must join the multicast group, so it must call one of the join() methods described earlier in *Problem 264*. Finally, the implementation should be written to receive datagrams as in the following code:

```
public class Main {

    private static final int SERVER_PORT = 4444;
    private static final int MAX_SIZE_OF_PACKET = 65507;
    private static final String MULTICAST_GROUP = "225.4.5.6";
    private static final String MULTICAST_NI_NAME
        = "ethernet_32775";

    public static void main(String[] args) {

        CharBuffer cBuffer;
        Charset charset = Charset.defaultCharset();
        CharsetDecoder chdecoder = charset.newDecoder();
        ByteBuffer dtBuffer
            = ByteBuffer.allocateDirect(MAX_SIZE_OF_PACKET);

        // create a channel
        try (DatagramChannel dchannel
            = DatagramChannel.open(StandardProtocolFamily.INET)) {

            InetAddress multigroup
```

```
            = InetAddress.getByName(MULTICAST_GROUP);

    // if the group address is multicast
    if (multigroup.isMulticastAddress()) {

      // if the channel was successfully open
      if (dchannel.isOpen()) {

        // get the multicast network interface
        NetworkInterface mni
          = NetworkInterface.getByName(MULTICAST_NI_NAME);

        // optionally, configure the client side options
        dchannel.setOption(
          StandardSocketOptions.SO_REUSEADDR, true);

        // bind the channel to remote address
        dchannel.bind(new InetSocketAddress(SERVER_PORT));

        // join the multicast group and receive datagrams
        MembershipKeymemkey = dchannel.join(
          multigroup, mni);

        // wait to receive datagrams
        while (true) {

          if (memkey.isValid()) {

            dchannel.receive(dtBuffer);
            dtBuffer.flip();
            cBuffer = chdecoder.decode(dtBuffer);

            System.out.println(cBuffer.toString());
            dtBuffer.clear();
          } else {
              break;
          }
        }
      } else {
        System.out.println("The channel is unavailable!");
      }
```

```
        } else {
            System.out.println("Not a multicast address!");
        }
    } catch (IOException ex) {
        System.err.println(ex);
        // handle exception
    }
  }
}
```

Next, let's talk about blocking/unblocking datagrams.

Blocking/unblocking datagrams

As you already know, blocking datagrams from a certain multicast group can be done via the block()
method, while unblocking via the unblock() method. Here is a snippet of code that blocks a list of
addresses that we don't like:

```
List<InetAddress> dislike = ...;
DatagramChannel datagramChannel = ...;

MembershipKey memkey = datagramChannel
  .join(group, network_interface);

if(!dislike.isEmpty()){
  for(InetAddress source : dislike){
    memkey.block(source);
  }
}
```

Or, if you have a list of addresses that you like, then you can connect to all of them as follows:

```
List<InetAddress> like = ...;
DatagramChannel dchannel = ...;

if (!like.isEmpty()){
  for (InetAddress source : like){
    dchannel.join(group, network_interface, source);
  }
}
```

Finally, let's test our application.

Testing the multicasting server/client application

First, start the server and wait until you see the following message in the console:

```
Server is ready ... sending date-time info soon ...
```

Then, you can start one or more instances of the client. At every 10 seconds, the server will send a datagram marked by the *Sending date-time ...* message:

```
Server is ready ... sending date-time info soon ...
Sending date-time ...
Sending date-time ...
Sending date-time ...
```

Every client that joined this multicast group will receive the datagrams from the server:

```
Fri Aug 25 08:17:30 EEST 2023
Fri Aug 25 08:17:40 EEST 2023
Fri Aug 25 08:17:50 EEST 2023
```

Done! Notice that this application suffers from some shortcomings. For instance, the server and the client are not aware of each other. The server sends datagrams even if no client is listening, and the client may wait for datagrams even if the server is offline. Challenge yourself to address these shortcomings by adding more control to each side. Moreover, feel free to experiment with blocking/non-blocking modes and connectionless/connected features for multicast applications.

267. Adding KEM to a TCP server/client application

In this problem, we attempt to write a TCP server/client application that communicates with each other via encrypted messages. The server side is referred to as the sender and the client as the receiver.

In this context, a sender can encrypt a message using its private key, and the receiver decrypts it using the sender's public key. In case you didn't recognize this scenario, then allow me to mention that we are talking about **Authenticated Key Exchange (AKE)** within **Public Key Encryption (PKE)** or, in short, about encrypting/decrypting messages based on the key exchange algorithms.

AKE within PKE is a popular choice, but it is not secure. In other words, AKE vulnerabilities can be speculated by quantum computers that are capable of altering most key exchange algorithms. JDK 21 can prevent such issues via the newly introduced KEM (https://en.wikipedia.org/wiki/Key_encapsulation_mechanism). This is a final feature delivered as JEP 452.

KEM schemes rely on a private-public keypair and, additionally, on a common secret key. KEM works on the following steps.

Generating a public-private keypair by the receiver

The receiver (client) generates a private-public keypair via the old-school approach known as the `KeyPairGenerator` API. The public key is obtained via `getPublic()` and the private key via `getPrivate()`. Here, we generate the keypairs for **Diffie-Hellman** (**DH**) key exchange with *Curve25519* as defined in RFC 7748:

```
private static PublicKey publicKey;
private static PrivateKey privateKey;
...
static {
  try {
    KeyPairGenerator kpg
      = KeyPairGenerator.getInstance("X25519");
    KeyPair kp = kpg.generateKeyPair();


    publicKey = kp.getPublic();
    privateKey = kp.getPrivate();
  } catch (NoSuchAlgorithmException ex) {...}
}
```

For now, we need only the public key.

Transmitting the public key to the sender

Next, the receiver sends the previously generated public key to the sender. This is done via the receiver's `SocketChannel`:

```
try (SocketChannel socketChannel = SocketChannel.open()) {
  ...
  socketChannel.write(
    ByteBuffer.wrap(publicKey.getEncoded()));
  ...
}
```

The sender needs the receiver's public key to generate a secret key.

Generating the common secret key by the sender

First, the sender needs to reconstruct the receiver's `PublicKey` instance from the received `byte[]` and for this, it can use the `KeyFactory` API as follows:

```
KeyFactory kf = KeyFactory.getInstance("X25519");
PublicKey publicKeyReceiver = kf.generatePublic(
  new X509EncodedKeySpec(buffer.array()));
```

The buffer.array() represents the byte[] containing the bytes of the public key. With the PublicKey in hand, the sender can rely on the KEM scheme to obtain the secret key. It starts by using the KEM class from JDK 21, which provides the functionality of a KEM:

```
KEM kemSender = KEM.getInstance("DHKEM");
```

The DHKEM built-in algorithm is an advanced version of the DH algorithm (https://en.wikipedia.org/wiki/Diffie%E2%80%93Hellman_key_exchange).

Next, the sender creates an Encapsulator and calls the encapsulate() method (known as the key encapsulation function), which generates (at each call) a secret key and a key encapsulation message:

```
private static SecretKey secretKeySender;
...
KEM.Encapsulator encorSender
  = kemSender.newEncapsulator(publicKeyReceiver);
KEM.Encapsulate dencedSender = encorSender.encapsulate(
  0, encorSender.secretSize(), "AES");
secretKeySender = encedSender.key();
```

If we call the encapsulate() method without arguments, then this is equivalent to encapsulate(0, encorSender.secretSize(), "Generic"). But, as you can see, we preferred the AES algorithm instead of Generic.

At this moment, the sender has the secret key and the encapsulation message via encedSender.

Sending the encapsulation message to the receiver

Now, the sender will transmit the key encapsulation message to the receiver via the encapsulation() method:

```
socketChannel.write(ByteBuffer.wrap(
  encedSender.encapsulation()));
```

The receiver is the only one capable of using their private key to decapsulate the received packet via a new Decapsulator. Once it does this, the receiver has the secret key:

```
private static SecretKey secretKeyReceiver;
...
KEM kemReceiver = KEM.getInstance("DHKEM");
KEM.Decapsulator decReceiver
  = kemReceiver.newDecapsulator(privateKey);
secretKeyReceiver = decReceiver.decapsulate(
    buffer.array(), 0, decReceiver.secretSize(), "AES");
```

The secret key of the sender (secretKeySender) and the secret key of the receiver (secretKeyReceiver) are identical.

Using the secret key to encrypt/decrypt messages

Now, the sender and receiver can continue the communication by encrypting/decrypting messages using the secret key and the well-known `Cipher` API:

```
Cipher cipher = Cipher.getInstance("...");
cipher.init(Cipher.ENCRYPT_MODE/DECRYPT_MODE,
  secretKeyReceiver/secretKeySender);
socketChannel.write(ByteBuffer.wrap(
  cipher.doFinal("some message".getBytes())));
```

For instance, the receiver can send an encrypted token to the sender:

```
Cipher cipher = Cipher.getInstance("AES/ECB/NoPadding");
cipher.init(Cipher.ENCRYPT_MODE, secretKeyReceiver);
socketChannel.write(ByteBuffer.wrap(
  cipher.doFinal("My token is: 763".getBytes())));
```

The sender may generate a password based on this token and send it back to the receiver:

```
// decrypt the token
Cipher cipher = Cipher.getInstance("AES/ECB/NoPadding");
cipher.init(Cipher.DECRYPT_MODE, secretKeySender);
String decMessage = new String(
  cipher.doFinal(message), Charset.defaultCharset());

// generating the password based on token

// encrypt the password and send it
cipher.init(Cipher.ENCRYPT_MODE, secretKeySender);
socketChannel.write(ByteBuffer.wrap(cipher.doFinal(
  "The generated password is: O98S!".getBytes())));
```

Finally, the receiver decrypts the received password. In the bundled code, you can find the complete code.

268. Reimplementing the legacy Socket API

The Socket API has been improved over time and it is still receiving attention for potential further improvements.

Prior to JDK 13, the Socket API (`java.net.ServerSocket` and `java.net.Socket`) relied on `PlainSocketImpl`. Starting with JDK 13 (JEP 353), this API has been replaced by `NioSocketImpl`.

As its name suggests, `NioSocketImpl` is based on the NIO infrastructure. The new implementation doesn't rely on the thread stack being capable of taking advantage of buffer cache mechanisms. Moreover, sockets can be closed via the `java.lang.ref.Cleaner` mechanism, which gives special attention to how socket objects are garbage collected.

Starting with JDK 15 (JEP 373, follow-on of JEP 353), the internal Socket API has been reimplemented at `DatagramSocket` and `MulticastSocket` APIs. The goal was to make these APIs simpler and easier to adapt to work with Project Loom (virtual threads).

Whenever you prefer to go for the old `PlainSocketImpl`, you should run your code with the JVM `-Djdk.net.usePlainSocketImpl=true` option.

269. Quick overview of SWS

SWS was added in JDK 18 under JEP 408 in the `jdk.httpserver` module. Basically, SWS is a minimalist implementation of a static file server capable of serving a single directory hierarchy. If the request points to a file, then SWS will serve that file. If the request points to a directory containing an index file, then the index file will be served; otherwise, the directory content will be listed.

SWS is very easy to set up and is available as a command-line tool (`jwebserver`) and as a suite of programmatic API points (`com.sun.net.httpserver`). SWS supports HTTP 1.1 only (not HTTPS or HTTP/2) and it can respond only to the idempotent `HEAD` and `GET` requests (any other request type will return a 405 or 501 HTTP code).

In addition, MIME types are set up automatically by SWS and no security mechanism (for instance, OAuth) is available.

Key abstractions of SWS

To better understand how SWS works behind the scenes, consider the following diagram:

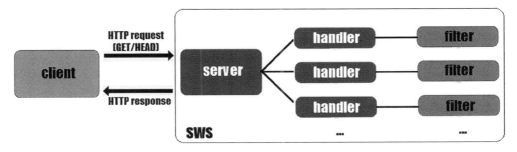

Figure 13.5: SWS key abstractions

On the left-hand side, we have a client for SWS (for instance, a browser) that triggers the HTTP requests and gets back HTTP responses. An HTTP request-response cycle is also known as an *exchange* – a client triggers a request and gets a response in exchange). On the right-hand side, there is an SWS containing the server, and a few *handlers* and *filters*. The server listens for incoming TCP connections. Next, each HTTP request is delegated to the proper handler (there can be one or more handlers). Here is where the request is practically handled by SWS. Finally, we have some filters. These are optional and they can be executed before processing the request (pre-processing filters) or after processing the request (post-processing filters – for instance, for logging purposes).

Going further, an HTTP request flows through SWS as in the following diagram:

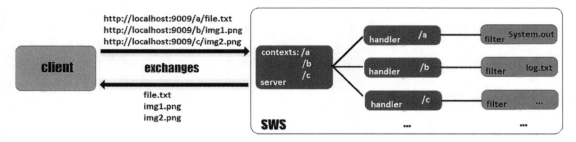

Figure 13.6: SWS handlers and filters

One of the abstractions used by SWS is *context*. A context is a mapping between a root URI part and a handler (/context/). For instance, the URL http://localhost:9009/a/file.txt has the context /a/, which is associated with a certain handler. This way, SWS knows how to dispatch requests to handlers. In other words, SWS inspects the incoming request, extracts the context, and tries to find a handler with a matching context. That handler will serve the requested resource (file.txt). Finally, after the request is handled, a post-processing filter will log the request details.

270. Exploring the SWS command-line tool

The only prerequisite for running the SWS command-line tool (jwebserver) is JDK 18 and the following syntax:

> **jwebserver [-b bind address] [-p port] [-d directory]**
> **[-o none|info|verbose] [-h to show options]**
> **[-version to show version information]**

Figure 13.7: jwebserver command-line tool syntax

The options of jwebserver are straightforward. Here is a short description of the most useful ones:

- -b addr: This is the binding address. It defaults to the loopback, 127.0.0.1 or ::1. For all interfaces, we can use -b 0.0.0.0 or -b ::. The –b addr is similar to--bind-address addr.
- -p port: This specifies the port on which the SWS will listen for incoming requests. The default port is 8000. The -p port option is similar to--port port.
- -d dir: The dir variable points out the directory to be served. The default is the current directory. The –d dir is similar to--directory dir.
- -o level: The level variable can be none, info (default), or verbose and it specifies the output format. The –o level is similar to --output level.

You can list all options and their description via the `jwebsever -h` command. Keeping these options in mind, let's start an SWS instance.

Starting SWS from the command line

Let's assume that we want to serve the files from a directory named `docs`, which contains a text file and a few image files (you'll find this folder in the bundled code). For this, we open a command prompt (in Windows) and navigate to the `docs` folder. Next, from this folder, we launch the `jwebserver` command as in the following figure:

```
Command Prompt - jwebserver                                          —    □    ×

C:\SBPBP\GitHub\Java-Coding-Problems-Second-Edition\Chapter13\P270_SWSCommandLineTool\docs>jwebserver
Binding to loopback by default. For all interfaces use "-b 0.0.0.0" or "-b ::".
Serving C:\SBPBP\GitHub\Java-Coding-Problems-Second-Edition
        \Chapter13\P270_SWSCommandLineTool\docs and subdirectories on 127.0.0.1 port 8000
URL http://127.0.0.1:8000/
```

Figure 13.8: Starting SWS via jwebserver command

Next, we need to copy the URL displayed on the command prompt into a browser address bar (here, the URL is `http://127.0.0.1:8000/`). Since our request points to the current directory (`docs`), we get back the listing of this directory in the following figure:

🌐 127.0.0.1:8000 ✕

← → C ⌂   ⓘ 127.0.0.1:8000

Directory listing for /

- books.txt
- Java Coding Problems 1st Edition.png
- Java Coding Problems 2nd Edition.png
- jOOQ Masterclass.png
- The Complete Coding Interview Guide in Java.png

Figure 13.9: SWS serving the current directory listing

If we click on `books.txt` or on any of the images then we will trigger a request to a file, so SWS will return the file content and the browser will render it accordingly.

Here is a screenshot of clicking on `books.txt` and `Java Coding Problems 2nd Edition.png`:

Figure 13.10: SWS serving two files (a text file and an image)

Meanwhile, SWS has logged each of our requests in the following image:

```
Command Prompt - jwebserver                                                          —  □  ×

C:\SBPBP\GitHub\Java-Coding-Problems-Second-Edition\Chapter13\P270_SWSCommandLineTool\docs>jwebserver
Binding to loopback by default. For all interfaces use "-b 0.0.0.0" or "-b ::".
Serving C:\SBPBP\GitHub\Java-Coding-Problems-Second-Edition
        \Chapter13\P270_SWSCommandLineTool\docs and subdirectories on 127.0.0.1 port 8000
URL http://127.0.0.1:8000/
127.0.0.1 - - [27/Aug/2023:17:21:14 +0300] "GET / HTTP/1.1" 200 -
127.0.0.1 - - [27/Aug/2023:17:21:20 +0300] "GET /books.txt HTTP/1.1" 200 -
127.0.0.1 - - [27/Aug/2023:17:21:49 +0300] "GET /Java%20Coding%20Problems%202nd%20Edition.png HTTP/1.1" 200 -
```

Figure 13.11: SWS has logged the GET requests

Done! Next, let's see how we can configure the server.

Configuring SWS from the command line

Configuring SWS from the command line can be done via the options listed earlier. For instance, if we want to change the default port then we use `-p port` (or `--port port`). In the following example, we use port 9009 instead of the default 8000. Moreover, we make our server available only to the address 172.27.128.1 via `-b addr` (this is an address specific to my machine representing a *Hyper-V virtual Ethernet adapter* supporting multicast):

```
jwebserver -b 172.27.128.1 -p 9009
```

This time, we open the browser and point it to `http://172.27.128.1:9009/`.

Feel free to test other options as well.

Stopping SWS from the command line

A SWS instance runs until it is explicitly stopped. In Unix/Windows, we can stop SWS from the command line by simply typing *Ctrl + C*. Sometimes, you have to wait a few seconds until the server is stopped and the command prompt is available for other commands.

271. Introducing the com.sun.net.httpserver API

Since 2006, next to the SWS command-line tool, we have the programmatic bridge represented by the com.sun.net.httpserver API. Practically, the goal of this API is to allow us to programmatically launch an SWS instance in a very easy way.

First, we have the SimpleFileServer, which is the main API for creating an SWS instance via three static methods, createFileServer(), createFileHandler(), and createOutputFilter(). We are especially interested in the createFileServer(InetSocketAddress addr, Path rootDirectory, SimpleFileServer.OutputLevel outputLevel) method. As you can see, via this method, we can create an SWS instance with a given port, root directory (this should be an absolute path), and output level as follows:

```
HttpServer sws = SimpleFileServer.createFileServer(
    new InetSocketAddress(9009),
    Path.of("./docs").toAbsolutePath(),
    OutputLevel.VERBOSE);


sws.start();
```

After running this application, an SWS will be available at http://localhost:9009/.

The default address is the loopback address, so you can also express the InetSocketAddress as new InetSocketAddress(InetAddress.getLoopbackAddress(), 9009). Moreover, we can bind the server after creation via bind(InetSocketAddress addr, int backlog).

For programmatically starting and stopping the SWS instance, we have the start() and stop() methods.

Using a custom HttpHandler

Another approach for programmatically creating a custom SWS instance relies on creating a file handler and passing it to the overloaded HttpServer.create() method. The file handler can be created as follows:

```
HttpHandler fileHandler = SimpleFileServer.createFileHandler(
    Path.of("./docs").toAbsolutePath());
```

This file handler can be passed to HttpServer.create(InetSocketAddress addr, int backlog, String path, HttpHandler handler, Filter... filters) next to the port, socket backlog (*maximum number of queued incoming connections to allow on the listening socket*), context path, and optional filters as follows:

```
HttpServer sws = HttpServer.create(
    new InetSocketAddress(9009), 10, "/mybooks", fileHandler);


sws.start();
```

This time, the server will be available at `http://localhost:9009/mybooks/`. If you want to achieve the same thing and still use `createFileServer()`, then you need to explicitly set the context and the file handler via `setContext()` and `setHandler()` after creating an SWS as follows:

```
private static final Path ROOT_DIRECTORY_PATH =
  Path.of("./docs").toAbsolutePath();
...
HttpHandler fileHandler
  = SimpleFileServer.createFileHandler(ROOT_DIRECTORY_PATH);

HttpServer sws = SimpleFileServer.createFileServer(
  new InetSocketAddress(9009),
  ROOT_DIRECTORY_PATH,
  OutputLevel.VERBOSE);

sws.createContext("/mybooks").setHandler(fileHandler);

sws.start();
```

There is also a `createContext(String path, HttpHandler handler)`.

Using a custom filter

Adding a post-processing filter for SWS logging can be done via `createOutputFilter(OutputStream out, OutputLevel outputLevel)`. So, we have to specify an output stream and the level of logging.

We can have multiple filters (via the filters array, `Filter...`), but here we create a single one that sends the log into a text file named `swslog.txt`:

```
HttpHandler fileHandler = SimpleFileServer.createFileHandler(
  Path.of("./docs").toAbsolutePath());

Path swslog = Paths.get("swslog.txt");
BufferedOutputStream output = new
  BufferedOutputStream(Files.newOutputStream(swslog,
    StandardOpenOption.CREATE, StandardOpenOption.WRITE));

Filter filter = SimpleFileServer.createOutputFilter(output,
  SimpleFileServer.OutputLevel.VERBOSE);

HttpServer sws = HttpServer.create(
  new InetSocketAddress(9009), 10, "/mybooks",
  fileHandler, filter);

sws.start();
```

This time, each request solved by our SWS will be logged into `swslog.txt`.

Using a custom executor

By default, all HTTP requests of an SWS instance are handled by the thread that was created by the `start()` method. But, we can specify any `Executor` for handling the HTTP requests via the `setExecutor()` method. For instance, we can rely on `newVirtualThreadPerTaskExecutor()` as follows:

```
HttpServer sws = SimpleFileServer.createFileServer(
   new InetSocketAddress(9009),
   Path.of("./docs").toAbsolutePath(),
   OutputLevel.VERBOSE);

   sws.setExecutor(Executors.newVirtualThreadPerTaskExecutor());

   sws.start();
```

Getting the current `Executor` can be done via the `getExecutor()` method. If no `Executor` was previously set, then `getExecutor()` returns `null`.

272. Adapting request/exchange

Adapting a request can be useful for testing and debugging purposes. Practically, we can adapt the request (`com.sun.net.httpserver.Request`) before the handler sees it, so we can modify the initial request and pass the result to the handler. For this, we can rely on the pre-processing `Filter`.`adaptRequest(String description, UnaryOperator<Request> requestOperator)` method. Besides the description, this method gets the effective request state of the exchange as `UnaryOperator<Request>`.

Here is an example that adds to each request the header `Author` next to a post-processing filter that logs the request details to the console:

```
HttpHandler fileHandler = ...;

Filter preFilter = Filter.adaptRequest(
  "Add 'Author' header", r -> r.with(
    "Author", List.of("Anghel Leonard")));

Filter postFilter = SimpleFileServer.createOutputFilter(
  out, SimpleFileServer.OutputLevel.VERBOSE);

HttpServer sws = HttpServer.create(
  new InetSocketAddress(9009), 10, "/mybooks",
    fileHandler, preFilter, postFilter);

sws.start();
```

We can see that the Author header is added to each request directly in the logs. In the following figure, you can see this header among other headers:

```
> Accept-language: en-US,en;q=0.9,ro;q=0.8
> Upgrade-insecure-requests: 1
> Author: Anghel Leonard
> If-modified-since: Tue, 29 Aug 2023 11:02:50 GMT
> Sec-ch-ua-mobile: ?0
> Cache-control: max-age=0
```

Figure 13.12: The Author header was added

Besides adaptRequest(), the Filter class defines the beforeHandler(String description, Consumer<HttpExchange> operation) pre-processing filter and the afterHandler(String description, Consumer<HttpExchange> operation) post-processing filter. In both cases, the operation argument represents the effective implementation of the filter. As you can see, these filters are acting as hooks for com.sun.net.httpserver.HttpExchange, which represents an *exchange* (an HTTP request and the response in exchange):

```java
Filter preFilter = Filter.beforeHandler("some description",
  exchange -> {
    // do something with the exchange before handler
  });

Filter postFilter = Filter.afterHandler("some description",
  exchange -> {
    // do something with the exchange after handler
  });
```

Via the exchange object, we have access to request/response headers and body.

273. Complementing a conditional HttpHandler with another handler

Let's assume that we want to choose between two HttpHandler instances based on a condition. For instance, for all GET requests, we want to use the following well-known HttpHandler:

```java
HttpHandler fileHandler = SimpleFileServer.createFileHandler(
  Path.of("./docs").toAbsolutePath());
```

For all other requests, we want to use an HttpHandler that always returns the same resource (for instance, the text *No data available*). Defining a HttpHandler that always returns the same code and resource (so, a *canned response*) can be done via the HttpHandlers.of(int statusCode, Headers headers, String body) method as in the following example:

```java
HttpHandler complementHandler = HttpHandlers.of(200,
```

```
Headers.of("Content-Type", "text/plain"),
  "No data available");
```

In addition, the `HttpHandler` class exposes a method that can decide between two `HttpHandler` instances based on a condition. This method is `handleOrElse(Predicate<Request> handlerTest, HttpHandler handler, HttpHandler fallbackHandler)`. As you can see, the condition is expressed as `Predicate<Request>`, so in our case, we can write it as follows:

```
Predicate<Request> predicate = request ->
  request.getRequestMethod().equalsIgnoreCase("GET");
```

Next, all we have to do is to pass this `Predicate<Request>` and the two handlers to the `handleOrElse()` method:

```
HttpHandler handler = HttpHandlers.handleOrElse(
  predicate, fileHandler, complementHandler);
```

If `predicate` is evaluated to `true` (so, an HTTP GET request was received), then `fileHandler` will be used; otherwise, `complementHandler` will be used. Finally, we create and start an SWS instance as follows:

```
HttpServer sws = HttpServer.create(
  new InetSocketAddress(9009), 10, "/mybooks", handler);


sws.start();
```

Notice that the passed `HttpHandler` is `handler`.

274. Implementing SWS for an in-memory file system

We already know that SWS can serve files from the default local file system. While this file system fits many scenarios, there are also use cases (for instance, testing scenarios) where it will be more practical to mock a directory structure in order to simulate certain expectations. In such scenarios, an in-memory file system will be more suitable than the local file system since we can avoid the creation/deletion of resources and we can use different platforms.

An in-memory file system implementation for Java 8 (based on the `java.nio.file` API) is provided by the Google project named *Jimfs* (`https://github.com/google/jimfs`). By following the instructions from the GitHub example, we wrote the following code for a simple in-memory file system:

```
private static Path inMemoryDirectory() throws IOException {

  FileSystem fileSystem
    = Jimfs.newFileSystem(Configuration.forCurrentPlatform());

  Path docs = fileSystem.getPath("docs");
  Files.createDirectory(docs);
```

```
    Path books = docs.resolve("books.txt"); // /docs/books.txt
    Files.write(books, ImmutableList.of(
      "Java Coding Problems 1st Edition",
      "Java Coding Problems 2nd Edition",
      "jOOQ Masterclass",
      "The Complete Coding Interview Guide in Java"),
      StandardCharsets.UTF_8);

    return docs.toAbsolutePath();
}
```

The path returned by the previous code is /docs/books.txt (you can easily create any kind of directory/files hierarchy). Since the SWS file handler supports any kind of path's file system that implements the java.nio.file API, we should be able to start an SWS instance for the in-memory path returned via inMemoryDirectory() as follows:

```
HttpServer sws = SimpleFileServer.createFileServer(
  new InetSocketAddress(9009), inMemoryDirectory(),
  OutputLevel.VERBOSE);

sws.start();
```

For testing, point the browser to http://localhost:9009.

275. Implementing SWS for a zip file system

Using a ZIP file system can also be a common use case for SWS. The following snippet of code creates a ZIP file system via the java.nio.file API and returns the corresponding path:

```
private static Path zipFileSystem() throws IOException {

  Map<String, String> env = new HashMap<>();
  env.put("create", "true");

  Path root = Path.of("./zips").toAbsolutePath();
  Path zipPath = root.resolve("docs.zip")
    .toAbsolutePath().normalize();

  FileSystem zipfs = FileSystems.newFileSystem(zipPath, env);
  Path externalTxtFile = Paths.get("./docs/books.txt");
  Path pathInZipfile = zipfs.getPath("/bookszipped.txt");

  // copy a file into the zip file
```

```
        Files.copy(externalTxtFile, pathInZipfile,
                StandardCopyOption.REPLACE_EXISTING);

    return zipfs.getPath("/");
}
```

The result is an archive named docs.zip with a single file named bookszipped.txt—this file was copied into the archive from the external /docs folder where it is stored under the name books.txt.

Next, we can write our SWS instance as follows:

```
HttpServer sws = SimpleFileServer.createFileServer(
    new InetSocketAddress(9009), zipFileSystem(),
    OutputLevel.VERBOSE);

sws.start();
```

After starting the SWS instance, just point the browser to the http://localhost:9009/bookszipped. txt URL and you should see the content of the text file.

276. Implementing SWS for a Java runtime directory

Starting with JDK 9 (JEP 220), the runtime images have been restructured to support modules and become more performant and secure. Moreover, naming stored modules, classes, and resources has received a new URI scheme (jrt). Via the jrt scheme, we can reference modules, classes, and resources contained in runtime images without touching the internal structure of the image. A jrt URL looks as follows:

```
jrt:/[$MODULE[/$PATH]]
```

Here, $MODULE is a module name (optional) and $PATH (optional) represents the path to a certain class/ resource file within that module. For instance, to point out the File class, we write the following URL:

```
jrt:/java.base/java/io/File.class
```

In the jrt file system, there is a top-level modules directory that contains one subdirectory for each module in the image. So, we can fetch the proper path for SWS as follows:

```
private static Path jrtFileSystem() {

    URI uri = URI.create("jrt:/");

    FileSystem jrtfs = FileSystems.getFileSystem(uri);
    Path jrtRoot = jrtfs.getPath("modules").toAbsolutePath();

    return jrtRoot;
}
```

Next, SWS can serve the `modules` directory of the given runtime image as follows:

```
HttpServer sws = SimpleFileServer.createFileServer(
  new InetSocketAddress(9009), jrtFileSystem(),
  OutputLevel.VERBOSE);


sws.start();
```

Finally, start SWS and point out the URL to a class/resource. For instance, the `http://localhost:9009/` `java.base/java/io/File.class` URL will download the `File.class` for local inspection.

Summary

This chapter covered 19 problems with Socket API and SWS. In the first part of this chapter, we covered NIO.2 features dedicated to TCP/UDP server/client applications. In the second part, we covered JDK 18 SWS as a command-line tool and as a suite of API points.

Leave a review!

Enjoyed this book? Help readers like you by leaving an Amazon review. Scan the QR code below for a 20% discount code.

Limited Offer

packt.com

Subscribe to our online digital library for full access to over 7,000 books and videos, as well as industry leading tools to help you plan your personal development and advance your career. For more information, please visit our website.

Why subscribe?

- Spend less time learning and more time coding with practical eBooks and Videos from over 4,000 industry professionals
- Improve your learning with Skill Plans built especially for you
- Get a free eBook or video every month
- Fully searchable for easy access to vital information
- Copy and paste, print, and bookmark content

At www.packt.com, you can also read a collection of free technical articles, sign up for a range of free newsletters, and receive exclusive discounts and offers on Packt books and eBooks.

Other Books
You May Enjoy

If you enjoyed this book, you may be interested in these other books by Packt:

Build Your Own Programming Language

Clinton L. Jeffery

ISBN: 9781804618028

- Analyze requirements for your language and design syntax and semantics.
- Write grammar rules for common expressions and control structures.
- Build a scanner to read source code and generate a parser to check syntax.
- Implement syntax-coloring for your code in IDEs like VS Code.
- Write tree traversals and insert information into the syntax tree.
- Implement a bytecode interpreter and run bytecode from your compiler.
- Write native code and run it after assembling and linking using system tools.
- Preprocess and transpile code into another high-level language.

Learn Java with Projects

Dr. Seán Kennedy

Maaike van Putten

ISBN: 9781837637188

- Get a clear understanding of Java fundamentals such as primitive types, operators, scope, conditional statements, loops, exceptions, and arrays.
- Master OOP constructs such as classes, objects, enums, interfaces, and records.
- Develop a deep understanding of OOP principles such as polymorphism, inheritance, and encapsulation.
- Delve into the advanced topics of generics, collections, lambdas, streams, and concurrency.
- Visualize what is happening in memory when you call a method or create an object.
- Appreciate how effective learning-by-doing is.

Packt is searching for authors like you

If you're interested in becoming an author for Packt, please visit authors.packtpub.com and apply today. We have worked with thousands of developers and tech professionals, just like you, to help them share their insight with the global tech community. You can make a general application, apply for a specific hot topic that we are recruiting an author for, or submit your own idea.

Share your thoughts

Now you've finished *Java Coding Problems, Second Edition*, we'd love to hear your thoughts! Scan the QR code below to go straight to the Amazon review page for this book and share your feedback or leave a review on the site that you purchased it from.

https://packt.link/r/1837633940

Your review is important to us and the tech community and will help us make sure we're delivering excellent quality content.

Index

Y

yield statement
using, in switch expressions 144

Z

zero-length memory segment 387

Z Garbage Collector (ZGC) 658, 663
colored pointers 664
concurrent 664
load barriers 665
region-based 666
tuning 674

zip file system
Simple Web Server (SWS),
implementing 740, 741

Zipper data structure 307-312

Download a free PDF copy of this book

Thanks for purchasing this book!

Do you like to read on the go but are unable to carry your print books everywhere?

Is your eBook purchase not compatible with the device of your choice?

Don't worry, now with every Packt book you get a DRM-free PDF version of that book at no cost.

Read anywhere, any place, on any device. Search, copy, and paste code from your favorite technical books directly into your application.

The perks don't stop there, you can get exclusive access to discounts, newsletters, and great free content in your inbox daily

Follow these simple steps to get the benefits:

1. Scan the QR code or visit the link below

https://packt.link/free-ebook/9781837633944

2. Submit your proof of purchase
3. That's it! We'll send your free PDF and other benefits to your email directly

Made in United States
Troutdale, OR
03/23/2025

29988107R00443